IMPACT OF MASS MEDIA

Current Issues

FOURTH EDITION

Edited by
RAY ELDON HIEBERT
University of Maryland

LONGMAN

An imprint of Addison Wesley Longman, Inc.

New York • Reading, Massachusetts • Menlo Park, California • Harlow, England
Don Mills, Ontario • Sydney • Mexico City • Madrid • Amsterdam

Publishing Partner: Priscilla McGeehon
Editor: Donna Erickson
Marketing Manager: John Holdcroft
Project Coordination and Text Design: York Production Services
Cover Designer/Manager: Nancy Danahy
Full Service Production Manager: Richard Ausburn
Print Buyer: Denise Sandler
Electronic Page Makeup: York Production Services
Printer and Binder: The Maple-Vail Book Manufacturing Group
Cover Printer: Coral Graphic Services, Inc.

For permission to use copyrighted material, grateful acknowledgment is made to the copyright holders on pp. 465–468, which are hereby made part of this copyright page.

Library of Congress Cataloging-in-Publication Data

Impact of mass media : current issues / edited by Ray Eldon Hiebert— 4th ed.
    p.   cm.
  Includes bibliographical references and index.
  ISBN 0-8013-3198-6
  1. Mass media—United States. 2. Mass media—Influence. 3. Mass media—Social aspects. I. Hiebert, Ray Eldon.
  P92.U5I46 1998   98-28394
  302.23′0973—dc21   CIP

Please visit our website at http://longman.awl.com

ISBN 0-8013-3198-6

12345678910—MA—01009998

CONTENTS

PREFACE

First published in 1985, *Impact of Mass Media* was has become widely used in many journalism, mass communication, and public communication courses. Given the fast changing world of mass communication, we have revised the book three times since 1985 in an effort to keep these readings current.

Carol Reuss, professor and associate provost at the University of North Carolina at Chapel Hill and a co-editor of the first two editions of this book, has written that nothing could be more important to a liberal education than an understanding of mass media: the way they affect our lives, the way they have changed, and the way they have changed the United States and the world. This book demonstrates the enormous impact that television, radio, newspapers, magazines, and the Internet have on our culture, society, politics, and government. The readings also shed light on mass media's effects on key current issues such as crime, violence, sexuality, war and conflict, minorities, culture, and gender. The readings show how mass media can be manipulated, and how they might manipulate us. This book takes up some of the basic issues of the impact of mass media, issues that are hotly debated, and it examines these issues from several different perspectives. Some of the authors presented here are vigorously in favor of mass media. Others are vigorously opposed and critical. And some try to take a balanced approach. We have not tried to suggest which view the reader should hold, but hope that each reader would make up his or her own mind.

Impact of Mass Media does not present simple answers but attempts to show many sides of the sometimes highly controversial legal, moral, ethical, economic, and political issues concerning the impact that mass media has on all of our lives. Each part of the book has four readings that we consider interesting, insightful, and thought-provoking. A few were written by scholars, but many were written by journalists and working professionals and deal with pertinent issues on subjects and themes generally of current interest. By noting the date on which each article was originally published, students are able to put the reading into some historical perspective. This book is not meant to be a comprehensive review or exhaustive statement about the themes and topics covered, but rather is meant to provide real examples of the impact of mass media taken from everyday life. Students and teachers need to discuss these issues and reach their own conclusions.

Seventeen important and often controversial issues are presented in *Impact of Mass Media:*

1. What are the effects of mass media in our society?
2. To what extent are we molded and shaped by the media?
3. Should mass media be as free as they are in our society?
4. What about those of us who are not a part of mass media?
5. What rights do we have to communicate to the masses?
6. How can we get access to media?
7. Can we bring pressure on media to get them to perform in a manner acceptable to us?
8. How can we exercise some control over the process?
9. Have we become a violent society because we read about crime in our newspapers and see violence on television and in films?
10. Has our sexual identity been altered by exposure to sexual explicitness in mass media?
11. Does the media present an accurate picture of our politicians?
12. To what extent does our government control mass media?
13. Has the nature of war been changed by mass communication?
14. Do mass media present a fair and accurate picture of minorities and women in our society?
15. Are we becoming a classless society as a result of mass media?
16. Are we becoming a society without culture or taste?
17. And finally, as media are changing as a result of new technologies, what impact will these changes have on media, on culture, and on society? How will the Internet change journalism and change the way we perceive our selves and the world?

And what can we do about all of these questions, if anything?

Features of *Impact of Mass Media*

Practical issues. This book is designed to deal with media issues in a practical, not theoretical, manner. Theory is important, and the curriculum of mass communication should provide students with theories that explain the impact of mass media. This book, though, provides snapshot views of the reality on which those theories are based.

The Internet as a mass medium. Many articles in this edition focus on new media, especially the Internet. In 1995, when the third edition of this book was published, the Internet was not yet a mass medium. Since then, however, the Internet has become a powerful addition to media that impact on our lives.

New articles in this edition—more than half—respond to the constantly changing issues in the media, and add to our understanding of media's impact, which is always evolving and increasing.

New introductions to each selection put the readings into a contemporary context for students.

New test questions, discussion topics, and suggested readings have also been added to each section to help students further explore the concepts in the text.

Significant videos on mass media are identified for the first time in this edition. Many wonderful and important video productions and documentaries about mass media are now available, including footage (especially on electronic media) that provide an important historical perspective to the study of mass media.

Since mass media are alive, changing, and part of the real, everyday world, we also suggest that students stay aware of current events to further illuminate their understanding of the changing nature and impact of mass media. Nearly every day some development in the news concerns the media itself.

Read these articles carefully, because only if we are fully informed about the media around us will we be able to make them work for us. In this way we will be empowered by information and not be victims of manipulation.

Acknowledgments

We are grateful for the review of the manuscripts by Kwadwo Anokwa, *Butler University;* Marlene Cowan, *Towson State University;* Tom Draper, *University of Nebraska—Kearney;* James Featherston, *Louisiana State University;* Diane Furno-Lamude, *University of New Mexico;* Katherine Heintz-Knowles, *University of Washington;* Mary Beth Holmes, *University of Scranton;* George Johnson, *James Madison University;* Bill Loges, *University of Denver;* Charles Lubbers, *Kansas State University;* Arvind Rajagopal, *Purdue University;* Peter Restivo, *Augusta College;* and Jan Whitt, *University of Colorado.*

Ray Eldon Hiebert

IMPACT
OF MASS MEDIA

Current Issues

PART · I
Changing Mass Media

Mass media are technology-based industries. They depend on machines to make them work—printing presses, broadcasting transmitters, cameras, projectors, radio and television receivers, and much more. Increasingly, they depend on high-tech equipment, especially computers. The technical developments that took place during World War II made mass television possible and greatly expanded the entire world of electronics. And since that time technological changes have been taking place in our society at an ever-increasing rate. Mass media technologies have changed many times, which have caused changes in mass media themselves, which have caused changes in content, which have caused changes in audiences, which have caused changes in mass media effects.

For print and electronic media, these changes have produced several important results: They have made the communication process faster, cheaper, and easier. This has led to a great proliferation of media, both mass and specialized. This has also reduced the role of the gatekeeper between the communicator and the audience. And perhaps most important, it has allowed the communicator to be far more accurate in directing information to a specific audience.

In printing, earlier technologies had produced giant presses that made possible large daily newspapers, but these production plants were so expensive that relatively few newspapers could afford to stay in business. Beginning in the 1960s, the introduction of photo-offset lithography reduced the cost of printing. In the 1970s and 1980s, the introduction of computers reduced the cost of printing and editorial production, and gave the writer/reporter more control over his or her work. In the late 1980s, the introduction of desktop publishing technologies, using personal computers, made the production of the printed word so inexpensive that the average person can now afford to be a publisher.

Similar changes have taken place in the electronic media. Before 1950, movies had to be made in large studios, using bright lights and large and expensive sound and camera equipment. Radio and television transmitters were large and ungainly. A television camera was the size of a desk, and lights in a TV studio had to be so bright that their heat was almost unbearable. The technological changes that began after World War II and have continued to the present have miniaturized and improved the equipment and made it available at a fraction of its earlier cost. Today, we can hold a TV camera in the palm of our hand; a radio transmitter can fit in a suitcase; high-speed film allows movies to be made with small cameras and lightweight sound equipment on location anywhere. As with print media, it is now possible for the average person to be in the electronic communication business.

Other technological developments have aided in the expansion of electronic media. FM broadcasting, which was developed in the 1950s and 1960s, more than doubled the frequencies available to radio. Cable TV, which was developed in the 1970s and 1980s, multiplied the TV possibilities by a factor of ten or more. Video cameras and tape recording—lightweight, inexpensive, and easy to operate—make it possible for anyone to be a movie producer.

Perhaps the most important technological development has been the computer, now an essential part of all mass communication. In the mid-1960s, computers were unheard of in the communication business. One computer was the size of a large classroom, used hundreds of vacuum tubes that had short lifetimes, and cost millions of dollars. Today, a small desk- or laptop computer that is faster and more reliable, with more memory and more functions, can be purchased for not much more than a thousand dollars. This technology is being put to use in almost every aspect of mass communication.

The computer has allowed another development that is changing mass communication as much as anything else—market research. Putting together our increased knowledge of human psychology, our use of statistical tools, and the computer to analyze data, we can now predict a number of communication outcomes with considerable reliability and solve a number of communication problems with considerable success. We can discern what audiences want, what they will pay attention to, and what they will pay for. We can find particular segments in a mass society who want a certain communication product or whom we want to reach with a particular message. And we can measure audience response to communicated messages.

All this has made the mass communication process more reliable. More messages can be communicated. Audiences are more likely to find particular messages that suit their interests and points of view. Communicators are more likely to be able to reach the audiences they seek.

In the last few years, another significant change has been the development of the Internet and online journalism. All of this is changing the landscape of mass media. This first section gives some examples of new global issues resulting from the new technologies and their impact on mass media.

I

The Growing Power of Mass Media

RAY ELDON HIEBERT

Editor's Note: This essay sets the stage for the readings in this book. It argues that mass media are changing and growing more powerful. It also sets forth the basic issues that confront mass communicators and mass audiences at the beginning of the twenty-first century and a new millennium.

The author—and editor of this book—is a professor at the University of Maryland, former dean of its College of Journalism, and former director of the American Journalism Center in Budapest, Hungary, and the Washington Journalism Center, in Washington, D.C.

If George Washington could return to the country he fathered 200 years ago, he would certainly ask what had happened to all the horses. He would be surprised to see they had nearly all been replaced by millions of horseless carriages, racing at unbelievable speeds, on a vast grid of highways connecting cities and their soaring skyscrapers, all lighted at night not with candles but with millions of electric bulbs glowing magically forever. He would find an unbelievable, fairy-tale world, different from anything he had known.

Certainly, Washington would be most impressed by change itself. His own world had changed little for many hundreds, maybe even thousands, of years before him. The speed of change would be difficult for him to comprehend, and it sometimes is even hard for us to understand and to accept. In the space of only 200 years, almost everything, even the basic facts of life, have been transformed in nearly every way. Time has a completely different meaning in this speeded-up life; everything is faster. Distance is not the same as Washington knew it, either; everything is shorter, nearer. Food is no longer the stuff you grow in your garden or shoot with your gun; it comes in packages, processed in some distant factory. Many people never even think that milk comes from cows, or that french fries are potatoes that were grown in the ground.

Many of the old truths that Washington believed in would be shattered for him now: his ideas about stars and planets, of endless frontiers, of jungles filled with exotic animals, of kings in royal splendor and savages in leopard skins, and of the nature of illnesses, the human mind, even of the substance of matter itself. He would find newspapers with stories about things that had happened in China or Europe or Africa only hours ago; live and instantaneous television pictures of scenes and events that his generation had never experienced; pictures of the surface of Mars, or of Earth from outer space, or of bacteria in a glass of water; telephone conversations with friends or family thousands of miles away; an almost endless cache of data on computer screens with the touch of just a few buttons and key words. All of what we take for granted at the end of the twentieth century would stun him into total disbelief. In short, it would have been impossible for him to imagine today's mass media.

A NEW WORLD OF COMMUNICATION

Certainly, the first president of the United States would be awed by the power of these new media to change ideas about the world, perceptions, and even life itself. At the end of the twentieth century and the beginning of a new millennium, there can be little doubt about mass media's impact on the way the world works. Consider a few examples: The communist world collapsed, and mass media played a key role. In the Persian Gulf War of 1991, the American government seemed to be as much concerned with influencing the media as with fighting the enemy. Our politicians have spent hundreds of millions of dollars on television advertising; they are no longer judged by their ideas or leadership but by their ability to project a telegenic image. Athletes no longer seem as engaged in sportsman-like competition as they are in competing for huge salaries as mass entertainers. The O. J. Simpson trials and the death and funeral of Diana, Princess of Wales, have shown us that celebrities often command the world's media attention more than real issues of life and death for the planet.

Most of us have had some direct experience with the impact of media on our lives, and we have witnessed their power in molding institutions and shaping events. What is still debatable, however, is whether that power is being used for good or for ill. In this discussion there are many sides—and that is what this book is all about.

Without question, the mass media in America are unique. Americans have the most mass media, spend the most time on them, and fulfill most of the mass media appetites of the world. Yet we have not necessarily become the best-informed citizens of the world, nor the most literate. In many ways, we are no longer even the most successful.

Television in America has become the most powerful of all mass media, which is why it gets more emphasis in this book. Simply put, we spend more time on television and are more concerned about its impact than all the other media together.

DEFINING MASS MEDIA

A sociological description of mass media in the United States can help to explain much of why they do what they do. We may like or dislike media, but unless we understand the rationales for their content and formats, we will be less able to criticize them constructively and to work for improvements.

We should begin by defining our terms. Basically, we divide mass media into two categories: *print,* or newspapers, magazines, and books; and *electronic,* or radio, television, sound recordings, motion pictures, and the Internet. These instruments must be able to carry messages quickly to audiences so large that they cannot be gathered together in any one place at any one time. Thus, mass audiences are apt to be diverse, heterogeneous, and multicultural. Mass communicators themselves are not people with whom these audiences have personal contact; they are remote and anonymous. The messages of mass communication are usually transient and impermanent as well. For radio and television, they are here one moment, gone the next. The messages of newspapers last only a day, and magazines only a week or a month. Books and films last a bit longer, but in an age of mass media, even they are displaced quickly.[1]

At the end of the twentieth century, about 1,550 daily newspapers are being published in the United States, down from about 2,600 at their peak earlier in the twentieth century. About 7,500 weekly newspapers that provide news about a local community are being published, a fairly stable number for the past few decades. Tens of thousands of other, special interest weeklies are published by religious, industrial, organizational, or institutional groups to further their own purposes. About 11,000 consumer magazines are published on a weekly, monthly, or quarterly basis (and a few even daily); these are publications available to the general public, either on the newsstand or through the mail. Thousands of others are published for special interests, on a regular or irregular basis. About 40,000 different book titles are published each year, and even if some are produced in only a few thousand copies, the total copies of books printed in the United States each year is in the hundreds of millions.

In the late 1990s in the United States, about 5,000 AM and 5,000 FM stations are broadcasting in local communities, as are about 1,550 commercial and 350 educational television stations. The sound recording industry is more centralized; only about 250 labels (or companies) are now responsible for 90 percent of all cassette, CD, video and disk sound recordings, and altogether, they produce about 1,14 billion pieces of recorded music a year, including music videos. The motion picture industry is the most concentrated of all; seven major production companies produce half of the 421 new, and 50 of the reissued, feature films per year in America.

THE ROLE OF GOVERNMENT

Government plays a unique role in American mass media. Unlike that in most other countries, the U.S. government does not own or operate any mass media that are readily available for public consumption within the country. (One exception is Voice of America, the federal government's international radio station, which is broadcast only in shortwave and aimed at foreign countries. Another exception is *Stars and Stripes,* a daily newspaper published with government funds for personnel on military bases who theoretically might not have access to privately published newspapers.) Also unlike that in many other countries, the American government rarely provides financial subsidy to mass media. (One exception has been government support for public broadcasting, to ensure that some educational programming will get on the airwaves.)

The American philosophy about *government's relationship to mass media* comes primarily from the tradition that government should not compete with private industry, and that citizens should get their information from private sources, to help ensure that government cannot manipulate information to suit its own purposes or to increase its own power. The philosophy about *government control of mass media* comes from the First Amendment to the Constitution, which says that "Congress shall make no laws abridging freedom of speech or of the press." (The primary exception are regulations governing broadcasting, but even these restrictions say relatively little about broadcast content.)

Thus, American government plays a minor role in legal control of the media. There are few laws and few institutional supports.

THE ROLE OF ADVERTISING AND PUBLIC RELATIONS

In any discussion of mass media, we must include advertising, which isn't a medium itself but is so inextricably woven into the fabric of most mass media that it cannot be ignored. By advertising we mean the purchase of time or space in print and electronic media to present a specific message. Advertisers are not employed by any medium, but since they provide critical financial support, they play a key role in the mass communication process.

Increasingly, public relations has become an essential part of mass media as well. Public relations people also are not employees of any medium; rather, they serve the special interests of those outside the mass media. They seek to influence the content of mass media by packaging news and information, by shaping personalities to fit media formats, and by creating or staging events to capture the attention of the media. Their goal is to achieve a particular mass message and (the public relations people would hope) a particular audience response. It is no longer possible to understand mass media without understanding public relations.

MASS MEDIA AS PRIVATE ENTERPRISES

We must understand that mass media in the United States are market-driven. They are private businesses, usually established to make a profit; to do so, they must provide a commodity that people want. To sell advertising time or space, any medium must have an audience that advertisers want to reach. If the medium does not attract a large enough audience to bring in enough money from subscriptions or advertising sales to cover its costs and make a profit, it will most likely go out of business unless its owners can cover its losses with profits from other businesses.

TWENTIETH-CENTURY PHENOMENA

Instruments of mass communication are relatively new to human history. Some, like electronic media, were inventions of the twentieth century. Print media, though invented earlier, were essentially reinvented in the last 100 years to reach a mass audience. Advertising developed much earlier, but in the twentieth century, it has became a massive and, to some extent, scientific industry. Public relations is the quintessential twentieth-century profession, perhaps the very symbol of our age; in fact, much of today's news has it origins in, or is somehow affected by, public relations efforts.

The impact of mass media is a fitting subject as we start a new century. For much of the 1900s, scholars argued about the real power of mass media. Now, most concede that mass media have powerful effects, even though questions remain about the precise nature of their impact or the actual cause-and-effect relationship.

LIMITED EFFECTS THEORIES

Do the media make things happen, or do they merely report what has happened? Do they make us act? Do they influence our opinions? Do they merely reflect our actions, thoughts, and feelings? Obviously, there are many variables for scientists to consider when trying to answer these questions. In the mid-1950s, many social scientists believed that mass media had limited effects, that they affected each individual differently. Two leading social scientists, Bernard Berelson and Morris Janowitz, concluded their examination of these questions with the following statement:

> The effects of communication are many and diverse. They may be short-range or long-run. They may be manifest or latent. They may be strong or weak. They may derive from any number of aspects of the communication content. They may be considered as psychological or political or economic or sociological. They may operate upon opinions, values, information levels, skills, taste, or overt behavior.[2]

Berelson and Janowitz didn't mean that it was useless to be concerned about the impact of mass media. They meant that every conclusion had to be qualified. They meant that one must be exceedingly careful in making generalizations and assigning blame. They believed that the effects of mass media must be measured and predicted on a case-by-case basis, taking into consideration all the variables in each situation.

POWERFUL EFFECTS THEORIES

The carefully guarded conclusions of Berelson and Janowitz, however, were stated at the middle of the twentieth century, before television had become such a powerful force. In the mid-1950s, television was still primarily a limited adult activity. Most people's values had already been shaped by other forces—namely, family, religion, teachers, and print media. By the end of the twentieth century, social scientists were ready to assign a more direct and powerful impact to television.

Most important, perhaps, has been the work of George Gerbner, whose "cultivation analysis" is based on the theory that television, as the dominant medium, has a cumulative effect, ultimately creating the culture in which we live. Today, according to Gerbner, it is television—not parents, teachers, or religious leaders—that establishes the values of young children, the ethics they will hold for their lifetime. Television tells the stories on which our society is based. Gerbner writes:

> Television is the overall socializing process superimposed on all the other processes. By the time children can speak (let alone go to school and perhaps learn to read) they will have absorbed thousands of hours of living in a highly compelling world. They see everything represented: all the social types, situations, art and science. Our children learn—and we ourselves learn and maintain—certain assumptions about life that bear the imprint of this most early and continued ritual. In our age, it is television mythology we grow up in and grow up with. . . . Those who tell stories hold power in society. Today television tells most of the stories to most of the people most of the time.[3]

Many scientific studies have confirmed that for the news and information we need about ourselves, our communities, and our world, we now turn more often to mass media, especially television, than to our families, friends, neighbors, religious organizations, or social institutions.

CHANGING TIMES

This book examines some of the current issues from several different perspectives. Some authors presented here vigorously support and defend the media. Others are opposed and critical. Still others try to take a balanced approach.

The issues are changing, and so is the world. It is a much different place today than it was only a few years ago, in 1985 and 1988, when the first and second editions of this book were published, or since the third edition was published in 1995. Since then, the Soviet empire has collapsed, the Iron Curtain has come down, the Berlin Wall has been demolished, and communism (which prevailed throughout much of the world in 1988) has been discredited as a viable political and economic system.

Other issues have also changed. We're not so concerned about the rights of citizens to have access to the mass media for their own views as we once were—though we probably should be—nor are we as concerned about business and the media, or religion and the media, which were covered in earlier editions. Other issues, however, such as responsibility, ethics, violence, sex, politics, government, war, minorities, gender, age, culture, and technology, remain important.

CHANGING HABITS

At the beginning of the twentieth century, the average American spent a few minutes each day reading a daily newspaper, a few minutes more reading magazines, maybe less than an hour reading a book—and no time at all watching movies or television, listening to radio or recordings, or surfing the World Wide Web, none of which existed as a public medium. By the end of the twentieth century, Americans are spending more than half their leisure time—activities other than eating, sleeping, or working—on mass media, and the majority of that time is spent watching television. Today, the numbers are 3,400 hours a year on media, or about 40% of our total time, more than we spent sleeping (2,900 hours, 33%) or working (2000 hours, 23%), or all the other things we do (only 460 hours, 5%).

In America today, young people spend more time in front of the television than they do in class. By the time an average American graduates from high school, he or she will have spent about 12,000 hours in class and about 19,000 hours watching the tube.

CHANGING MEDIA

The mass media themselves have changed, not just for former communists or citizens of the developing world but even for Americans. In fact, the media seem to be in a state of constant evolution, which sometimes is as baffling for us as if we had been dropped here like George Washington from the eighteenth century. Only fifty years ago, in the 1940s, most people in this world had never seen a television set. Only thirty years ago, in the 1960s, most had never seen color pictures on a TV screen. Only twenty years ago, in the 1980s, most could only receive a half-dozen different TV channels. Only ten years ago, in the late 1980s, most had never heard of the Internet, and only a few years ago, in the mid-1990s, only a small percentage of people were communicating online. Since 1995, an entirely new mass medium—the Internet—has emerged as a force in the world, and the changing media themselves have become a major issue.

The process of change for American media has been particularly explosive in the last decade-and-a-half of the twentieth century. In 1995, Robert Mac-Neil, former co-anchor of the *MacNeil/Lehrer News Hour* on public television, told an audience at the tenth anniversary of the Freedom Forum Media Studies Center in New York:

> About ten years ago our known media universe exploded with a big bang and everything flew into fragments that have since been coalescing into new galaxies: the old and new television networks, satellite and cable companies, movie and publishing empires, record companies and video rental chains, home shopping and telephone companies, are all still colliding and merging, or shattering and reconverging differently. We are probably still at too young a stage in the birth of this new media universe

to know which will come to rest as fixed stars and which will burn out, but the heavens are still trembling at their nativity, shareholders and employees from shock, and more detached observers from anxiety about what the new constellations will mean.[4]

Conformity, Not Diversity

To understand the changing media at the end of the twentieth century, it is important to analyze the anatomy of the "big bang" that MacNeil so poetically describes. Perhaps the best place to start is with history: America was expected to be a diverse society, and the mass media were supposed to represent and ensure that diversity. In fact, however, the mass media at the end of the twentieth century have become less diverse, less competitive, and more standardized despite more television channels to watch, more radio stations to listen to, and more printed material to read.

Media critic Richard Harwood points out that the "Golden Age" for diversity in the American press was the period from 1880 to 1930. During that time, some 2,600 dailies were published, and every major city had a half dozen or more competing papers. At one time, New York City had 30 dailies, with many different ideological and political persuasions. More than 1,000 foreign-language papers, including 160 dailies, were published in 24 different languages. In addition, the black press included 500 different periodicals and millions of readers.[5]

By the end of the twentieth century, only a handful of cities had competing dailies, and few independently owned newspapers remained. Nearly all daily papers in the United States had become politically "independent"—or "neutered," as Harwood characterizes them—with bland or conformist political convictions, or none at all. The ethnic press had declined to 236 papers and "lost much of its distinctiveness," Harwood writes, and the shrinking black press has been "enfeebled."

While newspapers are more profitable than ever today, they also are more efficient. They can operate with fewer employees, meaning that even within the newsroom, fewer voices are being heard. According to a study by the Freedom Forum, the newsroom labor force of 53,700 in the mid-1990s is expected to decline to 50,000 by the year 2001, even as the U.S. population continues to increase.

Radio and television have never been nonconformist, extremist, or highly partisan. They have always broadcast middle-of-the-road programming that would reach the largest possible audience. The Fairness Doctrine, which mandated that broadcasting give all sides equal time and opportunity, in fact discouraged stations from taking a strong stand on issues. Broadcast journalists frequently blamed the Fairness Doctrine for their bland coverage. But with the end of the Doctrine as a result of deregulation during the Reagan administration (1980–1988), programming content, including news and documentaries, has not become bolder. In fact, broadcast news has become less varied since deregulation, and at the end of the twentieth century, it is almost impossible to find a hard-hitting documentary anywhere on radio or television—even on public television.

Corporate Ownership, Not Family Businesses

Patterns of ownership have changed as well. Daily and weekly newspapers once were locally and family-owned enterprises. Of the 1,550 or so daily newspapers published in America today, more than three-fourths are owned by newspaper groups or larger corporations. And a relatively small number of these groups or corporations—about 145—account for more than four-fifths of the total circulation of U.S. dailies.

Book and magazine publishing has always been more centralized than newspapers, being headquartered mostly in New York, but it still was often family-owned or operated as small businesses. Now, most of the major book companies and magazines have been merged into larger corporations, many of them media conglomerates. Specialized magazine and book publishing operations have been launched across the country, and these have usually been feasible economic ventures only because they do not require the huge investment in equipment required to produce a daily newspaper. These specialized magazines and books, however, are also not likely to reach a mass audience.

Radio and television were also small and locally owned businesses, mandated as such by Federal Communication Commission regulations that limited ownership to seven AM, seven FM, and seven TV stations. No owner could operate more than one in any given listening area as well. When networks were started in the late 1920s, this began the trend toward centralized and nationalized programming content, but station owners themselves remained relatively small-business operators.

With the deregulation started during the Reagan years, limitations on ownership were relaxed. When deregulation became complete with the overhaul of the communications law in 1996 (including no limits at all on the number of radio stations an individual or corporation can own), mergers began almost immediately. Within a few months Rupert Murdoch's Fox network, with 22 TV stations (the largest number in history) became larger than ABC, CBS, and NBC, and its stations reached some 40 percent of all American homes, being located in 11 of the top 12 markets. (ABC, CBS, and NBC with their affiliate arrangements with local stations—the "networks"—were still massive, however, and provided more hours of programming than Fox.) Other organizations such as the Tribune Company also acquired new stations and was broadcasted in eight of the top 11 markets.

Ben Bagdikian points out that by 1989, 29 corporations controlled most of the business in daily newspapers, magazines, television, books, and motion pictures in the United States. By 1996, writes Robert McChesney, only about 50 firms controlled the overwhelming majority of the world's mass media, and nine of those 50—Time Warner, Disney, Bertelsmann, Viacom, Murdoch's News Corp., TCI, General Electric (NBC), Sony, and Seagram—held the dominant share. Immediately following are Westinghouse (CBS), New York Times, Hearst, Comcast, and Gannett.

Profit, Not Public Service

Quite naturally, the purpose of mass communication has shifted. When the businesses were locally and family-owned, community and public service was as important a motive as profit. The primary goal of any large, publicly held corporation, however, is simply to make a profit and provide income for shareholders. The mass media have become bottom-line oriented, and the bottom line is money.

This orientation has changed news judgment. News is no longer the information that people need; it is now the information that news executives believe that people want. The news media make enormous sums of money providing titillating information, usually about celebrities, to feed an enormous public appetite for gossip and rumor, especially if it involves crime, violence, sex, and famous people. Two of the biggest stories, and big money makers, of the mid-1990s were the trials of O. J. Simpson and the death and funeral of Princess Diana. Neither was news of serious consequence for their vast audiences, but the media exploited them—to the detriment of other, more important issues. As Robert MacNeil wrote about CNN's coverage of Simpson:

> Keeping the audience hooked led CNN, in my opinion, to overdo its coverage of the O. J. Simpson story. So did the commercial networks, operating on the same reasoning as CNN: If we do not do it, everyone else will and our audience will drain away. The result was that the O. J. Simpson story was hyped, hyperventilated and blown out of all proportion to its importance in the scheme of things. . . . The obsession paid off handsomely. One report estimated that the Simpson coverage goosed CNN's ratings to an extent that raised profits by an additional $70 million in one quarter.[6]

Nielsen Media Research says about 50 million Americans watched Princess Diana's funeral, at a very early hour on a Saturday morning. Nielsen also estimated that an incredible 2.5 billion viewers saw the rites worldwide, bringing in, of course, an equally astounding advertising revenue. Almost every medium in the world capitalized on Diana's death in some way—and made a profit from it. *Time* magazine, for example, produced a Diana commemorative issue that sold a million more newsstand copies than its usual weekly sale.[7] TV stations that concentrate most on violent and sensational news get the highest ratings and, thus, the highest profits. Wars, too, always make a lot of money for the mass media.

Entertainment, Not Information

We have reached the point at which television is almost exclusively an entertainment medium, without much non-entertainment content. Even the news and information selected for television by its gatekeepers emphasizes the vivid, the bloody, the sexy, and the emotional.

The same is increasingly true of newspapers and magazines. *USA Today,* the national newspaper started in 1982, has led the way in making newspapers more visual, more colorful, and more like television. Many other newspapers have followed its lead, and even the most popular magazines and books today are those that entertain rather than inform or analyze, express thoughtful opinions, or deal with philosophical issues.

Visual Imagery, Not Verbal Logic

In his four-part series for public broadcasting, *The Public Mind: Image and Reality in America,* Bill Moyers showed how we have become a society inundated with visual images, a barrage that pummels our senses daily. The average TV viewer is exposed to about 42,000 TV commercials a year. "Almost everywhere we look today," Moyers said, "creative expression serves a commercial goal." Advertising has become "the common wafer of the marketplace."

What does this cultural atmosphere say to and about us? And should we care? Moyers writes:

> Ever since the pioneers of public relations and advertising spoke about the "engineering of consent," critics have analyzed its effects. For some it reveals pure manipulation—the appropriation of language and meaning, the trivializing of life and thought. For others, it is the dawning of a new era—the printed word is dead and art and commerce are joined in ever more sophisticated ways.[8]

Some probable results: The U.S. literacy rate is declining; many countries now have a more literate population than America. Readership of newspapers also has declined steadily over the past thirty years, and was sharply down in the 1990s. Many Americans are woefully ignorant of politics and public affairs, and they are less and less active politically. And, interestingly, American distrust of mass media is increasing.

THE DECLINE OF DEMOCRACY

A discouraging fact about life in America has been the declining percentage of citizens who vote. By the end of the twentieth century, fewer than half of those eligible were voting in national elections. And with this reduction in the percentages of voters, it became easier for special interests to sway elections. All they had to do was spend a lot of money on television and other media advertising in a campaign to assure victory with a smaller number of votes. Thus, political success increasingly depended on fundraising, usually from well-financed special interest groups, to pay for media advertising.

Crucial issues were often fought at the state level between special-interest groups seeking legal status for their concerns, such as affirmative action, handgun control, or regulation of pornography on the Internet. In California, for example, more money was spent in 1996 on campaigns for special initiatives than on electing the president. In Washington state, in another example, citizens in the urban area of Seattle, concerned about accidental handgun deaths, supported an initiative in 1997 for trigger locks on handguns. Citizens in the rural eastern part of the state perceived this proposal as a threat to their constitutional right to bear arms, however, and the National Rifle Association joined their side, spent millions of dollars on media advertising, and defeated the trigger-lock initiative.

In the age of mass media, Americans have been made to think that democracy means having lots of consumer choices in the marketplace of products, rather than alternative choices in ideology, issues, or political leadership in the marketplace of ideas.

ILLUSIONS OF REALITY

When we realize that the illusions we receive from mass media are exactly that—illusions, not real or accurate or perfectly matched to our perceptions—we become disillusioned. The first time we read a newspaper story that describes an event about which we have personal knowledge, we are likely to say, "Hey, that's not the way it was; I saw it myself and it didn't happen that way at all." The first time we visit a television studio and see the painted sets for the local news show, we say, "Gee, I thought that was the real city skyline behind the anchorperson." The first time we go to Washington, D.C., and see the White House, we exclaim, "It's so small! It seemed so much bigger on television!"

This book is about the illusions we get from mass media—and our disillusionment when we find out that everything isn't the way we thought it was. Dispelling these illusions may be one of the most important responsibilities of modern education. The illusions and disillusionments of young people in our society are probably greater than they have ever been in any society before.

This book is not a scientific examination of the specifics of the impact of mass media. Instead, it presents current arguments about that impact by some leading thinkers, experienced observers, and thoughtful critics.

Questions about the impact of mass media usually engender heated debate. The arguments raised here may be among the most important of our age, because in one way or another we are all affected by mass media. And we have all debated these questions ourselves, ever since we emerged from behind the dark glass of childhood to realize that TV, the silver screen, and the printed word may not, after all, represent reality.

What can we believe? What is true, and what is not? Education must provide a way to answer these questions. We need to be educated about mass media if we want to steer a clear course between illusions on the one hand and disillusionment on the other.

REAL INFORMATION IS POWER

One thing seems certain: The power and reach of mass media at the beginning of the new millennium is greater than ever. The age of mass communication has made it possible for us to gain access to far more information than ever before. Information is indispensable to a complex and advanced civilization. We are an information-hungry society; we need an ever-increasing amount of facts to maintain and increase our standard of living. Information today is a commodity that we are willing to pay for. We also have more leisure time, and we depend on mass media to provide much of our information and entertainment.

We have often been told that information is power. The question is, are we getting the information we really need? And what must we do to ensure that the information we receive from mass media will meet our needs and not the purposes of someone else?

This book is designed to help readers reach their own conclusions about the role of mass media in their lives. Conflicting arguments are often presented here deliberately. These arguments should be discussed, and new facts and perspectives should be considered so that each person can arrive at an informed point of view. Only in this manner will truth—truth for each individual—emerge from this vast marketplace of facts and ideas.

Today, mass media are too essential to be ignored. The issues raised by them will no doubt continue to grow in importance throughout the twenty-first century. And even if George Washington were dropped from a time machine into our midst from the 1790s, it wouldn't take him long to understand and agree with those conclusions.

NOTES

1. For a good sociological definition of mass media, see Charles R. Wright, *Mass Communication: A Sociological Perspective,* 3rd ed. (New York: Random House, 1986).

2. Bernard Berelson and Morris Janowitz, *Reader in Public Opinion and Communication* (New York: Free Press, 1966), p. 379.

3. Quoted in "Society's Storyteller: How Television Creates the Myths by Which We Live," *Media & Values,* Fall 1992, p. 9.

4. Robert MacNeil, "Regaining Dignity," *Media Studies Journal,* Summer 1995, p. 105.

5. Richard Harwood, "The Golden Age of Diversity," *Washington Post,* July 22, 1994, p. A23.

6. Robert MacNeil, "More News, Lower Standards," *The Freedom Forum,* Oct. 16, 1996.

7. See Lance Morrow, "Journalism After Diana," *Columbia Journalism Review,* Nov./Dec. 1997, pp. 38–39.

8. Bill Moyers, "Consuming Images," *The Public Mind: Images and Reality in America,* Part One, Public Affairs Television Inc., Alvin Perlmutter Inc., the Corporation for Public Broadcasting, 1989.

2

The New TV: Stop Making Sense

MITCHELL STEPHENS

Editor's Note: Television is the world's most ubiquitous and influential medium, but it is also changing. In the past fifty years, television has gone through its birth pangs, childhood, adolescence, young adulthood, and maturity. It is only natural that is has been an evolving mechanism and institution, both technologically and linguistically. The technology is something everyone understands, but the new language is something we all need to comprehend.

It is the changed language of television that is changing the world, because it is changing our minds, our thinking, our feelings, even our way of relating to other people and to the world. Over the past fifty years, the makers of television content have learned to speak this new language. They've stopped trying to make television out of newspapers, magazines, books, and even radio. Now they are making television out of television, putting into the small screen a new language of vivid color and action, without regard to the linear thinking required by older media. As Mitchell Stephens says, "It's fast, hip and illogical. Welcome to the future."

Stephens is chairman of the Department of Journalism at New York University and author of *A History of News* (New York: Viking Penguin, 1988). This article is reprinted by permission from the *Washington Post,* April 25, 1993.

The commercial begins with a man in an apron fondling an artichoke and discoursing on its nature. Five seconds pass. The camera stays with him. Your remote-control finger begins to itch. "This is a fresh one, of course," the chef notes. Seven seconds, eight seconds. "They also come frozen . . ."

Then, just when you're about to zap the guy, the following words begin to roll across the screen: "One day this may be interesting to you. But until that day comes . . ." At that moment the screen explodes with frantic, often fuzzy images of tumbling, dancing, screaming young people—13 different shots, none of which last more than a second. Flitting between them are the words: "Be Young. Have Fun. Drink Pepsi."

This commercial, like the others in a recent series prepared by the BBDO Worldwide agency for PepsiCo, is ostensibly about the virtues of youth vs. age: Pepsi is fawning over the members of yet another new generation in a shameless attempt to get its corn syrup into their digestive systems. But the commercial has another meaning: It is also an attack by the new television on the old.

The old television, static and talky—that's what that simulation of a cooking show represents. It is the television most serious critics of the medium say they want to see more of: Ted Koppel, Robert MacNeil, or Alistair Cooke, talking to us, sticking to the subject, instructing us about Clinton's economic plan, Victorian England or artichokes. It is television for people whose minds were formed primarily by another medium: print.

The new television—television for people who grew up on television, television for people with itchy remote-control fingers—is hyper, disjointed and nonverbal. It cannot be found on PBS or the Sunday morning news shows. It got its start in music videos. ("Ninety percent of this has to do with MTV," BBDO creative director Don Schneider acknowledges.) You can catch glimpses of the new television in some action or sports shows—particularly in introductions and promos. But this style of television is now most visible in commercials, like that one for Pepsi—once the artichoke chef has been given the hook.

"I don't think there was ever a conscious attempt to say this commercial compares the old TV to the new," Schneider explains. "But in effect that's what it does." Pepsi's goal was, in Schneider's words, "to reclaim youth"—and the new TV is the television of the young. It is also likely to be the television of the future.

MOVING FROM OLD TO NEW

Every new medium seems to have begun by imitating older, more familiar media. This was true of print: The earliest printed books, with their illuminations and fancy letterings, were designed to look like handwritten manuscripts. And it has been true of television: The TV formats that are most familiar to us began as imitations of radio or theater or film. It takes time for a medium to develop new forms of its own. The first novels and the first printed newspapers did not appear for a century and a half after the invention of the printing press. In that Pepsi commercial, and in its cousins, we are seeing some of the first formats original to television.

Consider, for another example, a commercial for the Sega video game system. This ad is only 30 seconds long, yet it manages to hurl at the viewer 48 different images, including: a roller coaster, a rocket, a fireball, a touchdown, a rock concert, a collapsing building, an exploding house, a woman in a bikini (for that part of the audience that prefers such sights to house explosions), and a couple of dozen scenes from Sega video games themselves. That's an average of $1\frac{1}{2}$ images per second, making this perhaps the fastest half minute in television and—what?—five, 10 times as fast as anything we are likely to see elsewhere in our lives.

The makers of this Sega commercial, like almost all advertisers and most music-video producers, don't have much of interest to say. Their message can be boiled down to the usual: "Hot! Sexy! Unconventional but fashionable!" (a persistent contradiction). "Buy! Buy! Buy!" Nor do they deploy their plethora of images with any great intelligence or dexterity. Nevertheless, the feeling and the pacing of such commercials, and of the music videos that inspired them, is truly original. (The famous shower murder in Alfred Hitchcock's "Psycho" is cut just about this fast, but its many shots were all contained within one scene; in these commercials, almost every shot creates its *own* scene.)

While a few experimental films have played with techniques this radical, they have been seen only by small audiences. In contrast, "these commercials are widely distributed and understood," notes Jeffrey Goodby, co-chairman of Goodby, Berlin and Silverstein, the agency that produced the Sega ad. "They are not just happening in film schools."

ESCAPING FROM LOGIC

Another new Pepsi commercial uses as its foil a middle-aged professorial type sitting in a room piled high with dusty, colorless . . . books! (You can almost see the "focus groups" these commercials were tested on sneering.) Books represent the old order. This is television that finally—almost triumphantly—seems to be escaping their influence.

Sure, some commercials still make use of that venerable literary device, the narrative—albeit in radically condensed form: A man who has lost his legs in combat returns to play basketball; an attempt to "deprogram" a Coca-Cola drinker fails; a son is reconnected to his mother through the good graces of a telephone company. We know by now how narratives work: A scene is set, a conflict created; there is a crisis, a resolution. However, many, perhaps most, of the more adventurous new commercials employ none of the above. They are instead jumbles, like that Sega commercial, or hyperkinetic dances, like some of the other new Coke commercials. They have begun almost purposefully to shed the vestigial remnants of literary devices.

There is a telling moment in still another new Pepsi ad. A hip and decidedly young man sits in an easy chair on a beach wearing sunglasses. He brings his hands to his glasses. We never see him remove them. However, when this young man is next seen—less than a second later—the sunglasses are off. This is a violation of what filmmakers call "continuity." Sunglasses can't simply hop off a face; traditionally, there had to be some sort of "transition shot."

"We used to be real nervous about getting a transition shot," Schneider recalls. No more. Nowadays, many advertisers no longer worry about such things. The idea that events must happen in a logical sequence apparently belongs to the old television. (It probably harks back to the printed page, where words had no choice but to proceed in a straight line, one after another.) An obsession with framing shots symmetrically also seems dated, as does the compulsion to make sure that everything is in focus or that a picture has been held on screen long enough for viewers to figure out what is in it. Some images in this series of Pepsi commercials are instantaneous blurs.

NEW USE FOR WORDS

The new TV also has found a new—diminished—role for words. This is a development of some consequence. Words have been our primary means of communicating information for most of our history as a species. Images—a drawing in a cave, a photograph in a newspaper, an illustration in a textbook—have usually played a secondary role. But in the new television the role of words and images is being reversed.

Now, rapidly changing, moving images—exploding houses and undulating, underclad, underage people—carry most of the information. Words are reduced to simply underlining the image—"Be young"—a purpose better accomplished, in many cases, by a scream than by a disquisition. A recent Reebok commercial interrupts its parade of intrepid athleticism only for terse, written expressions of the rules on "Planet Reebok": "No Limits," "No Cupcakes," "No Wimps," etc. So much for prose.

The Sega commercial, typically, uses few spoken words and then only, Goodby explains, to change the rhythm, to momentarily "stop" the headlong rush of images. Among them is this deathless statement, lip-synched by football star Joe Montana: "I forgot what I was going to say." The old television encouraged people to chatter away. In the new television there is plenty to show but no longer much to say.

COMMERCIALS PROVIDE CUES

Is there not something frightening about all this? Is human communication to be reduced to a series of images of fiery explosions and attractive, gyrating people? To injunctions against "wimps"? Can we really find intellectual sustenance in such out-of-focus, off-center three-quarter-of-a-second, non-narrative blurs?

Well, no. Certainly not now, not yet. Pepsi commercials—no matter how fast and clever—hardly approach the profundity of books (or even *MacNeil/Lehrer* segments, for that matter). But the new television is still very young. People with higher motives than selling sweetened beverages are eventually going to get their hands on these forms. Artists will arrive who can squeeze larger meanings out of the relationships between their cascading images, who can use them to conjure up new ideas.

The value of the most daring commercials—no matter how empty-headed they seem—is in the clues they provide to what we can expect from the new TV when it matures. Here is a reading of some of those clues:

The New Television Will Be Very Fast

In the rush of images that ends Pepsi's artichoke commercial, the *de rigueur* woman-in-a-bathing-suit shot (in this case she is rotating a Hula-Hoop) *seems* to stay on the screen an awfully long time—"an eternity," Schneider calls it. Actually, it lasts slightly less than a second. The new commercials have altered our sense of time: In the land of half-second images, a second now seems almost languid.

Of course, television in general has altered our sense of time. We have been trained, in a process that began for the latest Pepsi generation with *Sesame Street,* to expect the perspective or the scene to change every 10 seconds or every five seconds or faster. Older documentaries, dramas and commercials, with their 15- or 20-second cuts, now look slow and boring. And one lesson of these recent commercials is that we can expect the pace to grow faster still—throughout television. Those who now bemoan the shallowness of the five- or 10-second sound bite in TV newscasts will have even shorter sound bites to bemoan soon.

How fast can TV become? "The shortest unit you can get on videotape is one-thirtieth of a second," Goodby answers, "and the eye can see that."

The New Television Will Have Rhythm

All this speed has created new kinds of organizational problems. For example, an ad produced by BBDO for General Electric's airplane engines shows 77 different images in 60 seconds. They include shots of a hockey goalie, a mother kissing a child, a computer screen, fast-motion traffic, a group of kids holding up a Sumo wrestler and, oh yes, airplanes. Some of the images are sepia in tone, some feature bright primary colors; in some the camera zooms or shifts focus, in some it remains still; some are close-ups, some long shots.

No existing grammar is of any value in organizing these disparate images: Viewers don't seem to care if images dangle or disagree. Nor are cinematic guidelines of much use: The fastest of these commercials waste no time on such things as "reaction shots." There are no "cutaways" to someone watching an airplane land. And it takes only a few seconds in that GE commercial to break a couple of other old cinematic rules, as a camera hurriedly pans from right to left across the front of an airplane and then, at a similarly dizzying pace, from left to right across its wing.

The "creatives" at these advertising agencies have only one sure guide as they arrange these images: rhythm. The shots in that GE commercial come and go to the beat of a peppy, if saccharine, ditty listing the many places airplanes with GE engines fly: "St. Petersburg and Uruguay and Malibu and Paraguay . . ."

Rhythm is crucial to these commercials. Even if advertisers get over their infatuation with youth and MTV, they will, consequently, still lean heavily on music. That ad for airplane engines, it should be noted, is certainly not intended for teenagers. The music is there, and will continue to be there as the new TV develops, because it is needed to help hold everything together. "It just works," Schneider comments. "The eye loves film cut to fast, heavy rock-and-roll."

The New Television Will Be Casually Surrealistic

Some strange things have been happening lately in TV commercials: A man suffering in the heat opens a beer bottle, and it begins to snow. Footballs sail in and out of TV sets. Trucks are transformed into race cars. Faces become cubelike in shape or merge into one another. The new television easily overcomes such trivialities as physical laws: You don't have to convince people, as you would in most books (or even in most movies) that there is a world where snow might suddenly fall on a hot day; you simply show it suddenly falling.

Such excursions beyond reality should have significant artistic uses. Words re-imagine the world primarily through metaphor: One thing—a dawn, say—is spoken of as if it were another—"rosy-fingered." In the new television, one thing can be shown to *be* another. Through this easily available surrealism, the world will be subject to new, perhaps even more stimulating, re-imaginings.

These methods might even have something to contribute to journalism. The administration's health care proposals might be illustrated by suspending reality for a couple of minutes and showing Hillary Rodham Clinton flying through hospitals, adding and subtracting patients, changing treatments, tackling paperwork and reaching into doctors' wallets. The new TV may not be willing to tarry for more than a few seconds over politicians' statements, but it might develop ways of explaining that are more powerful than simple statements.

The New Television Will Not Limit Itself to Following a Single Train of Thought

As our eyes have marched along the long, thin lines that are stacked on a printed page, they've gotten used to things happening one at a time: "They dismounted. Rodolphe tethered the horses. [Emma] walked ahead of him on the moss between the cart tracks." That's how things proceed most of the time on *Nightline* or *Masterpiece Theatre* too. And it leads to a certain kind of logic: one-thing-at-a-time logic, if/then, cause/effect logic—the logic on which most of us were brought up.

In these new television commercials, however, numerous things happen at once: Swarms of pictures fly by, there are patches of narration, music pounds away, slogans jump out at us. Because so much is going on, there is room in these commercials for odd juxtapositions, for wild digressions, for effects that seem to have no cause at all: A shot of Sadaam Hussein pops up in the middle of that Sega commercial.

"I've watched adults watch a Sega commercial," says Goodby. "They ask all these logical questions, and they get confused. They want it to make more sense than it's really going to make."

These commercials rarely make a simple one-thing-at-a-time sense. There is too much room in them for paradox: The last slogan flashed on the screen in that "Planet Reebok" ad is "No Slogans." There is too much room for irony and for unexpected bursts of self-consciousness: One recent Nike commercial, starring Michael Jordan and Bugs Bunny, pauses for an instant to place a sign reading "Product Shot" next to a picture of the sneakers it is hawking—then it's on to the next incongruous moment.

"This quick cutting really works to our benefit," notes Schneider. "We're trying to get a lot of information out there, and this way you can get more in." Because it allows "more in," this fast, jumpy TV eventually should also work to the benefit of serious artists who want to get more profound information "out there." Its capaciousness may allow them to cobble together ideas that would have been too oddly shaped, too multilayered, too freighted with contradictions to fit between the covers of a book. It may allow them to invent new ways of making sense.

Certainly nothing quite that challenging has shown up on television yet. We may not see it anytime soon; perhaps a language of imagery will first have to be invented and mastered. But the signs that television has the potential to help us say something new are already here—not so much in the programs themselves but in these 30- and 60-second spaces between them.

3

Identity Crisis of Newspapers

Doug Underwood

Editor's Note: Newspapers are in a state of transition. They are still the largest mass medium in terms of the number of people they employ and total annual revenues, but they have been sorely tried by the competition from television and new alternative media. Evening papers have been particularly vulnerable. Today, people seem to come home after work and watch TV news rather than read the evening newspaper. Many evening dailies have gone out of existence in the past decade.

The newspaper industry is now trying to reinvent itself in the age of electronics. Editors and publishers are brainstorming to discern how to keep their old readers and win new ones, especially the young. Part of this effort is inspired by new technologies, which newspaper people feel they must bring to their business. Another part is simply inspired by the success of television. In fact, some newspapers are trying to reinvent themselves as television.

Perhaps the first and most famous such effort was *USA Today*, founded in 1982. It uses satellite transmissions to beam electronic images of its pages to twenty-six printing plants around the United States, allowing it to be printed and distributed simultaneously nationwide, the first truly national newspaper, competing directly with national network television. The paper also makes heavy use of vivid color, striking graphics, and punchy writing of short news items, in the mode of TV news. Moreover, it sells its copies on the streets in newspaper boxes that have been deliberately designed to look like TV sets.

Many newspapers have copied *USA Today*, but in the 1990s newspapers have to do much more to reinvent themselves as viable mass media. This article summarizes such efforts. Doug Underwood is a former daily journalist who is now on the communications faculty at the University of Washington in Seattle. This article appeared in *Columbia Journalism Review*, March/April 1992.

Note: This was written before the advent of newspapers on-line, which in the late 1990s has changed newspapers even more.

Recently, readers of the *Kansas City Star* were treated to an intriguing new audio-electronic feature. In a box above a six-paragraph feature story about a rock band headed by Chicago White Sox pitcher Jack McDowell, readers were invited to dial a number to hear some of the band's music. Thirteen hundred people dialed into the newspaper's audio "Star Touch" system to hear brief samples of McDowell's songwriting, singing, and guitar playing.

These days boxed invitations abound as reporters at the *Star* strive to turn the newspaper into a "navigational tool" for readers using their telephones to gain access to the *Star*'s new audio system. "We're turning this technology over to the newsroom," says Scott Whiteside, until recently the *Star*'s vice-president for new product development. "We've told them, 'You have the privilege of redefining journalism. Nobody has done this before.'"

After decades of wringing their hands about the coming of the Information Age but doing little about it, newspaper executives are embarking on the "reinvention" of the daily newspaper—the newest buzzword in industry circles. They have been frightened into doing so by the persistence of their circulation problems, by setbacks in their fight to keep the Bell companies out of the information delivery business, and by the depth of the recession, which has sped the collapse of the industry's retail advertising base.

Gannett's "News 2000" program is a case in point. Editors of local Gannett newspapers are quite literally remolding their beat structures and newsroom organization to respond to perceived reader interests. The just-implemented program is part of Gannett's effort to encourage its local newspapers to pay greater attention to community issues. At the Gannett-owned daily in Olympia, Washington, for example, editors have replaced traditional beats with "hot topic" teams, slapped limits on story length and jumps, added extensive reader service lists, and replaced some reporters with news assistants who gather "news-you-can-use" data from local agencies.

EXPERIMENTING WITH ONLINE NEWS

Gannett has taken its cue from the trend-setting *Orange County Register,* which shook up newspaper traditionalists two years ago with its switch to reader-friendly beats like "malls" and "car culture," and from Knight-Ridder's experimental newspaper in Boca Raton, Florida, with its test-marketed formula of news nuggets, pastel hues, multiple graphics, and reader-grabbing features.

Newspapers are also experimenting once again with electronic videotext systems. Many journalists thought videotext was dead when Knight-Ridder shut down its pioneering Viewtron program in the mid-1980s because it couldn't sign up enough subscribers (see "What Zapped the Electronic Newspaper?" *CJR,* May/June 1987). These days newspapers in Albuquerque and Fort Worth are making a go of modest, low-investment videotext systems that give readers access to electronically archived material that can't be fitted into the daily newshole. At the same time, newspapers in Denver and Omaha shut down more elaborate and expensive videotext experiments, saying there was not yet a market for videotext in their cities. Meanwhile, newspaper executives are watching (nervously, in many cases) as new computer developments point toward the time when today's newspaper, television, computers, and the telephone will be blended into a single multimedia instrument.

Futurists say that all this is just the Information Age finally catching up with newspapers. Paul Saffo, a research fellow at the Institute for the Future in Menlo Park, California, argues that paper is becoming outmoded as computers become society's principal way of storing data. "We'll become paperless like we became horseless," he says. "There are still horses. But little girls ride them."

Amid all the flailing about as newspapers prepare for an uncertain tomorrow, three general strategies can be discerned: efforts to save the newspaper as it is, efforts to augment the newspaper electronically, and efforts to look beyond the newspaper-on-print.

THE FUTURE OF THE NEWSPAPER-AS-IT-IS

In recent years, front pages with more "points-of-entry" and "scannable" news, marketing programs developed in tandem with the news department, and "news-you-can-use" and reader-written features have proliferated. And yet there is no evidence that the focus on readers—and the fixation on marketing and packaging and redesigns associated with it—has done anything to improve newspapers' prospects. Indeed, even the industry's own consultants now caution against expecting circulation growth from redesigns or the adoption of reader-driven marketing formulas.

James Batten, the chairman of Knight-Ridder, a chain known for the high quality of its journalism, launched what he called a "customer-obsession" campaign, an important part of which was the redesigned *Boca Raton News.* It showed initial circulation jumps. However, last summer the *News* dismissed two circulation managers after their departments allegedly overstated the newspaper's paid circulation—a sign of the pressure the newspaper is feeling to show results for Knight-Ridder.

Today's editors, says Susan Miller, Scripps Howard's vice-president/editorial, have come to believe that reader-driven newspapering can be a "higher calling." The vast majority of staffers are becoming accustomed to the idea that "newspapers are to be of service to readers and are not staffed by a Brahmin class that was chosen to lecture the population." Miller says, adding, "People who refuse to be service-oriented will leave in disgust and say we're pandering and will call us bad names—but they will leave."

THINNING THE RANKS OF MIDDLE MANAGEMENT

Bill Walker, a former *Sacramento Bee* reporter, is one who left. In a piece titled "Why I Quit" in the *San Francisco Bay Guardian,* he wrote:

> "Nowadays, editors spend their days taking meetings in glass offices, emerging only to issue reporters instructions like this: "Get me a 12-inch A1 box on the city's reaction to the tragedy. Talk to teachers, kids, the mayor, the bishop. Focus on the shock, the sadness, the brave determination to move

on. And don't forget the homeless. We've got color art from the shelter." Meanwhile, the promotions director is already producing a cheery drive-time radio spot to plug the story. . . . We used to have a saying: no matter how bad journalism was, it beat selling insurance for a living. But no more.

Miller, for her part, predicts that the economics of the industry will lead to a thinning of the ranks of mid-level management. At many organizations those ranks were swollen as newspapers put more emphasis on the planning and packaging of the news product. Miller thinks that the leaner newsroom of the future will mean that more power will be placed in the hands of front-line troops. Bill Baker, Knight-Ridder's vice-president/news, says that the emphasis newspaper companies will be putting on innovation will make entrepreneurial thinking in the newsroom more valued. He adds that several new information products being developed by "The Edge of Knight-Ridder," an internal product-development program, were created by veteran reporters who have "the appetite to follow through on them."

Still, newspaper managers may find it difficult to abandon the traditional hierarchy or change their ways of thinking. Publishers oriented to the bottom-line and newspaper managers who made their way up in a safe, monopolistic environment tend to be wary of creative risk-taking. The temptation to hire another consultant, order up another readership survey, or let an industry organization do their thinking for them will, in most cases, win out over coming up with their own ideas and then investing in them.

BEEFING IT UP ELECTRONICALLY

Newspapers are making a marginal profit at best in their efforts to find an audience that wants access to an electronic menu of items like restaurant and movie reviews, expanded news stories, sports scores, advance classified ads, business news, and public records. The most popular form of access has been telephone info-lines, and newspapers like the *Kansas City Star* are integrating them into the full operation of the newspaper. Videotext systems are still considered risky, but even editors at newspapers that have abandoned videotext agree that the market for electronic newspapering is growing.

That's certainly the way Gerry Barker, marketing director for the *Fort Worth Star-Telegram*'s "Startext" electronic information service, sees it. "The generation coming out of school who are very computer-oriented—these are the readers of tomorrow," Barker says. "People have misjudged it. It's a social revolution that's happening out there. You can't throw dollars and technology at this and expect it to hatch. It's evolutionary. Just because we built a few Edsels doesn't mean the car is wrong."

Many analysts attribute the failure of early videotext efforts to the attempt by newspapers to transfer the newspaper-on-print too literally onto the computer. "The newspaper's approach to news has to change in order to be successful in transmitting information electronically," says Richard Baker, director of corporate communication for CompuServe, a twenty-two-year-old computer communications company with more than 900,000 customers. "Newspapers and magazines have to embrace the concept of sharing the creation of the news. There needs to be a willingness and openness to let the readers have a much greater hand in determining what's the news." Baker adds that the key to CompuServe's success is the development of customized information and interactive "bulletin boards."

The pressure on newspapers to become all-service information companies has grown recently as the newspaper industry has lost court efforts to keep the telephone companies out of the electronic information business. The experience of the French Minitel system, which gives telephone users in France access to telephone directories and a variety of interactive and communications services via mini-computers, is seen as the model for how U.S. telephone companies may use their monopoly powers to move in on newspapers' most lucrative business. Yet everything ultimately argues for a partnership between newspapers and the telephone companies—and that may already be happening. For example, the *Seattle Times* (whose publisher, Frank Blethen, has been one of the vocal critics of the Baby Bells) recently announced that the *Times* was negotiating to team up with US West to be a data provider on the telephone company's information network.

THE PAPERLESS NEWSPAPER

With the coming developments in electronic data delivery, many newspaper futurists believe the newspaper-on-print faces a perilous future. They say videotext operations and the new computer pagination systems—by means of which newspaper pages are fully designed and laid out on the computer screen—are simply crude, first steps toward the multimedia systems that will come to dominate the information industry. In software systems that are already on the market, computer users can pull from the computer's memory a variety of audio-visual material—including printed text, mobile graphics, video images, music, special effects—which let users create their own multimedia productions.

These developments—combined with the advances in computer-transmitted television—present enormous implications for both newspapers and broadcasters. Digital broadcasting—by means of which images are transmitted in a code used by computers—promises to provide a truly multimedia system that will allow text, graphics, and video images to be transmitted to the computer screen. It doesn't take a rocket scientist to see how this development will increase the pressures to blend the now-separate media forms, and companies in the U.S. and Japan have been hurrying digital technology to the marketplace much faster than many predicted.

Many communications conglomerates, now integrated across newspaper and broadcast divisions, are well structured to take advantage of those developments. Knight-Ridder officials are planning for the day (which they see happening within this decade) when these multimedia newspapers will be available on portable, touch-sensitive, flat-panel displays.

BRAVE NEW INFORMATION WORLD

Roger Fidler, the director of new media development for Knight-Ridder, predicts a "bright future" for the "essence" of the newspaper. "I don't see print disappearing," he says. "But I see it taking a different form. The question is not whether there will be newspapers in the next century, but who will publish them. I'm not convinced the majority of the newspaper companies today will be in business in the next century."

So what will it be like to be a journalist in the brave new information world? The minimalistic journalism brought about by reader-friendly newspapering has done much to turn news into just another commodity in the marketplace. And as newspapers join the electronic competition, newspaper journalists are likely to find themselves ever more subject to the forces of technological change, the demands of perpetually updating the news for electronic services, and the pressure to think of their work in marketing terms.

As with many other professions in the go-go 1980s, marketing and the bottom-line have become the by-words of newspapering, and new information technologies offer much to encourage that trend. In the years ahead, newspaper companies—and newspaper professionals—can probably expect to bump up and down on a rocky ride of diminished profit margins, failed efforts at experimentation, and intrusions into their markets.

REASONS TO BE OPTIMISTIC

That's the potential dark side. But there are also reasons to be optimistic. The endless newshole promised by computers does offer an answer to the ever-shrinking news columns—and could hold hope for journalists frustrated by the design gimmicks that have increasingly circumscribed the work life of those who produce the text. Newspapers have always been at the base of the information pyramid, providing much of the in-depth information that is then compressed and marketed by the electronic information purveyors. As the explosion of information continues, there will be even more need for highly skilled journalists to root through it, filter out what's important, and help put it into perspective. The demand for more specialty reporting skills, the opportunities for more creative and analytical writing, and the chance to use data bases to do more sophisticated investigative reporting are all potential upsides of electronic newspapering.

Newspaper journalists should also take heart from the fact that virtually none of those who gaze into the future are predicting the near-term demise of the newspaper-on-print. Technology, so far, has been unable to match the efficient way the eye can scan the newspaper page or the way a newspaper can be folded up and carried around—or the way it can be read while breakfasting over coffee and bagels on a Sunday morning.

Newspapers understand their local, or their specialty, markets. And they can offer an intelligent voice in a world where the cacophony of other media seems to be drowning the public in noise it doesn't want to hear. "There are things about a newspaper that are attuned to the human spirit," says Bill Baker of Knight-Ridder, "and it'll be there forever."

4

The Age of Multimedia and Turbonews

JIM WILLIS

Editor's Note: When news and information come in huge quantities and bewildering varieties, our ability to understand what's really going on is severely tested. Multimedia communication and the virtual workplace may profoundly alter the way we work in the decades ahead. We will get more information faster, and from more sources, than ever before, and we will have more to cope with, as media formats change and knowledge gaps grow, all requiring new skills and thought processes.

We will need new electronic literacy training to sort all the new media in our minds and not be overwhelmed by them. One problem will be to maintain our own identities in the welter of images, personalities, and messages. Another will be to remain broad and general enough to maintain normal relationships rather than become so specialized that we cannot communicate with our families and neighbors and friends.

Jim Willis is the Hardin Professor of Journalism at the University of Memphis and former chair of the Communication Department at Boston University. This article is reprinted by permission from *The Futurist,* September-October 1995.

What will society look like under the evolving institutions of interactive multimedia technologies, which are still in their infancy? One probable—if not inevitable—change resulting from advances in communications has to do with the nature of news: The media will transform both the message and what we do with it.

Turbonews is a term I coined to describe the vast masses of news and information that can now reach us at the speed of light. Rapid technological changes are occurring in mass communication, and media executives resemble drivers at the start of an Indy car race, rushing to jump-start their turbonews vehicles and push them onto the infobahn.

Turbonews is the result of these advances now being embraced by very new and different media. The birth and development of fiber optics, communication satellites, and CD-ROM technology will have far wider impacts on journalism than even television had. In fact, there is a definite sort of B.C./A.D. turning point represented here: *before computers* and *after disks.*

To be sure, the twentieth century has seen other important advances in technologies that affect the mass media. The past three decades have seen advances in newsgathering and processing technologies ranging from offset presses to electronic newsgathering equipment and satellite news vans. Why make such a bold statement about this latest round of technical wizardry? Because up to now, the changes all went together to produce the same *forms* of news product: either an ink-on-paper, hard-copy journal or a strictly electronic program. The latest round of changes promises a *new* multimedia format with characteristics of both print and electronic media. Another important difference is that print and television journalism produce information for mass audiences, while the new media de-massify—even personalize—information consumption.

CHANGING MEDIA FORMATS

By changing media formats, we change the way information is gathered, presented, processed, and quite possibly the way consumers are affected by it. For instance, with the turbonews-gathering process of *online* newspapers and magazines, the reporter is working under a more immediate deadline, much the same as the live television correspondent does. But accuracy and speed mix about as well as oil and water. The history of journalism is littered with examples of stories that would have been great if only they had been true. Unfortunately, with the advent of turbonews and real-time reporting, and the rush to create a medium that is instantly accessible by users, accuracy can suffer greatly.

Commenting on the effect that television's live coverage of the Gulf War was having on Americans, ABC television's media analyst Jeff Greenfield wrote in 1991:

> We watch almost hypnotically . . . and yet we watch with a growing sense of frustration, a hunger to hear every fragment of information linked with the knowledge that much of what we learn we will unlearn in the next half hour.

With turbonews, you take a product like a newspaper or magazine that relies on linear thinking and transmogrify it into what is essentially a nonlinear video program, such as the newsmagazines have experimented with via their CD-ROM versions, complete with video boxes and narrators. Turbonews thus imitates television in trying to deliver the text-image-sound-all-at-once experience. Yes, there are still words on the screen that could conceivably be read and printed out in the user's own home. But the use (and therefore success) of multimedia services often rises and falls on the video, graphics, and quality of color, speed, and movement of each.

THE KNOWLEDGE GAP

The new information media may actually be making us dumber. Communication theorist Marshall McLuhan warned that television is helping to destroy literacy. Turbonews could make things worse.

The power of CD-ROMs to store massive amounts of information and the hyperspeed ability of fiber-optic technology to deliver all this to the user is astounding. We *could* become a much more learned and informed society if we took advantage of all this information. But the average American now spends less than half an hour a day reading a newspaper. Will people really go to the trouble of accessing the vast amounts of information that may become available instantaneously in the years ahead? The gap between the knowledge available and the knowledge assimilated might actually increase instead of decrease.

Some observers conclude that, despite what information overload can do to us, having more information is better than having less. Others are not so sure.

Another widening knowledge gap—that between the haves and have-nots—is the result of the rising cost of accessing information. Television used to be free; now viewers must pay to subscribe to most of the channels. Users must also pay to subscribe to online databases such as Prodigy and CompuServe. Nexis and Lexis cost even more, and search time for most databases is very expensive. The average magazine sells for $3 or more, and even the daily newspaper costs 50¢. People with less income will likely receive much less information than people with higher incomes.

Each of these parallel gaps—income and knowledge—will increasingly exacerbate the other. A rising diffusion of information in a society will lead to increasing knowledge gaps among individuals who live in different socioeconomic sectors of society. Social groups occupying lower-strata positions may gain information, but not as fast as those people in higher-strata groups. Therefore, the predictive element here is socioeconomic class: The richer classes will be able to receive more information than the poorer classes.

THINKING SKILLS IN THE AGE OF TURBONEWS

The new media forms will also affect traditional critical thinking skills. In the pre-television era, when the print media were the dominant vehicle for news, information, and entertainment, one set of critical thinking skills was needed. Many assumed it was the only kind needed. It was a time when we could read the assertions of writers and take time to evaluate them for their veracity. The same was true in print advertising: Claims could be made, and we could sit and ponder their logic. Telling the difference between truth and lies has never been an easy matter, but it did seem easier when we were reading claims instead of being subjected to a multitude of fleeting images—many having a screen life of only a few seconds, or even fractions of seconds.

The kind of information media that people use exerts a strong influence on the type of education that society should be providing—if part of education's goal is to help students discern truth from lies. Television analyst Neil Postman writes:

> If, for example, we were living in a culture where all forms of important public discourse were a product of the printing press, and an oratory rooted in the printed word, then it would make sense to educate our students in logic, rhetoric, and semantics, and leave it at that.

He adds, however, that this type of education—while still useful—is inadequate to meet the needs that the age of turbonews has thrust upon us. We need electronic literacy for the electronic age.

ELECTRONIC LITERACY

Such electronic literacy training would provide insight into the ways and means television uses to create imagery and substantiate its assertions. Its purpose would be to provide a kind of behind-the-scenes look at how video images are made, much like an English teacher might diagram a sentence to show students its various components. It would be like showing how a magician performs tricks. The point of this training would be to demystify what seems to be a startling end result. Simply watching television doesn't provide this insight any more than watching a skillful magician shows audiences that what they see isn't really magic at all.

Such literacy training might also provide insight into the ways in which moving sights and sounds connect with our senses and how that is different from a more linear connection.

For example, Michael Deaver, media aide to former President Ronald Reagan, has explained how he manipulated the visual messages coming out of the White House. Deaver was in charge of providing the president's photo opportunities to the media on a daily basis. These photo ops were carefully created to present pleasing images of the president, and often they were used to counter-balance negative stories about him.

One example was when the day's news was going to be that housing starts were down nationwide. To counteract that, he arranged for Reagan to fly to Fort Worth, Texas, and walk through a new home that was being constructed. Television followed dutifully and matched that video with the reporter's story about housing starts. Even though the audio portion of the story was that housing was in a slump, what viewers saw was President Reagan touring a home under construction. The viewers may have heard the story, but what they saw was more powerful. Thus, the impression left in many minds was, "Hmm, housing starts must be up." Deaver concludes, "In the battle between the eye and the ear, the eye wins every time."

That is why educating students in a new kind of literacy—and new kind of critical thinking skills—is so important. Every election year, viewers choose their officeholders more on the basis of manipulated and carefully crafted visual imagery than on a more substantive basis. Postman recommends that students get a course in *media ecology,* which would focus on how the media control the form, distribution, and direction of information and thus the cognitive and behavioral patterns of viewers.

TURBO-CONSCIOUSNESS

Still another possible effect of the new media is what psychologist Kenneth J. Gergen has called *postmodern consciousness.* He uses this concept to describe the syndrome of Americans who are so bombarded with a multitude of media images, personalities, and relationships that they have trouble hanging on to their own personal identity and recognizing the authenticity of traditional reason and emotions.

Gergen believes the driving force behind postmodernism is technology— notably communication technologies "that shower us with social relationships both direct and vicarious." Included in these technological applications are the telephone, radio, television, motion pictures, mass publication, photo-copier, cassette recordings, CDs, satellite transmission, the VCR, computer, fax, and mobile telephone. These technologies give us instant access to the world at large.

"No longer is our social existence tied to a small town, a suburban community, or an urban neighborhood," Gergen warns. "Rather, as we wake to *Good Morning, America,* read the papers, listen to radio talk shows, . . . answer faxes and electronic mail, . . . take an evening graze through cable-TV channels, we consume and are consumed by a social world of unbounded proportion. We are exposed to more opinions, values, personalities, and ways of life than was any previous generation in history. . . . There is, in short, an explosion in social connection."

That explosion could result in the splintering of the self. For instance, Gergen and others warn that we could see the collapse of a centered self as the mass media must accommodate multiple audiences. A man in today's environment must simultaneously demonstrate professional responsibility, soft and romantic sensitivity, macho toughness, and family dedication; he must have expertise in sports, politics, software, the stock market, mechanics, food, and wine; he must have a circle of friends, a fitness program, the right CDs, interesting vacation plans, and an impressive car.

On the other hand, these expanding technologies also offer a large possibility for positive human development, Gergen points out. Women today have many strong role models depicted in the media that did not exist a half century ago. Some images are true and some are false, but at least there are more for women to choose from.

GLOBAL VILLAGE OR TOWER OF BABEL?

Will multimedia and turbonews give us the global village that Marshall McLuhan and his co-author Harold Innis envisioned would result from the growth and spread of television? Ideas and values would become more uniform as Western programming invaded other cultures and, over time, brought them in line with Western values and behavior. It would be a world shrunk by a ubiquitous medium that delivered a more uniform type of cultural language and set of values through popular programming and informational content.

On the other hand, communication technologies may create a Tower of Babel in which everyone, instead of speaking the same cultural language, is speaking radically different languages and pursuing radically different interests. This scenario can already be seen in magazines, which have moved from general-interest, mass-circulation to narrow-interest, small-circulation products.

This specialization, which began in earnest in the 1970s, has led to a plethora of magazines targeted at thousands of special interests and tastes, most of which are very narrowly defined. And the "de-massing" trend has been emulated by cable television and other media.

Someday soon, a typical family could come together around the dinner table, fresh from perusing distinctly different magazines and CD-ROMS, watching distinctively different cable-TV channels and videos, and conversing with e-friends on the Internet. And they will have absolutely nothing in common to talk about.

ADDITIONAL RESOURCES FOR PART I

Suggested Questions and Discussion Topics

1. According to "The Growing Power of Mass Media" by Ray Hiebert, the mass media are getting more powerful, but are they getting better? Discuss both sides of this question.

2. For one week, keep a diary of your mass media activities. List each thing you read everyday, each television program you watch, each radio program or sound recording you listen to, movie you attend, and the amount of time you devote to these activities each day. Write a brief essay comparing your media activities with others you know—your friends, parents, younger brothers and sisters, and so on. Draw some conclusions from your analysis.

3. In "The New TV: Stop Making Sense," what does the author, Mitchell Stephens, mean by "stop making sense"?

4. From "The New TV: Stop Making Sense," discuss two or three examples of the "new TV" already in existence.

5. In "Identity Crisis of Newspapers," why is the author, Doug Underwood, optimistic about the future of newspapers? Do you agree with him?

6. "Identity Crisis of Newspapers," considers how newspapers are changing to allow for more "reader-friendly" journalism. Give three examples of how this new type of journalism has changed content.

7. According to "The Age of Multimedia and Turbonews" by Jim Willis, what is the difference between the "global village" and the "tower of Babel"?

8. In "The Age of Multimedia and Turbonews," why does the author suggest that "turbonews" might be damaging to literacy?

Suggested Readings

J. Herbert Altshull, *Agents of Power.* New York: Longman, 1984.

William Barbour, ed., *Mass Media: Opposing Viewpoints.* San Diego, CA: Greenhaven Press, 1994.

W. Lance Bennett, *The Politics of Illusion,* 3rd ed. New York: Longman, 1996.

Daniel J. Czitrom, *Media and the American Mind: From Morse to McLuhan.* Chapel Hill, NC: University of North Carolina Press, 1982.

Ray E. Hiebert, Donald Ungurait, and Thomas Bohn, *Mass Media: An Introduction to Modern Communication,* 6th ed. New York: Longman, 1991.

Douglas Kellner, *Television and the Crisis of Democracy.* Boulder, CO: Westview, 1995.

Matthew Robert Kerbel, *Remote and Controlled.* Boulder, CO: Westview, 1990.

Dennis W. Mazzocco, *Networks of Power: Corporate TV's Threat to Democracy.* Boston: South End Press, 1994.

Marshall McLuhan, *Understanding Media: The Extensions of Man.* New York: McGraw-Hill, 1964.

Michael Parenti, *Inventing Reality: The Politics of News Media.* New York: St. Martin's Press, 1993.

Suggested Videos

"The Development of Mass Communication." New York: Insight Media, 1989. (26 minutes)

"The History of Mass Media." New York: Insight Media, 1997. (30 minutes)

"Newer Alternative Media, 1994." New York: Insight Media. (20 minutes)

"The Functions of Mass Communication." New York: Insight Media, 1989. (26 minutes)

"Mass Communication Versus Mass Media." New York: Insight Media, 1996. (99 minutes)

"The News Media Under Fire." New York: Insight Media, 1997. (15 minutes)

"Creating Critical Viewers." New York: Insight Media, 1992. (77 minutes)

"Tuning Into Media: Literacy for the Information Age." New York: Insight Media, 1993. (30 minutes)

"Signal to Noise: Life with Television." New York: Insight Media, 1996. (three volumes, 60 minutes each)

PART · 2

Mass Media and
a Changing World

Much has been made of the role mass media have played in the political changes that have occurred worldwide in the past few years. George P. Shultz, former secretary of state, told a Stanford student audience in 1990 that the recent dramatic upheaval in the Eastern bloc was a byproduct of the emergence of the information revolution. The world is changing rapidly and we are living in a new age, Shultz said: "I think it's been apparent for quite some time that the more open and more free [political] system works better [than a closed totalitarian system such as Soviet communism]. It works better from a moral standpoint, and it works better from an economic standpoint. But there has emerged over a period of time, and I think with increasing force in the 1980s, the information revolution, a change in the nature of how things work."

Shultz noted how the all-news cable television network, CNN, was readily available throughout much of the world and brought world events to a global audience: "Information goes around so readily that by now . . . whenever anything important happens anywhere, it is known about everywhere. When I traveled as Secretary of State . . . I would go to the Soviet Union and watch CNN. Go to China, and watch CNN. Go to our operations center for the State Department, which is a 24-hour, seven-day-a-week operation, and of course it's getting this huge flow, thousands and thousands of cables every day. But we also have on CNN."

Mass media recently played a key role in changing not only the totalitarian regime of the former Soviet empire but also many oppressive regimes in Africa, Asia, and Latin America and the apartheid policies of South Africa. But Eastern Europe has been the most striking example. Dana Braunova, a Czechoslovakian journalist, recalled the events as she watched them unfold:

> It all began [in Czechoslovakia] on November 20, 1989, when the non-party newspapers dared to denounce the brutal police attack on a student demonstration. Thus the "media revolt" got underway and Czechoslovakia's journalists began to report on events openly and honestly. It was not an easy job, especially for those working for hard-line directors in the state press, radio and TV agencies. Their determination proved to be decisive in communicating with the provincial population, since police had

taken steps to prevent the delivery of non-state newspapers outside Prague.

With the previously distorted TV and radio coverage, people outside the capital had no real knowledge of the situation in Prague, nor for the reasons for the students' strike and the subsequent rallies. This lack of information could well have isolated cities and towns and made it easy for the security forces to crush the movement for democracy and human rights.

In addition to the mass media, wall posters played a unique role in keeping information flowing. Distributed by students and opposition groups, the posters denounced police brutality and campaigned for human rights.[1]

Two days after the attack on students, nearly 400 journalists met in Prague, denounced police brutality, called for an investigation, rejected the monopoly of the Communist party, and called for a general strike. They then formed a syndicate of Czech journalists, the first nonpolitical journalistic organization in Czechoslovakia since the Communists had come to power.

What happened in Czechoslovakia was also taking place in Hungary, Poland, East Germany, Romania, Bulgaria, and the Soviet Union itself, all dramatically symbolized by the demolishment of the Berlin Wall. The forty-year Cold War had come to an end.

In 1989, Ted Koppel of ABC-TV produced a documentary called "Revolution in a Box." It showed how video cameras were being used to produce underground video news shows, which were then surreptitiously distributed to people eager to learn what was really going on in the closed society of communism. Koppel believed that the camcorder was democratizing the world because it was a tool of mass communication in the hands of ordinary people. It is no longer possible, in this new age of communication technology, said Koppel, for totalitarian regimes to exercise complete and absolute control over the lives of the people they rule. For if people can communicate, if they can get access to information, they can acquire control of their own lives.

Perhaps it is too early to tell whether Koppel's theory will continue to prevail. But the decade of the 1990s certainly started off in a way that would make us think he was right.

Since the early 1990s, however, when so many political changes took place, many of the mass media have become global conglomerates, raising a whole host of new issues for the new millennium.

NOTES

1. From *The Democratic Journalist,* as quoted in *Action,* January–February 1990, pp. 1–2.

5

The Global Media Giants

ROBERT W. McCHESNEY

Editor's Note: Mass media are becoming increasingly global empires with no national boundaries. In the past, most newspapers, radio stations, and television stations were owned locally and aimed at a local audience. Magazines began to become national media in the nineteenth century, as did the motion picture and sound-recording industries in the twentieth. Beginning in the late 1920s, broadcast networks began to establish national programs and audiences. In the 1980s, satellite transmission made newspapers such as *USA Today* into national—and even international—media; the same happened for broadcasting as well.

With these new technologies has come an increasing concentration of ownership. In the 1990s, international conglomerates of media companies are no longer bound by political ideologies or national orientation, only by the need to make a profit.

Robert W. McChesney is a professor in the School of Journalism and Mass Communication at the University of Wisconsin-Madison. This article is adapted from his book *The Global Media: The New Missionaries of Capitalism,* co-authored with Edward S. Herman (Cassell, 1997), and is reprinted with permission from *Extra! The Magazine of FAIR,* November/December 1997.

A specter now haunts the world: a global commercial media system dominated by a small number of super-powerful, mostly U.S.-based transnational media corporations. It is a system that works to advance the cause of the global market and promote commercial values, while denigrating journalism and culture not conducive to the immediate bottom line or long-run corporate interests. It is a disaster for anything but the most superficial notion of democracy—a democracy where, to paraphrase John Jay's maxim, those who own the world ought to govern it.

The global commercial system is a very recent development. Until the 1980s, media systems were generally national in scope. While there have been imports of books, films, music and TV shows for decades, the basic broadcasting systems and newspaper industries were domestically owned and regulated.

Beginning in the 1980s, pressure from the IMF, World Bank and U.S. government to deregulate and privatize media and communication systems coincided with new satellite and digital technologies, resulting in the rise of transnational media giants.

THE TOP FIVE

How quickly has the global media system emerged? The two largest media firms in the world, Time Warner and Disney, generated around 15 percent of their income outside of the United States in 1990. By 1997, that figure was in the 30 percent–35 percent range. Both firms expect to do a majority of their business abroad at some point in the next decade.

The global media system is now dominated by a first tier of nine giant firms. The five largest are Time Warner (1997 sales: $24 billion), Disney ($22 billion), Bertelsmann ($15 billion), Viacom ($13 billion), and Rupert Murdoch's News Corporation ($11 billion). Besides needing global scope to compete, the rules of thumb for global media giants are twofold: First, get bigger so you dominate markets and your competition can't buy you out. Firms like Disney and Time Warner have almost tripled in size this decade.

Second, have interests in numerous media industries, such as film production, book publishing, music, TV channels and networks, retail stores, amusement parks, magazines, newspapers and the like. The profit whole for the global media giant can be vastly greater than the sum of the media parts. A film, for example, should also generate a soundtrack, a book, and merchandise, and possibly spin-off TV shows, CD-ROMs, video games and amusement park rides. Firms that do not have conglomerated media holdings simply cannot compete in this market.

THE NEXT FOUR

The first tier is rounded out by TCI, the largest U.S. cable company that also has U.S. and global media holdings in scores of ventures too numerous to mention. The other three first-tier global media firms are all part of much larger industrial corporate powerhouses: General Electric (1997 sales: $80 billion), owner of NBC; Sony (1997 sales: $48 billion), owner of Columbia & TriStar Pictures and major recording interests; and Seagram (1997 sales: $14 billion), owner of Universal film and music interests. The media holdings of these last four firms do between $6 billion and $9 billion in business per year. While they are not as diverse as the media holdings of the first five global media giants, these four firms have global distribution and production in the areas where they compete. And firms like Sony and GE have the resources to make deals to get a lot bigger very quickly if they so desire.

Behind these firms is a second tier of some three or four dozen media firms that do between $1 billion and $8 billion per year in media-related business. These firms tend to have national or regional strongholds or to specialize in global niche markets. About one-half of them come from North America, including the likes of Westinghouse (CBS), the New York Times Co., Hearst, Comcast and Gannett. Most of the rest come from Europe, with a handful based in East Asia and Latin America.

FIFTY FIRMS WORLDWIDE

In short, the overwhelming majority (in revenue terms) of the world's film production, TV show production, cable channel ownership, cable and satellite system ownership, book publishing, magazine publishing and music production is provided by these 50 or so firms, and the first nine firms thoroughly dominate many of these sectors. By any standard of democracy, such a concentration of media power is troubling, if not unacceptable.

But that hardly explains how concentrated and uncompetitive this global media power actually is. In addition, these firms are all actively engaged in equity joint ventures where they share ownership of concerns with their "competitors" so as to reduce competition and risk. Each of the nine first-tier media giants, for example, has joint ventures with, on average, two-thirds of the other eight first-tier media giants. And the second tier is every bit as aggressive about making joint ventures.

LACK OF COMPETITION

Just how uncompetitive is the global media system? Consider the rampant use of equity joint ventures. Rupert Murdoch said it best when asked how he regards direct competition with one of the other giants when entering a new market: "We can join forces now, or we can kill each other and then join forces" (*Business Week*, 3/25/96). Murdoch and the other giants know there is only one rational choice.

To hear TCI major-domo John Malone, this is hardly the sort of ruthlessly competitive market that Milton Friedman and Jack Kemp lecture about. "Nobody can really afford to get mad at their competitors because they are partners in one area and competitors in another" (*Financial Times*, 5/28/96). And the largest media giants are also prime customers for each other.

NOT ENTIRELY NEGATIVE

In some ways, the emerging global commercial media system is not an entirely negative proposition. It occasionally promotes anti-racist, anti-sexist or anti-authoritarian messages that can be welcome in some of the more repressive corners of the world. But on balance the system has minimal interest in journalism or public affairs except for that which serves the business and upper-middle classes, and it privileges just a few lucrative genres that it can do quite well—like sports, light entertainment and action movies—over other fare. Even at its best the entire system is saturated by a hyper-commercialism, a veritable commercial carpetbombing of every aspect of human life. As the C.E.O. of Westinghouse put it, "We are here to serve advertisers. That is our *raison d'etre*." (*Advertising Age*, 2/3/97).

Some once posited that the rise of the Internet would eliminate the monopoly power of the global media giants. Such talk has declined recently as the largest media, telecommunication and computer firms have done everything within their immense powers to colonize the Internet, or at least neutralize its threat. The global media cartel may be evolving into a global communication cartel.

LITTLE PUBLIC DEBATE

But the entire global media and communication system is still in flux. While we are probably not too far from crystallization, there will likely be considerable merger and joint venture activity in the coming years. Indeed, by the time you read this, there may already be some shifts in who owns what or whom.

What is tragic is that this entire process of global media concentration has taken place with little public debate, especially in the U.S., despite the clear implications for politics and culture. After World War II, the Allies restricted media concentration in occupied Germany and Japan because they noted that such concentration promoted anti-democratic, even fascist, political cultures. It may be time for the United States and everyone else to take a dose of that medicine. But for that to happen will require concerted effort to educate and organize people around media issues. That is the task before us.

6

Global Mass Media Empires

CARL BERNSTEIN

Editor's Note: American mass media, especially the entertainment media, have become global industries, changing both those who consume
their products and those who create them. American mass media, for example, now get 85 percent of the world's revenue from pay-TV, 75 percent from television, 55 percent from home videos, 55 percent from
movies, 50 percent from sound recordings, and 35 percent from book
sales.

In European theaters, 70 percent of box-office receipts are for
American films. In India, half of all film imports come from the United
States. In Peru, 90 percent of all films shown are American. In Japan,
American movies produce long lines of customers at the movie theaters.

In television, U.S.-made movie videos bring in $1.9 billion from
abroad. In Europe, two-thirds of all programming is American. European
syndication of U.S. shows such as *Dallas* earned $1 billion in 1990.

The United States also dominates the sound-recording markets of
the world even though American recording firms lose more than $30
million annually to pirates. Michael Jackson's recording of "Bad" sold
135,000 copies in India alone.

Carl Bernstein, formerly an editor at *Time,* was a reporter at the
Washington Post when he and Robert Woodward made journalistic history by uncovering the Watergate scandal during the Nixon administration. Before joining *Time,* he was a broadcast executive at ABC. This article appeared in *Time,* December 24, 1990.

Just outside Tokyo 300,000 people troop through Japan's Disneyland each
week, while 20 miles outside Paris a new city is rising on 8 sq. mi. of formerly
vacant land. Once Euro Disney Resort opens for business in 1992, forget the
Eiffel Tower, the Swiss Alps and the Sistine Chapel: it is expected to be the
biggest tourist attraction in all of Europe. In Brazil as many as 70% of the
songs played on the radio each night are in English. In Bombay's thriving theater district, Neil Simon's plays are among the most popular. Last spring a
half-dozen American authors were on the Italian best-seller list. So far this
year, American films (mostly action-adventure epics like *Die Hard 2* and *The
Terminator*) have captured some 70% of the European gate.

America is saturating the world with its myths, its fantasies, its tunes and dreams. At a moment of deep self-doubt at home, American entertainment products—movies, records, books, theme parks, sports, cartoons, television shows—are projecting an imperial self-confidence across the globe. Entertainment is America's second biggest net export (behind aerospace), bringing in a trade surplus of more than $5 billion a year. American entertainment rang up some $300 billion in sales last year, of which an estimated 20% came from abroad. By the year 2000, half of the revenues from American movies and records will be earned in foreign countries.

IMPLICATIONS OF GLOBAL MEDIA

But the implications of the American entertainment conquest extend well beyond economics. As the age of the military superpowers ends, the U.S., with no planning or premeditation by its government, is emerging as the driving cultural force around the world, and will probably remain so through the next century. The Evil Empire has fallen. The Leisure Empire strikes back.

"What we are observing," says Federal Reserve Board Chairman Alan Greenspan, "is the increasing leisure hours of people moving increasingly toward entertainment. What they are doing with their time is consuming entertainment—American entertainment—all over the industrialized world."

For most of the postwar era, hard, tangible American products were the measure of U.S. economic success in the world. Today culture may be the country's most important product, the real source of both its economic power and its political influence in the world. "It's not about a number, though the number is unexpectedly huge," says Merrill Lynch's Harold Vogel, author of the 1990 book *Entertainment Industry Economics.* "It is about an economic state of mind that today is dominated by entertainment."

What is the universal appeal of American entertainment? Scale, spectacle, technical excellence, for sure: *Godfather Part III. Batman.* The unexpected, a highly developed style of the outrageous, a gift for vulgarity that borders on the visionary: a Mötley Crüe concert, for example, with the drummer stripped down to his leather jockstrap, flailing away from a calliope riding across the rafters of the Meadowlands Arena in New Jersey. Driving plots, story lines and narrative: a Tom Clancy hero or one of Elmore Leonard's misfits. Indiana Jones strength of character, self-reliance, a certain coarseness, a restless energy as American as Emerson and Whitman.

"People love fairy tales," observes Czech-born director Milos Forman, "and there is no country that does them better than the United States—whatever kind of fairy tales, not only princesses and happy endings. Every child dreams to be a prince: every adult has a secret closet dream to be Rambo and kill your enemy, regardless if it's your boss or communists or whoever."

Donald Richie, the dean of arts critics in Japan, sees a broader appeal. "The image of America radiates unlimited freedom, democracy, a home of the people," says Richie. "This certainly appeals to the Japanese, who live in a very controlled, authoritarian society." Jack Valenti, president of the Motion Picture Association of America, concurs, arguing that American entertainment—particularly movies, television and rock—was a primary catalyst in the collapse of communism in Europe and the Soviet Union.

On a recent visit to China, David Black, the supervising producer for *Law & Order,* watched young Chinese sell bootleg copies of Chuck Berry and Jerry Lee Lewis tapes in Shanghai. "In Hollywood," says Black, "we are selling them the ultimate luxury: the fact that people don't have to live the life they're born into. They can be a cowboy, a detective, Fred Astaire—and that's what America is selling now. The hell with cars. Cars are just wheels and gears. People want to be able to play at being other people more than they want transportation."

ADULATION OF GLOBAL STARS

The process exacts a spiritual cost. At work sometimes in the iconography of American popular culture is a complex nostalgia for the lost American soul. Madonna is not Monroe, Stallone is not Billy Wilder. But they are cultural forces with an authority and resonance uniquely American. Such gilded presences radiate signals of material success and excess on a scale heretofore unknown in popular entertainment. Perhaps more important, their influence—as models for imitation, objects of media attention—far outweighs that of the traditional heroes and heroines in what may have been an earlier and more accomplished age. The very adulation that the global stars receive simultaneously diminishes and trivializes them, as if they were mere image and electricity.

Money, lavish production, the big-budget blockbusters that only the American movie studios are willing to finance—these are part of the appeal. And of course the newness of it all, whether in music or film or TV. Only in the U.S. does popular culture undergo almost seasonal rituals of renewal.

Giovanni Agnelli, the Italian automobile industrialist, adds another factor: quality. "What is unique about American movies and popular music and television?" asks Agnelli. "They are better made; we cannot match their excellence."

Nor, it seems, can anyone else on the world stage right now. Matsushita's purchase of MCA, like Sony's ownership of CBS Records and Columbia Pictures, signals a recognition of the value of integrating the yin and the yang of leisure economics, the hardware of VCRs and DAT and the software of music and programming. "Our entertainment is the one thing the Japanese can't make better or cheaper than us," says David Geffen, the largest single shareholder in the recent MCA-Matsushita deal. "That's why they are buying in. But they will have zero influence in the product. Companies don't decide what gets made; the content of American entertainment is inspirationally motivated."

Michael Eisner, chairman of Walt Disney Co., and other industry executives argue that the unique character of American entertainment is the result of the polyglot nature of the society itself—and the clash of cultures and races and traditions within it. The U.S. is the only country in the world with such a heterogeneous mix, uniquely able to invent rap music, Disney World, Las Vegas, rock 'n' roll, Hulk Hogan, Hollywood and Stephen King.

INFATUATION WITH ENTERTAINMENT

A whole school of traditional economists is worried, however, that infatuation with the entertainment business and its glitzy success is symptomatic of a self-indulgent, spendthrift society deep into self-deceit. "The pre-eminence of entertainment is illusory success," warns Allen Lenz, economist for the Chemical Manufacturers Association. "It's no substitute for manufacturing. We need balance in our economy, not just the goods of instant gratification. The future of America is not in Michael Jackson records, $130 Reeboks and *Die Hard 2*. The fact is, you can't make it on Mickey Mouse."

Or can you? Disney's Eisner is part of a powerful cadre of modern-day Hollywood moguls who have acquired what their predecessors only hoped to have: real global power—economic, social, political.

They exercise it through their stewardship of global entertainment conglomerates in the midst of a communications revolution that has changed the nature of the world. Eisner, Fox's Rupert Murdoch, Paramount's Martin Davis, Steve Ross of Time Warner (which owns the parent company of *Time*), Ted Turner of Turner Communications, record executive Geffen, superagent Michael Ovitz and others have an astonishing influence on what the world sees, hears, reads and thinks about.

"The most important megatrend of the century is the availability of free time," maintains Italian Foreign Minister Gianni De Michelis, who is working on a book about the new dynamics of global economy. "This is the reason the U.S. will remain the most important economy in the world—because its GNP is increasingly geared to entertainment, communications, education and health care, all of which are about individuals 'feeling well,' as opposed to the 19th century concept of services intended to protect the workplace and production."

De Michelis' notion illustrates another aspect of today's entertainment business: the lines between entertainment, communications, education and information are increasingly blurred, and the modern U.S. entertainment company is uniquely positioned to provide software in all four areas.

ENTERTAINMENT AS MULTIPLIER

Just as the auto industry determines the basic health and output of a host of other industries (steel, plastics, rubber), the American entertainment business has become a driving force behind other key segments of the country's economy. As a result of this so-called multiplier effect, the products and profits of dozens of U.S. industries are umbilically tied to American entertainment: fast food, communications technology, sportswear, toys and games, sporting goods, advertising, travel, consumer electronics and so on. And the underlying strength of the American economy, many economists believe, has a lot to do with the tie-in of such businesses to the continued growth and world dominance of the American entertainment business and the popular culture that it exports.

"The role of entertainment as a multiplier is probably as great as, or greater than, any other industry's," observes Charles Waite, chief of the U.S. Census Bureau of Economic Programs. "Unfortunately, there's no exact way to measure its effect." But if the American entertainment industry's boundaries were drawn broadly enough to include all or most of its related businesses, some economists believe, it could be credited with generating more than $500 billion a year in sales.

Though the business is increasingly global, the domestic entertainment industry is still the backbone, and it is still thriving. The enormous profits of the '80s are being reduced by the recession. But the amount of time and money the average postadolescent American spends in the thrall of entertainment remains astounding: 40 hours and $30 a week, if industry statistics are to be believed. By the time U.S. culture goes overseas, it has been tried, tested and usually proved successful at home.

Americans this year will spend some $35 billion on records, audio- and videotapes and CDs, almost as much as they will spend on Japanese hardware manufactured to play them. In the air-conditioned Nevada desert, the opening of two gargantuan amusement centers dedicated to gambling and show business—the Mirage and Excalibur hotels—is leading Las Vegas toward its biggest year ever. In Nashville the country-music business is keeping the local economy afloat amid a tide of regional recession. Felix Rohatyn, the fiscal doctor, says the only hope for New York City, laid low by the collapse of the boom-boom Wall Street economy of the '80s, is to turn it into a tourist attraction keyed to entertainment. But the industry is also undergoing profound change in its essential financial and cultural dynamic: moving toward the European and Asian customer as a major source of revenue while moving away from American network television as the creative and economic magnet. *Rambo III* earned $55 million at home but $105 million abroad.

Another effect of globalization: rather than waiting months or years before being released outside the country, American movies and television programs are beginning to enter the foreign marketplace in their infancy and even at birth—and boosting profits. Universal opened *Back to the Future II* in the U.S., Europe and Japan simultaneously. The film made more than $300 million, and the receipts were available months earlier than usual, accruing millions of dollars in interest.

PROTECTIONIST MEASURES

The pervasive American presence is producing a spate of protectionist measures around the world, despite vigorous protests by American trade negotiators. The 12 members of the European Community recently adopted regulations requiring that a majority of all television programs broadcast in Europe be made there "whenever practicable."

Leading the resistance to the American invasion has been France and its Culture Minister, Jack Lang, a longtime Yankee basher who has proclaimed, "Our destiny is not to become the vassals of an immense empire of profit."

Spurred by Lang, who has gone so far as to appoint a rock-'n'-roll minister to encourage French rockers, non-French programming is limited to 40% of available air time on the state-run radio stations. But even Alain Finkelkraut, the highbrow French essayist and critic who is no friend of pop culture, concedes, "As painful as it may be for the French to bear, their rock stars just don't have the same appeal as the British or the Americans. Claude François can't compete with the Rolling Stones."

In Africa, American films are watched in American-style drive-in theaters to the accompaniment of hamburgers and fries, washed down with Coca-Cola. One of the biggest cultural events in Kenya in recent weeks has been the national disco-dancing championships. But in Nairobi last month, two dozen representatives of cultural organizations held a seminar on "Cultural Industry for East and Central Africa" and concluded that something must be done to roll back Western (primarily American) dominance of cinema, television, music and dance. "Our governments must adopt conscious policies to stop the dazzle of Western culture from creeping up on us," Tafataona Mahoso, director of the National Arts Council of Zimbabwe, told the gathering.

In Japan too, where the influence of American entertainment is pervasive, the misgivings are growing. "Younger people are forgetting their native culture in favor of adopting American culture," says Hisao Kanaseki, professor of American literature at Tokyo's Komazawa University. "They're not going to see No theater or Kabuki theater. They're only interested in American civilization. Young people here have stopped reading their own literature."

Though movie admissions cost about $12 in Japan, customers seem willing to pay that to stand in the aisles for American films. "To the Japanese, American movies are hip and trendy, and Japanese audiences would rather die than be unfashionable," says William Ireton, managing director of Warner Bros. Japan.

Aside from the Islamic world, where laws based on fundamentalist strictures often forbid access to *any* entertainment, there seem to be very few places where that is not the case. Even in secular Iraq, teenagers jam the half a dozen or so little shops in downtown Baghdad that sell pirated copies of American rock-'n'-roll tapes and where the walls are covered with posters of Madonna and Metallica.

GOODWILL TOWARD AMERICA

The exponential growth of the American entertainment industry since the late 1970s has taken place in an era of extraordinary affection and goodwill toward the U.S. in the industrialized world. In Europe, Asia and even Latin America, anti-Americanism is lower than at any time since the Vietnam War. The phenomenon is in part self-fulfilling: to a large extent that goodwill can be traced to the projection of America as seen through its popular culture rather than to the nation's actual political or social character. If anything, there is an increasing dissonance between what America really is and what it projects itself to be through its movies and music.

"Even in Nicaragua, when we were beating their asses in the most horrible way, they had this residual love for us," observes author William Styron, who visited the country during the *contra* war. "They love us for our culture, our books, our heroes, our baseball players, our sports figures, our comic strips, our movies, everything. They had this consummate hatred of Reagan, but underneath was enormous love and affection for us as a kind of Arcadia."

The American entertainment business captures much that is appealing, exuberant—and excessive—about the American character. The fantasies and limitless imaginations of Americans are a big part of who they are. It is also, ironically, the source of America's moral authority. For it is in the country's popular culture—movies, music, thrillers, cartoons, Cosby—that the popular arts perpetuate the mythology of an America that to a large extent no longer exists: idealistic, rebellious, efficient, egalitarian. In the boom time of their popular culture, Americans have found new ways to merchandise their mythologies. This is what America manufactures in the twilight of the Reagan era.

Christopher Lasch, the social historian who wrote *The Culture of Narcissism,* sees the development of an entertainment-oriented economy as the final triumph of style over substance in the U.S. Lasch believes the most singular American psychological characteristic—the desire for drama, escape and fantasy—has come to dominate not only American culture and politics but even its commerce. "It's all of a piece. Its effect is the enormous trivialization of cultural goods. Everything becomes entertainment: news, political commentary, cultural analysis," he says. "The most significant thing about the process is that it abolishes all cultural distinctions, good and bad, high and low. It all becomes the same, and therefore all equally evanescent and ultimately meaningless."

IMPERIALISM OF AMERICAN POPCULT

Is the imperialism of American popcult smothering other cultures, destroying artistic variety and authenticity around the world to make way for the gaudy American mass synthetic? "It's a horrible experience to go to the most beautiful place in the world only to turn on *Crossfire,*" says Leon Wieselthier, the literary editor of the *New Republic.*

"I've always felt that the export of our vulgarity is the hallmark of our greatness," says Styron, who lived for many years in Paris and whose books always sell well in France. "I don't necessarily mean to be derogatory. The Europeans have always been fascinated by wanting to know what's going on with this big, ogreish subcontinent across the Atlantic, this potentially dangerous, constantly mysterious country called the U.S. of A." American popular culture fills a vacuum, vulgar or not. "French television is a wasteland: ours is a madhouse. But at least it's vital," says Styron. "*Dallas* and *Knots Landing* and the American game shows are filling a need in France."

Susan Sontag, whose 1964 essay *Notes on "Camp"* broke new ground in interpreting American popular culture, expresses doubt that the vitality of European culture will be extinguished by America's onslaught. "The cultural infrastructure is still there," she says, noting that great bookstores continue to proliferate in Europe. Rather than regarding Americans as cultural imperialists, she observes wryly, "many Europeans have an almost colonialist attitude toward us. We provide them with wonderful distractions, the feeling of diversion. Perhaps Europeans will eventually view us as a wonderfully advanced Third World country with a lot of rhythm—a kind of pleasure country, so cheap with the dollar down and all that singing and dancing and TV."

HOW LONG WILL IT LAST?

How long will the American cultural hegemony last? "I think we are living in a quasi-Hellenistic period," says Chilean philosopher Claudio Veliz, a visiting professor of cultural history at Boston University, who is writing a book on the subject.

"In 413 B.C., Athens ceased to be a world power, and yet for the next 300 years. Greek culture, the culture of Athens, became the culture of the world." Much as the Greek language was the lingua franca of the world, Veliz sees the American version of English in the same role. "The reason Greek culture was so popular is very simple: the people liked it. People liked to dress like the Greeks, to build their buildings like the Greeks. They liked to practice sports like the Greeks; they liked to live like the Greeks. Yet there were no Greek armies forcing them to do it. They simply wanted to be like the Greeks."

If America's epoch is to last, the underlying character of American culture must remain true to itself as it is pulled toward a common global denominator by its entertainment engine. But danger signals are already present: too few movies characterized by nuance, or even good old American nuttiness; more and more disco-dance epics, sickly sweet romances and shoot-'em-up, cut-'em-up, blow-'em-up Schwarzenegger characters: rock 'n' roll that never gets beyond heavy breathing and head banging; blockbuster books that read like T shirts. The combination of the foreign marketplace and a young domestic audience nourished on TV sitcoms, soaps and MTV may be deadly.

The strength of American pop culture has always been in its originality and genuineness: Jimmy Stewart and Bruce Springsteen, *West Side Story* and *The Graduate,* Raymond Chandler and Ray Charles, the Beach Boys and Howdy Doody, James Dean and Janis Joplin. It would be a terrible irony if what America does best—celebrate its own imagination—becomes debased and homogenized by consumers merely hungry for anything labeled MADE IN THE U.S.A.

Another American century seems assured, though far different from the one now rusting out in the heartland. The question is, Will it be the real thing?

7

Video Killed the Red Star

Dave Rimmer

Editor's Note: Mass media have had a profound impact on the Soviet and post-Soviet world. Communist media were completely controlled by the Communist Party, and they were very effective in keeping society under the thumb of the old Soviet system. Western media have sometimes been given some credit for the breakup of the old system, as information leaped over the Iron Curtain in the form of international broadcasts, such as Voice of America and Radio Free Europe, and smuggled rock-and-roll records and video recordings.

Post-Soviet society has embraced much of Western mass media, and one of the most popular exports has been MTV. In fact, MTV has sometimes been given credit for creating a whole new culture in Central and Eastern Europe as well as in many other parts of the world.

A longer version of this article originally appeared in the *Guardian Weekend* magazine in the United Kingdom. This version is reprinted with permission from *Budapest Week*, August 26–September 1, 1993.

Checking into my room at the Savoy Hotel, Moscow, one of 164,208 European hotel rooms which offer the service, I thumb the button for MTV: some music while unpacking. It feels too quiet without it, the squeaky-clean five-star hush that money can buy in any major city.

Outside, it's another world. The streets swarm and bustle with all the chaos, desperation and excitement of radical change. Having caught a few glimpses on the way from the airport—flashes through the car window like pictures on a screen—I'm itching to get out and explore. The Lubyanka's round the corner, Red Square just a stroll away.

On the TV, images slide one into another: black women dancing in an alley, fingers on guitar strings, speeded up cityscape, audience reaction in solarized slo-mo. Video jockeys prattle before animated backdrops that hold the eye even as the words fly by the ear. A sponsor's logo cuts into a station ID Endings segue neatly into beginnings. Time passes in an eddying stream. Half an hour later, I realize I'm still watching. Anyone who's ever tuned into the pop video channel will recognize its mesmerizing effect. But today it's not just that which is holding me to the screen. I'm alone in a strange and slightly scary city. MTV, by contrast, is composed of familiar rhythms, familiar faces—such as those of the Pet Shop Boys, who will be arriving later at this same hotel. At one point there's a news item on Berlin's Love Parade, the annual techno house carnival along the Ku'damm, in which I'd participated the previous weekend. At that moment, MTV-land seems more my world than the city around me might ever be.

I am here, however, to cover the opening of MTV Russia: a point where the two worlds come together.

A NON-STOP YOUTH CHANNEL

The following night is one for the connoisseur of the bizarre media event. In an indoor arena of the Moscow Olympic complex that these days houses a disco for the young and *nouveau riche,* beneath a giant letter M styled in simulated lumber (a smaller T and V in pseudo-folkloric red and gold), hemmed in by a mad crush of camera-toting media representatives, four men are pretending to saw through a log.

Two of them are in business suits: William Roedy, Managing Director and CEO of MTV Europe, and Boris Zosimov, CEO and President of Biz Enterprises, the Russian media and entertainment company which has negotiated rights to syndicate a weekly 43 hours of MTV programming on Russian network television.

The other two are in bright yellow and blue costumes with tall pointed hats and look like they've just stepped from the pages of a Marvel comic. These are Pet Shop Boys Chris Lowe and Neil Tennant and their being here, dressed like this, is part of what Tennant caricatures as their "ruthless promotional strategy."

Sawing back and forth, stiff and awkward, the pair struggle to keep straight faces as their tall hats threaten to dislodge. Given the task at hand, they couldn't have been more impractically dressed, but that, of course, is the point of the exercise.

"I've always said," Tennant comments later, "that if you're going to make a fool of yourself, then do it in front of as large an audience as possible."

The log is quickly cloven. Applause and the flashing of cameras. The crowd surges behind the foursome as they pass beneath the M.

"MTV Music Television," a voice booms forth, "a non-stop youth channel for the global village reaching over 200 million homes in over 70 countries, including 45 million in Europe alone . . ."

THE MOST YOUNG VIEWERS IN EUROPE

Through the arch is MTV-land. Fake palm trees with fairy lights flank a stage waiting for the night's performances. The cavernous hall is festooned with sponsor logos, including an inflatable cola bottle the size of an ICBM. The voice thunders on.

"No channel in Europe has more 16–34-year-old viewers than MTV. Since MTV launched in 1987, the MTV logo has become the national flag of young Europeans."

MTV's U2 weekend is playing in the Savoy bar as William Roedy and I meet the next morning for coffee. A West Point graduate who always kept the television on while doing his homework, Roedy once commanded an American nuclear missile base and speaks of "launching" MTV in Eastern Europe "very actively and aggressively."

Russia is the last domino to fall. Ever since finding cable distribution in Hungary well in advance of the collapse of communism, MTV has been riding the waves of change in Eastern Europe.

"It culminated for me personally," says Roedy, "in hooking up MTV in East Berlin in November of '89, coincidentally, and within an hour the Politburo resigned and within 48 hours the Wall came down."

ENDING THE COLD WAR

He will happily claim some of the credit for MTV. "It probably played a very significant part in ending the Cold War. It is a window on the west which came to represent the free flow of expression. When we went into what was the Eastern bloc we found people already knew about us from pirating."

But in another version of history, the introduction of MTV by dying communist regimes was nothing but a failed attempt to placate dangerous aspirations that were already bubbling up—rather like the way they all organized elections only to get booted out. McDonald's hamburgers preceded MTV to both Hungary and Moscow. In a Europe that is both breaking up at one level and coalescing on another, the spread of youth culture and satellite media is just one part of an inexorable process.

And Russia is just the latest deal. Biz Enterprises is paying MTV hard currency for syndication rights (a one-year agreement, with an option on a further two) and aim to turn their own profit by inserting local advertising. Blocks of MTV programming will go out on various Moscow channels and, though at first only for two hours a week, nationally to 88 million households full of potential soft drink consumers and record buyers.

Looked at another way, a possible 210 million viewers, weaned on the bald over-simplifications of state propaganda, can now drink deep of the capitalist media's complex ambiguities. Bye bye, Big Brother and pass the soma. Forget history, give us Greatest Hits.

IMAGES PER MINUTE

Roedy smiles when I get on to the question of what a procession of three-minute videos with an IPM (images per minute) faster than the average advertisement does to the attention span.

"There's a wonderful new concept called twitch time. Have you heard of this? This is fun. Twitch time refers to the delayed hand reaction for, whatever, a video game, a PC or a remote control for a TV. For someone like myself it can be anywhere from 30 seconds to ten minutes. For someone who's five or seven years old," he snaps his fingers, "they're like that. It's not really short attention span. It's the ability to consume more information quicker. It's progress. It's the future."

But what about the nature and quality of that information? MTV has an occasional campaign which says "Feed your head, read books." Yet by so expertly marketing a format which ditches narrative and leaves little scope for rationality, MTV is in the vanguard of those cultural trends which lead away from literacy.

"I'm probably a bad example, but I'm a television junkie. When I'm home I never have the TV off. It's always on. Yet I am a compulsive reader. Compulsive. I read probably . . . oh, at least two or three newspapers a day. I read stacks of magazines. I try to read books . . ."

Does he read with the television on?

"Always. Always with the television on."

Hanging round in the dollar world of the hotel lobby, waiting to venture into the rouble world outside, the Pet Shop Boys and I are scanning the daily *Moscow Times.* On the back page, above an ad for (American) Smirnoff vodka, there's an interview with Wim Wenders, in town for the Moscow Film Festival.

"If you think back 10 or even 20 years," I read Wenders saying, "you'll realize the incredible influence images have today on our lives. We're all dealing with too much imagery trying to get our attention. And we don't have that much attention left.

MEDIA "BOOTLEGACY"

"Movies already look very much like publicity," [Wenders] continues. "The idea of selling has entered almost all areas, so images that were not intended to sell us anything in the beginning are now being used more and more to sell things. Not only products but also ideologies. Especially here in Russia and the former Soviet Union, the idea of images selling ideologies has been heavily pushed forward."

Chris Lowe waves his copy at me.

"Hey, this newspaper's free. Why isn't *The Guardian* free?"

Why aren't Pet Shop Boys records free?

"Actually," says Neil Tennant, "they are, here."

The Pet Shop Boys are popular in Russia—hence their invitation to perform the ceremonial log-sawing. On the street outside are some fans who've travelled all the way from Latvia, just to catch a glimpse. But there's a clause in their contract with EMI about "third countries." Russia is one and Brazil another.

"You don't get any money from them," says Tennant, "and unfortunately we're huge in all of them."

Later, in the crowded and appallingly tatty state-owned Melodia record shop on Kalinin Avenue, I get a sense of why. There's a long list of CDs, posted on four sides of a pillar. Although an intellectual property law was passed by the Russian parliament only the day before, people can still come in with a 90-minute cassette, hand over 1,000 roubles (today, about a dollar), and have them tape the two albums of your choice.

There's a long dissertation about this "bootlegacy" in the brochure Boris Zosimov hands me when I call round at Biz Enterprises for an interview. "As long as Russian bootleggers are making billions of roubles," he says, "Russian companies that do respect copyrights will remain the injured parties, even though they didn't create the problem."

Zosimov's office is tiny, with a rattling fan and curtains stitched from US and Soviet flags. But, dressed in Versace with a handful of gold discs on the wall next to a picture of him receiving a medal from Yeltsin, this former Komsomol employee and son of "a big government guy" looks anything but the injured party. Copyright he may respect, but as Zosimov guides me through a diagram of the network of 13 companies he owns—management, record companies, concert promotion, merchandising, music publishing, magazine publishing, TV—it becomes clear that, by Western standards, some of his other business practices are a little irregular.

Examining the sleeve of a double album heavy metal compilation he shows me, I seek some clarification. So Zosimov has released a record on his own label entirely of bands he also publishes and manages?

He shrugs. "I know, I know. It's forbidden all over the world. Except Russia." Later, a little sheepishly, he asks my advice. Would he really run into legal problems? I tell him about conflict of interest. He decides that, should the law change, he will give up management. Meanwhile, he demonstrates a perfect understanding of vertical integration.

"On MTV I have my own time and I will definitely promote my own products. If I will not sell, let's say, all minutes, or maybe if I need to sell this record again, I will promote this record, like a commercial."

If MTV's initial one-year deal with Zosimov looks a little cautious, this is probably the explanation. The first few days of MTV on Moscow television were notable for the frequent appearance of the Biz Enterprises logo.

"My dream is a Time-Warner." Zosimov concludes. "Somebody, somewhere started Time-Warner, so why not start one here?"

THERE IS ANOTHER LIFE

At one point Zosimov produces a brochure for his new magazine, *Imperial.* This is aimed at "the new social class" in Russia "who have potential and financial income to become a new aristocracy." Among its promised attractions are details of how to open a Swiss bank account.

At another point he remembers when he left the Komsomol. "One day I said I couldn't handle it. During the day I lived one way of life, working in this terrible Komsomol—you will never understand it—and during the night I had friends, parties, girls, all this music. It became a nightmare for myself. I was living two lives."

And later, expressing some clearly genuine enthusiasm at the prospect of Russian MTV: "When the kids and the people will see a really quality product, they will say, 'My God, there is another music, there is another life.'"

THE POWER OF VIDEO

"It's another world here," sings Neil Tennant on "The Theatre," a track on the forthcoming Pet Shop Boys album, *Very.* "Below shop windows, on the pavement . . ." It's a song about the homeless in London's West End—"the bums you step over as you leave the theatre." But retitle it Savoy Hotel, rejig the lyrics a little, and it could just as easily be set in central Moscow.

Tennant and I make several sorties into the surrounding streets. Everywhere are piles of discarded banana skins. People stand around trying to sell individual items: a bottle of vodka, some fruit, a street atlas. Crossing back from the Children's World department store, where everything is dirt cheap but involves queuing four times—as opposed to the hotel, where all is easily available, yet extortionate—we see a man with a bag being chased by another with murder in his eyes. At first it looks like the first guy stole the second guy's bag. Then we learn that the second guy was mafia, and the first was trying to sell on the street without paying for his pitch.

One afternoon, in a long, smelly underpass, we pause to listen to a string quintet. The music is sad and beautiful. The musicians, who've obviously all spent years in some academy, are in tatty, filthy denims. It's a poignant contrast: the pop star here to open MTV Russia, the highly-trained classical players busking for hyperinflatory roubles.

Everywhere we are trailed by the Latvian fans. In the small McDonald's on Tsverskaya, we buy them all Big Macs. Behind the counter are scores of workers. One of them recognizes Tennant and then order breaks down completely as they all start waving napkins to be autographed, looking for proof that this creature from the MTV world has truly landed here among them.

It's a small measure of the power of video that while Tennant gets spotted, Lowe—who always wears hat and sunglasses in any photo or video—can, bareheaded, slip in and out of the hotel unnoticed, go for rides on the Metro, visit the city baths, and never get bothered at all.

Another morning at the Savoy and MTV's U2 weekend continues remorselessly as Tennant and I meet for breakfast. There is footage of one of U2's Zooropa concerts (an MTV viewer from Warsaw has won a competition to videotape them live on stage), in which the band play before a huge battery of video monitors sputtering irksome slogans and a restless, baffling montage of imagery. This has been sold as an "ironic comment" on the media age but ends up simply replicating all the most irritating aspects of contemporary culture. It's distracting, confusing, overwhelming.

VIDEO-FED EXPECTATIONS

Here's another measure of video power. Go to any large concert these days and you'll probably end up watching, not the band, but some kind of giant monitor. These are usually used for a mix of performance close-ups and other imagery the band have commissioned to make their stage show more interesting. For an audience with video-fed expectations, the fleshy charisma of a group and their instruments is rarely enough any more. And for the artists who make those videos, being photogenic is at least as important as the ability to sing, dance or play.

"There's plenty of great singers in the world," shrugs Tennant, "but if an artist is a great singer and songwriter and doesn't know what else to do, it's very, very difficult to make it work."

In the late '70s and early '80s, a fundamental shift occurred in the workings of the pop industry. In Tennant's opinion: "There's not a record company in London that can find an artist, get her or him the songs, put together the image—this classic, manipulative thing record companies are always supposed to do—sell it to the public and have a huge success. A record company has to have a management team or the band themselves, as in our case, which comes to them with the whole package and plonks it down on the table. The record company fronts the money, like a bank, but also acts as a distribution and marketing company. But you have to give them the marketing tools to work with as well."

This is a truth that stretches all the way from Malcolm McLaren with the Sex Pistols to, say, Clive Davis of Arista choosing songs for Whitney Houston. Sometimes artists hire consultants, like U2 with Brian Eno.

"It's a Hollywood star system way of doing things," reflects Tennant, "which, to be fair, when it works, produces stars. I happen to like stars."

And MTV?

"It's the shop window."

DIGITAL MONEY

For all but the very hugest of celebrities, it's impossible to make any money from video. Tennant, when I ask him, doesn't even know if he gets royalties from MTV. "I'm sure we do get paid something and I'm sure it's probably not very much." (An MTV press officer later confirms that the sum per play is "pennies. Most people ask us how much artists pay us," she says.) The 22 videos Pet Shop Boys have made since 1985—each costing around $5,000–60,000—represent an investment on which they will never see any direct financial return.

In business terms, for the artist, a video is a promotion for a pop single and a single a promotion for an album. In America MTV played two videos off the Pet Shops' first album, *Please.* It sold a million. Then they played three off the next one, *Actually.* It sold another million. Only one was shown from *Introspective.* It sold 600,000. That was in 1988. Since then MTV America has not shown one Pet Shop Boys video and sales of the 1990 album, *Behaviour,* dipped to 250,000.

In the UK, with its lively domestic pop media and only three million households connected to MTV (even Belgium has more), video is not so important—although the recent Pet Shop Boys' "Top Of The Pops" performance of "Can You Forgive Her?" was essentially a kind of video done live.

"It's fair to say that now we make videos for MTV Europe and MTV America, in the vague hope that MTV America will one day play one again," says Tennant "And MTV Europe—we're doing it for Germany."

Everything one now thinks of as the Pet Shop Boys—silent Chris walking two steps behind singing Neil and so on—stems from discussions the group had with photographer/videomaker Eric Watson at the very beginning of their career. For the latest round of material, though, they have tried something different. "One-dimensional" is the buzzword. No more mini costume dramas, no more Chris walking two steps behind. Their videos are no longer "about" anything. Instead there are simple shapes and strong colors, SF costumes in non-naturalistic computer-animated realities, an absence of narrative or personality. The current Pet Shop Boys image—and they don their costumes for any occasion involving cameras—is as abstract as the digital money that these days also flies from market to market by satellite.

INCESTUOUS MEDIA EVENTS

"It's quite interesting," says Tennant, "that with MTV you're going to get teenagers growing up in Russia with the same musical memories as teenagers growing up in Spain or Germany or England. If you think about what is the West, culturally it's a shared memory of famous people, music, film stars, automobiles and, now, I suppose, everyone using the same technology. There's a sense in which it's very medieval. Once again, Durham has the same culture as Rome. I mean, what I like about the EC is that it's the Holy Roman Empire all over again."

Where there was once the Catholic Church and the international language of Latin, now there are technological media and the international language of American English.

"I am an internationalist and I like to think that people in Durham and people in Rome, in theory at any rate, more or less have the same opportunities in the same way that a young novice might once have travelled from Rome to Durham because he was a Benedictine monk. But I always come back to the problem: what is the ideology that holds it all together?"

The work we're all doing in Moscow continues as one long incestuous media event. I interview MTV. MTV interviews me. I take notes about the photographer snapping an NBC crew filming an MTV crew filming Steve Blame doing a link for the MTV News about the launch, the towers of the Kremlin behind him. Moscow, in all this, is nothing but a backdrop. The colorful onion domes of St. Basil's Cathedral in Red Square—the one image that instantly says "Russia"—is used as a set for both MTV links and for part of the video for the next Pet Shop Boys single. "Go West."

TWO WORLDS COMING TOGETHER

Surrounded by a coachload of excited New Jersey schoolchildren who scream at the MTV logo but have never heard of Tennant and Lowe. I take more notes about the photographer now snapping the MTV crew filming director Howard Greenhaulgh filming the Pet Shop Boys standing there, a little self-conscious, in their yellow and blue costumes.

Around the edges of this bizarre crowd, a small boy—foxy-faced, ragged shorts—runs round trying to sell everyone a battered packet of postcards. No one has time to pay him any attention. Tears of desperation squeeze from the corners of his eyes. He's oblivious to it all, oblivious to anything but his own need for a bit of hard currency, in another world entirely.

A few days later, in Budapest, I go to the Burger King at Oktogon to watch the finished MTV news item. This is the largest Burger King in the world, successful as a place for teenagers to meet and eat. Not only does MTV play here all the time, but the whole decor—cheerful pastels, soft shapes, decorative dummies in designer sportswear—seems to have been fashioned in the style of the station.

The news item winks on. First an intro in front of St. Basil's, then another talking head, then me, billed as "music journalist," waxing glib about rock and Russia. Before I even recognize myself, a tableful of teenagers turns around pointing: "That's you! That's you!" Their excitement last only about five seconds, but for that brief instant of twitch time, their world and the MTV world have come, quite meaninglessly, together.

8

TV Once Again Unites
the World in Grief

TOM SHALES

Editor's Note: The funeral of Princess Diana in September 1997 was perhaps the most widely watched event in the history of mankind. More than 50 million Americans got up at an early hour on Saturday morning to tune in their television sets, and an estimated 1.2 billion were watching around the globe. Live television, says Tom Shales, united the world in a good cry. More important than the cry, however, was showing that the world can be a global village—given the right event—and that television alone can make it happen.

Shales characterizes the ceremony as dignified and the television coverage as mostly dignified, climaxing "a week of wallowing by the American networks that seemed excessive and often snide . . ." The press itself was the subject of much debate because many blamed Diana's death on the pursuit by the *paparazzi,* freelance photographers who chase celebrities to sell their photographs for high figures to the gossip-hungry tabloids—print and electronic alike. In the end, however, there might have been some redemption for the media through their impressive coverage of Diana's funeral.

For many years, Shales has been the television critic for the *Washington Post,* in which this article originally appeared on September 7, 1997. It is reprinted by permission.

If the whole world was watching, then the whole world was probably weeping, too. The globally televised funeral of Princess Diana could well rank as the most widely seen event in history—proving perhaps that nothing unites the world quite so effectively as grief.

Cameras showed people mourning in Hong Kong, in Canada, in Paris, and throughout the United States, a gathering via satellite in honor and memory of an internationally popular figure. Even watching at home, one felt like a participant in a story that now had achieved painful but definitive closure. Diana lived most of her adult life in the public eye, the heroine of a great nonfiction novel that now drew to a dramatic close.

And what a close—a combination of pageantry and intimacy, of grandiose spectacle and the close-ups of those who mourned her, whether similarly famous or merely part of the ever-peeping public.

All the American broadcast networks, even Fox, offered extensive coverage yesterday with big-name anchors like Dan Rather, Peter Jennings and Tom Brokaw signing on at 4 a.m. or earlier to report on events from London. Several cable channels had full-length coverage as well.

The British showed their customary aplomb at staging massive ceremonial occasions, and the American networks showed admirable and entirely uncharacteristic restraint in their approach, at least during the service from Westminster Abbey.

UP BEFORE DAWN

Before that, the anchors and reporters and as-yet-untold millions of viewers were up before dawn to watch the funeral procession make its way through London to the historic church. In addition to the broadcast networks and cable's CNN, which all aired most of the proceedings without commercials, viewers could see BBC coverage relayed by C-SPAN and by the Arts & Entertainment cable network, which rarely offers live news coverage of anything.

Pictures from inside Westminster Abbey, supplied by the BBC and ITN to American networks, were stunning, and many of the images inside and outside immensely poignant—especially a card inscribed simply "Mummy" that rested among white flowers at the head of the casket. This gesture from William and Harry, the sons of Diana, was in its way more moving than all the shots of tearful mourners huddled outside the church.

And yet for all the eloquence of what was shown, it was the speech given by Diana's brother, Charles, Earl Spencer, that was probably the most memorable part of the ceremony. It was hardly a typical eulogy, though it included such observations as "All over the world she was a symbol of selfless humanity, a standard-bearer of the rights of the downtrodden, a very British girl who transcended nationalities."

The more surprising portions were those referring to the tabloid press that hounded Diana, and criticism of the British royal family, whose faces were never shown inside the church, per their request to the British networks. Spencer said Diana never needed a title to prove her worth—her title was taken away from her upon her divorce from Prince Charles—and he made a vow to help protect her sons from the royals as well as from the press.

On the subject of paparazzi and England's trashy tabloid papers, he said of his dead sister, "I don't think she ever understood why her genuinely good intentions were sneered at by the media," and said he himself wondered "why there appeared to be a permanent quest on their behalf to bring her down."

KEEPING SILENT

Perhaps, he speculated, "genuine goodness is threatening to those at the opposite end of the moral spectrum." The eight-minute speech was impeccably delivered and prompted applause when it was over from those inside the church as well as those outside.

Rather, Jennings and Brokaw managed to keep silent through almost all of the service itself. They had plenty of other opportunities to talk, before and after, and had plenty of cohorts and experts on royalty to help them. Probably the most helpful was Jeffrey Archer on NBC, while the least helpful was also on NBC: New Yorker Editor Tina Brown, mumbly and aloof.

The dignified ceremony and mostly dignified coverage climaxed a week of wallowing by the American networks that seemed excessive and often snide, with lots of wild speculation about how the popularity of Diana was somehow going to destroy the British monarchy, if not what was left of the empire itself. Reporters appeared gleeful in passing along each new criticism of the royal family, including the preposterous idea that they should parade their grief in public as a way of somehow satisfying their critics.

UNCONTROLLABLE WEEPING

Reporters and commentators also tried to outdo one another in characterizing Diana as a Cinderella-like working-class waif with whom the lowly masses could identify, when in fact she was born into one of England's oldest aristocratic families.

Over and over, the British were castigated, essentially for having been insufficiently Americanized and for not following the new rules of emotional exhibitionism as dictated by Oprah Winfrey and Sally Jessy Raphael. When the queen made a nationally televised speech Friday, picked up by networks here, that quieted some of the clamor, reporters scoured the streets to find people who felt that this, too, was an insufficient display.

Apparently nothing less than uncontrollable weeping and the rending of garments would do.

ABC's coverage of the death of Diana began last Sunday with an incompatible trio on the screen: Jennings, Barbara Walters and Diane Sawyer. They all appeared to hate one another, and Sawyer had little of value to contribute. She was nowhere to be seen in ABC's London coverage yesterday; apparently Walters had won a strategic victory. It made ABC's broadcast better, though Walters came across at times as too gabbily gossipy for such a solemn occasion.

CLUTTERING THE SCREEN

Another odd touch by ABC: giving the screen over to stat sheets on certain of the participants when the time came for them to take part. These graphics were like baseball cards, or something out of "Wide World of Royalty." Tastelessly enough, Diana's older sister Sarah McCorquodale was identified with these phrases plastered on the screen: "Born 1955," "Former girlfriend of Prince Charles" and "Suffered from anorexia nervosa." And this while she read a poem in memory of her late sister.

Jennings had tacky moments as well—such as when he referred to the 97-year-old Queen Mother Elizabeth as "a genteel doddering aunt" ("genteel" was one of the most overused words of the day) or when he noted that the ceremony would not touch upon "the more reckless or darker side of Diana." It hadn't been touched upon all week (if it existed at all); why would it be brought up now?

NBC and CBS competed to see which network could clutter the screen with the largest number of graphics. NBC had a large blue box that said "Live" (or, later, "Recorded Earlier') in the upper left corner, plus the obnoxious peacock logo in the lower right, plus, sometimes, logos identifying the source of the video (Sky TV, for example) in the lower left.

CBS devoted almost the bottom third of the screen to its graphic "CBS News Live Coverage—Princess Diana's Funeral" along with some sort of ugly electronic bunting and not one but two representations of the trademark CBS Eye.

ADVERTISING, OF COURSE

The funeral of a cherished public figure hardly seems the time or place to advertise, but network promotion departments are almost vicious in their relentlessness.

Tom Brokaw and Katie Couric never quite seemed coordinated with one another on NBC, and Brokaw exhibited his usual impervious chilliness. Rather, on the other hand, is the anchor who's unafraid to get emotionally involved. His voice broke last Sunday when he concluded the special edition of "60 Minutes" devoted to Diana's death, and he appeared to be choking up again as he read closing comments yesterday morning, just before signing off at 10:58 a.m.

Among them:

"It is the nature of modern life that, by the time a great event has arrived, there is almost nothing left to be said about it. . . . What any American must say who has been here the past week is this: The great British people, who are more than allies to America, have been profoundly touched by the loss of their princess. Touched—and changed."

RACE FOR SIGNIFICANCE

At least these remarks seemed reasonable and not as hyperbolic as much of the commentary that aired on the networks during the days between the fatal car accident and the funeral. The race was to see who could attach the most extravagant social and political significance to the princess's death. When network newscasts ended their orgies of melodrama each night, tabloid shows like "Extra" and "American Journal" picked up the story and kept it going.

It was hard to tell the network newscasts from the tabloid tattlers.

As guests filed into Westminster Abbey before the service, cameras caught such superstars as Tom Hanks, Tom Cruise, Steven Spielberg and Sting, making this seem less a funeral for a princess than a gathering of pop stars. Singer George Michael wore a long frock coat, choosing to make a fashion statement at a memorial service. Elton John, who sang a rewritten version of "Candle in the Wind," was dressed, for him, relatively conservatively.

THE WHOLE WORLD IS CRYING

The simple point of the whole amazing international ordeal may be that the entire world felt it needed a good cry, and the ceremony and its coverage were certainly designed to inspire one. As John sang, the networks tried to turn his song into a music video, with misty shots of a happy Diana as people want to remember her. ABC News whipped up a new montage of Diana shots to conclude its coverage, accompanying them with emotionally charged orchestral music from, of all things, the film "Black Beauty." But corny as it may sound, it was strikingly well edited and quite effective.

One might have wondered as one watched, and watched, and watched, what alien beings from other worlds might have thought of the spectacle if they were watching, too. They might find it bizarre and outlandish. Or they might understand that someone much loved on her home planet had died and this is the way we global villagers convene, via television and satellite hookups, to demonstrate grief and affection.

It is impressive, and encouraging, that so many millions could stop and watch and listen in honor and memory of someone most of them had never met. Certainly it's one of the finer purposes to which the much-maligned and much-abused medium of television could ever be put.

ADDITIONAL RESOURCES FOR PART 2

Suggested Questions and Discussion Topics

1. According to Robert W. McChesney's "The Global Media Giants," who are these giants, and what do they have in common?
2. According to "The Global Media Giants," what role does competition play between these giants, and why?
3. From "Global Mass Media Empires" by Carl Bernstein, list six statistics that would support the idea that American mass media have become a global industry.
4. In "Global Mass Media Empires," the role of the U.S. entertainment industry as a "multiplier" is discussed. Explain how, and on what industries, this multiplier effect works.
5. From "Video Killed the Red Star" by Dave Rimmer, discuss the different perspectives presented on the role of MTV in the demise of the Soviet Union.

6. From "Video Killed the Red Star," discuss some of the differences pointed out between the market for television in Russia and in the United States.

7. From "TV Once Again Unites the World in Grief" by Tom Shales, discuss the way Shales characterizes the network news coverage of Princess Diana's funeral.

8. In "TV Once Again Unites the World in Grief," what did the author find good and what not so good about network coverage of Princess Diana's funeral?

Suggested Readings

Mark D. Alleyne, *News Revolution: Political and Economic Decisions About Global Information.* New York: St. Martin's Press, 1996.

John Downing, *Internationalizing Media Theory: Transition, Power, Culture: Reflections on Media in Russia, Poland, and Hungary, 1980–1995.* Thousand Oaks, CA: Sage Publications, 1996.

Howard H. Frederick, *Global Communications & International Relations.* Belmont, CA: Wadsworth, 1993.

Richard A. Gershon, *The Transnational Media Corporation: Global Messages and Free Market Competition.* Mahwah, NJ: Lawrence Erlbaum Associates, 1996.

Tomasz Goban-Klas, *The Orchestration of the Media.* Boulder, CO: Westview Press, 1994.

Peter Golding and Phil Harris, *Beyond Cultural Imperialism: Globalization, Communication, and the New International Order.* Thousand Oaks, CA: Sage Publications, 1997.

Cees J. Hamelink, *The Politics of World Communication.* Thousand Oaks, CA: Sage Publications, 1997.

Edward S. Herman and Robert W. McChesney, *The Global Media: The New Missionaries of Global Capitalism.* London: Cassell, 1997.

Carla Brooks Johnson, *Winning the Global TV News Game.* London: Focal Press, 1995.

John C. Merrill, *Global Journalism: Survey of International Communication,* 3rd ed. New York: Longman, 1995.

Hamid Mowlana, *Global Information and World Communication.* Thousand Oaks, CA: Sage Publications, 1997.

Dolores V. Tanno and Alberto Gonzalez, eds., *Communication and Identity Across Cultures.* Thousand Oaks, CA: Sage Publications, 1997.

Philip M. Taylor, *Global Communication, International Affairs, and the Media Since 1945.* London: Routledge, 1997.

Suggested Videos

Noam Chomsky and Edward Herman, "The Propaganda Model of News, Part One: The Filters of News; Part Two: Domestic Issues; Part Three: International Issues." Northampton, MA: Media Education Foundation, 1997. (60 minutes)

"Global Media." New York: Insight Media, 1997. (30 minutes)

"The Theories of the Press." New York: Insight Media, 1991. (25 minutes)

"The Dish Ran Away With the Spoon: U.S. TV in the Caribbean." New York: Insight Media, 1992. (60 minutes)

PART · 3

Mass Media and a Changing America

As we saw in the last section, mass media have played a powerful role in bringing about what appears to be a smaller world. But have mass media really made the world better for everyone?

Looking at the United States, many critics say that mass media are making America worse, not better. The particular villain is television, but motion pictures, advertising, slick magazines, cheap novels, and even daily newspapers are given a share of the blame as well.

Of course, we can ask the age-old question, who is really to blame? Is it the media themselves? Is it the owners, producers, directors, and editors—the so-called gatekeepers—of mass media? Is it the creative writers and artists and reporters? Is it the advertisers and PR firms who try to get their messages into mass media and to influence media for their own purposes? Is it lawmakers, who should be passing laws to bring about stricter control of mass media, or the government, which should be administering those laws? Or is it—some might say, God forbid!—the consumer, the mass majority, the great American audience that influences media content by its choices in the marketplace?

Many would say the ultimate responsibility rests with customers—readers, listeners, and viewers. They make their selections from a great variety of options; they can turn off the television or switch channels; they can choose from any number of newspapers, magazines, movies, radio programs, and books. They can also choose to avoid mass media; they can converse with family and friends, work in the garden, play games, or do aerobic exercises.

As we have pointed out, Americans spend more than half their leisure time on mass media, most of it mediocre fare. It is their choice. They are not required to do so, and there are plenty of other options.

When we examine what people choose when they have a free choice, the results are not particularly helpful. For example, the *National Enquirer,* a tabloid sold in supermarkets that deals mainly in sex, sleaze, gossip, half-truths, and total lies, sells about 20 million copies a week. *The New York Times* doesn't sell that many copies in a week of daily issues. In the Washington, D.C., area, for example, recent Audit Bureau of Circulations figures show the number of people who subscribe to each of the following publications:

National Enquirer	54,731
New Yorker	26,898
Soap Opera Digest	22,302
Scientific American	17,820
Weight Watchers	17,784
Guns & Ammo	9,688
Harper's	7,799

Perhaps children and the poor have fewer options, and studies show that these two population groups are most likely to spend the most time watching television—with disastrous results, according to some critics, especially for children, who are most vulnerable to the impressions they get from television.

Should the government exercise some degree of authority over children's television, in an otherwise free society, to protect the young? Many people think so. Others see such a move as an opening for government encroachment in all other areas of personal and civil liberties. For these people, the solution might better be family control, in which parents dictate what and how their children watch television and join with their children to help them interpret the fantasies and fictions of television from a normal point of view.

A problem here is that fewer and fewer households have parents at home during the early years of a child's life; more and more children are spending those most impressionable preschool years in day-care centers, where television is often used as an easy baby-sitter and pacifier.

A corollary problem is that adults themselves don't seem to have better taste than children. For example, studies show that adults are turning away from newspapers. Is this because they don't want factual reporting and intelligent analysis? Or are newspapers themselves trying too much to be glitzy products to keep up with television? One thing is sure: The power of the news media at the beginning of the 1990s seems to have declined considerably from the days when journalists exposed the scandal of Watergate and brought about the resignation of an American president.

9

So Many Media, So Little Time

RICHARD HARWOOD

Editor's Note: Americans spend more time on mass media than do people in most other societies. The average American spends 21 percent of his or her time working 31 percent sleeping, and 48 percent in other activities. Of these other activities, 78 percent is spent on mass media, or eight hours and fifty-two minutes per day. More than half of that media time, actually, 58 percent—is spent on television, not even including home videos.

Unfortunately, by far the largest percentage of our mass media time is devoted to entertainment, not information. News time and news audiences seem to be shrinking in America. Where will it all lead?

Richard Harwood is a long-time Washington journalist, columnist, and former ombudsman for the *Washington Post,* a job that required him to be the newspaper's conscience. This column was published in the *Washington Post* on September 2, 1992.

There are 8,760 hours in a 365-day year. Adolescents, according to the folklore, spend most of that time thinking or dreaming about sex. Adults have other, although not necessarily more interesting, demands on their time.

Adjusting for vacations, weekends, holidays and illness, the average full-time worker in the course of a year puts in about 1,824 hours at the job. Sleep, at $7\frac{1}{2}$ hours a night, accounts for 2,737 hours.

The largest share of our time, however, is claimed by the "media"—3,256 hours a year, or about nine hours a day. This estimate comes from Veronis, Suhler & Associates, a reputable investment banking house in New York, specializing in the communications industry.

Where does this "media" time go? These are the daily average calculations, based on the Veronis, Suhler data:

Television including cable: Four hours and nine minutes.
Radio including drive time: Three hours.
Recorded music: 36 minutes
Daily newspapers: 28 minutes.

Consumer books: 16 minutes.

Consumer magazines: 14 minutes.

Home video: Seven minutes.

Movies in theaters: Two minutes.

This is a big business, the nation's ninth largest, ranking just below aerospace and just above electronic equipment and its components. The adult consumers of all this amusement and information spent last year $108.8 billion on the "media"—about $353 per person. Advertisers spent another $80 billion to bring it to us.

RETHINKING JOURNALISM

Our lives and our economy are affected in many ways. The "media" are a great engine in our consumer society. They provide the jobs for hundreds of thousands of technicians, writers, artists, performers, intellectuals, pseudo-intellectuals and the orally accomplished. They shape our attitudes and beliefs and put pictures of the world into our heads.

We can't quantify those influences or rank them in any order of importance. Does rap music or the editorial page of the *New York Times* have greater impact on the minds of our youth? Which history of the assassination of John Kennedy is a greater popular "truth"—the Warren Commission report or the film *JFK?* Are "family values" more affected by speeches from George Bush and Dan Quayle or by TV sitcoms, soap operas, hillbilly music, Ann Landers and Oprah?

James Carey, dean of the College of Communication at the University of Illinois, ruminates on these questions in an essay published in the Kettering Review:

> We have inherited . . . a journalism of the expert and the conduit, a journalism of information, fact, objectivity and publicity. It is a scientific conception of journalism: it assumes an audience to be informed, educated by the journalist and the expert. . . . [But] today the most important parts of our culture are in the arts, in poetry, in political utopianism, in the humanities. . . . The [scientific] metaphor that has governed our understanding of journalism in this century has run into trouble. Neither journalism nor public life will move forward until we actually rethink, redescribe, and reinterpret what journalism is; not the science or information of our culture but its poetry and conversation.

WHAT THE MARKETPLACE SAYS

I'm not sure I understand what he is saying. Not all of us can or necessarily ought to be minstrels, poets, troubadours or conversationalists. But it is obvious from the Veronis, Suhler data that he is right in one sense—newspapers, books and magazines are now marginal claimants on our time and attention, occasional voices in the noise of the crowd. The marketplace is saying that other "media" occupy the large spaces in our lives.

It is also obvious that the politicians [in 1992]—Bill Clinton and Al Gore, in particular—understand that there may be more effective ways than an hour on *Meet the Press* to get into our heads and hearts. Clinton does a saxophone recital on the *Arsenio Hall Show.* Gore evokes Elvis Presley in his acceptance speech. Murphy Brown is the year's new political icon. Major Dad is summoned to certify the legitimacy of the president of the United States. The Walter Lippmanns and James Restons of journalism once commanded audiences with the great men of public affairs, men (and women) who now pander to Katie Couric and CNN.

UNDERSTANDING THE CHANGES

The Public Broadcasting Service, the most "scientific" and information-driven medium in the television wasteland, struggles against MTV and *Entertainment Tonight* to maintain a 2 percent share of the prime-time minutes. Its blood cousin, National Public Radio, attracts only 10,000 of the 2.5 million teenagers tuned in at any time to the radio spectrum. The audience erodes for the evening news as portrayed by the major networks. General Electric, owner of NBC, contemplates the sale of its money-losing news division to an independent syndicator. Newspapers remain profitable, but their audience share has declined steadily for three decades. The news magazines are reinventing themselves in fits and starts in an uncertain quest for greater relevance.

Our understanding of these changes is limited. The new media world was never planned; it came upon us largely through technological mutations and unforeseen opportunity. We don't know where it is headed, whether "journalism and public life will move forward" under its influence or will undergo greater trivialization.

The historical data from Veronis, Suhler contain a very faint suggestion that we are entering a withdrawal phase in our addiction to the media. We gave them 59 fewer hours of our time on Earth [in 1991] than in 1986. This may reflect more discriminating standards of consumption. On the other hand, it could be the cumulative result of these many years of sleep deprivation.

10

Tuning Out Traditional News

HOWARD KURTZ

Editor's Note: Audiences of mass communication have more information available than ever before in human history. Although choices in local daily newspapers are limited, there seems to be no limit on specialized daily and weekly newspapers and magazines for every special interest. The average American can listen to between thirty and forty different AM and FM radio stations, and the average American household with cable TV can receive forty to fifty—or more—different programs at any one time.

  Unfortunately, this doesn't seem to have made Americans more interested or more informed. Howard Kurtz says that many Americans have simply "tuned out" traditional news. Kurtz is a media reporter and critic for the *Washington Post,* where this article was originally published on May 15, 1995. It is reprinted with permission.

LUTHERVILLE, Md.—Elizabeth Yarbrough, a school cafeteria worker here, hadn't heard that Republicans in Congress want to end the federal school lunch program and turn it over to the states.

She doesn't know the name of her congressman. And she's "not real familiar" with the "Contract With America," which Republicans made the centerpiece of the first 100 days they controlled the House. She watches some television news and listens to Howard Stern, but buys the *Baltimore Sun* only on Sundays, for the want ads.

"I unfortunately don't pay much attention," said Yarbrough, 35. "I haven't seen any improvement of anything in this country for so long. It doesn't really matter who's in power. The little guy is just squashed like a bug."

It seems, on the surface, like a paradox. At a time when there are more media outlets providing more news and information than ever before, why is so little of it getting through to a sizable segment of the population?

The plain fact is that much of the American public has simply tuned out the news—that is, the kind of traditional news, heavily laden with politicians and official proceedings, routinely covered by the mainstream press. These people see journalists as messengers from a world that doesn't much interest them.

Some of the reasons for this disconnect emerged in a recent series of conversations here in the Baltimore suburbs. Some people say they are simply too busy with work and family to follow the news. Others are rather suspicious of the media. Still others see a depressing sameness to the drumbeat of headlines.

"If they'd put more happy stories in the news, I'd read it more," said Rhonda Burris, 28, a clerk for the Baltimore welfare department who also cleans offices at night. "It's usually someone got killed, someone's baby fell out the window. I don't want to hear it."

LACK OF INTEREST

Jean Langston, 44, an insurance claims examiner who often works a second job until midnight, is too busy to bother with newspapers. "I've bought papers and carried them around for three or four days and never gotten to it," she says.

Len Pross, 48, a letter carrier who likes talk radio, finds most news organizations slanted. "Too many news people want to be Rush Limbaughs," he says. "The news is chopped up into bits and pieces. You don't get a whole story."

Norman Brown, 51, a furniture salesman, says he is too busy for daily news reports—but he makes time for such programs as "The Oprah Winfrey Show" and "Geraldo!" "They have interesting topics, daughters running around with their mother's boyfriend. It's entertaining," he says.

Some of this lack of interest may stem from the way that media organizations define and package the news, news that many people find irrelevant to their daily lives. Some of it may involve a new generation of well-educated, well-compensated journalists who identify more with society's elite than with working-class Americans.

But much of it has to do with a growing sense of alienation from the political system, and the belief that the major media are an integral part of that system. Some of those interviewed say they are not angry at the press, but disgusted with what the press, in their eyes, represents.

"A vicious circle may be at work: cynical coverage tailored to a cynical public, which makes the public more cynical and begets more cynical coverage," Paul Starobin of the National Journal wrote recently in Columbia Journalism Review.

POLL HIGHLIGHTS

All this has contributed to a striking degree of ignorance about national affairs. According to recent polls for various news organizations:

- Only half of those surveyed could name Newt Gingrich as the speaker of the House, although 64 percent knew that Judge Lance Ito is presiding over the O.J. Simpson trial.
- Just four in 10 are familiar with the Republicans' Contract With America, despite an avalanche of publicity since the 1994 campaign.

- Only half know that Congress approved the North American Free Trade Agreement, one of the biggest political battles of the Clinton presidency.
- Only 24 percent said Congress has cut the federal budget deficit by billions of dollars; nearly half said it had not. Since Clinton took office the deficit has declined by nearly $100 billion.
- Just one in three said Congress had raised taxes on the very rich; half said it had not. The Clinton economic package raised income taxes on the wealthiest 1 percent of taxpayers.

MORE HEAT THAN LIGHT

Political strategists, whose job is to break through the media static, say news reports are competing for attention with the likes of "Roseanne," "Hard Copy" and "Cops," which apparently resonate more with some viewers than Dan Rather, Tom Brokaw and Peter Jennings, the main networks' nightly news anchors.

"The problem with the Contract With America is there's no visual," said Frank Luntz, the Republican pollster who helped shape the contract. "There's no blood, no guns going off, no policemen knocking down people's doors. There's nothing to make people look up and stamp it on their brain."

Many analysts say the media, with their emphasis on conflict, convey more heat than light about public issues. They say too many journalists cover public affairs as a sort of insider's game in which all politicians are assumed to be scheming and devious.

Others see the press as a willing conveyor belt for propaganda. "There's a lot of misinformation in political campaigns that gets quoted in the press without the press providing a refereeing function," said Kathleen Hall Jamieson, dean of the Annenberg School of Communications at the University of Pennsylvania. "The he-said-she-said style of journalism minimizes the likelihood the public will know whether he or she is telling the truth."

SPLIT ALONG DEMOGRAPHIC LINES

On issue after issue, news stories—such as those reporting that Clinton raised income taxes on the wealthy—seem to have little impact. A Wall Street Journal poll last year found that 43 percent expected to pay more in income taxes. Even among those making less than $20,000—a group whose taxes were cut—26 percent expected to pay more.

"There was a largely knee-jerk response that whenever government does something, I'm going to end up paying the bill," said Stanley Greenberg, Clinton's pollster.

When it comes to news, the country is split along demographic lines. Those who are vitally interested in the sort of news carried by the *Baltimore Sun* or other papers are older, more affluent and better educated.

According to a survey by the University of Chicago's National Opinion Research Center, only a third of those under 30 read a newspaper every day, compared to three-quarters of those over 65. Less than half of those without a high school diploma read a paper every day, compared to more than two-thirds of those who have attended graduate school. And regular readers include fewer than four in 10 of those earning $15,000 to $20,000 a year, but seven in 10 of those earning more than $60,000.

NEW FORMS OF MEDIA

Newer forms of media are filling the vacuum. Many people who don't bother with newspapers listen to talk radio or watch daytime talk shows or tabloid television. These programs deal in a more emotionally charged way than the mainstream press with such issues as sex, race, welfare and affirmative action.

The *Washington Post* recently asked a research firm to select a dozen Baltimore-area residents who do not read a newspaper every day and are interested in talk radio or daytime talk shows. These people, none of whom has a college degree, seemed distinctly uninterested in the Republican revolution on Capitol Hill. Although the Contract With America has received an avalanche of news coverage, most knew nothing about it.

Clarence Lowery, 65, a retired asbestos worker, could not name any provision in the contract but nonetheless dismissed it as "politician lies. They always say they're gonna do something and they can't."

Rhonda Burris, the city clerk, knew only that the Republicans are "trying to cut this and cut that. . . . It doesn't seem like they can do anything for me. They just talk."

Melissa Sharrow, 32, a sales representative, thought the contract involved trading with other countries. "I don't pay much attention [to politics] because it upsets me," she said.

SOME NEWS PENETRATES

Clearly, the daily clamor of charges and countercharges between the White House and Congress is but a faint echo by the time it penetrates the lives of many Americans.

Over dinner one recent evening, four Baltimore County residents said they were unaware of the recent congressional battle over term limits, or that the House had voted on it the previous month. "That's one of the things Newt won't bring up now because he wants to keep his job," said Len Pross, the letter carrier.

Still, some news manages to permeate pop culture. All those at the dinner knew that Gingrich's mother had told CBS's Connie Chung that her son had called Hillary Rodham Clinton "a bitch." And all knew that Clinton had said on television that he wears briefs, not boxers.

Elizabeth Yarbrough recalled Gingrich saying on television that "women could not possibly go into battle because they'd get infections in the trenches," as she put it. But she could not identify any policy Gingrich advocates.

Many people trust news reports far less than their own experience, or what they have heard from acquaintances and relatives. "I have a friend who works for the government and he says he hardly does anything and he gets a raise every year," said Norman Brown, the furniture salesman.

Yarbrough has two children, and her husband is unemployed after working 15 years for a bakery equipment company that moved to Florida. About stories she reads on an improving economy, Yarbrough said, "I don't believe that. I go to the grocery store and see the price of everything going up. My husband calls these places, there's no contracts, no jobs."

Several people suggested that journalists and politicians do not understand the welfare issue. Jean Langston, the claims examiner, said her sister, a school secretary with four children, had to go on welfare temporarily after losing her job. "They don't know about these situations," Langston said.

SELECTIVE MEMORY

Many people tend to remember colorful news reports that confirm what they already believe. Pross, a Christian activist who is educating his 11-year-old at home, said he heard on the conservative radio show "Focus on the Family" that Hillary Clinton is working on a U.N. treaty under which "children's rights could supersede the rights of parents."

Burris said she recalls reading that members of Congress receive free private school scholarships for their children. Yarbrough still talks about a pair of "Prime Time Live" reports on government waste that are more than two years old.

"They were showing these people who do idiotic things like measure the flow rate of ketchup, making $40,000 to $50,000 a year," she said. "I never realized there were that many unnecessary jobs."

Yarbrough also recalls reading in a newspaper that "they were thinking of getting rid of this department where they sit around collecting $80,000-a-year paychecks for doing absolutely nothing." Reminded that as a cafeteria worker she is also a government employee, she said: "I'm feeding kids. I'm doing something productive."

Many of these folks grew up reading the *Baltimore Sun* or *Baltimore News American* in their parents' homes. But somewhere along the way they lost the habit.

"A newspaper is not something I relish reading," Pross said. "It's much easier to sit in front of the tube and have someone tell you something." Langston said it "just drives me crazy" when front-page stories jump to an inside page.

MEDIA FIX ON THE RUN

When she was growing up, Langston says, her father would chew over the news with the egg man and the bread man as they made deliveries to the house. Today, she and others say, they almost never discuss politics with friends or relatives.

Their lives revolve around work, children and church, not news cycles. Burris is always driving her children to sporting events and dance recitals. For Langston, who cares for her daughter and niece, it's dance practice and choir rehearsal. Brown is single and self-employed. "My job takes up all my time," he said. "I have a tremendous amount of paperwork. I listen to the news, but it goes in one ear and out the other. You hear the Republicans and the Democrats saying the same things."

They get their media fix on the run; in limited doses. Langston keeps an eye on "Good Morning America" or "Today" while getting ready for work, and reads *Good Housekeeping* on the supermarket checkout line. Pross listens to Rush Limbaugh while delivering the mail. Burris watches "Entertainment Tonight" and reads *People* because she likes to keep up with the movie stars. Brown reads *Time*—"I like the pictures"—and *Money,* and listens to Baltimore radio host Tom Marr.

They use words like "repetitive" and "monotonous" to describe the news. And they have pet peeves that seem to encapsulate their doubts about the media.

SKEPTICAL ENVIRONMENT

Pross says he finds ABC's Sam Donaldson "arrogant" and doesn't like the way he covers the White House, although Donaldson has been off that beat since 1989. Langston objects to the O.J. Simpson trial coverage. "The reporters give their opinions and it's as if he's already guilty," she said. "Because of the experience of black people and the problems we've had, we don't want to say he's guilty until we've seen all the facts."

Pross says he finds Limbaugh entertaining but that "I don't agree with him about everything. I don't like the way he puts down everyone just because they may be a liberal. Of course, that's what sells him. He's puffed up."

In this highly skeptical environment, few had kind words for the president. Burris said it seems like Hillary Clinton is running the White House. Yarbrough says she was excited by Bill Clinton during the 1992 campaign but that the last time he was on television, "I kind of wandered off and said, 'What else is on?'"

Like several of her neighbors, Yarbrough feels slightly guilty about being poorly informed. But, she said. "It's more trouble than it's worth to listen to the news and get your hopes up."

11

Is TV Ruining Our Children?

Richard Zoglin

Editor's Note: Although a number of groups are pressing for laws to bring some control to children's television, over the past forty years the way children grow up has already been profoundly changed. Children are introduced to the real world—and taught their ABCs—earlier than ever. But they may be affected by an overdose of TV violence. Even sitcoms change childhood notions by showing that adults don't always know what they're doing.

Richard Zoglin covers media issues for *Time.* He was aided in this article, which appeared in *Time* on October 15, 1990, by the reporting of William Tynan.

Behold every parent's worst nightmare: the six-year-old TV addict. He watches in the morning before he goes off to school, plops himself in front of the set as soon as he gets home in the afternoon and gets another dose to calm down before he goes to bed at night. He wears Bart Simpson T shirts, nags Mom to buy him Teenage Mutant Ninja Turtles toys and spends hours glued to his Nintendo. His teachers says he is restless and combative in class. What's more, he's having trouble reading.

Does this creature really exist, or is he just a paranoid video-age vision? The question is gaining urgency as the medium barges ever more aggressively into children's lives. Except for school and the family, no institution plays a bigger role in shaping American children. And no institution takes more heat. TV has been blamed for just about everything from a decrease in attention span to an increase in street crime. Cartoons are attacked for their violence and sitcoms for their foul language. Critics ranging from religious conservatives to consumer groups like Action for Children's Television have kept up a steady drumbeat of calls for reform.

EFFORTS TO REFORM

[In 1990] Congress took a small step toward obliging. Legislators sent to President Bush a bill that would set limits on commercial time in children's pro-

78

gramming (a still generous $10\frac{1}{2}$ minutes per hour on weekends and 12 minutes on weekdays). The bill would also require stations to air at least some educational kids' fare as a condition for getting their licenses renewed. Bush has argued that the bill infringes on broadcasters' First Amendment rights, but (unlike President Reagan, who vetoed a similar measure [1988]) he is expected to allow it to become law.

Yet these mild efforts at reform, as well as critics' persistent gripes about the poor quality of children's TV, skirt the central issue. Even if the commercialism on kidvid were reined in, even if local stations were persuaded to air more "quality" children's fare, even if kids could be shielded from the most objectionable material, the fact remains that children watch a ton of TV. Almost daily, parents must grapple with a fundamental, overriding question: What is all that TV viewing doing to kids, and what can be done about it?

INSEPARABLE COMPANION

Television has, of course, been an inseparable companion for most American youngsters since the early 1950s. But the baby boomers, who grew up with Howdy Doody and Huckleberry Hound, experienced nothing like the barrage of video images that pepper kids today. Cable has vastly expanded the supply of programming. The VCR has turned favorite shows and movies into an endlessly repeatable pastime. Video games have added to the home box's allure.

The average child will have watched 5,000 hours of TV by the time he enters first grade and 19,000 hours by the end of high school—more time than he will spend in class. This dismayingly passive experience crowds out other, more active endeavors: playing outdoors, being with friends, reading. Marie Winn, author of the 1977 book *The Plug-In Drug,* gave a memorable, if rather alarmist, description of the trancelike state TV induces: "The child's facial expression is transformed. The jaw is relaxed and hangs open slightly; the tongue rests on the front teeth (if there are any). The eyes have a glazed, vacuous look . . . ."

Guided by TV, today's kids are exposed to more information about the world around them than any other generation in history. But are they smarter for it? Many teachers and psychologists argue that TV is largely to blame for the decline in reading skills and school performance. In his studies of children at Yale, psychologist Jerome Singer found that kids who are heavy TV watchers tend to be less well informed, more restless and poorer students. The frenetic pace of TV, moreover, has seeped into the classroom. "A teacher who is going into a lengthy explanation of an arithmetic problem will begin to lose the audience after a while," says Singer. "Children are expecting some kind of show." Even the much beloved *Sesame Street* has been criticized for reinforcing the TV-inspired notion that education must be fast paced and entertaining. Says Neil Postman, communications professor at New York University and author of *Amusing Ourselves to Death:* "*Sesame Street* makes kids like school only if school is like *Sesame Street.*"

INFLUENCING BEHAVIOR

Televised violence may also be having an effect on youngsters. Singer's research has shown that prolonged viewing by children of violent programs is associated with more aggressive behavior, such as getting into fights and disrupting the play of others. (A link between TV and violent crime, however, has not been clearly established.) Other studies suggest that TV viewing can dampen kids' imagination. Patricia Marks Greenfield, a professor of psychology at UCLA, conducted experiments in which several groups of children were asked to tell a story about the Smurfs. Those who were shown a Smurfs TV cartoon beforehand were less "creative" in their storytelling than kids who first played an unrelated connect-the-dots game.

But the evidence is flimsy for many popular complaints about TV. In a 1988 report co-authored for the U.S. Department of Education, Daniel Anderson, professor of psychology at the University of Massachusetts in Amherst, found no convincing evidence that TV has a "mesmerizing effect" on children, overstimulates them or reduces their attention span. In fact, the report asserted, TV may actually increase attention-focusing capabilities.

Nor, contrary to many parents' fears, have the new video technologies made matters worse. Small children who repeatedly watch their favorite cassettes are, psychologists point out, behaving no differently from toddlers who want their favorite story read to them over and over. (The VCR may actually give parents *more* control over their kids' viewing.) Video games may distress adults with their addictive potential, but researchers have found no exceptional harm in them—and even some possible benefits, like improving hand-eye coordination.

LOSS OF CHILDHOOD

Yet TV may be effecting a more profound, if less widely recognized, change in the whole concept of growing up. Before the advent of television, when print was the predominant form of mass communication, parents and teachers were able to control just what and when children learned about the world outside. With TV, kids are plunged into that world almost instantly.

In his 1985 book *No Sense of Place,* Joshua Meyrowitz, professor of communication at the University of New Hampshire, points out that TV reveals to children the "backstage" activity of adults. Even a seemingly innocuous program like *Father Knows Best* showed that parents aren't all-knowing authority figures: they agonize over problems in private and sometimes even conspire to fool children. "Television exposes kids to behavior that adults spent centuries trying to hide from children," says Meyrowitz. "The average child watching television sees adults hitting each other, killing each other, breaking down and crying. It teaches kids that adults don't always know what they're doing." N.Y.U.'s Postman believes TV, by revealing the "secrets" of adulthood, has virtually destroyed the notion of childhood as a discrete period of innocence. "What I see happening is a blurring of childhood and adulthood," he says. "We have more adultlike children and more childlike adults."

VIGILANCE ESSENTIAL

What all this implies is that TV's impact is pervasive and to a large extent inevitable. That impact cannot be wished away; all that can be done is to try to understand and control it. Reforms of the sort Congress has enacted are a salutary step. Networks and stations too—though they are in the business of entertainment, not education—must be vigilant about the contents and commercialization of kids' shows.

The ultimate responsibility still rests with parents. The goal should not be—cannot be—to screen out every bad word or karate chop from kids' viewing, but rather to make sure TV doesn't crowd out all the other activities that are part of growing up. These counterbalancing influences—family, friends, school, books—can put TV, if not out of the picture, at least in the proper focus.

12

Crack and the Box

PETE HAMILL

Editor's Note: Americans have the money to buy drugs, says the author of this article, and the supply is plentiful. But almost nobody in power asks why people spend good money on them.

Pete Hamill here suggests that the drug plague coincides with the unspoken assumption of most TV shows: that life should be easy. Such a view encourages people to pop a pill, smoke some dope, inhale some powder, or inject some liquid for an easy way out of the problems of life. He suggests that watching television itself can be addictive and, thus, encourages addictive behavior of all sorts.

Hamill is a columnist for *New York Newsday.* The original version of this article first appeared in *Esquire* magazine in May 1990.

One sad rainy morning [in 1990], I talked to a woman who was addicted to crack cocaine. She was 22, stiletto-thin, with eyes as old as tombs. She was living in two rooms in a welfare hotel with her children who were two, three and five years of age. Her story was the usual tangle of human woe: early pregnancy, dropping out of school, vanished men, smack and then crack, tricks with johns in parked cars to pay for the dope. I asked her why she did drugs. She shrugged in an empty way and couldn't really answer beyond "makes me feel good." While we talked and she told her tale of squalor, the children ignored us. They were watching TV.

Walking back to my office in the rain, I brooded about the woman, her zombielike children, and my own callous indifference. I'd heard so many versions of the same story that I almost never wrote them anymore: The sons of similar women, glimpsed a dozen years ago, are now in Dannemora or Soledad or Joliet; in a hundred cities, their daughters are moving into the same loveless rooms. As I walked, a series of homeless men approached me for change, most of them junkies. Others sat in doorways, staring at nothing. They were additional casualties of our time of plague, demoralized reminders that although this country holds only two percent of the world's population, it consumes 65 percent of the world's supply of hard drugs.

WHY ADDICTION?

Why, for God's sake? Why do so many millions of Americans of all ages, races and classes choose to spend all or part of their lives stupefied? I've talked to hundreds of addicts over the years; some were my friends. But none could give sensible answers. They stutter about the pain of the world, about despair or boredom, the urgent need for magic or pleasure in a society empty of both. But then they just shrug. Americans have the money to buy drugs; the supply is plentiful. But almost nobody in power asks, *Why?* Least of all, George Bush and his drug warriors.

William Bennett talks vaguely about the heritage of '60s permissiveness, the collapse of Traditional Values and all that. But he and Bush offer the traditional American excuse: It Is Somebody Else's Fault. This posture set the stage for the self-righteous invasion of Panama, the bloodiest drug arrest in world history. Bush even accused Manuel Noriega of "poisoning our children." But he never asked why so many Americans demand the poison.

IS TV THE ANSWER?

And then, on that rainy morning in New York, I saw another one of those ragged men staring out at the rain from a doorway. I suddenly remembered the inert postures of the children in that welfare hotel, and I thought: *television.*

Ah, no, I muttered to myself: too simple. Something as complicated as drug addiction can't be blamed on television. Come on. . . . But I remembered all those desperate places I'd visited as a reporter, where there were no books and a TV set was always playing and the older kids had gone off somewhere to shoot smack, except for the kid who was at the mortuary in a coffin. I also remembered when I was a boy in the '40s and early '50s, and drugs were a minor sideshow, a kind of dark little rumor. And there was one major difference between that time and this: *television.*

We had unemployment then. illiteracy, poor living conditions, racism, governmental stupidity, a gap between rich and poor. We didn't have the all-consuming presence of television in our lives. Now two generations of Americans have grown up with television from their earliest moments of consciousness. Those same American generations are afflicted by the pox of drug addiction.

Only 35 years ago, drug addiction was not a major problem in this country. We had some drug addicts at the end of the 19th Century, hooked on the cocaine in patent medicines. During the placid '50s, Commissioner Harry Anslinger pumped up the budget of the old Bureau of Narcotics with fantasies of reefer madness. Heroin was sold and used in most major American cities, while the bebop generation of jazz musicians got jammed up with horse.

TV GENERATION

Until the early '60s, narcotics were still marginal to American life; they weren't the $120 billion market they make up today. If anything, those years have an eerie innocence. In 1955 there were 31.7 million TV sets in use in the country (the number is now past 184 million). But the majority of the audience had grown up without the dazzling new medium. They embraced it, were diverted by it, perhaps even loved it, but they weren't *formed* by it. That year, the New York police made a mere 1,234 felony drug arrests; in 1988 it was 43,901. They confiscated 97 *ounces* of cocaine for the entire year; [in 1990] it was hundreds of pounds. During each year of the '50s in New York, there were only about a hundred narcotics-related deaths. But by the end of the '60s, when the first generation of children *formed* by television had come to maturity (and thus to the marketplace), the number of such deaths had risen to 1,200. The same phenomenon was true in every major American city.

In the last Nielsen survey of American viewers, the average family was watching the television seven hours a day. This has never happened before in history. No people has ever been entertained for seven hours a *day.* The Elizabethans didn't go to the theater seven hours a day. The pre-TV generation did not go to the movies seven hours a day. Common sense tells us that this all-pervasive diet of instant imagery, sustained now for 40 years, must have changed us in profound ways.

Television, like drugs, dominates the lives of its addicts. And though some lonely Americans leave their sets on without watching them, using them as electronic companions, television usually absorbs its viewers the way drugs absorb their users. Viewers can't work or play while watching television; they can't read; they can't be out on the streets, falling in love with the wrong people, learning how to quarrel and compromise with other human beings. In short, they are asocial. So are drug addicts.

One Michigan State University study in the early '80s offered a group of four- and five-year-olds the choice of giving up television or giving up their fathers. Fully one-third said they would give up Daddy. Given a similar choice (between cocaine or heroin and father, mother, brother, sister, wife, husband, children, job), almost every stone junkie would do the same.

MIND-ALTERING INSTRUMENT

There are other disturbing similarities. Television itself is a consciousness-altering instrument. With the touch of a button, it takes you out of the "real" world in which you reside and can place you at a basketball game, the back alleys of Miami, the streets of Bucharest, or the cartoony living rooms of Sitcom Land. Each move from channel to channel alters mood, usually with music or a laugh track. On any given evening, you can laugh, be frightened, feel tension, thump with excitement. You can even tune in *MacNeil/Lehrer* and feel sober.

But none of these abrupt shifts in mood is *earned.* They are attained as easily as popping a pill. Getting news from television, for example, is simply not the same experience as reading it in a newspaper. Reading is *active.* The reader must decode little symbols called words, then create images or ideas and make them connect; at its most basic level, reading is an act of the imagination. But the television viewer is *passive* and doesn't go through that process. The words are spoken to him by Dan Rather or Tom Brokaw or Peter

Jennings. There isn't much decoding to do when watching television, no time to think or ponder before the next set of images and spoken words appears to displace the present one. The reader, being active, works at his or her own pace; the viewer, being passive, proceeds at the pace determined by the show. Except at the highest levels, television never demands that its audience take part in an act of imagination. Reading always does.

In short, television works on the same imaginative and intellectual level as psychoactive drugs. If prolonged television viewing makes the young passive (dozens of studies indicate that it does), then moving to drugs has a certain coherence. Drugs provide an unearned high (in contrast to the earned rush that comes from a feat accomplished, a human breakthrough earned by sweat or thought or love).

And because the television addict and the drug addict are alienated from the hard and scary world, they also feel they make no difference in its complicated events.

THE EASY LIFE?

The drug plague also coincides with the unspoken assumption of most television shows: Life should be *easy.* The most complicated events are summarized on TV news in a minute or less. Cops confront murder, chase the criminals and bring them to justice (usually violently) within an hour. In commercials, you drink the right beer and you get the girl. *Easy!* So why should real life be a grind? Why should any American have to spend years mastering a skill or craft, or work eight hours a day at an unpleasant job, or endure the compromises and crises of a marriage? Nobody *works* on TV (except cops, doctors and lawyers).

Love stories on television are about falling in love or breaking up; the long, steady growth of a marriage—its essential dailiness—is seldom explored, except as comedy. Life on television is almost always simple: good guys and bad, nice girls and whores, smart guys and dumb. And if life in the real world isn't that simple, well, hey, man, have some dope, man, be happy, feel good.

Most Americans under the age of 50 have now spent their lives absorbing television; that is, they've had the structures of drama pounded into them. Drama is always about conflict. So news shows, politics and advertising are now all shaped by those structures. Nobody will pay attention to anything as complicated as the part played by Third World debt in the expanding production of cocaine; it's easier to focus on Manuel Noriega, a character right out of *Miami Vice,* and believe that even in real life there's a Mister Big.

JUST SAY NO

What is to be done? Television is certainly not going away, but its addictive qualities can be controlled. It's a lot easier to "just say no" to television than to heroin or crack. As a beginning parents must take immediate control of the sets, teaching children to watch specific television *programs,* not "television," to get out of the house and play with other kids. Elementary and high schools must begin teaching television/media literacy as a subject, the way literature is taught, showing children how shows are made, how to distinguish between the true and the false, how to recognize cheap emotional manipulation. All Americans should spend more time reading. And thinking.

For years, the defenders of television have argued that the networks are only giving the people what they want. That might be true. But so is the Medellin cartel.

ADDITIONAL RESOURCES FOR PART 3

Suggested Questions and Discussion Topics

1. According to "So Many Media So Little Time," by Richard Harwood, what is the approximate difference between the amount of time we watch television and read newspapers?

2. From "So Many Media, So Little Time," list the top three media that get most of the average person's attention, with No. 1 being the medium to which people give most of their time, followed by No. 2 and No. 3. Choose from these options: newspapers; television, including cable; books; magazines; recorded music; and radio.

3. From "Tuning Out Traditional News" by Howard Kurtz, discuss some of the reasons according to those Kurtz interviewed, why people seem to be tuning out the news.

4. According to "Tuning Out Traditional News," how do demographic factors affect news consumption?

5. According to "Is TV Ruining Our Children?" by Richard Zoglin, TV may be changing the whole concept of growing up. How so?

6. List at least three characteristics according to Richard Zoglin in "Is TV Ruining our Children?" of children who are heavy TV watchers.

7. According to "Crack in the Box" by Pete Hamill, what does television do to viewers that might have some connection with the growing drug problem in our society?

8. In "Crack and the Box," Pete Hamill draws a parallel between addiction to drugs and addiction to television in the United States. Give three reasons why Hamill believes such a connection exists.

Suggested Readings

Joy Keiko Asamen and Gordon L. Berry, *Research Paradigms, Television, and Social Behavior.* Thousand Oaks, CA: Sage Publications, 1997.

James L. Baughman, *The Republic of Mass Culture: Journalism, Filmmaking, and Broadcasting in America Since 1941.* Baltimore: Johns Hopkins University Press, 1997.

Jennings Bryant and Dolf Zillman, eds., *Media Effects: Advances in Theory and Research.* Mahwah, NJ: Lawrence Erlbaum Associates, 1994.

John William Cavanaugh, *Media Effects on Voters: A Panel Study of the 1992 Presidential Election.* Lanham, MD: University Press of America, 1995.

James W. Dearing and Everett M. Rogers, *Agenda-Setting.* Thousand Oaks, CA: Sage Publications, 1996.

Richard Jackson Harris, *A Cognitive Psychology of Mass Communication,* 2nd ed. Mahwah, NJ: Lawrence Erlbaum Associates, 1997.

Tannis M. MacBeth, *Tuning in to Young Viewers.* Thousand Oaks, CA: Sage Publications, 1996.

Neil Postman, *Amusing Ourselves to Death: Public Discourse in the Age of Show Business.* New York: Viking Press. 1986.

Victor C. Strasburger, *Adolescents and the Media: Medical and Psychological Impact.* Thousand Oaks, CA: Sage Publications, 1995.

Ella Taylor, *Prime-Time Families: Television Culture in Postwar America.* Berkeley, CA: University of California Press, 1991.

Judith Page Van Evra, *Television and Child Development,* 2nd ed. Mahwah, NJ: Lawrence Erlbaum, 1997.

Suggested Videos

George Gerbner, "The Electronic Storyteller: Television and the Cultivation of Values." Northampton, MA: Media Education Foundation, 1997. (30 minutes)

George Gerbner, "The Crisis of the Cultural Environment: Media and Democracy in the 21st Century." Northampton, MA: Media Education Foundation, 1997. (30 minutes)

"Tube Babies." New York: Insight Media, 1994. (35 minutes)

"Trial by Television." New York: Insight Media, 1993. (50 minutes)

"The Glitter: Sex, Drugs, and the Media." New York: Insight Media, 1995. (23 minutes)

"Television and Human Behavior." New York: Insight Media, 1992. (26 minutes)

"Hollywood's Role in Shaping Values: David Putnam." Princeton, NJ: Films for the Humanities & Sciences. (52 minutes)

PART · 4
Freedom and Responsibility

In the United States, mass media probably have more freedom than in any other country. Even those similar to the United States in legal systems and political philosophies—such as Canada, the United Kingdom, New Zealand, and Australia—have all adopted, since World War II, public policies that are more restrictive of press and mass media than anything in America.

Britain and Australia, for example, have an Official Secrets Act, which allows the government to withhold information it deems threatening to its security, and the government can prosecute the press if it publishes or broadcasts such information. In the United States, we have a Freedom of Information Act, which carefully limits what the government can withhold and forces the government to divulge any other information that citizens and the press might want. But the main difference is this: If mass media publish or broadcast information that the U.S. government has legally withheld, they cannot be prosecuted for doing so. In general, in the United States, the burden of responsibility to protect government secrets rests with the government, not with the press.

In our most kindred countries—Britain, Canada, Australia, and New Zealand—broadcasting is much more restricted than in the United States. These countries all have large national broadcast systems that are quasigovernmental institutions, funded largely by taxpayers. Even though they might pride themselves on their independence, these institutions—the BBC in Britain, CBC in Canada, ABC in Australia—often bend to the direct orders of their governments.

The U.S. government owns no public broadcasting except the Voice of America (VOA), our external broadcast service allowing America to inform the world about our policies and our version of the news. Since there is little chance of making a profit from this kind of venture, it must be supported by the government or it wouldn't exist. Congress, which provides the subsidy for the VOA, also insists that it broadcast only on shortwave aimed abroad, not at American audiences, because we don't want government interference in the information process.

The government does provide some financial support for public broadcasting, again largely because there hasn't been enough profit in educational programming in the past. PBS and NPR, the television and radio services of public broadcasting, are trying to raise their own funds from sponsors, viewers, and listeners to reduce their dependence on the government.

All other broadcasting in America is strictly private business. Radio and television operate within guidelines set by the Federal Communications Commission, but the print media have virtually total freedom from government interference. Nonetheless, U.S. broadcasters with a license to broadcast can do almost anything they want to make a profit.

Many people, perhaps a growing number, feel that American mass media are too free, that some limits should be imposed on some of their actions. Even a majority of journalism students, in a poll recently taken at the University of Maryland, indicated that the press had too much freedom, which many antimedia groups seek to limit. Many others want to force mass media, through legal means, to be more responsible.

At the same time, from another direction, there are those who would set limits on the freedom of speech if what is said belittles a particular group, especially if that group is a minority in society and has traditionally been denigrated. We have come to be concerned about the "political correctness" of our speech.

Does the near absolute legal freedom of speech and of the press in the United States give individuals or the press the freedom to be irresponsible? And what is irresponsibility? Most of us would agree that it is irresponsible to falsely yell "Fire!" in a crowded theater, but is it irresponsible to use derogatory language when referring to minority groups, women, or anyone? Where should the line be drawn on freedom?

Clearly, if mass media operate in an irresponsible manner in the opinion of the majority, that majority can insist on laws that would place limits on their actions. Even the Constitution, and its First Amendment guaranteeing freedom of speech and of the press, can be changed by a two-thirds majority of all the states. It has already been amended twenty-six times.

For the journalist, the demand for press responsibility has often been perceived as a way of controlling the press. Who determines what is responsible and what is irresponsible? The journalist would like to have that determination made by readers, listeners, and viewers, through their choices of media in an open marketplace, rather than by the government. Yes, the journalist would say, without controls there may be some irresponsibility in the media, but an irresponsible press is much less to be feared than an irresponsible government. Only an absolutely free press, even if it is occasionally irresponsible, can guarantee freedom from an irresponsible, corrupt, or despotic government.

13

Reflections on the First Amendment

GEORGE E. REEDY

Editor's Note: "If the press didn't tell us, who would? A simple question; and its answer is as old as the nation: No one." This statement by Robert H. Wills, president in 1990 of the Society of Professional Journalists, Sigma Delta Chi, reflects the sentiments of most American journalists.

Protection for such sentiments comes from the First Amendment to the Constitution, which says, in part, "Congress shall make no law abridging freedom of speech or freedom of the press." Yet the absolute freedom that the First Amendment guarantees has come under increasing attack.

In this article, George E. Reedy defends the First Amendment. He was President Lyndon Johnson's press secretary in 1964–1965, but he started his professional career as a journalist and is now the Nieman professor emeritus at Marquette University. This article was first published in *The Quill* in March 1990.

What is badly needed in the United States today is a simple statement chiseled in stone over the entrance to every public building and every educational institution and inscribed on indestructible billboards along every major highway. It should read:

> Freedom of speech is freedom of the press and freedom of the press is freedom of speech; if either is cut, both will bleed and personal freedom will die.

It is more than passing strange that Americans need such a reminder. We have lived as free men and women with that principle for nearly two centuries while personal freedom in every nation that has controlled the press has gone down the drain.

Perhaps freedom has in some sense been too successful in the United States, because most of us have come to take it for granted.

There are even those today who believe that a free press is a luxury that we can discard temporarily when it appears to conflict with our needs in time of crisis. This philosophy cropped up nearly 16 years ago in the chief minority opinion on the Pentagon Papers ease and, while it did not control the final decision of the Supreme Court, only three justices rejected it in its entirety.

NO ILLUSIONS ABOUT FREEDOM

Those Founding Fathers, led by James Madison, who forced adoption of the First Amendment, had no illusions regarding "temporary" press restraints. They knew that even a short-term suspension of press freedom would always become permanent, and it would not be confined to the press alone. Freedom is a package in which the various elements gather strength from each other, and none of them can be surgically excised, like an inflamed appendix, without all collapsing.

The First Amendment, which everyone talks about but which few read, says: "Congress shall make no law respecting an establishment of religion, or prohibiting the free exercise thereof; or abridging the freedom of speech, or of the press; or the right of the people peaceably to assemble, and to petition the Government for a redress of grievances."

This is remarkably lucid language. It says in unmistakable terms that we Americans can believe what we want to believe, say what we want to say, publish our thoughts in an effort to convince others, and assemble those who agree with us to try to persuade our government to do what we think it should do.

Obviously, freedom to speak and publish also means freedom to inquire. Control the chain at any point and we become helpless subjects of arbitrary rule.

NO SPECIAL PRIVILEGES

What is equally important in modern times is that the First Amendment does not confer a special privilege on the press. The privilege is *freedom to publish,* on paper or by electronic means, and it is a privilege that belongs to every American—whether he or she writes books, newsletters or ordinary letters.

The press is an institution that publishes daily and therefore resorts to the First Amendment more often than do other institutions and individuals. But the freedom to publish is still a privilege that belongs to all of us, without which freedom of speech would be meaningless.

In a mass society, it does little good for me to whisper my political views to close friends. If I hope to accomplish anything, I must find a way of publishing my opinions so they can be read or heard by others.

I have never been able to decide in my own mind whether a free society produces a free press or a free press produces a free society. I suspect that the two go together, along with protections against arbitrary administration of the laws.

History, however, is very revealing on the relationship. Every dictatorship that has come to power in our memory has begun by seizing the press as the first step toward abolishing personal liberty. Men and women who cannot publish cannot fight back. Furthermore, without a press free to dig out facts without governmental supervision, we have no means of calling governmental officials to account. We cannot change—nor can we protest against—that which we do not know.

THE NEED FOR A FREE PRESS

The right to learn, to investigate, to express opinions, to demand accountability—these rights were vital at the time the First Amendment was written. They are even more crucial now in an era of big government in which unsavory or merely incompetent deeds can be concealed in the labyrinthian corridors of buildings that house tens of thousands of federal workers, and in which telling facts and plans and statistics can be tucked away in impenetrable footnotes to trillion-dollar budgets.

Without a full-time corps of journalists intensively analyzing the workings of the governmental machine, we are helpless against a bureaucracy that, however well intentioned it may be, is certainly not going to inform us of its shortcomings.

People in power do not like to be disturbed, and freedom of speech and press is always disturbing.

THE CASE OF NATIONAL SECURITY

In modern times, the most popular rationale for restraining the press involves "national security." I am placing the phrase in quotes deliberately because it is usually voiced in the same tones of reverence as those employed when reciting the Lord's Prayer. National security is a phrase intended to put an end to thought rather than to stimulate discussion.

Most of us are somewhat uncertain as to the exact meaning of the phrase, national security, but we all know that it somehow involves our survival as a people. In a world of atomic bombs, space stations, and potential laser-beam weapons, we are very quick to buy any proposals to guarantee our future. It seems to make a lot of sense for us to take steps that withhold from possible enemies information as to how we can fight back if attacked.

No one can seriously argue that there is no information whose publication should be withheld temporarily at certain times. But that is not really a problem. In this century, our nation has fought four major wars with no compulsory press censorship. When those wars are reviewed, it is apparent that in no instance did we suffer any setback because national security secrets were revealed by the press.

American journalists are as patriotic as anyone else and do not want to see their country defeated. In the name of national security, they have in the past entered into voluntary agreement to defer publication, and the voluntary agreements have worked.

Nevertheless, journalists who value their craft and trust the American people do not knowingly lie to protect someone's conception of the national interest. There have been charges that news correspondents painted an overly gloomy picture of what happened in Vietnam and thus sapped our morale. But that smacks of an alibi invented for covering up the pursuit of a disastrous national policy. If we are to censor the press for being "downbeat," we might as well give up freedom altogether.

THE PRICE OF SECRECY

There is another side to the national security issue, however. It is that even in instances where deferring information can be justified, we pay a heavy price for it. First, if something should go wrong, the American people will not be prepared for it and can easily panic. At the first publicly known setback in a previously secret national policy, the morale of the people will suffer and confidence in the government will begin to shrink.

Second, if some things are censored that should be censored, the people then would have no means of knowing whether other things that should *not* have been censored have been censored.

Third, and most important, is that secrecy limits the number of minds that can be brought to bear on a subject. It prevents genuine, adversarial discussion, which is the only process that gives us conclusions in which we can have confidence.

DAMAGES FROM SECRECY

There is ample, historical precedent to establish the importance of all three of these points. One of the great strengths of the Allies in World War II was the absolute insistence of the British Broadcasting Corporation that it be the first to announce every defeat. As a result, the British were able to take setbacks calmly. And when the BBC announced victories, those reports were believed all over the world—and the inhabitants of the Axis countries were disheartened no matter what their own governments said.

When we finally entered Japan at the end of the war, we discovered that the Japanese had realized that their government was feeding them censored news and consequently the rumor mills were working overtime. The people knew they were on the losing end when their government told them they were winning.

To my mind, the most direct argument against censorship, official or self-imposed, can be derived from the tragic series of events of 1961 labeled "the Bay of Pigs." The plan to invade Cuba was absolutely harebrained and any genuine adversarial discussion would have blown it out of the water. But it was kept secret within a small circle, and it is amazing what follies can be contrived by the minds of even the most brilliant men and women when they are thinking in isolation. The failure of the invasion held us up to scorn and ridicule, and to this day our standing in Latin America suffers.

One important American newspaper got hold of the story in advance but soft-pedaled it at the request of the State Department. Had the account been placed on page one, the invasion would have been called off and today we would be a stronger nation.

DAMAGES FROM SECRET GOVERNMENT AGENCIES

Secrecy in any form damages a nation. I have travelled extensively in Latin America and Asia. Everywhere, on both continents. I have encountered a disturbing attitude. It is that every American—journalist, businessman or even tourist—is thought to be a probable CIA agent who is to be trusted only after thorough investigation.

I cannot but wonder whether the CIA can ever have accomplished anything in those areas that makes up for what we have lost in standing. I was in Chile before the election that made Salvador Allende president, and it was apparent from ordinary conversations in Santiago that his only real strength with the people was the widespread belief that United States agents were trying to keep him from the presidency.

There is, unfortunately, an all too widespread belief that our security rests upon our ability to spring unexpected surprises upon other nations that may become hostile. This is a belief that can be held only by ignoring the real world in which we live. It fails to account for a key development of the modern age: that science and technology have abolished secrecy or any possibility of attaining it.

INEFFICIENCY OF SECRECY

In modern times, it is possible to withhold information from ordinary citizens who do not have the necessary background to understand what they are looking at. But we are wasting our time if we think we can withhold such information from governments.

The modern reality encompasses teams of scientists in the Soviet Union, in Great Britain, in France, in mainland China, in the United States—men and women who have all read the same books and, in many instances, studied under the same professors. These scientists and technicians and analysts read the same publications and talk to each other at international congresses. They have access to satellites that constantly report to them construction projects of any size in other countries.

Furthermore, when we speak of the weapons of today, we are talking about objects of massive size that are being manufactured in enormous plants employing tens of thousands of people. There is nowhere a basement where a scientist with long hair is peering through a cracked microscope to come up with a death ray. The marvels of the last quarter of the 20th Century are the results of team effort—team efforts on such a massive scale that the process and the results cannot be hidden.

SECURITY IN OPENNESS

Our real security lies in intelligent and open use of our resources, including the men and women who adapt and direct the new technologies, and who are willing to work because they feel themselves to be a vital part of our society.

There is only one way such people can function effectively, and that is through the fullest and freest discussion. In the modern world, that means the public must be fully informed as to what its government is doing. Dictatorships can stay in power as long as they are successful. But they crumple at the first setback. Free people have the resiliency that enables them to recover from defeat.

It would be idle not to recognize the current reality. There are many people who say they have lost their confidence in a free press. Some think that the press spends too much time "taking out after people" and treating them with arrogance if not with insolence. Others believe that the press is too gloomy and is printing too much "bad news"—with the implication that "good things" would happen if "good news" were printed.

It is not difficult to sympathize with those points of view. The only trouble is that bad news is created by bad or misguided people. It is not printed because the press wants to "get" somebody but because we cannot make a better world unless we know what is wrong.

FREEDOM BELONGS TO THE PEOPLE

While the press is a "watchdog," in that it alerts the rest of us to what is happening in the world, when it comes to doing something about a matter, I am my own watchdog, as is every other American. It is not the press that takes after political leaders, but the people themselves when they find that the leaders have done something wrong. No newspaper or news magazine or network has ever brought down a president or caused a governor to be tossed out of office.

There is little doubt that we live in a world where most of the news is bad. We face crushing debts; irresponsible dictators who somehow must be kept in check; famine conditions in many parts of the world; and the ever present shadow of nuclear war. It is little wonder that a free press is required to bring us bad news under such circumstances.

If the press does *not* bring us bad news, the bad events will not go away. All that will happen is that we, the American people, will lose our ability to act and react intelligently. Much as we would like to do so, we cannot dig a hole and hide.

The First Amendment to the Constitution speaks with elegant simplicity. It belongs to me, to you, to every American. It does not establish a kind of subsidy for an industry nor is it a device for an evasion of responsibility.

There are some people, of course, who will use the First Amendment responsibly and others who will use it irresponsibly. But if we start giving pieces of it away, it will all perish—what we like and what we don't like.

Freedom of the press means freedom to obtain and to publish the knowledge without which we cannot manage our own affairs. We have done very well as a free people. Let's keep it up.

14

Keeping The Free Press Free

WILLIAM RENTSCHLER

Editor's Note: Freedom of the press in America is guaranteed by the First Amendment to the Constitution. The Constitution can be amended, however, as it has been twenty-six times already. If public outcry about the irresponsibility of the press should reach such force that changes to the First Amendment are proposed, the press and mass media could be placed under more stringent legal limitations.

Many claim that the extraordinary freedom enjoyed by mass media in this society carries with it unusual responsibilities. That is the argument put forward here by William Rentschler, a long-time journalist and author living and writing in Lake Forest, Illinois. This article is reprinted with permission from *Editor & Publisher,* October 25, 1997.

I know of no serious politician who would speak out for the curtailment of personal freedom. But I do know some who—in ways both subtle and blatant—would restrict freedom of the press. They are dead wrong.

To shackle the press is to assure ultimately the demise of freedom, perhaps at first only in fragments—but then, after all, isn't freedom indivisible?

"Our liberty," said Jefferson in 1786, "depends on the freedom of the press, and that cannot be limited without being lost."

I believe there were clumsy, occasionally sinister, attempts by some members of the Nixon administration to muzzle and frustrate the press during the Watergate scandal.

I would literally fight to my last breath to preserve the sacred right of the press to pursue the truth with its full vigor. I believe a press that is unshackled and responsible is the one dependable bulwark against encroachment on our personal liberties.

That applies as much to a small weekly newspaper as to a press giant like the *Chicago Tribune.*

A FREE PRESS MUST BE RESPONSIBLE

A critical point is that the free press must also be responsible. Yet even in instances of obvious irresponsibility—and they are not all that uncommon—I would continue to oppose vigorously any and all shackles, government control, or oppression of the press in any form.

The prime burden that guarantees a responsible free press must fall on the press itself. The responsible free press must look at itself with an eye at least as critical and objective as that which it trains on others. It must "investigate" itself with a zeal that would reflect credit on its best investigative reporters. It must truly listen and respond to constructive outside influences. It must make a conscientious effort to "connect" with its readers and freely offer redress to those who believe they have been wronged or unfairly defamed.

FREEDOM BRINGS CHALLENGES

What I am saying is that freedom of the press in its purest state imposes on the press itself an immense challenge, yes, an obligation to do right, to do better, to serve its readers and the public better than any other medium of communications.

The question then becomes: How and where can the daily press improve itself, how can it dispense the news and inform the people reliably and accurately, how can it help upgrade the quality and performance of government and our public servants, how can it contribute most effectively to the creation and preservation of a just, decent and free society?

Here are my thoughts:

- Much of the press today operates on the premise that the public figure is guilty until and unless proven innocent. Recent events tend to give credence to this notion, but it does conflict with deep-etched concepts of fairness and justice, and it does keep many of our very best people out of the public arena. It also tends to nurture the over-whelming cynicism and anti-politician mood which pervades the nation today. The press must curb its anti-politician posture without abandoning a responsible adversarial role.

CONCERNED WITH CELEBRITY STATUS

- Too many reporters today seem far more concerned with achieving superstar, even celebrity, status than with covering the news objectively, factually, fairly, with restraint and without sensationalism. Too many reporters seem to be angling for instant status as a Clarence Page or Bob Greene, a Kup or Bill Zwecker, for invitations to appear on *Meet the Press* or any of the overflow of tabloid TV shows. Or they're cranking up to write a million-dollar book, join the press staff of an established politician (the *Tribune*'s Tom Hardy recently became press chief for retiring Gov. Edgar) or do almost anything but report the news carefully and fairly. There was a time when the reporter was a reporter, only that, fairly obscure, but a dependable, professional craftsman. Perhaps that was as it ought to be.

• With some justification, the press claims to be "intimidated" by government. But intimidation is a two-way street. Today, in many respects, the power of the press literally outweighs that of government, for the press wields enormous power—the power to do good, but also the power to smudge a reputation, to end or at least derail a career, to destroy a life, even to alter society's course

Many in public life feel it is suicidal to take on the press, even to right a glaring wrong. The press has its ways of dealing with the complaining politician, the persistent critic, occasionally by the simple but deadly expedient of cutting his or her name out of its columns unless he murders his mother-in-law, gets indicted, or dies. Or the press can get on the back of a specific target—such as recently defrocked Chief Justice James Heiple of the Illinois Supreme Court or Chicago City Council Finance Chair Ed Burke—and ride him unmercifully with the ferocity of a pursuing wolf pack.

What I am saying is that the unfettered press must go to extreme lengths to be fair, to avoid all that's unfair, unbalanced unverified. The press must be as careful as government to avoid any course which might reasonably be interpreted as intimidation.

Editors are especially critical. Strong editors of high principle with the courage on occasion to "cross" their prima donna staff members—reporters and columnists in particular—are essential to maintaining and ever-implementing the integrity of the press.

JOURNALISTS AND POLITICIANS

For a metropolitan reporter—sometimes green, untrained, unleavened by any real depth of background or sense of history, at other times seasoned, but venal, arrogant, unresponsive to reason or enthusiasm—has influence which may exceed that of all but a handful of individuals across the whole spectrum of our society. To permit a green medic to perform delicate brain surgery could be akin to murder. Yet a green reporter's slant can kill a good bill, stall a vital project, elevate a dolt, or blacken undeservedly a reputation.

A few of the most biased, unprincipled, nastiest people I have known are journalists and politicians. Interestingly I would say the ratio of good to bad in each category is roughly comparable. Yet both groups include more people who are more deeply committed to the common good than most segments of our society.

My point is that it comes down to the editor who, in the final analysis, is most likely, most qualified, to provide the judgment, experience, depth and perspective that a reporter may lack.

A FAIR AND BALANCED PRODUCT

It is, as I see it, the obligation of the responsible, first-rate editor to exercise to the utmost his/her discretion, discrimination, influence—and, if necessary, veto power—even at the risk of offending prized staffers, often proud and defensive, to produce ultimately a fair and balanced editorial product.

- Among the most constructive contributions the press can make is a faithful recounting of the positive performance of most public officials. The almost unrelieved downgrading of politicians has resulted in a serious erosion of confidence and respect for those in public life. The public servant has become "fair game" to the extent that many of our most able and qualified citizens are unwilling to subject their families and reputations to the abuse and disrespect they would inevitably suffer. This is hardly a revelation, and the "adversary" relationship between press and government makes good sense unless carried to destructive extremes. The press must continue to investigate and unearth and criticize, but it has at least an equal obligation to add to public understanding of the public sector and its people by factual, fair reporting, backgrounding, explaining and interpreting in a rational, unsensational manner. Virtually every major newspaper I know has room for improvement in meeting this near-sacred obligation.
- The intelligent public, from which the press draws its most loyal and consistent readership, craves straight talk. Many papers today straddle and waffle, and seem bent on avoiding tough, unequivocal editorial stands on tough issues. Media critic Hodding Carter III says U.S. newspapers suffer from "the blands." People sense and often deplore this fence-sitting and discount the commitment of the press to any genuine set of journalistic principles. Syndicated columnists mostly tackle the same topics and sound pretty much alike, allowing for their ideological distinctions. Most spring from the New York/Beltway corridor and tap pretty much the same sources.

THE COOKIE-CUTTER EFFECT

This cookie-cutter effect may explain in part continuing circulation declines by the daily press. Without relying on focus groups and consultants, newspapers today must carve out their own distinctive profiles to regain their influence and appeal.

- Finally, it is the trust of ordinary people that assures a press freedom, a concept that loses its meaning if it loses the trust of the public. People, various polls and surveys show, are highly skeptical of the fairness, independence and trustworthiness of the nation's biggest dailies.

Rebecca W. Rimel, president of the Pew Charitable Trusts of Philadelphia, blames the "moat mentality" of owners, publishers and editors—their arrogance, condescension, high-and-mighty attitude—for the yawning gap, the moat, if you will, which separates the press from its readers and the general public, and turns many to other media for their enlightenment and entertainment. This poses an ominous threat to the otherwise bright future of America's major newspapers.

The press must be able to function without external restraint, without fear, without cause to fear. But at the same time a truly free press cannot reject or escape the restraints of conscience and responsibility.

15

The Totalitarianism of Democratic Media

DAVE BERKMAN

Editor's Note: The free media of democratic nations are more effective in promoting government policies, says author Dave Berkman, since unlike the controlled media of non-democratic states, their views are trusted by the public. Berkman argues that most media in democratic nations are owned by corporate and business groups that depend on government support for success and, therefore, help to promote official policies. He maintains that the U.S. government, aided by the media, must share the blame with totalitarian states such as the Soviet Union for past violations of world peace and stability.

Dave Berkman is a professor in the Department of Mass Communication, University of Wisconsin-Milwaukee, and a media columnist for the *Shepherd Express,* an alternative newspaper in Milwaukee. This article appeared in both *Media Ethics,* Fall 1993, and the *St. Louis Journalism Review,* March 1994, and is reprinted with permission.

It's always been taken on faith that, given their monolithic nature, totalitarian media are far more effective in promoting support for government actions and policies than are the non-governmentally controlled, free media in democratic nations such as the United States.

No media were more monolithic than the strictly party/government-controlled, agitprop-focused press in the Soviet Union. But because the populace knew that all they read, heard or viewed was strictly controlled by the Communist Party, few believed what they were told. The proof of this is the widespread opposition to everything which the Soviet government practiced and stood for, which manifested itself immediately on the heels of the Communist regime's collapse. This was also true, though perhaps to a lesser extent, with the Nazi press which held sway in Germany from Hitler's ascension to power in 1933 through the defeat of the Third Reich in 1945. For, if Nazi industry czar Albert Speer is to be believed, one of Hitler's constant fears was that support for the (ceaselessly propaganda-promoted) German war effort was so shallow, that he resisted all attempts to place the German economy on a full war footing until well after it became clear the Axis was doomed to defeat.

FREE MEDIA PROMOTING GOVERNMENT POLICY

Here in the United States, our Constitutionally guaranteed right to a free press allows the existence of alternative media such as the *Village Voice, Bay Guardian, The Nation,* and the book you're now reading. It also permits the presence of dissenting voices in our mainstream media such as Anthony Lewis in the *New York Times* and Bill Moyers on Public TV. And because these occasionally dissenting voices are allowed expression, this has given rise to a generally held belief that the American government can never succeed in achieving public acceptance of anything like an official party line.

Which is exactly why the ostensibly free American media have become so effective as promoters of American government policy and action: Clearly, a press over which there exists no governmental censorship apparatus telling it what it may or may not state must, by definition, be free—and therefore can be believed. But, what it turns out that the press's predominant tenets reflect—varying, except for the rare dissenters cited above, only in degree— are the policies, actions and beliefs which are held by the corporate interest/government oligopoly which has ruled America since the rise of big business in the last quarter of the nineteenth century. Those other two ostensibly free institutions in our society—public education and religion—equally reflect these values.

AMERICANS HAVE HAD NO DOUBT ABOUT ENEMIES

The Russians, apparently, never really accepted Americans as what their government-controlled media insisted as their enemies. But, except for a ragtag-left remnant, who in America, during the 40 years of Cold War, ever doubted what the government and our free press unilaterally proclaimed: the threat to American freedoms represented by the Soviet Union?

As any objective history of the second half of the twentieth century will reveal, we were at least as guilty as was the Soviet Union in the military and hegemonic excesses which wreaked gross havoc on the world. So why did we so mindlessly accept that we were the unsullied good guys and they were the evil empire?

Why have so many of us, who have been the victims of an exploitative economic system designed to benefit those who own and manage it at the expense of the rest of us, so mindlessly bought off on the belief that what benefits the few at the top is the system that benefits the rest of us? This, despite the unemployment, underemployment, poor pay and lack of such basic economic rights as health care that so increasingly result from this economic system.

CARRYING GOVERNMENT'S LINE WITHOUT FORCE

It's because when a nominally free media keep repeating in lockstep unison such absurdities as an America that leads a "Free World"—the dominant bromide of the pre–Soviet Collapse Era—or that "free market" is a synonym for "democracy"—the dominant bromide of the post–Soviet Era—why shouldn't we believe?

No one can point to any evidence, after all, that anyone in government is forcing a free media monolith to parrot such absurdities. Clearly, if without coercion, so many media voices seem to agree on such "truths," why should we disagree?

It makes you wonder—given the skepticism of those who've lived under totalitarianism—whether intellect doesn't manifest itself most freely where totalitarian media hold sway!

16

Stop Making Sense

CHRISTOPHER LASCH

Editor's Note: Some critics say mass media are failing to meet their responsibilities by being too bland and too objective. In this article, a widely published historian and media critic aments the current state of American journalism and calls for a return to the fiery partisan prose that characterized newspapers in the past.

Some of the blame, according to this author, lies with advertising and public relations. "Responsibility came to be equated with the avoidance of controversy," partly because of advertising and public relations. "The decline of the partisan press and the rise of a journalism professing rigorous standards of objectivity do not assure a steady supply of usable information," which is what is really necessary to make democracy and freedom possible.

The original version of this article first appeared in the Spring 1990 issue of the *Gannett Center Journal*. This version was published in *NewsInc.*, December 1990.

Let us begin with a simple proposition: What democracy requires is public debate, not information. Of course it needs information too, but the kind of information it needs can be generated only by vigorous popular debate. We do not know what we need to know until we ask the right questions, and we can identify the right questions only by subjecting our own ideas about the world to the test of public controversy. Information, usually seen as the precondition of debate, is better understood as its by-product. When we get into arguments that focus and fully engage our attention, we become avid seekers of relevant information. Otherwise, we take in information passively—if we take it in at all.

From these considerations it follows that the job of the press is to encourage debate, not to supply the public with information. But as things now stand the press generates information in abundance, and nobody pays any attention. It is no secret that the public knows less about public affairs than it used to know. Millions of Americans cannot begin to tell you what is in the Bill of Rights, what Congress does, what the Constitution says about the powers of the presidency, how the party system emerged or how it operates. Ignorance of public affairs is commonly attributed to the failure of the public schools, and only secondarily to the failure of the press to inform. But since the public no longer participates in debates on national issues, it has no reason to be better informed. When debate becomes a lost art, information makes no impression.

THE PRESS AND THE END OF DEBATE

Let us ask why debate has become a lost art. The answer may surprise: Debate began to decline around the turn of the century, when the press became more "responsible," more professional, more conscious of its civic obligations. In the early nineteenth century the press was fiercely partisan. Until the middle of the century papers were often financed by political parties. Even when they became more independent of parties they did not embrace the ideal of objectivity or neutrality. In 1841 Horace Greeley launched his *New York Tribune* with the announcement that it would be "a journal removed alike from servile partisanship on the one hand and from gagged, mincing neutrality on the other." Strong-minded editors like Greeley, James Gordon Bennett, E. L. Godkin, and Samuel Bowles did not attempt to conceal their own views or to impose a strict separation of news and editorial content. Their papers were journals of opinion in which the reader expected to find a definite point of view, together with unrelenting criticism of opposing points of view.

It is no accident that journalism of this kind flourished during the period from 1830 to 1900, when popular participation in politics was at its height. Eighty percent of the eligible voters typically went to the polls in presidential elections. After 1900 the percentage began to decline sharply, Torchlight parades, mass rallies, and gladiatorial contests or oratory made nineteenth-century polities an object of consuming popular interest.

JOURNALISM AS TOWN MEETING

In the midst of such politics, nineteenth-century journalism served as an extension of the town meeting. It created a public forum in which the issues of the day were hotly debated. Newspapers not only reported political controversies but participated in them, drawing in their readers as well. And print culture rested on the remnants of an oral tradition: Printed language was still shaped by the rhythms and requirements of the spoken word, in particular by the conventions of verbal argumentation. Print served to create a larger forum for the spoken word, not yet to displace or reshape it.

The "best men," as they liked to think of themselves, were never altogether happy with this state of affairs, and by the 1870s and 1880s their low opinion of politics had come to be widely shared by the educated classes. The scandals of the Gilded Age gave party politics a bad name. Genteel reformers—"mugwumps," to their enemies—demanded a professionalization of politics, designed to free the civil service from party control and to replace political appointees with trained experts.

The drive to clean up politics gained momentum in the Progressive Era. Under the leadership of Theodore Roosevelt, Woodrow Wilson, Robert La Follette, and William Jennings Bryan, the Progressives preached "efficiency," "good government," "bipartisanship," and the "scientific management" of public affairs, and declared war on "bossism." These reformers had little use for public debate. Most political questions were too complex in their view, to be submitted to popular judgment. They liked to contrast the scientific expert with the orator—the latter a useless windbag whose ranting only confused the public mind.

THE RISE OF PROFESSIONALISM

Professionalism in politics meant professionalism in journalism. The connection between the two was spelled out by Walter Lippmann in the Twenties, in a series of books that provided a founding charter for modern journalism—an elaborate rationale for a journalism guided by the new idea of professional objectivity. Lippmann held up standards by which the press is still judged.

In Lippmann's view, democracy did not require that people literally govern themselves. Questions of substance should be decided by knowledgeable administrators whose access to reliable information immunized them against emotional "symbols" and "stereotypes" that dominated public debate. The public, according to Lippmann, was incompetent to govern itself and did not even care to do so. A complex industrial society required a government carried on by officials who would necessarily be guided—since any form of direct democracy was now impossible—by either public opinion or expert knowledge. Public opinion was unreliable because it could be united only by an appeal to slogans and "symbolic pictures." Truth, as Lippmann conceived it, grew out of disinterested scientific inquiry; everything else was ideology. Public debate was at best a disagreeable necessity. Ideally, it would not take place at all; decisions would be based on scientific "standards of measurement" alone.

The role of the press, as Lippmann saw it, was to circulate information, not to encourage argument. The relationship between information and argument was antagonistic, not complementary. He did not take the position that argumentation was a necessary outcome of reliable information; on the contrary, his point was that information precluded argument, made argument unnecessary. Arguments were what took place in the absence of reliable information.

ONLY DEBATE LEADS TO UNDERSTANDING

Lippmann had forgotten what he learned (or should have learned) from William James and John Dewey: that our search for reliable information is itself guided by the questions that arise during arguments about a given course of action. It is only by subjecting our preferences and projects to the test of debate that we come to understand what we know and what we still need to learn. Until we have to defend our opinions in public, they remain opinions in

Lippmann's pejorative sense—half-formed convictions based on random impressions and unexamined assumptions. It is the act of articulating and defending our views that lifts them out of the category of "opinions," gives them shape and definition, and makes it possible for others to recognize them as a description of their own experience as well. In short, we come to know our own minds only by explaining ourselves to others.

The attempt to bring others around to our own point of view carries the risk, of course, that we may adopt their point of view instead. We have to enter imaginatively into our opponents' arguments, if only for the purpose of refuting them, and we may end up being persuaded by those we sought to persuade. Argument is risky and unpredictable—and therefore educational. Most of us tend to think of it (as Lippmann thought of it) as a clash of rival dogmas, a shouting match in which neither side gives any ground. But arguments are not won by shouting down opponents. They are won by changing opponents' minds.

If we insist on argument as the essence of education, we will defend democracy not as the most efficient but as the most educational form of government—one that extends the circle of debate as widely as possible and thus forces all citizens to articulate their views, to put their views at risk, and to cultivate the virtues of eloquence, clarity of thought and expression, and sound judgment. From this point of view, the press has the potential to serve as the equivalent of the town meeting.

RISE OF PUBLICITY AND PROMOTION

The rise of the advertising and public-relations industries, side by side, helps to explain why the press abdicated its most important function—enlarging the public forum—at the same time that it became more "responsible." A responsible press, as opposed to a partisan or opinionated one, attracted the kind of readers advertisers were eager to reach: well-heeled readers, most of whom probably thought of themselves as independent voters. These readers wanted to be assured that they were reading all the news that was fit to print, not an editor's idiosyncratic and no doubt biased view of things. Responsibility came to be equated with the avoidance of controversy because advertisers were willing to pay for it. Some advertisers were also willing to pay for sensationalism, though on the whole they preferred a respectable readership to sheer numbers. What they clearly did not prefer was "opinion"—not because they were impressed with Lippmann's philosophical arguments but because opinionated reporting did not guarantee the right audience. No doubt they also hoped that an aura of objectivity, the hallmark of responsible journalism, would rub off on the advertisements that surrounded columns of print.

In a curious historical twist, advertising, publicity, and other forms of commercial persuasion themselves came to be disguised as information and, eventually, to substitute for open debate. "Hidden persuaders" (as Vance Packard called them) replaced the old-time editors, essayists, and orators who made no secret of their partisanship. And information and publicity became increasingly indistinguishable. Today, most of the "news" in our newspapers consists of items churned out by press agencies and public-relations offices and then regurgitated intact by the "objective" organs of journalism.

DECLINE OF PARTISANSHIP

The decline of the partisan press and the rise of a journalism professing rigorous standards of objectivity do not assure a steady supply of usable information. Unless information is generated by sustained public debate, most of it will be irrelevant at best, misleading and manipulative at worst. Increasingly, information is generated by those who wish to promote something or someone without arguing their case on its merits or explicitly advertising it as self-interested material. Much of the press, in its eagerness to inform the public, has become a conduit for the equivalent of junk mail. When words are used merely as instruments of publicity or propaganda, they lose their power to persuade. Soon they cease to mean anything at all. People lose the capacity to use language precisely and expressively, or even to distinguish one word from another. The spoken word models itself on the written word instead of the other way around, and ordinary speech begins to sound like the clotted jargon we see in print. Ordinary speech begins to sound like "information"—a disaster from which the English language may never recover.

ADDITIONAL RESOURCES FOR PART 4

Suggested Questions and Discussion Topics

1. In "Reflections on the First Amendment," George Reedy makes three key arguments about why the First Amendment should prevail if officials cite "national security reasons" when they desire secrecy. What are they?

2. From "Reflections on the First Amendment," do you agree with the author about national security? Why?

3. According to William Rentschler's "Keeping the Press Free," freedom comes with some responsibilities. According to the author, with whom should the responsibilities ultimately lie, and why?

4. According to "Keeping the Press Free," how would Rentschler argue with Reedy about journalistic coverage of political figures?

5. In "The Totalitarianism of Democratic Media," what does David Berman suggest about the "adversarial role" of the news media in America?

6. From "The Totalitarianism of Democratic Media," discuss your own ideas about Berman's point of view.

7. From "Stop Making Sense," why does the author, Christopher Lasch, feel that "objective" journalism does not really enlarge the public forum?

8. In "Stop Making Sense," Lasch traces the decline in public debate to a change in the press at the turn of the century. What was that change?

Suggested Readings

J. Herbert Altschull, *From Milton to McLuhan: The Ideas Behind American Journalism.* New York: Longman, 1990.

Margaret A. Blanchard, *Revolutionary Sparks: Freedom of Expression in Modern America.* New York: Oxford University Press, 1995.

Ted Galen Carpenter, *The Captive Press: Foreign Policy Crises and the First Amendment.* Washington, DC: Cato Institute, 1995.

Commission on Freedom of the Press, *Freedom of the Press: A Framework of Principle.* New York: Da Capo Press, 1972.

Elizabeth Blanks Hindman, *Rights vs. Responsibilities: The Supreme Court and the Media.* Westport, CT: Greenwood, 1997.

William E. Hocking, *Freedom of the Press: A Framework of Principle.* Chicago: University of Chicago Press, 1947.

John C. Merrill, *The Dialectic in Journalism: Toward a Responsible Use of Press Freedom.* Baton Rouge, LA: Louisiana State University Press, 1993.

William L. Miller, ed., *Alternatives to Freedom: Arguments and Opinions.* New York: Longman, 1995.

Roy L. Moore, *Mass Communication Law and Ethics.* Mahwah, NJ: Lawrence Erlbaum Associates, 1998.

John C. Nerone, ed., *Last Rights: Revisiting Four Theories of the Press.* Chicago: University of Illinois Press, 1995.

Lucas A. Powe, *The Fourth Estate and the Constitution: Freedom of the Press in America.* Berkeley, CA: University of California Press, 1992.

Frederick S. Siebert, Theordore Peterson, and Wilbur Schramm, *Four Theories of the Press.* Urbana, IL: University of Illinois Press, 1956, 1963.

Oliver Trager, ed., *The Arts and Media in America: Freedom or Censorship.* New York: Facts on File, 1991.

Suggested Videos

"Media Rights and Responsibilities." New York: Insight Media, 1997. (30 minutes)

"Media Law." New York: Insight Media, 1995. (30 minutes)

"The Communications Decency Act." New York: Insight Media, 1996. (102 minutes)

"First Amendment Freedoms." New York: Insight Media, 1989. (30 minutes)

"Anatomy of a Libel Case: Business vs. the Media." New York: Insight Media, 1985. (120 minutes)

"Cultural and Media Messages: Response and Responsibility." New York: Insight Media, 1996. (58 minutes)

"The Hollywood Censorship Wars." New York: Insight Media, 1993. (50 minutes)

PART · 5

Ethical Values

It is important to say at the outset of any discussion about ethical values that these are matters of social norms, not of laws. One isn't obligated by law to comply with a social norm; to do so is a voluntary and personal matter. Since few laws govern mass media, given the First Amendment guaranteeing press freedom, most of our legitimate concerns about media deal with ethics. For example, there is no law against telling a lie by mass media, but it would be unethical to do so. There is no law against doctoring a photograph, but that would be unethical as well.

Of course, mass communicators cannot violate normal laws (murder, theft, bribery, etc.) in doing their work. Yet some of their legal activities may strike some people as unethical because they might seem to be violations of social norms. Nevertheless, communicators are free to violate such norms because they are only voluntary.

There is probably a difference between the social norms accepted by journalists and those accepted by some of their critics. Most journalists in American society seem to be motivated by the idea that the public has a right to know what is going on in any sphere of activity. There are others (perhaps even some journalists, too) who feel that the public shouldn't know everything. Journalists frequently believe that whatever they do is justified if the end result is to inform the public. For example, using stolen documents might be justified if the information they contain is essential to the public. Some would call this behavior unethical, but it is not illegal.

There are journalistic behaviors, however, that society in general, including journalists, would consider unethical. Such behavior can be divided into two categories. First is exploitation of others for one's own gain. Sensationalizing news, not for the purpose of keeping people informed but to sell media, would be unethical to most journalists. Invading a person's privacy, not to reveal some essential information but to sell that information, would also be unethical to most journalists. Causing persons embarrassment or even harm by identifying them publicly when it is not essential to do so, such as in a rape case, would be considered unethical, particularly if the motive for the revelation is to attract an audience and thus make a greater profit from the information. For the press or mass media to do these things is not illegal, but many would rightly question the ethics of such behavior.

Second is the problem of allowing outsiders to exploit the mass media for their own gain or purposes. Journalists who allow themselves to be used so that others can influence the public have broken an unwritten contract with their audiences. They have not broken any laws, but we would certainly question their ethics. Conflict of interest is one of the most frequent problems here. Journalists might put forth information as if it were balanced, fair, accurate, and objective when in reality it represents a biased point of view because of the journalists' own involvement with one side of an issue. Again, they have not broken any laws, but they have committed what many would regard as unethical behavior.

Journalists who allow others with special interests to influence their work, whether deliberately or out of laziness and inattention to their job, also have not violated a law, but we should question their ethics. If an item released by some PR office is published or broadcast as if it were a balanced and objective account, no law would be broken, but we could legitimately question the ethics of such behavior.

Most American news media have codes of conduct for their employees that deal with ethical standards. An organization might discipline employees for violating its code of conduct, but the employee could not be charged with breaking any law. Many journalistic associations, such as the Society of Professional Journalists and the Radio Television News Directors Association, maintain codes of conduct. These are not laws by which communicators must live; they are voluntary guidelines. Even so, there are growing concerns about the ethical behavior of mass media, and the articles in this section describe some of the current problems.

17

Are Journalists People?

JAMES FALLOWS

Editor's Note: The death of Princess Diana in the late summer of 1997 caused a great deal of hand-wringing and soul-searching about the ethics of the mass media. The *paparazzi* were blamed for chasing Diana to her fatal auto accident, and by implication, the media were accused of buying *paparazzi* photographs and of encouraging their activity. Some said it was all the public's fault through having such a voracious appetite for celebrity.

The event did cause many thoughtful journalists and analysts to look at the ethics of mass media more closely. Journalists have a particular view that their professional role is to give the public information that it needs and wants. In filling that job, they must do so without feeling, or their emotions will lead them to bias or short-change the information. How can journalists do their job while doing less harm?

That is the question James Fallows tries to answer in this thoughtful and philosophical look at the problem. A long-time journalist and media critic, he is a former editor of *U.S. News & World Report*, in which this article originally appeared on September 15, 1997. It is reprinted with permission.

Doctors take the Hippocratic oath, saying that their first duty is to "do no harm." But it's not that simple. In their training, doctors learn that duty can require sawing open a skull to fix a brain, administering poison to combat cancer, scarring flesh to cut out disease. To do their job, they must set aside part of their humanity—the part that makes them hesitate to put a knife through skin. They can live with themselves, and we can respect them, in the knowledge that the harm is toward a valued end. While they set aside part of their humanity, they have not rejected it all. We call the ones who do monsters, like the Nazi sadist Dr. Josef Mengele.

With doctors as with other groups authorized to do harm—soldiers, police, judges who deprive people of their liberty, business competitors who deprive rivals of markets and their employees of jobs—there are outside constraints meant to contain the social damage. A soldier who goes too far may face court-martial. An army unit that goes too far may face war-crime trials.

Rogue police officers know that review boards exist. For doctors, the constraints range from licensing requirements to the threat of malpractice suits.

JOURNALISTS ARE REGARDED AS CALLOUS

Yet for all these groups, the internal constraints are more important: the daily judgments, by individuals whose daily decisions may harm others, about how many normal "human" sympathies they can maintain and still do their job. Through World War II and the 1950s, Gens. George C. Marshall and Curtis LeMay were both professional soldiers. Both were bound by the same code of honor and rules of war; both were devoted to the security of the United States. But they are remembered very differently now, because of the way each balanced his soldierly and "human" sensibilities. During the war, LeMay supervised the firebombing of Tokyo, which killed more people than died in Hiroshima; afterward, he advocated keeping U.S. nuclear forces on hair-trigger alert. Marshall, having mobilized a fighting and killing force as Army chief of staff, argued when the war was over that rebuilding the beaten enemy was the wisest course. LeMay is now seen as a dogged but limited warrior; Marshall, as a great man—the only career soldier to have won the Nobel Prize for peace. Marshall's concept of duty left room for other aspects of human sympathy. LeMay's idea of professional duty blotted out most everything else.

Today's journalists might ask themselves: Which is the better example of true tough-mindedness? Which suggests the right way to carry out hard professional obligations without forgetting every other moral claim? Journalists should ask, because others will be asking for them in the aftermath of Princess Diana's death.

Despite her own tangled relationship with fame and the media, despite the complex chain of specific blame for the high-speed crash, the instantaneous world-wide reaction against the *paparazzi* suggests that people think journalists are callous and cavalier about the harm we do. We are believed to hound attractive celebrities, to be more interested in human weakness than in anything else, to chew up private lives for short-run entertainment. The car crash was a painfully literal illustration of the damage that people believe the press can cause.

JOURNALISTS CAN DO HARM

Like doctors, soldiers, and police, journalists are among the select groups authorized to do harm. Those of us in this business may tell ourselves that it's not true—that we're just putting out tomorrow's fish wrap (updated version: "It's only TV!"), that the charges and countercharges we print will sort themselves out, that it doesn't matter what we say as long as we spell the names right. No one outside the business believes that. We give people labels—Richard Jewell, "Atlanta bomber"—and the labels stick long after our attention has moved on. Through the way they treat their friends and families, people try over the decades to define how they prefer being known. The words, pictures, truths, and lies we present about them can obliterate that identity forever. For people outside the business, dealing with reporters is like dealing with police: There is no such thing as a fair fight.

As with doctors, police, and soldiers, the harm we do is necessary—on the whole. You need only live in one of the world's many countries without a free press to see damage on a different scale. Government corruption goes uncontested. Cronies flourish, uncriticized. Torture, official murder, even slavery persist—whispered about, but officially uncondemned. In societies with an aggressive press, by contrast, the daily fear of exposure is an unavoidable and healthy part of government and corporate life. Like able doctors, the best journalists have learned to set aside parts of their humanity—the part that mainly makes them feel sorry for the cabinet official whose career is ruined through his own greed, the part that makes them reluctant to ask the impolite question of someone who has been nice to them. As with the police, the good that journalists do is usually on behalf of society at large, not the person they are dealing with (who often resents them). This is an important line of work, but not a healing art.

FEW LIMITS ON JOURNALISTS

Because there are so few external limits on what journalists can do (mainly libel laws, a remote concern for most in the news business in most of their work), and because we know we must anesthetize part of our humanity, many influential people in this business take a further step. They begin to assume that there is *no* balance, no tradeoff, no limit to what we should do. Our duty, we tell ourselves, is exclusively to be tough, and then to let the public sort out the consequences. The ethic is like that of lawyers willing to use any courtroom trick to help their clients. But in court there is someone fighting back from the other side.

The truth is that in viewing any of the occupations whose members are allowed to do harm, the public wants to see evidence of the internal struggle. They want to see police officers considering whether deadly force is necessary, soldiers and statesmen worrying about the harm they might cause civilians, doctors wondering at what cost to prolong life—and reporters wrestling with whether it's necessary to invade someone's privacy or damage someone's reputation and, if so, why.

That is why the most damaging allegation against the *paparazzi*—the one detail the photographers broke silence to rebut—is that when they came across the crash they simply took pictures and did nothing else to help. That was apparently an offense under French law, which obliges passersby to render aid. More important, it is a violation of what we would expect of human beings, no matter what their professional role.

JOURNALISTS CAN FACE HARD CHOICES

In times of emergency, journalists—and especially photographers—face truly hard moral choices. Twenty-five years ago, in Vietnam, it was of greater human benefit for the AP's Nick Ut to get a photo of nine-year-old Kim Phuc running naked down a highway with napalm burning her back, forever dramatizing the effects of war, than for him to have dropped his camera and rushed to her aid. In drought-stricken Sudan, photographer Kevin Carter saw an even younger girl about to starve to death. He took a picture, showing a vulture waiting in the background; afterward, the girl died. The picture, which won the 1994 Pulitzer Prize, did more than any other news story to draw attention to the famine. But Carter was racked by criticism that he should have tried to save the girl. Three months after receiving the award, he killed himself.

Carter's story is tragic, but in less catastrophic ways the public would like to see the struggle, would like journalists to show that we know these are hard choices and that we are mindful when inflicting harm. There was little sign of this in Paris. The only visible moral struggle was about whether it was right for journalists to embarrass members of their trade. Other photographers declined to snap photos of their seven colleagues under investigation. "If it's clear they don't want me to take their pictures, I won't, out of professional solidarity," a staff photographer for the newspaper *Le Parisien* was quoted as saying. "Information is light," proclaims a photojournalist in Tom Stoppard's play *Night and Day,* when asked to justify his business. But only when the information is about someone else.

Why do we resist showing the struggle and pretend that the choices aren't hard? There are two reasons: one we'll admit in public, one we won't.

The public reason is that we're giving the audience what it demands—the market makes us do it. The *paparazzi* chased Diana because pictures of her are so valuable; they are so valuable because newspapers know they will boost sales; *ergo* the people who buy the tabloids to see photos of Diana helped chase her to her death.

DRIVEN BY THE MARKET?

Satisfying the market is part of the story, and a newspaper that no one buys or a broadcast that no one watches might as well not exist. The problem with relying on this excuse is that except in Cuba or North Korea, everyone lives with market pressures. The police must respond to a political market that demands safe streets (and doesn't much care how that happens). Politicians answer a relentless market of opinion polls and election returns. Sitcom producers need big audience numbers. So does anyone who puts out a movie, or a record, or a book.

Yet as soon as people in these other categories say they have no choice about what they do because of the market, editorialists and columnists jump all over them. How dare you sell cigarettes, just because people want to buy them? How can you publish pornography indiscriminately, just because you know it will sell? To journalists, politicians who "pander"—that is, respond to a market—are more contemptible than pornographers. Our editorials and analysis pieces tell them that they should shape and push and lead political markets—lift people up, like FDR or Lincoln, rather than follow them down, like Joe McCarthy. The press's tools for changing public opinion are nearly

identical to politicians'. And if senators or presidents are expected to sur-
mount the immediate demands of the electoral market—which threatens to
put them out of work, not just cut into profits—then the same standard
should apply to the press. What people care about is at least partly shaped by
what the press serves up. This market, like the one for political ideas, works
both ways.

The other reason, which we're less comfortable admitting, is that thinking
about consequences and humanity is considered weak. In our business even
mentioning it is soft minded and sentimental—a sign that you are too squea-
mish for the real work, like a police officer who falls for hard-luck tales from
cons or a surgeon afraid to see blood.

There is something real to this concern, too. A crucial part of journalistic
work is being willing to "pull the trigger" and do stories that will make powerful people mad. The Army did not want to read Seymour Hersh's stories about
My Lai. Neither Al Gore nor Haley Barbour wants to see one more story, ever,
about their sources of political funds. But there is a difference between knowing you have to act like a prosecutor sometimes and always acting that way.
Even prosecutors choose not to prosecute, sometimes proving their respect
for the law by closing a file after an investigation.

THE LUKAS EXAMPLE

Surgeons cause problems when they assume that every ailment can be cured
by cutting. Journalists cause problems when they ignore the examples of colleagues who are tough without being bullies and show that toughness partly
by restraint.

Three months before journalists shocked the world with news of the death
of Diana, many in the business gathered to mourn J. Anthony Lukas, a legen-
darily thorough reporter for the *Baltimore Sun* and the *New York Times* and
author of five books. At a memorial service in Manhattan, one well-known
writer after another expressed admiration for Lukas's craft. But the most powerful tributes came from people who, if they were known, were known because of Lukas: They were real-life characters in his most celebrated book,
Common Ground.

Colin and Joan Diver were portrayed in the book as once idealistic young
white liberals who, though consumed with guilt, moved to the white suburbs
from their home in a South Boston neighborhood filled with blacks when their
exasperation with crime and racial strife became too great. The book ended with
a barbed description of Colin Diver (who has since become dean of the University
of Pennsylvania Law School) obsessively painting and repairing the white picket
fence that separated his new suburban house from the ominous world beyond.

In the eight years he spent researching the book, Lukas intruded more
deeply on the Divers (and two other families, the poor black Twymons and
poor Irish McGoffs) than any photographer tracking Diana. He wanted to
know everything about them. The book chronicled, in intimate detail, the failure of the Divers' grand dream. Yet when Lukas died, a dozen years after the

book came out, Joan Diver rose to "celebrate your giant presence in our lives" and her husband read aloud the very description of him and his fence that ended the book.

PROVING IT CAN BE DONE

Then Rachel and Cassandra Twymon spoke. They are two members of a family whose every difficulty and weakness—as well as aspiration—had also been chronicled in *Common Ground*. They broke down in tears as they described how fully Lukas had entered their family's existence—"it seemed like Tony just lived with us"—and how much they would miss someone so deeply curious about their lives. The sorrow of Lukas's subjects said much about him as a man. The significance for the craft of journalism was what he proved: that a tough, pushy, hard-minded investigator could commit himself to telling the whole awkward truth about a situation without making his subjects feel used. Instead, they felt understood and honored by the record he made of their lives.

Lukas had years to research and write his book, as do others who take on similar projects. Daily and weekly journalism, tyrannized by limits of space and time, can never treat anything with the same exhaustive nuance. Everything on TV has the same problem. Yet limits of imagination hold more reporters back than do those of space and time. On-the-spot coverage of breaking stories can have these noble aspirations. It takes only an instant to snap an unforgettable picture like the ones taken after the Oklahoma City bombing.

An astounding piece of newspaper reporting came three years ago from Leon Dash of the *Washington Post*. He inserted himself totally into the life of a family that, on paper, belongs in the depths of the American underclass. The central character, Rosa Lee Cunningham, was a drug addict, thief, welfare cheat, and terrible mother, who taught her children to steal and turned tricks with her babies in the next room. Most of the children, when grown up, ended up in jail or on welfare. Dash neither sentimentalized the family nor demonized them. He presented every humiliating truth in an illuminating way. For his work, he won a Pulitzer Prize, along with photographer Lucian Perkins, whose pictures of Rosa—lost in thought at her apartment window, appraising the quality of sweaters stolen by her son in a burglary, leading a congregation in song at a Baptist church—are unvarnished, poignant, remarkable.

Winners of Pulitzers are considered the best in the newspaper business, and the list is full of exemplars. This year, a joint prize went to a reporter, Michael Vitez, and a photographer, Ron Cortes, for their series in the *Philadelphia Inquirer* about chronically ill patients who wanted to die with dignity.

But the examples aren't limited to prizewinners and once we start down the list, we could go on for pages, with admirable work from newspapers around the country, radio, and television. And that is the point: not that everything is so great in the news business just because there are a number of good stories, but that a number of our colleagues have disproved those who argue that balanced coverage is impossible in our business. They do not operate under different rules from anyone else. The constraints and incentives come from within. An inner awareness of the struggle to remain human is what has made police, soldiers, and doctors respectable. It can make the public respect the value of our work again.

18

Methods of Media Manipulation

Michael Parenti

Editor's Note: The claim that media bias results from innocent error or deadline pressure is overstated, according to Michael Parenti. He writes that many important stories are under-reported—or completely ignored—because the media refuse to take on powerful interests such as corporations. He maintains that the media have suppressed important news about the military and CIA, have not told all sides of many crucial stories, and often have framed information to create a particular impression without explicit advocacy or lack of objectivity.

Michael Parenti is the author of thirteen books, including *Inventing Reality: The Politics of News Media.* This article is reprinted with permission from *The Humanist,* in which it originally appeared in July/August 1997.

We are told by people in the media industry that news bias is unavoidable. Whatever distorsions and inaccuracies found in the news are caused by deadline pressures, human misjudgment, budgetary restraints, and the difficulty of reducing a complex story into a concise report. Furthermore—the argument goes—no communication system can hope to report everything; selectivity is needed.

I would argue that the media's misrepresentations are not all the result of innocent error and everyday production problems, though such problems certainly do exist. True, the press has to be selective, but what principle of selectivity is involved?

Media bias usually does not occur in random fashion; rather, it moves in the same overall direction again and again, favoring management over labor, corporations over corporate critics, most whites over low-income minorities, officialdom over protesters, the two-party monopoly over leftist third parties, privatization and free market "reforms" over public sector development, U.S. dominance of the Third World over revolutionary or populist social change, national security policy over critics of that policy, and conservative commentators and columnists like Rush Limbaugh and George Will over progressive or populist ones like Jim Hightower and Ralph Nader (not to mention more radical ones). The built-in biases of the corporate mainstream media faithfully reflect the dominant ideology, seldom straying into territory that might cause discomfort to those who hold political and economic power, including those who own the media or advertise in it.

SUPPRESSION BY OMISSION

Manipulation often lurks in the things left unmentioned. The most common form of media misrepresentation is suppression by omission. Sometimes the omission includes not just vital details of a story but the entire story itself, even ones of major importance. As I just noted, stories that might reflect poorly upon "the powers that be" are the least likely to see the light of day. Thus, the Tylenol poisoning of several people by a deranged individual was treated as big news, but the far more sensational story of the brown-lung poisoning of thousands of factory workers by large manufacturing interests (who themselves own or advertise in the major media) remained suppressed for decades, despite the best efforts of worker safety groups to bring the issues before the public.

We hear plenty about the political repression perpetrated by left-wing governments such as Cuba (though a recent State Department report actually cited only six political prisoners in Cuba), but almost nothing about the far more brutal oppression and mass killings perpetrated by U.S.-supported right-wing client states such as Turkey, Indonesia, Saudi Arabia, Morocco, El Salvador, Guatemala, and others too numerous to mention.

Often the media mute or downplay truly sensational (as opposed to sensationalistic) stories. Thus, in 1965 the Indonesian military—advised, equipped, trained, and financed by the U.S. military and the CIA—overthrew President Achmed Sukarno and eradicated the Indonesian Communist Party and its allies, killing half a million people (some estimates are as high as a million) in what was the most heinous act of political mass murder since the Nazi Holocaust. The generals also destroyed hundreds of clinics, libraries, schools, and community centers that had been opened by the communists. Here was a sensational story if ever there was one, but it took three months before it received passing mention in *Time* magazine and still another month before it was reported in the *New York Times*. (The April 5, 1966, piece was accompanied by an editorial that actually praised the Indonesian military for "rightly playing its part with utmost caution.")

Information about the massive repression, murder, and torture practiced by U.S.-sponsored surrogate forces in the Third World, and other crimes committed by the U.S. national security state, simply are omitted from the mainstream media and thereby denied public debate and criticism. They are suppressed with an efficiency and consistency that would be called totalitarian were it to occur in some other countries.

ATTACK AND DESTROY THE TARGET

Sometimes a story won't go away. A congressional investigation begins or information is circulated around the world on the Web, as recently happened with the CIA-crack expose. In any case, it begins to reach larger publics and gain visibility despite the suppression perpetrated by "our free and independent media." When omission proves to be sufficient, the media move from ignoring the story to vigorously attacking it. So we get the hit pieces in the print and broadcast media—a barrage, unrelenting, repetitive, unforgiving, backed by a cascade of outright lies.

Thus, at one time or another over the course of forty years, the CIA involved itself with drug traffickers in Italy, France, Corsica, Indochina, Afghanistan, and Central and South America. Much of this activity was the object of extended congressional investigations—by Senator Frank Church's Foreign Relations Committee and Congressman Otis Pike's House Select Intelligence Committee in the 1970s, and Senator John Kerry's Select Committee on Intelligence in the late 1980s—and is a matter of public record. But the media seem not to have heard about it.

In August 1996, when the *San Jose Mercury News* published an in-depth series about the CIA-contra crack shipments that were flooding East Los Angeles, the major media held true to form and suppressed the story. But after the series was circulated around the world on the Web, the story became too difficult to ignore, and the media began its assault. Articles in the *Washington Post* and *New York Times* and reports on network television announced that there was "no evidence" of CIA involvement, that the *Mercury News* series was "bad journalism," and that the public's interest in this subject was the real problem, a matter of gullibility, hysteria, and conspiracy mania. In fact, the *Mercury News* series, drawing from a year-long investigation, cited specific agents and dealers. When placed on the Web, the series was copiously supplemented with pertinent documents and depositions that supported the charge. In response, the mainstream media simply lied, telling the public that such evidence did not exist. By a process of relentless repetition, the major media exonerated the CIA from any involvement in drugs.

LABELING

Like all propagandists, media people seek to predetermine our perception of a subject with a positive or negative label. Some positive ones are "stability," "the President's firm leadership," "a strong defense," and "a healthy economy." Indeed, who would want instability, weak presidential leadership, a vulnerable defense, and a sick economy? The label predefines the subject and does it without having to deal with actual particulars that might lead us to a different conclusion.

Some common negative labels include "leftist guerrillas," "Islamic terrorists," "conspiracy theories," "inner-city gangs," and "civil disobedience." These, too, are seldom treated within a larger context of social relations and issues. The press itself is facilely and falsely labeled "the liberal media" by the hundreds of conservative columnists, commentators, and talk show hosts who crowd the communication universe while claiming to be shut out of it.

FACE-VALUE TRANSMISSION

One way to lie is to accept at face value what are known to be official lies, uncritically passing them on to the public without adequate confirmations. For the better part of four years, in the early 1950s, the press performed this function for Senator Joseph McCarthy, who went largely unchallenged as he brought charge after charge of "treason" and "communist subversion" against people whom he could not have victimized without the complicity of the national media.

Face-value transmission has characterized the media's performance in almost every area of domestic and foreign policy, so much so that journalists have been referred to as "stenographers of power." (Perhaps some labels are well deserved.) When challenged on this, reporters respond that they cannot inject their own personal ideology into their reports. Actually, no one is asking them to. My criticism is that they already do. Their conventional ideological perceptions usually coincide with those of their bosses and with officialdom in general, making them faithful surveyors of the prevailing orthodoxy. This influence of bias is perceived as "objectivity."

FALSE BALANCING

In accordance with the canons of good journalism, the media are supposed to tap competing sources to get both sides of an issue. In fact, both sides are seldom accorded equal prominence One study found that on National Public Radio, supposedly the most liberal of the mainstream media, right-wing spokespersons are often interviewed alone, while liberals—on the less frequent occasions they appear—are almost always offset by conservatives.

Furthermore, both sides of a story are not necessarily all sides. During the 1980s, television panel discussions on defense policy pitted "experts" who wanted to maintain the existing high levels of military spending against other "experts" who wanted to increase the military budget even more. Seldom, if ever heard, were those who advocated drastic reductions in the defense budget. Progressive and radical views are almost completely shut out.

FRAMING

The most effective propaganda is that which relies upon framing rather than on falsehood. By bending the truth rather than breaking it, using emphasis and other auxiliary embellishments, communicators can create a desired impression without resorting to explicit advocacy and without departing too far from the appearance of objectivity. Framing is achieved in the way the news is packaged, the amount of exposure, the placement (front page or buried within, lead story or last), the tone of presentation (sympathetic or slighting), the headlines and photographs, and, in the case of broadcast media, the accompanying visual and auditory effects.

Newscasters use themselves as auxiliary embellishments. They cultivate a smooth delivery and try to convey an impression of detachment that places them above the rough and tumble of their subject matter. Television commentators and newspaper editorialists and columnists affect a knowing style and tone designed to foster credibility and an aura of certitude—or what might be called authoritative ignorance—as expressed in remarks like "How will this situation end? Only time will tell," or "No one can say for sure" (better translated as, "I don't know and if I don't know then nobody does"). Sometimes the aura of authoritative credibility is preserved by palming off trite truisms as penetrating truths. So newscasters learn to fashion sentences like "The space launching will take place as scheduled if no unexpected problems arise," and "Because of lagging voter interest, election-day turnout is expected to be light," and "Unless Congress acts soon, this bill is not likely to go anywhere."

We are not likely to go anywhere as a people and a democracy unless we alert ourselves to the methods of media manipulation that are ingrained in the daily production of news and commentary. The news media regularly fail to provide a range of information and commentary that might help citizens in a democracy develop their own critical perceptions. The job of corporate media is to make the universe of discourse safe for corporate America, telling us what to think about the world before we have a chance to think about it for ourselves. When we understand that news selectivity is likely to favor those who have power, position, and wealth, we move from a liberal complaint about the press' sloppy performance to a radical analysis of how the media serve the ruling circles all too well with much skill and craft.

19

Photographs That Lie

J. D. LASICA

Editor's Note: In a free press system, there are few laws against telling a lie. Today it is easy to rearrange a photograph so it has no connection to reality, yet people will believe it to be a true representation of reality because it is a photograph. Isn't that telling a lie? And while not illegal (unless it is in an advertisement and the altered photograph would make a fraudulent claim), most of us would say it is unethical.

Even in advertising, it is rare that an altered photograph in an ad can be proved to be so blatant as to be fraudulent. And in news, doctored photographs would be totally protected by the First Amendment, although certainly a photo changed so as to damage a person's reputation could be subject to a libel action in court.

This wide latitude to alter pictures raises a host of issues about the ethical dilemma of digital retouching of photographs for publication. These same issues are a concern for the visual representation of reality on television and motion picture screens as well.

This article explains technological developments in photography and examines the resulting ethical concerns. It should be noted that all the technical innovations the author suggested would take place when he wrote this article in the late 1980s have subsequently become common practice by the end of the 1990s.

Author J. D. Lasica is a features editor and columnist at the *Sacramento Bee.* This article was originally published in the *Washington Journalism Review* in June 1989, and is reprinted with permission.

A few years ago I wandered into a seminar touting the wonders that technology would bring to the photographs of tomorrow. Up on the screen, a surreal slide show was in progress. One slide showed Joan Collins sitting provocatively on President Reagan's lap. *Click.* Joan was now perching, elfishly, on the president's shoulder. *Click.* Reagan had grown a third eye. *Click.* Now he was bald. *Click.* And so on.

A representative from the Scitex Corporation, a Bedford, Massachusetts, company that manufactures digital retouching equipment, said that computers could now alter the content of photographs in virtually any manner. The slides had all been produced electronically—with no trace of tampering.

The audience, clearly dazzled, tossed off a dozen or so questions about whether the machines could do this or that. Finally a hand shot up. "Nobody's said a word about the potential for abuse here. What about the ethics of all this?"

"That's up to you," said the representative.

Welcome to journalism's latest ethical nightmare: photographs that lie.

THE NEW DIGITAL ARTISTRY

In the past few years, this razzle-dazzle digital artistry has begun to turn up at the nation's largest newspapers, magazines and book publishing houses. The trend has a lot of people worried.

Consider what has taken place already:

- Through electronic retouching *National Geographic* slightly moved one of the Great Pyramids at Gîza to fit the vertical shape of its cover in 1982.
- An editor at the *Asbury Park Press,* the third-largest newspaper in New Jersey, removed a man from the middle of a news photo and filled in the space by "cloning" part of an adjoining wall. The incident prompted the paper to issue a policy prohibiting electronic tampering with news photos.
- The *Orange County Register,* which won a Pulitzer Prize for its photo coverage of the 1984 Summer Olympics, changed the color of the sky in every one of its outdoor Olympics photos to a smog-free shade of blue.
- The editors of the book *A Day in the Life of America* could not choose a cover photo from the thousands of pictures taken by the world's leading photojournalists. They solved the problem electronically by taking a photo of a cowboy on horseback, moving him up a hillside and, for good measure, enlarging the crescent moon. "I don't know if it's right or wrong," says co-director David Cohen. "All I know is it sells the book better."
- For one of its covers, *Popular Science* used a computer to place an airplane from one photo onto the background of another aerial photo. And a number of magazines have combined images of people photographed at different times, creating composites that give the false appearance of a single cover shot.
- The *St. Louis Post-Dispatch* used a Scitex computer to remove a can of Diet Coke from a photo taken of Ron Olshwanger, winner of the 1989 Pulitzer Prize for photography.

WHAT IS REALITY?

Faster than you can say "visual credibility gap," the 1980s may be the last decade in which photos could be considered evidence of anything.

"The photograph as we know it, as a record of fact, may no longer in fact be that in three or five years," warns George Wedding, director of photography for the *Sacramento Bee.*

Jack Corn, director of photography for the *Chicago Tribune,* one of the first papers to buy a Scitex system, says the stakes are enormous. "People used to be able to look at photographs as depictions of reality," he says. "Now, that's being lost. I think what's happening is just morally, ethically wrong."

Digital technology's impact will be no less dramatic in other areas.

Within a decade, consumers will be able to buy a hand-held digital camera that uses a microchip instead of film, allowing the owner to "edit" photos. Soon you'll be able to remove your mother-in-law from that otherwise perfect vacation snapshot.

In the cinema, some experts are predicting the day when long-dead movie stars will be re-animated and cast in new films. "In 10 years we will be able to bring back Clark Gable and put him in a new show," John D. Goodell, a computer graphics consultant, told the *New York Times.*

Beyond such fanciful applications of digital technology, Goodell raises a dark scenario. Consider what might happen if the KGB or a terrorist group used such technology to broadcast a fabricated news bulletin about a natural disaster or an impending nuclear attack—delivered by a synthetic Dan Rather.

TV'S CREDIBILITY AT STAKE

More likely than an assault by the Islamic Jihad on our airwaves will be an assault on our trust in visual images. Will photos be admissible evidence in a courtroom if tampering cannot be detected? Can newspapers rely on the truthfulness of any photo whose authenticity cannot be verified? As the price of these machines comes down, what will happen when the grocery-store tabloids start using—or abusing—them?

In television, too, the potential for abuse is great. Don E. Tomlinson, assistant professor of journalism at Texas A&M University, foresees the day when news producers try to re-create news events that they failed to capture on camera using exotic technology whose use was once confined to cinematic special effects. Airing such a simulation on a nightly newscast could confuse viewers about whether they're watching the real thing.

Tomlinson goes so far as to suggest that an unscrupulous TV reporter might use digital technology to fabricate an entire story because of ratings pressure, for career advancement or simply to jazz up the news on a slow day. A shark lurking near a populated beach, for example, could be manufactured using the file footage and a digital computer.

PRINT MEDIA ALSO LIABLE

While digital machinations on television may pose the greatest threat to the credibility of visual images in the long run, today the war is being waged in print.

Ironically, publishers are snapping up these systems not for their photoaltering capabilities but for economic reasons. Newspapers and magazines are using digital computers to achieve huge savings in labor and materials, enhance the quality of color photo reproduction, push back editorial dead-lines (because of the time saved) and transmit color separations to remote printing plants via satellite.

Among the publications already employing the technology are *Time, Newsweek, U.S. News & World Report, USA Today, Newsday,* the *Atlanta Journal* and *Constitution,* the *Providence Journal-Bulletin* and, most recently, the *New York Times.* (Incidentally, while Scitex is the industry leader in producing these machines, it is not alone in the field. Crosfield Electronics of East Rutherford, New Jersey, and Hell Graphics Systems of Port Washington, New York, also manufacture digital retouching systems.)

"People have no idea how much alteration is going on," says Michael Morse of the National Press Photographers Association. "When you're looking at that *Redbook* or *Mademoiselle* or *Sports Illustrated* tomorrow, there's a good chance somebody has done something to that picture."

Of course, some of this photo modification is familiar terrain. Pictures have been faked since the earliest days of photography in the 1850s. Retouching photos by hand was once common practice in many newsrooms, and photographers can change the composition of a black-and-white print in the darkroom. But over the years, ethical standards have tightened. Today retouching a news photo is forbidden at most publications, and faking a photo can be grounds for dismissal.

RULES ARE CHANGING

As the tools of the trade change, however, the rules of the game evolve as well. Altering a photo has never been so fast and seamless. Digital systems allow an editor or art director to capture, display, alter, transmit and publish a picture without it ever seeing photographic paper.

A photographer in the field is now able to capture an image on a light-sensitive semiconductor chip and send it to the newsroom via telephone line, microwave or even satellite. The image—a collection of hundreds of thousands of pixels, similar to the makeup of a TV screen—is then reassembled on the video monitor of a picture editing station, or "electronic darkroom," where an editor can size it, crop it, enhance the contrast and tone and correct minor flaws. From there the image is sent to a color laser plotter, which converts the pixels into signals of zeros and ones (representing the densities of magenta, cyan, yellow and black printing inks) and produces a color separation. While conventional processing reads a transparency or photo by exposing it to light, electronic scanning creates an instant digital representation of an image. *Voilà!* A process that would normally take hours is accomplished in minutes. With a plaything this seductive, it's easy to understand the temptation to "improve" a news photo at the stroke of a few keys.

Rolling Stone magazine used a digital computer to erase a pistol and holster shing over the arm of "Miami Vice" star Don Johnson after he posed for a 1985 cover shot. Editor Jann Wenner, an ardent foe of handguns, ordered the change; using a computer saved the time and expense of having the cover re-shot.

WHERE DO YOU DRAW THE LINE?

Unquestionably, this high-tech process is here to stay. The question thus becomes: Where do you draw the line?

"If someone wants to remove a tree from a photo or move two people closer together, that's crossing the line," says Dennis Copeland, director of photography for the *Miami Herald*. "The media's image has been hurt because of those few people who've abused the technology."

While a spot survey of editors, art directors and picture editors at major newspapers nationwide found no one who supported the notion of using digital technology to tamper with the integrity of a documentary news photograph, there was far greater acceptance of using it to create conceptual or illustrative photos.

The distinction is far from academic. Documentary photographs aim to portray real events in true-to-life settings. Conceptual photos are meant to symbolize an idea or evoke a mood. Because a studio shot of, say, a truffle is more akin to a still life than to the hard-edge realism of photojournalism—indeed, because the shot is staged in the first place—art directors and page designers are given wide latitude in altering its content.

What is happening, many photographers and picture editors fear, is that the distinction between the two styles is blurring, partly due to the new technology. Scott Henry, chief photographer for the *Marin County* (California) *Independent-Journal,* detects in photojournalism "a quiet shift toward pictures as ornamentation or entertainment rather than reportage."

And George Wedding of the *Bee* says of tampered photographs, "Fabricated images that look authentic or first glance sometimes taint the believability of the pictures around them."

Wedding sees a trend toward increased reliance on conceptual photos, caused in part by the recent influx into newsrooms of art directors and designers who take their visual cues from art schools and the advertising field, where manipulation is the name of the game. "These people have not been taught the traditional, classic values and goals of documentary photojournalism," he says.

Joseph Scopin, assistant managing editor for graphics at the *Washington Times* (which uses the Scitex system), thinks those fears are overblown. "If you run a photo of someone holding a 4-foot-tall, 300-pound strawberry, it's pretty obvious to the reader we're playing with the images," he says.

READERS DON'T ALWAYS UNDERSTAND

Sometimes, however, the distinction can be lost on the reader.

The *Asbury Park Press* ran into that difficulty in 1987 when it ran a cover story in its "Health and Fitness" section on a new kind of beef with lower cholesterol. Says Nancy Tobin, the paper's design director, "We had a head-on shot of a cow munching hay and a studio shot of a beautiful salad, and [we] combined the two images on Scitex. People came up to us afterward and said, 'How'd you get that cow to eat that salad?' We labeled it *composite photo illustration,* but some people were left scratching their heads."

Readers may grow more accustomed to digital photography's use as it spreads from the feature sections to the rest of the paper. Last summer the *Hartford Courant* ran a Page One color photo that showed how the city's skyline will look after several new skyscrapers go up; the feat was accomplished with *Newsday's* Scitex equipment. Experts say it won't be long before newspapers' real estate pages display computer-created photos, rather than rough "artist's conceptions," of planned developments.

But some observers worry that increased use of digital retouching will make readers skeptical about the integrity of even undoctored images.

"People believe in news photographs. They have more inherent trust in what they see than what they read," says Kenneth Kobre, head of photojournalism studies at San Francisco State University. "Digital manipulation throws all pictures into a questionable light. It's a gradual process of creating doubts in the viewer's mind."

NEW SELF-RESTRAINT

It was precisely that concern that led *National Geographic,* the magazine that moved a pyramid, to rethink its position. Jan Adkins, former associate art director, explains: "At the beginning of our access to Scitex, I think we were seduced by the dictum, 'If it can be done, it must be done.' If there was a soda can next to a bench in a contemplative park scene, we'd have the can removed digitally.

"But there's a danger there. When a photograph becomes synthesis, fantasy rather than reportage, then the whole purpose of the photograph dies. A photographer is a reporter—a photon thief, if you will. He goes and takes, with a delicate instrument, an extremely thin slice of life. When we changed that slice of life, no matter in what small way, we diluted our credibility. If images are altered to suit the editorial purposes of anyone, if soda cans or clutter or blacks or people of ethnic backgrounds are taken out, suddenly you've got a world that's not only unreal but surreal."

Adkins promises that, at *National Geographic* anyway, "the Scitex will never be used again to shift any one of the Seven Wonders of the World, or to delete anything that's unpleasant or add anything that's left out."

But even if other publications begin to show similar self-restraint, critics warn, digital technology is making additional inroads that threaten the credibility of visual images.

TEMPTING TECHNOLOGIES

Already, there are a half dozen software programs on the market, such as "PhotoMac" or "Digital Darkroom" for the Macintosh, that allow the user to edit photographs digitally. The programs retail for about $700.

And then there is the digital camera, a sort of hand-held freeze-frame video camera that should be in stores within a decade, at a price within reach of the average buyer. What disturbs many people about this device is that the original image exists in an electronic limbo that can be almost endlessly manipulated. The camera differs from Scitex digital retouching equipment, which works with an original photo or negative.

"The term *photographic proof* may already be an archaic term," says the *Bee's* Wedding. "You used to be able to hold up a negative and see that the image is real. With the advent of digital technology, you're going to hold up a floppy disk and you're not going to see anything."

Adds Tobin of the *Asbury Park Press:* "This is scaring everyone, because there's no original print, no hard copy. From the moment the shutter is snapped, it exists only as a digitized electronic impulse. Talk about the ability to rewrite history! It literally will be possible to purge information, to alter a historic event that occurred five years ago because no original exists. There's enormous potential for great wrong and great misuse."

Scitex spokesperson Ned Boudreau says the digital industry addressed such concerns long ago. "To hear the critics tell it," he says, "it's like we've unleashed Joe McCarthy all over again. We haven't."

He says safeguards, such as an archiving system that stores originals where no one can get at them, can be built into the digital equipment. At present, however, manufacturers do not provide such options unless requested.

ACCEPTANCE, OR THE LOSS OF TRUST

John Derry, director of graphic services for Chromaset, a San Francisco creative-effects studio that has used digital retouching for dozens of corporations advertising campaigns, thinks Americans will learn to accept the technology as it becomes pervasive. "Maybe it's generational," he says. "My mother could never tell the difference between videotape and movies, between the hard, sharp edge of Johnny Carson and the soft look of motion picture film.

"As we move into this new technology, perhaps there will be people who won't be able to discern electronically manipulated images from undoctored images. But I think most of us are already pretty savvy about this stuff. If you show someone a picture of Reagan punching Gorbachev, most people won't think it's real. They'll think, Oh, look at this doctored photo. How'd they do that?"

None of this assuages the critics of digital technology, but even its detractors concede this much: It's not the technology itself that's the culprit. Machines aren't ethical or unethical; people are.

"You've got to rely on people's ethics," says Brian Steffans, a top graphics photography editor at the *Los Angeles Times.* "That's not much different from relying on the reporter's words. You don't cheat just because the technology is available."

Wedding of the *Bee* is less sanguine about the future of news photography: "I hope that 10 years from now readers will be able to pick up a newspaper and magazine and believe what they read and see. Whether we are embarking on a course which will make that impossible, I don't know. I'm afraid we have."

20

Where We Went Wrong

JULES WITCOVER

Editor's Note: One of the biggest media stories of the 1990s has been the press coverage of President Clinton's sex scandals. In its eagerness to cover the Monica Lewinsky episode, for whatever motive, the news media have been seen by much of the American public to be grossly unethical. In fact, many would say that the press has suffered more than the president as a result of the coverage.

In this article, long-time Washington reporter Jules Witcover analyzes what caused the news media to make their judgments, and there are many lessons to learn.

Witcover is new a Washington correspondent for the *Baltimore Sun* and has been a reporter and columnist covering Washington for forty-three years. He is the author of thirteen books on U.S. presidential politics and history. This article was published in the *Columbia Journalism Review*, March/April 1998, and is reprinted with permission.

In the sex scandal story that has cast a cloud over the president, Bill Clinton does not stand to be the only loser. No matter how it turns out, another will be the American news media, whose reputation as truth-teller to the country has been besmirched by perceptions, in and out of the news business, about how the story has been reported.

The indictment is too sweeping. Many news outlets have acted with considerable responsibility, especially after the first few frantic days, considering the initial public pressure for information, the burden of obtaining much of it from sealed documents in legal proceedings and criminal investigations, and the stonewalling of President Clinton and his White House aides.

But the explosive nature of the story, and the speed with which it burst on the consciousness of the nation, triggered in the early stages a piranha-like frenzy in pursuit of the relatively few tidbits tossed into the journalistic waters by—whom? That there were wholesale leaks from lawyers and investigators was evident, but either legal restraints or reportorial pledges of anonymity kept the public from knowing with any certainty the sources of key elements in the saga.

Into the vacuum created by a scarcity of clear and credible attribution raced all manner of rumor, gossip and, especially, hollow sourcing, making the reports of some mainstream outlets scarcely distinguishable from supermarket tabloids. The rush to be first or to be more sensational created a picture of irresponsibility seldom seen in the reporting of presidential affairs. Not until the story settled in a bit did much of the reporting again begin to resemble what has been expected of mainstream news organizations.

WHITE HOUSE DAMAGE CONTROL

The Clinton White House, in full damage-control mode, seized on the leaks and weakly attributed stories to cast the news media as either a willing or unwitting collaborator of sorts with independent counsel Kenneth Starr's investigation of alleged wrongdoing by the president. Attacking the independent counsel and his office was a clear diversionary tactic, made more credible to many viewers and readers by suggesting that the overzealous news business, so suspect already in many quarters, was being used by Starr.

Unlike the Watergate scandal of twenty-five years ago, which trickled out over twenty-six months, this scandal broke like a thunderclap, with the direst predictions from the start. Whereas in the Watergate case the word impeachment was unthinkable and not uttered until much later in the game, the prospect of a premature end to the Clinton presidency was heard almost at once. "Is He Finished?" asked the cover line on *U.S. News & World Report*. Not to be outdone, *The Economist* of London commanded, "If It's True, Go."

ABC News's White House correspondent Sam Donaldson speculated on *This Week with Sam and Cokie* on January 25 that Clinton could resign before the next week was out. "If he's not telling the truth," Donaldson said, "I think his presidency is numbered in days. This isn't going to drag out. . . . Mr. Clinton, if he's not telling the truth and the evidence shows that, will resign, perhaps this week."

NEWS AROUND THE CLOCK

After Watergate, it was said that the president had been brought down by two reporters, Bob Woodward and Carl Bernstein, and their newspaper, *The Washington Post,* and they were widely commended for it. This time, after initial reporting by Michael Isikoff of *Newsweek,* there was a major piling-on by much of American print and electronic journalism, for which they have been widely castigated. A *Washington Post* poll taken ten days after the story broke found 56 percent of those surveyed believed the news media were treating Clinton unfairly, and 74 percent said they were giving the story "too much attention."

The advent of twenty-four-hour, all-news cable channels and the Internet assured the story of non-stop reportage and rumor, augmented by repeated break-ins of normal network programming and late-night rehashes. Viewing and listening audiences swelled, as did newspaper and magazine circulation, accommodated by special press runs.

Not just the volume but the methodology of the reporting came in for sharp criticism—often more rumor-mongering than fact-getting and fact-checking, and unattributed appropriation of the work and speculation of others. The old yardstick said to have been applied by the *Post* in the Watergate story—that every revelation had to be confirmed by two sources before publication—was summarily abandoned by many news outlets.

As often as not, reports were published or broadcast without a single source named, or mentioned in an attribution so vague as to be worthless. Readers and listeners were told repeatedly that this or that information came from "sources," a word that at best conveyed only the notion that the information was not pure fiction or fantasy. As leaks flew wildly from these unspecified sources, the American public was left as seldom before in a major news event to guess where stories came from and why.

Readers and listeners were told what was reported to be included in affidavits and depositions in the Paula Jones sexual harassment case—information that supposedly was protected by a federal judge's gag order—or presented to independent counsel Starr. Leakers were violating the rules while the public was left to guess about their identity, and about the truth of what was passed on to them through the news media, often without the customary tests of validity.

NEW ROLE OF THE INTERNET

In retrospect, it was sadly appropriate that the first hint of the story really broke into public view not in *Newsweek,* whose investigative reporter, Isikoff, had been doggedly pursuing for more than a year Paula Jones's allegations that Clinton had made inappropriate sexual advances to her when he was governor of Arkansas. Rather, it surfaced in the wildly irresponsible Internet site of Matt Drudge, a reckless trader in rumor and gossip who makes no pretense of checking on the accuracy of what he reports. ("Matt Drudge," says Jodie Allen, Washington editor for Bill Gates's online magazine *Slate,* "is the troll under the bridge of Internet journalism.")

Drudge learned that *Newsweek* on Saturday, January 17, with its deadline crowding in, had elected not to publish. According to a February 2 *Newsweek* report, prosecutors working for Starr had told the news-magazine they needed a little more time to persuade former White House intern Monica Lewinsky to tell them about an alleged relationship she had with the president that had implications of criminal conduct.

Early Saturday morning, according to the same *Newsweek* report, the magazine "was given access to" a tape bearing conversations between Lewinsky and her friend Linda Tripp. But the *Newsweek* editors held off. Opting for caution of the sort that in earlier days was applauded, they waited.

The magazine also reported that publication was withheld because the tapes in themselves "neither confirmed nor disproved" obstruction of justice, because the magazine had "no independent confirmation of the basis for Starr's inquiry," and because its reporters had never seen or talked with

Lewinsky "or done enough independent reporting to assess the young woman's credibility." If anything, such behavior if accurately described resonated with responsibility, although holding back also left *Newsweek* open to speculation by journalists that its action might have been a quid pro quo for information received.

Drudge, meanwhile, characteristically feeling no restraints, on Monday morning, January 19, jumped in and scooped *Newsweek* on its own story with a report that the newsmagazine had "spiked" it after a "screaming fight in the editors' offices" on the previous Saturday night. Isikoff later said "there was a vigorous discussion about what was the journalistically proper thing to do. There were no screaming matches."

Drudge was not without his defenders. Michael Kinsley, the editor of *Slate,* argued later that "the Internet beat TV and print to this story, and ultimately forced it on them, for one simple reason lower standards . . . There is a case to be made, however, for lower standards. In this case, the lower standards were vindicated. Almost no one now denies there is a legitimate story here." Kinsley seemed to harbor the crazy belief that had Drudge not reported that *Newsweek* had the story, the newsmagazine never would have printed it the next week, and therefore the Internet could take credit for "forcing" the story on the mainstream news media.

Newsweek, not going to press again until the next Saturday, finally put the story on its America Online site on Wednesday, January 21, after *The Washington Post* had broken it on newsstands in its early Wednesday edition out Tuesday night, under the four-column banner atop page one CLINTON ACCUSED OF URGING AIDE TO LIE. The story was attributed to "sources close to the investigation." ABC News broadcast the gist of it on radio shortly after midnight Wednesday.

THE STORY SPREADS LIKE WILDFIRE

The *Los Angeles Times* also had the story in its Wednesday editions, but *The New York Times,* beaten badly by the *Post* on the Watergate story a quarter of a century earlier, was left at the gate again. The lead on its first story on Thursday, January 22, however, was a model of fact: "As an independent counsel issued a fresh wave of White House subpoenas, President Clinton today denied accusations of having had a sexual affair with a twenty-one-year-old White House intern and promised to cooperate with prosecutors investigating whether the president obstructed justice and sought to have the reported liaison covered up."

The story spread like an arsonist's handiwork. *The Washington Post* of Thursday reported from "sources familiar with the investigation" that the FBI had secretly taped Lewinsky by placing a "body wire" on Tripp and had got information that "helped persuade" Attorney General Janet Reno to ask for and receive from the three-judge panel overseeing the independent counsel authorization to expand the investigation.

On that same Thursday, the *Times* identified Lucianne Goldberg, the literary agent who later said she had advised Tripp to tape her conversations with Lewinsky. But *The Washington Post* continued to lead the way with more information apparently leaked by, but not attributed specifically to, lawyers in the case, and in the Paula Jones sexual harassment lawsuit that had caught Lewinsky in its web.

GOOD TASTE AS VICTIM

On network television on Friday, taste went out the window. ABC News correspondent Jackie Judd reported that "a source with direct knowledge of" Lewinsky's allegations said she "would visit the White House for sex with Clinton in the early evening or early mornings on the weekends, when certain aides who would find her presence disturbing were not at the office." Judd went on: "According to the source, Lewinsky says she saved, apparently as a kind of souvenir, a navy blue dress with the president's semen stain on it. If true, this could provide physical evidence of what really happened."

That phrase "if true" became a gate-opener for any rumor to make its way into the mainstream. Judd's report ignited a round of stories about a search for such a dress. Despite disavowals of its existence by Lewinsky's lawyer, William Ginsburg, stories soon appeared about a rumored test for tell-tale DNA by the FBI.

The *New York Post,* under the headline MONICA KEPT SEX DRESS AS A SOUVENIR, quoted "sources" as saying the dress really was "a black cocktail dress that Lewinsky never sent to the cleaners," adding that "a dress with semen on it could provide DNA evidence virtually proving the man's identity—evidence that could be admissible at trial." The newspaper also reported that "Ken Starr's investigators searched Lewinsky's Watergate apartment, reportedly with her consent, and carried off a number of items, including some clothing," which Ginsburg subsequently confirmed. He later said that the president had given Lewinsky a long T-shirt, not a dress.

The Village Voice, in a scathing retracing of the path taken by the ABC News report of a semen-stained dress, labeled Judd's account hearsay and noted it had nevertheless been picked up by other news organizations as if such a dress existed. Six days after the original ABC story, CBS News reported that "no DNA evidence or stains have been found on a dress that belongs to Lewinsky" that was "seized by the FBI from Lewinsky's apartment" and tested by "the FBI lab."

ABC, the next day reported that "according to law enforcement sources, Starr so far has come up empty in a search for forensic evidence of a relationship between Mr. Clinton and Lewinsky. Sources say a dress and other pieces of clothing were tested, but they all had been dry cleaned before the FBI picked them up from Lewinsky's apartment." In this comment, ABC implied that there had been stains, and it quoted a ABC spokesperson as saying, "We stand by that initial report" of a semen-stained dress.

A close competitor for the sleaziest report award was the one regarding the president's alleged sexual preference. On Wednesday, January 21, the Scripps Howard News Service reported that one person who has listened to the Lewinsky-Tripp tapes said Lewinsky "described how Clinton allegedly first urged her to have oral sex, telling her that such acts were not technically adultery."

THE WHITE HOUSE CRISIS

That night, on ABC News's *Nightline,* Ted Koppel advised viewers gravely that "the crisis in the White House" ultimately "may come down to the question of whether oral sex does or does not constitute adultery." The question he insisted, was neither "inappropriate" nor "frivolous" because "it may bear directly on the precise language of the president's denials. What sounds, in other words, like a categorical denial may prove to be something altogether different."

Nightline correspondent Chris Bury noted Clinton's "careful use of words in the matter of sex" in the past. He recalled that in 1992, in one of Gennifer Flowers's taped conversations offered by Flowers in her allegations of a long affair with the then governor of Arkansas, she "is heard discussing oral sex with Clinton. Bury went on, "during this same time period, several Arkansas state troopers assigned to the governor's detail had said on the record that Clinton would tell them that oral sex is not adultery."

The distinction came amid much speculation about whether Clinton, in his flat denial of having had "sexual relations with that woman," might be engaging in the sort of semantic circumlocution for which he became notorious in his 1992 presidential campaign when asked about his alleged affair with Flowers, his draft status, smoking marijuana, and other matters.

The Washington Post on Sunday, January 25, reported on the basis of the Tripp tapes that "in more than 20 hours of conversations" with Tripp, "Lewinsky described an eighteen-month involvement that included late-night trysts at the White House featuring oral sex." The story noted in its second paragraph: "Few journalists have heard even a portion of these audio tapes, which include one made under the auspices of the FBI. Lewinsky herself has not commented on the tapes publicly. And yet they have been the subject of numerous news accounts and the fodder for widespread speculation." Nevertheless, it then added: "Following are descriptions of key discussions recorded on the tapes, information that *The Washington Post* has obtained from sources who have listened to portions of them."

SUITABLE FOR CHILDREN?

The story went on to talk of "bouts of 'phone sex' over the lines between the White House and her apartment" and one comment to Tripp in which Lewinsky is alleged to have said she wanted to go back to the White House—as the newspaper rendered it—as "special assistant to the president for [oral sex] " The same story also reported that "Lewinsky tells Tripp that she has an article of clothing with Clinton's semen on it."

On television, these details led some anchors, such as Judy Woodruff of CNN, to preface some reports with the kind of unsuitable-for-children warning usually reserved for sex-and-violence shows like *NYPD Blue*. But comments on oral sex and semen may have been more jarring to older audiences, to whom such subjects have been taboo, than to viewers and readers from the baby boom and younger.

The tabloids were hard-pressed to outdo the mainstream, but they were up to the challenge. Borrowing from *The Sun* of London, the *New York Post* quoted Flowers in an interview saying "she reveals that Clinton once gave her his 'biblical' definition of oral sex: "It isn't 'real' sex." The headline on the story helped preserve the *Post*'s reputation: GOSPEL ACCORDING TO BUBBA SAYS ORAL SEX ISN'T CHEATING.

Meanwhile, the search for an eyewitness to any sexual activity between Clinton and Lewinsky went on. On Sunday, January 25, Judd on ABC reported "several sources" as saying Starr was investigating claims that in the spring of 1996, the president and Lewinsky "were caught in an intimate encounter" by either Secret Service agents or White House staffers. The next morning, the front-page tabloid headlines of both the *New York Post* and the New York *Daily News* shouted, CAUGHT IN THE ACT, with the accompanying stories attributed to "sources."

BREAKDOWN IN SOURCING

Other newspapers' versions of basically the same story had various attributions: the *Los Angeles Times:* "people familiar with the investigation"; *The Washington Post:* "sources familiar with the probe"; *The Wall Street Journal:* "a law enforcement official" and "unsubstantiated reports." The *Chicago Tribune* attributed ABC News, using the lame disclaimer "if true" and adding that "attempts to confirm the report independently were unsuccessful." *The New York Times,* after considering publication, prudently decided against it.

Then on Monday night, January 26, *The Dallas Morning News* reported in the first edition of its Tuesday paper and on its Web site: "Independent counsel Kenneth Starr's staff has spoken with a Secret Service agent who is prepared to testify that he saw President Clinton and Monica Lewinsky in a compromising situation in the White House, sources said Monday." The story, taken off the Internet by The Associated Press and put on its wire and used that night on *Nightline,* was retracted within hours on the ground that its source had told the paper that the source had been mistaken (see box, page 21).

Then there was the case of the television talk show host, Larry King, referring to a *New York Times* story about a message from Clinton on Lewinsky's answering machine—when there was, in fact, no such story. Interviewing lawyer Ginsburg the night of January 28, King told his guest that the story would appear in the next day's paper, only to report later in the show: "We have a clarification, I am told from our production staff. We may have jumped the gun on the fact that *The New York Times* will have a new report on the phone call from the president to Monica Lewinsky, the supposed phone call. We have no information on what *The New York Times* will be reporting tomorrow."

Beyond the breakdown in traditional sourcing of stories in this case, not to mention traditional good taste, was the manner in which a questionably sourced or totally unsourced account was assumed to be accurate when printed or aired, and was picked up as fact by other reporters without attempting to verify it.

LOOSE ATTRIBUTIONS

For days, a report in *The Washington Post* of what was said to be in Clinton's secret deposition in the Paula Jones case was taken by the press as fact and used as the basis for concluding that Clinton had lied in 1992 in an interview on *60 Minutes.* Noting that Clinton had denied any sexual affair with Gennifer Flowers, the *Post* reported that in the deposition Clinton acknowledged the affair, "according to sources familiar with his testimony."

Loose attribution of sources abounded. One of the worst offenders was conservative columnist Arianna Huffington. She offered her view on the CNBC talk show *Equal Time* that Clinton had had an affair with Shelia Lawrence, the widow of the late ambassador whose body was exhumed from Arlington National Cemetery after it was revealed he had lied about his military record. Huffington, in reporting on the alleged affair, confessed that "we're not there yet in terms of proving it." So much for the application of journalistic ethics by journalistic amateurs.

With CNN and other twenty-four-hour cable outlets capable of breaking stories at any moment and Internet heist artists like Drudge poised to pounce on someone else's stories, it wasn't long before the Internet became the venue of first resort even for a daily newspaper. *The Wall Street Journal* on February 4, ready with a report that a White House steward had told a grand jury summoned by Starr that he had seen Clinton and Lewinsky alone in a study next to the Oval Office, posted the story on its World Wide Web site and its wire service rather than wait to break it the next morning in the *Journal.* In its haste, the newspaper did not wait for comment from the White House, leading deputy press secretary Joe Lockhart to complain that "the normal rules of checking or getting a response to a story seem to have given way to the technology of the Internet and the competitive pressure of getting it first."

POUNCING ON JUICY MORSELS

The Web posting bore the attribution "two individuals familiar with" the steward's testimony. But his lawyer soon called the report "absolutely false and irresponsible." The *Journal* that night changed the posting to say the steward had made the assertion not to the grand jury but to "Secret Service personnel." The story ran in the paper the next day, also saying "one individual familiar with" the steward's story "said that he had told Secret Service personnel that he found and disposed of tissues with lipstick and other stains on them" after the Clinton-Lewinsky meeting. Once again, a juicy morsel was thrown out and pounced on by other news outlets without verification, and in spite of the firm denial of the *Journal* report from the steward's lawyer.

One of the authors of the story, Brian Duffy, later told *The Washington Post* the reason the paper didn't wait and print an exclusive the next morning was because "we heard footsteps from at least one other news organization and just didn't think it was going to hold in this crazy cycle we're in." In such manner did the race to be first take precedence over having a carefully checked story in the newspaper itself the next day.

White House press secretary Michael McCurry called the *Journal*'s performance "one of the sorriest episodes of journalism" he had ever witnessed, with "a daily newspaper reporting hour-by-hour" without giving the White House a chance to respond. *Journal* managing editor Paul Steiger replied in print that "we went with our original story when we felt it was ready" and "did not wait for a response from the White House" because "it had made it clear repeatedly" it wasn't going to respond to any questions about any aspect of the case.

Steiger said at that point that "we stand by our account" of what the steward had told the Secret Service. Three days later, however, the *Journal* reported that, contrary to its earlier story, the steward had not told the grand jury he had seen Clinton and Lewinsky alone. Steiger said "we deeply regret our erroneous report of the steward's testimony."

COMPETING FOR NEWS BREAKS

On a less salacious track, the more prominent mainstream dailies continued to compete for new breaks, relying on veiled sources. *The New York Times* contributed a report on February 6 that Clinton had called his personal secretary, Betty Currie, into his office and asked her "a series of leading questions such as: 'We were never alone, right?'" The source given was "lawyers familiar with her account."

The *Post,* "scrambling to catch up," as its media critic Howard Kurtz put it, shortly afterward confirmed the meeting "according to a person familiar with" Currie's account. Saying his own paper used "milder language" than the *Times* in hinting at a motivation of self-protection by the president, Kurtz quoted the *Post* story that said "Clinton probed her memories of his contacts with Lewinsky to see whether they matched his own." In any event, Currie's lawyer later said it was "absolutely false" that she believed Clinton "tried to influence her recollection."

The technology of delivery is not all that has changed in the reporting of the private lives of presidents and other highranking officeholders. The news media have traveled light years from World War II days and earlier, when the yardstick for such reporting was whether misconduct alleged or proved affected the carrying out of official duties.

In 1984, when talk circulated about alleged marital infidelity by presidential candidate Gary Hart, nothing was written or broadcast because there was no proof and no one willing to talk. In 1987, however, a *Newsweek* profile reported that his marriage had been rocky and he had been haunted by rumors of womanizing. A tip to *The Miami Herald* triggered the stakeout of his Washington townhouse from which he was seen leaving with Donna Rice. Only after that were photographs of the two on the island of Bimini displayed in the tabloid *National Enquirer* and Hart was forced from the race. Clearly, the old rule—that questions about a public figure's private life were taboo—no longer applied.

But the next time a presidential candidate ran into trouble on allegations of sexual misconduct—Bill Clinton in 1992—the mainstream press was dragged into hot pursuit of the gossip tabloids that not too many years earlier had been treated like a pack of junkyard dogs by their supposedly ethical betters. The weekly supermarket tabloid, *Star,* printed a long, explicit first-person account of Flower's alleged twelve-year affair with Clinton. Confronted with the story on the campaign trail in New Hampshire, Clinton denied it but went into extensive damage control, culminating in his celebrated *60 Minutes* interview. With the allegations quickly becoming the centerpiece of his campaign, the mainstream press had no recourse but to report how he was dealing with it. Thus did the tail of responsible journalism come to wag the dog.

BLURRING THE LINE

From then on, throughout Clinton's 1992 campaign and ever since, the once-firm line between rumor and truth, between gossip and verification, has been crumbling. The assault has been led by the trashy tabloids but increasingly accompanied by major newspapers and television, with copy-cat tabloid radio and TV talk shows piling on. The proliferation of such shows, their sensationalism, bias and lack of responsibility and taste have vastly increased the hit-and-run practice of what now goes under the name of journalism.

The practitioners with little pretense to truth-telling or ethics, and few if any credentials suggesting journalistic training in either area, now clutter the airwaves, on their own shows (Watergate felon G. Gordon Liddy, conspiracy-spinner Rush Limbaugh, Iran-Contra figure Oliver North) or as loudmouth hosts and guests on weekend talkfests (John McLaughlin, Matt Drudge).

In the print press and on the Internet as well, journalism pretenders and poseurs feed misinformation, speculation, and unverified accusations to the reading public. The measure of their success in polluting the journalism mainstream in the most recent Clinton scandal was the inclusion of Drudge, as a guest analyst on NBC News' *Meet the Press.* The program also included Isikoff, the veteran *Newsweek* investigative reporter.

Playing straight man to Drudge, moderator Tim Russert asked him about "reports" that there were "discussions" on the Lewinsky tapes "of other women, including other White House staffers, involved with the president." The professional gossip replied, dead-pan: "There is talk all over this town another White House staffer is going to come out from behind the curtains this week. If this is the case—and you couple this with the headline that the *New*

York Post has, [that] there are hundreds, hundreds [of other women] according to Miss Lewinsky, quoting Clinton—we're in for a huge shock that goes beyond the specific episode. It's a whole psychosis taking place in the White House."

Drudge officiously took the opportunity to lecture the White House reporters for not doing their job. He expressed "shock and very much concern that there's been deception for years coming out of this White House. I mean, this intern relationship didn't happen last week. It happened over a course of year and a half, and I'm concerned. Also, there's a press corps that wasn't monitoring the situation close enough." Thus spoke the celebrated trash-peddler while Isikoff sat silently by.

RESPONSIBILITIES TO THE READER

Such mixing of journalistic pretenders side-by-side with established, proven professional practitioners gives the audience a deplorably disturbing picture of a news business that already struggles under public skepticism, cynicism, and disaffection based on valid criticism of mistakes, lapses, poor judgment, and bad taste. The press and television, like the Republic itself, will survive its shortcomings in the Lewinsky affair, whether or not President Clinton survives the debacle himself. The question is, has the performance been a mere lapse of standards in the heat of a fast-breaking, incredibly competitive story of major significance? A tapering off of the mad frenzy of the first week or so of the scandal gives hope that this is the case.

Or does it signal abandonment of the old in favor of a looser regard for the responsibility to tell readers and listeners where stories come from, and for standing behind the veracity of them? It is a question that goes to the heart of the practice of a trade that, for all its failings, should be a bulwark of a democracy that depends on an accurately informed public. Journalism in the late 1990s still should be guided by adherence to the same elemental rules that have always existed—report what you know as soon as you know it, not before. And if you're not sure, wait and check it out yourself.

Those news organizations that abide by this simple edict, like a disappointed *Newsweek* in this instance, may find themselves run over by less scrupulous or less conscientious competitors from time to time. But in the long run they will maintain their own reputations, and uphold the reputation of a craft that is under mounting attack. To do otherwise is to surrender to the sensational, the trivial and the vulgar that is increasingly infecting the serious business of informing the nation.

ADDITIONAL RESOURCES FOR PART 5

Suggested Questions and Discussion Topics

1. According to James Fallows ("Are Journalists People?"), what is one of the main differences between journalists and other professions, and why are journalists often perceived as callous?

2. Also according to Fallows, what are some reasons for thinking that giving the people what they want might not be a good excuse for journalistic excesses, such as the paparazzi's zeal in their pursuit of Princess Diana?

3. In "Methods of Media Manipulation," author Michael Parenti is much harsher about the nature of unethical behavior in the media than Fallows. Discuss any three elements of Parenti's argument supporting his notion that media behavior is deliberately, not accidentally, unethical.

4. In "Methods of Media Manipulation," what does Parenti mean by "framing"? From your own experience with media, discuss an example that you think illustrates this principle.

5. From J. D. Lasica's "Photographs That Lie," discuss two or three examples from well-known publications that illustrate the author's contention.

6. Give four examples of cases when photos have been manipulated digitally to alter the photo's content, as described in "Photographs That Lie."

7. In light of subsequent events in the White House in the summer and fall of 1998, how would you assess Jules Witcover's analysis of press coverage of the Lewinsky-Clinton scandal in his article "Where We Went Wrong," published in March/April 1998.

8. From the points made by Jules Witcover in "Where We Went Wrong," discuss why you think the news media were either right or wrong in the way they handled coverage of the Monica Lewinsky case.

Suggested Readings

G. Clifford Christians and Mark Fackler, *Media Ethics: Cases and Moral Reasoning,* 5th ed. New York: Longman, 1998.

G. Clifford Christians and Michael Traber, *Communication Ethics and Universal Values.* Thousand Oaks, CA: Sage Publications, 1997.

Louis A. Day, *Ethics in Media Communications: Cases and Controversies.* Belmont, CA: Wadsworth, 1996.

Conrad C. Fink, *Media Ethics.* Englewood Cliffs, NJ: Prentice-Hall, 1995.

Jack Fuller, *News Values: Ideas for an Information Age.* Chicago: University of Chicago Press, 1996.

David Gordon, John Kittross, Carol Reuss, John Merrill, and A. David Gordon, *Controversies in Media Ethics.* New York: Longman, 1996.

J. Vernon Jensen, *Ethical Issues in the Communication Process.* Mahwah, NJ: Lawrence Erlbaum, 1997.

Richard T. Kaplar and Patrick D. Maines, *The Government Factor: Undermining Journalistic Ethics in the Information Age.* Washington, DC: Cato Institute, 1995.

Val E. Limburg, *Electronic Media Ethics.* Newton, MA: Butterworth-Heinemann, 1994.

Caryl Rivers, *Slick Spins and Fractured Facts: How Cultural Myths Distort the News.* New York: Columbia University Press, 1996.

Ted Schwartz, *Free Speech and False Profits: Ethics in the Media.* Cleveland, OH: Pilgrim Press, 1996.

Suggested Videos

"Ethical Considerations in Journalism." New York: Insight Media, 1989. (20 minutes)

"Media Ethics." New York: Insight Media, 1997. (30 minutes)

"Media Ethics: Ethical Issues in Professional Life, 1992." New York: Insight Media. (30 minutes)

"Eye on the Media: Private Lives, Public Press." New York: Insight Media, 1983. (60 minutes)

"The Ethics of Journalism." New York: Insight Media, 1995. (two parts, 30 minutes each)

PART · 6

Profit versus Service

One of the most uncomfortable developments in American mass media during the past decade has been the move toward centralized ownership. Thomas Jefferson, James Madison, and other Founding Fathers of our system envisaged a journalism of competition. They believed truth would emerge from an open marketplace of ideas, but only if there were competing ideas. If only one voice were heard, we could not judge the truth of what was being said. Many different newspapers, each with their own perspectives, are necessary for us to get all the facts so we can make up our own minds.

Throughout American history we have feared the concentration of power that made our forebears flee their native lands. They came here to avoid religious, political, economic, or cultural domination. They fled from despotic kingdoms and religions, and they set up a political system that would minimize the chances for any one person or group to become all-powerful. The three branches of government that were devised—executive, legislative, and judicial—were to provide checks and balances on one another, lest any one become too strong. And a free press was essential as a watchdog of all three branches.

The Founding Fathers also believed that newspapers should be published because their owners had something important to say. Only then would such publication perform a valuable service to the health and freedom of the community. The Founding Fathers without doubt did not ratify the First Amendment to give the press the freedom to make money. Freedom was to allow the press to publish the truth needed by the community, a service that only a competitive press could provide.

That notion still prevails among many mass media, but not all. An increasing number seem to be motivated not by public service but by profit. In the rush to profit, mass media businesses have increasingly joined forces, merged their operations to be more efficient, and catered to the common denominator.

Corporate journalism, however, has not come about simply because of greed. It is also the product of economic forces over which media owners have little control. Costs of everything have skyrocketed, from paper and equipment to salaries and benefits. A case can be made that without mergers and conglomerations, even more small media would be forced to go out of business.

News media, rather than entertainment media, have been most affected by corporate journalism and economic recession. Throughout the world of journalism, news staffs and news bureaus have been "down-sized," to use a 1990s corporate word, and news has been turned into entertainment to attract larger audiences to replenish the owners' dwindling coffers.

Fortunately, as we can learn elsewhere in this book, new technologies in print and broadcasting are making the process less expensive and more accessible to a larger number of people. To some extent, this may help to offset the rise of corporate journalism and the decline of competition among mass media.

21

The Empire Strikes

BEN BAGDIKIAN

Editor's Note: "It is quite possible," writes Ben Bagdikian, "that by the 1990s a half-dozen large corporations will own all the most powerful media outlets in the U.S." As we have already seen in Chapter 5 ("The Global Media Giants"), Bakdikian's prediction has certainly come true.

In this article, taken from his book, *The Media Monopoly,* Bagdikian describes what happens when fewer and fewer owners take over more and more mass media channels. He says America has become a game show. "Winning is all that matters . . . cash prizes . . . get rich quick. We are turning the commonweal into the Commorwheel of Fortune."

America is not alone in this dilemma. Bagdikian points out that concentration of ownership is happening elsewhere in the world, too. In Canada, three chains now control 90% of French-language daily newspaper circulation, and three other chains control two-thirds of all English-language newspaper circulation. In seven provinces two-thirds or more of provincial circulation is controlled by a single chain.

Bagdikian, former dean of the Graduate School of Journalism at the University of California at Berkeley, was for many years a newspaper editor and reporter. This article originally appeared in *The Media Monopoly* (Beacon Press, 1983, 1987, 1993). This version was published in *Media & Values,* Summer 1989 and is reprinted with permission.

If all major media in the United States—every daily newspaper, magazine, broadcasting station, book publishing house and motion picture studio—were controlled by one "czar," the American public would have reason to fear for its democracy.

The danger is not that this single controller would necessarily be evil, though this kind of extravagant power has a grim history. Whether evil or benevolent, centralized control over information, be it governmental or private, is incompatible with freedom. Modern democracies need a choice of politics and ideas, and that choice requires access to truly diverse and competing sources of news, literature, entertainment and popular culture.

Fortunately, no single corporation controls all the mass media in the United States. But something is happening that points in that direction. If mergers and acquisitions by large corporations continue at the present rate, one massive firm will be in virtual control of all major media by the 1990s. Given the complexities of social and economic trends, that is not inevitable. It is, however, quite possible—and serious corporate leaders predict—that by the 1990s a half-dozen large corporations will own all the most powerful media outlets in the United States.

A FEW CORPORATIONS CONTROL MOST MEDIA

The predictions are not groundless. They are based on extraordinary changes in recent years. At the end of World War II, for example, more than 80 percent of the daily newspapers in the United States were independently owned, but by 1986 the proportion was almost reversed: 72 percent were owned by outside corporations and 15 of those corporations had most of the business. The pace of takeovers by large national and multinational corporations is increasing. In 1981, 20 corporations controlled most of the business of the country's 11,000 magazines, but only five years later that number had shrunk to six corporations.

Today, despite 25,000 media outlets in the United States, 29 corporations control most of the business in daily newspapers, magazines, television, books and motion pictures.

But there is something strange about leaders of the media acquisition drive. Most would agree that one "czar" in control would be disastrous for democracy, yet they praise the march toward that unhealthy end. The media they control take every opportunity to report the beauties of corporate bigness. And while there is much news and commentary about media mergers and acquisitions, it is reported almost exclusively as a financial game without social consequences. The general public is told almost nothing of the dangers.

THE MOTIVE IS PROFIT

Compounding the trend has been the practice of companies already dominant in one medium, like newspapers, investing in a formerly competitive medium, like television. Ownership in every major medium now includes investors from other media—owners of newspapers, magazines, broadcasting, cable systems, books and movies mixed together. In the past, each medium used to act like a watchdog over the behavior of its competing media. The newspaper industry watched magazines, and both kept a public eye on the broadcasting industry. Each was vigilant against the other industries' lobbying for unfair government concessions or against questionable business practices. But now the watchdogs have been cross-bred into an amiable hybrid, with seldom an embarrassing bark.

Corporations do not purchase local newspapers and broadcast stations for sentimental reasons. They buy them as investments that will yield a maximum return as quickly as possible. When they buy a local monopoly, which is typical of newspapers, or an assured share of the market, typical of television, few investors can resist the spectacular profits that can be made by cutting quality and raising prices. The magnitude of this temptation is not what media executives talk about in public. But in private they and their acquisition agents are unequivocal. Christopher Shaw, the merger expert, for example, speaking at a session of potential media investors in October 1986, said that a daily monopoly newspaper with a 15 percent annual operating profit can, within two years of purchase, be making a 40 percent profit by cutting costs and raising advertising and subscription prices. The investors were told, "No one will buy a 15 percent margin paper without a plan to create a 25–45 percent margin."

NO PUBLIC ACCOUNTING

During most of this century the process of media consolidation remained quiescent, but beginning in the mid-1960s large corporations suddenly began buying media companies. The financial trigger was Wall Street's discovery of the best-kept secret in the business of American newspapers.

For decades American newspaper publishers cultivated the impression that they presided over an impoverished institution maintained only through sacrificial devotion to the First Amendment. This image helped reduce demand from advertisers for lower rates and agitation by media employees for higher wages. The truth was that most daily papers were highly profitable. But that was easy to conceal when newspapers were privately owned and no public reports were required.

The golden secret was disclosed by an odd combination: the fertility of founding families and the inheritance taxes.

Most of the country's established newspapers were founded or began major growth in the late 19th Century, including *The New York Times,* the *Washington Post,* and the *Los Angeles Times.* At the time they were modest operations. But by the 1960s, thanks to the country's population growth, affluence and heightened literacy, as well as to mass advertising and local monopolies, they had become substantial enterprises. Papers that once represented small investments (Adolph Ochs bought *The New York Times* in 1896 with only $75,000 of his own money) were now worth millions.

TELEVISION IS A "SEMI-MONOPOLY"

Inheritance taxes for family owners can be avoided for about three generations; a person could leave the estate in trust to someone alive at the time the will takes effect, often a grandchild, plus 21 years. By the end of the 1960s, the grace period for hundreds of papers was about to end and owners looked for a way to avoid overwhelming taxes (and possible forced sale of the papers) on the death of the heirs and the imposition of postponed estate taxes. One answer was to spread the ownership by trading shares on the stock market, thereby relieving family members of inheritance taxes on the entire property. Or the family could sell the paper outright to an outside corporation.

Major papers began offering their stock publicly in the early 1960s, thus opening their financial records to scrutiny by the Securities and Exchange Commission and Wall Street. So, suddenly, in the 1960s the investing world discovered that the newspaper industry was fabulously wealthy. The media race was on.

Television in the 1960s was already concentrated in ownership, but was to become even more so. Television, in the jargon of Wall Street, is a "semi-monopoly," not only because of the limited number of owners, but because in most cities the dominant stations have virtually guaranteed high profits; the ratings simply determine which company gets the most.

MORE MEDIA IN CORPORATE MIX

Recent events in broadcasting have further concentrated ownership in television. Initially, no company was permitted to own more than seven radio and seven television stations. Under the political drive for deregulation, the FCC in 1984 permitted each company to expand its holdings to 12 AM and 12 FM radio stations and 12 television stations, and said it would lift all restrictions in 1990.

In the past decade, magazine groups, book companies, even Hollywood studios, were added to the corporate mix when conglomerates came to appreciate the power to create national styles and celebrities (and extra profits) when combinations of different media reinforced each other in unified corporate promotional campaigns.

Magazine articles could become books, which could become television programs that could become movies from which a novelized version could join the parade of accompanying T-shirts, posters, cosmetics and stylized clothing. Owning properties in all the media concentrated the profits from them all.

PUBLIC IN THE DARK

It is possible that large corporations are gaining control of the American media because the public wants it that way. But there is another possibility: the public, almost totally dependent on the media to alert them to public problems, has seldom seen in their standard newspapers, magazines or broadcasts anything to suggest the political and economic dangers of concentrated corporate control. On the contrary, for years the media have treated mergers and acquisitions as an exciting game that poses no threat to the national pattern of news and information.

Most owners and editors no longer brutalize the news with the heavy hand dramatized in movies like *Citizen Kane* or *The Front Page.* Only a few bosses still storm into the newsroom to order outrageous lies into the headlines. Most of the time, professional journalistic standards and public sophistications are high enough to make gross suppression of dramatic developments ineffective.

Far more effective in creating public opinion is the pursuit of events or ideas until they are displayed in depth over a period of time, until they form a coherent picture and become integrated into public thinking. It is this continuous repetition and emphasis that create high priorities among the general public and in government. It is in that power—to treat some subjects briefly and obscurely but others repetitively and in depth, or to take initiatives unrelated to external events—that ownership interests most effectively influence the news they create.

CONFLICTS OF INTEREST ARE INEVITABLE

Media conglomerates have become larger, they have been integrated into higher levels of American banking and industrial life as subsidiaries and within their boards of directors. Half the dominant firms are members of the Fortune 500 largest corporations in the country. They are heavy investors in, among other things, agribusiness, airlines, coal and oil, banking, insurance defense contracts, automobile sales, rocket engineering, nuclear power and nuclear weapons. Many have heavy foreign investments affected by American foreign policy decisions.

It is normal for all large businesses to make serious efforts to influence the news, to avoid embarrassing publicity, and to maximize sympathetic public opinion and government policies. Now they own most of the news media that they wish to influence.

22

Cutting Out the Heart and Soul of Newspapers

Sally Lehrman

Editor's Note: Are newspapers ruining themselves in their pursuit of profit? Many say yes. Thus, the question becomes: Is it possible to have profitable newspapers in the age of television without cutting the heart and soul out of them?

Sally Lehrman maintains that newspapers have new opportunities they are not exploiting and communities with which they have lost touch. She feels that the problem can be solved, however, if newspapers take a more quality-oriented approach to their production, become more involved with their communities, insist on better reporting and writing, and create new audiences for their product.

Lehrman is a reporter for the *San Francisco Examiner* and was a 1995–1996 John S. Knight Fellow at Stanford University. This article is reprinted with permission from *Outlook*, the publication of the Robert C. Maynard Institute of Journalism Education, Vol. 8, No. 1, Spring 1996.

Newspapers across the country are enacting stringent cost controls to counter declining readership and mounting competition from other media. Company executives maintain that they've applied the knife with utmost care, with an eye to preserving quality coverage. But industry analysts say the papers' ardent drive to slim down operations has reversed strides toward more inclusive coverage and may permanently undermine reader appeal.

In the interest of streamlining, they warn, newspapers have become homogenized, superficial, even boring.

"You can cut quality and readers may not notice for a while," says John Morton, newspaper analyst at Lynch, Jones & Ryan in New York. "I worry about cutting to the point of being detrimental."

In the spirit of last hired, first fired, Morton says newspapers often make their first cuts to their newest programs—most recently to expanded coverage of traditionally underserved audiences such as ethnic groups and specific geographic areas.

SPECIAL EDITIONS NOW POSSIBLE

Improved distribution and production capabilities have enabled papers to construct special editions to compete head-to-head with shoppers, free distribution weeklies and direct mailers. As their reward, the papers get income from smaller advertisers who want to reach a particular demographic or geographic zone. But such projects are expensive, so they're the first to go.

In 1992, the *Los Angeles Times* launched *City Times,* a weekly to serve the racially and economically diverse core areas of Los Angeles. Last year, the paper canned it. The newspaper also dropped its Spanish-language newsweekly, started in the fall of 1993, in favor of a joint venture with *La Opinion,* a Spanish-language daily. The new publication relies mainly on advertising to drive editorial.

Last year, *Newsday* shut down its satellite New York City edition, which had been widely praised by media critics for its feisty coverage of the city and its minority populations. The paper was near breakeven after a decade of growth, but parent company Times Mirror's profit margin was below the industry average, at about 9 percent.

Karen Howze, a Washington management consultant, conducts content audits for newspapers, television stations and the Maynard Institute. Howze says cost containment is just the latest excuse for the industry's ongoing failure to address a changing world. News organizations, entrenched in their own definition of what is news, often overlook children, gays and lesbians, people with disabilities or middle-class people of color, she says.

MANAGEMENT DOESN'T KNOW ITS COMMUNITY

"We're still operating as if it were 1950," Howze says. "For the most part, newspaper staff and newspaper managements have no idea who is in their communities. We're still doing things like it's a white world out there, and that's all."

The soaring price of newsprint—typically, 60 percent of a newspaper's cost—triggered the current round of cost-cutting. Newsprint costs climbed by up to 40 percent over the past year, pushing profit margins down by several percent to the mid-teens.

Publishers responded by trimming outlying circulation and cutting back the number of papers in their newsracks. They reduced web width, shrunk newsholes and compressed staff size. *The Miami Herald,* for example, is cutting staff by about 8 percent and focusing coverage more locally with the aim of boosting its profit margin from 16 percent to 18 percent. *The Philadelphia Inquirer,* another Knight-Ridder paper, is reducing staff by about 9 percent and cutting its newshole in an effort to boost its profit margin from 8 percent to 12 percent.

Some cuts have been healthy, strengthening papers that were overly fat. They'll be in better shape to compete when newsprint prices flatten over the next couple of years. And some are using the sense of crisis to restructure their pages into a more relevant, readable package, even to expand into novel territory and to develop new revenue streams.

Many newspapers, however, are taking actions likely to cost them their long-term franchise, warns Philip Meyer, a University of North Carolina journalism professor and former Knight-Ridder director of news and circulation research. The health of a newspaper depends on delivering advertising in the context of a trustworthy, informative environment. Most papers are abandoning this ideal in order to protect their profit margins, he says. He predicts that papers will either have to give up their comfortable profits or give up publishing.

"They're getting locked into a downward spiral where they will keep cutting costs and lowering service until they just disappear," Meyer says. "It's the economic reality."

CHANGES IN STAFFING AND COVERAGE

Acquisitions and consolidations have also driven sharp changes in staffing and coverage throughout the industry. A number of regional newspaper companies have streamlined their operations, sometimes to the point of sharing news pages from city to city.

The Journal Register Co. manages five dailies and a number of weeklies in Connecticut. In an article on the company, the *New Haven Advocate,* an alternative weekly, mourned the loss of investigative reporting, attention to public notice filings and coverage of local commission and Board of Aldermen committee hearings. Many media critics fear such meat-and-potatoes reporting, or what the *New Haven Advocate* calls the "grunt work of democracy," is being lost in the environment of short-term financial decision-making.

Ben Bagdikian, former dean of the Graduate School of Journalism at the University of California at Berkeley, says reporters around the country tell him they are pressured to write shorter and spend less time on stories. "If you weaken your reporting power and cut down your newshole, you're saying [to the reader], 'We don't care,'" Bagdikian says.

Local coverage loses out—and so does public knowledge and government participation. "This country depends more on local decision-making than any other industrialized country in the world," Bagdikian says, adding that public journalism—the routine, systematic coverage of important events as they occur—is vital to democracy.

Media critics say the shift toward austerity has also harmed access to the workings of democracy. In a study conducted by Women, Men and Media, a Virginia-based news analysis group, front-page references to women in a sampling of 20 newspapers dropped substantially in 1995. News references to women and quotes by women on the front page fell from 25 percent to 19 percent.

The media watchdog group, Fairness and Accuracy in Reporting (FAIR), criticizes newspapers and magazines for relying on inflammatory terms such as "quota" and "preferential" in their coverage of affirmative action. The group says the press not only neglects to discuss the continuing racism in society, but also has failed to point out recent examples of corporate racism in hiring and customer service.

The organization also reviewed three months of welfare coverage by six influential news outlets, including newspapers, television and news magazines. It found that reporters most often turned to men for comment, although welfare policies primarily affect women. Of sources whose gender could be identified, 71 percent were male. The coverage reinforced stereotypes, focusing on women under age 20 even though only 6 percent of mothers who receive Aid to Families with Dependent Children are in that age group.

ON-LINE NEWS MAY WORSEN TRENDS

FAIR and others worry that the new medium of on-line news may only further such trends. Readers can narrow their exposure to other cultures and ideas through their selection of on-line news areas. And on-line publishers, apparently convinced that people of color aren't in their market, conclude that there's no need to serve them, according to media critics.

"The potential for damage is greater on line," says management consultant Howze. "The potential for segregation is worse, because you choose what you want [to read]."

Andy Beers, news director at Microsoft's MSN News, however, views electronic media as an opportunity to provide more inclusive coverage. Beers says Microsoft's interactive multimedia news service is able to offer more cultural and ethnic diversity than print and broadcast media, which are concerned about disenfranchising their mainstream audience, the most affluent 60 percent of the nation's population.

MSN News offers a greater variety of international coverage, he argues, and is developing ways to provide very specific local information. The company hopes to convert the "chat-room" model into a full-blown town hall, where citizens can interact directly with their political representatives.

Beers says the nonlinear mode of on-line media, where subscribers easily can choose to move deeper into certain sections of the news site, means electronic news services can develop niches and ease away from homogenous, promotional-oriented content. While "quality" is still a value to be defined in the new medium, a growing number of people are getting into on-line news with content issues in mind, Beers says.

CONFRONTING HARD TIMES AGGRESSIVELY

At the same time, Beers admits that his newsroom of about 40 editors is primarily white and male. "Every news organization needs to do better," he says.

Bruce Koon, managing editor of the Mercury Center, the *San Jose Mercury News'* on-line forum, says the newness of the medium and the perception that the audience is largely young, white and male limits the ability of on-line news services to strengthen inclusive coverage.

Says Koon, "Is it the newspaper's responsibility to try to diversify the on-line community? I think it is, but at this point I'm not sure how they'd do it."

Koon says newspapers are struggling to identify appropriate material for their on-line publishing ventures. "The only kind of content that's working right now is specialized content. It's still unclear if generalized newspaper content is going to work here," he says.

The *Mercury News* is among a cadre of newspapers that have chosen to confront hard times aggressively, with varied success.

The San Jose, Calif., paper recently launched a free Spanish-language weekly, *Nuevo Mundo.* The paper has a staff of 11 editorial and sales people under Editor Angelo Figueroa, and will generate its own content, rather than rely on translations from the *Mercury News.* Jay T. Harris, publisher of both papers, pointed to the region's growing number of Latinos—projected at 20 percent of the population by the year 2000—and told his readers, "It's something we have to do for our future. We want to be the newspaper for all the people here."

Harris is considering a Vietnamese-language paper as well. And in the daily's newsroom, people of color make up nearly one quarter of the staff.

QUALITY EDITORIAL CAN HELP

John Toth, publisher of the small *Half Moon Bay Review,* serving a coastal town south of San Francisco, has found that quality editorial can counteract weakening revenue.

A year ago, he met with his salespeople and said, "We've got to do something different." One woman suggested starting a bimonthly magazine and Toth liked the idea. The paper, which is owned by Wick Communications, published six magazine issues last year and doubled its special section revenue. "In a year's time, it will have tripled," Toth says.

Toth also took a gamble and started a Spanish-language page to serve the large immigrant and Spanish-speaking population in Half Moon Bay—nearly 20 percent of the region is Latino. Many English-speaking readers responded angrily, arguing that the section discouraged non-native speakers from improving their English. The section has received little advertising support and Toth doubts the page will ever become a moneymaker. "Every once in a while we get an ad," Toth says. "Our whole goal was to simply inform people so they wouldn't be lost."

He's now looking for a Portuguese interpreter in order to add a section that would serve the 2,000 people in the community who are of Portuguese descent or newly immigrated from that country.

In Atlanta, the Cox Newspaper Group has responded to the current cost pressures by expanding staffing and newsholes over the past year. Arnold Rosenfeld, the group's editor in chief, says Cox has concentrated on developing savings companywide, not just in editorial, an easy target because of its high labor costs. As newsprint prices increased, department heads considered new revenue streams and ways to cut without getting into muscle and bone.

"Editorially, I won't say there has been no impact, but it has been lessened greatly by measures taken in advance" of the newsprint hike, Rosenfeld says. Cox, which owns the *Atlanta Journal-Constitution* along with 17 other papers throughout the South and Midwest, went ahead with several large projects, including a computer-based Medicare investigation that involved an 18-month court battle to obtain documents, as well as ambitious coverage of the Olympics.

TOUGHEN REPORTING AND IMPROVE WRITING

The *Newark Star-Ledger* also has countered the trend to cut back. Under the direction of editor Jim Willse, the large New Jersey paper has expanded its staff and launched a plan to toughen reporting and improve writing. Willse has said a more interesting paper will lure more readers and advertisers. So far, however, circulation has continued to erode.

The *Los Angeles Times,* faced with struggling retail revenues and a dismal regional economy, decided it had no choice but to retrench, according to Senior Editor Carol Stogsdill. "It was all money. We couldn't continue to carry the losses," she says.

The paper handed off three of its suburban editions to a subsidiary and dropped two others. It discontinued *City Times,* which it had distributed free each week. And it closed *Nuestro Tiempo,* also a free weekly with its own editorial staff.

Stogsdill regrets the loss, especially in serving the people of central Los Angeles and those who speak primarily Spanish. But she argues that the regular *Los Angeles Times* reader is actually getting a better paper as a result.

The community news that had formed the special editions now goes into two pages, appearing four days a week, within the metro section. The regions that had been segregated out of the daily now get more regular news coverage, including more frequent front-page stories, Stogsdill says. Experienced metro reporters are on the beat, increasing the visibility of local issues.

"We look at it more like a national beat," she says. "We don't run listings anymore."

The paper offers fewer opportunities for entry-level reporters. The *Los Angeles Times* cut its staff by about 10 percent, to a total of 1,080 last year. The proportion of minority employees in editorial remains flat at about 20 percent of the staff, and women make up a little over 34 percent.

CARVING A NEW MASS AUDIENCE

Stogsdill says newspapers must begin to use the cost-cutting environment as a way to become more focused, rather than to offer less to the reader and hope no one notices.

"Too often, cutting means we just have fewer pages, everyone throws their hands up in the air, and nothing else changes," Stogsdill says.

"Every time we cut back, we need to look not at what pages are we not going to run, but to regroup and look at it almost as a whole new product, what things can we run that are important to our community."

Harris, at the *Mercury News,* says newspapers may be making a critical mistake by choosing to cut into areas that hurt the coverage of diverse communities. "If we do not carve a new mass audience out of a collection of communities, our future does not have bright prospects," Harris says. "That is our future."

23

Profit and Quality Are Inseparable

LEADING NEWSPAPER CEOS

Editor's Note: In June 1990, the *Washington Journalism Review* (now the *American Journalism Review*) published a lengthy special report by Jonathan Kwitny entitled "The High Cost of Profits." Highly critical, it said that "corporate newspapers lay golden eggs for Wall Street. And CEOs pressure editors, sometimes with bonuses, to cut news staffs and keep dividends rising." It asked whether the constant pressure to increase profits focused newspapers too much on the short term, and was that threatening news coverage and journalistic quality?

The *Washington Journalism Review* sent advance copies of the articles to more than a dozen of the nation's top newspaper company executives with a request for their comments.

The executives, seven of whom responded, were asked the following questions:

1. Kwitny describes economic conditions—including monopoly status, stockholder expectations and high newspaper acquisition prices—that pressure management to increase profits. Do you see any changes ahead that could ease the severity of the profit pressure?
2. Various editors and reporters told Kwitny that emphasis on short-term profits is forcing news cuts and lowering newspaper quality. Under these conditions, will newspapers be able to maintain the quality and the sense of public service that journalists traditionally feel to be part of their calling?

Here are the answers, allowing the CEOs to speak for themselves. This article is reprinted from the *Washington Journalism Review,* July/August 1990.

JAMES K. BATTEN
CHAIRMAN AND CEO,
KNIGHT-RIDDER, INC.

Newspapers, not unlike other American businesses these days, do indeed face significant economic pressures. But to suggest that profit-crazed infidels from the countinghouse are massing at the newsroom door is a little farfetched.

Through my more than 30 years in this business, conscientious editors, publishers and corporate people have struggled to strike a wise and proper balance between obligations to readers and communities, and to their newspapers' owners. It's not a perfect or painless process, but in Knight-Ridder at least, it works. Over the years we have become ever more convinced of this article of faith: Ultimately, journalistic quality and financial success go hand in hand.

Finding the right balance at any newspaper in any given year is rarely simple. That job gets tougher when business is sluggish, as it has been for much of the last three years. In 1989, due mainly to a soft retail economy, newspaper revenues did not even keep up with the cost of living. That generates stress for all concerned.

But contrary to Jonathan Kwitny's implication, Knight-Ridder is controlling costs without harming the quality of our newspapers. In fact, newsroom spending will be up more than 5 percent company-wide this year—and more than 23 percent over the last four years, above the rate of inflation and the rate of newspaper revenue growth. News spending as a percent of total revenue has been steady over that period. Full-run news space, despite careful trimming at some papers, is up about 5 percent compared to 1986.

WJR readers unfortunately did not get this picture from Mr. Kwitny's article, even though we tried to explain it to him.

None of this is to suggest that life is easy at the moment, or that every decision is unanimous. But we don't simply resolve things by business-side fiat. We encourage honest debate, and because we have excellent and deeply caring people, we usually get it. That makes for better final decisions.

When the U.S. economy becomes healthier, as it will, newspapers' health will follow suit. That will help, but the pressures will not disappear. Profit growth is important if newspapers are to remain an attractive investment and, ultimately, retain their vitality and independence. Financially stagnant newspapers are at best uncertain guardians of a free press. In addition, another set of pressures—for improved performance on behalf of newspapers' customers—will continue to escalate. Readers and advertisers are more demanding than they were a generation ago. Longer term, newspapers' prosperity—and First Amendment vigor—will depend heavily on the editors' and reporters' ability to hold the attention of an American audience increasingly distracted from public affairs, the traditional centerpiece of excellent journalism.

Newspapers whose journalists disdain that challenge—feeling their high calling *entitles* them to reader attention and respect—will not do well. Such papers inevitably will erode both in public-service effectiveness and in profitability.

Our profession in the 1990s needs editors and reporters with talent and relish for *communicating* with busy and easily diverted Americans already awash in news and information—even before they reach for a newspaper. Wafting earnest journalistic messages into the air is not enough. They have to land somewhere to matter to anybody.

The choice is not between fluff and substance, as some believe. Our need is for newspapers so compelling, so varied, so enlightening, so well-written and designed, that they maintain daily print journalism's invaluable role in American life and public discourse.

I see heartening examples of that kind of newspapering increasingly around the country. Even in these tough times.

JOHN J. CURLEY
CHAIRMAN, PRESIDENT AND CEO,
GANNETT COMPANY

You must consider the nation's economic climate when you pose this question [about the possibility of profit pressures easing]. We see little evidence that the economy continues its endless expansion, despite the rosy government data. The imperative to control cost derives less from ownership status or stockholder expectations than it does from the deteriorating consumer economy and restructuring in the retail industry. These two factors have combined to produce the poorest advertising environment in almost 20 years, and we're feeling its effects on the revenue side.

To counter this, we're prudently spending money, not socking it away. We put a lot of money into appropriate programs in circulation and advertising, and the result is that we've been successful in stemming the slide of household penetration at our newspapers. We expect to see the returns on that down the road.

I said this to stockholders at our annual meeting in April, and I'll say it again here: We're building for the year 2000, not the short-term fixes. We continue to be very frugal at corporate headquarters, but we've spent more on salaries and news holes to hire and retain quality people and improve the newspapers. There's no question that today's economic conditions require editors to be more strategic in their allocation of newsroom resources. But doing things differently doesn't mean doing them less well, and I believe news executives throughout Gannett understand that.

Through ANPA's circulation and readership steering group, which I've chaired, we are working to develop ways to increase public interest in coverage of public affairs and vital issues. This is, of course, the heart and soul of news coverage and our responsibility under the First Amendment.

MICHAEL JOHNSTON
PRESIDENT AND CEO, THOMSON
NEWSPAPER CORPORATION

Very few journalists work for nonprofit newspapers. It is important for everyone to realize that we are in a business, and it's called the newspaper business. As in any other business, the purpose of the stockholder's investment is to make a profit. It seems obvious to us at Thomson Newspapers that it is in every employee's best interest that the enterprise be profitable, as that is the only way employment can be maintained, and also to understand that profit and quality are not at odds but complement each other. It is also important to keep in mind that the best way to increase profit is by increasing market share and penetration. That comes about only through better newspapers, which seems to us to mean that high standards must be maintained if the market is going to let the newspaper grow.

A good newspaper holds up a mirror to the community it serves, not to the face of a single reporter or journalist, although a good reporter can become that mirror. Where the conflict always develops is when the journalist determines that he knows, by some divine right, what that community needs to know. Journalism prizes awarded by peers represent only one of many measures of quality. Newspapers have an obligation to present to their subscribers a balanced report, but they must develop a product their market wants to read and is willing to buy. Those two interests can be, and often are, in conflict. At Thomson Newspapers, we feel strongly that, over the long term, the market is the arbiter of quality standards, and success in the marketplace is a genuine award of merit.

JIM KENNEDY
CHAIRMAN AND CEO,
COX ENTERPRISES

Our newspapers are businesses and, as such, I don't see any prospects for the reduction in emphasis on profitability. In the case of newspapers with adequate profit margins, I would suspect management to be more concerned with maintaining those margins while at the same time seeking new ways to grow revenue. In newspapers with unsatisfactory margins, I suspect the focus would be in eventually improving those margins to satisfactory levels. I do believe, though, that both public and private newspaper companies are willing to accept short-term reductions in profit to better position themselves to achieve long-term goals.

In fact, most of us will have to do just that in order to reclaim some of the circulation penetration we have lost over the past two decades. As we try to rebuild the basic foundation of our business, circulation (hopefully the goal of both editors and publishers), we must also contend with a much more complex business environment. Not only do we face increased competition from shoppers, weeklies, direct mail, radio and television but also from new businesses that seem to surface daily. Addressing the issue of quality is a terribly subjective enterprise. How do you define quality in a daily newspaper? Certainly a newspaper that isn't profitable, and therefore unlikely to survive, could not be considered a good newspaper. Also a newspaper that continues to lose market share, in my opinion, should not be considered a good newspaper.

We must find effective ways to reach the mass audience and at the same time tailor our newspaper to smaller, highly targeted audiences. The zoning of news and advertising copy is an obvious example. In my opinion, newspapers will have to get better to do all this, and when I say "better," in many cases that's going to mean doing things in different ways than they have been done before. Our society is changing, and so must our newspapers.

Editors must continue to shoulder the historic responsibility of journalism to serve a free people and safeguard the workings of our democracy. Journalists must continue to honor the sense of public service that they feel is their calling. They must also be men and women who are open-minded and willing to listen to what their readers say they want from a newspaper. Editors who understand both their "Fourth Estate" obligations and the realities of the marketplace will be the successful leaders of our newspapers as we go into the new century. Those who refuse to change with the public they serve and who don't master the totality of their responsibilities will fail, as might their newspapers.

PHILLIP J. MEEK
PRESIDENT, PUBLISHING GROUP,
CAPITAL CITIES/ABC

Management's obligation is to balance profit optimization, franchise strengthening, community service and employee development within the context of whatever external conditions exist. Excessive multiples [ratios of newspaper purchase prices to revenue and cash flow], which are coming down, require a shorter-term view and more emphasis on profits near term. Otherwise, use of the word "pressure" twice in the question is about as subjective as Kwitny's inescapable point of view—and terribly unfair.

Too many journalists are driven by, but vehemently deny, acceptance and recognition by their peers. When times are good, it is easier, but not necessarily right, for publishers to accommodate those desires. Witness the increasingly absurd assemblage of professionals at the World Series, Super Bowl and political conventions. One's presence assures acceptance in the fraternity. Declining market penetration, not profit levels, is forcing an analysis of priorities. What information readers want to cope with—with the increasing demands on their daily lives—must be the constant objective of any newspaper, not what the newsroom professionals think the readers need and the newsroom wants!

D. R. SEGAL
PRESIDENT AND CEO,
FREEDOM NEWSPAPERS, INC.

Until we overhaul the human race and delete the greed chromosome, I suspect there will be unremitting pressure to increase all profits. Of course, greed being the engine that drives progress, when we eliminate cupidity we can go back to trading stone axes for flint knives, and who is to say we wouldn't enjoy all that?

I do not think there is anything on the subject of profits that is particular to owners of newspapers. Most of them have a nice sense of self but so do the owners of shoe stores and practitioners of medicine. I don't think I caught the name of the newspaper CEO who was rewarded with a substantial raise when he announced the winning of a Pulitzer Prize and the diminution of the operating net by 25 percent, especially if his company was highly leveraged.

Of course, it's not fair. I mean, my situation is far different from, say, Jim Batten's or John Curley's. They have thousands of investors, some of them little widow women in Boise and teachers' pension funds. (The latter, to quote an investment banker I know, "don't buy stocks, they rent them.") These passive and even transient investors might not read newspapers nor even like them. Very likely few of them hold voting stock, but they vote with their feet, and when their computers tell them to. I don't think the element of quality or responsibility to the Republic figure in the computer software. The CEOs of the huge public companies live their lives in three-month increments, and I venture to guess that they reach for a Tums every morning when they turn to the stock pages. My God, it's down a point. Maybe I can call in sick.

My company is family-owned. We think in terms of generations, not quarters. The pressure on management is there, but apparently more benign and kinder. I think we are structured to react cautiously to downturns. What's best for the grandkids? Go for the buck now or build value for the long term? Usually the verdict comes down for the latter.

What a luxury! And what motivation to keep up the quality of products and services for a very selfish reason: It's good business for the grandchildren.

Those are the realities. Whether by attrition or the Saturday Night Unpleasantness, we'll all try to tighten up. Except for that company whose name escapes me, that is going at 100 percent efficiency, certain economies might not substantially reduce quality. And on Sunday we can take flowers over to Boot Hill and put them so solemnly on the graves of such heroes as the old *Herald-Tribune,* which died of an excess of devotion.

W. DEAN SINGLETON
VICE CHAIRMAN AND CEO,
MEDIANEWS GROUP

Upon reading Jonathan Kwitny's provocative piece on modern newspaper economics vis-a-vis editorial quality, I was somehow reminded of the man who loved the taste of sausage until he found out how it was made.

In this day and time, when you scrutinize profitability and the myriad parts of newspaper economics, there is, I suppose, something suddenly distasteful about a profession we all prefer to believe is noble, compassionate and critical to the democratic process.

Clearly something is wrong when newspaper profits in many places—but certainly not everywhere—are soaring while the number of daily newspapers is dwindling, readership is falling at an alarming rate and credibility in the public's eye is said to be at an all-time low.

I, for one, am not ready to lay the blame for these dismaying trends entirely at the feet of profit-taking, although in the industry some of us—perhaps all of us—may indeed have some soul-searching to do with respect to the profit question.

There is a Catch-22 at work here, certainly so for those publicly held media companies. With growing profit, you cannot reinvest—without investors, you cannot grow—and without attractive earnings, you cannot dazzle the Wall Street analysts who push the stocks.

I have some problems with that last part. It is the main reason why I am glad our newspapers are privately held. We aren't under any analysts' guns. But we are in business just the same and we begin each day mindful that there simply is no way to be an artistic success without first being a financial success.

Mr. Kwitny's piece does not address some tough realities that every publisher faces today.

1. Newspapers and newspaper groups must be profitable enough to handle the huge capital expenditures needed to modernize, especially in the larger markets. Advertisers want perfect color, for example, and readers are now dead set against having inky newspapers in their homes. Readers also want full-time, on-time delivery. Adult carriers are paid more than teens.

2. Today's publishers, to compete for readers and advertisers with other information sources, namely television, must spend as much as 5 or 6 percent of annual revenues on marketing, promotion and research. That wasn't the case a generation ago when most publishers would have laughed off today's "promote or die" thesis. To some degree, at least, the need to promote cuts heavily into monies that would be put into newsroom staffing and news hole.

One complaint I have with Mr Kwitny's piece is that I think he makes the age-old mistake commonly seen when our industry tries to cover itself—viewing newspapers strictly from the eyes of reporters and editors. To wit: Never mind *how* the money is spent, never mind *how* good the news staff might be—just *how many* people work in the newsroom and *how much* are they paid?

Also of great concern to me is the arrogance I see in too many newsrooms and among too many editors. "Editorial quality," in my estimation, also has a lot to do with understanding readers and what they say they need and understanding the hard-for-reporters-to-swallow fact that readers buy newspapers for advertising as well as for news.

There is nothing more odious to me, as a publisher, than the specter of an editor hell-bent for the almighty Pulitzer Prize at the expense of the local news, or a supercilious newsroom that ignores reader-research data that begs for a new direction.

Corporate dividends will not kill our industry—arrogance and history might!

24

Learning to Love Lower Profits

Philip Meyer

Editor's Note: In this age of growing competition, newspapers that only seek to make the largest possible profit will fail their communities and may not even survive. In this article, veteran journalist Philip Meyer warns that unless newspapers adjust to changing realities, accept more modest profit margins, and nurture their products, they will lose out to new, rival media that might better serve the reader and the community. Meyer writes that information can now be transmitted to audiences in many different ways, but that the medium that moves it will not be as important to audiences as the reputation of the content's creators.

Meyer holds the Knight Chair in Journalism at the University of North Carolina at Chapel Hill. He spent twenty-three years working for Knight-Ridder as a reporter and Washington correspondent and as the company's director of news and circulation research. This article is reprinted with permission from the *American Journalism Review*, December 1995.

To understand the American newspaper industry, visit the Rock of Chillon. It sits on the eastern edge of Lake Geneva, and it was fortified in the ninth century. In the 12th century, the counts of Savoy built a castle on the rock. With the lake on the west side and a mountain on the east, the castle commands the north-south road between. Any traveler on that road who did not pay a toll to the owner of the castle had to climb the mountain or swim the lake. It was such a sweet deal that the lords of Savoy and their heirs clung to that rock for three centuries.

U.S. newspaper publishers are like the Savoy family because a monopoly paper is a tollgate through which information passes between the local retailers and their customers. For most of this century that bottleneck has been virtually absolute. Owning the newspaper was like having the power to levy a sales tax.

But today's newspaper culture is the victim of that history of easy money. For perspective, consider the following comparison: In most lines of business there is a relationship between the size of the profit margin—the proportion of revenue that trickles to the bottom line—and the speed of product turnover. A business whose product has high turnover and consequently huge revenue can do nicely with a low margin. A low turnover product needs a high margin.

EASY MONEY LED TO BAD HABITS

Supermarkets can prosper with a margin of 1 to 2 percent because their buyers consume the products continually and have to keep coming back. Sellers of diamonds or yachts or luxury sedans build much higher margins into their prices to compensate for low turnover. Across the whole range of retail products, the average profit margin is in the neighborhood of 6 to 7 percent.

In turnover, newspapers are more like supermarkets than yacht dealers. Their product has a one-day shelf life. Consumers and advertisers alike have to pay for a new version every day if they want to stay current. Absent a monopoly, newspaper margins would be at the low end. But because they own the bottleneck, the opposite is true. Before technology began to create alternate toll routes, a monopoly newspaper in a medium-size market could command a margin of 20 to 40 percent.

That easy-money culture has led to some bad habits that still haunt the industry. If the money is going to come in no matter what kind of product you turn out, you are motivated to turn it out as cheaply as possible. If newspapers are under pressure, you can cheapen the product and raise prices at the same time. And, most important, innovation is not rewarded.

Before newspapers were controlled by publicly held companies, their economic condition was not well known. Some retailers may have noticed that the publisher's family was going to Europe while they took theirs to the mountains or the beach, but publishers were usually careful not to flaunt their wealth so as not to arouse resentment from their less favored clientele.

CHANGING THE HABITS

When newspaper companies began going public in the late 1960s, the books were opened, and Wall Street was delighted with what it saw. The only drawback was the cyclical nature of the business. Because it is tied to retail sales plus real estate and help wanted ads, the newspaper business is sensitive to the vagaries of the business cycle. The financial analysts who advise institutional investors make their reputations on their ability to predict the near future. So they prefer companies whose growth patterns are steady year in and year out.

It was Gannett's Al Neuharth who found the solution to this problem. Under his guidance, Gannett concentrated on acquiring monopoly newspapers in medium-size markets where the threat of competition was remote. Neuharth motivated his publishers to practice earnings management, which simply meant holding earnings down during the cyclical upswings by making capital investment, refurbishing the plant and filling holes in the staff while boosting them in the down cycles by postponing investment, shrinking the news hole and reducing staff.

Gannett papers did this aggressively enough to produce a long period of steady quarter-to-quarter growth that satisfied the analysts' lust for predictability. The long term costs to these behind-the-scenes contortions that smoothed the bumps in the trend line did not bother them. Neither, for that matter, did the fact that some of the growth was unreal, because analysts and accountants alike are accustomed to looking at nominal dollar values rather than inflation-adjusted dollars. Neuharth's glory days were also a period of high inflation, and that helped to mask some of the cyclical twists and turns.

ROOM FOR NON-MONOPOLY NEWSPAPERS

The price of Gannett stock soared, putting pressure on the managers of the other public companies to practice earnings management. One of the devices was the contingency budget, a budget more like a decision tree than a planning tool. An editor is told how much he or she can spend on the news product in a given year provided that revenues remain at a certain level. If revenue falls below expectations, leaner budget plans are triggered at specified points on the downward slope.

It worked just long enough to raise everyone's expectations about the value of newspapers. Today, despite some heroic efforts, not even Gannett can match Neuharth's record of "never a down quarter." Inflation is no longer high enough to mask the fluctuations in real return, readers are drifting away, and advertisers are finding other routes for their messages.

The readership decline was first taken seriously in the late 1960s, when new information sources began to compete successfully for the time of the traditional newspaper reader. Competition spawned by technology began long before talk of the electronic information highway. Cheap computer typesetting and offset printing led to the explosive growth of specialized print products that could target desired audiences for advertisers. Low postal rates combined with cheap printing and computerized mailing lists spurred the growth of direct mail advertising. In short, the owners of the traditional toll road have been in trouble for some time now, and they know it.

Some observers draw a line on the chart of newspaper decline, use a straight edge to extend it into the future and foresee the death of newspapers. The reality could be quite different. There is room for newspapers in the non-monopoly environment of the newspaper future. They will not be as profitable, and that is a problem for their owners—whether they be private or public shareholders—but it is not a problem for society.

EXPECT LOWER PROFITS

Imagine an economic environment in which newspapers earn the normal retail margin of 6 or 7 percent of revenues. As long as there are entrepreneurs willing to produce a socially useful product at that margin—and trust me, there will be—society will be served as well as it is now. Perhaps they will not be the same entrepreneurs who are serving us now, and that is not necessarily a concern to customers—except for one problem.

The problem is that there is no smooth, non-chaotic way to get from a newspaper industry used to 20 to 40 percent margins to one that is content with 6 or 7 percent. The present owners have those margins built into their expected return on investment, which is to say their standard of living.

It is return on investment that keeps supermarket owners content with 2 percent margins. And it is return on investment that makes newspaper owners, whether they be families, sole proprietors or public shareholders, want to preserve their 20 to 40 percent. If I sell you a goose that lays a golden egg every day, the price you pay me will be based on your expectation that the goose will continue to produce at the same rate. If under your roof the goose drops its production to one golden egg a week, you will be a major loser.

But it will still be a pretty good goose, and somebody will be proud to own and house and feed it. And that new owner can, of course, get a comparable return on investment by paying one-seventh of the price you paid. What happened to the rest of the goose's value? I captured it when I sold it to you on the basis of the seven-day production schedule. Neither I nor the third owner of the goose loses. Neither does society. Only you.

ACCEPT NEW REALITIES

Avoiding the fate of the second owner of the goose is the central problem facing newspaper owners today. They know they have to adjust to the reduced expectations that technology-driven change has brought them. They just don't know how. To understand the range of possible adjustments, consider two extreme scenarios:

Scenario 1: The present owners squeeze the goose to maintain profitability in the near term at the risk of killing it in the long term.

Under this scenario, the owners raise prices and simultaneously try to save their way to profitability with the usual techniques: cutting news hole, reducing staff, peeling back circulation in remote or low-income areas of less interest to advertisers, postponing maintenance and capital improvement, holding salaries down.

A good newspaper, some sage once observed, is like a fine garden. It takes years of hard work to build and years of neglect to destroy. The advantage of the squeeze scenario for present-day managers is that it has a chance of being successful in preserving their accustomed standard of living for their career lifetimes. Both advertisers and readers are creatures of habit. They will keep paying their money and using the product for a long time after the original reasons for doing so have faded.

Scenario 2: The present owners—or their successors—will accept the realities of the new competition and invest in product improvements that fully exploit the power of print and make newspaper companies major players in an information marketplace that includes electronic delivery.

Under this scenario, they will build, not degrade, their editorial products. As Tufts University political scientist Russell Neuman says in "The Future of the Mass Audience," there is a way to preserve at least some of the monopoly aspect enjoyed by newspapers. He calls it the "upstream strategy." Find another bottleneck further back in the production process.

GETTING BACK TO TRUST

Historically, the natural newspaper monopoly has been based on the heavy capital cost of starting a hot-type, letterpress newspaper operation. That high entry cost discouraged competitors from entering the market. Today, computers and cold type have made entry cost low, but the tendency toward one daily umbrella paper per market has continued unabated. That is because the source of the monopoly involves psychological as well as direct economic concerns. In their efforts to find one another, advertisers and their customers tend to gravitate toward the dominant medium in a market. One meeting place is enough. Neither wants to waste the time or the money exploring multiple information sources.

This is why the winner in a competitive market can be decided by something as basic as the amount of classified advertising. One paper becomes the marketplace for real estate or used cars. Display advertisers follow in what, from the viewpoint of the losing publisher, seems a vicious cycle. From the viewpoint of the winner, of course, it is a virtuous cycle.

Neuman's thesis is that the competitive battle across a wide variety of media and delivery systems will make content the new bottleneck. "What is scarce," he says, "is not the technical means of communication, but rather public attention." Getting that attention depends on content. He cites the victory of VHS over Betamax for home video players. Betamax had superior technology, but the makers of VHS made sure that the video stores had their tapes.

How would that principle apply to newspapers? The most effective advertising medium is one that is trusted. Thus the newspaper's product is not information so much as influence, a concept promoted by Hal Jurgensmeyer during his years at Knight-Ridder. The quickest way to gain influence, however, is by becoming a trusted and reliable provider of information.

Trust, in a busy marketplace, lends itself to monopoly. If you find a doctor or a used car dealer that you trust, you'll keep going back without expending the effort or the risk to seek out alternatives. If Walter Cronkite is the most trusted man in America, there can be only one of him. Cathleen Black, head of the Newspaper Association of America, was getting at the same idea when she exhorted her members to capitalize on the existing "brand name" standing of newspapers. Brand identity is a way of capturing trust.

THE PUBLIC JOURNALISM MOVEMENT

And newspapers are in a good position to win that role of most trusted medium based on their historic roles in their communities. Under Scenario 2, they would define themselves not by the physical nature of the medium, but by the trust that they have built up. And they would expand that trust by improving services to readers, hiring more skilled writers and reporters, taking leadership roles in fostering democratic debate.

Which scenario are we moving toward—squeezing the goose or nurturing it? While the signals are mixed, most of the decisions making business page headlines point to the squeeze scenario. Layoffs, closing bureaus, shrinking news holes are the order of the day. On the other hand, the public journalism movement represents an effort to build civic spirit in a way that will emotionally bind citizens to the newspaper. Whether very many newspapers will spend the money to wholeheartedly practice genuine public journalism remains to be seen. The short term economic pressures are against them. The first scenario produces visible and immediate rewards while the costs are hidden and distant. The second yields immediate costs and distant benefits.

The dilemma cuts across all forms of newspaper ownership, but publicly held companies bear a special burden because of Wall Street's habit of basing value on short term return. Take the case of a long term-oriented, nurturing company like Knight-Ridder. With total average daily circulation of 3.6 million, its newspapers would bring a total of $6.5 billion if sold separately at an average value of $1,800 per paying reader. (McClatchy paid the Daniels family more than $2,400 per unit of circulation for Raleigh's *News & Observer,* but Raleigh is a better than average market.) With 52.9 million shares outstanding at the 1994–95 high price of $61 per share, the entire company, including its non-newspaper properties, is valued by its investors at only $3.2 billion or around half the break-up value.

How would a successful takeover bidder tap that other $3.3 billion? By selling the papers to squeeze-oriented publishers who would slash costs and build the bottom line by putting out a bare-bones product. And how can public companies avoid such takeovers? By slashing and squeezing themselves in the same manner.

MOST VALUE IS IN GOOD WILL

That's in the near term. Now stretch your time horizon beyond anything seen by Wall Street and imagine the final stages of the squeeze scenario. A newspaper that depends on customer habit to keep the dollars flowing while it raises prices and gives back progressively less in return has made a decision to liquidate. It is a slow liquidation and is not immediately visible because the asset that is being converted to cash is intangible—what the bean counters call "good will."

Good will is the organization's standing in its community. More specifically, it is the habit that members of the community have of giving it money. In accounting terms, it is the value of the company over and above its tangible assets like printing presses, cameras, buildings, trucks and inventories of paper and ink. I asked two people who appraise newspapers for a living, John Morton of Washington, D.C., and Lee Dirks of Santa Fe, to estimate the proportion of a typical newspaper's value represented by good will. Both gave the same answer: 80 percent. That leaves only 20 percent for the physical assets.

This is vital intelligence for an entrepreneur interested in entering a market to challenge a fading newspaper. As an existing paper cuts back on its product and its standing in the community falls, there must come an inevitable magic moment when a competitor can move in, start a paper and build new good will from scratch, and end up owning a paper at only 20 percent of the cost of buying one.

Such a scenario is overly simplified, of course. The entry of competition could be just what it takes to get the existing paper to switch to a Scenario 2 strategy. But the newcomer would have a tremendous advantage, and that is its lower capitalization. Because its investment outlay is only one-fifth that of the existing paper, the challenger can get the same return at a 6 percent margin as the old paper gets with a 30 percent margin. Voila! A happy publisher with a 6 percent margin! Here is a publisher who can cheerfully pour money into the editorial product, expand circulation, create new bureaus, heavy-up the news hole and do the polling and special public interest investigations that define public journalism.

Precedent exists for this wild dream. Remember Al Neuharth. One of the factors that propelled him to the top at Gannett was his astuteness in recognizing a parallel situation in east-central Florida. Rapid population growth stimulated by space exploration had created a community that needed a new newspaper. He founded *Florida Today* for significantly less than the cost of buying an existing paper. The only obstacle is finding the right time and place—plus an opposition that is greedy and either short-sighted or slow-footed enough to continue squeezing out the old margins in the face of a challenge.

THE OLD WAY MAY NOT SURVIVE

To old newspaper hands, the prospect of battles between the newspaper squeezers and the newspaper nurturers has a definite charm. Some of us old enough to remember the fun of working in competitive markets would line up to work for the nurturer against the squeezer. But the threat to companies that are liquidating their good will might come from another direction. It might not come from other newspaper companies at all.

The race to be the entity that becomes the institutional Walter Cronkite in any given market will not be confined to the suppliers of a particular delivery technology. How the information is moved—copper wire, cable, fiberglass, microwave, a boy on a bicycle—will not be nearly as important as the reputation of the creators of the content. Earning that reputation may require the creativity and the courage to try radical new techniques in the gathering, analysis and presentation of news. It might require a radically different definition of the news provider's relationship to the community, as well as to First Amendment responsibilities.

These possibilities do not bode well for existing newspaper organizations. Their inherent conservatism, a consequence of their easy-money history, places them at a disadvantage in attempts at innovation. The pressures to keep squeezing out historic margins in the short term will make them inflexible. But sooner or later some business entity will find the formula, and the castle that it builds on its rock will shelter the best and the brightest creators of content.

ADDITIONAL RESOURCES FOR PART 6

Suggested Questions and Discussion Topics

1. In "The Empire Strikes," what does Ben Bagdikian predict about the ownership of the mass media in the United states in the 1990s? To what extent has he been accurate in his predictions?

2. In "The Empire Strikes," what does Bagdikian suggest as reasons for the lack of public knowledge about the economic situation of the mass media?

3. From "Cutting Out the Heart and Soul of Newspapers" discuss three or four of author Sally Lehrman's main reasons why newspapers have changed in recent years.

4. From "Cutting Out the Heart and Soul of Newspapers," discuss three or four of Lehrman's main suggestions for saving newspapers.

5. In "Profit and Quality Are Inseparable." Dean Singleton suggests two "tough realities" that every publisher faces today. What are they?

6. In "Profit and Quality Are Inseparable," Philip J. Meek suggests that journalists are different from management. How does he summarize these differences?

7. In "Learning to Love Lower Profits," what does author Philip Meyer mean by the "public journalism movement"?

8. In "Learning to Love Lower Profits," why does Meyer suggest that trust is a more important element in selling newspapers than in selling other commodities?

Suggested Readings

Alison Alexander, James Owers, and Rodney Carveth, *Media Economics: Theory and Practice,* 2nd ed. Mahwah, NJ: Lawrence Erlbaum, 1998.

Patricia Aufderheide, Erik Barnow, and Richard M.Cohen, eds., *Conglomerates and the Media.* San Francisco: New Press, 1997.

Ben Bagdikian, *The Media Monopoly,* 4th ed. Boston: Beacon Press, 1992.

Thomas W. Bonnet, *Telewars in the States: Telecommunications Issues in a New Era of Competition.* Mahwah, NJ: Lawrence Erlbaum, 1996.

George Gerbner, Hamid Mowlana, and Herbert Schiller, *Invisible Crises: What Conglomerate Control of Media Means for America and the World.* Boulder, CO: Westview Press, 1996.

Kevin Maney and Kevin Manley, *Megamedia Shakeout: The Inside Look at the Leaders and Losers in the Exploding Communications Industry.* New York: John Wiley & Sons, 1995.

Robert W. McChesney, *Corporate Media and the Threat to Democracy.* New York: Seven Stories Press, 1997.

John H. McManus, *Market-Driven Journalism: Let the Citizen Beware?* Thousand Oaks, CA: Sage Publications, 1994.

Herbert Schiller, *Information and the Crisis Economy.* New York: Oxford University Press, 1986.

Herbert Schiller, *The Mind Managers.* Boston: Beacon Press, 1973.

George Seldes, *Lords of the Press.* New York: Blue Ribbon Books, 1941.

Suggested Videos

"Fear and Favor in the Newsroom." San Francisco: California Newsreel, 1996. (57 minutes)

"The Book Industry." New York: Insight Media, 1997. (30 minutes)

"The Film Industry." New York: Insight Media, 1997. (30 minutes)

"The Newspaper Industry." New York: Insight Media, 1997. (30 minutes)

"The Magazine Industry." New York: Insight Media, 1997. (30 minutes)

"The Broadcast Television Industry." New York: Insight Media, 1997. (30 minutes)

"The Radio Industry." New York: Insight Media, 1997. (30 minutes)

"Tell the Truth and Run: George Seldes and the American Press." Hohokus, NJ: New Day Films. 1997. (111 minutes)

PART · 7

Public Relations:
Manipulating Mass Media

For a variety of reasons, mass media can be manipulated by outside forces who would seek to use the media for their own purposes, usually to influence the public. Let's examine some of the causes before we look at some of the effects.

One cause is the inequity in personnel. News media can rarely afford to employ enough reporters and editors to cover any situation thoroughly, so they must depend on outsiders for help. At the University of Maryland, for example, only two daily newspapers have large enough staffs and budgets to cover the university full time. Even those two reporters, one for the *Baltimore Sun* and one for the *Washington Post,* cannot keep up with all the news on the campus. Local TV and radio stations and weekly newspapers cannot afford to assign full-time reporters to the university.

At the same time, the university employs several dozen people in its public relations (PR) office. When something happens on campus, these people provide information to the news media, but because the news media are understaffed, they cannot always determine whether the information provided by the university is fair, accurate, balanced, and objective, or whether it has been deliberately or even accidentally shaped to serve the interests of the university.

If the PR people are ethical, of course, that won't happen, and it probably doesn't happen at the University of Maryland. But there is no law to prevent it from happening, and not everyone is ethical.

A second reason for manipulation is inequity in knowledge, experience, and access to information. Fewer than fifty reporters cover the U.S. Defense Department on a regular basis, and that department employs more than a thousand people who deal with the press. Moreover, journalists who cover the Pentagon are usually generalists. A few have covered military affairs long enough to have acquired some expertise in the subject, but none of them could have the skills and knowledge and access to data and information that would characterize the department's PR specialists. Because journalists must often depend on these specialists for the facts and their interpretation, the Defense Department can put out its own interpretation on any matter of national defense. Perhaps the best example of this ability to manipulate the news is the 1991 war in the Persian Gulf. (See Part 12 for further details.)

A third reason for mass media manipulation is greed and laziness. It is cheaper for news organizations to let others do their work, and of course it is easier on reporters if they only have to look over someone's press release rather than doing extensive research and writing themselves. The result is that what might seem like an objective and factual news story might instead be only part of the facts, and told in a way that would serve some special interest.

Another form of manipulation comes from using news to serve the interests of advertisers. In most mass media, news and advertising are separate parts of the organization, and one should not influence the other. But this separation has been breaking down in some organizations, and the lines between news and advertising have been blurred.

The articles in this section develop these problems with specific examples.

25

The Manufacture of Opinion

Scott M. Cutlip

Editor's Note: Without a doubt, PR has become an integral part of contemporary mass media. Every institution and organization must understand its public relationships to survive and increasingly must employ trained and experienced specialists to do this work. Much of the content of mass media today originates in PR offices, and much of our news is a reaction to events staged to serve a particular purpose.

PR became an organized activity because of the rise of powerful media. In a democracy, everyone, not just the press or mass media, has the right to express an opinion. Getting one's opinion expressed in the media, however, or using the media to influence other people's opinions, is not a simple task, and the process can be easily abused.

In this article, Scott M. Cutlip explores the reasons why PR has grown and some of the problems that have resulted. He is dean emeritus of journalism at the University of Georgia and co-author of *Effective Public Relations* (Englewood Cliffs, NJ: Prentice-Hall, 1994), now in its sixth edition. This article is reprinted with permission from the *Gannett Center Journal,* in which it originally appeared in Spring 1989.

Persuasive communication is as old as Plato's *Republic,* but what started in the early 1900s as a little-accepted vocation in our own country has reached the size, scope and power of an industry. America's public relations practitioners, some 150,000 strong, wield major influence in the public opinion game. Propagandist, press agent, public information officer, public relations or public affairs officer, political campaign specialist, lobbyist—all are protected in our democratic system by the same First Amendment rights that journalists enjoy, enabling them to play a far more important opinion-making role than the public perceives, or than journalists (who themselves are only about 130,000 strong) are usually willing to admit.

By one estimate, 40 percent of all "news" content today comes from the desks of public relations specialists. The thrust of their work is always the same—to mobilize public attention and support according to the aims of a paying client. Their hope is to set the public agenda. Professional case-pleaders play to win, usually using ethical and above-board means to get their message across, sometimes using false fronts known as "third-party techniques." To hidden persuaders, the nation's media are merely the conduit that legitimizes their opinion machine. Often their clients are the same business interests that buy the advertising that supports the media financially. When the distinction between "free" and "paid" media coverage breaks down, the idea that America's press is wholly independent does too.

HOW DID IT GROW

A Yale professor once told his students years ago: "The way to get at the nature of an institution that is alive, is to see how it has grown." Long before public relations became an industry, persuasive communicators played a decisive role in this country's growth.

The Revolution of 1776 was brought about by the propaganda of Samuel Adams and a small band of Massachusetts-based agitators struggling against great odds. The strong Tory loyalties of many powerful citizens and the political indifference of residents preoccupied with eking out a living in an untamed land were formidable obstacles to overcome. America's revolutionaries were the first public relations specialists: they demonstrated the influence an organized, articulate minority could bring to bear on an unorganized, apathetic majority. The Declaration of Independence, "written out of a decent respect for the opinions of mankind," was the most successful propaganda document of the 18th century.

There is no way to measure with certainty the effect of public relations campaigns, but most historians, including Frederick Jackson Main, agree that popular sentiment was running against the Federalists until Hamilton and Madison, assisted by John Jay, wrote and circulated the Federalist Papers to the nation's press. Historian Allan Nevins termed the turnaround in this political debate "the best public relations job in the nation's history." Surely it was one of the most decisive.

From the ratification of the Constitution to the Civil War, Amos Kendall, President Jackson's ghostwriter and publicist, led the fight against the rechartering of Nicholas Biddle's U.S. Bank. (Biddle's own publicist was Mathew St. Clair Clarke.) Kendall was as able a public relations person as to ever serve in the White House. Unlike Michael Deaver, who served Ronald Reagan, Kendall's exploits were based on substance, not perceptions.

HISTORY'S GREAT COMMUNICATORS

History offers abundant examples of the power exerted by "great communicators." Public relations programs are most often born of crises in public opinion, but many begin in order to promote causes or business interests. The nation's first public relations agency was the Publicity Bureau, established in Boston in 1900 by George V. S. Michaelis, Herbert Small, and Thomas Marvin, all ex-newspapermen. They were soon joined by a fourth journalist, James Drummond Ellsworth, who later worked for Theodore N. Vail, the president of AT&T, fashioning its pioneering public relations program. Newspapers (and later the broadcast media too) were the primary source of recruits for this burgeoning vocation. The Publicity Bureau obtained as its first clients Harvard University, the Fore River Shipyard and the Boston Elevated. It disappeared into the mists of history sometime after 1911.

Charles W. Eliot, then president of Harvard, understood the importance of public opinion. In his inaugural address in 1869 he described his university job as "the necessity of influencing opinion toward advancement of learning." Two years after hiring the Publicity Bureau, Eliot refused to pay for its services. The prestige of having Harvard as a client, he shrewdly saw, was recompense enough. He was right. The Massachusetts Institute of Technology soon signed on as a Publicity Bureau client to compete with its sister institution. More than any other factor, competition has spurred the growth of the public relations battalions.

It was not long before the Publicity Bureau, serving mostly business clients, collided with the leading force in government public relations—Theodore Roosevelt. Roosevelt used the White House as a "bully pulpit," and his battle to reform the nation's railroads (represented by the Publicity Bureau) presaged the struggle between government and special interests that has grown more intense since.

DOMINATING THE FRONT PAGES

Roosevelt was a master of the art and power of publicity and quickly came to dominate the nation's front pages. One of his first acts upon assuming the presidency was to work out a cooperative arrangement with wire service reporters, providing them with a press room in the White House. Roosevelt is said to have invented "Monday," for he knew that Sunday was a slow news day and saved big stories for that day. The newsman David Barry, who covered the presidency, observed that Roosevelt "knew the value and potent influence of a news paragraph written as he wanted it written and disseminated through the proper influential channels." He exploited the news media as a tool of leadership and managed the news in his favor.

Roosevelt's reformist tendencies not only indirectly stimulated the growth of the public relations industry but also shifted the balance of governmental power from Congress to the presidency. As political scientist Elmer E. Cornwell, Jr. has noted: "[The] interaction between the developing media of communication and their generalized impact . . . and growing presidential use of them . . . altered . . . the center of gravity of the national government system." The White House, with its powerful PR machinery and presidential mystique came to dominate the public perceptions of government.

The PR-minded president who followed Roosevelt sustained and strengthened this "presidential government." Woodrow Wilson, a stiff and austere scholar, nonetheless understood the importance of public opinion to leadership. As governor of New Jersey, as a candidate for the White House in 1912, and as a first-term president, Wilson was served ably by Joseph Tumulty, a gregarious Irishman. Tumulty's influence was destroyed at the end of the first term by the second Mrs. Wilson; he had tried to postpone her marriage until after the 1916 election. During World War I, Wilson had at his side George Creel, director of the Committee on Public Information, conducting a massive propaganda campaign to convert a divided citizenry into fervent war patriots. Creel's abrasive relations with Congress destroyed his influence by the war's end, and the only public opinion battle that Wilson ever lost—his failure to gain ratification for the League of Nations—was the only one he had ever waged alone, without a PR person at his side.

Perhaps the most dramatic story of public relations' impact on public opinion is Louis McHenry Howe's 20-year campaign to put Franklin D. Roosevelt into the White House. In 1912, as a candidate for the New York State Senate, FDR hired Howe as his campaign manager, and from that day forward Howe was a constant political and public relations mentor. "Dear Mr. Future President," he addressed a letter to FDR in 1912! When Roosevelt was stricken by polio in 1921, most people close to him expected him to lead the life of an invalid squire at Hyde Park. Howe refused to give up the dream of the presidency. Roosevelt never made a serious political blunder as long as Howe was there to tell him, "Hell no, dammit, it won't work." Howe died in 1936; it is not by chance that Roosevelt's two greatest blunders—his failure to pack the Supreme Court in 1937 and to defeat conservative Democratic senators in 1938—came after.

A LOGICAL OUTGROWTH OF MASS MEDIA

The public relations skills of Teddy Roosevelt and of his successors forced their political and commercial adversaries to counter with similar weapons, and thus began the growth of today's massive public relations system. In retrospect, it is a logical outgrowth of the development of America's mass media. The Associated Press, the world's largest news-gathering organization, dates from 1900. E.W. Scripps' United Press began in 1907. William Randolph Hearst started his International News Service in 1909. The newfound power of mass media outlets served by these and other organizations was set to work by special interests, political leaders and the muckrakers who spearheaded the Age of Reform.

The Publicity Bureau reached its zenith of feverish activity in 1905, when the railroads hired it in an attempt to head off regulatory legislation. Threatened by the growing clamor for public relief from railroad abuses, the railroads organized a counter-campaign. The Publicity Bureau immediately expanded, increasing its Boston staff and opening offices in New York, Chicago, Washington, St. Louis, Topeka and points west. In Chicago alone, 43 people, mostly experienced newspaper reporters, were employed. The Chicago office subscribed to every newspaper published in the Midwest and began clipping them as an early, primitive way of keeping tabs on public opinion. Traveling agents made the rounds of newspaper offices to talk to editors. A card file (known internally as The Barometer) was set up on each newspaper. The Publicity Bureau saturated the press with articles favorable to the railroads, prepared and distributed millions of pamphlets and books, and flooded existing channels with arguments against the legislation. But, like many a propaganda campaign before and since, the whole effort came to naught when the Hepburn Bill passed into law on June 29, 1906. The Bureau's work, which included unmarked, paid-for news items, was no match for President Roosevelt's nationwide stump-speaking tour.

EXPLOITATION OF POWERFUL MEDIA

Ray Stannard Baker, a contemporary muckraker, raised questions about the role of PR agents in this battle that nag us to this day. Baker argued first that the Publicity Bureau had conducted its operations secretly instead of frankly appearing before the court of public opinion as an agent of the railroad. Second, he asked: "Against such an organization as this, supplied with unlimited money, representing a private interest that wishes to defeat the public will, to break the law, and enjoy the fruits of unrestrained power, what chance to be heard have those who believe the present conditions are wrong?" The powerful National Rifle Association, which repeatedly carries the day against the will of the majority of Americans who want gun control, is a current example.

That the exploitation of powerful print outlets with million-plus circulations by Ida Tarbell, Lincoln Steffens, Upton Sinclair and other muckrakers added to the impetus for controlled publicity in the early 1900s can be seen in the careers of two early public relations pioneers, Ivy Lee and Pendelton Dudley. After working in the 1904 Democratic presidential campaign, Lee was employed by the anthracite coal operators of Pennsylvania, led by the ruthless George Bauer, to help them cope with a difficult strike. In 1906 Lee moved on to the Pennsylvania Railroad, which, like all other roads, was under heavy political fire. In 1914 he was appointed as a personal advisor to John D. Rockefeller, Jr., who (along with his father) was under attack for the strike-breaking tactics of the Colorado Fuel and Iron Company, culminating in the Ludlow Massacre. Lee died in 1934 with his name clouded by his representation of the I. G. Farben Co. in Hitler's Germany. At Lee's urging, Pendleton Dudley opened an office in Wall Street in 1909. (Only last November did his name disappear from the PR marquee.) Dudley denied in later years that the field was started in response to the muckrakers. But his "first client of note" was the historic Trinity Church in lower Manhattan, which was under public scrutiny in the *New York World* for its exploitation of tenants, including prostitutes, living in cold-water flats. Lee and Dudley were the prototypes of today's PR practitioners, some of whom represent the new robber barons of mega-mergers, junk bond dealing and leveraged buyouts.

INFORMATION REPLACES PROPAGANDA

Ivy Lee represented a change from the ex-journalists hired by corporations to counter the muckrakers with whitewash press agentry. As the late historian Eric Goldman observed, Lee's pledge to work in the open and to supply journalists with the information they needed marked "the second stage of public relations." The public, Goldman wrote, was no longer to be ignored by business nor fooled by their press agents. The "propagandist" (a word which earned its sinister connotations only after World War I) gave way to the "public information official."

From PR's beginning to its present, public relations practitioners and journalists have functioned in a mutually dependent relationship, sometimes as adversaries and sometimes as colleagues. Journalists are often captives of practitioners, who tend to have not only abler manpower—public relations generally pays better than journalism—but also news control. Small wonder that Bill Moyers, who served as President Johnson's press secretary, once called the White House press corps "the highest-paid stenographers in Washington." Veteran Sam Donaldson admitted "the most insular, sterile place for a television reporter to be in Washington is in the White House press room." The artillery of the press can be muffled or diverted toward decoy targets by skillful public relations ploys—holding an unfavorable story until another, bigger story breaks; or releasing the news late Saturday, when the Sunday papers have already been put to bed and TV stations are operating with skeleton crews.

Equally often, public relations practitioners and their clients or employers are unable to disseminate information because of inadequate news staffs and the frozen patterns of news. The relationship of practitioners and journalists, consequently, is often a stormy one. Suspicions and resentments exist on both sides. Although neither can function alone effectively, the public's interest is for the relationship to be adversarial.

Reporters and editors naturally tend to spotlight the strange, the destructive and the novel at the expense of detailed explanations of the issues. As the *Boston Globe's* Marty Nolan says, "The reporter has a vested interest in chaos."

PSEUDOEVENTS AND PACKAGED NEWS

Public relations staffs, on the other hand, load our channels of communication with the clutter and noise of prefabricated stories, omitting some facts and, occasionally, deliberately obfuscating others. Historian Daniel Boorstin, borrowing from Walter Lippmann, terms such stories *pseudoevents.* They serve to blur rather than clarify public issues. "The disproportion between what the informed citizen needs to know grows with the increase of the official's power of *concealment and contrivance,*" Boorstin wrote in *The Image.* "Inevitably our whole system of public information produces always more *packaged news,* more psuedoevents."

Much of what Boorstin calls "packaged news" content goes through American journalism unfiltered. Nobody likes to admit to being "kept," so many journalists and editors pretend this is not the case. But the news media are outnumbered and outgunned by the public relations industry on several fronts. Consider the Associated Press. With 6,500 news outlets in the United States, the AP is the main supplier of news for newspapers, newsmagazines, and radio and TV stations. Yet even the mighty AP can afford only one reporter at the Pentagon, which annually spends $300 billion in citizens' tax money. This lone reporter must rely heavily on the handouts, "Blue Tops" and "guidance" of the more than 200 public affairs officers who are based in the Pentagon and on the public payroll. The public affairs budget of the Department of Defense for 1989 alone totals more than $47 million and provides for nearly 1,000 information officers.

Paid publicity-wire networks are growing rapidly too. Today, in the majority of the nation's news rooms, publicity-wire teleprinters and fax machines stand alongside clattering AP, UPI, *New York Times* and Reuters terminals, bringing in publicity releases fed from a central office. Since the PR Newswire started this practice in New York in March 1954, free publicity wires have spread across the nation. Businesswire, headquartered in San Francisco, has some 1,700 outlets. The London-based Universal News, which operates some 1,400 outlets, transmits news releases around the world. These paid publicity wires serving the U.S., Canada, Europe and other parts of the world have come to constitute a third international news service. Electronic handouts are easier than old-fashioned legwork

EVERYONE HAS A RIGHT TO PUBLIC EXPRESSION

Most pseudoevents are staged spectacles so transitory that they do little more harm than wasting newsprint. Some have more lasting effects. Consider the natural environment, perhaps the most vital issue of our time. Jim Sibbison, a former public affairs officer, wrote in the *Columbia Journalism Review:*

> For most Washington reporters, press releases are all there is time for. . . . The once-eager band of reporters in the 1970s has dwindled to a handful. The pollution problem the EPA is supposed to be coping with is as vast as ever, but most Washington bureau chiefs no longer keep a close watch on the agency.

A former wire service reporter assigned to a statehouse wrote some years ago:

> I watched my state government grow and grow until there were twice as many agencies to cover yet the same personnel to do the job. Finally, the only people you had time to see were the PR people who were developing stories and putting them in shape for the newsman. You finally felt more like a garbage collector than a reporter.

The social justification of public relations in a free society is to ethically, effectively plead the cause of a client or organization in the forum of public debate. It is a basic democratic right that every idea, every individual, industry or institution shall have a full and fair hearing. In today's media system, more-over, individuals, ideas and industries must have the expertise of skilled advocates to gain media access.

THE STRUGGLE FOR TRUTH

But today the armies of public relations grapple with truth and falsehood on many fronts. The Surgeon General of the United States, the American Cancer Society and the National Cancer Institute have been waging a 25-year campaign of information to lengthen lives by combatting the counter-campaign by the tobacco lobby. The Tobacco Institute and its public relations staff spend upwards of $20 million a year trying to soften the fact that 350,000 die annually of causes linked to cigarette smoking. Philip Morris spent $5 million alone on its publication: "The American Smoker—An Economic Force." And the media are not unwitting bystanders in this public opinion drama. Tobacco advertising represents a large share of newspapers' and magazines' revenue. The Tobacco Institute campaign recalls the chemical industry's attack on the late Rachel Carson after the publication of her book *Silent Spring*. Monsanto went so far as to show once-fertile land rendered barren by lack of pesticides.

These "no holds barred" struggles, even those involving deliberate deception, are protected by the First Amendment on the principle enunciated by the late William O. Douglas: "When ideas compete in the market for acceptance, full and free discussion exposes the false and they gain few adherents."

As the Supreme Court has more recently extended the First Amendment's protection to commercial speech, "free and full discussion" has increasingly led to the use of paid advertisements as a public relations toll. Exxon spent more than $2 million on full-page newspaper ads in the nation's dailies to apologize for the tanker disaster at Valdez. The ads were late off the mark and flawed because Exxon failed to accept responsibility for the accident. The company will learn that events, far more than advertisements, mold public opinion.

AN IMPORTANT FUNCTION, IF PROPERLY PERFORMED

When I began teaching public relations at the University of Wisconsin in 1946, just 25 other colleges and universities offered such a course. Today more than 300 colleges and universities offer one or more courses in public relations—most of them, appropriately, in courses allied to the journalism curriculum.

The Public Relations Society of America, one of the two major associations of practitioners, has long had a Code of Professional Conduct. It requires that "A member shall adhere to truth and accuracy and to generally accepted standards of good taste." The code is enforced unevenly and infrequently, but at least the organization makes an enforcement attempt. The American Society of Newspaper Editors backed off from its own Canons of Journalism in the mid-1920s.

The public relations industry, despite its astonishing growth in the last 90 years, currently has a black eye. The criminal convictions of Reagan aides Michael Deaver and Lyn Nofziger, both on felony counts, and the guilty pleas of Carl "Spitz" Channell and Richard R. Miller, two practitioner fund-raisers who were involved in the Iran-Contra scandal, are representative of the industry's cynicism and "credibility gap." (Polls, however, show that journalism's reputation is hardly better.) When the aim of public relations is to confuse and obscure rather than to clarify and explain, it deserves our disgust. Only by linking the need for public approval to improvements in the conduct of the organizations they serve, including their own, can public relations practitioners use their talents to serve the interests of all. In 1923 Edward L. Bernays, one of the field's pioneers, defined the role of public relations as that of interpreting the public's views to the organization and interpreting the organization's policies and programs to its constituent publics, in order to arrive at an accommodation of mutual interests. This mature view of the function of public relations has taken hold slowly in management in the last 66 years. Where this concept is practiced, both the organization and the public are well served.

26

Is the Press Any Match for Powerhouse PR?

ALICIA MUNDY

Editor's Note: Public relations firms seem to be getting much more sophisticated about managing the news media. This article analyzes the "new and improved" devices that big PR firms in Washington, D.C., are using to manipulate journalism and thus control the public agenda.

Alicia Mundy was national correspondent for *Regardie's* and is now contributing editor of *The Washingtonian*. This article appeared in the *Columbia Journalism Review*, September/October 1992.

The use and abuse of journalists by PR flacks and lobbyists has long been a fact of life in Washington. In the past couple of years, though, media manipulation has been taken to a new level. How have the spinmeisters come to play such an important part in our political life, and why do the media go along with them?

Media manipulation has evolved considerably since the days when a well-connected flack could place a story simply by calling up a columnist or editor. Power has been diluted among the government and lobbyists, GOP and Democratic factions, and an array of interest groups. And the rise of new media outlets, together with increased competition among Washington bureaus of many papers, has made it almost impossible for a single media connection to decide whether a story lives or dies. As a high-ranking Hill and Knowlton executive said, "You can't just show up with a bottle of Wild Turkey and get your topic on the hearing schedule anymore. You have to work with staffers, and you have to be more aware of alliances and petty fights on the Hill. It's just not easy." To which a former H&K media specialist adds, "You can't just pick up a phone and call Scotty Reston and get a story out, because there *are* no Scotty Restons."

The '90s bag of tricks includes such time-honored ploys as using media foibles and competition to keep a story alive, as well as "media assistance" and "image enhancement"—slicker versions of the apocryphal call to Reston. It also includes a new emphasis on keeping a client's name *out* of the news.

THE NEW AGGRESSIVENESS

And then there's the New Aggressiveness, consisting of threats veiled and un-veiled. Hill and Knowlton's Bob Gray began advising controversial clients sev-eral years ago that they should "Go after the little lies in a big way." In other words, attack any and all flaws in a reporter's story, then use them to discredit the whole piece. His philosophy, as summed up by clients, is: if you get them to back down on the minor details they've screwed up on, they're unlikely to fight you on the major ones.

There's also a new and worrisome emphasis on official forums to jump-start a news story when you can't get it launched independently in the media. Though reporters interviewed insisted that no one can create a story if it isn't genuine "news," a good lobbyist can make news happen by putting it in the right months. At least one crucial congressional hearing on Kuwait in the fall of 1990 was prompted by H&K, according to Gray, because of concerns within the Kuwaiti royal family that Americans just weren't "upset enough" by the invasion by Iraq. As foreign countries keep hiring American lobbyists to handle diplomatic issues in Washington, you can expect to see more "official stories" on the front page and the evening news that have a hidden agenda.

And there's the latest wrinkle in PR—"De-Keatingization," a combination of vaccination and crop dusting that allows a public official to do what he wants to do (such as voting his conscience on an issue), without appearing to be contaminated by impure motives (such as money).

A MINEFIELD FOR REPORTERS

Oh, a few PR firms say they're trying something completely different: the New Honesty. "It's something we recommend to corporate clients, especially on en-vironmental and health issues," says a media consultant, as though suggesting a new hem length or hair color. "In some cases, we really push directness with the media, openness. And," he adds, "it sometimes disarms them. When they think you're being up front, they'll let you tell your story your way."

It's a minefield out there for reporters, and the good news is that many of the lobbyists interviewed insisted that we Washington reporters have gradu-ally become sophisticated, less likely to fall for a spin. But if that's really true, a hell of a lot of flacks are making a hell of a lot of money in Washington for do-ing nothing.

Hill and Knowlton is not the biggest firm spin-doctoring in the capital these days, but it's the first company that comes to mind when media practi-tioners and observers discuss how news is shaped and how the Washington press corps helps out. The bookends at H&K's Washington operation (the main office is in New York) are Bob Gray and Frank Mankiewicz.

Perhaps the most successful campaign Gray has run is the Richard Nixon Rehabilitation Campaign, on which he's left as many fingerprints as a five-year-old on a jelly jar. It's no accident that Nixon the Monster has become Nixon the Elder Statesman, appearing in your living room in the Sunday op-ed pages, on *Nightline,* before the American Newspaper Publishers Association, and at a dinner at the liberal Carnegie Endowment for International Peace in Washington. Ask Gray who got 500 foreign affairs writers to believe they were among the "50" elites selected to receive Nixon's comments on aid to the Soviet Union, and he will only smile. Ask who helped arrange the Washington affair at which President George Bush gave his imprimatur to the Nixon resurrection, and Gray's smile grows wider.

A CLASSIC CAMPAIGN

An inside look at a "classic propaganda campaign" by Hill and Knowlton was recently provided by *The Daily Record,* a business and legal newspaper in Maryland, in the form of a memorandum—one of several confidential documents released in court as the result of a lawsuit over the installation of asbestos in public buildings in Baltimore. The memo was drawn up in 1983, but the PR strategy outlined in it is timeless.

Representing U.S. Gypsum, which for years had used asbestos in some products, H&K advised Gypsum that "the spread of media coverage must be stopped at the local level and as soon as possible." One focus of this strategy was to plant stories on op-ed pages "by experts sympathetic to the company's point of view." The plan included placing articles attesting to the safety of asbestos.

Although a Gypsum spokesman told *The Daily Record* that the company did not implement the advice, court papers show that Gypsum planted op-ed pieces in papers in Baltimore and Detroit. An interoffice Gypsum memo reads: "Attached is an excellent series run over four days, beginning March 3 [1985] in the Detroit News. Our consultant, Jack Kinney, very actively fed much of this information to the special writer, Michael Bennett. SBA is exploring ways of more widely circulating these articles." (As recently as June 30, 1991, the *Baltimore Sun* published an article by Bennett which claimed that the risk of asbestos exposure was comparable to "smoking one half a cigarette in a lifetime.")

The memo further recommended that Gypsum set up an industry group to handle media inquiries and "take the heat from the press and industry critics," and suggested that Gypsum should enlist scientists and doctors as "independent experts" to counter claims that asbestos is a health risk. "It can then position the problem as a side issue that is being seized on by special interests and those out to further their own causes," the twenty-five-page memo continued.

"The media and other audiences important to U.S. Gypsum should ideally say, 'Why is all this furor being raised about this product? We have a non-story here.'"

Ideally, such articles would not only have influenced the public, but would also have worked their way into court exhibits in the lawsuit and swayed the jury. But this past May, U.S. Gypsum and the Asbestospray Corporation were ordered to pay the City of Baltimore $23 million for compensatory and punitive damages.

H&K executives call the strategy outlined in the 1983 memo "old-fashioned," but recent H&K blitzkreigs show it's still state of the art.

PACKAGING THE *JFK* MOVIE

Asked for a success story to demonstrate the effectiveness of H&K, Mankiewicz preferred two: the packaging of the movie *JFK,* and the repackaging of the Wall Street law firm Kaye, Scholer. In this case, there's no memo; just Mankiewicz.

As director Oliver Stone was finishing filming *JFK* last spring, an article by *Washington Post* reporter George Lardner, Jr., appeared, fiercely attacking Stone's adaptation of history for his movie. That fall, a *New York Times* piece by Bernard Weinraub reported that "Warner Brothers . . . has taken the unusual step of hiring Frank Mankiewicz, the Washington press-relations executive and former campaign manager for Robert F. Kennedy, to promote the film and seek support in the news media for Mr. Stone. Last week," the November 7, 1991, piece continued, "Mr. Stone flew to Washington and had dinner with representatives from the *New York Times,* the *Washington Post, People* magazine, and CBS." Mankiewicz coached Stone in writing and, suddenly, thoughtful pieces by Stone began springing up like dandelions in bluegrass all over the nation's op-ed pages. (Sound familiar?)

Did Stone himself pen those pieces? "Sure, he did," Mankiewicz hrrmmpps. Then he winks. "Most of them."

If a journalist had the gall to question a scene from the upcoming movie (versions of the script were floating around the country), Stone pounced on him with a full-fledged attack, out of proportion to the comment by the reporter ("Go after the little lies in a big way"). He and Mankiewicz fought back on every negative article, even threatening to take out a full-page ad in the *Washington Post* if the paper wouldn't print Stone's rebuttal to an unfavorable article—a concession executive editor Benjamin Bradlee had opposed. Ultimately the *Post* printed an edited form of the rebuttal. "We couldn't let anything go unchallenged," Mankiewicz explains.

Then he pitted *Newsweek* and *Time* against each other, convincing each magazine that it had an exclusive. Both responded with overkill—arranging cover stories, historical perspectives by veteran reporters, and later, in the case of *Time,* a contempo essay by Ron Rosenbaum on America's fascination with JFK assassination theories. The ploy worked beautifully up to the last minute, when *Time* had to change its cover for its exclusive Gorbachev interview. "But they gave it a big line on the cover anyway," Mankiewicz says, smiling.

When the film was about to premiere, Mankiewicz arranged meetings with influential congressmen such as Lee Hamilton of Indiana and Louis Stokes of Ohio. He also arranged a few cozy dinners in Georgetown for friends in politics and movies. After screenings of the film for selected journalists and others, he made the legendary recluse Stone available for questions. Finally, he helped to get Stone invited as a speaker at the National Press Club.

"Frank just knows how Washington works," Stone says. "He got us into the right audience, got the movie presented as a serious historical statement. He knows how to work the press establishment here, and got us a fair hearing with the right congressmen. I think he's a genius."

REPOSITIONING A LAW FIRM

The second success story cited by Mankiewicz in an interview in May was what he saw as the repositioning of the Wall Street firm Kaye, Scholer as victim, not perpetrator, in the S&L scandal. Kaye, Scholer had represented Charles Keating in his S&L dealings with the Lincoln thrift in Arizona. Earlier this year, Kaye, Scholer was forced by the Office of Thrift Supervision to pay $41 million and to bench its senior partner because the firm had allegedly helped Keating conceal his financial dealings from Lincoln's shareholders. Kaye, Scholer called in Hill and Knowlton, and soon pieces contending that the firm had been wronged began to crop up in legal journals and on newspaper op-ed pages.

"Kaye, Scholer was a mugging. We have shown that they have been unfairly attacked by the Justice Department and victimized by the threat of publicity," says Mankiewicz, handing me a two-inch stack of articles defending the law firm.

All this is designed to "target our audience," which he defines as other law firms, accounting firms, and potential clients.

It's not a bad scheme, says media reporter Howard Kurtz of the *Washington Post*. "All these op-ed pieces may not save the day at the time, but they can change the debate or raise the possibility of another side of the story, which may come back later to a client's benefit."

Meanwhile, Mankiewicz tells me, there's more on the way. "And there's a piece coming out in *The American Lawyer* soon," he says, smiling.

Weeks later, the new issue of *The American Lawyer* hits the stands. On the cover, inch-high red type declares: U.S. V. KAYE, SCHOLER: THEY GOT WHAT THEY DESERVED.

Asked about this unexpected setback, "So what?" Mankiewicz snarls. "I hear they've got an article coming out saying the Rodney King verdict was justified. Here's my quote: '*The American Lawyer* supports police brutality in all forms—from the Justice Department to the Los Angeles police.'"

MAKING A FEDERAL CASE: LOBBYING OR PLANTING STORIES

"Op-ed plants are bullshit," say a chorus of Hill and Knowlton competitors, many of whom cut their teeth working with Mankiewicz. The "new" media management doesn't waste time with opinion articles read by "five people drinking coffee in a newsroom," as one consultant puts it.

"The real work today is done behind the scenes on issues," says a former H&K executive. "You have people of substance going to regulators and assistant secretaries," he explains. "Then you notify the press in advance that the government is taking a certain action, and why, and who you represent, and why your client deserved to have this regulation changed.

"You make your client's story a *government* story, showing how the government's action—by now a quiet fait accompli—has not only helped your client, but is good for the people. That's how you get the story out the right way in the media," he says, smiling, before going on to cite several environmentally incorrect clients who, thanks to adept manipulation, survived encounters with the feds, the media, the "greenies," even a sing-in by aging rocker Jackson Browne.

The executive reviewed the Gypsum asbestos situation. "Listen, the client's alibi was that asbestos isn't bad. Asbestos is one product that is uniformly feared, maybe more than cigarettes. You don't do the op-ed drill."

What he would have recommended would have included more elements of lobbying: "Admit the error. Talk to city officials privately. Explain your financial situation and offer the cheapest way out to remove the stuff. This avoids the costly suit. Then tell the world what a good-neighbor company you are and come back for another contract."

H&K, like other large firms, has tried to adjust to the differences between the two functions—PR and lobbying—as they are defined in Washington. On such controversial issues as Kuwait and *JFK,* for example, it was faced with the choice between targeting the media directly or using official channels to spin the story and *then*—as in the case of Kuwait—going after the media. The choice will determine how the press will play the story. Meanwhile, with Washington firms now pushing foreign policy agendas for China, Italy, Haiti, and many other countries, the Capitol Hill approach has gained more acceptance.

"Using Congress is an old tack, but I've never seen it done so openly as I did with H&K and Kuwait," says a former White House official who lobbies, but does not flack, in Washington. "What astounds me is that the press just went along with it. In this case, it was a legitimate story. But it makes you wonder about the other stories that get built up the same way."

The press often has little choice. When a representative or senator calls a press conference or a hearing, somebody has to cover it.

DE-KEATINGIZATION: MAKING THE CLIENT BOMB-PROOF

As Mankiewicz recalls, "A member of Congress told me he'd support me on [business legislation that would benefit a client] if I'd de-Keatingize him first. I didn't know what he meant, but he explained he didn't want his constituents, especially the press, saying he was supporting it just because he'd gotten contributions from one of the parties involved."

The object of "de-Keatingizing" someone, Mankiewicz explains, is to make your target, the person you want to support your issue publicly, invulnerable to negative press coverage. "You have to make the issue bomb-proof. 'De-Keatingize,' meaning get rid of any taint. You have to give your guy the ammunition to show the press that the issue he's backing is inherently something the public—specifically your target's constituents—wants." An easy way to do that, Mankiewicz says, is to produce a favorable poll on the issue. The best recent example of this tactic says a key member of the White House team that oversaw the Clarence Thomas nomination, was the handling of the Senate Judiciary Committee. The senators found it a lot easier to support Thomas once they'd seen *USA Today* polls showing that a majority of African-Americans approved of Thomas's nomination. "We used media polls—which appear unbiased—to give the senators their out on the matter. And the senators used the polls to explain their vote to the media," this source says.

"The polls de-Keatingized Thomas," Mankiewicz sums up.

THE HERNIA STRATAGEM

This is a new technique not currently taught in PR texts. Mankiewicz has used it to considerable effect in response to questions about H&K's representation of Kuwait and BCCI. If you interview him in person about such issues he will chase you with a six-inch-thick pile of clips, rebuttals, and op-ed pieces showing what a bum rap H&K took—and he won't let you leave until you've promised to take the clips and read them all.

Don't knock this. This past May, Daniel Schorr found himself on the receiving end of a Mankiewicz missive on Kuwait. In a lengthy piece for the *Washington Post* titled "See It Not: True Confessions of a Lifetime in TV Journalism," Schorr had referred—in a single sentence—to "public relations 'video releases' or outright hoaxes, like the tearful recital of atrocities in Kuwait by the carefully coached daughter of the Kuwaiti ambassador in Washington"—whose appearance at a congressional hearing was arranged by Hill and Knowlton. Mankiewicz responded by sending a pile of clips that persuaded Schorr that he was in error in using the word "hoax."

"I sent a letter to the *Post* correcting myself, and a copy to Frank," Schorr says. "He called and asked if he could circulate it." Shortly thereafter (and well before the *Post* ran it), the letter became a lead story in a PR newsletter, which benefitted Hill and Knowlton if no one else. "I think it was cheap," says Schorr.

By forcing the journalist to retreat on one detail, the counterattack served to blunt the point of Schorr's original article—the lack of suspicion among the media about staged "news."

LOBBING BACK THE LOBBY CHARGE

In its handling of the Bank of Commerce and Credit International, Hill and Knowlton had more at stake than the bank's reputation; it had its own. After former Customs Commissioner William von Raab testified in 1991 that "influence peddlers" had prevented federal regulators and prosecutors from moving in on BCCI, H&K went on the offensive. The firm was registered at the Justice Department as a lobbyist for BCCI from 1988 to March 1990 and had taken charge of blocking any negative publicity about an affiliated institution, First American Bank of Washington.

In response to charges that H&K had "lobbied" for BCCI, Mankiewicz resorted to the hoary ploy "The Public Testimonial"; he wrung from von Raab a carefully phrased letter (which now hangs behind his desk) stating, "I do not have any information that Mr. Gray or you spoke to any official in either our federal government's executive or legislative branch on behalf of BCCI."

True. According to Mankiewicz, all of the work on behalf of BCCI done by H&K was handled by offices in London and Tampa. True, too, lobbying, in the technical Washington sense, means that someone officially registered as a firm's representative officially visited a member of Congress on behalf of that client. Of course, if the PR person mentioned the client over dinner, got a few pieces placed in the *Post,* or placed a few calls to the White House, that wouldn't officially count as lobbying.

In fact, when *Regardie's* magazine, my employer, was going to press in April 1990 with a cover story called "Who Really Owns First American Bank" (about BCCI, Clark Clifford, and First American), we were deluged with calls from Mankiewicz on behalf of First American and copies of letters to congressmen denouncing the story. Still, he can legitimately wave von Raab's letter like a vaccination certificate to ward off an outbreak of skeptical reporters.

THE PREEMPTIVE STRIKE

"It's more common now for PR firms to try to stop a negative story *before* it's in print," says the *Washington Post's* Howard Kurtz. "Correcting a story afterwards is rarely as effective as shutting it down, or turning it around a little."

One increasingly popular way of aborting a story is to launch an ad hominum attack on the reporter. An H&K executive who insisted on anonymity confirmed that one of the standard procedures these days when a client anticipates negative press involves digging up the reporter's previous stories, then alleging that the reporter has already shown malice towards the subject. A former H&K executive provides an example. He says that when *Time* was preparing its cover story on the Church of Scientology, H&K employees dug up the reporter's previous work, trying to document disputes between the reporter and church leaders. In April, the church filed a $416 million libel suit against *Time,* Time Warner, and reporter Richard Behar, claiming among other things that *Time* had assigned a biased reporter to write the story.

Other tactics include dredging up the number of corrections that can be traced to a reporter as proof of negligence-to-be. Or alleging that the reporter has some conflict of interest in connection with the subject.

"Like the little-lies approach, the anti-reporter tactics are all red herrings," says the former H&K media specialist, who insisted on anonymity. "But if you make enough noise about them, you can make an editor in Washington think twice about how hard he'll let the reporter write the story. And that's your goal."

THE NEW HONESTY

Public relations firms "always say, It could have been worse without our help, when a PR problem blows up in their faces," says an H&K competitor. "And that way you can never call their bluff and say, Prove it."

But in the case of United Way of America, failure to accept Hill and Knowlton's advice clearly did make matters worse. Last December, Washington reporters began calling to ask about the UWA president's travel, expenses, subsidiary commercial for-profit ventures, and his personal liaisons. United Way hired Mankiewicz to field "inquiries." He in turn urged UWA to hire a respected D.C. investigative firm to look into UWA itself. The investigators looked, gasped, and gave Mankiewicz the bad news: the allegations were true. The top echelon of UWA had been living in the lap of luxury on donors' dollars.

Mankiewicz urged the board of directors and UWA president William Aramony to follow the simplest rule of PR: Tell the Truth. Tell it All. Tell it Now.

But, informed sources say, Mankiewicz was overruled by the board and Aramony, who weren't prepared to let the public know what was happening. The result was that when the UWA stories broke in February, affiliates across the country responded with devastating effect by withholding their dues.

"We could have controlled the story, given it our spin, if they'd let us," says Mankiewicz.

"THERE'S NO SUCH THING AS A BAD CLIENT"

It's fine for Alan Dershowitz to insist on the innocence of some of his more notorious clients, but media types wonder how lobbyists and flacks justify plugging the causes of some of theirs.

It wasn't always like this. Loet Velmans, president of Hill and Knowlton from 1978 to 1986, remembers when the firm had the "luxury" of turning down clients. "Let's call it pragmatism," he says. "But we wouldn't take on clients who would upset our most important people—our employees—or other clients." He cited the tobacco industry, which H&K dropped as a client in the 1960s. "We couldn't do anything for them because they wouldn't take our advice—to research what smoking would do to you, and to invest in cancer research. They couldn't publicly do anything to suggest the link between cigarettes and cancer, and it was useless to represent them."

Velmans also recalls an era when H&K refused unsavory political clients: Ferdinand Marcos, South Africa.

Nowadays the list of foreign clients of prominent firms such as H&K; Black, Manafort, Stone and Kelly; Van Kloberg & Associates; Neill & Company; and Sawyer/Miller includes Zaire, Peru, El Salvador, Colombia, Kenya, and Saddam Hussein. With a good spin, Eva Peron could have been packaged as a victim of sexual harassment.

"Things have changed now. The competition is so fierce, hardly anyone turns away paying customers," Velmans says. Mankiewicz wishes that some *had* been turned away. He was infuriated when he learned in 1990 that H&K

had been hired by the Catholic bishops to push the church's anti-abortion position. "That's what they have priests for," he says. The controversy briefly raised the issues of legitimacy in clientele, but last year an executive told the Washington staff at H&K, "We'd represent Satan if he paid."

Maybe, but they may have to be careful what they say about him. Last year, H&K was sued by investors in BCCI; plaintiffs claimed H&K had portrayed the bank as pure. The suit was dismissed, but it raised questions of how far a PR firm can go with a controversial client.

"If asbestos is safe, China is a democracy, and BCCI is clean, how can you believe these guys on anything?" asks a fierce-featured news show host who doesn't like H&K but often goes along with its spin, like the rest of us. "There should be more backlash."

CAN THE MEDIA DO ANYTHING?

What steps can the media take to, if not lash back, at least make it clear that the emergence of certain issues reflects the handiwork of a spinmeister? Kurtz of the *Washington Post* believes that more stories exposing how a PR firm has been brought in to effect policy on a grand scale will help to alert the public to possible manipulation.

It's a warm and fuzzy sentiment. But as long as we need stories, and as long as we rely on outsiders to do the legwork, and as long as we're afraid of being beaten, says a newsmagazine editor in Washington, we are going to give spinmeisters more credence than we should.

There's some good news: "You won't get a story placed by having a flack call a reporter anymore," says Kurtz. "Most reporters would prefer to hear from the source or subject themselves."

"You are your best spokesperson," says Mankiewicz. "There's an American prejudice against having someone else field your questions. That's starting to come into it more."

So how can Mankiewicz charge $350 an hour for doing what he does? "*Some*body has to do it," he says.

As for the bottom line: "Can you manipulate the Washington media?" Mankiewicz muses, "Can I? Well, if I could I wouldn't tell you."

"And I can't," he hrrmmpps. And winks.

27

The CEO and the Reporter

Harold Burson

Editor's Note: Of course, not all PR workers are devious, and not all
reporters are free from their own biases and special interests and ignorance. Often PR consultants are necessary because the press isn't doing
a good job.

   This is the view of Harold Burson, founder and chair of one of the
world's largest PR firms, Burson-Marsteller Ltd. This article originally appeared in the *Emory Business Magazine,* Spring 1989, and this version was
published in *Across the Board,* July/August 1989.

Today's typical *Fortune*-500 chief executive officer is, at best, suspicious of
the motives of reporters covering him, his company, his industry, or business
in general. At worst, he has a deep-seated antagonism that keeps him removed
from or inaccessible to the press.

   Horror stories that have the media as centerpiece abound among CEOs.
Regrettably, some of these stories have a basis in fact: a reporter's biased point
of view reinforced by selective out-of-context quotes, ill-prepared reporters
writing on complex business issues for which they lack even rudimentary
grounding, a predilection for the controversial and "sensationalizing the trivial."

   True enough, it's not always the reporter who's at fault when an article
contains information the CEO considers better left unsaid or unwritten. More
frequently than most CEOs want to admit, they themselves are the sources or
otherwise bear responsibility for less-than-favorable articles. Some (fewer today than in years past) arrive for interviews without having thought through
what they want to say; others simply talk too much—they say things, forgetful
of the reality that a reporter's job is to report.

SUSPICIOUS OF EACH OTHER

Talk to business reporters and you'll find the suspicious are not one-sided.
They have their own versions of the relationship: CEOs talk with reporters

only when they have something positive to say; in times of adversity, they simply cannot be reached; you can't get a straight answer—and when you do, it's too late.

There is truth to both points of view. Yet CEOs and business reporters need one another. Business today requires all of the understanding it can muster. And who better to help create and promote that understanding than the media, both print and electronic, that report the news?

My observation is that, during the past decade, progress has been made on both sides of the equation. And this bodes well for a public better informed about business and the workings of the private sector.

Increasingly, CEOs have come to recognize both the needs of the reporter and the process that moves news from the reporter's notebook to the printed page or the television screen. Many have come to appreciate the need for speed in responding to questions posed late in the afternoon; there's better understanding of deadlines. Many have even taught themselves to respond in quotable terms, in terms of television's 10-second sound bite.

BOTH SIDES NEED EACH OTHER

More significant, some CEOs have begun to look at the press as a communications vehicle that is available to help them achieve their own corporate objectives. After all, the media, individually and certainly collectively, have a wide audience. What better vehicle to reach customers, employees, shareholders, or government leaders with a specific message? A few CEOs now view the media as potential partners in their own communications process. And they are learning how to work with the media to better advantage.

Speaking for the media, today's business reporters are better equipped for their jobs than their eager counterparts of the decade of the '70s. Many, if not most, have broad general knowledge of business; many have become specialists in the industries and business disciplines they cover.

Most important, the media have made a major commitment to business news coverage. Each of the network evening news shows now has a segment on business; each of the networks has set aside time and committed resources for business news shows. Newspapers are devoting more space to business news coverage; a lot of it has moved from the business page to the front page.

All of this is for the good. Our free market economy requires the underpinning that only the public can give it—as consumers, as employees, as investors, and as voters. Anything that contributes knowledge and understanding of how business operates in a democratic society is worth working for.

28

Big Brother Gets Wired: The Dark Side of the Internet

JOHN STAUBER AND SHELDON RAMPTON

Editor's Note: Public relations has turned increasingly not only to market research but also to the latest technologies to find ways to reach and persuade target audiences. This article describes some ways in which computer software and the Internet can now be used to control the political activities of employees so they will become lobbyists on behalf of corporate interests, how automated systems can feed news releases and other information to target reporters, how any mention in the media can be tracked, and how any target audience member's behavior can be predicted.

John Stauber is a writer specializing in criticism of PR and co-author of *Toxic Sludge Is Good for You! Lies, Damn Lies, and the Public Relations Industry* (Monroe, ME: Common Courage Press, 1995). This article was published in *PR Watch,* First Quarter, 1997, a publication of the Center for Media & Democracy, which is devoted to criticism of public relations. It is reprinted with permission.

Your boss calls you into his office and hands you a phone number. "Call your senator," he says. "I've got a piece of legislation that I need killed, and I want you to lobby against it for me. Here's a script spelling out what I want you to say. I'll just sit right here and listen in on your conversation."

This scenario—a vision of dictatorial hell for employees, heaven for corporate lobbyists—is not only possible but happening today on a mass scale, thanks to companies like Gnossos Software.

In a leaflet for a product called "Net Action," Gnossos gives an example of the way computer database and Internet technologies are giving corporations unprecedented control over the political activities of their employees:

"Susan Michaels, Grassroots Director for ABC Corporation, comes to work on Tuesday morning and is greeted with e-mail from the Washington office regarding an urgent legislative effort," the leaflet begins. "An amendment is being offered to the telecommunications reform bill which is against ABC Corporation's interests. The Washington Office requests a Net Action alert for the House of Representatives. Time is now 9 a.m.

"Susan drafts an email and reviews it with the Washington office until 10 a.m. At 10 a.m. Susan sends a corporate-wide email broadcast which hits 10,000 desktops throughout the United States within 30 minutes, using the internal email system. Susan requests immediate Net Action messages to be sent to congress@gnossos.com to be forwarded to Congress.

"Between 10 a.m. and 1 p.m. 1,000 employees (10%) take 5 minutes and send an email with their name, address, and message to congress@gnossos.com, Net Action properly formats the email and routes it to the office of each constituent's legislators.

"At 5 p.m. Susan receives a thankful call from the Washington office stating that the primary proponents of the planned amendment have decided to pull the controversial amendment, in part due to grassroots activity.

"The next morning Susan receives a file with the full list of the 1,000 respondents to the Net Action. In 10 minutes, she processes these responses..."

NOT A FANTASY

This Orwellian scenario is no futuristic fantasy. It is a chilling example of the dark side of modern technology in actual current practice. Using the combined power of computer databases and Internet communications, corporations are "empowering" their employees by ordering them to lobby en masse, while digitally recording their activities so they can be "processed" and monitored.

This type of technological trickery was not only tolerated but celebrated at the Public Affairs Council's "National Grassroots Conference for Corporate and Association Professionals" in Key West. In workshop after workshop, presenters stressed the importance of using modern computer and communications technologies to the fullest extent possible.

The sophistication of a company or trade association's database and communications system is the key to the "grassroots" lobbying technique. The first step is to store data on company employees and retirees in a computerized database which is "enriched" with 9-digit zip codes and matching state and federal legislative districts, enabling the company to identify each employee's state and federal legislators are, along with his or her voter precinct. Databases also keep track of employee phone numbers, e-mail addresses, history of political activity and contributions, special connections and potential influence over specific politicians.

This database in turn is integrated into "campaign management software," which keeps a record of each individual's political lobbying on behalf of the company. Through the Internet and automated telephone technology, companies can rapidly "patch through" employees to the offices of their elected officials.

"CORPORATE ACTION NETWORKS"

The pharmaceutical giant Merck & Co. is one of the companies that is using the information superhighway to mobilize a "Merck Action Network" of 8,800 company employees and retirees. Participants receive a quarterly Grassroots Update and "Action Alert," and participate in their industry-wide trade association lobbying network, the Health Care Leadership Council.

Merck's Laura Romeau described how Merck leads the troops using its own Internet website. According to Romeau, the company deliberately has avoided registering the website (http://congress.nw.dc.us/merck/) on any Internet search engine, so as "to preserve it as a membership privilege" and to prevent "anyone else from going into it."

Merck's recent actions include generating 800 individual telephone calls to Congress in order to lobby for "FDA Reform" (i.e. speeding up pharmaceutical drug approvals), along with gathering 80,000 names in a petition drive.

Romeau emphasized that Merck, in contrast to some corporations, is "very careful about who, what, and how much we ask people to do," although she qualified this by saying "except during the health care reform debate, when everything was on the line."

MONITORING SUCCESS

Whatever "very careful" means, it does not mean that Merck avoids pressuring its workers into supporting its political positions. "Get employees to see that they're not just volunteering their time, but that it's part of their job," Romeau advised. She also advised fellow PR pros to monitor the success of their grassroots efforts by "asking employees for copies of letters and responses."

Upon first perusal, Merck's website looks indeed like an appealing model of computer-enhanced individual empowerment. It includes a database enabling visitors to type in their zip code and see a list of their congressional representatives. Other features make it easy to quickly compose and send e-mail. Rather than going directly to the congressperson in question, however, the e-mail gets routed through the company's web server—a subtle way of signaling employees that their messages can be easily monitored.

During a "Fundamental Grassroots" workshop, PAC staffer Leslie Swift-Rosenzweig kept a straight face as she described employee participation in company grassroots lobbying as "voluntary." She added, however, that "some companies are putting grassroots activities into their job descriptions."

Jack Mongoven of Mongoven, Biscoe & Duchin was even more blunt. Asked how public affairs officers could get more employees active in company lobbying programs, Mongoven replied bluntly, "Get a letter from the CEO or a company vice-president. . . . People will be anxious to please you. They remember the one who hired them."

THE FLIP SIDE

Merck's annual grassroots budget is "$200–300 thousand per year," Romeau said—small in comparison to the company's lobbying and Political Action Committee donor programs. At first glance, therefore, the scale of Merck's Action Network may not seem terribly significant. Keep in mind, however, that one out of every six workers in the United States is now employed by a large corporation such as Merck and that nearly all of the Fortune 500 are presently gearing up to "go grassroots" with a vengeance.

Multiply the impact of the Merck Action Network by 500 and you start to get a sense, not only of why corporations presently "rule," but also how they plan to remain in charge well into the 21st century.

Corporations realize, however, that computer and Internet technologies also threaten to create forces beyond their control. "Many public interest activist groups are way ahead of corporations," warned Samuel A. Simon, President of Issue Dynamics, in a seminar titled "Learning How to Harness the Power of the Internet for Your Grassroots Program."

To illustrate his point, Simon used an overhead projector to display the interactive web sites of the Sierra Club (http://www.sierraclub.org) and the League of Conservation Voters (http://www.lcv.org).

AN INTER-MODAL WAY

Simon noted that information overload is increasingly making it difficult to find anything or, conversely, to persuade the public to pay attention to information broadcast via the Internet. The solution, he argued, is to "push your information in an inter-modal way, to reach out to people in the way that they want to be reached (i.e. by fax, pager, phone, or computerized e-mail.)"

Bell Atlantic, for example, uses an automated list server to feed customized information to over 700 reporters across the country. When registering with Bell Atlantic through Bell's internet site (http://www.ba.com), reporters fill out a registration form that specifies what kind of news story and angle interests them and how they want to receive news releases, advisories, graphics and other background materials. Armed with this information, Bell is able to spoonfeed reporters just the information they need to write their story.

"Have any companies here been attacked on the Internet?" Simon asked. Several people raised their hands, including a representative from Brown & Williamson Tobacco Co. "Then you understand," Simon said, "the importance of having ongoing monitoring of what is being said about your company."

Fortunately, he added, companies can "hire a young person knowledgeable about computers for very little money" to help the monitor what's being said about them on the Internet.

Services like Nexis-Lexis and Alta-Vista enable corporations to track virtually every instance in which they are mentioned in the news or on the Internet. If corporations don't want to do this in-house, they can hire other companies to do it for them. In fact, as Scott Farven from Aetna Insurance pointed out, sometimes companies prefer to "hire vendors to avoid tainting yourself."

WE HAVE YOUR DNA

Dr. Verne Kennedy, president of the Pensacola, Florida-based Marketing Research Institute, offered a keynote address on yet another high-tech corporate intrusion into citizens' lives. Looking every bit the part of the absent-minded professor, Kennedy started off his speech with a rather peculiar apology.

"I feel a bit guilty, because some of these new technologies smack of Big Brother," he said as he described what he calls "DNA Grass Roots Targeting."

"DNA," in Kennedy's usage, stands for "demographic niche attributes," which MRI specializes in collecting from surveys, census records, election voting data, consumer and credit data. A person's "DNA profile" includes information such as his or her age, marital status, number of children, length of residence, homeowner or renter status, house value, net worth, number of years of schooling.

"Based upon a person's DNA, we can predict their reaction to a specific message," Kennedy said. DNA profiles are "extremely good at predicting behavior."

MRI specializes in selling this information to rightwing and Republican Party political candidates, along with corporate marketing groups.

Kennedy denied that his company uses confidential information such as the bank credit records, but he admitted that "some less scrupulous companies" are already providing this type of personal information to their clients.

ADDITIONAL RESOURCES FOR PART 7

Suggested Questions and Discussion Topics

1. In "The Manufacture of Opinion," what does author Scott Cutlip mean by "psuedo events" and "packaged news"? Discuss some examples of both from the current news media.

2. In "The Manufacture of Opinion," why does Cutlip consider public relations to be a logical outgrowth of mass media? Explain.

3. From "Is the Press Any Match for Powerhouse PR?" by Alicia Mundy, discuss several examples of Hill & Knowlton's "spin-doctoring" in Washington.

4. According to "Is the Press Any Match for Powerhouse PR?", what is "the hernia strategem"?

5. From "The CEO and the Reporter," how does author Harold Burson characterize the relationship between business and the press?

6. Do you think business suspicion of reporters is justified, or is it just an excuse to bully reporters into doing what business wants? Discuss.

7. According to John Stauber's "Big Brother Gets Wired: The Dark Side of the Internet," the automated list server has become a new tool to influence public communication. Explain how Bell Atlantic uses it.

8. From "Big Brother Gets Wired: The Dark Side of the Internet," how can services such as Nexis-Lexis and Alta-Vista be used by businesses when dealing with the news media? Explain.

Suggested Readings

Stephen P. Banks, *Multicultural Public Relations: A Social Interpretive Approach.* Thousand Oaks, CA: Sage Publications, 1995.

Stuart Ewen, *PR! A Social History of Spin.* New York: Basic Books, 1996.

Edward Herman and Noam Chomsky, *Manufacturing Consent.* New York: Pantheon Books, 1988.

Ray E. Hiebert, *Courtier to the Crowd: The Story of Ivy Lee, Father of Public Relations.* Ames, IA: Iowa State University Press, 1965.

Ray E. Hiebert, ed., *Precision Public Relations.* New York: Longman, 1982.

Jacquie L'Etang and Magda Pieczka, *Critical Perspectives in Public Relations.* London: International Thomson Business Press, 1996,

Jon V. Pavlik, *Public Relations: What Research Tells Us.* Thousand Oaks, CA: Sage Publications, 1987.

Stan Sauerhaft and Chris Atkins, *Image Wars: Protecting Your Company When There's No Place to Hide.* New York: John Wiley & Sons, 1989.

Fraser P. Seitel, *The Practice of Public Relations,* 7th ed. Upper Saddle River, NJ: Prentice-Hall, 1998.

Christopher Spicer, *Organizational Public Relations: A Political Perspective.* Mahwah, NJ: Lawrence Erlbaum, 1997.

John Stauber and Sheldon Rampton, *Toxic Sludge is Good for You! Lies, Damn Lies, and the Public Relations Industry.* Monroe, ME: Common Courage Press, 1996.

Suggested Videos

Stuart Ewen, "Managing Democracy: The Rise of Public Relations." Northampton, MA: Media Education Foundation. 1998. (forthcoming)

John Stauber and Sheldon Rampton, "Toxic Sludge is Good for You: The Selling of Corporate Propaganda." Northampton, MA: Media Education Foundation. 1998. (forthcoming)

"Manufacturing Consent: Noam Chomsky and the Media." New York: Insight Media. (two parts, 166 minutes) 1994.

"Public Relations." New York: Insight Media, 1996. (23 minutes)

"The Psychology of Mass Persuasion." New York: Insight Media, 1981. (45 minutes)

Bill Moyers, "The Image Makers." New York: PBS. (55 minutes)

PART · 8

Advertising: Manipulating the Public

News should be accurate, fair, balanced, and objective, but as we learned in the previous section, it is often loaded or slanted by those inside and outside the media to influence rather than to inform. Advertising is something we expect to be more manipulative, but we don't expect it to be misleading or false.

In the 1990s, misleading advertising appeared to be increasing in mass media. Federal government efforts to police standards diminished during the Reagan/Bush years, causing a number of consumer groups to express growing concern about deceptive advertising.

Reporting on this issue in *The Washington Post,* Paul Fahri said that the debate is "rarely over flagrantly fraudulent practices like selling snake oil as medicine; rather, the most frequent complaints concern potentially misleading information or lack of information." He points out that health organizations, for example, "decry such common practices as touting reduced-calorie products as 'lite' because there are no generally accepted standards for making such a claim. There is also much debate over nutritional claims such as cereal advertising that proclaims to reduce cancer." Car rental and airfare advertisers have been accused of not fully disclosing additional charges and restrictions. Auto ads cram detailed information about safety features, options, and prices into fine print.

Of course the debate has two sides. According to Fahri, the advertising industry's self-regulatory group claims that the perceptions of increased deceptive ads are just perceptions, not supported by real evidence. In the advertising business, says William V. Weithes, chairman of a large world-wide ad agency, "If you're not on the up and up, your competitors will jump all over you."[1]

Perhaps a bigger problem than deceptive advertising is the misuse and abuse of human needs and emotions to sell a product, or advertisements that appeal to children and youths who are particularly vulnerable to such appeals. Cigarette advertising has been especially guilty, according to consumer and feminist groups.

"Bored? Lonely? Restless? What you need," says a four-page R. J. Reynolds Tobacco Company ad campaign, is a Camel cigarette. It features a sexy blond on the cover and the face of Camel's mascot, Old Joe, inside. It offers tips on "how to impress someone at the beach," including a suggestion to "run into the water, grab someone and drag her back to shore, as if you've saved her from drowning. The more she kicks and screams, the better." The ad includes a coupon for a free pack of cigarettes and urges the would-be coupon users to "ask a kind-looking stranger to redeem it." A Reynolds company spokesperson said the ad series was intended to be tongue-in-cheek, but the company's CEO apologized and said it would never run again.[2]

In the 1990s, cigarette smoking has been the target of much criticism from anti-smoking groups, medical scientists, and government agencies, and to-bacco companies have made some concessions, such as withdrawing the Joe Camel character from Camel cigarette ads, in the hopes of preventing further legislative restriction on its advertising. But as we see in this section, the to-bacco companies are finding new ways to promote their products.

Advertising aimed at children is a special problem. According to *Adweek,* the number of children's magazines has grown in the 1990s. Most of them carry advertising, and much of that advertising blurs the line between editorial and product pitch. One example is an Instant Quaker Oatmeal ad that appears to be a full-page Popeye comic strip. Popeye proclaims, "Can the spinach. I want me Instant Quaker Oatmeal."

Product-related television programs are also proliferating. Syndicated programs such as *G.I. Joe* and *Transformers* are "toy-driven," and the entire program is a commercial for the product.

These ads have an impact on kids. A survey of 1500 children aged 8 to 15, by the Yankelovich Youth Monitor, asked kids what influenced them the most to buy a product: 41 percent said TV commercials; 41 percent said a peer who owned the product; parent suggestions influenced only 20 percent.[3]

This unit provides a few examples of some of the issues being raised in the 1990s about mass media advertising's manipulation of the public.

NOTES

1. Paul Fahri, "Misleading Ads Seen on Rise as Federal Policing Efforts Diminish," *The Washington Post,* May 23, 1989, p. C5.

2. Brooke A. Masters, "Camel Ad Ignites Opposition," *The Washington Post,* July 26, 1989, p. C1.

3. Daniel M. Gold, "The Backlash Over Clutter in Kidland," *Adweek,* October 8, 1990, p. 4.

29

Cigarettes Under Fire

Richard W. Pollay

Editor's Note: Cigarette advertising usually provides glowing visions of the good life. Everyone is young and healthy, the women are thin and sexy, the men are virile and strong, the setting is usually the clean outdoors.

This vision, says George Gerbner, former dean of the Annenberg School of Communication at the University of Pennsylvania, "counters and overwhelms all other information about an addiction that kills more than a thousand people a day, more than heroin, crack, alcohol, fire, car accidents, homicides, and AIDS combined."

During the late 1990s much discussion has been raised in public forums about the manipulation of the public in cigarette advertising, with Congress and various state legislatures drafting legislation to restrict tobacco companies, restrict smoking in public places, and restrict cigarette advertising that uses images of human beings to sell the product.

Author Richard W. Pollay is a teaching and research professor at the business school of the University of British Columbia and curator of its History of Advertising Archives. This article originally appeared in *Media & Values*, Spring/Summer 1991 and is reprinted with permission.

Although inseparable from the act of smoking, cigarette smoke is one substance that is hardly ever seen in ads and commercials for cigarettes. Evidently, its haze would obscure the illusion of youth and vigor advertisers attempt to project with healthy models and pure and pristine environments.

In a way that's ironic, because the "PR smokescreen" the industry has been producing for decades has been highly effective in camouflaging the pernicious nature of its activities. Even in these days of anti-smoking awareness, tobacco producers have been fighting a highly effective rear guard action aimed at reassuring and retaining concerned smokers and recruiting new ones to replace an increasing number of quitters. The industry's own records show how it's done. A closer look at 50 years of ads shows how good they have been at turning a pernicious product into a symbol of health and good times.

SMOKESCREENS

"Tobacco industry says it wants to halt kids' smoke," say headlines reporting public relations from the Tobacco Institute. Don't believe it. No matter how privileged or persuasive, this cigarette smokescreen is totally contradicted by facts emerging from archives and trials. The facts show that cigarette firms research the starting process and preferences of kids as young as 15 extensively, design ads to appeal to their emotional needs and are well aware of teen nicotine addiction.

For every dollar spent on PR activities denying an interest in kids, many hundreds more will advertise cigarettes and recruit starters. More millions are spent to support a decades-long effort to minimize and obscure consumer judgments about smoking risks, reach new markets by appealing to women and minorities and reassure troubled "pre-quitters."

Thanks to recent ground-breaking suits seeking liability compensation for cancer victims, records of the industry's public relations firm, Hill & Knowlton, are now open at the Wisconsin State Historical Society. In addition, boxes of incriminating corporate records for virtually all cigarette makers and affiliates have been subpoenaed and reviewed by experts. They expose in detail what the cigarette firms seek to accomplish and how they go about it.

Since smoking dropouts from quitting—and dying—are high, continued success depends on a steady flow of recruits. The industry is dominated by the companies who recruit the most new, young smokers. "Young smokers represent the major opportunity group for the cigarette industry," said Canada's Imperial Tobacco Limited. A marketing executive quoted by the FTC said: "Market expansion in this industry means two things—kids and women. I think that governs the thinking of all the companies."

Much research and marketing effort is aimed at teenagers beginning at age 15. Memos about industry plans bear titles like "Youth Target Study" or "Project 16." Hidden camera interviews and surveys gather data on demographics (e.g. age, sex, family size), lifestyle (taste in music, clothes, movies, hobbies, etc.), health (knowledge, rationalizations and concerns), and personality. The psychological research is highly sophisticated, measuring factors like ego strength, submissiveness, shrewdness, tendency toward guilty feelings and self-discipline. Different personality types are targeted, like Dakota's current efforts to reach "virile females."

MOLDING THE IMAGE

One of the purposes of cigarette advertising is to shape how others perceive the nicotine user, and his or her own social and self image. Advertisers know that peer group pressure is an important factor in kids' decision making. Thus they work consciously to use ads to shape group, as well as individual, perceptions.

According to corporate studies, adolescents' urge to display symbols of their desired independence can be turned into a motivation for smoking. Ads for Marlboro fit this model, since the cowboy is self-sufficient with no boss (parent/teacher). Selling a drug like nicotine—documented by the Surgeon General as addictive as well as lethal—as a symbol of independence is ironic and tragically deceptive.

Many studies have shown that media that carry cigarette ads do a poor job with the health story. Editors are naturally reluctant to bite the hands that feed them, and the cigarette firms don't hesitate to use their clout if necessary. The world's largest ad agency, Saatchi & Saatchi, offended R. J. Reynolds Nabisco in 1989 by writing an ad for Northwest Airlines announcing a no smoking policy. The ad agency lost $84 million dollars of business, not from cigarettes, but from Nabisco Brands, owned by RJR. Cigarette firms also own all brands made by Kraft, Miller Beer and General Foods, keeping them among the top 10 advertisers, even on TV.

Promotional spending by U.S. cigarette manufacturers has more than tripled in the two decades since cigarette ads were banned on American radio and television—perhaps the clearest evidence of advertising's importance to these corporations. Instead of adding their TV advertising budgets to their profits they chose to invest instead in free sample distribution, billboards magazine ads and sport and concert promotion.

UNDERESTIMATING THE RISKS

The addictiveness and health risks of smoking are underestimated by even the well educated, thanks to advertising and the relative lack of media exposure to the medical catastrophe represented by lung cancer and other smoking-related illnesses. About 90 percent of today's college students, for example, underestimate the risks of smoking. Corporate research finds that starters "almost universally assume these risks will not apply to themselves because they will not become addicted." R. J. Reynolds found that: "However intriguing smoking was at 11, 12 or 13, by the age of 16 or 17 many regretted their use of cigarettes for health reasons and because they felt unable to stop smoking when they want to." Other research documents discuss how teens become "slaves to their cigarettes."

Firms also know that warnings are little noticed by kids and, if and when seen, go unheeded. But it's ironic that the 1964 U.S. law requiring warning labels on cigarette packages is seen as a triumph for consumer advocates.

Of the 15 proposals considered by Congress at the time, only the industry-sponsored bill passed. Even *Advertising Age* called the legislation that finally emerged—a version of the industry-sponsored proposal—"a shocking piece of special interest legislation." It weakened the warning wording, let the industry decide placement and type, did *not* apply to ads until the next decade (1972), handcuffed the FTC's regulatory powers for many years and blocked cities or states from passing more stringent laws. Political astuteness, media contacts and lobbying experience helped tobacco producers work a "damage control" victory.

Despite Congressional intentions, the warning formula that finally emerged from the legislative process is far from effective. The placement and printing of warnings on tobacco packages and ads minimizes the attention they get. Research shows that the warnings are rarely noticed and poorly re-called. Recent changes require a rotation of four different warnings and less ambiguous language, but even these are all but illegible in billboards or transit ads, and are totally absent in sponsored sports events, like Virginia Slim-sponsored tennis. They actually do have one unintended effect—helping firms avoid lawsuits because they can tell courts and grieving families that smokers were warned.

Not all ads are aimed at kids, of course. Women have been targeted since the 1920s, when Marlboros were called "Mild as May" in an attempt to position them as a product for the growing women's market. Public relations photos from the era identified women smoking in public as lighting a "torch of liberty." As in many modern ads, some brands were portrayed as symbols of fashionable slimness. Virginia Slims tells today's women that "You've Come a Long Way Baby!" But in truth things have changed very little. Women, like men, are sold addiction and death by ads positioning cigarettes as symbols of freedom and style. Blacks, too, have long been targeted, but were years late in being offered filter products as an appeal to safety concerns.

Now ads from Philip Morris Companies Inc. feature endorsements from prominent African Americans for "Free Speech" ads. The company poses as a defender of freedom and liberty, while in reality protecting its record profits as a promoter of nicotine addiction.

A LEAKY PAIL

Frequent industry claims that cigarette advertising is merely intended to promote brand switching also don't stand up to analysis. Switchers are a small and unattractive market segment. Only about 10 percent or less of smokers are switchers in any given year, and these are mostly fickle "pre-quitters." Corporate documents identify efforts aimed at switchers as third in their priority list, behind advertising designed to attract new starters and reassure existing smokers. This is exactly what might be expected. If you had a leaky pail (business) and wanted to hold as much water (dollars spent on cigarettes) as possible, you would try to stop the leaks (block quitting) and/or open the taps to fill the pail faster (recruit starters). Stirring the water (promoting switching) would do you no good at all.

Ads are developed and carefully tested to insure that viewers get the intended message of an image, such as "self-reliance," "intelligent choice," or "no need to quit." Pictures in this case are worth far more than a thousand words. Because seeing is believing, they are experienced, not analyzed. Regulatory laws, which deal with the meanings of words, are ill-prepared to deal with the consequences of visual persuasion. Thus, pictures of healthy smokers are permissible and potent in a context in which verbal health claims would be regulated or ridiculed.

ADS AIMED AT HEALTH CONCERNS

Ads aimed at smokers concerned about health risks, a vast majority of adult smokers, appeal to their fears, offering reassurances about health and safety. The majority show pure, pristine environments with healthy, robust smokers fit for athletic challenges because "positive life-style images . . . effect the continued social acceptability of smoking." Most ads for filtered products imply relative safety, an idea sometimes ludicrously false. Kent filters were initially made from asbestos, trade named "micronite." The 1954 ads implied an American Medical Association endorsement that the AMA called "outrageous hucksterism." The tar and nicotine levels for filtered Pall Mall, Chesterfield and Lucky Strikes were once higher, not lower, than the unfiltered versions of the very same brands.

Cigarette firms complain that they are heavily regulated. In truth, they need *not* comply with the Consumer Products Safety Commission, the Controlled Substances Act, the Federal Hazardous Substances Act, the Food and Drug Administration, or the Toxic Substances Act. Only the FTC has had periodic and limited authority over the years, and it has been frustrated, defeated and handcuffed. Well-meaning Congressional initiatives over the years rarely get out of committee, or survive the lobbying counter-attack.

Other countries are taking far more substantial initiatives to control the ads and other promotional inducements to smoke. Partial or nearly total bans of cigarette promotion already exist or are now before legislatures in Canada, New Zealand, Norway, France, Italy and the entire European Common Market to name a few.

As a Canadian, I have direct experience with Canada's cigarette advertising ban, which became effective in January 1989. Canada's initiative to ban tobacco advertising could be a model for the United States because of the two countries' similar smoking history, shared tobacco suppliers, related cultures and free trade relationship. But at the moment, unfortunately, the Canadian ad ban is locked in controversy.

As soon as it took effect it was instantly challenged by separate suits from each and every cigarette firm. Legal challenges alleged that the ban violates freedom of commercial speech, grounds that would likely be used in the U.S. to fight similar restrictions. A trial spanned nearly a year and a decision from the Quebec Superior Court is pending.

The decision is uncertain, in part because the judge and lawyers are themselves addicted smokers, but no matter what the outcome, the case is certain to go to the nation's Supreme Court. The stakes are enormous both for cigarette firms enjoying record profits, and the Canadian public, currently experiencing 40,000 smoking-related deaths a year, according to statistics from the Canadian Health and Welfare Department. Canada's cigarette sales dropped seven percent during the first year of the ban. A comparable drop in the smoking-related death rate would represent a savings of 2,800 lives a year.

AD BANS

Ad bans work, because advertising works. As long as advertising continues to be part of tobacco industry policy, they should be a necessary part of public policy, if only because of the message of warning they send. Unfortunately, many American residents, especially smokers, think that the U.S. would ban cigarette ads if smoking were highly hazardous, and that the lack of a ban implies that the product's hazards are not all that great. This faith in the U.S. government is sadly misplaced to date.

Unlike other products, cigarettes are deadly when used exactly as intended. The advertising images, and their intended meanings, are inherently false. Media need to develop a sense of responsibility for disseminating them. Western society needs to re-examine the commercial ethos that made them possible for so many decades—and is still keeping them going in the United States.

30

Rock 'Til They Drop: Tunes, Teens, and Tobacco

WILLIAM NOVELLI

Editor's Note: Advertising comes in many forms because different audiences respond to different kinds of media. If you want to reach young people, for example, there is little point in using traditional advertising in newspapers, and some products, such as tobacco, can't be advertised on radio or television. Young people, however, listen to a lot of music, but since CD and tape cassettes do not have space on their covers for extensive ads, influencing or selling to young people through music requires innovative promotional techniques.

This article by William Novelli explores some of the techniques employed by tobacco companies to use music as a medium to advertise and promote smoking. Novelli is president of the Campaign for Tobacco-Free Kids. This article is reprinted with permission from the *Washington Post,* in which it appeared originally on May 11, 1997.

THE WAY OF DOING BUSINESS IN AMERICA

In the forefront of the new effort is soap opera actress Martha Byrne, who says she has long dreamed of becoming a pop-rock icon. Philip Morris hired a major producer and high-priced instrumentalists to put together Byrne's first album, then launched her on a nationwide tour. But the CD wasn't designed to be purchased in music stores. Instead, the tobacco company is marketing its own record label. Woman Thing Music, named after the new slogan for Virginia Slims. Customers can only get the CD at Byrne concerts or free with the purchase of two packs of cigarettes.

Byrne apparently didn't face any moral struggle in making the decision to sign on with Philip Morris. "I don't feel that I am being used, I feel that I am being elevated to the next step," Byrne told the *Wall Street Journal.*

Similarly, Art Collins, Iggy Pop's manager, expressed no concern about peddling smokeless tobacco with his band's music. "I know it's an issue to lots of people, but not to me—I'm a smoker," he told the *Los Angeles Times.* "It's not the PC thing—it's just the way of doing business in America right now."

IT'S NOT TOO LATE TO STAND UP

Fortunately, not every entertainer approached by Big Tobacco feels the same way. Leslie Nuchow, a New York City-based singer, turned down an offer to appear with Byrne because of the tour's tobacco taint. A former smoker whose grandmother died from emphysema, Nuchow is planning her own protest concert, "Virginia Slam," in June to "show girls you don't have to sell out and be manipulated," according to the *Atlanta Journal-Constitution.*

A band listed on Skoal's ROAR tour recently wrote the Campaign for Tobacco-Free Kids to say that they had never agreed to participate. "60ft Dolls was offered a place on the tour, and although 60ft Dolls could really do with a major tour we turned it down purely because of its involvement with tobacco," wrote Natasha Hale, the group's manager. "60ft Dolls already have two cigarette addicts in its own group and thus know what a disgusting unhealthy addictive habit it is and would never do anything to support it. The fact that we are on the billing is a mistake and we are doing all we can to get our name off the promotional material as soon as possible."

It's not too late for other performers to stand up and make the only right choice: Don't tour.

Of course, U.S. Tobacco and Philip Morris could also do the right thing and cancel the tours. But based on the ethics displayed by tobacco industry leaders like James Morgan, that is highly unlikely.

HANGING OUT TO DO COOL STUFF

The Web page also heralds another feature of these concerts, the ROAR LEV, or Lifestyle Experience Village, which promoters are billing as a "multimedia, interactive compound, unprecedented in the history of touring music. In between our unbelievable line-up of bands, the LEV will provide a place to hang out and do some cool stuff." No doubt that cool place will highlight the alluring, but highly addictive and deadly taste of smokeless tobacco, if U.S. Tobacco's previous efforts are any indication. The company has long handed out free samples at rodeos, at hunting and fishing expositions, and on college campuses.

Smokeless tobacco, or snuff, is pulverized tobacco that you "dip" from a tin and put between your cheek and gum. It's a cheap way to get a nicotine high (federal taxes are minuscule). The Surgeon General says that the use of oral snuff can lead to mouth cancer, gum disease and nicotine addiction. Routine use causes leukoplakia, a disease characterized by lesions on the cheeks, gums and tongue—and 50 times the likelihood of oral cancer.

The highest prevalence of smokeless tobacco use is among young males. Twenty percent of high school boys currently use smokeless, according to the most recent study by the Centers for Disease Control and Prevention.

PARTNERSHIP WITH THE MUSIC INDUSTRY

Lloyd D. Johnston, a University of Michigan specialist in teen drug use, says that one notable factor in the increase in tobacco use is the industry's aggressive use of advertising and promotional giveaways. In the case of snuff, a doubling of advertising expenditures since 1985 has resulted in a 50 percent increase in sales, according to the Federal Trade Commission.

U.S. Tobacco is not alone in its efforts to use hip, youth-oriented musicians as a way to hook a new generation. And, perhaps not surprisingly, teen smoking has been rising. In 1991, 28 percent of high school students smoked in the month preceding the CDC survey. Just four years later, that rate had increased to 35 percent. CDC has concluded that as many as 5 million teens will die prematurely from smoking-related diseases unless current trends are reversed.

The rate of smoking is now highest among white teen females, with 40 percent having smoked in the month preceding the 1995 survey. That number will no doubt grow if the Virginia Slims "It's a Woman Thing" partnership with the music industry is successful. Previous marketing efforts by Virginia Slims, a Philip Morris brand, have substantially increased smoking by young women.

You've got to give them credit for audacity. With the noose of federal regulations and state lawsuits beginning to tighten around them, tobacco companies continue to find new, sneaky ways to promote their products—particularly to kids.

In some of their most immoral marketing initiatives to date, conglomerates such as Philip Morris and U.S. Tobacco have recently teamed up with singers and alternative rock groups to promote cigarettes and smokeless tobacco to teenagers. The slate of concert tours could not be more aggressively aimed at the youth market: From creating a slick Web page, to advertising in youthful magazines, to offering interactive games, Big Tobacco has impressionable 12- to 18-year-olds squarely in its cross hairs.

I'm not surprised at the tobacco executives—they're capable of anything. On *60 Minutes* last Sunday, I watched the videotaped deposition of Philip Morris president James Morgan as he was asked if he would stop selling tobacco if scientists determined conclusively that it caused cancer. His answer was a simple "no."

ENTERTAINERS BEING USED AS PITCHMEN

But I am surprised at the entertainers, who have allowed themselves to be turned into tobacco pitchmen. The latest outrage is the ROAR tour, a 40-city rock show that is being underwritten by U.S. Tobacco's Skoal brand of moist snuff—the most popular form of smokeless tobacco, a product whose use by teenage boys and young men has exploded in recent years. U.S. Tobacco sells a carefully graduated line of products intended to bring their young users all the way from cherry-flavored to full-blown addiction.

The ROAR (Revelation of Alternative Rhythms) tour, which makes local stops in Manassas and Baltimore, includes '70s throwback Iggy Pop, and alternative rock groups like the Rev. Horton Heat, Sponge, Tonic, the Bloodhound Gang and others. It is being advertised on a Web site and in national magazines such as *Details* and *Rolling Stone.*

While it is illegal to sell tobacco products to anyone under the age of 18, the appeal of these bands to youth is unmistakable. Those under the age of 20 are the biggest purchasers of rock music. The companies are using the universal teen language of music to create the impression that tobacco is stylish, cool and acceptable. Studies show that virtually all tobacco habits begin well before the age of 20, often in the 12- to 14-year-old range.

31

The Squeeze

RUSS BAKER

Editor's Note: A long-standing tradition in American journalism has been the separation between advertising and editorial or program content. Advertising is expected to be clearly labeled as such; the reader, listener, or viewer will understand that someone has paid for the message to influence or persuade. Traditionally, advertising and editorial staffs have been separated as well, to diminish the influence of the advertiser on editorial or program content.

Today, that tradition is being challenged by some big advertisers who want more say about the content of the medium in which they place their ads. This article explores how some major advertisers have stepped up the pressure on magazines to alter their content and asks if future editors will give in to this kind of pressure.

Russ Baker is a free-lance writer in New York and frequent contributor to the *Columbia Journalism Review*, in which this article originally was published in September/October 1997. It is reprinted with permission.

In effort to avoid potential conflicts, it is required that Chrysler Corporation be alerted in advance of any and all editorial content that encompasses sexual, political, social issues or any editorial that might be construed as provocative or offensive. Each and every issue that carries Chrysler advertising requires a written summary outlining major theme/articles appearing in upcoming issues. These summaries are to be forwarded to PentaCom prior to closing in order to give Chrysler ample time to review and reschedule if desired ... As acknowledgement of this letter we ask that you or a representative from the publication sign below and return to us no later than February 15.

> —from a letter sent by Chrysler's ad agency, PentaCom, a division of BBDO North America, to at least fifty magazines

Is there any doubt that advertisers mumble and sometimes roar about reporting that can hurt them? That the auto giants don't like pieces that, say, point to auto safety problems? Or that Big Tobacco hates to see its glamorous, cheerful ads juxtaposed with articles mentioning their best customers' grim way of death? When advertisers disapprove of an editorial climate, they can—and sometimes do—take a hike.

But for Chrysler to push beyond its parochial economic interests—by demanding summaries of upcoming articles while implicitly asking editors to think twice about running "sexual, political, social issues"—crosses a sharply defined line. "This is new," says Milton Glaser, the *New York* magazine cofounder and celebrated designer. "It will have a devastating effect on the idea of a free press and of free inquiry."

Glaser is among those in the press who are vocally urging editors and publishers to resist. "If Chrysler achieves this," he says, "there is no reason to hope that other advertisers won't ask for the same privilege. You will have thirty or forty advertisers checking through the pages. They will send notes to publishers. I don't see how any good citizen doesn't rise to this occasion and say this development is un-American and a threat to freedom."

Hyperbole? Maybe not. Just about any editor will tell you: the ad/edit chemistry is changing for the worse. Corporations and their ad agencies have clearly turned up the heat on editors and publishers, and some magazines are capitulating, unwilling to risk even a single ad. This makes it tougher for those who do fight to maintain the ad-edit wall and put the interests of their readers first.

SOME RECENT EXAMPLES

- A major advertiser recently approached all three newsweeklies—*Time, Newsweek,* and *U.S. News*—and told them it would be closely monitoring editorial content. So says a high newsweekly executive who was given the warning (but who would not name the advertiser). For the next quarter, the advertiser warned the magazines' publishing sides, it would keep track of how the company's industry was portrayed in news columns. At the end of that period, the advertiser would select one— and only one—of the magazines and award all of its newsweekly advertising to it.
- An auto manufacturer—not Chrysler—decided recently to play art director at a major glossy, and the magazine played along. After the magazine scheduled a photo spread that would feature more bare skin than usual, it engaged in a back-and-forth negotiation with that advertiser over exactly how much skin would be shown. CJR's source says the feature had nothing to do with the advertiser's product.
- Kimberly-Clark makes Huggies diapers and advertises them in a number of magazines, including *Child, American Baby, Parenting, Parents, Baby Talk,* and *Sesame Street Parents.* Kimberly-Clark demands—in writing in its ad insertion orders—that these ads be placed only "adjacent to black and white happy baby editorial," which would definitely not include stories about, say, Sudden Infant Death Syndrome or Down's syndrome. "Sometimes we have to create editorial that is satisfactory to them," a top editor says. That, of course, means something else is likely lost, and the mix of the magazine is altered.

- Former Cosmo Girl Helen Gurley Brown disclosed to *Newsday* that a Detroit auto company representative (the paper didn't say which company) asked for—and received—an advance copy of the table of contents for her bon voyage issue, then threatened to pull a whole series of ads unless the representative was permitted to see an article titled "How to Be Very Good in Bed." Result? "A senior editor and the client's ad agency pulled a few things from the piece," a dispirited Brown recalled, "but enough was left" to salvage the article.

BOWING TO NEW WINDS

Cosmo is hardly the only magazine that has bowed to the new winds. Kurt Andersen, the former *New York* magazine editor—whose 1996 firing by parent company K-III was widely perceived to be a result of stories that angered associates of K-III's founder, Henry R. Kravis—nonetheless says that he always kept advertisers' sensibilities in mind when editing the magazine. "Because I worked closely and happily with the publisher at *New York,* I was aware who the big advertisers were," he says. "My antennae were turned on, and I read copy thinking, 'Is this going to cause Calvin Klein or Bergdorf big problems?'"

National Review put a reverse spin on the early-warning-for-advertisers discussion recently, as the *Washington Post* revealed, when its advertising director sent an advance copy of a piece about utilities deregulation to an energy supplier mentioned in the story, as a way of luring it into buying space.

And Chrysler is hardly the only company that is aggressive about its editorial environment. Manufacturers of packaged goods, from toothpaste to toilet paper, aggressively declare their love for plain-vanilla. Colgate-Palmolive, for example, won't allow ads in a "media context" containing "offensive" sexual content or material it deems "antisocial or in bad taste"—which it leaves undefined in its policy statement sent to magazines. In the statement, the company says that it "charges its advertising agencies and their media buying services with the responsibility of pre-screening any questionable media content or context."

AUTO COMPANIES LEAD THE PACK

Procter & Gamble, the second-largest advertising spender last year ($1.5 billion), has a reputation as being very touchy. Two publishing executives told Gloria Steinem, for her book *Moving Beyond Words,* that the company doesn't want its ads near anything about "gun control, abortion, the occult, cults, or the disparagement of religion." Even nonsensational and sober pieces dealing with sex and drugs are no-go.

Kmart and Revlon are among those that editors list as the most demanding. "IBM is a stickler—they don't like any kind of controversial articles," says Robyn Mathews, formerly of *Entertainment Weekly* and now *Time*'s chief of makeup. She negotiates with advertisers about placement, making sure that their products are not put near material that is directly critical. AT&T, Mathews says, is another company that prefers a soft climate. She says she often has to tell advertisers, "We're a *news* magazine. I try to get them to be realistic."

Still, the auto companies apparently lead the pack in complaining about content. And the automakers are so powerful—the Big Three pumped $3.6 billion into U.S. advertising last year—that most major magazines have sales offices in Detroit.

After *The New Yorker,* in its issue of June 12, 1995, ran a Talk of the Town piece that quoted some violent, misogynist rap and rock lyrics—along with illustrative four-letter words—opposite a Mercury ad, Ford Motor Company withdrew from the magazine, reportedly for six months. The author, Ken Auletta, learned about it only this year. "I actually admire *The New Yorker* for not telling me about it," he says. Yet afterwards, according to *The Wall Street Journal,* the magazine quietly adopted a system of warning about fifty companies on a "sensitive advertiser list" whenever potentially offensive articles are scheduled.

OTHERS MAY BE TEMPTED TO FOLLOW

It is the Chrysler case, though, that has made the drums beat, partly because of Chrysler's heft and partly because the revelation about the automaker's practice came neatly packaged with a crystalline example of just what that practice can do to a magazine.

In the advertising jungle Chrysler is an 800-pound gorilla—the nation's fourth-largest advertiser and fifth-largest magazine advertiser (it spent some $270 million at more than 100 magazines last year, behind General Motors, Philip Morris, Procter & Gamble, and Ford). Where it leads, other advertisers may be tempted to follow.

The automaker's letter was mailed to magazines in January 1996, but did not come to light until G. Bruce Knecht of *The Wall Street Journal* unearthed it this April in the aftermath of an incident at *Esquire. The Journal* reported that *Esquire* had planned a sixteen-page layout for a 20,000-word fiction piece by accomplished author David Leavitt. Already in page proofs and scheduled for the April '97 issue, it was to be one of the longest short stories *Esquire* had ever run, and it had a gay theme and some raw language. But publisher Valerie Salembier, the *Journal* reported, met with then editor-in-chief Edward Kosner and other editors and voiced her concerns: she would have to notify Chrysler about the story, and she expected that when she did so Chrysler would pull its ads. The automaker had bought four pages, the *Journal* noted—just enough to enable the troubled magazine to show its first year-to-year ad-page improvement since the previous September.

TAKING MARCHING ORDERS

Kosner then killed the piece, maintaining he had editorial reasons for doing so. Will Blythe, the magazine's literary editor, promptly quit. "I simply can't stomach the David Leavitt story being pulled," he said in his letter of resignation. "That act signals a terrible narrowing of the field available to strong, adventuresome, risk-taking work, fiction and nonfiction alike. I know that editorial and advertising staffs have battled—sometimes affably, other times savagely—for years to define and protect their respective turfs. But events of the last few weeks signal that the balance is out of whack now—that, in effect, we're taking marching orders (albeit, indirectly) from advertisers."

The Chrysler letter's public exposure is a rough reminder that sometimes the biggest problems are the most clichéd: as financial concerns become increasingly paramount it gets harder to assert editorial independence.

After the article about *Esquire* in the *Journal,* the American Society of Magazine Editors—the top cops of magazine standards, with 867 members from 370 magazines—issued a statement expressing "deep concern" over the trend to give "advertisers advance notice about upcoming stories." Some advertisers, ASME said, "may mistake an early warning as an open invitation to pressure the publisher to alter, or even kill, the article in question. We believe publishers should—and will—refuse to bow to such pressure. Furthermore, we believe editors should—and will—follow ASME's explicit principle of editorial independence, which at its core states: 'The chief editor of any magazine must have final authority over the editorial content, words, and pictures that appear in the publication.'"

SOME HAVE NO PROBLEM

On July 24, after meeting with the ASME board, the marketing committee of the Magazine Publishers of America—which has 200 member companies that print more than 800 magazines—gathered to discuss this issue, and agreed to work against prior review of story lists or summaries by advertisers. "The magazine industry is united in this," says ASME's president, Frank Lalli, managing editor of *Money.* "There is no debate within the industry."

How many magazines will reject Chrysler's new road map? Unclear. Lalli says he has not found any publisher or editor who signed and returned the Chrysler letter as demanded. "I've talked to a lot of publishers," he says, "and I don't know of any who will bow to it. The great weight of opinion among publishers and editors is that this is a road we can't go down."

Yet Mike Aberlich, Chrysler's manager of consumer media relations, claims that "Every single one has been signed." Aberlich says that in some cases, individual magazines agreed; in others a parent company signed for all its publications.

CJR did turn up several magazines, mostly in jam-packed demographic niches, whose executives concede they have no problem with the Chrysler letter. One is *Maxim,* a new book aimed at the young-men-with-bucks market put out by the British-based Dennis Publishing. "We're going to play ball," says *Maxim*'s sales manager, Jamie Hooper. The startup, which launched earlier this year, signed and returned the Chrysler letter. "We're complying. We definitely have to."

At *P.O.V.,* a two-and-a-half-year-old magazine backed largely by Freedom Communications Inc. (owners of *The Orange County Register*) and aimed at a similar audience, publisher Drew Massey says he remembers a Chrysler letter, can't remember signing it, but would have no problem providing advance notice. "We do provide PentaCom with a courtesy call, but we absolutely never change an article." Chrysler, alerted to *P.O.V.*'s August "Vice" issue, decided to stay in. Massey argues that the real issue is not about edgy magazines like *P.O.V.,* but about larger and tamer magazines that feel constrained by advertisers from being adventurous.

Hachette Filipacchi, French-owned publisher of twenty-nine U.S. titles, from *Elle* to *George,* offered Chrysler's plan for a safe editorial environment partial support. Says John Fennell, chief operating officer: "We did respond to the letter, saying we were aware of their concern about controversial material and that we would continue—as we have in the past—to monitor it very closely and to make sure that their advertising did not appear near controversial things. However, we refused to turn over or show or discuss the editorial direction of articles with them."

DECIDING YOUR NEIGHBORHOOD

It has long been a widely accepted practice in the magazine industry to provide "heads-ups"—warnings to advertisers about copy that might embarrass them—say, to the friendly skies folks about a scheduled article on an Everglades plane crash, or to Johnnie Walker about a feature on the death of a hard-drinking rock star. In some instances, advertisers are simply moved as far as possible from the potentially disconcerting material. In others, they are offered a chance to opt out of the issue altogether, ideally to be rescheduled for a later edition.

In the 1980s, Japanese car makers got bent out of shape about news articles they saw as Japan-bashing, says *Business Week*'s editor-in-chief, Stephen B. Shepard, a past ASME president. Anything about closed markets or the trade imbalance might be seen as requiring a polite switch to the next issue.

Chrysler, some magazine people argue, is simply formalizing this long-standing advertiser policy of getting magazine executives to consider their special sensitivities while assembling each issue. But Chrysler's letter clearly went beyond that. PentaCom's president and C.E.O., David Martin, was surprisingly blunt when he explained to *The Wall Street Journal* the automaker's rationale: "Our whole contention is that when you are looking at a product that costs $22,000, you want the product to be surrounded by positive things. There's nothing positive about an article about child pornography."

Chrysler spokesman Aberlich insists the brouhaha is no big deal: "Of the thousands of magazine ads we've placed in a year, we've moved an ad out of one issue into the next issue about ten times a year. We haven't stopped dealing with any magazine." He compares placing an ad to buying a house: "You decide the neighborhood you want to be in." That interesting metaphor, owning valuable real estate, leads to other metaphors—advertisers as editorial NIMBYs (Not In My Back Yard) trying to keep out anybody or anything they don't want around.

As for the current contretemps, Aberlich says it's nothing new, that Chrysler has been requesting advance notice since 1993. "We sent an initial letter to magazines asking them to notify us of upcoming controversial stuff—

graphic sex, graphic violence, glorification of drug use." But what about the updated and especially chilling language in the 1996 letter, the one asking to look over editors' shoulders at future articles, particularly *political, social* material and *editorial that might be construed as provocative?* Aberlich declines to discuss it, bristling, "We didn't give you that letter."

SUCCESS BREEDS INDEPENDENCE

How did we get to the point where a sophisticated advertiser dared send such a letter? In these corporate-friendly times, the sweep and powers of advertisers are frenetically expanded everywhere. Formerly pure public television and public radio now run almost-ads. Schools bombard children with cereal commercials in return for the monitors on which the ads appear. Parks blossom with yogurt- and sneaker-sponsored events.

Meanwhile, a growing number of publications compete for ad dollars— not just against each other but against the rest of the media, including new media. Those ads are bought by ever-larger companies and placed by a shrinking number of merger-minded ad agencies.

Are magazines in a position where they cannot afford to alienate any advertiser? No, as a group, magazines have done very well lately, thank you. With only minor dips, ad pages and total advertising dollars have grown impressively for a number of years. General-interest magazines sold $5.3 billion worth of advertising in 1987. By 1996 that figure had more than doubled, to $11.2 billion.

Prosperity can enhance independence. The magazines least susceptible to advertiser pressures are often the most ad-laden books. Under its new editor-in-chief, David Granger, the anemic *Esquire* seems to be getting a lift, but *GQ* had supplanted it in circulation and in the serious-article business, earning many National Magazine Awards. This is in part because it first used advertiser-safe service pieces and celebrity profiles to build ad pages, then had more space to experiment and take risks

PROSPERITY DOES NOT ALWAYS BRING VIRTUE

Catherine Viscardi Johnston, senior vice president for group sales and marketing at *GQ*'s parent company, the financially flush Condé Nast, says that in her career as a publisher she rarely was asked to reschedule an ad—perhaps once a year. Meddling has not been a problem, she says: "Never was a page lost, or an account lost. Never, never did an advertiser try to have a story changed or eliminated."

At the other extreme, *Maxim,* which signed the Chrysler letter, does face grueling ad-buck competition. The number of new magazine startups in 1997 may well exceed 1,000, says Samir Husni, the University of Mississippi journalism professor who tracks launches. And *Maxim*'s demographic—21- to 34-year-old males—is jam-packed with titles.

This is not to say that prosperity and virtue go hand in hand. Witness Condé Nast's ad-fat *Architectural Digest,* where editor-in-chief Paige Rense freely admits that only advertisers are mentioned in picture captions. The range of standards among magazines is wide.

And that range can be confusing. "Some advertisers don't understand on a fundamental level the difference between magazines that have a serious set of rules and codes and serious ambitions, and those that don't," says Kurt Andersen. "The same guy at Chrysler is buying ads in *YM* and *The New Yorker.*"

If it is up to editors to draw the line, they will have to buck the industry's impulse to draw them even deeper into their magazines' business issues. Hachette Filipacchi's U.S. president and C.E.O., David Pecker, is one who would lower the traditional ad-edit wall. "I actually know editors who met with advertisers and lived to tell about it," he said in a recent speech. Some editors at Hachette—and other news organizations—share in increased profits at their magazines. Thus, to offend an advertiser, it might be argued, would be like volunteering for a pay cut. So be it; intrepid editors must be prepared to take that.

CONSUMERS SHOULD DECIDE

Ironically, in fretting over public sensibilities, advertisers may not be catering to their consumers at all. In a recent study of public opinion regarding television—which is even more dogged by content controversies than magazines—87 percent of respondents said it is appropriate for network programs to deal with sensitive issues and social problems. (The poll was done for ABC, NBC, and CBS by the Roper Starch Worldwide market research firm.) Asked who should "have the most to say about what people see and hear on television," 82 percent replied that it ought to be "individual viewers themselves, by deciding what they will and will not watch." Almost no one—just 9 percent—thought advertisers should be able to shape content by granting or withholding sponsorship. Even PentaCom admitted to the *Journal* that its own focus groups show that Chrysler owners are not bothered by Chrysler ads near controversial articles.

So what's eating these folks? Partially, it may be a cultural phenomenon. Ever since magazines began to attract mass audiences and subsidize subscription rates with advertising, many magazines have chased readers—just as networks chase viewers now—with ever more salacious fare. But corporate executives have often remained among the most conservative of Americans. Nowhere is this truer than in heartland locations like Chrysler's Detroit or Procter & Gamble's Cincinnati.

FEAR OF ACTIVIST GROUPS

Ad executives say one factor in the mix is sponsors' fear of activist groups, which campaign against graphic or gay or other kinds of editorial material perceived as "anti-family." Boycotts like the current Southern Baptist campaign against Disney for "anti-family values" may be on the rise, precisely because advertisers do take them seriously. This, despite a lack of evidence that such boycotts do much damage. "Boycotts have no discernible impact on sales. Usually, the public's awareness is so quickly dissipated that it has no impact at all," says Elliot Mincberg, vice-president and general counsel of People For the American Way, a liberal organization that tracks the impact of pressure groups. Why, then, would advertisers bother setting guidelines that satisfy these groups at all? "They're trying to minimize their risk to *zero*," says an incredulous Will Blythe, *Esquire*'s former literary editor.

Yet not every advertiser pines for the bland old days. The hotter the product, it seems, the cooler the heads. The "vice" peddlers (booze & cigarettes), along with some apparel and consumer electronics products, actually like being surrounded by edgy editorial copy—unless their own product is zapped. Party *on!*

Even Chrysler's sensitivities appear to be selective. *Maxim*'s premier issue featured six women chatting provocatively about their sex lives, plus several photos of women in scanty come-hither attire, but Chrysler had no grievances.

THE REAL PROBLEM IS SELF-CENSORSHIP

The real danger here is not censorship by advertisers. It is self-censorship by editors. On one level, self-censorship results in omissions, small and large, that delight big advertisers.

Cigarettes are a clear and familiar example. The tobacco companies' hefty advertising in many a magazine seems in inverse proportion to the publication's willingness to criticize it. Over at the American Cancer Society, media director Susan Islam says that women's magazines tend to cover some concerns adequately, but not lung cancer: "Many more women die of lung cancer, yet there have hardly been any articles on it."

To her credit, *Glamour*'s editor-in-chief, Ruth Whitney, is one who has run tobacco stories. She says that her magazine, which carries a lot of tobacco advertising, publishes the results of every major smoking study. But Whitney concedes they are mostly short pieces. "Part of the problem with cigarettes was—we did do features, but there's nobody in this country who doesn't know cigarettes kill." Still, everybody also knows that getting slimmer requires exercise and eating right, which has not prevented women's magazines from running that story in endless permutations. Tobacco is in the news, and magazines have the unique job of deepening and humanizing such stories.

Specific editorial omissions are easier to measure than how a magazine's world view is altered when advertisers' preferences and sensitivities seep into the editing. When editors act like publishers, and vice versa, the reader is out the door.

Can ASME, appreciated among editors for its intentions, fire up the troops? The organization has been effective on another front—against abuses of special advertising sections, when advertisements try to adapt the look and feel of editorial matter. ASME has distributed a set of guidelines about just what constitutes such abuse.

ENFORCING GUIDELINES

To enforce those guidelines, ASME executive director Marlene Kahan says the organization sends a couple of letters each month to violators. "Most magazines say they will comply," she reports. "If anybody is really egregiously violating the guidelines on a consistent basis, we'd probably sit down and have a meeting with them." ASME can ban a magazine from participating in the National Magazine Awards, but Kahan says the organization has not yet had to do that. In addition, ASME occasionally asks the organization that officially counts magazine ad pages, the Publishers Information Bureau, not to count advertising sections that break the rules as ad pages—a tactic that ASME president Lalli says tends to get publishers' attention.

Not everyone in the industry thinks ASME throws much of a shadow. "ASME can't bite the hand that feeds them," says John Masterton of *Media Industry Newsletter,* which covers the magazine business. During Robert Sam Anson's brief tenure as editor of *Los Angeles* magazine, the business side committed to a fifteen-page supplement, to be written by the editorial side and called "The Mercedes Golf Special." Mercedes didn't promise to take any ads, but it was hoped that the carmaker would think kindly of the magazine for future issues. The section would appear as editorial, listed as such in the table of contents. Anson warned the business side that, in his opinion, the section would contravene ASME guidelines, since it was in effect an ad masquerading as edit. A senior executive told him not to worry—that at the most they'd get a "slap on the wrist." The section did not run in the end, Anson says, because of "deadline production problems."

CONTENT THAT BORES THE CUSTOMERS

The Chrysler model, however—with its demand for early warnings, and its insistence on playing editor—is tougher for ASME to police. Special advertising sections are visible. Killed or altered articles are not. And unless it surfaces, as in the *Esquire* case, self-censorship is invisible.

One well-known editor, who asks not to be identified, thinks the problem will eventually go away. "It's a self-regulating thing," he says. "At some point, the negative publicity to the advertisers will cause them to back off."

Of course, there is nothing particularly automatic about that. It takes an outspoken journalistic community to generate heat. And such attention could backfire. The *Journal*'s Knecht told the audience of public radio's *On the Media* that his reporting might actually have aggravated the problem: "One of the negative effects is that more advertisers who weren't aware of this system have gone to their advertising agencies and said, 'Hey, why not me too! This sounds like a pretty good deal!'"

Except, of course, that it really isn't. In the long run everybody involved is diminished when editors feel advertisers' breath on their necks. Hovering there, advertisers help create content that eventually bores the customers they seek. Then the editors of those magazines tend to join the ranks of the unemployed. That's just one of the many reasons that editors simply cannot bend to the new pressure. They have to draw the line—subtly or overtly, quietly or loudly, in meetings and in private, and in their own minds.

32

Woolly Times on the Web

Robin Goldwyn Blumenthal

Editor's Note: The Internet poses new challenges to old traditions about the separation of news and advertising because there are few rules—and even fewer traditions—on the World Wide Web. The president of the American Society of Magazine Editors calls it "the Wild West of publishing . . . anything goes." Ultimately, it may come to the question of whether the web can be a place for legitimate journalism.

Robin Goldwyn Blumenthal, a former reporter at *The Wall Street Journal,* is currently a free-lance writer and editor at *Barron's.* This article was published by the *Columbia Journalism Review,* September/October 1997, and is reprinted with permission.

Web-based publishing may be technologically advanced, but when it comes to drawing the line between advertising and editorial, some new media are re-opening very old dilemmas and debates.

Says Jeff Chester, executive director of the Center for Media Education, a new-media watchdog group: "In a world where marketing, advertising, and editorial are all being rolled up into one, the already frayed distinctions or safeguards are being obliterated."

And Josh Schroeter, director of strategic planning at the Center for New Media at Columbia's Graduate School of Journalism, predicts that in the digital medium, unlike in the old-style media where advertising seems almost incidental to the content, "what you're going to see is a marketing vehicle with the editorial content inserted into that."

Many of the purveyors of news and information—and purveyors appears to be the apt word for this medium—also seem genuinely concerned about how they are going to maintain journalistic integrity. There's a widespread sense that "this is the Wild West of publishing right now—sort of anything goes," as *Money* managing editor Frank Lalli puts it. This has led to efforts to bring a sheriff to Dodge City. Lalli is also the president of the American Society of Magazine Editors, which recently issued some journalistic rules of conduct for presenting information and advertising online.

BIGGEST ISSUE IS DISCLOSURE

Online advertising in 1996—the first full year of large-scale advertising on the World Wide Web—totaled about $300 million, says Jupiter Communications, an online ad tracking firm. That is merely a blip on the screen compared with the $38.2 billion of advertising in newspapers and $9.2 billion in magazines. But Alan Braverman, an analyst at Credit Suisse First Boston, projects Internet advertising will swell to $3.1 billion by the year 2000, while others have put it as high as $5 billion.

With that kind of money at stake, one of the biggest issues for readers is disclosure. ASME declares that Web sites must clearly and prominently identify who is controlling or paying for their content or copy. The ASME rules also call for online publishers to clearly distinguish between editorial and ad content on all Web pages. The rules discourage embedding advertising links in editorial copy or displaying logos in conjunction with another company's, except in custom publishing. But there are plenty of gray areas to contend with.

Feed, an online magazine of culture, politics, and technology, has been experimenting with something called "commerce links" in its articles. These links, which usually appear in the margins, take the reader to a commercial site where he or she can buy related books. But the commerce links are always printed in green to distinguish them from other content-related links, and *Feed* doesn't accept payment for its link choices. In a very small number of cases, it has embedded commerce links in the body of text.

WEB SURFERS MAY NOT UNDERSTAND

When the idea was conceived, "we did a lot of soul-searching," says Steven Johnson, co-founder and editor in chief. "If you set the commercial links off, as long as the relationships are understood, linking makes a lot of sense, and enhances the experience of the reader."

Though banner ads are still the most popular form of advertising on the web, co-branding—joint ventures and cross promotions between advertisers and publishers or their affiliates—has become increasingly popular, and increasingly complicated as well. For instance, Time Warner Cable and Procter & Gamble together run a site called ParentTime. It's to be found on Time Inc.'s Pathfinder site, which is also the gateway to CNN, *Money,* and *Time,* among others. Web surfers who don't look to the fine print at the bottom of ParentTime's home page probably won't realize that the parenting guide they're reading is co-produced by one of the nation's largest advertisers, the maker of everything from Vicks cough syrup to Pampers.

Daniel Okrent, editor of new media at Time Inc., says that Pathfinder rents space on its home page to ParentTime just as it does to the Zagat restaurant survey—as a service to its readers. Although Okrent licenses the space, he exerts no editorial control over the ParentTime site. But he would, he says, consider distinguishing on the Pathfinder home page between *Time*'s branded titles and its licensees. And he maintains he would remove from the site any publication that "publishes lies, things dangerous, or obscene" by his standards.

WHERE ASSOCIATIONS MIGHT LEAD

Joint ventures and pairings raise important questions about their effect on the media partner's coverage. When *The Wall Street Journal Interactive Edition* teamed with Microsoft in late 1996 to offer free online *Journal* subscriptions to users of Microsoft's Internet Explorer web browser, some skeptics wondered whether they'd see a difference in how the paper treated news of Microsoft's fierce battle-of-the-browsers with its archrival Netscape. But the *Interactive Journal*'s editor, Neil Budde, dismissed those concerns. Microsoft, he says, spends "far more money advertising in print and it doesn't influence our news coverage." He maintains that "there's never going to be a case where we'll let advertising or business relationships affect our news judgment or the way we cover the news."

Other questions can arise in areas such as the advertisers' microsites on *The New York Times on the Web,* where companies or brands like Maxwell House and Delta have had their logos displayed right next to the *Times*'s. A user who enters the site through the home page can click on an ad banner that constantly rotates the message: "Visa and *The New York Times* bring you good eats, cool shows, hot flicks/click here for weekly reviews"—and access the same movie, theater, and restaurant reviews that appear in the editorial section. The strip at the top of the microsite says it is "presented by Visa as a supplement to *The New York Times on the Web,*" although what kind of supplement isn't clear, because it is filled with editorial content that has already been written by *Times* staffers. Some critics wonder where these associations might lead.

ANALOGY TO TELEVISION

"The analogy is to television, where you have the brand sitting there in the background, like the Jeep Eagle score-board at the Yankee games," says Peter Storck, group director of online advertising at Jupiter Communications. "I think it would be okay to have a sponsor for a crossword puzzle, but if it were international news sponsored by IBM, I might get a little concerned."

Martin Nisenholtz, president of The New York Times Electronic Media, says the company is "very careful in creating microsites to delineate between what is advertiser content and what is editorial content," and that it defines such sites as pages where the *Times* is "working with an advertiser to bring certain parts of the editorial into view." Nisenholtz maintains that the *Time*'s mantra—to report the news "without fear or favor"—is still in force online, and he points out that the content has already been written and can be accessed elsewhere on the site. "We're not going to create any kind of environment where our editorial content is compromised in any way," he says. "We'll get off the Web before we do that."

USA Today online has co-branding relationships with advertisers in its Marketplace sections. Not only does it display joint logos with advertisers, it also shares revenue with its partners for every product or service bought from Marketplace. The commercial sections, which are organized around such topics as travel, automotive, and finance, display headlines that link to relevant staff-written stories elsewhere on the site. On the Marketplace Tech page, for instance, a reader can click on a staff-written story about Disney's free introductory offer of its Daily Blast Internet service, and then click from there straight to the Disney site.

ABANDONING SOME PRINCIPLES

Lorraine Cichowski, vice president and general manager of The USA Today Information Network, which produces *USA Today* online, isn't concerned that coverage of these advertisers might be compromised, pointing out that the stories have already been written. The site has also been experimenting with prime advertising space on its home page. The paper's logo has morphed, for instance, into animated ads for cars. But Cichowski says a recent car ad that ran for a week drew only three responses from readers, two negative, one positive. "The logo's integrity wasn't compromised at all," she says, "It just got out of the way for awhile."

But even if the electronic media are clear about what constitutes an ad, readers may not always be, and that confusion should be of concern to journalists. "It's vital not only to avoid a conflict of interest but to avoid the appearance of conflict, because in the long run the appearance is what determines people's opinions of the credibility," says Lewis Perdue, the chairman of the web publisher SmartWired Inc. Perdue, who has a background in journalism and public relations, is advocating a stringent code of journalistic ethics on the Web through a site called webethics.com.

New media should take care how closely they work with advertisers because, says Phil Lemmons, editorial director of *PC World,* "with co-branding, what's being sold is implied endorsement." Lemmons, whose August issue examined some instances of deception on the Web, helped draft the ASME principles for digital media. He is concerned that traditional publishers on the Web may abandon some of their principles because they must compete with other sites, many of them non-journalistic, that use such over-the-top tactics as product placement.

A RISK IN ANY MEDIUM

So what's the solution? James Kinsella, general manager of MSNBC on the Internet, a joint venture of Microsoft and NBC, says his company is "actually changing the entire model" for Web advertising: the ad pops up in a separate window and the viewer can push a button to stop it. Although he says he shares the fear that advertising may subvert content on the Internet, he and others maintain that it's a risk in any medium. He thinks that privacy and the tracking of information about consumers are larger problems.

Concerning the blurred lines between content and advertising online, Abe Peck, acting dean of Northwestern's Medill School of Journalism, says that to some extent, "the Web's taking a lot of heat the traditional media should be taking."

Still, he cautions that online publishers "have to decide about their brand identity." They should ask themselves: "Is the Web a place where they can do legitimate journalism, or put on fishnet stockings and stiletto heels and tart around?"

ADDITIONAL RESOURCES FOR PART 8

Suggested Questions and Discussion Topics

1. In "Cigarettes Under Fire," what does author Richard W. Pollay think about the total banning of cigarette ads in any and all media? What country has done that so far?

2. According to "Cigarettes Under Fire," why should cigarette manufacturers be so interested in marketing to teenagers?

3. From "Rock 'Til They Drop: Tunes, Teens, and Tobacco," discuss author William Novelli's description of the tobacco industry's partnership with the music industry. Why would it be a useful partnership for tobacco? Why for music?

4. From "Rock 'Til They Drop: Tunes, Teens, and Tobacco," discuss Martha Byrne's rationale for working with Philip Morris and your own opinions about it.

5. In "The Squeeze," what does author Russ Baker mean by self-censorship, and what does he think about it?

6. From "The Squeeze," briefly summarize "the Chrysler model" for a relationship between mass media and advertiser. Even though the American Society of Magazine Editors (ASME) is deeply concerned about this practice, why is it difficult to police?

7. What, according to "Woolly Times on the Web" by Robin Goldwyn Blumenthal, are the main differences between advertising on television and advertising on the Internet?

8. What, according to "Woolly Times on the Web," do many web surfers not understand about advertising on the Internet?

Suggested Readings

Stuart and Elizabeth Ewen, *Channels of Desire: Mass Images and the Shaping of American Consciousness.* New York: McGraw-Hill, 1982.

Jib Fowles, *Advertising and Popular Culture.* Thousand Oaks, CA: Sage Publications, 1996.

Katherine Toland Frith, ed. *Undressing the Ad: Reading Culture in Advertising.* New York: Peter Lang Publishing, 1997.

Jerry Kirkpatrick, *In Defense of Advertising: Arguments from Reason, Ethical Egoism, and Laissez-Faire Capitalism.* Westport, CT: Quorum, 1994.

D. M. Krugman, L. M. Reid, S. W. Dunn and A. M. Barban. *Advertising: Its Role in Modern Marketing.* Orlando, FL: Dryden Press, 1994.

Martin Mayer, *Whatever Happened to Madison Avenue? Advertising in the '90s.* Boston: Little, Brown, 1991.

Vance Packard, *The Hidden Persuaders.* New York: Van Rees Press, 1965.

Frank Presbrey, *The History and Development of Advertising.* Garden City, NY: Doubleday, Doran & Co., 1929.

Randall Rothenberg, *Where the Suckers Moon: An Advertising Story.* New York: Alfred A. Knopf, 1995.

Vincent Vinikas, *Soft Soap, Hard Sell: American Hygiene in an Age of Advertisement.* Ames, IA: Iowa State University Press, 1992.

Barton C. White, *The New Ad Media Reality.* Westport, CT: Quorum, 1993.

Suggested Videos

"Advertising and the End of the World." Northampton, MA: Media Education Foundation. 1997. (50 minutes)

"Pack of Lies: The Advertising of Tobacco." Northampton, MA: Media Education Foundation. 1992. (35 minutes)

Bill Moyers, "Consuming Images." Princeton, NJ: Films for the Humanities & Sciences. 1989. (60 minutes)

"The Fine Art of Separating People from Their Money." New York: Insight Media. 1997. (115 minutes)

"Advertising, 1997." New York: Insight Media. 1997 (30 minutes)

"30-Second Seduction, 1985." New York: Insight Media. 1985. (25 minutes)

"Invisible Persuaders: The Battle for Your Mind, 1994." New York: Insight Media. 1994. (22 minutes)

"Why Ads Work: The Power of Self-Deception." New York: Insight Media. 1995. (21 minutes)

PART · 9

Sex, Crime, and Violence

The United States is the most violent country in the world, with the highest rates of interpersonal violence and homicide, whose children are becoming increasingly involved in violence at a younger age. Every eight seconds of the school day, a child runs away from home; every 47 seconds, a child is abused or neglected; every 67 seconds a teenager has a baby; every seven minutes a child is arrested for a drug offense; every 36 minutes a child is injured by a gun; every hour and a half a child is killed by a gun; and every day, 135,000 children bring a gun to school. Between 1988 and 1998, the adolescent homicide rate has more than doubled, to become the second leading cause of death overall among Americans ages 15 to 24.[1]

What is wrong with America? Why are there so many more violent deaths by handguns in this country than any other society on this planet? Is it because handguns are so readily available? Is it because we've had a history of the violent use of guns going back to the settlement of a new continent and a lawless frontier? Or is it because of mass media, especially television and motion pictures? Many experts would say it is some combination of these factors, plus the stress of modern, fast, harried and competitive society.

Yet statistics on crime and violence show a dramatic rise since the advent of television. Is television more to be blamed than the other factors? A University of Washington study concluded that without television, there would be half the number of homicides each year in America. The study was based on a comparison of homicide rates in Canada, U.S., and South Africa, both before and after the introduction of television. Homicide rates doubled in Canada and America in the first 20 years of TV. During the same 20-year period in South Africa, before television was available, homicide rates increased only 7 percent. In the first 10 years of TV in South Africa, from 1974 to 1984, homicides increased 56 percent, and have grown ever faster in the 1990s.[2]

By the end of the twentieth century, more than a thousand studies had been done that have determined a causal link between violence depicted in the media and aggressive behavior among those exposed to it. In a 1993 report, the American Psychological Association concluded: "There is absolutely no doubt that higher levels of viewing violence on television are correlated with increasing acceptance of aggressive attitudes and increased aggressive behavior."[3]

One thing is certain: American mass media are full of violence. A study by the National Coalition of Television Violence showed that 37 percent of all programming on American cable and network TV features themes high in violence; on HBO it was 86 percent; on USA Network it was 85 percent. Hollywood movies make up the majority of the most violent programming, although violent TV series were prominent on the major networks, according to the study.

In a radio address after a tragic school shooting in 1998, President Clinton said, "We must face up to the fact that these [school shootings] are more than isolated incidents. They are symptoms of a changing culture that desensitizes our children to violence."[4]

Why should television be so taken with violence? Perhaps the answer lies in the nature of the medium itself. Television isn't made up of letters and words and sentences that must have a logic to them. It is made up of images to which we are more apt to respond emotionally than rationally. Those images must move, especially on a tiny screen, in order to attract our attention, and the more violent the movement, the more we are compelled to watch.

Crime and violence are not only major themes of entertainment media; they are an essential part of news, and as we show in another unit of this book, part of advertising, too. And they are not limited to the small screen of television. The movies have become more violent since the advent of TV (compare current movies to the ones that were made prior to TV), perhaps to keep up with the competition of TV. Newspapers and magazines deal with more violent issues than they used to, especially crime, accident, and disaster stories, again perhaps to compete with TV.

The murder of Nicole Simpson and Ron Goldman and the subsequent trial of O. J. Simpson in the summer and fall of 1994 further underlined the public's intense interest in violent crime, especially when celebrities are involved. That murder case received newspaper headlines of a size usually reserved for a declaration of war, while network television gave it nearly round-the-clock coverage and even preempted the president of the United States and world sports events. Some said more people viewed the O. J. Simpson hearings than had watched the moon landing in 1968.

Even video games may be part of the problem. About a third of all American homes now have some kind of video game, and children are spending up to 40 hours a week playing such games, according to *Computer Magazine*. Roughly 80 percent of the games have violence as a theme. "When a kid plays a violent video game, he is getting trained to pull the trigger," says Carole Lieberman, a Media consultant at the University of California at Los Angeles.[5]

Sex, which is often combined with violence, is more explicit on television and in all mass media now than ever before. Is it because we have become less puritanical, and the media are reflecting us? Or are we less puritanical because we watch and hear and read more explicit sexual messages than ever before?

In New Zealand, as in much of the world now, young people watch a lot of music TV, much of it American, most of it full of sex and violence. A New Zealand woman described it: "A young black woman, long and lean, wearing a tight miniskirt, sheer bustier, fishnet stockings and stillettos, leans forward and pouts. Then she gyrates her hips and throws back her head, exposing her bare throat and cleavage. A young white man in jeans and T-shirt stands singing and watching the woman. He reaches out to grab her, perhaps he chases her, but she slips from his grasp. Sound familiar? It could be the outline of any one of thousands of popular music videos that screen on TV each year."[6]

World-wide, MTV is the fastest growing mass medium.

NOTES

This unit discusses how and why sex, crime, and violence are so much a part of mass media today.

1. See Elliott, Delbert (1994). *Youth Violence: An Overview.* Boulder, CO: Center for the Study and Prevention of Violence.

2. Study of Three Countries Links TV and Homicide Rate," *The Chronicle of Higher Education,* May 17, 1989, p. A6. See also, "Murder Rate Has Jumped in South Africa." *Jet,* May 13, 1996, p. 33. (Some critics have claimed that apartheid was responsible for the rise of violence in South Africa, but apartheid started in 1948, and violence did not rise until 1974, the year television appeared for the first time in that country. Violence has spread even faster since the end of apartheid and the more widespread use of television sets throughout the country in the 1990s.)

3. American Psychological Association Commission on Youth and Violence, *Violence and Youth: Psychology's Response, Volume One: Summary Report.* Washington, American Psychological Association, 1993.

4. See "Clinton Says School Shooting Incidents Reflect 'Changing Culture.'" *The Washington Post,* May 24, 1998, p. A10.

5. Milloy, Courtland, "Video Wars: The Next Generation." *The Washington Post,* July 3, 1991, pp. 16–20.

6. Sabbage, Lisa, "Video Vararies," *Broadsheet,* July 1991, pp. 16–20.

33

Growing Up Violent

DAVID S. BARRY

Editor's Note: For several decades, social and behavioral scientists have been studying the relationship between mass media and human behavior, especially violent and abnormal behavior. This article reviews that research and concludes that there is a link between "screen mayhem" and an increase in aggressive behavior.

Author David S. Barry is a journalist and free-lance writer as well as a TV screenwriter. This article first appeared in the *Journal of the Writers Guild of America West,* and the version reprinted here appeared in slightly condensed form in *Media & Values,* Summer 1993.

If you were a teenager in the 1950s, you remember the shock effect of news headlines about the new specter of juvenile delinquency. The book *The Amboy Dukes* and the movies *Blackboard Jungle* and *Rebel Without a Cause* were deeply alarming in their portrayal of teenagers willing to defy their school teachers and beat up other students. The violence portrayed in those stories terrifying as it was, consisted almost entirely of assaults with fists and weapons which left victims injured, but alive. It was nonlethal violence. The notion of American teenagers as killers was beyond the threshold of credibility.

Since the 1950s, America has [become] almost unrecognizable in terms of the level of criminal violence reported in everyday news stories. In looking for a root cause, one of the most obvious differences in the social and cultural fabric between postwar and prewar America is the massive and pervasive exposure of American youth to television. Behavioral scientists and medical researchers have been examining screen violence as a causative element in America's crime rate since the 1950s. Study after study has been published showing clear evidence of a link. And researchers say that the evidence continues to be ignored as the violence steadily worsens.

The statistics about children and screen violence—particularly that shown on television—are grim. You've probably seen figures that show an average of 28 hours of weekly TV watching by children from ages two to 11. For prime-time programming, which contains an average of five violent acts per hour, that works out to 100 acts of violence each week, 5,000 a year. But children also watch cartoons, which contain far more violence than adult programming. For Saturday morning cartoon shows, the violence rate spikes up to 25 acts per hour, the highest rate on TV. With children's programming added to the mix, the average child is likely to have watched 8,000 screen murders and more than 100,000 acts of violence by the end of elementary school. By the end of the teenage years, that figure will double. Those numbers are not mere statistics. They do not occur in a social vacuum, but in a culture and society with a murder rate increasing six times faster than the population. Whether we like to acknowledge it or not, America is in the grip of an epidemic of violence so severe that homicide has become the second leading cause of death of all persons 15 to 24 years old (auto crashes are the first)—and the leading cause among African-American youth. In 1992, the U.S. Surgeon General cited violence as the leading cause of injury to women ages 15 to 44, and the U.S. Centers for Disease Control consider violence a leading public health issue, to be treated as an epidemic.

A HOSTILE AMERICA

From the 1950s to now, America has gone from being one of the safest to one of the most violent countries on earth. Here are some numbers: In 1951, with a population of 150 million, federal crime reports showed a national total of 6,820 homicides, 16,800 rapes and 52,090 robberies. For 1980, with a population of 220 million (a 47 percent increase), the numbers were 23,000 murders, 78,920 rapes and 548,220 robberies.

In big cities, changes were more drastic. In Detroit, for instance, the 1953 murder total was 130, with 321 in New York and 82 in Los Angeles. Thirty years later, the Detroit murder tally was up to 726, the New York toll 1,665—and the Los Angeles murder total was 1,126. The fastest climbing sector of the rising crime rate is youth, with the past 10 years showing a 55 percent increase in the number of children under 18 arrested for murder. America now loses more adolescents to death by violence—especially gun violence—than to illness.

The reason these numbers belong in this discussion is that the medical community sees a direct link between screen violence and criminal behavior of viewers. In panel discussions on this subject, we usually hear claims from TV and movie industry spokespersons that opinion is divided in the medical community. Different conclusions can be drawn from different studies, so the arguments go, and no clear consensus exists. Yet, the American medical establishment is clear—in print—on the subject of just such a consensus. The American Medical Association, the National Institute of Mental Health, the U.S. Surgeon General's Office, the U.S. Center for Disease Control and the American Psychological Association have concluded that study after study shows a direct causal link between screen violence and violent criminal behavior.

CAUSAL LINKS

The research goes back decades. The 1968 National Commission on the Causes and Prevention of Violence cited screen violence as a major component of the problem. The 1972 *Surgeon General's Report on TV and Behavior* cited clear evidence of a causal link between televised violence and aggressive behavior by viewers. A 10-year followup to the Surgeon General's report by the National Institute of Mental Health added far more data in support of the causal link. The NIMH report, a massive study covering an additional 10 years of research, was clear and unequivocal in stating: "The consensus among most of the research community is that violence on television does lead to aggressive behavior by children and teenagers who watch the programs."

A 1985 task force for the American Psychological Association Commission on Youth on Violence came to the same conclusion. A 1992 study for the APA Commission on Youth and Violence took the issue further, examining research evidence in light of its effects or implementation. The finding was that the research evidence is widely ignored. The APA report was authored by Edward Donnerstein, Ph.D., chair of the Department of Communications, University of California Santa Barbara, by Leonard Eron, Ph.D., University of Chicago and Ron Slaby of the Education Development Center, Harvard University. Their 39-page report, about to be published, states definitively that, contrary to arguments of people in the TV and motion picture industry, there is consistency and agreement in the conclusions drawn by the major medical organizations' studies of media violence.

After discussing a massive number of studies and an extensive body of research material, Donnerstein's study quotes from the 1982 NIMH report: "In magnitude, television violence is as strongly correlated with aggressive behavior as any other behavioral variable that has been measured."

Specifically, the report noted the agreement by the NIMH, the APA and the Centers for Disease Control that research data confirms that childhood watching of TV violence is directly related to criminally violent behavior later on.

DAILY ASSAULT

Adding scope to the APA report is a study recently conducted for the non-profit Center for Media and Public Affairs in Washington, D.C. The CMPA tabulated all the violence encountered during an 18-hour broadcasting day (a Thursday) in Washington, including cable TV. The tally showed an overall average of 100 acts of violence per hour for a total of nearly 2,000 acts of violence in the 18-hour period. Most of the violence involved a gun, with murder making up one-tenth of the violent acts recorded. A breakdown by channel, or network, showed cable to be far more violent then network broadcasting. WTBS was clocked at 19 violent acts per hour, HBO at 15 per hour, USA at 14 and MTV, the youth-oriented music video channel, at 13 violent acts per hour.

The networks (except for CBS, whose violence content was skewed by the reality show *Top Cops*) were as low in violence content as PBS, which showed two violent acts per hour. ABC showed three violent acts per hour and NBC two. CBS, because of *Top Cops,* was tallied at 11 violent acts per hour. But only one-eighth of the violence occurred in adult-oriented TV entertainment. The bulk of the violence occurred in children's TV programming, with cartoons registering 25 violent incidents per hour—six times the rate of episodic TV drama. Toy commercials ranked with cartoons in violent content. Next were promos for TV shows and movies, which were four times as violent as episodic drama.

The most violent period of daily TV programming was mornings from 6 to 9 A.M. where 497 scenes of violence were recorded for an hourly rate of 165.7. Next was the 2 P.M. to 5 P.M. afternoon slot with 609 violent scenes, or 203 per hour. The morning and afternoon slots compared to 320 violent scenes in prime time, from 8 P.M. to 11 P.M. or 106 per hour, and a late-night rate (from 11 P.M. to 12 A.M.) of 114.

NO CONSEQUENCES

In addition to recording totals, the CMPA examined the context in which the screen violence occurred. The finding was that most TV violence was shown with no visible consequences, nor any critical judgment. A significant amount of the violence occurred in movie promos, where it was shown out of context. Music videos generally present violence without comment or judgment. Similarly, violence in cartoons and toy commercials usually occurs without consequences or comment. More than 75 percent of the violence tallied in the study (1,640 of the nearly 2,000 violent acts) was presented with no judgment as to its acceptability as behavior. Violence was judged criminal in fewer than one-tenth of the incidents. And, ironically, while violence in episodic TV drama and TV movies for adult viewers is subject to close scrutiny for context and suitability, the bulk of the screen violence viewed by children is not.

The studies mentioned above make a compelling argument, particularly when looked at as a group. But a new study, by Dr. Brandon Centerwall of the University of Washington Department of Epidemiology and Psychiatry, takes the discussion much farther. In a study published in the June, 1992 *Journal of the American Medical Association,* Centerwall looked for statistical connections between the change in violent crime rates following the introduction of TV in the United States.

Centerwall found this: murder rates in Canada and the U.S. increased almost 100 percent (92 percent in Canada, 93 percent in the U.S. corrected for population increase) between 1945 and 1970. In both countries, the ownership of TV sets increased in almost the same proportion as the homicide rate.

Centerwall's stark and unmistakable conclusion is this: white homicide rates in Canada, the U.S. and South Africa were stable or declining until the advent of television. Then, in the course of a generation, the murder rates doubled.

The APA study by Donnerstein Slaby and Eron also makes the point that research evidence of TV violence effects has "for decades been actively ignored, denied, attacked and even misrepresented in presentations to the American public, and popular myths regarding the effects have been perpetuated." Consequently, Donnerstein says, a major education gap exists regarding television's contribution to the problem of violence in America.

The discouraging point made in both studies is that, despite the massive research evidence of screen violence as a direct contributing factor to America's homicide rate, the screen violence level continues to rise.

As a writer deeply committed to the Constitutional guarantees against censorship, I don't like to hear the suggestion of government regulation of movies or TV. But it's time we at least face the evidence of what screen violence is doing to our children, and come to some sober conclusions about our responsibilities to the common good.

34

Armageddon—Live at 6!

Larry Platt

Editor's Note: Car crashes, body bags, and chalk outlines. Counting on blood, guts, and violence to grab viewers, WSVN, a television station in Miami went to the top in the rating wars. Its standard features on its news shows were hurricanes, murders, and tragedies. Even while Congress debated a fiercely contested federal crime bill, this station covered local crime stories but rarely mentioned the substance of the legislation.

Unfortunately, WSVN is not untypical; most local television news in America emphasizes violence in its local news coverage. Not all stations have been as focused on crime and violence, but as WSVN showed that crime and violence were good for ratings, others have followed its example.

For WSVN, the only complaints came from Miami hotels, whose owners felt that TV's emphasis on crime and violence was frightening customers and hurting Miami's tourist business. Since this article was written, the hotels have put some pressure on Miami television stations, including WSVN, to tone down the crime. But most viewers would agree that WSVN is still a leader in sensational coverage.

Larry Platt writes about the media for *Philadelphia Magazine* and is a contributor to *The Philadelphia Inquirer*'s commentary page. This article is reprinted with permission from *Forbes MediaCritic,* Summer 1995.

On August 17, 1994, national drug czar Lee Brown was lobbying for President Bill Clinton's beleaguered crime bill during a campaign-style appearance at a Miami, Florida police station. Across the nation, the fate of the bill was one of the top news stories of the day. WSVN-TV, Miami's Fox affiliate, was talking about crime that day, too. During three hours of news coverage that evening, Channel 7's viewers saw scenes involving crime or violence or both—car crashes, body bags, chalk outlines, and the like. Dramatic background music blared while dizzying jump cuts, slow-motion footage, glitzy graphics, and in-your-face close-ups kept viewers from channel-surfing. Throughout the broadcast, flamboyant correspondents reported gory details with an "end-of-the-world" urgency.

WSVN has on average a 16-minute "news hole" to fill during each of its 30-minute news broadcasts. On August 17, when I tuned in, the station devoted a full 10 minutes of that time to crime and other tragedies, or "mean world" stories as they have been called. Missing from these broadcasts, however, was any mention of the crime bill being debated in Congress.

At 'SVN crime is in, but crime-fighting is out; all things violent, lurid, or catastrophic get air time; solutions get no time. *Miami Herald* columnist Carl Hiaasen has called 'SVN "sensationalistic, lubricious, and irresponsibly gruesome," adding that if Jeffrey Dahmer had lived there, Channel 7 undoubtedly would have been his favorite station.

IF IT BLEEDS, IT LEADS

Of course, crime and violence on the local news is nothing new. Nearly 30 years ago ABC affiliate WPVI-TV in Philadelphia, one of the most commercially successful local stations in the country, pioneered the "If It Bleeds, It Leads" format. A random scan of a week's content of 'PVI news revealed the station devoted 44 percent of its coverage to crime. Nowadays, if it bleeds it apparently fills the rest of the news slot as well. In Chicago, CBS affiliate WBBM opens with screaming headlines about sex and violence, delivered by a bevy of twentysomething reporters who try to create on-air drama. In Los Angeles, KCBS switches live to hovering helicopters at the first sign of a high-speed chase. During one week last fall KCBS's evening newscast devoted 54 percent of its coverage to crime. As one media observer notes, in the '90s Miami's WSVN has turned this type of "street news" into an art form.

"For some time now, everyone in Miami has known that WSVN was irresponsible and went for drama over substance and covered a disproportionate amount of crime news," says University of Miami journalism professor Joseph Angotti, a former senior vice-president of NBC News who has released two studies of Miami TV news in the last two years. According to Angotti's data, in November 1993, 'SVN's six o'clock newscast devoted nearly half its coverage to crime-related stories, more than double the amount of its competitors. Six months later, the figure had temporarily dropped to a still market-leading 30 percent. Even with this decrease, "our findings still concerned people," Angotti said, "because it became clear that the station wasn't helping the community and was detrimental to Miami's image in and out of state." Indeed, 'SVN received dubious national attention last year when nine South Florida hotels blacked out some or all of the station's programming in their 2,640 guest rooms, claiming that, as one hotelier put it, tourists "look at Channel 7 and they're afraid to go out on the street."

YOU CAN'T KNOCK SUCCESS

Professors and hoteliers aren't the only ones worried about the journalism practiced by 'SVN. Countless media observers passionately lament the station's ascendancy. And publications ranging from *Newsweek* to the

Washington Post to *The American Prospect* have printed articles critical of its format. Still, there has been little discussion of the "whys" and "hows" of its success. And successful it is. In the five years since 'SVN news went tabloid after it lost its NBC affiliation, noted *The American Prospect,* the station has climbed from fourth to second in the South Florida market and has begun making a run at numberone WPLG, the ABC affiliate. Last October, according to the Nielsen service, 'SVN took top honors and was the market's only station to see its ratings increase from the same period in 1993. On election night in November, 'SVN blew away the competition, posting a 13.8 rating to 'PLG's 10.9. And last year it was again one of the most profitable stations in the U.S., to the tune of more than $20 million.

Advertisers have been flocking to the station because 'SVN has carved out a unique niche in South Florida, attracting legions of viewers—mostly young, many female—who have traditionally ignored the local news. Those who call 'SVN's newscast a journalistic nightmare have to confront the inconvenient reality that it is a whopping financial success. Amid all the handwringing, one ironic fact looms: If imitators borrow 'SVN's compelling glitz while maintaining journalistic integrity, the station could ultimately be the salvation of local TV news rather than its executioner. A contradiction? Perhaps. A fascinating case study? Definitely.

South Florida is a huge area with a diverse population of some 3 million people. It includes the cities of Miami, Fort Lauderdale, and Hollywood. How does a station attract viewers in such a diverse market? By playing to the common denominator: anxieties about crime, urban decay, and human tragedy. The danger, of course, lies in blurring the fine line between informing viewers and exploiting their fears. "We don't exploit anything," says 'SVN General Manager Joel Cheatwood. "The fact is, this is South Florida. Things like crime are on everybody's mind."

"WE HAVE TO BE ENTERTAINING"

But there's no denying that such issues are easier to cover than, say, the budget for the city of Miami. With limited editorial personnel, local news programs like 'SVN's are capable of unearthing, or even reporting on, only a small fraction of the newsworthy stories taking place in their markets' neighborhoods. Other news outlets such as the *Miami Herald* and smaller-circulation city papers are more equipped to cover news from these communities. And for Miami's immigrant population there are two Spanish-language newscasts, on Telemundo and Univision.

While 'SVN might not be able to cover some important local stories, it can provide its viewers with breaking national news. Thanks to an agreement with CNN, 'SVN carries footage, often live, of national and international events of interest to South Florida residents. On August 17, 1994, for instance, in the middle of all the blood and gore, more than eight minutes were devoted to Janet Reno's Washington press conference on the Cuban refugee crisis. And in September, 'SVN carried live footage of U.S. troops landing in Haiti. It's a cost-effective way for a local station like 'SVN to bring the world to its viewers and to give them a convenient news package. With fewer people tuning in to the Tom Brokaws and Dan Rathers of the world, it's also an efficient way to expand market share.

But what the architects of 'SVN news seem to understand better than most is that local newscasts don't have the luxury of an information monopoly anymore. Viewers no longer have to wait until six o'clock to get information on major events. The early evening is no longer exclusively dominated by news programs; now entertainment alternatives also fill that time slot. News directors find themselves competing with dozens of TV and radio talk shows, cable programs, newsmagazine shows, sitcoms, infotainment—you name it. "The fact is there are not enough news junkies out there to watch a dry and boring presentation," says Cheatwood, who has often seen himself vilified in the press for promoting his flashier, more dramatic type of news product. "I make no bones about it—we have to be entertaining because we compete with entertainment options as well as other news outlets."

A COPY-CAT INDUSTRY

While there is general accord that Cheatwood's concessions to entertainment have relaxed some long-held journalistic standards, the station's effort to liven up the look of the news has paid big dividends. And while the success of 'SVN hasn't yet spawned any carbon copy duplicates, a whole host of stations across the country are, to one degree or another, borrowing from the format. At Boston's WHDH, 'SVN's sister station (both are owned by entrepreneur Ed Ansen), the ratings have increased by a point across the demographic board since the CBS affiliate revamped its format in November of 1993 and began mimicking 'SVN's fast pace. Other stations that have borrowed heavily from 'SVN are WPRI in Providence, Rhode Island, and Oklahoma City's KFOR.

"This is a copy-cat industry," says Bruce Northcott, president of Frank Magid Associates, a TV news consulting firm. With increasing competition among the affiliates and independents, he adds, "I'm sure we're going to see more and more 'SVNs. To compete . . . stations have to do something to get noticed. The 'SVN format gets noticed. And now that it's a proven money-maker, the die is cast."

Indeed, 'SVN's newscast is ripe for copying because of its appeal to an important demographic group. Traditionally, 18- to 34-year-olds, who are attractive to advertisers because they are mostly single with plenty of disposable income, have not tuned in to the nightly news. Last October, 'SVN almost drew more viewers in this age group than the three local affiliates combined. Journalism professor Kevin Hall of Florida International University says his students "cannot tell you the name of ABC's anchor; they literally don't know who Peter Jennings is. But all of my students can name Rick Sanchez. And they can tell you all about him."

Sanchez is 'SVN's bigger-than-life anchor, an on-air presence who rolls up his sleeves and breathlessly delivers the news as if his life depended on it. Sanchez, writes columnist Hiaasen, "can make a routine domestic shooting sound like a sniper attack on an orphanage." The anchor's casual, working-Joe style, along with 'SVN's use of MTV-like production gimmicks, have created a package attractive to a younger demographic. "I don't watch it to get information," says 31-year-old Ian Levinson, who works in a Miami restaurant. "I watch it 'cause it's cool to come home, get a beer, and watch such self-parody. It's like watching *Saturday Night Live*'s 'Weekend Update.'" While such comments do not bode well for 'SVN's reputation among media watchers, Professor Hall, who says he's alternately "charmed and appalled" by the station's newscasts, points out that "'SVN has grabbed what's good from MTV—its energy—and applied it to news." For instance, on election night last November, while Miami's other stations soberly relayed the latest returns, those watching 'SVN literally saw fireworks with each new strand of information.

AFRAID TO GO OUT AT NIGHT

WSVN's Cheatwood believes critics overlook the fact that his station has succeeded in attracting viewers, like Miami's Levinson, who have never before shown interest in the nightly news, national or local. "We've created a brand new audience for news and pulled them into the tent," he boasts. True enough. But others question the tradeoff.

"'SVN offers the most mindless programming ever. It's one 7-11 knockoff after another," says Hall. "But when Rick Sanchez comes on and is all excited and the graphics are filling up your screen and they're switching to remote cams across the state, it becomes infectious. I just wish they'd direct this wonderful energy to things that matter more. If a station comes along that can address a topic like the economy with the type of pizzazz 'SVN uses, we'd all be better served."

But the fact is 'SVN's reporters don't spend much time on topics like the economy. Instead, the world portrayed in its broadcast each night is far more violent and dangerous than the real one. Though crime is a major political and social issue in South Florida, Miami's crime rate has remained roughly constant over the past three years, with a substantial jump only in car theft.

"Most people are afraid to go out at night and to go into the city, both of which are safer than getting into your car," says Dr. George Gerbner of the University of Pennsylvania's Annenberg School of Communication, who has spent 30 years studying the effects of TV violence, both real and fictional. "Our findings indicate that the violence on the news exploits an already existing sense of fear and apprehension."

HAS JOURNALISM BEEN SACRIFICED?

Gerbner's research shows that even if you haven't personally been the victim of crime, the more TV violence you watch, the more likely you are to feel vulnerable, mistrustful, and even paranoid. Violent crime coverage on TV news is particularly harmful, he says, because the steady procession of body bags and chalk outlines—not to mention accident and natural disaster coverage—contains the not-so-subtle threat that something awful is about to happen to you. "Is a person less fearful if he or she doesn't watch local news? Of course," responds Cheatwood. "But the same could be said if I picked up a medical journal. I mean, if I didn't know that cancer existed, sure, I'd be less fearful, but I'd also be less informed." But does 'SVN's news inform, or merely frighten or emotionally jar? In its search for a market niche, has the station sacrificed journalism? Though Cheatwood argues that his station's news product is "journalistically sound," Hall and others say that the primary problem with its editorial content is that it presents a series of disconnected events without any context.

Consider, for instance, a two-minute report that appeared on 'SVN last fall. It focused on the mother of one of three young children who had contracted encephalitis, then recovered. The camera tight to her face, the mother managed to say of her daughter through her tears: "I'm going to love her from now on, because you don't know from day-to-day or minute-to-minute what can happen."

EYE-CATCHING AND EMOTIONAL

The moment's raw emotion made for riveting TV. But vital information was missing. No soundbites from health department officials explained whether this was an isolated incident or part of an outbreak. No one explained how encephalitis is contracted or what the symptoms and health risks are. In fact, beyond exposing viewers to a touching story, 'SVN conveyed nothing substantive about this threatening disease. "Putting stories into some kind of perspective is something we talk to news managers about all the time," says Cheatwood. "Now, maybe the encephalitis story didn't have the perspective I would like, but that would just be due to producer oversight. Overall, we want to give context to the news." If that's the case, Cheatwood's management team isn't doing a great job of getting this point across; lack of context appears to be the rule, not the exception.

Cheatwood defends 'SVN by explaining, "I work in an industry that fears change and that looks upon anything that is different as no good. We won't be deterred by that." If the success of 'SVN has proven anything, it's that, in the words of *Miami Herald* TV critic Hal Boedeker, people tune in out of "fascination. . . . There really are people who can't wait to see what WSVN is going to do next."

There is no doubt that the bobbing and weaving of cameras, the slo-mo, the background music, the frantic voiceovers, and the blood and guts make for compelling TV. It's eye-catching. It's emotional. And it's here to stay because people are watching. Someday, a station will take the best of the format—its excitement and energy—and combine it with information people need to know. Just imagine how many viewers would tune in if the kind of drama that so enthralls Miami had some substance to it.

35

What You See Is What You Think

Diana Workman

Editor's Note: More and more, prime-time television uses sex to draw viewers. But rather than enlightening the audience, television serves to more deeply entrench discomfort about sex and contributes to continued ignorance in society about love, sex, and responsibility, according to the author of this article.

The author ends the article, which was written in the late 1970s, by asking what would be "in store for the '90s?" By the late 1990s, we know the answer: more sex than ever. A mid-1990s analysis showed that top-rated soap operas averaged 6.6 sexual incidents per hour, compared to half that number in the mid-1980s. Talk about safe sex and contraception was still relatively rare: only 6 references in 50 episodes. Extramarital sex outnumbered married sex acts 120 to 36. On talk shows and their promos, the rate of sexual behaviors increased from about 10 to more than 15 an hour. Prime time major network broadcasts contained an average of 10 instances of sexual behavior per hour and the consequences were rarely discussed. And a study of shows most watched by children and adolescents found than one in four of the interactions coded per episode conveyed some sort of sexual message.

Diana Workman, M.P.H., is a health education and family planning specialist. She is president of Family Planning Alternatives in Sunnyvale, California. This article was originally published in *Media & Values*, Spring 1989 and is reprinted with permission.

A 12-year-old caught spreading a telephone sex number around school can expect a lecture from his parents.

So it isn't surprising that that's what happened to Ben, a leading character on the show *Growing Pains,* during one of the sitcom's 1986 programs.

But the episode featuring his crime and punishment should strike other chords among television viewers. Its storyline provides a good example of television's increasing tendency to present sexual themes—many of them involving young people—without fully facing the consequences.

Intensive analysis of three weeks of 10 top prime-time shows from late 1986 as part of a study sponsored by the Center for Population Options and the University of California/Berkeley led my co-researcher Kim Bloomfield and myself to some uncomfortable conclusions about television sex.

Our months of laboriously counting and then decoding sexual references and behavior during our sample time made one thing perfectly clear: there is a tremendous amount of sexual activity and innuendo on television. And its pervasiveness as a means of drawing viewers, which began to accelerate in the late 1970s, has continued and even increased.

HOW MUCH SEX?

Our focused viewing of 10 popular shows tallied physical, verbal and implied acts or references to sex, before further analyzing them according to the program type, network and time frame. Age and gender of initiators were also recorded.

The following brief summaries represent the frequency of many types of sexual behavior:

- "Touching behaviors," including kissing, hugging, and other affectionate touching were presented at the rate of 24.5 acts per hour.
- "Suggestions and innuendo" involving flirtatious behavior or general allusions to sexual behavior appeared at a rate of 16.5 times per hour.
- Sexual intercourse was suggested 2.5 times per hour.
- A range of "discouraged sexual practices" such as sadomasochism and exhibitionism were suggested at a rate of 6.2 times per hour.
- On the other hand, educational information about sex was infrequently presented, occurring at a rate of 1.6 times per hour.

Although portrayal of sexual intercourse is still taboo, virtually every program in our sample contained at least one sexual reference. We also found more sexual content than one might expect in programming that aired during the supposedly family-oriented, mid-evening viewing hour (8–9 P.M./Eastern and Pacific and 7–8 P.M./Central and Mountain time). Some of the emphasis in this time frame was explained by the heavy use of sexual references and innuendo on sitcoms, where they seem to be regarded as a sure-fire laugh. The sitcom format tends to distort the treatment of serious issues even when shows are brave enough to attempt serious themes.

In the *Growing Pains* example, Ben was ahead of many of TV's sexually confused young people in one way: he did talk to his Dad about the phone-sex incident. And even when meting out punishment, his father, Jason, appeared very supportive. But in other ways the show matched our profile of television's sexual references, which were clear enough to enable us to map their characteristics and identify several recurring themes

FIVE PROBLEMS WITH TV SEX

1. *Children, especially young boys, are often "straight men" in jokes about sex and sexuality. Either they lead in to an adult's joke or they make it themselves.*

   The "phone sex" show, in which one adolescent not only participates in, but underpins, a kinky sex episode, is not unusual. More typical, perhaps, is a joke that arises on *Who's the Boss,* when eight-year-old Jonathan breaks his arm.

   "I broke my toe and couldn't walk," says his sister. When his grandmother, Mona, portrayed as very sexually active, says "I broke my pelvis . . . ." "She couldn't walk!" interrupts Tony, Jonathan's embarrassed father. In this case, the eight-year-old's broken arm sets the stage, the thirteen-year-old sister provides the lead-in, and the adults deliver the punchline to this sexual joke.

2. *TV children avoid discussing problems with their parents, and they discuss sex least of all.*

   Very few shows in our sample feature parent–child sexual discussion. When it does occur, it is only because an incident or problem forced the issue, as in the phone-sex segment. Interestingly, although father Jason of *Growing Pains* is a psychiatrist and he and his wife appear very understanding, the young characters usually try to prevent their parents from discovering what they're going through. As a result, the parents have a minimal role in solving their children's problems. An episode of *Family Ties* in which Mallory is prevented from eloping by brother Alex provides another example. Although faced with a serious life issue and blessed with understanding, low-key parents, she discusses her motivation and feelings with them only after the incident is closed.

   No interaction is one-sided, and TV's parents are often equally uncomfortable. Although on *Who's the Boss?* father Tony is upset to hear his daughter got a C, he's *relieved* to learn it was in sex education. The message here is twofold. As a father, Tony is uncomfortable about his daughter taking sex education. He also concludes that the better she does in sex education class, the more likely she is to be or become sexually active. Thus, the program reinforces the misconception that sex education causes promiscuity and implies that most parents are uncomfortable with it.

   Unlike most TV families, *The Cosby Show's* Huxtables were approached by their children before, not after, a crisis in their relationships with boy and girlfriends. Although the problems were perhaps not as serious as in some other shows, the parents were able to contribute their experience and play an active role in their resolution. Unfortunately, this seems to be the exception, not the rule, on prime-time television.

3. *Sex and sexual issues are usually presented in an exploitative way, rather than a loving and meaningful one.*

Of the six implied acts of intercourse in our sample, four were described as "lustful," one "routine" or involving sex out of habit, and only one was clearly "loving." In only one case, involving impotence, did any sort of sexual discussion take place before or after intercourse.

4. *Tender, loving sexual behavior is rarely portrayed between people in committed relationships. Instead, sexual references are presented in a context that makes even normal sexual practices appear extreme.*

Relationships on recent shows like *thirtysomething* have made loving sex between committed couples more common. In our sample, an episode of *Murder, She Wrote* in which a young husband picks up his wife and lovingly carries her into the bedroom and shuts the door was about as graphic as most television intercourse gets (and more loving and committed than most).

By contrast, most of the few references to intercourse we observed were made among friends, co-workers and strangers, demonstrating a focus on sexuality not preceded, projected or sustained by a loving relationship.

Even more problematic were the large numbers of sexual references to a variety of sexual practices besides intercourse, including some usually considered to be socially discouraged. Shows like *Night Court, Golden Girls, Moonlighting* and *Murder, She Wrote* refer with relative frequency to masturbation, voyeurism, transvestitism, transsexualism, homosexuality, sadomasochism, oral sex, prostitution and pornography.

In our sample, the farcical *Night Court* features the largest number of sexual references of this type. In almost every episode, Dan, the prosecuting attorney, searches relentlessly for sexual partners. When a woman asks him if he ever has sex at work, he replies, "Well, never with another person." In one scene, an offstage sexual episode ends with him bound and gagged in a closet, implying a sadomasochistic encounter. Such references fail to separate the kinky from the normal; instead, they tend to view all sexual behavior with a leer.

5. *If sexual intercourse is implied, precautions or discussions of birth control are avoided. Unintended pregnancies almost never occur, and sexually-transmitted diseases and contraception are seldom discussed or portrayed.*

Maddie's pregnancy on *Moonlighting,* ending in a miscarriage, is typical of TV's unwillingness to focus on the consequences of sexual behavior. Rare as they are, TV pregnancies are apt to end in miscarriages and stillbirths, leaving the characters apparently unchanged by the experience. Even more common are sexual relationships untroubled by worries about pregnancy and sexually transmitted diseases, even though safe sex, contraception and sex education are rarely discussed.

In our sample, a reference by *Moonlighting*'s David Addison to a pregnancy resulting from his first sexual experience (once again, "the kid didn't make it"), and a fantasy pregnancy arising from *Growing Pains'* father Jason's fears about his son's first car are the only acknowledgment that sex can have consequences. The first did not result in a real baby, and the second wasn't real at all!

In the shows we watched, sexually transmitted diseases were never mentioned and contraceptive use was neither depicted nor discussed. Pressures to be sexually active and issues related to it (self-esteem, peer pressure, boy/girlfriend anxieties) were never addressed. Although fears about AIDS have recently broken the taboo against discussion of condoms and safe sex practices, such instructive programming remains an exception rather than the rule.

SEX AND CONSEQUENCES

Our study confirms that prime-time television has created a market for itself by taking shocking, often humorous sexual material and packaging it as family entertainment. But what children learn from TV sex is still open to discussion.

That they are learning something seems indisputable. Most children spend more time with television than they do in school. The screen inevitably becomes a classroom for lessons about life.

Perhaps TV's most profound lesson is its reflection of the continuing sexual discomfort of our society. Thus, today's frequent, but veiled, sexual references become the flip side of the sexless TV of the '50s and early '60s. It just makes one wonder what's in store for the '90s.

36

The V-Chip Story

MARY ANN BANTA

Editor's Note: Violence on television has become the subject of great hand-wringing, much national debate, some legislation, and token action by the industry to forestall further social and governmental restriction. A number of pressure groups have formed to seek solutions to the problem, and one such group is the National Coalition on Television Violence (NCTV), which maintains that the public needs more information about the effects of television violence. The broadcast industry has long maintained that television violence has no effect.

One action taken by the government has been to require all new TV sets to have a "V-Chip" installed, but that too has been surrounded by controversy and debate. In this article, Mary Ann Banta, a member of the NCTV board of directors, explains the V-Chip, how it came about, and what it will and will not do.

This article is a public statement made by the NCTV following enactment of the V-Chip legislation in 1995.

Almost from its inception, television has attracted critics concerned with violence portrayed in prime-time and Saturday morning children's programs. Spokesmen for the broadcast industry took the position that television and the violence portrayed on television had no affect on behavior of the viewer. To many this was a strange position for an industry that was also selling commercial time with the specific intent to influence the viewer's purchasing behavior.

Both broadcasters and media activists have collected research data on the number of violent acts portrayed during entertainment programming and the effects of viewing television violence. More important, the industry conducted research and subscribed to rating systems to ascertain what people were watching. Numbers were most important because network and station revenues were not impacted by the effects of television, but by the numbers of people of a specific age range (market segment) who were watching television.

As time went on, it became clear to media researchers that no single study points to television violence as a "cause" of aggressive or violent behavior, but that television is certainly a "contributing factor" to an individual's aggressive behavior and to the problem of violence in society. The research also pointed to two other effects:

- Developing insensitivity to violence.
- Developing an excessive fear of violence.

Dr. George Gerbner described the latter as a "mean world syndrome" where the viewer perceives the world as more violent than it actually is.

REPORTS AND TASK FORCES

The summer of 1993 marked an important milestone for the issue of television violence. Due to the work of Senator Paul Simon (D-IL), the industry met and discussed the issue media violence with media activists. For the first time the industry leaders acknowledged that there may be some reason for concern. The broadcast industry and the cable industry both agreed to monitor their offerings for levels of violence. While organizations such as National Coalition on Television Violence (NCTV) had been monitoring for years, the industries had tended to disregard these efforts as tainted. They assumed that groups concerned about television violence could not or would not conduct unbiased, reliable research. UCLA was chosen to monitor broadcast television, while Mediascope was contracted to do the same for cable television. When their reports were issued, both found levels of televisions violence that corresponded to what had been reported by NCTV. Both reports also agreed that the level of violence was too high and much of what was broadcast was inappropriate for young children.

Also, during the summer of 1993, Senator Kent Conrad (D-ND) began to organize a task force dealing with the issue of television violence. Ultimately this group included both media activist groups and large national organizations like the American Medical Association and the National PTA. Initially the Senator's intention was not for legislative action but to merely put the broadcast and cable industry on notice that this was a serious problem and required action on their part. Rep. Edward Markey (D-MA) had been actively working for the passage of V-Chip legislation in the house. Senator Conrad introduced the Children's Media Protection Act of 1995 in the Senate. As a result of their collaborative efforts a section of this proposed legislation, popularly known as the V-Chip legislation, became part of the Telecommunications Act.

WHAT DOES THE LAW REQUIRE?

The law requires manufacturers to install a "V-Chip" in new television sets and requires that, if the networks establish ratings, they must transmit these ratings so they may be recognized by the V-Chip. The networks are urged to devise their own rating system within 1 year. The FCC is required to review the rating system devised and if the system is not established, or if the FCC rejects it, the FCC is permitted to choose a panel to develop a rating system for the networks.

The law does not require the networks to APPLY the system, just to establish a system This may be a moot question. If the cable industry uses a rating system, or if any one of the four broadcast networks use it public pressure would force the other networks to go along with the rating system.

WHAT IS THE V-CHIP?

The legislation requires insertion of microchip circuitry in new TV sets allowing parents to screen out shows that have been rated for violent and "objectionable" content. The electronic blocking device is known as the V-Chip, with the "V" standing for "violence." There is no V-chip, per se, because nobody has had to make one, according to William Posner, president of EEG Enterprises Inc. as quoted by Roger Fillion (Reuters).

The final product may not be a chip, but a modification of existing technology in TV sets, i.e., the closed-captioning system. According to industry spokesmen, modification to the existing closed-caption to include the V-chip rating would not be difficult. A rating code would be carried within an unused portion of the television signal, the black bar that appears when the horizontal hole on a television set goes out of whack and the picture rolls. It would be an improvement over existing technology that allows parents to block an entire channel, since the V-chip could automatically block selected programs. The Electronic Industries Association has been working on a V-Chip technical standard for more than 3 years.

COMMENTS ON THE V-CHIP

President Bill Clinton looks on the V-Chip as giving the remote control back to the parent. The administration supported the V-Chip and has aided in the formation of a means to create a rating system. Senator Paul Simon, a long time critic of the industry, surprised and disappointed many when he opposed the concept of the V-Chip and the legislation which incorporates it into new television set. In an article written for *Business Wire* and also in a speech on the floor of the Senate he argues that:

- The V-chip is no substitute for the industry disciplining itself.
- In areas of high crime where children watch 50% more TV, the V-chip would not be used.
- Teenagers will find a way around the V-Chip.
- They will see the programs at the homes of other children.
- It will take years for the V-Chip to be in all TV sets. TV needs to be cleaned up now.
- Will the V-Chip distinguish between gratuitous, glamorized violence and other types?
- Will broadcasters shy away form any programming deemed to be violent?
- It will be a pro for cable and a negative for broadcast television. Yet it is broadcast television that has made the most progress in lessening violence.
- For 10- to 14-year-old males a negative rating will have drawing effect.

• In short the V-Chip is a gimmick.

Donald Wildmon president of the American Family Association said the V-Chip "sounds like a good step on the surface, but in the long run would absolve the entertainment industry of their responsibility." Ted Turner, chief executive of Turner Broadcasting, noted movies have become more violent despite a rating system. He predicted that advertisers' concern will change the face of television: "I think it is going to result in more Brady Bunch-type programming."

In mid-January America Online (AOL) asked members whether they supported the concept of a V-Chip. Of the 24,890 responses received, over 55% said they supported the concept of a V-Chip, almost 40% were against, and about 5% did not care. AOL stresses that this is not a scientific survey. Many expressed concern over the government's intervention by requiring the industry to install the V-Chip, suggesting that it be optional. Others were concerned about the cost.

The cable industry is receptive to an industry-devised rating system, perhaps because shows with coarse language, excessive violence, and sexually suggestive scenes are more common on cable than on broadcast television. There are so many cable networks that the industry as a whole is less averse to labeling than broadcast networks that rely on a "broader" audience than cable. The broadcasters rely on advertising for revenue, whereas cable revenue comes from subscriber fees and advertising.

INDUSTRY COMMENTS

NBC West Coast president, Don Ohlmeyer, was quoted often by Brian Lowry of *Variety*. He says that the networks air relatively little violent programming. He also pointed out that a network loses anywhere from $250,000 to $1 million every time it airs a movie with a viewer discretion advisory. He was also quoted: "It is not the role of network television to program for the children of America. . . . Television's obligation is not [to be] the nation's baby-sitter."

This view that television has no public service responsibility is not supported by Barry Diller who was quoted by Frank Rich of the *New York Times*. Diller thinks the V-Chip is a "genuinely dumbbell idea." But Diller believes that broadcasters will make a real, long-term commitment to public-interest TV only if forced to do so as part of a trade-off for the "spectrum"—the additional airwaves that broadcasters want for digital television—and want for free. "If broadcasters are going to get new channels and have reinvigorated public responsibility, they should get them free." If not, "they should pay whatever the government can gouge out of them."

Prior to the meeting between the Clinton administration and industry leaders, a source was quoted by Dennis Sharton of *Variety* as saying, "You can't win the public relations battle on this . . . when it's obvious there is bipartisan congressional support for doing something on an issue, when you have an FCC chairman talking about this, and when public opinion is not in your favor, it's just not smart to thumb your nose and run to court."

In 1993, Jack Valenti, the president of the Motion Pictures Association of America, was an outspoken critic of the V-Chip. In the press conference that followed the industries' meeting with the President, he announced that the industry plans to have a rating system in place by January 1997. He stressed that rating was going to be a "humongous," even Herculean, task for the industry. Even after stressing what difficulty the industry would have, he did not let go of the idea that it is the parent who should be the guardian of what a child watches. "There has to be some kind of renaissance of individual responsibility that's accepted by parents, by the church, and by the school so that you build inside a youngster what we call a moral shield—it's fortified by the commandments of God—so that that child understands clearly what is right and what is clearly wrong."

It has been suggested that the real reason for the industry's lack of a court challenge to the V-Chip may be political. The decision may have more to do with the threat of auctioning the broadcast spectrum. If it appears that the industry is intransigent on the issue of program ratings, it may be easier to require the networks to pay full freight on the spectrum. The FCC, which has raised about $19 billion through nine auctions for other parts of the airwaves since mid-1994, estimates a digital TV sale could raise anywhere from $11 billion to $70 billion. At present, stations do not pay for their lucrative use of the publicly owned airwaves.

PROBLEMS WITH THE V-CHIP

- There will certainly be problems related to the implementation of the rating system and the use of the V-Chip.
- Will the rating be carried just at the beginning of the program, or will the rating be carried throughout the program so if a program is turned on in progress the rating will be read by the chip and the program will be blocked?
- Would each episode of a show be rated, or would shows be given just one rating, regardless of content from week-to-week?
- If "R" ratings are limited to a post-9 P.M. would that mean that reruns of those shows could not air in the lucrative 7 P.M. and 8 P.M. time known as prime access, when the studios make their money back on programming?
- Some worry that a more detailed rating system could be used by pressure groups to target certain television programs. Advertisers could be forced not to advertise certain rating categories.
- It will be a huge job to rate 300,000 hours a year, plus the programs that are available for re-runs.

NCTV'S POSITION ON THE V-CHIP

The new study of media violence done under the auspices of network television shows that the concern about media violence is well founded. These findings reflect earlier findings by NCTV. The V-Chip is needed. Mediascope's

National Television Violence Study found that 57% of television programs aired in 1994 and 1995 contained some violence. Further, the aggressors went unpunished in 73% of all violent scenes, while the negative consequences of violence were not shown, e.g., 58% of violent acts did not show the victim feeling any pain, and anti-violent messages were few, showing up in only 4% of programs about violence. One in four violent scenes involve a handgun; 39% of violent scenes were portrayed as humorous.

Senator Simon's dismissal of the V-Chip was discouraging. He has been a friend too long. While we agree that the V-Chip is not the answer, it has an important role to play. His dismissal of parents in high-crime areas is unfair to economically poor parents. To be economically poor does not, in fact, make you an unconcerned parent. The truth is the use of blocking by low-income parents will not disturb advertisers nearly as much as its use by affluent parents.

Of course teens can "get around" the blocking technology. The very young child, the audience for whom the chip is really intended, will be protected. It is alarming that the Senator thinks that the entertainment industry will do more than study themselves as the result of his actions. There will be a V-Chip in every television set before the industry disciplines itself. Yes, the V-Chip will be able to rate for "acceptable" violence, such as a documentary portrayal of the Civil War. The question will be: Can the entertainment industry be convinced that cartoons need to be rated for violence? Again, it cannot not be over-stressed, the V-Chip is intended to help parents of YOUNG children. Should the Senator be more concerned about the incomes of the broadcasters vs. the cable industry at the expense of our children? He fails to mention that the broadcasters have failed to live up to and, in some cases, even acknowledge their licensed responsibility to children.

Newton Minow, former FCC Chairman and author of the phrase "vast wasteland," calls for stronger measures to protect children. Television operators should be required to air a specific amount of educational programming. He also favors banning commercials in programs aimed at young children. The Clinton administration favors airing three hours a week of educational programming for children, but Reed Hundt, current Chairman of the FCC, has been unable to convince a majority of the five commissioners to agree to this minimal standard.

The V-Chip is neither a solution nor a "dumbbell idea." It is a tool that a parent can use to help monitor a child's television viewing. Parents will still have the responsibility. Parents will need to become more aware of what types of programs are suitable for particular ages of children. Until now, television programs were aimed at a general audience. The problem is a program, suitable for a "general audience" is often not suitable for a 5-year-old.

The real effect of the V-Chip will not be known for a long time, because the real effect of the V-Chip may or may not be economical. There is much speculation about how a profit making industry will respond to ratings and a parent's ability to block programs. Much will depend on how the industry chooses to rate programs. The reality is that it is impossible to predict how this action will turn out.

ADDITIONAL RESOURCES FOR PART 9

Suggested Questions and Discussion Topics

1. According to David S. Barry in "Growing Up Violent," what is the basic difference between violent action in movies of the early 1950s and in TV of the early 1990s? What is the most violent time in daily TV programming?

2. In "Growing Up Violent," what does Barry mean by "no consequences," and what do you think are the consequences of "no consequences"?

3. In "Armageddon—Live at 6!" by Larry Platt, what does the success of WSVN-TV in Miami say about American TV audiences?

4. In "Armageddon—Live at 6!" by Larry Platt, what does the author mean by "copy-cat industry"? Is there any solution to this problem? Discuss.

5. In "What You See Is What You Think," Diana Workman analyzes five problems with TV sex. Discuss any one of them.

6. In "What You See Is What You Think," Workman says that what children learn from TV sex is still open to discussion. From your own experience, what do you think children learn? Discuss.

7. In "The V-Chip Story," author Mary Ann Banta describes various problems with the V-chip technology. Discuss the two or three you think are most important.

8. In "The V-Chip Story," Banta suggests that the TV industry is ambivalent about the V-chip. Discuss some of the possible reasons for this ambivalence.

Suggested Readings

Martin Barker and Julian Petley, eds., *Ill Effects: The Media/Violence Debate*. London: Routledge, 1997.

Cynthia A. Cooper, *Violence on Television: Congressional Inquiry, Public Criticism, and Industry Response—A Policy Analysis*. Lanham, MD: University Press of America, 1996.

Wilson Bryan Key, *Media Sexploitation: You Are Being Sexually Manipulated at This Very Moment. Do You Know How?* Englewood Cliffs, NJ: 1976.

John Leonard, *Smoke and Mirrors: Violence, Television, and Other American Cultures*. San Francisco: New Press, 1997.

Madeline Levine, *Viewing Violence: How Media Violence Affects Your Child's Adolescent Development*. New York: Doubleday, 1996.

Marian Meyers, *News Coverage of Violence Against Women: Engendering Blame.* Thousand Oaks, CA: Sage Publications, 1996.

National Television Violence Study, Vols. 1 and 2. Thousand Oaks, CA: Sage Publications, 1996 and 1997.

Marcia Pally, *Sex & Sensibility: Reflections on Forbidden Mirrors and the Will to Censor.* Hopwell, NJ: Ecco Press, 1994.

Kevin W. Saunders, *Violence as Obscenity: Limiting the Media's First Amendment Protection (Constitutional Conflicts).* Raleigh, NC: Duke University Press, 1996.

Carol Wekesser, ed., *Violence in the Media.* San Diego, CA: Greenhaven Press, 1995.

Suggested Videos

"Dreamworlds: Desire, Sex, and Power in Music Video." Northampton, MA: Media Education Foundation. 1990. (55 minutes)

George Gerbner, "The Killing Screens: Media and the Culture of Violence." Northampton, MA: Media Education Foundation. 1994. (37 minutes)

"The Date Rape Backlash: Media and the Denial of Rape." Northampton, MA: Media Education Foundation. 1994. (60 minutes)

"Sexual Harrassment: Building Awareness on Campus." Northampton, MA: Media Education Foundation. 1995. (23 minutes)

"Teen Sexuality in a Culture of Confusion." Northampton, MA: Media Education Foundation. 1995. (40 minutes)

"TV Violence and You." Princeton, NJ: Films for the Humanities & Sciences. (30 minutes)

"Crime, Violence, & TV News." New York: Insight Media, 1993. (83 minutes)

"If It Bleeds It Leads." New York: Insight Media, 1986. (14 minutes)

PART · 10

Politics

Politicians seem to have won the war against mass media. It used to be a pretty even match, although politicians usually were winners in the long run, with the exception, perhaps, of Richard Nixon. Yet even Nixon was elected twice to the vice presidency and twice to the presidency before his own troubles with Watergate brought him down.

In many ways television has helped politicians win the war. TV has become absolutely essential to American politics and has changed the whole nature of the process. It took awhile for politicians to discover how to use and control the medium, but by the 1980s, the lessons had been well learned. By the 1990s, it no longer seemed to be a contest.

Television is more about show business than it is about information. And as television has become the most powerful medium for Americans, politicians have adapted to show biz tactics and strategies. News coverage in all the media has been influenced by the power of television, so news has become show biz, too, with the result that real political issues and debates have been given short shrift in the mainstream media while concentrating on the glamourous, sexy, and sensational lives of politicians.

First of all, television requires politicians to have certain kinds of physical characteristics and personality traits. Abraham Lincoln probably would not have been elected in an age of television; he may have been too ugly. Theodore Roosevelt was probably too boisterous; TV requires a low-key, cool approach. Franklin D. Roosevelt could project a strong image on radio because of his booming voice, but as a paraplegic his disability would probably have been overwhelmingly negative on television. Ronald Reagan, however, was just right. By the 1980s it seemed as though one should be a movie star, or at least comfortable in front of cameras, in order to win high political office. Bill Clinton brought to the presidency a movie star-type of telegenic good looks, glamour, physical energy, and presence to his candidacy. He was good in front of a camera and in a crowd. Even his rumored sexual history stimulated media coverage.

Secondly, television requires a lot of money. In nominating candidates to run in elections, political parties have learned not only how to choose those who are reasonably telegenic, but also to pick nominees who can raise money. Fund raising has become a major part of campaigning because it costs so much to use television. Those who are already wealthy have a great advantage. Where the party stands seems less important than how much money it has raised to make an issue of its policies in campaign advertising. Money itself determines the issues; if money can't be raised to push a particular issue, it probably won't get into the party's platform. One of the biggest issues during the Clinton administrations has been the lengths to which political parties have gone to raise money to win elections.

Television is a medium that can be more thoroughly controlled than most other media. The industry is more concentrated, with fewer reporters than newspapers have, fewer stations, and in fact three major networks still count the majority of Americans in their audiences each evening. Thus television is easier to deal with. There is also the subtle problem that television stations must be licensed by government and subject to FCC regulations, which some critics say have been chilling factors for bold and blunt political reporting.

Politicians have learned they can now control political dialogue. They no longer have to answer tough questions from reporters. All they have to do is craft speeches containing a few snippets designed for TV, thirty seconds long. That's all television can use on the nightly news. And when these "sound bites" get used on national television, they dictate the coverage of print media as well, especially if the candidate has been "too busy" to meet with reporters during the campaign day. All the candidate has had time to do is set up some "photo opportunities" for TV and the front pages. An entire campaign can be conducted with sound bites and photo ops, without the intrusion of fact, argument, policy, or answers to hard questions about a candidate's stand.

Television deals with impressions rather than facts. A politician doesn't have to have a lot of reason on his side, but he must make a good impression. By the same logic, he can more easily smear his opposition and cause much damage to his opponent's image on television before there is a demand for the facts. Indeed, negative advertising has become a staple in contemporary politics.

Perhaps one result has been the growing disillusionment of American voters and the steady decline of the percentage of Americans who fill out their ballots in election years. Can America recover? That question remains to be answered, but perhaps changes in technologies in the future could return America to a more participatory democracy. Just as television has changed American politics in the 1990s, so perhaps will interactive telecommunications technology change politics in the twenty-first century.

37

No Business Like Show Business

ELLIOT CARLSON

Editor's Note: In this interview with a long-time journalistic observer of American politics at the highest levels in Washington and the White House, *Time* magazine's veteran commentator, Hugh Sidey, worries that big media are turning the American presidency into a soap opera, mostly because of television. And show biz is changing presidential politics, he says.

Sidey says it will be necessary for Americans to be a lot more skeptical of the images we see in news pictures and political advertising if we are to put politics into proper perspective at the end of the twentieth century.

The author, Elliot Carlson, is editor of *AARP Bulletin,* a publication of the American Association of Retired Persons, reaching one of the largest audiences of any publication in the U.S. It was published during the 1996 election primaries, March 1996, and is reprinted with permission.

You've just come across what seems a little-appreciated political fact: No sitting Democratic president has won re-election since Franklin D. Roosevelt.

You think you're on to one of the great truths of America's post-World War II political era: Only Republican presidents win re-election. Witness Eisenhower, Nixon, Reagan.

No doubt a clue to the outcome of the 1996 presidential election. Clinton is doomed. The historical pattern, after all, is unmistakable.

Or is it?

Just when you think it's all perfectly clear, you sit down with one of Washington's legendary journalists, veteran political commentator Hugh Sidey, who has covered presidents since Eisenhower and written about the presidency for *Life* and *Time* magazines.

Relaxing in his cluttered, book-lined office in *Time*'s Washington bureau, leaning back in his big leather chair, Sidey pauses a moment, bemused by the proposition put forward. Cocking his head, smiling gently, he assures you that your facts are correct.

AMERICAN POLITICS HAVE CHANGED

Trouble is, he suggests, your facts may no longer be all that relevant. American politics have changed.

"The pattern [you cite] is one that was established in the old politics," Sidey tells his visitor. "I think the media now are so pervasive and so strong, and politics is so much a part of show business now, that that old formula may not be valid."

What's happening, Sidey says, is that America's huge media empires—governed increasingly by entertainment and "show biz" values—are rendering invalid many of the old axioms about how politics works. "My gosh," Sidey says, "we've personalized the presidency so much—it's a soap opera. And the swings are incredible."

Sidey recalls that in 1991 George Bush's approval rating exceeded 90 percent. "Then he was beaten," he says, "by a man who was crippled, politically, but who came back because of Perot and other factors."

For that matter, "A year ago Clinton looked pretty much down in the dumps," Sidey says. "And he's come back. Now it's Dole, who seemed to be pretty steady, who is faltering."

Talking with a Bulletin reporter before the New Hampshire primary and the Iowa caucus, Sidey stresses that Dole's fortunes—and those of the other candidates—could change again, one way or the other, overnight.

PERVASIVENESS OF MEDIA

Everything hinges not only on events, but on the bombast of big media, with all their legions of reporters, commentators, anchor people and camera crews, generating what Sidey calls "total communication," a smothering coverage that focuses on everything, sometimes capturing the important, often magnifying the trivial.

A political sideshow here, a quirky development there (say, a Buchanan upset in Louisiana), can "suddenly resonate through [the system]," unraveling the toughest of front-runners. "Again, it's the pervasiveness [of the media]," he says. "It's every big network and every big commentator piling in on something."

As an example, he cites the media troubles that started plaguing the Dole campaign in January. "Big media would just love to kill Dole," Sidey says. "You can hear it on all the shows. Look at *Newsweek*—the cover is, 'Doubts about Dole.' And on 'Meet the Press' you hear, 'What's wrong with Dole?' 'Can Dole do it?' 'He's too old.'"

Whatever the outcome of the New Hampshire and Iowa votes, the point, Sidey says, is that the media are altering the political system, and thus setting the stage for a primary season—and a presidential election—in which almost anything can happen.

HISTORY UP CLOSE

Sidey says he feels a little guilty about all this—especially the enormous media attention focused on the presidency these days. And the current tendency to glamorize the office.

"I guess I'm somewhat to blame." Sidey says ruefully, referring to his long-time column in *Time* magazine. "I was the first guy to write a column exclusively about the presidency."

Responsible or not for what he thinks is a regrettable preoccupation with the presidential personality, he has earned the right to talk about presidents.

Since 1957, when he covered Eisenhower, Sidey has written about nine presidents, first for *Life* and then for *Time,* for which he served as a White House and political correspondent and later as Washington bureau chief.

In these roles he has often seen history close up. He was with Kennedy when he was assassinated in Dallas and he traveled the world with Lyndon Johnson. He was on board when Richard Nixon jetted into China in 1972 and he reported on Nixon's exit from Washington two years later.

At age 68, Sidey is now a contributing editor for *Time,* and contemplating new books to add to the five he has already written on the presidency.

SATURATION COVERAGE

Sitting in his high-tech, *Time* office, Sidey remains an anomaly, straddling various worlds, surrounded by books. his old Royal typewriter and a modern computer. But Sidey's distinctly thoughtful, ironical and bemused style remains unchanged. As does his preoccupation with the presidency.

Again and again, he returns to America's obsession with the office—and what the media are doing to it.

With so many networks and various clusters of TV groups now covering the White House, the result is saturation coverage of the presidency—"The news has to be updated every 15 minutes," Sidey says. "So you get this crescendo building up during the day. It starts out in the morning. You have these famed anchor people who need a drama for the evening news."

And as a result of this, "the news gets distorted," Sidey says, "because they force issues and kind of shade things, adding emotion here and there. You end up with a kind of a nightly docudrama, rather than straight reporting."

And recent presidents. Sidey points out, have caught on and learned to use the media's need for nightly drama to their own advantage. He cites the "soap opera" encounters between President Reagan and TV reporter Sam Donaldson back in the 1980s.

Walking to his helicopter, "Reagan would turn off his hearing aid while Sam shouted his questions," Sidey recalls. "Reagan would say, 'Can't hear you, Sam,' and give that wonderful grin. Reagan's ratings would go up and Sam's salary would go up."

NOT ONLY SHOW BIZ VALUES

Clinton, in Sidey's view, has become virtually "a vagabond president," flying more miles, he thinks, than any other president.

"The American presidency in that airplane is a spectacle in itself. My gosh," Sidey adds, "he's here one day and then I pick up the paper and he's in Atlanta or Houston the next. So [the presidency] has become a big media event as Clinton seeks out MTV or CSPAN or Larry King. He uses all these guys. That's a huge change."

To be sure, Sidey adds, media's "show biz" values aren't the only factors driving politics—and won't be the only factors, or even the chief factors, deciding the 1996 election.

"If the economy collapses, or the stock market loses 1,000 points, or if, God forbid, there's a disaster in Bosnia, then that changes everything," he says. Any incumbent president would suddenly be in trouble.

Yet, if the country remains calm, Sidey says, an incumbent Democrat can win re-election, despite historical patterns to the contrary. "I think the 1996 election is up for grabs."

OUTWITTING BIG MEDIA

But, Sidey contends, you can be sure of one thing: Big media will be playing a role, adding to the volatility, generating swings that may favor one candidate today, another tomorrow.

How should people respond to all this? Question everything. Sidey advises. Be skeptical. Don't jump to conclusions, or trust all the images

Unhappy as he is with media's "show biz" approach to news, all is not lost. Sidey says he remains optimistic about politics, insisting there's "a common wisdom among responsible people" that will help Americans, in the long run, outwit big media.

"I worry about some things, but actually I'm quite upbeat," Sidey says. "At least the ideals are out there. I still have great faith as Abraham Lincoln did and as Thomas Jefferson did in this society. I do think we have a notion of what's right—and that most people want to do what's right."

38

The Phantom Liberal

JUSTIN LEWIS, MICHAEL MORGAN, AND SUT JHALLY

Editor's Note: One result of the "show biz" quality of the coverage of American politics has been the skewed view of political leaders and their stands on the real issues that confront our society.

This article says that the kind of news coverage given to President Clinton, especially the landslice coverage of sexual scandals during his presidency, has obscured discussion of Clinton's position on various ideological and crucial issues of his administration. The same analysis could no doubt be made of any politician in an age of television, except, perhaps, those politicians who avoid showmanship and concentrate solely on the issues. But those politicians don't get the coverage, and thus their concerns are infrequently raised to the level of public discussion.

The authors are all professors in the Department of Communication at the University of Massachusetts at Amherst. This article was published in *Extra*, the magazine of Fairness & Accuracy in Reporting, in May/June 1998, and is reprinted with permission.

The media provide us with a nonstop stream of public opinion polls, but what does all the survey data really tell us? Are the polls an authentic expression of independently formed attitudes, or merely a reflection of the opinions favored by the mainstream media? The answer is a bit of both: There are moments when people are apparently following a well-established media agenda, as well as times when most people seem to disregard the positions promulgated by media elites.

The media's role in public opinion becomes less murky if we ask people not only what they think (which is as far as most polls go) but also, more importantly, what they know. This enables us to see what people have learned from the mass media, and to therefore understand something about the basis upon which people construct opinions.

When the Monica Lewinsky scandal broke, coverage of President Clinton escalated to extraordinary levels in every nook and cranny of the media. This was accompanied by the obligatory slew of polls, just about all of which were strongly favorable to the president. This curious mix of prurience and popularity prompted us to take a closer look at what Americans "know" about their president.

We surveyed 600 respondents across the United States, using a sample that was broadly representative in terms of age, gender, education, political persuasion and media habits (and with a margin of error of about 3 percentage points). The results of our study raise some "scandalous" questions about public knowledge, opinions and mass media.

DISTINGUISHING CHARACTERISTICS

Given the news media's preference for scandal over substance, no one should be very surprised by our finding that people know more about the president's presumed peccadilloes than about his policies. Nevertheless, the gap between the two—and the consistent, systematic misperceptions it reveals—is remarkable. So, for example, while 81 percent were aware of Gennifer Flowers' claims to have had an affair with (then-Governor) Clinton, and 75 percent were able to identify Linda Tripp's role in the Monica Lewinsky affair, only 13 percent knew that Clinton signed the welfare reform bill passed by the Republican-led Congress, and only 26 percent had even a vague notion of where he stands on healthcare reform. (These are, needless to say, hardly insignificant or obscure policy areas.)

While the better-publicized aspects of recent allegations received scores as high as one might expect to find in this kind of survey (93 percent could identify Monica Lewinsky and 89 percent Paula Jones), even some of the less salacious details of the Clinton scandals seemed more familiar than most of his policy positions. Over half of the sample was able to answer an open-ended question asking which case precipitated Kenneth Starr's investigation (i.e. Whitewater).

SCANDAL WINS

And yet, even when given a choice of just two answers, only 24 percent were able to identify the position taken by the Clinton administration on the recent international treaty on the banning of land mines. (The administration opposes the treaty.) While such treaties generally receive less attention than their importance warrants, the late Princess Diana's advocacy of this cause—as well as the award of the most recent Nobel peace prize to a North American who helped initiate the campaign—might have been expected to make the issue more visible.

Significantly, the only scandal-related question we posed that a majority had trouble with was the only overtly political one: Only 39 percent were aware that Independent Counsel Kenneth Starr is a Republican. On the six purely scandal-related questions, 62 percent of our sample gave five or six correct responses. For the nine policy-related questions, only 40 percent scored above 3 and less than 20 percent scored higher than 4. Even so, this low level of overall political understanding disguises what is, in our view, the most notable aspect of these findings: Most people are aware of those instances when Clinton has behaved as a progressive or "traditional" Democrat, but unaware of those times when he has adopted conservative or "new" Democrat positions.

WHO'S LEFT?

On the policy side, the questions that received the most correct responses suggest a very particular pattern: When Clinton has taken a position on the left or liberal side of an issue, people get the answer right. So, for example, 69 percent know that he is generally in favor of a woman's right to an abortion, and 74 percent know that in his 1998 State of the Union address he advocated spending the surplus on Social Security rather than tax cuts. However, when Clinton has adopted more conservative positions, people are not only unaware of this, they tend to assume he has taken a progressive or left stance.

In every case in which the correct response involves President Clinton taking or preferring a conservative position over a more progressive one, the proportion of right answers—between 13 and 31 percent—is lower than it would have been if respondents had been randomly guessing.

When asked about President Clinton's position on healthcare reform, for example, respondents were given two options:

a. That he promoted a universal system of national health insurance; or
b. That he favored adjustments to the existing system of private insurance in order to give more people access to the system.

Since becoming president, Bill Clinton has never advocated the first option and has consistently proposed the second—and yet 26 percent chose the correct answer while a much higher percentage (59 percent) chose the incorrect (but further left) version.

In addition to the healthcare, welfare and landmines questions, we found a succession of mistaken assumptions in which Clinton is cast as a progressive Democrat:

- More assume he opposed the deregulatory 1996 Telecommunications Bill than knew he supported it.
- More significantly overestimate the proportion of Democratic Party funds coming from labor (rather than business) than those who correctly identify business as the biggest donor.
- More say he is identified with the "liberal" wing of his party than know his affiliation to its more conservative "new Democrat" wing.

WILLING IGNORANCE

None of the questions were obscure and all might have been guessed by someone with a basic knowledge of Clinton's political inclinations. Yet out of seven questions of this type (in which Clinton's actual position is the more conservative one), only one person in our entire sample, or 0.17 percent, got all of them right, and only 8 percent got more than half right. Recall that as many as 74 percent responded correctly when the right answer involved Clinton taking a more progressive position.

The only case in which correct answers outnumbered those assuming a more progressive answer was a question about President Clinton's position on the death penalty. Overall, 28 percent correctly said that he supports the death penalty, and 21 percent said that he opposes it. In this instance, however, more than half (51 percent) admitted that they did not know the answer, and the number of correct responses is not much higher than one would expect with random guesses. What is striking about this question is that it suggests some willingness for respondents to declare ignorance (something that, we know from other studies, many are disinclined to do). In all the other instances, a majority (between 67 percent and 85 percent on five of the seven) claimed to know the answer.

Our findings suggest, in other words, that regardless of his attempts to frame himself as a "new Democrat" prepared to work with a Republican Congress and take "bipartisan" positions, the public still tends to think of Bill Clinton as an unreconstructed liberal, willing to take on the health insurance companies, the telecommunications industry and the Pentagon. And for all the negative connotations often attached to the "L-word," most people seem to approve of their imaginary left-wing president.

RUNNING TO THE CENTER

Equally interesting, in our view, are the implications of our findings for the conventional wisdom that politicians—particularly Democrats—need to run to the center to be popular. Many commentators suggested, for example, that President Clinton needed to sign the welfare bill to show he was prepared to support Republicans on apparently popular legislation. In fact, Clinton won the election with most people apparently believing that he *didn't* sign it.

At this moment in history, it is hard to argue that President Clinton's excellent approval ratings come from admiration of his character or personal integrity. And yet they also appear to coincide with the widespread assumption that he is a strongly liberal Democrat.

This is not to say that the public takes uniformly liberal positions on policy matters; there is clearly public support for some conservative positions (such as the death penalty). What our survey suggests is that many people seem to be prepared to buy the whole package for the sake of those parts of a progressive agenda—such as on education, healthcare or the environment—they do support.

UNINFORMED OR MISINFORMED?

What emerges here is not so much an uninformed public as a misinformed one.

Most of our respondents are not only able to distinguish between "liberal" and "conservative" positions on the issues, they feel confident enough to guess which positions are favored by the president. The problem is that the idea that Clinton is on the left is so powerful that their guesses are frequently wrong.

What is it about media coverage of President Clinton that has created such a systematically misleading impression? Why is it that, despite all of Clinton's attempts to situate himself in the center, he is still seen as on the left?

The answer involves an understanding of the nature of media influence. Research suggests that people are less likely to be informed by particular moments or details in news coverage than by an overall, oft-repeated framework.

MISLEADING IMPRESSIONS

For example, someone following the news closely may have been given information suggesting that in the recent showdown between the U.S. and Iraq, it was negotiators on the U.S. side who were notably unwilling to compromise on the principle of unconditional inspections. But the overall framework of the story was weighted so heavily in favor of the U.S. that these details were unlikely to dislodge the impression that it was the Iraqi side who must be guilty of inflexibility.

This was certainly the case in our survey: When asked which side had been less willing to compromise, an overwhelming 85 percent blamed Iraq, while only 10 percent saw inflexibility on the U.S. side or on both sides.

So although the media covered events such as Clinton's signing of the welfare bill, this failed to dislodge a framework in which we heard a great deal about Clinton the liberal and very little about Clinton the conservative—both from centrist corporate outlets and right-wing media strongholds such as talk radio. Indeed, it would appear that the most significant under-reported story in contemporary U.S. politics is Clinton's embrace of a range of conservative positions and the subsequent narrowing of the political spectrum.

Although the areas of agreement between Bill Clinton and his Republican opponents in both 1992 and 1996 were substantial, particularly on economic policy, the media characterize elections in strictly partisan terms. The pro-corporate agenda (and corporate funding base) that Clinton and the Republicans had in common—an agenda that most Americans do not support—received very little attention. Indeed, the fact that both Clinton and the leadership of the GOP are more conservative on a range of issues than most Americans remains the best-kept secret of American politics.

THE APPEARANCE OF CHOICE

This is, of course, exacerbated by a Republican Party that tends to routinely label their opponents as "liberal." (This strategy was used against Clinton even at times when many Republicans were complaining—with some justification—that he was stealing parts of their platform.) There are many conservative partisans with access to mainstream media who are happy to echo these Republican claims, but few forthright progressives in a position to criticize both Clinton and the Congress as too far right.

If the leadership of both major parties is to the right of the general public on important issues, that would call into question the democratic nature of the U.S. political process—an issue mainstream media are extremely reluctant to raise. It is much easier to make the political arena fit the format than it is to question the format itself. This is particularly so when leaders of both parties embrace generally pro-corporate positions that are congenial to most media owners.

In sum, what we are offered is the appearance of a choice between left and right. And that, our study suggests, is what most people think we get. What we are actually given is often more like Tweedledum and Tweedledee—a class of political elites in which positions on the left are routinely excluded.

39

The Alienated American Voter: Are the News Media to Blame?

RICHARD HARWOOD

Editor's Note: The increasing apathy of American voters toward politics and government has raised questions about the media's role. Some recent studies show that the news media play a key role in shaping voter attitudes.

Richard Harwood concurs that negative stories and political ads do encourage cynicism and discourage political participation, and that people are so confused that they avoid anything relating to politics and government. Harwood suggests, however, that the system works better than any other, despite its deficiencies.

Harwood was a writer and editor at the *Washington Post* for twenty-two years and is now a nationally syndicated columnist who often writes about media problems. This article was adapted from the keynote address he gave at a Brookings Center for Public Policy Education Forum and the Media and American Democracy. It is reprinted with permission from *Brookings Review,* Fall 1996.

The attention of the American public is not riveted on government. As we are constantly reminded by polls and academic studies, millions of our people can't name their city council members, their representatives in state government, or their representatives in Congress. Ten times more people can identify Judge Ito or Judge Wapner of TV's *People's Court* than can identify the Chief Justice of the United States. Half our people don't vote in presidential elections. Some 80–90 percent don't vote in many local elections. The Pew Research Center for People and the Press never lets us forget that people pay little attention to the latest happenings in Washington or in Bosnia and China. Most of us are pretty much oblivious to something called the "Contract with America" and other hot button issues of the day in Washington. One of the endearing anecdotes from my days as a political reporter in Kentucky involved a congressional candidate who was asked to state his position on the Taft-Hartley Bill. He did not equivocate: "By God, if we owe it we ought to pay it!"

THE MAN IN THE BACK ROW

Seventy years ago, in "The Phantom Public," Walter Lippmann gave us a sketch of the democratic condition. "The private citizen," he wrote, "has come to feel rather like a deaf spectator in the back row, who ought to keep his mind on the mystery off there, but cannot quite manage to stay awake. He knows he is somehow affected by what is going on. Rules and regulations continually, taxes annually, and wars occasionally remind him that he is being swept along by great drifts of circumstance.

"Yet these public affairs are in no convincing way his affairs. They are for the most part invisible. They are managed, if they are managed at all, in distant centers, from behind the scenes by unnamed powers. As a private person he does not know for certain what is going on, or who is doing it, or where he is being carried. No newspaper reports his environment so that he can grasp it; no school has taught him how to imagine it; his ideals, often, do not fit with it; listening to speeches, uttering opinions, and voting do not, he finds, enable him to govern it. He lives in a world in which he cannot see, does not understand, and is unable to direct.

"In the cold light of experience, he knows that his sovereignty is a fiction. He reigns in theory, but in fact he does not govern. Contemplating himself and his actual accomplishments in public affairs, contrasting the influence he exerts with the influence he is supposed according to democratic theory to exert, he must say of his sovereignty what Bismarck said of Napoleon II: 'At a distance it is something, but close to, it is nothing at all.'"

It is not, I think, entirely cynical, to conclude that these sentiments are as relevant now as then. We may be born equal in the sight of the divinity and we may possess certain inalienable rights. But equal status in the political system and in the economic order is not among them. According to the dictum in Washington, your Rolodex defines who you are. I would add that it is not only the names on your Rolodex that count but the names—especially your own—on the Rolodexes of the people we call. After unanswered phone calls following his retirement, a journalistic colleague said he had made a discovery: "I'm not a has-been. I'm a never-was."

In terms of political access, that is the normal plight of the average man and woman. They know, like Lippmann's man in the back row, that real political power is as unequally distributed as wealth and health in our democracy. The Friends of Bill are not on the same row with the Friends of Joe Six-Pack. This gets our attention in the press every few years, but it is unclear if we in the media bear responsibility for this state of affairs or, if we do, how we can repair the system.

In any case, the large promises implicit in the idea of "one man, one vote" have never been realized whatever the roles the press has assumed in political affairs over the history of our country. In an earlier age when the concepts of self-government and citizen legislators became our foundation stones, it was taken for granted that the tasks of governing should be assigned to a small element of society—men of property and learning. We attached many qualifications for voting and other participation in public affairs—sex, race, literacy, age, residency, and property ownership. It was also taken for granted that newspapers on the whole would be controlled subsidiaries of the political parties.

ONCE UPON A TIME, A PASSION FOR POLITICS

Many of the requirements for voting and office holding eventually were discarded and a commercially successful press emerged, a press no longer financially dependent on the parties but still capable of partisan practices that today would shock journalistic critics and practitioners out of their socks. We entered a long era in which great numbers of the unwashed and less privileged not only gained the franchise but gained office. A passion for politics stirred the masses as Tocqueville and other travelers noted. Not everyone was pleased. In Boston, having the Irish in City Hall was comparable to having barbarians in the Temple. Others elsewhere had similar reactions as rewards for political activism became more and more visible and political participation became more common. There was job patronage on a large scale. There were also turkeys, coal, and bail money from the precinct captain; immunity from arrest for barkeeps, gamblers, and prostitutes, as well as flexible judges if you wound up in court; construction contracts and franchises for loyalists and high bidders.

This was more democracy than the country had ever seen, and it was inspired not only by greed or hope of material gain but by the partisan fraternalism and sense of belonging that we now call communitarianism, and by lasting emotional intensities arising out of shared experiences, most especially the Civil War. An obvious legacy was the Solid South's century-long commitment to the Democratic party and Republican voting patterns that have endured even longer. The poorest county in Appalachia for a long time was the most Republican county in America, and still is so far as I know.

The rituals and celebrations of politics strengthened and sustained these bonds. Thousands gathered for grand feedings where the suds and whiskey flowed all night. Spectacular rallies at the precinct club house featured songs and banners, hours of speechmaking, exciting parades with bands and torchlights, dances and games of chance. Newspapers stoked these fires for a public in which education, as we define it today, was a scarce commodity.

When the first popular election for president was held in 1824, the turnout of eligible voters was about 27 percent. By the end of the century turnouts of 70–80 percent were common. They then fell off precipitously.

PROGRESSIVE REFORM

Speculation about the fall-off in popular political participation in this century abounds. One theory assigns blame to the ever-present reformers who concluded that too much raw democracy was ruining the country. In response there arose among the middle and upper classes a strong Progressive movement designed to destroy the city political machines and the patronage and corrupt practices on which they thrived. The movement involved such radical proposals as a merit system for public employment; the use of trained accountants and auditors to keep the books in order; anti-nepotism laws; universal suffrage coupled with foolproof voter registration systems and various other safeguards against electoral fraud. These proposals coincided with the rise of social science as a legitimate field of scholarly endeavor and the rise of credentialism as a panacea for many ills. Doctors, lawyers, architects, teachers, and engineers, among others, would henceforth be credentialed by colleges and universities and licensed to pursue their professions or vocations. Eventually, licensing boards were set up for hairdressers, barbers, morticians, cabdrivers, the building trades, and so on. So why not credentialed public employees?

The thrust of it all was that the nation should have "clean" government and "clean" elections and should bring to government businesslike management of its financial affairs and to government and business alike "professional" management and skills. Even newspapers began talking about the need for an educated newsroom labor force and for journalism schools to provide the training.

A generation of "muckrakers," led by such figures as Lincoln Steffens, Ida Tarbell, and Ray Stannard Baker, exposed the inner workings of the corrupt political machines and the corrupt use of economic power by corporations such as Standard Oil and American Sugar. Their work inspired newspaper people all over the country to emulation.

The results of the Progressive movement were mixed. Many reforms were achieved with lasting beneficial effects on society—child labor and antitrust laws, for example. But they had some unintended consequences.

EXIT THE VOTERS

Cleaning up government and elections greatly diminished the rewards of political activism for those whose credentials were nonexistent. One had now to pass a test or have a diploma to get a job; political loyalty was no longer enough. The Progressives and their muckraking allies had hoped that an "aroused public opinion would fulfill the promises of democracy," clean up the mess, and move society toward a more utopian state. Instead, what followed was apathy and disillusionment. Voter turnout fell 40 percent from 1896 to 1920. Steffens's marvelous book on the underside of politics, *The Shame of the Cities,* sold only 3,000 copies. Peter Finley Dunne's character, Mr. Dooley, asked a salient question: "Is there an institution that isn't corrupt to its very foundations? Don't you believe it."

The years since the mid-1960s are regarded by many journalists as the Second Muckraking Era. All institutions have been fair game for investigative reporting and critical assessment. In part, because of these efforts, the political process in one sense has been "purified" as Progressive reforms have been realized. The spoils system is by and large a thing of the past. Barriers to voting have been eliminated. Political party bosses are extinct, the smoke-filled room an archaic memory. The party machines that once provided the foot soldiers of politics have been replaced by a professional class of political consultants who in 1992 were paid $250 million to manage the elections of congressional candidates. That does not include the tens of millions of dollars paid consultants that year for presidential campaign services. They create the propaganda, raise the money, train and market the candidates, define issues and election strategies, organize rallies, get out the vote, and write the script for party conventions. They perform virtually all the functions once performed by ordinary people who now sit on the sidelines viewing elections, as Peter Shapiro has written, either with indifferent detachment or as "shameful exercises in mudslinging, obfuscation and demagoguery." The primary elections and caucuses that were intended to open up the system have been no cure for political alienation and mistrust. The participation rate in the primaries of 1992 and 1996 was barely 20 percent of the population. The rich vote far more than the poor, except in unusual settings such as the District of Columbia, where Mayor Marion Barry's vision of government—jobs for loyalists and the needy—has drawn enormous support in low-income wards.

ARE THE MEDIA RESPONSIBLE?

There are two important questions here. The first is whether apathy and lack of participation constitute a "problem" for American democracy. The second is this: If it is a problem, are the media responsible in one degree or another?

On the first point, some would argue with Lippmann and others that nonvoting by uninterested and uninformed people is not a problem at all. It was their view that instead of grading democracy on the basis of popular participation, we should judge the system by the well-being of its citizens: their health, education, safety, housing, and material standards of living. If those tests are met, this argument goes, the system works regardless of the numbers who participate in elections or otherwise take part in the political life of the nation.

That is not a popular argument. Academicians, politicians, and journalists tend to view the indifference or nonengagement of the electorate as a crisis. They are looking for causes, and one of the suspects is the press.

Professor Thomas Leonard, a student of the media's influence on the Progressive Movement, concluded that the work of the muckrakers was a major factor in the decline of political activism in that era. "It was," he wrote, "the discrediting of some basic assumptions about how democracy worked that made muckraking both shocking . . . and a message to pull back from political life." He based this judgment on circumstantial evidence, not academic science or research into the psyches of voters by professional pollsters and psychologists. Those tools weren't available then. In fact, the scholar Michael Robinson tells us that as late as the 1960s, "most political scientists clung to the theory of minimal consequences . . . which relegates television and all mass media to a position of relative impotence in shaping opinion and political behavior."

That theory is now suspect as evidence accumulates that the media—television in particular—exert political power. In his doctoral dissertation in 1972,

Robinson concluded that news and public affairs programs of the television networks were, in a broad sense, consistently propagandistic and sometimes malign. They evoked images of American politics "which are inordinately sinister and despairing," causing the viewer to "turn against the social and political institutions involved, or against himself, [for] feeling unable to deal with a political system like this."

More recent studies have reached similar conclusions: "Negative" news stories and "negative" political ads create cynicism, drive people away from political participation, and often confuse them to such a degree that they refuse to vote or even read about politics and government.

KEEPING POLITICS IN PERSPECTIVE

In pondering the implications of all this it is helpful to maintain a proper perspective. The fact that there are villains in government and politics and that the press is often wayward is not proof that political and governmental institutions are necessarily villainous or that journalists are always bad actors. That the American electorate includes many apathetic and politically ignorant people is not proof that the system is in terminal decline. A hundred million people went to the polls in 1992. The 80–90 million who didn't vote might very well have made a rational decision that they had little stake in the outcome.

A big ad in *The Wall Street Journal* last spring informed readers that "Without legislation correcting the BIF/SAIF premium disparity, SAID's deposit base will almost certainly decline to the point that SAIF premiums would not cover FICO interest payments, resulting in a FICO default as early as 1997." What is the guy in the back row to make of that? It is well to remember that while politics is central in the lives of the political class and in the professional lives of journalists, that is not the case with all of us. As Austin Ranney wrote some years ago, "The fact is that for most Americans, politics is still far from being the most interesting and important thing in life. To them, politics is usually boring, repetitious, and above all, largely irrelevant to the things that really matter in their lives, such as making friends, finding spouses, getting jobs, raising children, and having a good time." So on election days, they may simply prefer to go fishing, secure in the knowledge, as Annie sings in her showstopper, the sun will come up tomorrow.

It is certainly true that many imperfections in our democracy remain despite the best and well-meaning efforts of reformers. It is also true that the media have, in a large sense, much to answer for. Their own cynicism about politics and government has been infectious and often destructive. Their failure to put things in perspective is perhaps their greatest sin. But we have and will survive all that. As we deplore the state of democracy it clears the mind to ask: compared with what and with whom?

We can profitably remember and apply to the gloomy speculations and fears about the future Winston Churchill's great message to his country in 1940: "We are waiting for the long-promised invasion. So are the fishes."

40

The Electronic Republic

LAWRENCE K. GROSSMAN

Editor's Note: This article addresses the power of mass media to re-shape political values in the Information Age. It argues that an interactive telecommunications technology has the capability of transforming the American political system into an electronic republic. This means that the public not only receives instant information about politics and government but can give instant feedback on their attitudes and opinions about current political issues and government policies.

The people can now play a direct role in public life. The speedy flow of communications from people to government, however, may heighten the public's dissatisfaction with government.

Lawrence K. Grossman is the former president of PBS and NBC News and is currently president of PBS Horizons Cable Network. This article is excerpted from his book *The Electronic Republic: Reshaping Democracy in the Information Age* (Viking, 1995). This version was published in the *Media Studies Journal,* Summer 1995, and is reprinted with permission.

A new political system is taking shape in the United States. As we head into the twenty-first century, America is turning into an electronic republic, a democratic system that is vastly increasing the people's day-to-day influence on the decisions of state. New elements of direct democracy are being grafted on to our traditional representative form of government, transforming the nature of the political process and calling into question some of the fundamental assumptions about political life that have existed since the nation was formed more than two hundred years ago.

The irony is that while Americans feel increasingly powerless, cynical, and frustrated about government, the distance between the governed and those who govern is actually shrinking dramatically. Many more citizens are gaining a greater voice in the making of public policy than at any time since the direct democracy of the ancient Greek city-states some twenty-five hundred years ago. Populist measures such as term limits, balanced budget amendments, direct state primaries and caucuses, and expanding use of ballot initiatives and referenda reduce the discretion of elected officials, enable voters to pick their own presidential nominees, bypass legislatures, and even empower the people to make their own laws. Incessant public-opinion polling and increasingly sophisticated interactive telecommunications devices make government instantly aware of, and responsive to, popular will—some say, too responsive for the good of the nation. As the elect seek to respond to every twist and turn of the electorate's mood, the people at large are taking on a more direct role in government than the Founders ever intended.

This democratic political transformation is being propelled largely by two developments—the two-hundred-year-long march toward political equality for all citizens and the explosive growth of new telecommunications media, the remarkable convergence of television, telephone, satellites, cable and personal computers. This is the first generation of citizens who can see, hear, and judge their own political leaders simultaneously and instantaneously. It is also the first generation of political leaders who can address the entire population and receive instant feedback about what the people think and want. Interactive telecommunications increasingly give ordinary citizens immediate access to the major political decisions that affect their lives and property.

DIRECT PARTICIPATION

The emerging electronic republic will be a political hybrid. Citizens not only will be able to select those who govern them, as they always have, but increasingly they also will be able to participate directly in making the laws and policies by which they are governed. Through the use of increasingly sophisticated two-way digital broadband telecommunications networks, members of the public are gaining a seat of their own at the table of political power. Even as the public's impatience with government rises, the inexorable progress of democratization, together with remarkable advances in interactive telecommunications, are turning the people themselves into the new fourth branch of government. In the electronic republic, it will no longer be the press but the public that functions as the nation's powerful Fourth Estate, alongside the executive, the legislative and the judiciary.

The rise of the electronic republic, with its perhaps inevitable tendency to respond instantaneously to every ripple of public opinion, will undercut—if not fundamentally alter—some of our most cherished Constitutional protections against the potential excesses of majority impulses. These protections were put in place by the Founders, who were as wary of pure democracy as they were fearful of governmental authority. The Constitution sought not only to protect the people against the overreaching power of government but also to protect the new nation against the overreaching demands of ordinary people, especially the poor.

Telecommunications technology has reduced the traditional barriers of time and distance. In the same way it can also reduce the traditional Constitutional barriers of checks and balances and separation of powers, which James

Madison thought the very size and complexity of the new nation would help to preserve. "Extend the sphere, and you take in a greater variety of parties and interests; you make it less probable that a majority of the whole will have a common motive to invade the rights of other citizens." However, as distances disappear and telecommunications shrink the sphere, and as the executive and legislative branches of government become more entwined with public opinion and popular demand, only the courts may be left to stand as an effective bastion against the tyranny of the majority. The judiciary, the branch of government that was designed to be the least responsive to popular passion, will bear an increasingly difficult and heavy burden to protect individual rights against popular assault.

REPRESENTATIVE GOVERNMENT

Direct democracy, toward which we seem to be inexorably heading, was the earliest form of democracy, originating during the fifth century B.C. in the small, self-contained city-states of classical Greece. During the two hundred years of Athenian direct democracy, the ancient city-state whose governance we know most about, a privileged few citizens served at one and the same time as both the rulers and the ruled, making and administering their own laws. "Although limited to adult males of native parentage," writes Donald Kagan, "Athenian citizenship granted full and active participation in every decision of the state without regard to wealth or class." Democracy in Athens was carried as far as it would go until modern times.

By contrast, representative government—democracy's second transformation—is a relatively recent phenomenon, originating in the United States a little more than two centuries ago. Under representative democracy, Americans—at first a privileged few and now every citizen over age 18—can vote for those who make the laws that govern them. Unlike the ancient Greeks, our Constitution specifies a government that separates the rulers from the ruled. It connects people to the government by elections, but distances the government from the people by making the elected the ones who actually enact the laws and conduct the business of government. As political scientist Harvey C. Mansfield put it, that "Constitutional space is the genius of American republicanism. It keeps the process of democratization under control and prevents our democracy from ruining itself by carrying itself to an extreme."

Today, that Constitutional space is shrinking. New populist processes and telecommunications technologies amplify the voice of the people at large and bring the public right back into the middle of the decision making processes of government. As the power of public opinion rises, the roles of the traditional political intermediaries—the parties, the mass media experts, and the governing elite—decline. Institutions that obstruct the popular will or stand between it and the actions of government get bypassed.

Telecommunications technologies—computers, satellites, interactive television, telephones and radio—are breaking down the age-old barriers of time and distance that originally precluded the nation's people from voting directly for the laws and policies that govern them. The general belief holds that representative government is the only form of democracy that is feasible in today's sprawling, heterogeneous nation-states. However, interactive telecommunications now make it possible for tens of millions of widely dispersed citizens to receive the information they need to carry out the business of government themselves, gain admission to the political realm, and retrieve at least some of the power over their own lives and goods that many believe their elected leaders are squandering.

REDEFINING ROLES

The electronic republic, therefore, has already started to redefine the roles of citizenship and political leadership. Today, it is at least as important to reach out to the electorate—the public-at-large—and lobby public opinion, as it is to lobby the elect—the public officials who make the laws and administer the policies. In the words of literary critic Sven Birkerts in *The Gutenberg Elegies,* "The advent of the computer and the astonishing sophistication achieved by our electronic communications media have together turned a range of isolated changes into something systematic. The way that people experience the world has altered more in the last fifty years than in the many centuries preceding ours." The emergence of the electronic republic gives rise to the need for new thinking, new procedures, new policies, and even new political institutions to ensure that in the century ahead majoritarian impulses will not come at the expense of the rights of individuals and unpopular minorities.

We need to recognize the remarkable changes that the interactive telecommunications age is producing in our political system. We need to understand the consequences of the march toward democratization. We need to deal with the promise and perils of the electronic republic. It can make government intensely responsive to the people. It also can carry responsiveness to an extreme, opening the way for manipulation, demagoguery or tyranny of the majority that, in the words of *The Federalist Papers,* "kindle[s] a flame . . . [and] spread[s] a general conflagration through the . . . States."

Most studies of government, politics, and the media start at the top by examining the qualities of leadership that define political life. However, in the coming era, the qualities of citizenship will be at least as important as those of political leadership. In an electronic republic, it will be essential to look at politics from the bottom up as well as from the top down.

What will it take to turn the United States into a nation of qualified citizens who are engaged not as isolated individuals pursuing their own ends but as public-spirited members who are dedicated to the common good? In an electronic republic, finding the answer to that question is essential. In the words of Thomas Jefferson, "I know no safe depository of the ultimate powers of the society but the people themselves, and if we think them not enlightened enough to exercise their control with a wholesome discretion, the remedy is not to take it from them, but to inform their discretion."

ADDITIONAL RESOURCES FOR PART 10

Suggested Questions and Discussion Topics

1. From "No Business Like Show Business," by Elliot Carlson, what are the main reasons given for the changes in American politics?

2. Discuss the Clinton-Lewinsky affair and media coverage in the light of Carlson's thesis in From "No Business Like Show Business."

3. In "The Phantom Liberal," by Justin Lewis et al, suggest the reasons the authors suggest for the misinformation of the public about political matters.

4. "The Phantom Liberal" suggests that the average American did not have an accurate understanding of Bill Clinton's political policies and positions. What are the reasons given for this?

5. To what extent does Richard Harwood in "The Alienated American Voter: Are the News Media to Blame?" think the media are responsible for the rising political apathy of Americans? Discuss both sides of this question.

6. According to "The Alienated American Voter: Are the News Media to Blame?" by Richard Harwood, what can be done by the mass media to stimulate more citizen participation in politics? Discuss.

7. According to Lawrence Grossman's "The Electronic Republic," what are the two key developments in the democratic political transformation now taking place?

8. From "The Electronic Republic," what does the author mean by convergence, and how does he suggest the new convergence of media might change politics from the older age of television? Discuss.

Suggested Readings

Edwin Diamond and Stephen Bates, *The Spot: The Rise of Political Advertising on Television.* Cambridge, MA: MIT Press, 1984.

Edwin Diamond and Robert A. Silverman, *White House to Your House: Media and Politics in Virtual America.* Cambridge, MA: MIT Press, 1995.

Calvin F. Exoo, *The Politics of the Mass Media.* St. Paul, MN: West Publishing Co., 1994.

Doris A. Graber, *Mass Media and American Politics.* Washington, DC: CQ Press, 1993.

Doris A. Graber, *Media Power in Politics.* Washington, DC: CQ Press, 1994.

Ray Hiebert, Robert Jones, John Lorenz, and Ernest Lotito, eds., *The Political Image Merchants: Strategies in the New Politics,* 2nd ed. Washington, DC: Acropolis Books, 1976.

Lynda Lee Kaid and Dianne Bystrom, *The Electronic Election: Perspectives on the 1996 Campaign Communication.* Mahwah, NJ: Lawrence Erlbaum, 1998.

Lynda Lee Kaid and Christina Holtz-Bacha. *Political Advertising in Western Democracies.* Thousand Oaks, CA: Sage Publications, 1995.

Sidney Kraus, *Televised Presidential Debates and Public Policy,* 2nd ed. Mahwah, NJ: Lawrence Erlbaum, 1998.

Kathleen Hall Jamieson, *Packaging the Presidency: A History and Criticism of Presidential Campaign Advertising.* New York: Oxford University Press, 1984.

Sig Mickelson, *From Whistle Stop to Sound Bite: Four Decades of Politics and Television.* New York: Praeger, 1989.

Ralph Negrine, *The Communication of Politics.* Thousand Oaks, CA: Sage Publications, 1996.

Richard M. Perloff, *Political Communication: Politics, Press, and Public in America.* Mahwah, NJ: Lawrence Erlbaum, 1997.

Austin Ranney, *Channels of Power: The Impact of Television on American Politics.* New York: Basic Books, 1983.

Larry J. Sabato, *The Rise of Political Consultants: New Ways of Winning Elections.* New York: Basic Books, 1981.

Gerald Sussman, *Communication, Technology, and Politics in the Information Age.* Thousand Oaks, CA: Sage Publications, 1997.

Paul A. Winters, *The Media and Politics.* San Diego, CA: Greenhaven Press, 1996.

Suggested Videos

"Election Coverage: Free Elections and a Free Press?" Boston: Global Links Production, 1991. (45 minutes)

"The Made for TV Election." Washington, DC: News Analysis Associates, 1988. (90 minutes)

Theodore White, "Television and the Presidency." New York: Guber-Peters Ailes Communication Production, 1984. (90 minutes)

PART · II

Government

The Founding Fathers of America tried to establish a government in which no one person nor any one office could ever become all-powerful. They were reacting primarily to the absolute power of the monarchs of Europe, from which they and their families had fled to the New World. To prevent the concentration of power, they pursued the principle of balance of powers among various government entities. That is, they divided government into different parts, each with separate responsibilities. Local, state, and federal governments each had their own jurisdictions. Each was divided further into three branches, executive, legislative, and judicial, with various checks and balances built into the system to keep any one branch from becoming too powerful.

The Founding Fathers also realized that citizens needed information about government, and only with an informed vote at the ballot box could people turn out of office a government that had become corrupt, despotic, or too powerful. Only a free press could provide this information, and then only if there was no government censorship or interference with the press, only if there were competing voices in the marketplace, and only if government did not itself have a voice in that marketplace.

On these basic notions rest the foundation of all American journalism, at least for our first 200 years. Throughout our history, the press has viewed itself as the watchdog of government. Journalists are supposed to bark if the government does anything wrong. Furthermore, the news media are not supposed to support the government in any way; journalists are supposed to be neutral, just as they are in politics. Often, over the past 200 years, the press and mass media have actually seemed to many people to be unpatriotic; some have even called them treasonous in pursuing a policy of being neutral informers and critics of government.

At the same time, of course, government offices and officials must communicate with citizens. In fact, leadership requires the ability to communicate, and much of the government's responsibilities revolve around the collection, interpretation, and communication of information people need. Today we need more information than ever before to survive in a complicated society.

Increasingly, especially in the twentieth century, the government and the press have clashed over these roles. The government has tried to get information to the people or to keep information from them, sometimes for reasonable, and other times for questionable, motives. The press has felt a responsibility to question government motives and actions, to dig out all the information, to uncover all secrets, to ask tough and embarrassing questions, to go into any office, to look through any file—in the name of keeping the people informed.

The power of the press as a watchdog of government probably reached its peak in the 1960s and 1970s, especially with regard to the war in Vietnam and the Nixon administration. In Vietnam, news media had the absolute freedom to report anything and everything that happened. The judicial branch of government, in the Pentagon Papers decision, upheld the right of the press to be such a watchdog, even when it harmed government interests. What was reported was not always in the interests of the government, and many regarded the journalists as unpatriotic in the war effort.

During the Nixon administration, the press doggedly pursued the strange events one night in the Watergate office building until the facts led to the Oval Office and the involvement of President Nixon in unlawful activity and its cover-up. The result was the first and only resignation of a sitting American president.

Although the media war between the press and the government has been going on for 200 years, there are increasing signs that the government is winning. Today it can keep more things secret than ever before. The Freedom of Information laws, first passed in 1967, require the government to reveal much information, but these laws also establish areas where the government can legitimately withhold news from the public. The government is also getting much more sophisticated about using the techniques of public relations to present information with its own spin or to stage situations to make the kind of news it wishes to be communicated by mass media.

Congress passed a law in 1913 supposedly preventing the federal government from employing publicity or PR agents. But the American government today, at all levels and in every department or agency, employs tens of thousands of people who do the work of publicity or PR agents, even if they don't use those titles. Congress itself has become one of the branches of government best able to promote itself.

All of this leaves us with some doubts about the balance of powers and the role of mass media as the "fourth branch of government."

41

The Art of Bulldogging Presidents

SAM DONALDSON

Editor's Note: In the White House, rooms have been provided specifically for the news media. Some reporters work there full time, all year around. Their job is to keep an eye on the American president, to tell the people what that executive is doing, and why. Each day the president's press secretary gives White House reporters a briefing on events. Occasionally the president holds a press conference at which reporters can ask questions.

There is no law requiring the president to provide reporters with office space, to give them daily briefings, or to allow them to meet with the president. These things are done as a matter of tradition, but probably also because they serve the president's interests as much as the media's.

When Sam Donaldson was the White House correspondent for ABC News, he gained much national visibility and a reputation as the reporter with the tough (sometimes seemingly rude) questions. Here he tells why. He returned to his position as White House correspondent in 1998. This article was originally published in the book *Hold on, Mr. President,* by Samuel A. Donaldson Jr. (New York: Random House, 1987). The excerpt here was published by *The Quill,* May 1987.

Many people find it extremely difficult to talk to presidents. They get nervous. They are tongue-tied, intimidated by the larger-than-life quality we've built up around presidents, particularly, I think, in this television age. Jimmy Carter once told me he found it strange and disconcerting to have people from his hometown whom he'd known all his life stammer with awestruck admiration when they visited him in the Oval Office.

But reporters can't afford to remain in awe of those they cover. People expect the press to hold the mayor's feet to the fire and to bore in on the city council and to make sure the governor doesn't get away with a thing. It doesn't make any sense to let up on the one public servant whose official conduct affects us all the most. Presidents have a greater responsibility than other public servants and deserve a compassionate understanding of the difficulty of discharging that responsibility. But they are not due worship.

I know that's easier said than done. I trembled with nervousness when I met my first president, John F. Kennedy. But you get over it and come to realize that presidents put their pants on one leg at a time like everyone else. I think you talk to presidents just the way you talk to anyone else. And reporters can't be timid about it.

Nine months into his administration, I asked Jimmy Carter to defend himself against charges that "your administration is inept" and to comment on the recurring Washington undercurrent that "as a Georgian, you don't belong here."

Two years into his administration, I asked Ronald Reagan to comment on the perception that "disarray is here in the White House, that you have been out of touch, that you have had to be dragged back by your staff and friends on Capitol Hill to make realistic decisions on the budget. There was even a newspaper column saying that your presidency is failing."

LOOKING FOR STRAIGHT ANSWERS

I suppose neither man liked hearing those things. But those things were being said about them, and it was legitimate to ask them to respond.

A lot of people want to know what I'm after when I ask questions of the president. Well, it's simple. I'm looking for straight answers on topics the public has an interest in, most of them important, some of them not. With a nod to Will Rogers, I've never heard a question I didn't like. Sure, some were more relevant, important, interesting, more artfully or tactfully phrased than others. But I don't believe there's any such thing as a bad question, only bad answers.

So when I ask questions, I think it's important to challenge the president, challenge him to explain policy, justify decisions, defend mistakes, reveal intentions for the future, and comment on a host of matters about which his views are of general concern. I try to put my questions in a courteous manner, but I try also to make them specific, and pointed.

"Mr. President," I asked Ronald Reagan in October 1983, "Senator [Jesse] Helms has been saying on the Senate floor that Martin Luther King, Jr., had communist associations, was a communist sympathizer. Do you agree?" The president replied, "We'll know in about 35 years, won't we?" (That was a reference to the fact that certain records that might shed light on the subject would be sealed for that length of time.) In the same answer, the president went on to defend Senator Helms's sincerity for wanting to unseal the records. He had not delivered a direct reply to my question "Do you agree?" But he had nevertheless spoken volumes about his feelings.

Reagan later called Dr. King's widow, Coretta Scott King, to apologize for what he said was the press's distortion of his remark. There was no distortion, just an embarrassing insensitivity, and that was his, not the press's.

ASKING THE RIGHT QUESTIONS

The wording of questions is very important. If you say to a president, "Would you care to comment on X," he can always answer, "No, thanks," or he can say anything he wants to and call it a comment. As Reagan mounted the stairway of *Air Force One* in Texas one day in July 1986, we tried to get his reaction to the razor-thin victory he'd won that day in the Senate on confirmation of one of his judicial nominees.

"What about [Daniel] Manion?" someone yelled.

"He's going to be judge," replied Reagan with a smile, which was hardly a reaction, only a statement of fact. But having established that he could hear us above the noise, I sang out, "What about Tutu?" an obvious reference to Bishop Desmond Tutu's criticism the day before that "the West, for my part, can go to hell" because of its reluctance to embrace economic sanctions against the white minority government of South Africa.

"He's not going to be a judge," replied the president solemnly as he disappeared through the doorway of his plane. All right, pretty funny, but then in neither case had we asked the president a specific question, so it's fair to say we had only ourselves to blame.

Once I cried out in exasperation as Reagan retreated across the White House lawn, "What about the Russians?"

"What about them?" he shot back. As he ducked into his helicopter, I could only stammer that I'd ask the questions around here.

SPECIFIC AND SHORT

To be effective, questions must be specific and, preferably, short. They should invite a direct answer. I once asked Jimmy Carter, referring to former CIA director Richard Helms, "Mr. President, Mr. Helms's attorney says that his client will wear his conviction on charges of failing to testify fully before Congress as a badge of honor. Do you think it's a badge of honor, and do you think a public official has a right to lie in public about his business under any circumstances?"

Carter replied, "No, it is not a badge of honor, and a public official does not have a right to lie . . . ." Direct question. Direct answer.

Of course, presidents don't always agree with the way questions are framed, as Carter did in that one. But when they don't, that too can be most revealing.

In March 1985, I asked Reagan about the death of 17 South African blacks who were shot by government authorities the day before, in what I said "appears to be a continuing wave of violence by the white military government against the black majority population." Reagan was having none of my characterization. ". . . I think to put it that way—that they were simply killed and that violence was coming totally from the law-and-order side—ignores the fact that there was rioting going on in behalf of others there," he corrected me, making it perfectly clear who he thought was right and who was wrong in South Africa.

Reagan is always looking for a way to support existing authority, no matter whose, unless, of course, it is communist authority. So his attitude about the unrest in South Africa may not spring from racism. But, of course, to blacks the effect is the same as if Reagan meant it personally.

TRAPPING THE PRESIDENT?

Occasionally, I'm told I ask mean questions, that I'm always trying to "trap the president," and trying to make him "look bad." Not so. Consider the question I asked Reagan at his first press conference as president; there were no barbs, no hooks: I said, "Mr. President, what do you see as the long-range intentions of the Soviet Union? Do you think, for instance, that the Kremlin is bent on world domination that might lead to a continuation of the Cold War, or do you think that under other circumstances détente is possible?"

And out came his view that the Soviets "reserve unto themselves the right to commit any crime, to lie, to cheat, in order to attain" their goal of world revolution. That answer created an uproar, not matched until his speech two years later in which he called the Soviet Union an "evil empire."

And why did I ask him the question in the first place? After all, there was nothing startling about hearing such a view from Ronald Reagan. He had been offering it for years. But he hadn't been president then, and now that he was, it was important for people to know where the president stood. In fact, one of the main objectives in questioning a president is to put him on the record. Of course, sometimes presidents don't want their views on the record. Let me give you an example:

In February 1985, I asked Ronald Reagan at one of his infrequent news conferences, "Mr. President, on Capitol Hill . . . Secretary Shultz suggested that a goal of your policy now is to remove the Sandinista government in Nicaragua. Is that your goal?"

FOLLOWING UP

From the beginning of his presidency, Reagan has been working to overthrow the Sandinista government—officials of his administration freely admit it when they know their names will not be used—but for reasons of international law, foreign relations, and domestic policies, no one wants to admit it on the record. Following the advice of his aides, Reagan had always publicly denied any intention of "overthrowing" the Sandinistas.

But when I asked Reagan that night about "removing" the Sandinista government, he replied, "Well, remove in the sense of its present structure, in which it is a totalitarian state and it is not a government chosen by the people . . . ." Ah, I thought: It's out at last! The word *remove* had not triggered the same warning bell in Reagan's mind that the word *overthrow* would have, and he had delivered the unvarnished truth about his policy.

I pursued it.

"Well, sir," I followed up. "When you say *remove* . . . aren't you then saying that you advocate the overthrow of the present government of Nicaragua?" Now, the alarm bells went off in Reagan's head. He threw up a massive barrage of familiar rhetoric about the Sandinistas having betrayed the original revolution.

I pressed on, violating the one follow-up rule.

"Is the answer yes, sir?" I asked.

"To what?" replied the president.

"To the question 'Aren't you advocating the overthrow of the present government if you substitute another form of what you say was the revolution,'" I answered.

Cornered. But when Ronald Reagan is cornered, he stands and fights. "Not if the present government would turn around and say, 'All right,' if they'd say 'uncle.' . . ." he replied.

That seemed clear enough to me. The choice for Nicaragua was on the record: surrender or die. Reagan's zealous pursuit of the Sandinistas led to the illegal diversion of funds from his Iranian arms sales to supply the anti-Sandinista *contra* rebels. Presidents set direction for those who serve under them through many channels. Sometimes they give direct orders; other times subordinates get the message by simply listening to their public declarations. "Cry uncle," indeed!

PUTTING PRESIDENTS ON THE RECORD

Getting presidents to put their policy on the record is very important. Lyndon Johnson increased U.S. participation in Vietnam from a military advisory force of 16,000 to a full-scale battlefield force of about 542,000 men while maintaining throughout that there had been no change in policy. Given that reminder, reporters now try very hard to get presidents to keep the record straight about policy changes and the reasons for those changes.

Take the case of the U.S. Marines and Lebanon. In the fall of 1983, with U.S. Marines dying in Lebanon, Reagan declared that the "credibility of the United States would suffer on a worldwide scale" if the U.S. peace-keeping force of marines were withdrawn.

And one Friday in early 1984, the *Wall Street Journal* published an interview with Reagan in which he told the paper's Washington bureau chief, Albert Hunt, when asked about House Speaker Thomas P. "Tip" O'Neill's call for the Marines to be brought home, ". . . he may be ready to surrender [in Lebanon], but I'm not."

You can imagine the consternation in some quarters when the *very next* Tuesday, Reagan announced the withdrawal from Lebanon of the U.S. Marines.

At his April press conference, I asked him about it.

"Mr. President," I said, "last October you said the presence of U.S. Marines in Lebanon was central to our credibility on a global scale. And now you've withdrawn them. . . . To what extent have we lost credibility?"

"We may have lost some with some people," replied the president, ". . . but situations change, Sam. . . . I can, I think, explain." And off he went with the patented Ronald Reagan version of the history of the Middle East conflict. It always takes him several minutes to recite it, and he tells it differently each time.

When the recitation was over, I pressed him.

"You began your answer by saying we lost some credibility. Are you to blame for that? Or, like Secretary Shultz, do you blame Congress?"

I had made a tactical mistake. I had given him an out instead of simply asking, "Are you to blame for that?"

He seized it. ". . . they must take a responsibility . . . with the Congress demanding—'Oh, take our, bring our men home. Take them away'—all this can do is stimulate the terrorists and urge them on to further attacks because they see a possibility of success in getting the force out which is keeping them from having their way . . ." said the president, thus shifting all blame, escaping my question, but at the price of provoking a fearful row with Congress.

ARE TOUGH QUESTIONS BIASED?

Sometimes, people say that my questions reflect a political bias. It may seem hard to believe, but reporters' questions are not necessarily indicative of their own point of view.

A lot of people thought I was personally opposed to Jimmy Carter because of the questions I asked him, and a lot of people think I'm opposed to Ronald Reagan because of the questions I ask him. It's a reporter's job to challenge a president—every president—to explain and defend his policies whether you agree with them or not. Still, a lot of people, including presidents, seem to think the questions are personal.

In the summer of 1980, at a news conference devoted to Billy Carter's business relationship with the Libyan government, I asked President Carter to respond to an underlying widespread criticism "that this Billy Carter case is another example of a general aura of incompetence that hangs over your presidency . . . ." Carter began his response by saying, "I've heard you mention that on television a few times, but I don't agree with it . . . ."

If he had heard me mention that on television, it was because I had often reported what *others* were saying. As a rule, critics should be named when asking for a response, which helps to make it clear the reporter isn't expressing a personal view. But if I had tried that day to name all the people who were accusing the Carter administration of being incompetent, there would not have been a 1980 election; we would all still be in that room listening to me recite names.

Loyal admirers of the chief executive in office frequently demand that I stop asking critical questions and "support our president." Well, if I ever do decide to try to "get" a president, one way to do it would be to stand up and inquire, "Sir, please tell us why you are such a great man," and then watch the "great man" try desperately to keep from making a fool of himself as he tried to handle that softball. Good politicians, like any good batter, want something they can swing at.

Consider the hardball from House Speaker Tip O'Neill I tossed at Reagan in June 1981. "Tip O'Neill says you don't know anything about the working people, that you have just a bunch of wealthy and selfish advisers," I told him.

Reagan, who had already started from the room because the press conference had officially ended, turned back to the microphone with relish. "I'm trying to find out something about [Tip's] boyhood,' said Reagan. ". . . I grew up in poverty and got what education I got all by myself and so forth, and I think it's sheer demagoguery to pretend that this economic program which we've submitted is not aimed at helping the great cross-section of people in this country . . . ."

Now you may or may not agree with O'Neill's assessment of Ronald Reagan, but it's hard not to agree that Reagan took that question and hit it out of the ball park.

POLITICIANS CAN MAKE POINTS

Not only do good politicians like to swing at tough questions, but they also use them for their own purposes. Reagan did this once in Tokyo even before any questions had been asked.

He and leaders of other industrialized non-communist nations meeting at one of their yearly economic summits were trying to hammer out a statement on terrorism in May of 1986. Everyone was against state-sponsored terrorism, but some of the leaders did not want to specifically identify Libya as one of the chief culprits. Reagan told them that if Libya wasn't named, the very first question the press would ask would be, Why not? And in light of Libya's highly spotlighted activities, that would be a hard question to answer. Reagan's argument carried the day. Libya was put in but, of course, those of us waiting outside didn't know it.

Sure enough, when the leaders emerged, I sang out as if on cue, "Mr. President, your statement on terrorism does not mention Libya by name. Why not?" Reagan's face lit up in a wide smile. "Read the final statement," he said triumphantly, and, I was told later, once out of earshot of the press he turned to the other leaders and crowed, "See, didn't I tell you, the very first question!" Oh, well. I'm always glad to be of service.

PRESIDENTS RESPONDING TO CRITICISM

No matter how such questions are handled, getting the president to respond to the criticism of others is one of our main jobs in the White House press room. And sometimes, not often enough in my view, reporters ask questions that zero in on people who are not important figures but are still deserving of his attention. The champion of this calling is the legendary Sarah McClendon, who has been badgering, some would say terrorizing, presidents for 40 years.

Once, Sarah sharply berated Reagan for pulling back a promised appointment because the candidate for the job had criticized cutting the budget for an agency that protects consumers. ". . . Did you mean to give a signal to other Republicans that if they don't conform that off would go their heads?" asked Sarah.

Reagan, looking properly chastened, began his reply, "How can you say that about a sweet fellow like me?" That drew a laugh, but then, he had to go on and answer the question. Sarah, more power to her, is always sticking up for the underdog and asking presidents to explain why they are not.

That seems to me the right approach for a reporter. It's the people who don't have the power or whose thinking isn't in the mainstream who most need help in being heard.

When I said earlier that you ought to talk to presidents the way you talk to anyone else, I wasn't referring only to asking questions. I think that also applies to light banter at appropriate times.

Once, in the Oval Office, Ronald Reagan signed a congressional spending resolution and thanked senators Baker and Hatfield and congressmen Conte and "Michelle" for their "strong leadership" on this.

There is no Congressman Michelle. Reagan was clearly referring to Bob Michel of Illinois, the Republican leader in the House. So I said to the president, "That's Michel, sir, Michel."

"Oh, Michel, yes," he said. "Don't tell anyone, will you?" This while five television cameras were shooting away.

"No deals, Mr. President," I replied sternly.

"Now, Sam, haven't you ever made a mistake?" he pleaded.

"Sir," said I, "The last time I called someone Michelle, she was a blond." He laughed.

SPARRING WITH PRESIDENTS

Later, I was told one of the VIPs present from Capitol Hill thought it outrageous that a mere reporter had dared to banter with the president of the United States. To his credit, Reagan doesn't seem to share this attitude. Whereas others around Reagan often seem to be striving to put him on some kind of imperial pedestal, he seems to have his feet on the ground. In fact, he can even be a little pixieish. Once, as he stood on the pavement at Checkpoint Charlie looking into communist East Berlin, I yelled out to him to be careful not to cross the line. "You don't want to get captured by the commies," I admonished with a grin.

On hearing this, Reagan lifted his leg and, with a devilish smile on his face, swung it in the air across the line. Fortunately for the safety of the free world, he didn't fall over.

And he laughed loudly at himself when, having fulminated to newspaper editors against the Shiite Muslim leader he identified as Nabih Berra, I later told him out of their earshot, "Listen here, Berra was a catcher for the New York Yankees. The man you're after is named Berri."

Reagan spars better with reporters than Carter did, because of this ability to laugh at himself. Carter preferred to laugh at the other fellow. We noticed this trait early in the Carter campaign. Curtis Wilkie, a reporter for the *Boston Globe,* brought it up on the press plane one day, "Why don't you ever engage in any self-deprecating humor?" Wilkie asked.

The next day, Carter tried to poke fun at himself at every stop. Somehow, he didn't manage to sound convincing. But Carter does have a quick wit when it comes to casting humor in an outward direction. And one day in the Rose Garden he got me good. As I sat relaxing on one of the lawn chairs at the back of the garden, waiting for a scheduled presidential appearance, Carter, suddenly and early, came out of the Oval Office, walked up to the rope line behind which other reporters were waiting, and started talking.

I ran up as quickly as I could, but by the time I got there, Carter had turned away and headed back inside. "What did he say, what did he say?" I asked a little frantically.

"He said," replied one of the reporters, "he just wanted to see if he could get Donaldson off his lawn chair."

On another occasion. Carter hit home in a brief exchange in India. We had been taken to a small village near New Delhi (renamed Carterpuri by the Indians for the occasion) to see how the village solved its energy problem. This was at the height of concern over the energy crisis. Carterpuri solved its energy problem by throwing all the cow manure from its herds into a large pit, then siphoning off the methane gas to light the village lamps. So it came to pass that we all stood on the lip of the manure pit inspecting the process.

"If I fell in, you'd pull me out wouldn't you, Mr. President?" I joked.

"Certainly," Carter replied—pause—"after a suitable interval."

COVERING EVERY MOVE

It's not every day that presidents take reporters to the lip of a manure pit (literally, that is), but when they do. that's all right: It's our job to follow them wherever they go. And when presidents try to give us the slip, it's war.

A week or so after Jimmy Carter took office, he let it be known that he didn't see the need to take along a press pool in his motorcade every time he left the White House grounds, as had been the custom for years. We in the press were alarmed. We think there is a great, overriding public interest in covering the president when he's out and about, including in motorcades and on airplane rides.

Consider the day James Salamites, a young man out on the town, accidentally drove through an unguarded intersection in Hartford, Connecticut, and slammed into the side of the limousine carrying President Gerald R. Ford. Fortunately, no one was seriously hurt (one of Ford's aides suffered a broken finger), but it was one of those unplanned events that make the case for full-time press coverage of the president.

Jody Powell, Carter's press secretary, set up a meeting in the cabinet room, and I was chosen by lot as one of the press representatives to argue the case with Carter. The president opened by saying he understood the public interest in his activities, but he saw no need to take the press along on purely personal outings, such as taking his daughter, Amy, to the Washington zoo, for instance.

The headline flashed through my mind: "President Mauled by Runaway Lion, *It Is Suspected.*"

So I told him in so many words that he was wrong; that he no longer could expect to be left alone as an ordinary citizen might, because of the overriding interest in him as president, a position, I reminded him politely, no one had forced him to seek.

"You can take us along in your motorcade or we can stake out every one of the gates 24 hours a day and chase you through the streets, but we're going to cover you one way or the other," I told him. After all, no one dragged Carter or Reagan to the Oval Office and made them serve in the presidency. They fought long and hard for that job and the publicity glare that goes with it. Presidents must understand they live in a glass house when they move into the White House. Carter took the point and agreed to continue the motorcade press pool.

THE PUBLIC'S RIGHT TO KNOW

The fact is, the public is curious about everything presidents do, even when no great public issues are involved. A reporter once asked John F. Kennedy why he had a bandage on his finger, and Kennedy replied he had cut it with a knife down in the White House kitchen the night before as he was slicing sandwich bread. People found it fascinating.

During the Carter presidency, much of the copy turned out by news organizations and avidly gobbled up by readers had to do with Carter's family—his mother, Lillian, his sister, Gloria, who rode a motorcycle, his sister, Ruth, who was a faith healer, and of course his brother, Billy. And the comings and goings of young Amy Carter were chronicled and commented on unrelentingly. The same goes, of course, for Reagan's family.

One morning after the serious questioning at one of Reagan's mini-press conferences in the White House briefing room had ended and he was leaving the podium, I asked him, "Are you and your son Michael closer to resolving your differences?" He ducked the question by replying that he would give me the same answer his wife, Nancy, had given me the day before, when I had put the question to her during a Christmas tree photo opportunity: "Merry Christmas."

Well, you would have thought by the outrage registered in some quarters that I had inquired as to the First Couple's sex life—something *Los Angeles Times* reporter George Skelton once did in an interview with Reagan (more power to you, George). A Nixon appointee on the Federal Communications Commission, James Quello, thundered that I had asked the nastiest, most underhanded, most vicious question ever heard. I thought Quello's nomination of my humble effort a little too generous, as well as ham-handed, coming from the FCC.

But balanced against Quello's blast came a flood of letters from ordinary citizens wanting more information on the first family's domestic dispute. They said they had been reading about the dispute (it was in all the papers and news magazines) and wondered why the president hadn't answered the question.

UNCOMFORTABLE QUESTIONS

And when Patti Davis, the Reagans' daughter, wrote a novel that reflected an unflattering view of her parents, it was natural for me to ask Reagan if he had read his daughter's book and what he thought about it. Reagan replied that he found it "interesting fiction." Quello has yet to weigh in on that exchange.

I have a reputation for putting uncomfortable questions to presidents, but I am certainly not alone. One of the most relentless interrogators is the White House bureau chief for United Press International, Helen Thomas, the dean of the White House press corps. Helen has been taking dead aim at the first magistrate of the land since Kennedy's days. Two of my favorite examples of Helen's techniques are: to Jimmy Carter, ". . . was it worth it to you to cause some destabilization of the dollar and demoralization of the federal government, spreading doubt through the land, in order to repudiate much of your Cabinet?"; and to Ronald Reagan, ". . . how high does unemployment have to go and how much does the economy have to deteriorate before you are willing to accept cuts in the defense budget?"

Thomas is particularly effective because she is always working. I found that out one day early in the Carter administration, when I stumbled onto a birthday party for deputy press secretary Rex Granum in Granum's office, right off the press room. Carter himself was there having a piece of cake with Rex and other staff members. A moment later, Ed Bradley of CBS discovered the group.

Bradley and I began reminiscing with Carter about his presidential campaign, which we had both covered. Suddenly, Thomas appeared. And after the polite hellos, she immediately whipped out her notebook and began asking Carter about the details of his forthcoming energy program. Carter fled. At first, I was unhappy that Thomas had ruined the light conversation. But upon reflection, I realized she was absolutely right to do it. Reporters are there to get information and do it at every opportunity.

A DANGEROUS JOB

That principle, noble though it may be, once almost cost me my job, however. It came about this way.

In November 1981, the ABC News Washington bureau moved into a new building, and Reagan came to dedicate it. All the top executives of the company were there, led by ABC board chairman Leonard Goldenson. Roone Arledge, president of ABC News, presided at the ceremony in our newsroom. President Reagan delivered a short speech, after which I started shooting questions at him. I'm sure it came as no surprise to him, because he had seen me standing 10 feet away with a microphone in my hand.

"Can David Stockman continue to be effective after saying such damaging things about your economic program?" I asked, referring to the Office of Management and Budget director's famous admission to William Greider in *The Atlantic* that the administration had cooked the budget figures and really didn't know what it was doing.

The president began dodging and weaving in his answers but did reveal that he would be seeing budget director Stockman right after he returned to the White House—it turned out to be the famous meeting in which Stockman said Reagan had taken him to the "woodshed."

I kept on, and Helen Thomas joined me in popping questions.

"I was only joking when I said the first question would be by Sam Donaldson," Roone Arledge snapped in a decidedly non-joking voice, aware that the majesty of the dedication ceremony was rapidly disappearing.

"So, fire me," I interjected in what I hoped was a lighthearted tone.

"You know, that's not a bad idea," replied Arledge in a tone he may have meant to be similarly lighthearted but somehow sounded more like the whistle of a Katyusha rocket about to crash through the roof.

The official party moved backstage. I am told that Michael Deaver, then White House deputy chief of staff, immediately turned on Arledge. "You mouse-trapped us," said Deaver. "We agreed to come here to dedicate the building, and you tried to turn this into a press conference." It was a terribly embarrassing moment for the top management of the American Broadcasting Company and a terribly dangerous moment for me.

Before Arledge could reply—thank God, before he could reply—another voice interrupted. "Oh, that's all right, that's just the way Sam is," said Ronald Reagan with a chuckle.

Reagan may regret that moment of generosity. The give and take of years of intense and often critical press coverage can change a president's feeling toward the press. Carter, whose national career was made possible by early favorable press coverage, left the presidency convinced that many Washington reporters had been viciously unfair to him.

QUESTIONS AREN'T DAMAGING—ANSWERS ARE

By early 1986. Reagan publicly spoke of reporters as "sons of bitches," and by the end of the year, as his Iranian arms sale policy collapsed about him, he complained that we were circling like "sharks . . . with blood in the water." Such reactions are regrettable but understandable. No one likes to be criticized, especially presidents, who are surrounded by people telling them they are beyond reproach.

Let me sum up my philosophy on covering presidents. It's important work, and it never stops. Neither the press nor the president is ever off duty. I want to put questions to presidents directly, not just to their press secretaries and other aides. As to what questions are appropriate and how they should be asked, well, let's put it this way: If you send me to cover a pie-baking contest on Mother's Day, I'm going to ask dear old Mom whether she used artificial sweetener in violation of the rules, and while she's at it, could I see the receipt for the apples to prove she didn't steal them.

I maintain that if Mom has nothing to hide, no harm will have been done. But the questions should be asked. Too often, Mom, and presidents—behind those sweet faces—turn out to have stuffed a few rotten apples into the public barrel.

So when I cover the president, I try to remember two things: First, if you don't ask, you don't find out; and second, the questions don't do the damage. Only the answers do.

42

The Media May Devour Democracy

SEN. GEORGE J. MITCHELL

Editor's Note: Of course, politicians and journalists are frequently at war with each other. Journalists believe that the First Amendment guarantees them the freedom to pursue the truth. Some use that to defend their rights to be critical of politicians in the interests of the public; others use it for the pursuit of political ends, or profit, or fame.

But whatever their motives, journalists often come into conflict with politicians, and sometimes even the best of politicians cannot hold back their anger at the press and mass media. George J. Mitchell, a former Democratic senator from Maine and majority leader in the U.S. Senate, accuses the press of unnecessarily raising public doubts and thereby damaging the political process.

These remarks by Senator Mitchell were adapted from a statement made on the *MacNeil/Lehrer NewsHour* on public television in March 1994 and are reprinted here from the *Los Angeles Times,* March 13, 1994.

There is a culture of disbelief in America. I actually had a reporter say to me this past weekend, "I don't believe anything any politician says at any time, including you."

If you are an elected official in our society, for a very large number of people anything you say must be untrue on its face. This is a reversal of what I think ought to be the proper standard.

The presumption of disbelief is caused by a combination of things. For one, there exists in this country an enormous news machine. There is a huge demand for news that's 24 hours a day and into it must be fed something on a daily basis. If something doesn't exist to be fed in, then it must be made up. And the reality is that much of the commentary, analysis, criticism is highly speculative, often false, usually tinged with sensationalism.

This is a sad commentary on the state of the current coverage of the political process, but I believe that increasingly in America what is news is defined by what is or is not controversial. If it's not controversial, it's not news. If it lends itself to sensationalism, it achieves a high level of attention.

We bear a lot of the responsibility, we elected officials, who make mistakes and create the kind of unfortunate attitude that exists. So I don't think it's any one individual or group.

But let me give an example. In the last two years, we've passed significant legislation involving federal assistance to young people who want to go on to college. This is a very important aspect of our society—the education of young people, the opening up of higher education to people of all backgrounds. Nobody knows about the legislation—because it wasn't controversial, it wasn't news.

I'll never forget, two weeks after we passed the bill in the Senate, I went home to Maine and held a series of town meetings. I was at a school and people asked, "Senator, when are you guys going to do something about the student-aid program?"

I said, "Well, we just did two weeks ago, but you don't know about it because it literally didn't—it literally was not reported because it was not controversial." On the other hand, something like, dare I say the word *Whitewater*—it's now every night on the news, dominating the news. Why is that? Because, of course, it's controversial and sensational.

I'm not suggesting that all this is made up by the press; there are errors. I don't think there's much malice, frankly.

We use the words *press* and *media* to describe what we know not to be a monolith, but, in fact, thousands of people making millions of decisions in a highly competitive atmosphere, in which you'd better go with the story even though you've only got 6 percent of the facts, because if you don't, the other guy might go, so you can't wait till you get 60 percent of the facts.

We ought not to suspend the critical faculties, the sense of judgment and fairness, that exist in all of life outside of politics when we deal with politics, because it is, in fact, a part of our society, and it's part of the process. Not all the problems can be blamed on the press. But it is *a* contributing factor to this culture of disbelief.

43

Government Secrecy: Easy, Dangerous, and Undemocratic

JESSICA MATHEWS

Editor's Note: Although the United States has been committed for some time to declassifying old secrets, the process is slow and cumbersome. More than 1.5 *billion* pages of government documents remain classified as secret—and because it is so easy to make things secret, the problem of secrecy is growing, not diminishing.

As we've seen earlier in this book, the price of secrecy is high. Secrecy can destroy democracy itself, as E. J. Dionne comments at the end of this article.

Jessica Mathews is president of the Carnegie Endowment for International Peace and has been an occasional columnist for the *Washington Post*. E. J. Dionne is an editorial writer for the *Washington Post* and occasional columnist. Both of these articles were published in the *International Herald Tribune,* March 19, 1997, and are reprinted with permission.

Washington—If you want to understand what out-of-control government secrecy means, consider what happened to one of its heroes, Glenn Seaborg, Nobel laureate in chemistry, co-discoverer of plutonium and chairman of the U.S. Atomic Energy Commission for 10 years.

During that time Mr. Seaborg kept a journal—more than 18,000 pages of a diary plus correspondence, minutes of meetings and other documents—intended as a historical record. He rigorously excluded anything that could be considered classified, but to be doubly sure he had the whole thing reviewed and cleared when he left the AEC.

For 12 years all was well. Then, in 1983, the Department of Energy asked to make a copy for its own historical use. Mr. Seaborg mistakenly agreed. A year and a half later the department informed him that the journal contained classified information.

It ordered that his other copy be picked up, and threatened him with arrest if he resisted. He could be accused, he was told, of having removed classified material from the Atomic Energy Commission, because there was no written record of declassification. (Of course, since the material was not classified to begin with.) He could go to court, he was told, but the government had never lost such a case.

FAMILY LORE

Over the next years the journal was "sanitized" three separate times. Each time the reviewers made different deletions, from words to entire documents—1,000 in all.

Some were "bits of family lore." Another "particular speciality," Mr. Seaborg writes, were items already in the public record, such as the code names of nuclear tests, which the Department of Energy had itself published.

Other deletions were entries that could be embarrassing but in no way threatened security. It was "an arbitrary, capricious and frivolous process, almost devoid of objective criteria." (The whole awful story can be found in *Science* magazine, June 3, 1994.) Mr. Seaborg is still waiting for the original to be re-released.

FEEDING ON ITSELF

How to explain this mindless, autopilot style of operation? In part, there are too many secrets. Everyone who has ever worked in government knows that stamping something "Top Secret" makes people pay attention. If you work in the Defense Department, State, Justice, Energy or in the several intelligence agencies and you want to matter, you don't send unclassified memos.

So the system feeds on itself. It produced 3.6 million new classifications up to Top Secret in 1995. More than 1.5 billion pages of government documents more than 25 years old remain classified.

The report of a commission chaired by Senator Daniel Patrick Moynihan, Democrat of New York, identifies other huge costs. One is that when there are so many secrets, it is much harder to protect the relative few that count; leaking classified material becomes no big deal. Another is that when so much is classified, anything that is not is presumed to be unimportant.

SPARING THE U.S.

A survey of Cuban public opinion made at the time of the Bay of Pigs invasion showed public support for Fidel Castro so strong that any hope of an uprising against him was fantasy. The findings could have spared the United States one of its most costly blunders. "It is difficult not to think," Mr. Moynihan writes, that the poll "might have had greater impact had it been classified."

Or consider the intelligence community's colossal failure to detect the Soviet Union's imminent collapse, for which there is still no satisfactory explanation. General Ervin Rokke served in that time as defense attaché in Moscow. His highly classified reports on the usual national security subjects, he believes, provided less insight into the Soviet threat than the picture his wife could have drawn from the signs of economic ruin she encountered daily. But who at a high level would have paid attention to information so mundane and so freely available?

IMPOVERISHING ANALYSIS

The isolation that secrets impose on those who handle them impoverishes analysis. It perverts judgment, silences dissent and protects poor performance. Particularly when documents are presumed to be classified forever, excessive secrecy can breed arrogance and extreme abuses of authority.

In the nuclear establishment, where by law all information is born classified, the government killed, lied to and then stonewalled Americans for decades behind secrecy's impenetrable shield. Radioactive fallout, the Atomic Energy Commission asserted in 1955, "does not constitute a serious hazard to any living thing outside the test site." It knew this to be false then, and for years of successful lawsuits against radiation victims thereafter.

DEEPLY ROOTED

In his foreword to the new report, Mr. Moynihan highlights one more cost: the atmosphere of suspicion that too much secrecy creates between Americans and their government, a fertile breeding ground for conspiracy theories and domestic terrorism and a threat to healthy democracy.

As the remedy, the commission urges that secrecy henceforth be seen as a second system of government regulation and be provided "the discipline of a legal framework." Statutory standards should be set for what may be declared secret, and secrets should have, from the outset, a fixed lifetime, unless specific harm can be demonstrated. Declassification should have equal status, made routine and efficient.

It might not work. A culture as deeply rooted as this one changes slowly and painfully at best. There can be no doubt, however, that even partial success would be worth the effort.

MORE OPENNESS AND FEWER MISTAKES

—E.J. Dionne Jr., commenting in the *Washington Post*.

Unlike the other government regulations, the secrecy system operates, by definition, outside the public view. Accountability and secrecy are implacable foes.

Secrecy's most damaging blow is to democracy and the capacity for reasoned deliberation. Keeping too many secrets feeds paranoia and conspiracy mongering. ("Why isn't the government putting out that information? What is it hiding?") Facts that might explode conspiracy-spinning are withheld.

More openness about just what Soviet spies were and were not doing in America might have led us to be somewhat more wary in the 1930s and early 1940s, but less paranoid in the McCarthy era. Soviet espionage success, according to Senator Moynihan, "was waning by the time we began to be aware of it."

Disclosure of what the government knew, or thought it knew, could have avoided large policy errors by subjecting mistaken assumptions to public debate.

Intelligence vastly overestimated the strength of the Soviet economy, so that almost no one expected the Soviet collapse in 1989.

America went to war in Vietnam fearing that the Soviet Union and the People's Republic of China were seeking to extend Communist control into South Asia and beyond. But that war escalated at the very moment when the Russian-Chinese alliance, to the extent that it ever existed, had thoroughly fractured.

Secrecy within the government (agencies keeping secrets from each other) robs top officials of information they need.

Senator Moynihan's solution is straightforward: Keep fewer secrets, and safeguard the ones that matter. Some declassification has already begun, but the Moynihan commission proposes legislation to push this further and make it harder for government officials to label things secret in the first place.

We are talking a lot about deregulation in the part of the regulatory system that is most open. We need more deregulation in the part that is most closed.

44

News of the Congress
by the Congress

MARY COLLINS

Editor's Note: Congress has been able to put its spin on congressional news to a greater degree than ever before. Television stations and newspapers are increasingly allowing their local House members to cover themselves. It saves money for the press—and the representatives love having their version of the news published and broadcast, unfiltered by journalists.

Mary Collins is an associate editor of the *Washington Journalism Review*. News aides John Murawski and John Stetson provided research for this article, which was published in the *Washington Journalism Review* (now the *American Journalism Review*) in June 1990.

Every Wednesday at one o'clock the Democratic and Republican National Congressional Committees haul high-quality television equipment to the "Swamp," a patch of grass on the east side of the Capitol. Against the patriotic backdrop, House members tape short interviews with their press secretaries for the committees to send via satellite to stations in the members' districts.

"And the local stations often run the stuff," says Wesley Pippert, former press secretary for Rep. Paul Henry (R-MI) and one-time UPI reporter. "You can ponder the implications of that."

Because of this growing electronic flackery, many newspapers and television stations are dropping their independent political correspondents, choosing instead to get their Washington coverage from press secretaries and understaffed D.C. bureaus run by large parent companies. Some of them don't even bother with bureaus or independent news services. Lured by low costs, convenience and a deceptive patina of journalistic professionalism, an ever-growing portion of the Fourth Estate is relying entirely on canned congressional news.

THE WORK OF PRESS SECRETARIES

In the last 20 years the number of House press secretaries has quintupled from 54 in 1970 to more than 250 today [in 1990]. Armed with the latest technology—

including fax machines and television equipment—these image-makers have access to more media outlets than ever before. "The P.R. machinery is overwhelming," says Ron Cohen, executive editor of Gannett News Service. So much so that political reporters in all forms of media have been giving ground.

At WJMC-AM, a radio station in Jacksonville, North Carolina, News Director Glenn Hargett often uses tapes and releases prepared by Rep. Martin Lancaster's (D-NC) press secretary, Marshall "Skip" Smith. "Skip asks the member the questions himself and then sends us down a response. I see nothing wrong with a press secretary controlling the interview," he says. "I'll tell you, there were times in the past when I had to rely on Skip heavily. He was my only source. I had to trust him."

Smith himself says he uses his releases to "cut off bad publicity—to put our own spin on things."

Like most press secretaries on the Hill, Smith is a former journalist who puts his experience as an editor and news director to good use for his congressmen. He knows how to sell stories to thirsty media outlets. He knows reporters and deadlines. "He knows our operation," says Hargett.

Morgan Broman, press secretary for Rep. Richard Neal (D-MA), also makes good use of the connections he developed as a reporter/producer for WWLP-TV, a station in Neal's district in Springfield. "I call my old boss, and they'll generally write it [the press release] into the text" of the evening news, he says. WWLP News Director Keith Silver acknowledges that the station sometimes uses Broman's PR. "He knows what buttons to press," Silver says. "He knows who to talk to."

THE DEPENDENCE OF NEWS MEDIA

The ties are even tighter between Tina Kreischer, press secretary for San Diego's Congressman Bill Lowery (R-CA) and the *San Diego Union*. Her husband, Otto, reports on the Pentagon for the *Union* out of the Copley News Service's Washington bureau. Sometimes he works with his wife on stories because Lowery is on the Military Construction Subcommittee.

"When I have to go to them for comments or facts it's weird," he says. "The situation becomes interesting when she and I go to the National Press Club for dinner. She's there in a dual capacity [wife/press secretary]. The [Copley] reporters on her beat get to talk shop with her, so in that sense she is treated differently."

Tina Kreischer believes that at least 75 percent of the stories about Lowery that appear in the *Union* are based on her press releases. Though the paper rarely runs them verbatim, former Copley reporter Mark Ragan, who covered the Hill for the *Union*, says that the bureau does rely on them "heavily." "They're all so busy," he says. "Tina is very helpful."

Steve Green, managing editor of Copley's Washington bureau, describes the Kreischers' situation as an "odd-couple relationship. But I don't know what to do with it," he says. "You can't say he should divorce his wife or leave his job."

Copley's Washington office and other parent company news bureaus say they make a conscious effort not to rely on press secretaries for their congressional coverage. So do such independent bureaus as Potomac News Service and States News Service. Many smaller media outlets, on the other hand, depend almost entirely on press secretaries for Hill news. Case studies abound, particularly in the broadcast media.

One station in Rep. Porter Goss's (R-FL) district in Fort Myers, Florida, WINK-TV, gave up on Potomac News Service, an independent agency that provides Capitol Hill news for stations across the country, because "the cost is prohibitive," says Jim McLaughlin, managing editor and anchor. He estimates that one 30-second sound bite can cost as much as $500. "With Senate feeds and House feeds we pretty much have it covered," he says. According to News Director John Emmert the station now links up with news services only on an on-need basis. "It is more reactive," he concedes. "We no longer have a service hounding out a story."

KLBK-TV in Lubbock, Texas, also has a reactive relationship with the House member from its district, Larry Combest (R-TX). According to News Director Michael Sommermeyer, the fact that Combest's current press secretary, Keith Williams, is a former local reporter makes having a D.C. correspondent or using a news service superfluous. "As a small-market television station, we have to skimp and save and try to convince other people to help us out. That's why it's good to have Keith there. The only problem is the slanted view."

THE SURGE IN VIDEO NEWS RELEASES

"Capitol Hill press secretaries often send out daily feeds of an hour or more," says Bruce Finland, president and founder of the Potomac News Service. "It's not bad to have that, but more and more it's the *only* thing TV stations are taking out of Washington. That's what bothers me."

Business is booming for television crews at the Republican and Democratic National Committees and at the House's own TV studio in the basement of the Rayburn building. Costs are low—often 60 percent below the commercial rate—and equipment is top quality.

The demand is so high that use of the House studio has quadrupled since 1980, even though the political parties expanded their own television facilities during the same period. The House Administration Subcommittee is currently considering a request for $203,000 for additional personnel at the Hill studio.

This sudden surge in video press releases has put several independent television news services in Washington out of business. Finland says that at least three of a dozen or so services have died in the last five years. "Soon, I expect there will be only one or two left," he says. "Basically, the free satellite feeds have killed an industry. They've supplanted real news coverage."

This is not to say, however, that relying on parent bureaus like Hearst Broadcasting, or on news services like CONUS or Potomac News, is a cure-all. These bureaus provide Hill coverage to countless small stations that can't afford their own Washington correspondents. But most of these bureaus are chronically understaffed, using two general assignment reporters to cover *all* of Washington for six to 10 clients. Congress must compete for attention with the president, the U.S. Supreme Court, demonstrators and more. House coverage in particular gets short shrift.

Potomac News Service, for example, has just seven people in its bureau, only three of whom are full-time reporters. "On any given day," says Bureau Chief Eileen Cleary, "we do anywhere from one to 20 stories."

There is a case to be made that some station budgets just don't permit original Washington coverage. There is also some validity to the argument that tapes made by members of Congress may contain legitimate news. But it's not so easy to justify another aspect of this conveyance of incumbent propaganda: Few of the stations tell their viewers they are dispensing material prepared, not by the station, but by a politician. The viewer is left free to assume that the congressman's words are in response to a reporter's questions when, in fact, they are worked up by the congressman in collusion with his own paid press representative.

POTENTIALLY ILLEGAL, BUT NO ONE CARES

This practice is not only ethically suspect, it's potentially unlawful. According to the Federal Communications Commission (FCC), the public should be informed when any "records, transcriptions, talent, scripts, or other material or services of any kind are furnished by a candidate as an inducement to the broadcast of the program. . . . An announcement shall be made both at the beginning and conclusion of such program."

Practically speaking, the law is not enforced, because the FCC depends on complaints to trigger official monitoring, and viewers—unfamiliar with the law and unaware they're viewing congressional hand-outs—don't complain. Uncertainty about when a congressman is a "candidate" also clouds the issue. The FCC is now revising these regulations to include specific guidelines for video news releases (VNR).

But many news directors appear untroubled by either ethical or legal doubts. Based on an informal *WJR* survey of 26 stations, 87 percent say they rarely if ever notify viewers when "news" footage is provided by a congressman's office.

"I find that surprising and disturbing," says David Bartlett, president of the Radio-Television News Directors Association. "It's RTNDA's view—and the [view of a] vast majority of the people in the industry—that identification of a video is vital.

"Failing to identify the source of a VNR is a terrible breach of journalistic practice."

Stations that don't label political VNRs sink into a corrosive coziness with House members. A congressman gets to control his own 15-second appearance on the evening news—all the more effective because viewers consider it straight news. And the news director gets a free clip out of Washington relating to current events—all the more effective because viewers assume it's news coverage by the station, not the transmission of a political message. The only loser in the deal: the public.

The situation among newspapers, while also bleak, contains one bright aspect. According to media critic Ben Bagdikian, professor of journalism at the University of California, Berkeley, the concentration of ownership of print media in the hands of a few companies has improved congressional coverage. Many small papers now have access to Washington reporters via their parent bureaus. "They end up with a certain amount of delegation coverage that they've never had before," he says. And unlike Potomac News Service, business at States News Service has improved, says Managing Editor Rem Rieder.

NEWSPAPERS CAN'T DO THE JOB, EITHER

But newspaper bureaus in Washington are also short staffed. The typical reporter in these bureaus is expected to track eight to 10 House and Senate members for several newspapers.

States News, for example, covers U.S. representatives from more than 30 states with 31 reporters. According to Rieder, a state like California—which has 45 members in its congressional delegation—is assigned three reporters; most others get just one.

High staff turnover and low budgets also constrict the Hill reporting of these news services. Editor David Greenfield of the *Charleston* (West Virginia) *Daily Mail* says that when he was a Washington correspondent from 1979 to 1984 he saw four or five people from States News come and go on the Hill beat for the rival *Charleston Gazette.* "It's so low budget and has such a high staff turnover rate that reporters leave before they get to know the state. There's no continuity," he says.

Rieder, however, feels that things are changing—at least at States News, where the average reporter now stays two years, he says. Other staffers claim the average is closer to a year.

Many bureaus for newspaper parent companies are also stretched thin. At Knight-Ridder Newspapers two reporters provide congressional coverage for 28 dailies in 16 states; Scripps Howard News Service has one Hill reporter for 20 dailies.

"Flacks with faxes have real sway with local dailies," says David Hawkings, a Hill reporter for the Thomson Newspaper Group who covers 14 members for 14 papers. "A fax in the hand of a small local newspaper editor can be better than a bureau story in the bush."

Print reporters from the home districts could easily complement the House news provided by the understaffed D.C. bureaus, or even generate stories on their own, by making a few long distance phone calls. But few do.

A comparison between two dailies in Charleston, West Virginia, with roughly equal circulation, the *Gazette* and *Daily Mail,* dramatizes the difference a paper's own correspondent can make.

The morning *Gazette* (circulation, 55,000) closed down its independent Washington bureau in the 1960s and signed up the States News Service instead. Now it has dropped States News as well and relies on "the national wires and the PR people of congressmen for its Hill coverage," says City Editor Rosalie Earle.

The *Gazette*'s Joint Operating Agreement-partner and rival, the *Daily Mail* (circulation, 51,700), has taken a different approach. This evening paper has had its own full-time political correspondent for 12 years, even though Thomson Newspapers, which owns the paper, has a Washington bureau. "It's difficult to get a pertinent local story out of a bureau," says *Daily Mail* Editor David Greenfield.

When Congress gave itself a pay raise in November, for example, the *Gazette* relied on UPI for its Page One story, which included remarks from Senate Majority Leader Robert Byrd (D-WV) but nothing from Charleston's less renowned House member, Bob Wise. On the same day, the *Daily Mail*'s Hill correspondent, John Kimelman, also had a cover story, but it quoted extensively from the entire West Virginia House delegation, which had split its vote on the pay-raise issue.

BUT NOTHING IS REALLY FREE

The *Daily Mail* regularly carries localized front-page stories about such topics as Wise's decision to cut back on press releases, his family's response to the swearing-in ceremonies for the 101st Congress and his latest proposed legislation. The *Gazette,* by contrast, rarely publishes such specific stories on the representative, relying instead on the more generic news that comes over the wire. And even when the *Gazette* does play up congressional stories, it seldom mentions West Virginia's House members, because wire services tend to focus on politicians with national reputations.

Dailies that provide the *Gazette*'s type of off-the-shelf House coverage make it difficult for voters to learn about the doings or misdoings of their U.S. representatives. "There's such a lack of interest," says congressional press secretary Morgan Broman, "that opponents must educate the public on the failings of an incumbent at election time."

But the "educational" opportunities for challengers range from slim to none. For two years prior to election day, incumbents shape the flow of "news" from Washington to many of the newspapers and TV stations in their districts. Then at campaign time, incumbents outspend their opponents—on TV spots in particular—by more than three to one. The right question here may not be why 98.5 percent of House members seeking re-election in 1988 retained their seats, but how 1.5 percent managed to lose.

The problem, says Bruce Finland, of the Potomac News Service, is that the media have become accustomed to getting House coverage for free. And news organizations are bothered less and less by the fact that a press secretary's releases do not provide an objective, critical account of a congressman's activities.

"The genie is out of the bottle," Finland says. "I don't know of an instance where someone who gets something for free will suddenly turn around and pay for it."

But the "something for free" amounts to a hidden media contribution to the political welfare and safety of every incumbent U.S. representative, good, bad or indifferent. At a time when the media are concerned about their own credibility, this genie is a good candidate for grabbing, squeezing and stuffing—back into the bottle.

ADDITIONAL RESOURCES FOR PART II

Suggested Questions and Discussion Topics

1. In "The Art of Bulldogging Presidents," how does Sam Donaldson sum up his philosophy of reporting on government? Do you agree with his philosophy? Why?
2. In "The Art of Bulldogging Presidents," what does Sam Donaldson mean by suggesting that questions aren't damaging, answers are? Do you agree? Discuss.
3. In "The Media May Devour Democracy," what does Sen. George J. Mitchell say is the main reason the press is causing the growing culture of disbelief?
4. In "The Media May Devour Democracy," Sen. George J. Mitchell suggests that disbelief is dangerous for democracy. What do you think? Discuss.
5. In "Government Secrecy: Easy, Dangerous, and Undemocratic," what does author Jessica Mathews mean by "secrecy impoverishing" analysis? Discuss.
6. In "Government Secrecy: Easy, Dangerous, and Undemocratic," what does Mathews suggest are some of the silly reasons that documents get stamped as "secret"?
7. From Mary Collins' article "News of the Congress, By the Congress," describe three ways in which Congress tries to control news about its activities.
8. According to "News of the Congress, By the Congress," why are reporters dependent on congressional press secretaries?

Suggested Readings

Douglas Cater, *The Fourth Branch of Government.* Boston: Houghton Mifflin, 1959.

Timothy E. Cook, *Governing with the News: The News Media as a Political Institution.* Chicago: University of Chicago Press, 1998.

Everette E. Dennis and Robert W. Snyder, eds., *Covering Congress.* New Brunswick, NJ: Rutgers University Press, 1997.

Sen. J. W. Fulbright, *The Pentagon Propaganda Machine.* New York: Liveright, 1970.

Phil G. Goulding, *Confirm or Deny: Informing the People on National Security.* New York: Harper & Row, 1970.

Michael Grossman and Martha Kumar, *Portraying the President: The White House and the News Media.* Baltimore: Johns Hopkins University Press, 1981.

Stephen Hess, *The Government/Press Connection: Press Officers and Their Offices.* Washington, DC: Brookings Institution, 1984.

Stephen Hess, *The Ultimate Insiders: U.S. Senators in the National Media.* Washington, DC: Brookings Institution, 1986.

Stephen Hess, *The Washington Reporters.* Washington, DC: Brookings Institution, 1981.

Ray E. Hiebert, *The Press in Washington.* New York: Dodd, Mead, 1966.

Ray E. Hiebert and Carlton E. Spitzer, eds., *The Voice of Government.* New York: John Wiley & Sons, 1968.

Shanto Iyengar, *Do the Media Govern? Politicians, Voters, and Reporters in America.* Thousand Oaks, CA: Sage Publications, 1997.

Judith Lichtenberg, *Democracy and Mass Media.* New York: Cambridge University Press, 1990.

John Anthony Maltese, *Spin Control: The White House Office of Communications and the Management of Presidential News.* Chapel Hill, NC: University of North Carolina Press, 1992.

Dale Minor, *The Information War: How the Government and the Press Manipulate, Censor, and Distort the News.* New York: Hawthorn Books, 1970.

Clark Mollenhoff, *Washington Cover-Up.* New York: Doubleday, 1962.

Dan Nimmo and Michael W. Mansfield, *Government and the News Media: Comparative Dimensions.* Waco, TX: Baylor University Press, 1982.

Elaine S. Povich, *Partners & Adversaries: The Contentious Connection Between Congress & the Media.* Arlington, VA: The Freedom Forum, 1996.

William Rivers, *The Adversaries: Politics and the Press.* Boston: Beacon Press, 1970.

John Whale, *Journalism and Government. A British View.* Columbia, SC: University of South Carolina Press, 1972.

Suggested Videos

"Television and the Presidency." Nashville, TN: Freedom Forum First Amendment Center, 1997. (three parts, 30 minutes each)

"The Presidency, the Press, and the People." San Diego, CA: KCBS, 1990. (130 minutes)

Ted Koppel, "Bashing: The Press and the President." *ABC Nightline,* 1986. (30 minutes)

PART · 12
War and the Military

In the clash between the press and the government, the coverage of a war raises some particularly vexing questions. First, governments need to control information more during wartime than at other times. Information about military strategies that gets into enemy hands will certainly damage a war effort. Second, governments usually need to make a special attempt to win support for a military action. War is always costly in lives and property. Why should people make such a sacrifice? Governments must win a war for the minds of their people before they can effectively fight a war against an enemy. Thus, they must promote the war to their citizens, primarily through mass media.

If there is significant opposition to a war, however, the American press feels obligated to tell the public about it. Most American journalists feel strongly that they should never lie or cover up what their government does. If the government makes a mistake, journalists regard it as their responsibility to reveal it to the people. They feel that citizens need to know everything the government does, even when such information might jeopardize that government.

Moreover, wars are fought by two sides, not one, and American journalists are trained to tell both sides of any story. The enemy version is sometimes given equal time and space with the American version. From time to time journalists have been regarded as traitors when they have not blindly supported a government action, but the journalists themselves regard such reporting as faithful to their journalistic traditions.

The problem was not so severe in World War II and the Korean War, the purposes of which were generally well accepted by the people. In addition, print media could be controlled to some extent to serve the government's purposes, perhaps because they were slower and thus easier to manipulate or censor.

The issue came to the fore primarily during Vietnam, the first "TV war." Television was harder to control; it was faster and more compelling. It could bring the war almost instantaneously into the living rooms of all Americans. When citizens for the first time saw on television some of the war's brutality and horror first-hand, many were repulsed and withdrew their support of the war. Some critics say that America lost the war in Vietnam because television damaged public support for it at home.

Since Vietnam, the military has made a greater effort to control the news media as a way of winning the war for people's minds. The military had long paid attention to its public relations as an aspect of a war effort. In the past two decades it has become much more sophisticated about limiting the role of mass media. In the 1970s, the British limited media access to the war in the

Falklands, with considerable success. In the 1980s, Reagan was able to control media coverage of the skirmishes in Grenada and Libya, and in 1990, Bush was able to do so in Panama.

No American war was ever as thoroughly successful from a PR point of view as the Persian Gulf War in 1991. It was a short war, and the mass media would probably not have been so successfully managed by the military had it gone on much longer. But it provided some classic examples of new issues about mass media and the military in a war.

In some respects, mass media themselves have become weapons of modern warfare, and they are being used by both sides.

45

Mass Media as Weapons
of Modern Warfare

RAY ELDON HIEBERT

Editor's Note: Mass communication has become an essential part of modern warfare, and therefore the military has increasingly used public relations in fighting wars today. The Persian Gulf War in 1991 is an excellent example and demonstrates how the military's use of PR techniques successfully managed the news flow.

This article was first presented as the Robert Godlonton Commemorative Media Lecture in Pretoria, South Africa, on March 20, 1991, shortly after the war ended. Much additional information supporting this thesis has been made public since that time. Godlonton, a nineteenth-century South African editor, is regarded as the father of press freedom in that country.

Hiebert, the first American to deliver the Godlonton Lecture, is a professor at the University of Maryland and the editor of this book. This article was published in the *Public Relations Review,* Summer 1991.

We have witnessed, in the war in the Persian Gulf, either history's most impressive use of military weapons, or history's most thorough use of words and images as weapons of war, or both.

As a democratic society, Americans have always believed in the public's right to know, and the press's freedom to seek the truth. We have always felt that the people have a right to learn all the facts about government, to make sure government is serving the people's interests. And to that end we have not wanted government to play too big a role in telling us what is going on. We believe the facts should come from a free and independent press. We believe government should not operate any newspapers, magazines, radio or television stations or any other mass media, lest such ownership and control would allow government to hide or distort the facts in its favor. But that doesn't mean governments should not exercise leadership, because without leadership, including the leadership of public opinion, democracy becomes anarchy.

War provides a good case in point. Wars are waged today by governments, and in democratic societies governments must win public support from their own citizens before they can fight and win a war against the enemy. To win the minds at home in the recent war, the American government launched a public relations campaign on an unprecedented scale, and with unprecedented success. The smart bombs of the war succeeded in part because of smart words.

It is my thesis that mass communication is today an essential part of modern warfare, that public relations is a primary weapon of war—increasingly for all sides. In the Gulf War, both sides attempted to manage the words and images of battle. There is nothing new about that. Propaganda has always been a part of war. What was new about "Desert Storm" was the extent to which the American government and its military concerned itself with fighting the war for public support at home by using all the classic practices of public relations, including political strategies, media relations, community relations, employee relations, and crisis management. There were times, of course, when the practice was not perfect.

WHEN GOVERNMENTS ARE THREATENED

Today, even in democratic societies, governments under threat must exercise political leadership in order to survive. The problems for such leadership sometimes seem almost insurmountable. The French writer Alexis de Tocqueville, a shrewd observer, wrote the following about the new phenomenon of American democracy in his journal in 1831:

> In thus pressing democracy to the utmost limits, we have in actual fact handed over control of society to those who have no interest in stability since they possess and have but little understanding. Also, we have built our social order on ever moving ground. With us, every year, not only do public officials change, but principals, maxims of government and parties succeed to power at an incredible rate. Social standing and wealth are everlastingly caught up in this all-embracing change. There is no continuity in undertaking.[1]

In the war in Vietnam, Americans had relatively little understanding of the government's position, and little or no interest in the stability of the government's role or the continuity of its undertaking. Many blamed the press for this destabilization. Others blamed the government for not assuming better leadership, for not taking charge of the crisis, for not controlling the communication. Many in leadership roles have been saying since Vietnam, "never again."

When the British fought their war in the Falkland Islands, they did take charge. They put the war off limits to the press, moved in quickly and finished the job, before the public back home could destabilize the effort and destroy the continuity needed to get the task done. The British handling of the press in the Falklands War has become the model for all American military action since then.

I would suggest that to insure some continuity, which is essential for stable government, and especially for winning a war, public officials must exercise leadership in winning the collective mind of the people. And political leaders today use public communication and public relations to do just that—to inform, influence, change, or at least neutralize public opinion.[2]

MEDIA RELATIONS FOR A MEDIA EVENT

In many ways, the war in the Gulf was a media event. It was, without doubt, the most widely and certainly most instantaneously covered war in the history of mankind. In no other war had people been able to see the action in real time, at precisely the moment the battle was taking place. Sometimes, in fact, the military depended on mass media reporting to learn what was going on.

Nearly a thousand reporters thronged to Saudi Arabia, hundreds of times more than covered the Allied invasion of Normandy on D-Day during World War II. Newspapers and magazines were saturated with war news and comment. Radio and television made it the major story day after day. CNN provided nearly round-the-clock coverage throughout the war, and the coverage was seen worldwide. I was in a hotel room in Budapest, Hungary, when the war started, and I watched the same CNN coverage of the war that my wife was seeing in Silver Spring, Maryland, back in the United States. If Marshall McLuhan's global village was ever a reality, this was it.

But the news about the war was carefully managed by the government in a variety of ways. First of all, there were security guidelines about what kind of news was too sensitive to be covered, such as troop movements, future operations, and the like. No journalist objected to these kinds of guidelines. But military public relations sometimes went awry, especially when elements of news management seemed to have more to do with political policy than with the military security.

POOLS, ESCORTS, AND CENSORS

The military required the media to "pool" their reports, meaning that only a few reporters could ever visit a sensitive area, and their reporting was then shared with all the media. This certainly gave the government greater control over press access to information. Only a fraction of the journalists, and those mostly from the largest media organizations, were able to qualify for the pools. Unfortunately, reporters who broke the rules and went to forbidden zones on their own were sometimes taken into custody and shipped out of the area. (At least two dozen reporters suffered this fate.)[3]

Today it is standard operating procedure for a public relations person to accompany an official who is giving an interview to the press. The purpose is to help the official with facts and figures and make sure that the interview goes well. This PR policy was adopted by the military in the Gulf, requiring all reporters to be accompanied by an escort officer for all interviews. Sometimes this policy, too, went astray. One *New York Times* reporter had his press credentials taken away because he was conducting, without an escort, an "unauthorized" interview with Saudi shopkeepers 50 miles from the Kuwaiti border.[4]

At the same time, all reports had to be submitted to a "Joint Information Bureau (JIB)," which would review it for sensitive security information. Not a great deal was censored, because reporters were careful. But often copy was delayed, sometimes unconscionably. One reporter writing about an interview with a returning pilot used the word "giddy" to describe him. The escort officer objected, and the story was delayed two days while it was sent to the JIB for a ruling. An overzealous military sometimes found other delaying tactics. They used motorcycles—in an age of high-speed helicopters—to bring back pool reports from the reporters at the front line 600 miles from Riyadh. The long trip meant the news was old by the time the motorcycles arrived with the copy.[5]

Sometimes news subjects put off limits seemed to have little to do with military security. One regulation banned all photographs of coffins arriving at Dover Air Force Base in the States, presumably to reduce the coverage of U.S. casualties. Other facts were classified as top secret that seemed to have little to do with the war. For example, General Norman Schwarzkopf's body weight was a military secret. Photographs of the bombings in Iraq were not given to the press because "it would show the Iraqis how good we were."[6] Of course, the Iraqis had the photographs to begin with. They knew all about the precision of our smart bombs first-hand.

WAR AS CRISIS MANAGEMENT

Crisis management has come to be a very important part of public relations. In the U.S. today, there are at least a dozen current books available on the subject, and everyone in PR is either taking or offering a crash course on dealing with emergencies. It is not surprising that the military, too, should have learned the lessons of crisis management.

The public relations rules for crisis management are relatively simple: tell as much as you can and tell it fast; centralize the source of information with an effective and well-informed spokesman, usually the chief executive; deal with rumors swiftly; make as much available to the press as possible; update information frequently; stay on the record; and never tell a lie.

The military in the Gulf War followed this prescription almost to the letter. They quickly organized regular briefings for the press. They had a bit of trouble at first finding the best spokesman, but they finally settled on General Neal, who played the role brilliantly. Ultimately they found that the commander himself, General Schwarzkopf, was the best briefer of the lot. He had all the information at his fingertips, had an authoritative presence, and was wonderfully articulate in explaining details. In Washington, General Kelly proved to be equally adept as the briefing officer. It is interesting to note that his formal training wasn't in military science; he has a degree in journalism.

In fact, one important element of this war was the high level of intelligence and education of the American military. *Time* magazine noted the "remarkable professionalism . . . exemplified most visibly by the smooth TV performances of top military officers. . . . Intelligent, frank, sometimes eloquent, these men seemed to personify a new class of American military leaders who not only have a thorough grasp of their trade but also demonstrate broad political and worldly sophistication—not to mention PR savvy."[7]

Many of the military officers today have advanced degrees, often doctorates, and that is true as well of the officers whose primary duty is public relations. In the Navy, for example, more than 80 percent of the public affairs officers have advanced degrees, most in the subject of public relations itself.[8] In fact, the Armed Forces have their own post-graduate course, the Defense Information School, where officers and enlisted men and women can get advanced training in public relations.

DEPENDENT AND OVERWHELMED

Thus the military was able to articulate its facts and its point of view in its dealings with the press. Said *Time:* "With little access to the battlefield, reporters had to depend on the daily briefings in Riyadh and Washington for news. Those were handled with extraordinary skill. The briefings were filled with facts and figures (number of missions flown, Scuds fired), and the men who conducted them were cooperative, usually candid and, when it came to estimates of enemy damage, very cautious. The goal was to avoid excessive optimism and reduce expectations."[9]

If anything, the military overwhelmed the press with information. Reporters could not keep up with or digest the enormous quantities of details from briefings and press releases. Of course, all the detail was only that which the military wanted to make public.

One of the cardinal sins of public relations is to tell a lie. In an open marketplace of news, we hold, the truth will always come out, and if you've told a lie, it will ultimately hurt more than help. Of course, there are slips, deliberate and accidental. But for the most part, the press in the Gulf War was never able to catch the military in an outright lie. The reporters had great faith in the veracity of what they were being told. They might have been often overwhelmed with facts about some things, and underwhelmed about others, but they were not the victims often of outright lies.[10]

Reporters looked for lies, suspecting them at every turn. At one point, word got out—it later proved to be from a Saudi official—that six Iraqi helicopters had defected to the Allies. When the helicopters were not immediately found, the press shouted that the government had deliberately lied in order to encourage Iraqi defections. Later, after it was no longer news, it turned out that six "Iraqi" helicopters had indeed flown into Saudi Arabia, but they were in fact American helicopters camouflaged to look like Iraqis, returning from a spy mission.[11]

SOUND BITES AND PHOTO OPS

Gulf War public relations made use of the same techniques that had been so successful in the last presidential election campaign. In the 1988 campaign, the two major candidates, George Bush and Michael Dukakis, both followed a strategy of limiting access by the press to the candidates. Few spontaneous interviews of the candidates were granted to reporters. Tough questions about taxes, government spending, a declining economy, and other hard issues, were never dealt with.

Instead, reporters were allowed to cover carefully prepared and rehearsed speeches. The speeches were written so they would contain pithy statements of the kind that television uses for a "sound bite," a 20- and 30-second snippet of the candidate saying something that sounded important and meaningful for the evening TV news. And newspapers had to settle for these same concocted quotes.

In addition, the candidates would arrange for photo sessions with media photographers and cameramen, carefully staged to convey the proper image to deal with the current problem on the front page or the evening news. Thus, when Dukakis was attacked as a man who had little experience managing a major nation or knew nothing about defense and war, his handlers arranged a "photo op" showing the candidate riding in an army tank. This one backfired, but the sound bite and photo op campaign in general was a public relations success.

These same strategies were brought to the public relations of "Desert Storm." In many ways, this was the world's first war based on sound bites and photo opportunities. What we read were the carefully chosen words and what we saw were the carefully selected images, sanitized of blood and gore and death and destruction.

ORCHESTRATING A SPORTING EVENT

Almost every television news show every day carried pictures of the sleek instruments of war, silver jet fighters, bombers floating through the air like hawks playing a summer breeze, powerful tanks treading through the desert sands. One had to view all this with a mixture of pride and awe and admiration.

The fighting men who got on television were also orchestrated to present the best possible side of the war. When pilots returned from a bombing mission, we got thirty seconds of handsome young men standing in front of their airplanes, and the quotes we heard over and over again were sound bites of about how exhilarated they were, how easy it had been for them to score, how victory was in their grasp. The war was reported as if it were a sporting event and these key players were caught by TV for a few moments during a time-out in the game, a break in the action.

No hard questions were ever asked, or at least the answers were never shown on TV.

Television was allowed frequently to show us the video pictures taken by the cameras in noses of smart bombs. A whole nation watched mesmerized, looking at targets coming into view on the screen and then seeing the explosion. But, naturally, no more pictures followed; the camera was blown up together with the smart bomb and of course the target. The death and destruction that occurred were never shown. At least not until Saddam gave the world some other kinds of pictures. But we'll come back to that later.

COMMUNITY RELATIONS AND EMPLOYEE RELATIONS

The American military did not deal exclusively with the press in Riyadh and Washington in the conduct of its public relations campaign. They properly realized that there were many publics which had to be served. One of these publics was their own troops—soldiers, sailors, airmen and women, and marines who have opinions that need to be informed, influenced, changed, or at least neutralized.

The military has long provided its own employee media—newspapers, magazines, and broadcasts—for troops serving abroad. One of the first things the Americans did was to establish a radio station in Saudi Arabia for its troops, later TV and print media as well. Every navy ship had its own internal closed circuit TV system for information and entertainment.

All of the military people had families back home, and those families help to form opinions. So the military had elaborate home port and hometown news operations. Whenever anything happened to a member of the military— new assignment, special duty, commendation, battle action, or whatever—a news release was generated by computer and targeted at the home port or hometown media of the person involved. Although these releases were not apt to be used by large daily newspapers or major television stations, they were widely picked up by small town dailies and weeklies and local radio.[12]

Most of the personnel in the American military today are older than they were in World War II, Korea, or Vietnam. They are all volunteers, not draftees. They are in the military by their choice, are more professional, and most have families. The military has taken a strong stand on having an effective family re- lations program as one way to maintain loyalty and well-being of its employees.

PUBLIC RELATIONS AND THE OTHER SIDE

The Americans were not only concerned with communicating their message to the citizens and their soldiers. They also sent many messages, directly and indi- rectly, to the rest of the world and especially to the Iraqis. Sometimes those messages literally fell from the sky. We not only dropped bombs, but also hun- dreds of thousands of leaflets, in Arabic, urging the Iraqis to give up, to defect, to turn their backs on Saddam. Unfortunately, when an American reporter asked to see some of these leaflets, he was told that they were classified as se- cret. Just why wasn't he told? Certainly the enemy knew all about them.[13] Who was the potential enemy from whom these secrets must be kept? Could it have been the people back home, who might have destabilized the situation if they had known about these leaflets?

The Allies, of course, were not alone in using information and communica- tion as a weapon in the war. Saddam Hussein thought of himself as a great com- municator, too. He had the ability to have a commanding presence on televi- sion and often used it to his advantage. He liked to perform to the camera. And he understood the dynamics of using public relations on the American public.

After the August invasion, Iraq allowed more than 1,800 journalists from all over the world to work out of Baghdad.[14] Early in the crisis, Saddam got considerable sympathetic coverage. When he was holding hostages from Kuwait in Baghdad, he frequently posed on television with small children of the hostage families. He appeared to be a benign grandfather, patting the chil- dren on the head, holding them on his knee He conducted a well-orches- trated campaign to show himself to be a champion of the Arabs and a victim of unfair U.S. aggression. His army was presented as a formidable, perhaps unbeatable force.

A producer for a U.S. television network said, "It's obvious why they let [foreign reporters] in. It's like when ABC correspondent Sam Donaldson did a piece that really creamed former President Ronald Reagan, and the next day Reagan shook his hand. People don't listen to the words. They see the images. and these guys in Baghdad realize that."[15]

That statement was echoed by an Iraqi official, Sa'doun al Janabi. "We know the Western media, and we know something about what they want, so we try to give it to them. We decided to be open, to answer questions, to tell the truth." Janabi serves as public relations director for the Iraqi Ministry of Information. He speaks fluent English, and from August to February, he held court each day with the hordes of Western reporters who came to his ministry for information. He also carefully monitored the Western coverage coming out of Iraq. At one point, Saddam Hussein was quoted as saying, "We watch CNN, too."[16]

Saddam's biggest public relations coup came when the Allies dropped a smart bomb on a bunker near Baghdad, thinking it was a military operation. But in fact it had been a bomb shelter for families, resulting in the killing and maiming of dozens of women and children. The world's TV cameras were brought to the scene as the bodies were removed from the smoking wreckage, and this became world news.

WAR AS A POLITICAL CAMPAIGN

What is interesting about the recent war is the extent to which it was conducted as a political campaign. Five of eight of President Bush's closest advisors on the war had played major roles in Republican presidential campaigns over the past fifteen years. One of these senior officials told the *Washington Post* that, in the war, they used "the same basic tenets that would be used in managing the closing weeks of an intensely fought presidential campaign."[17] The President and his key advisors all used the language of politics in arguing how answers to Baghdad should be framed and timed. This is what they advised:

> You answer everything quickly and aggressively, put no trust in your opponent, and prevent him from ever gaining the initiative.[18]

They were not talking about the battlefield here; they were talking about the war of words, even though it might sound like military actions. In an age of almost instant communication, it is widely accepted in political campaign circles that charges by opponents must be answered within a few hours, or the charge becomes the dominant and unanswered news story for the better part of a day.

So for example, when the Soviets announced that Iraq had agreed to "unconditional" withdrawal, the White House quickly indicated Bush had serious reservations. Three hours later, officials concluded they needed a more definitive answer to the Soviet initiative and began planning for the next day's announcement of a deadline and demands, and they began putting out the word that the Soviet plan was "unacceptable," lest it remain unchallenged and would begin to gain momentum in Europe, where it was already daytime.

John Sununu, White House Chief of Staff, told the *Washington Post,* "There is an old political maxim that you can't beat somebody with nobody. In the same way, you can't beat a bad plan with no plan. And the President had a real sense—and others did—that we had to put out our plan, our requirements, quickly so the two could be compared. You could not allow the Soviet plan to be the only one in the public domain."[19]

On the last Monday night of the war, when Baghdad Radio reported that Saddam had finally ordered a withdrawal of his troops from Kuwait, the White House immediately put out a statement that "the war would go on." The officials needed to make that clear while the early evening television news programs were still on. An even harsher statement followed for the late evening TV news. As one official said, "We did not want the Baghdad Radio report to hang out [unanswered] for 10 or 12 hours."[20]

THE END GAME

In the end, the Iraqis lost both the military war and the media war. From my point of view, they were not good enough at either. One of Saddam's biggest public relations gaffes of the war was his last minute threat that this would be "the mother of all wars," perhaps the hollowest and flakiest bit of hype since Adolph Hitler's boast of a super race, proving once again that words have to match reality to be effective as public relations weapons.

It must be said, although I haven't said it yet, that words alone will not win a war. All the best public relations in the world may not overcome smart bombs, sophisticated weaponry, and highly trained professional military. But, on the other hand, those weapons alone might no longer win it, either.

We live in a world today where people's opinions count, because they can get translated into action. We also live in a world where the means of communication have become as sophisticated as the means of war. We have "smart media" that can deliver messages to target audiences across local, regional, and national boundaries, across racial, ethnic, and cultural barriers. Unless governments take these developments into consideration, they will fail in exercising the leadership that de Tocqueville found missing in the democratic United States in the early nineteenth century.

The effective use of words and media today, in times of crisis, is just as important as the effective use of bullets and bombs. In the end, it is no longer enough just to be strong. Now it is necessary to communicate. To win a war today, government not only has to win on the battlefield; it must also win the minds of its publics. Or, put in another way, when the government has to win, it also has to explain *why* it has to win. Stability, continuity, and even victory in the long run will only come when both action and communication are effective. The war in the Gulf has just given us a case in point. It may well be a scenario for all future wars to come.

NOTES

1. Alexis de Tocqueville, *Democracy in America,* Bradley ed. (Anchor Books, 1945), first published in 1835.

2. The best simple definition of public relations comes from two leading current practioners, Stan Sauerhaft and Chris Atkins, in their book *Image Wars: Protecting Your Company When There's No Place to Hide* (John Wiley & Sons, 1989, p. 13), i.e., "Public relations is the art and science of creating, altering, strengthening, or overcoming public opinion."

3. Sydney H. Schanberg, "Censoring for Political Security," *Washington Journalism Review,* March 1991, p. 24.

4. Ibid.

5. Interview with Juan Walte, Pentagon correspondent for *USA Today,* March 13, 1991.

6. Ibid.

7. *Time,* March 11, 1991, p. 58.

8. Interview with Gordon Peterson, Deputy Chief of Information, U.S. Navy, March 11, 1991.

9. *Time,* March 11, 1991, p. 56.

10. Interview with Juan Walte, op. cit.

11. Ibid.

12. Interview with Gordon Peterson, op. cit.

13. Interview with Juan Walte, op. cit.

14. *Virginia Pilot and Ledger Star,* December 30, 1990, p. A9.

15. Ibid.

16. Ibid.

17. *Washington Post,* February 27, 1991, p. A27.

18. Ibid.

19. Ibid.

20. Ibid.

46

The Pentagon Position on Mass Media

PETE WILLIAMS

Editor's Note: Whereas the previous article raises some of the issues that might concern a journalist, it is only fair and appropriate to give the government's point of view as well.

This article is the statement made by Pete Williams, the assistant secretary of defense for public affairs. It was given during hearings on the Persian Gulf War conducted by the Committee on Governmental Affairs in the U.S. Senate on February 20, 1991.

Some of the most enduring news reports during World War II came from Edward R. Murrow, who stood on a London rooftop and reported the German bombing raids. Fifty years later, Americans watched reporters on the rooftops of hotels in Riyadh and Dhahran—and their colleagues with gas masks on in Tel Aviv—describing incoming Scud missile attacks from Iraq.

It was the writer Henry Tomlnson who said, "The war the generals always get ready for is the previous one." The same might be said of journalists: the coverage arrangements for military operations in the Persian Gulf are frequently compared to what's remembered from Vietnam, Korea, or World War II.

But Edward R. Murrow's proposal to talk without a script so concerned the military that he had to record a series of trial runs on phonograph discs. He submitted them for approval, but they were lost. So he had to record six more before he persuaded the authorities that he could speak off the cuff without violating the censorship rules. Today, Arthur Kent, Sam Donaldson, Eric Engberg, and Charles Jaco can describe what they see—and show it on television—with no military censorship of any kind. And there are two other notable differences: they are live, and, at least in the case of CNN, their reports can be seen by the commanders of enemy forces just as easily as they can be seen by American viewers at home in their living rooms.

Operation Desert Storm isn't taking place in the jungles of Vietnam, or the hills of Korea, or across the continents and oceans of World War II. The campaign on the Arabian Peninsula has been designed to get a specific and unique job done. The press arrangements are also suited to the peculiar conditions there. But our goal is the same as those of our predecessors—to get as much information as possible to the American people about their military without jeopardizing the lives of the troops or the success of the operation.

ORIGIN OF THE PERSIAN GULF PRESS ARRANGEMENTS

Saddam Hussein stunned the world when his troops rolled across the northern border of Kuwait last August 2nd. Within five hours, his army had taken Kuwait City. And from that day forward, the number of Iraqi troops in occupied Kuwait continued to grow and to move south, stopping only at Kuwait's southern border with Saudi Arabia.

That weekend, August 5th, President Bush sent [Defense] Secretary Cheney to Saudi Arabia for discussions with King Fahd on how best to defend Saudi Arabia and the stability of the Persian Gulf. As history now knows, the first U.S. forces began to arrive a few days after their meeting, joining U.S. Navy ships already in the region. On Wednesday, as the first U.S. Air Force F-15's landed on sovereign Saudi territory, there were no western reporters in the Kingdom. We urged the Saudi government to begin granting visas to U.S. news organizations, so that reporters could cover the arrival of the U.S. military.

On Friday of that week, Secretary Cheney again called Prince Bandar, the Saudi Ambassador to the United States, to inquire about the progress for issuing visas. Prince Bandar said the Saudis were studying the question but agreed in the meantime to accept a pool of U.S. reporters if the U.S. military could get them in. So we activated the DOD National Media Pool, a structure that had been in use since 1985.

THE NATIONAL MEDIA POOL

The pool was set up after the 1983 U.S. military operation in Grenada. While Grenada was a military success, it was a journalistic disaster, because reporters were kept off the island until the fighting was over. So a retired army major general, Winant Sidle, from whom this committee will hear later today, was asked to head up a panel of military officers and journalists to work out a plan for news coverage of future military operations. The result of their work was the Department of Defense National Media Pool, a rotating list of correspondents, photographers, and technicians who could be called up on short notice to cover the early stages of military missions.

It was this pool that covered the U.S. Navy's escort of oil tankers in the Persian Gulf in 1987. Its first big test in ground combat came in December of 1989, during Operation Just Cause in Panama. Just Cause was a mixed success for the pool. It arrived within four hours of when the shooting started, but it took too long to get reporters to the scene of the action. I think we learned some important lessons from what happened in Panama, and we've applied them to what's going on in the Gulf.

The true purpose of the National Media Pool is to enable reporters to cover the earliest possible action of a U.S. military operation in a remote area where there is no other presence of the American press, while still protecting the element of surprise—an essential part of what military people call operational security. Of course, Operation Desert Shield was no secret. The President made a public announcement that he was ordering U.S. forces to the Gulf. But because there were no western reporters in Saudi Arabia, we flew in the DOD media pool.

FIRST REPORTERS CAME ON THE DOD POOL

We moved quickly, once we received permission from the Saudi government on Friday, August 10th. We notified the news organizations in the pool rotation that Friday night. They brought in their passports Saturday morning, and I took them to the Saudi embassy myself that afternoon, where the appropriate staff has been brought in to issue the necessary visas. One reporter had run out of pages in his passport, so we carried it across town so that the State Department could add some more.

The pool left Andrews Air Force base early Sunday morning, August 12th, stopping off to see the U.S. Central Command operation in Tampa, Florida. The reporters interviewed General Schwarzkopf, who had not yet moved his headquarters to Riyadh. So the press pool got to Saudi Arabia before the commander of the operation had even set up shop there. The reporters arrived Monday afternoon, August 13th, and continued to act as a pool until August 26th. After the pool began filing its reports, the Saudis started to issue visas to other reporters. But the news organizations in the Pentagon pool asked that we keep it going until the visa picture cleared up.

Jay Peterzell was *Time* magazine's representative on the pool. Afterward, he wrote this: "The Pentagon people worked hard to keep the press in the country." And he offered this assessment:

> The pool did give U.S. journalists a way of getting into Saudi Arabia and seeing at least part of what was going on at a time when there was no other way of doing either of those things. Also, in the first two weeks after the wave of TV, newspaper, and magazine correspondents flooded into the country, they did not produce any story that was essentially different from what we in the pool had filed.

Starting with those initial 17—representing AP, UPI, Reuters, CNN, National Public Radio, *Time,* Scripps-Howard, the *Los Angeles Times,* and the *Milwaukee Journal*—the number of reporters, editors, photographers, producers, and technicians grew to nearly 800 by December. Except during the first two weeks of the pool, those reporters all filed their stories independently, directly to their own news organizations. They visited ships at sea, air bases. Marines up north, and soldiers training in the desert. They went aboard AWACS radar warning planes. They quoted generals who said their forces were ready and privates who said they were not. They wrote about helicopter pilots crashing into the sand, because they couldn't judge distances in the flat desert light. And reporters described the remarkable speed with which the U.S. military moved so many men and women to the Gulf with so much of their equipment.

PLANNING FOR COMBAT COVERAGE

The mission given U.S. forces in Operation Desert Shield was to deter further aggression from Iraq and to defend Saudi Arabia if deterrence failed. After the President in mid November announced a further buildup in U.S. forces, to give the coalition a true offensive option, my office began working on a plan that would allow reporters to cover combat while maintaining the operational security necessary to assure tactical surprise and save American lives.

One of the first concerns of news organizations in the Pentagon press corps was that they did not have enough staff in the Persian Gulf to cover hostilities. Since they did not know how the Saudi government would respond to their request for more visas, and since they couldn't predict what restrictions might be imposed on commercial air traffic in the event of a war, they asked us whether we'd be willing to use a military plane to take in a group of reporters to act as journalistic reinforcements. We agreed to do so.

A U.S. Air Force C-141 cargo plane left Andrews Air Force base on January 17th, the morning after the bombing began, with 127 news media personnel on board. That plane left at the onset of hostilities, during the most intensive airlift since the Berlin blockade. The fact that senior military commanders dedicated one of their cargo airplanes to the job of transporting another 127 journalists to Saudi Arabia demonstrated the military's commitment to take reporters to the scene of the action so they could get the story out to the American people.

The plan for combat coverage was not drawn up in a vacuum. We worked closely with the military and with the news media to develop a plan that would meet the needs of both. We had several meetings at the Pentagon with the bureau chiefs of the Pentagon press corps. We talked with the reporters who cover the military regularly. And we consulted with some of the people you'll hear from later today—General Sidle and Mr. Hoffman—and several of my predecessors in the public affairs office at the Pentagon. Because an important part of our planning was working with the news media, our drafts and proposals frequently became public. We did our planning in Macy's window, which meant that our false starts and stumbles were in full view.

SAFEGUARDING MILITARY SECURITY

The main concern of the military is that information not be published which would jeopardize a military operation or endanger the lives of the troops who must carry it out. The preamble to the rules of reporters covering World War II summarized the issue by saying that editors, in wondering what can be published, should ask themselves, "Is this information I would like to have if I were the enemy?"

In formulating the ground rules and guidelines for covering Operation Desert Storm, we looked at the rules developed in 1942 for World War II, at those handed down by General Eisenhower's chief of staff for the reporters who covered the D-Day landings, and at the ground rules established by General MacArthur for covering the Korean war. We carefully studied the rules drawn up for covering the war in Vietnam.

The rules are not intended to prevent journalists from reporting on incidents that might embarrass the military or to make military operations look sanitized. Instead, they are intended to prevent publication of details that could jeopardize a military operation or endanger the lives of US troops.

Some of the things that must not be reported are:

- Details of future operations,
- Specific information about troop strengths or locations,
- While a specific operation is underway, the details of troop movements or tactics,
- Specific information on missing or downed airplanes or ships while search and rescue operations are underway, and
- Information on operational weaknesses that could be used against U.S. forces.

American reporters understand the reasoning behind these ground rules. They are patriotic citizens, and they don't want anything they write to endanger lives. The ground rules are the least controversial aspect of the coverage plan for the war in the Persian Gulf. Mr. Chairman, I'd like to ask that a copy of the ground rules and the guidelines be inserted at this point in the record.

THE GROUND RULE APPEAL PROCESS

The reporters covering World War II wrote their stories and submitted them to a military censor. The censors cut out anything they felt broke the rules and sent the stories on. The decisions of the censors were final. There is no such system of censorship in Operation Desert Storm. There is, instead, a procedure that allows us to appeal to news organizations—before the harm is done—when we think material in their stories would violate the ground rules. And the final decisions belong to journalists.

Stories written by reporters who are out with troops in the field are reviewed by military public affairs officers to ensure troop safety and operational security, then sent on to the press center in Dhahran, Saudi Arabia for release. If, after talking things over with the reporter, the field public affairs officer believes information in a story violates the ground rules, public affairs officers at the press center review it before release. If they, too, believe the story would break the ground rules, they appeal it to us at the Pentagon for our opinion.

If we, too, think there's a problem, we call bureau chiefs or editors stateside and discuss the story with them. We understand that news must move quickly, and we act as fast as we can. Our appeal process is intended only to allow us to discuss potential ground rule violations with editors and bureau chiefs and to remind them of the need to protect sensitive information. But unlike a system of censorship, the system now in place leaves the final decision to publish or broadcast in the hands of journalists, not the military.

Since Operation Desert Storm began on January 16th, over 820 print pool reports have been written. Of those, only five have been submitted for our review in Washington. We quickly cleared four of them. The fifth appeal came to us over the weekend, involving a story that dealt in considerable detail with the methods of intelligence operations in the field. We called the reporter's editor-in-chief, and he agreed that the story should be changed to protect sensitive intelligence procedures. This aspect of the coverage plan is also working well.

Only the pool stories, from reporters in the field, are subject to this review, not live television and radio reports or the thousands of other stories written in Dhahran and Riyadh, based on pool reports, original reporting, and the military briefings.

GETTING ACCESS TO THE TROOPS

As the number of troops in the desert grew, so did the number of reporters to cover them. The U.S. and international press corps went from zero on August 2nd, to 17 on the first pool, rising to 800 by December. Most of those reporters, the good ones anyway, want to be out where the action is, just as they've done in previous conflicts. But with hundreds of fiercely independent reporters seeking to join up with combat units, we concluded that when the combat started, we'd have to rely on pools.

Before the air phase of the operation began a month ago, news organizations were afraid that we wouldn't get the job done. They reminded us of their experience in Panama. But as viewers, readers, and listeners know, we had the pools in place before the operation started. Reporters were on an aircraft carrier in the Red Sea to witness the launching of air strikes, onboard a battleship in the Persian Gulf that fired the first cruise missiles ever used in combat, on the air force bases where the fighter planes and bombers were taking off around the clock, and with several ground units in the desert.

Carl Rochelle of CNN was asked on the air if he felt he had been allowed access to everything he wanted onboard the ships, and he said, "I must tell you I am more satisfied with the pool shoot I just came off than any of the others I've been on." Four days into the air campaign, Molly Moore of the *Washington Post* said, "It's gone a lot smoother than any of us thought."

Those first days were not without problems. We know of cases where stories were approved in the field only to be delayed for over a day on their trip back to the press center in Dhahran. The first stories written about the stealth fighters were, for some reason, sent all the way back to the F-117's home base in Nevada to be cleared. I'm sure some of the reporters you'll hear from later today will have examples of their own.

The biggest complaint from journalists right now is that more of them want to get out into the field. They are worried about how much access they'll have to the Army and the Marines in the event the President decides to proceed with the next phase of the campaign, intensifying action on the ground. And here's where the contrasts with World War II and Vietnam are especially strong.

ACCESS TO THE GROUND TROOPS

Unlike World War II, this will not be an operation in which reporters can ride around in jeeps going from one part of the front to another, or like Vietnam where reporters could hop a helicopter to specific points of action. If a ground war begins on the Arabian Peninsula, the battlefield will be chaotic and the action will be violent. This will be modern, intense warfare. Reporters at the front will have to be in armored vehicles or on helicopters. They'll have to carry their own gas masks and chemical protective suits along with all their other gear. Those with front line troops will be part of a highly mobile operation. It will be deadly serious business, and our front line units simply will not have the capacity to accommodate large numbers of reporters.

To cover the conflict, reporters will have to be part of a unit, able to move with it. Each commander has an assigned number of vehicles with only so many seats. While he can take care of the reporters he knows are coming, he cannot keep absorbing those who arrive on their own, unexpectedly, in their own rented four wheel drives. The pool system allows us to tell the divisional commanders how many reporters they'll be responsible for. And the reporters in these pools are allowed to stay with the military units they're covering, learning as much as they can about the unit's plans and tactics.

Our latest count shows that over 1400 reporters, editors, producers, photographers, and technicians are now registered with the joint information bureaus in Dhahran and Riyadh, representing the US and the international press. Not all of them want to go to the front. But more want to go than we can possibly accommodate. That's why we've had to rely on pools of reporters—rotating groups whose stories and pictures are available to all.

Of course, the ground war hasn't started yet. U.S. military units are repositioning, some of them moving nearly every day. And if the ground war does start, it won't be like Vietnam, with minor skirmishes here and there and a major offensive every now and then. It will be a set piece operation, as carefully orchestrated as possible. In this sense, it will be like D-Day. It's useful to remember that 461 reporters were signed up at the Supreme Headquarters, Allied Expeditionary Force to cover D-Day. Of that number, only 27 US reporters actually went ashore with the first wave of forces.

So the situation on the ground in the Arabian Peninsula is a little like the picture before D-Day, with reporters waiting for the action to start. Even so, when Desert Storm began, 43 reporters were already out with ground units, and the number has been growing. By the end of this week, 100 reporters will be with Army units, 33 with the Marines on land, and 18 more will be out with the Marines on amphibious ships. That's in addition to the 19 covering the

Navy on ships at sea, the 14 who have been roving around to air bases, covering the Air Force part of the campaign, and eight more covering the medical part of the story. So that's a total of 192 reporters who will be out with combat forces by the end of the week.

POOLS ARE A COMPROMISE

The news business is an intensely competitive one. Journalists are accustomed to working on their own. The best are especially independent. In the setup imposed now in the Persian Gulf, each correspondent files a story that becomes available to everyone else. Pools rub reporters the wrong way, but there is simply no way for us to open up a rapidly moving front to reporters who roam the battlefield. We believe the pool system does three things: it gets reporters out to see the action, it guarantees that Americans at home get reports from the scene of the action, and it allows the military to accommodate a reasonable number of journalists without overwhelming the units that are fighting the enemy.

The system we have now in Operation Desert Storm—with two briefings a day in Riyadh and one in the Pentagon, pools of reporters out with the troops, a set of clear ground rules, and a procedure of ground rule appeal—is intended to permit the most open possible coverage of a new kind of warfare. When it's all over, we very much want to sit down with representatives of the military and the news media to see how well it worked and how it might be improved.

I cannot deny that there have been problems. I know reporters are frustrated that they can't all get out to see the troops. But I believe the system we have now is fair, that it gets a reasonable number of journalists out to see the action, and that the American people will get the accounting they deserve of what their husbands and wives, and sons and daughters, are doing under arms half a world away.

When reporters arrived at General Eisenhower's headquarters in 1944, they were handed a book called *Regulations for War Correspondents.* In the foreword, he spelled out in three sentences the logic for the kind of system I've described to you today. Here's what he said to those journalists: "The first essential in military operations is that no information of value should be given to the enemy. The first essential in newspaper work and broadcasting is wide-open publicity. It is your job and mine to try to reconcile these sometimes diverse considerations."

47

Missed Story Syndrome

KATE MCKENNA

Editor's Note: Not only was the Persian Gulf War largely reported from the government's point of view, but some of its aftermath was not fully reported, either. The media largely ignored medical problems stemming from the war. Many journalists feel that news media should have pushed the Pentagon harder on this issue before an embarrassed Defense Department made a public announcement, forcing the journalists into action.

In this article, Kate McKenna searches for answers to why this important story was missed and delayed. She concludes that both the press and the government bungled.

McKenna is a free-lance writer who has written about Gulf War syndrome for *Playboy* and *People* magazines, and she is a frequent contributor about media to the *American Journalism Review*, in which this article was published in May 1997. It is reprinted with permission.

It was a warm, sleepy Friday in June, just the kind of afternoon to sneak out of the newsroom early and get a jump on the weekend. When word came that there would be a late-afternoon Pentagon press conference, the timing seemed suspicious to David Martin, who has covered the beat for CBS since 1983. "That," Martin says, "seems to be when bad news gets delivered in Washington."

And so it was on this Friday, June 21, 1996. After five years of steady and at times indignant denials from every corner of the Pentagon, Department of Defense officials came before the press to announce a dramatic reversal of their position on U.S. troop exposures during the Persian Gulf War. The government's repeated statements to Congress and Desert Storm veterans had been wrong: Chemical weapons had in fact been present on the Iraqi battlefield. Hundreds of troops—possibly more—may have been exposed during the 1991 demolition of the huge enemy ammunition depot called Khamisiyah, where nerve and mustard agents were stored. Other possible incidents of exposure also were under investigation.

Patrick J. Sloyan, *Newsday*'s senior Washington correspondent, was stunned. And a little angry. "It was, 'WHAT???!!'" he says. "Remember, the

Pentagon had been denying this the whole time. And I don't mean denying it cautiously. They denied it sweepingly: 'It did not happen.'"

Until that point, Sloyan hadn't written a word about the baffling illnesses that have plagued many veterans of the Persian Gulf War or about the possibility that some veterans had been exposed to chemical agents. Nor had many reporters in that Pentagon briefing room. The health problems of Gulf War veterans—tens of thousands of whom had been reporting symptoms ranging from muscle fatigue to rashes to neurological problems—had not emerged as a major national issue. That was about to change in a hurry.

Why the abrupt Pentagon reversal? There were a number of reasons, among them the resurfacing of a 1991 United Nations report, seemingly filed by U.S. officials and forgotten years before, describing the presence of chemical weapons at Khamisiyah. At the briefing, top Pentagon spokesman Kenneth Bacon and Assistant Defense Secretary Stephen Joseph cited "new information" as the reason for the turnabout.

Reporters raced for the phones. Suddenly, the Gulf War was a hot story again.

"ALL IN THEIR HEADS"

For more than five years after the conflict, the Pentagon maintained that U.S. troops had not been exposed to chemical weapons. Even as hundreds, then thousands, then tens of thousands of Gulf War soldiers reported health problems, the Defense Department did not budge. DOD officials had commissioned a special Defense Science Board task force to study the matter. It concluded that there was no evidence of the presence of chemical weapons on the Gulf War battlefield—and certainly no evidence that troops had been exposed.

Since the veterans had not been exposed to them, chemical weapons could not be making soldiers sick. So what was? Defense officials said all of the vaccines the vets had received, including nerve-agent pretreatment pills, were safe. They largely ruled out many of the pollutants the vets had encountered from oil well fires and the like.

The long-standing answer? Veterans must simply be suffering from stress-related ailments; it was "all in their heads."

The Pentagon retreat, says *New York Times* reporter Philip Shenon, "changed everything. First, they said there may have been chemical exposure, and secondly, they left open the possibility that there could be health consequences as a result."

No one has established a definitive link between chemical weapons and the ailments that have plagued the veterans. But the fact that the deadly agents had been present in the desert war zone, and that the Pentagon denials had been completely off base, transformed the problems of the veterans into a major news story.

Why hadn't anyone been listening?

WHY WAS THE STORY MISSED?

After the Gulf War, the press coverage was harshly criticized. There was a feeling that many reporters simply had written what they had been spoon-fed, that the media's vaunted skepticism had been overwhelmed by patriotic fervor.

And now, it seemed, the same thing had happened in coverage of Gulf War illness. Why did it take so long for the mainstream media to see this as a major story? Why had much of the press simply accepted the Pentagon line? Why did an issue resulting from our last major global conflict remain the near-exclusive domain of a handful of local and regional reporters for five years?

Certainly, there's little controversy about most of the chemical exposure the 700,000 U.S. soldiers encountered during the war: billowing benzene from oil well fires, diesel-soaked drinking and shower water, pesticide-coated uniforms and careless use of insecticides to ward off disease-carrying sandflies. Depleted uranium lay exposed across the battle-fields. Troops spit up black oily substances and sneezed what looked like axle grease. But the DOD and CIA vehemently ruled out the possibility of exposure to chemical weapons during Operation Desert Storm.

Yet in six months, the Pentagon went from stridently insisting that *no* soldiers had been exposed to chemical weapons in the Gulf War to admitting that 300 or 400 may have been exposed, later upping that figure to over 20,000. It's now clear that military intelligence had known of the presence of chemical weapons (although not, officials say, that U.S. troops had been exposed to them) since 1991, and that years of Pentagon statements smacked of, at best, misinformation, at worst, lies. What's more, key wartime records are missing, their loss attributed to a computer virus that seemed to only infect records from the week of weapons destruction at Khamisiyah.

If you talk to journalists who have watched this story develop, you'll find widespread agreement on one matter: The media should have pushed the Pentagon harder before the June 21 announcement. But there's little consensus about how the press has played catch-up since then. In particular, the *New York Times* and *Washington Post* have taken dramatically differing approaches to the question of what might have made the veterans sick.

SOME EFFORTS WERE MADE

Gulf War Veterans groups have long maintained that the Pentagon knew more than it was saying. Since 1992, it's been their rallying cry—heard over the years by only a few members of the press, notably by reporters at the *Birmingham News,* the *Dallas Morning News,* the *Hartford Courant* and Gannett News Service. Their stories played big regionally, but couldn't crack the Pentagon's facade—or muster much national attention.

In Birmingham, Dave Parks started reporting in 1992 on local veterans who were sick with health problems that seemed "mysterious"—except that their symptoms began soon after the start of Operation Desert Storm on January 16, 1991 (see "Tracking Gulf War Illness," page 31). The veterans described in detail an apparent chemical weapons attack near their camp at the Port of Jubayl in Saudi Arabia and said that their commanders had ordered them not to discuss it. Immediately after the attack, the Seabees said, they experienced a variety of symptoms: Some felt a burning sensation on their skin, some felt their lips go numb, some had their breathing passages clog up. Later, the veterans said, they were variously plagued by respiratory problems, dizziness, blackouts, rashes, muscle aches, fatigue.

Parks, joined by the paper's Washington correspondent, Michael Brumas, talked to veterans, doctors and government officials, trying to find out why these veterans were sick. Parks' stories explored a variety of possible causes. Brumas was told about the presence of chemical weapons in the Gulf theater during interviews in Paris and Prague.

Ed Timms and Steve McGonigle of the *Dallas Morning News* interviewed sick local veterans, including one who returned from the Gulf with a life-threatening sensitivity to chemicals. (Today, he's under a doctor's care, living in a sterilized glass chamber.) Thomas D. "Dennie" Williams of the *Hartford Courant* reported on defective Army equipment, including chemical masks and suits, and interviewed sick veterans whose lives had depended on them.

Brian Cabell of CNN, which gave Gulf illnesses more air time than the three major networks, quickly followed up on Parks' interviews with the Seabees and also reported on a New Orleans doctor who had had some success treating Gulf vets.

BUT MOST WERE SPORADIC

But most news outlets covered the issue sporadically, running spot news stories after a hearing or the release of a report.

"There was never any follow-up," says James J. Tuite III, a former congressional staffer and now director of the Gulf War Research Foundation. "You'd get the initial flash in the mainstream press, but unless you continue to do something spectacular, you're not on the radar screens anymore."

And those short attention spans had an effect, as cyclical news coverage raised and lowered public expectations for answers about Gulf War illness. Everyone seemed to be searching for the magic bullet. First, it was oil well fires. But a study would show that that didn't explain everybody's problems. Next it was leishmaniasis, a disease carried by desert sandflies. But fewer than 40 veterans were found to actually have leishmaniasis. Then it was depleted uranium; again, not every sick soldier had been exposed.

"Each time we went through this, it seemed harder to get Congress or the general public or the media to focus on it," says Phil Budahn, media relations manager of the American Legion. "And that's where the Dave Parks and the Dennie Williams of the world did an amazing service, because they were able to keep the issue alive by telling the stories of veterans in their areas and tracking their cases. They were also devoting the resources that, frankly, the *New York Times* and *Washington Post* weren't."

The few who took the time to investigate found there was plenty lurking beneath the surface. When the DOD reported that its medical exams of

10,000 Gulf War veterans showed the soldiers were no sicker than the general population, the *Courant*'s Williams posed a follow-up question: Exactly whom were the sick soldiers being compared to? It took nearly three months of pushing before the Pentagon admitted that the "general population" used as a comparative group for the Gulf War fighting force, mostly men in their 30s, was a group of mostly women over 60.

But generally, the press simply printed what the DOD said. "Reporters would just see the DOD study come out and they'd write their little stories: Here's what the DOD program is, some quotes; here's what the veterans have to say about it: They say it's crap," Williams says.

In the absence of national media interest, a few energetic veterans became investigative journalists themselves. They hit the phones, solicited expert testimony and held their own hearings. More important, they filed Freedom of Information Act requests and fed key documents—wartime military logs showing reports of mustard and nerve gas at the front—to the press and Congress. Their persistence prompted several congressional investigations of Gulf War illness.

The Senate Banking Committee's hearings were the first public forums to raise the question of low-level chemical exposure as a possible cause of Gulf War illness. The committee also looked into whether a chemical weapons attack in the Port of Jubayl could have made some veterans sick, as the *Birmingham News* had suggested. The senators probed whether nerve-agent pretreatment pills—actually nerve agents themselves—taken by veterans as protection against possible chemical exposure may have caused neurological damage. And they heard the anguished appeals of veterans' family members: wives who said they were also showing symptoms of "gulf war syndrome" or wondered if their children's birth defects were connected to their husbands' sickness.

But by the end of 1994 the investigations had ended inconclusively. Once again it fell to the veterans to try to encourage the media to take their health woes seriously. But at the national level, this was an uphill struggle.

COMPLEXITIES WERE DISCOURAGING

Like many major newspapers, the *New York Times* published few stories on Gulf War illness—less than a dozen from 1993 until the Pentagon announcement last June. It generally ran Associated Press stories on DOD or National Institutes of Health reports ("Health Panel Finds No Single Cause for Gulf War Veterans' Ills") or the occasional staff-written piece on spot news. But it did little serious enterprise reporting on the subject.

The *Los Angeles Times* largely relied on spot news stories on Senate investigations and Pentagon reports, although it also did some enterprise pieces. The paper reported on an unreleased Senate survey that found a high number of spouses also exhibited symptoms of "Gulf War syndrome." In another story it examined miscarriages and birth defects among Gulf War families. But there was little follow-up.

The *Washington Post* followed the story more consistently than most of the national media. The paper also devoted a lot of space to a thoughtful three-part series in 1994 by science writer David Brown. Brown's series gave an overview of possible Gulf War exposures, including exposure to environmental toxins and stressful situations. He also tended to debunk what the veterans were saying and reflect the Pentagon view that there was no evidence to show Gulf War veterans were suffering from anything but stress.

"Years after the fact, these exposures can't be reproduced experimentally," says Brown, who has a medical degree. "So you have to look at, what do the statistics show? What are the biological possibilities? What can be gleaned from general knowledge in medicine about toxicity of certain substances?"

The complexity of such questions—and the time and investment it would take to sort through them—no doubt discouraged many reporters and editors. After all, scientists had never before studied what happens when 700,000 people are exposed to a multitude of chemicals, including pesticides, multiple vaccines and possibly nerve or mustard agents.

"I don't think newsrooms ever said, 'Ah, let's take a pass on that story. We don't believe these guys,'" says Drex Heikes, a *Los Angeles Times* assignment editor in Washington. "But Congress was getting into it, they had subpoena power, they were bringing in witnesses, they were truly going after this. So you kind of see that one's getting done, that's not where we need to be spending our resources. In hindsight, not a great decision—because there was something more there."

SOME COVERAGE HAD IMPACT

There is no reason to think that more aggressive coverage would have solved the mystery. We may not know for years precisely which, if any, battlefield poisons made the veterans sick. But more media attention probably would have forced the government to take the situation more seriously.

"It would have been nice to have had more coverage early," says Norm Brewer, who began covering Gulf War illness for Gannett News Service in late 1993, "because it seems like, since the briefing on Khamisiyah, the weight of all the new coverage resulted in the Pentagon and the Veterans Administration taking a much more serious look at what could be happening here."

Not that the issue was entirely ignored. The occasional magazine article and infrequent network news spot would examine the plight of the veterans. The AP and Reuters filed bread-and-butter stories on congressional hearings and government studies. Those hearings and Pentagon announcements might occasionally crop up on the network news shows, and maybe rate a segment on a morning news program.

CNN was the only network providing regular coverage of the issue. The veterans and their illnesses became grist for the likes of Leeza Gibbons and Montel Williams.

But pieces like those by *Nightline* and *People* magazine on Gulf War families whose postwar children were born with birth defects did have impact. They attracted the attention of Hillary Rodham Clinton in 1995, and her concern led to the formation of the Presidential Advisory Committee on Gulf War Veterans' Illnesses, which began looking into what could be making soldiers sick.

The veterans' plight also caught the interest of *60 Minutes* anchor Ed Bradley. "This issue was something that was worth saying, 'Let's look into this and see if there's anything to it.'" Bradley says. "Instead, all we got really was obfuscation from the Pentagon." A *60 Minutes* segment featuring interviews with veterans aired in March 1995.

Intrigued by this multifaceted subject—with its battlefield drama, postwar dilemmas and the pathos of sick veterans desperately searching for answers— Bradley wondered why the press wasn't jumping all over the story. "I don't want to be critical of my colleagues, and there have been a few reporters who have been persistent in going after it," Bradley says. "But, generally, it hasn't been a hot-button issue and for the life of me, I don't know why."

TALKING ONLY TO GENERALS

Why were the big national newspapers and the networks so slow to embrace the story of Gulf War illness?

Birmingham's Dave Parks has a simple answer. "The Washington media just didn't have access to the information we had," he says. "They didn't have a parade of guys going through their newsroom going, 'I'm sick. Aren't you going to do something to help me?'" He adds, "The snowball was rolling here, it wasn't rolling there."

His Gulf War reporting partner agrees. "This was not an inside-the-Beltway story," says Brumas. "It was big where sick veterans live and work. And since the Department of Defense was not admitting anything on this, there was nowhere for most Washington media to go."

What the DOD was saying, and what much of the media were repeating, was that the illnesses were probably due to stress. No one, not in the mainstream press and certainly not in the military, was considering the possibility of nerve-agent poisoning at below lethal levels or the dangerous interaction of chemicals from all of those battlefield toxins.

Says Rep. Christopher Shays (R-CT), chairman of a House subcommittee that looked into the subject, "The Washington crowd was pretty much asleep. The media wasn't listening to veterans, and that goes for Congress as well. Congress had hearings, then just kind of let up on them. And one reason why is that the media wasn't paying attention either."

And perhaps the Washington press corps was simply too sophisticated for its own good. "Maybe the problem is that the major outlets all have Pentagon reporters," says Phil Budahn of the American Legion. "I don't see that as an indication that they were all co-opted. But they were talking to the generals, the military experts, who were saying, 'If these soldiers were really hit by nerve gas, they'd be dead immediately, not sick years later.' They were not thinking about low-level chemical exposures or multiple chemical exposures or synergistic interactions."

And there's the question of a news peg. "This is a story that's been going on for a while," says *Nightline* producer Leroy Sievers. "Short of saying, 'These guys have been sick, they're still sick and we still don't know what the answer is' . . . the question is, why do this now?"

Nightline has done three stories on Gulf War illness, one before the Khamisiyah announcement and two since. "It's really one of those stories that can suck you in," Sievers says. "It's incredibly compelling, it really breaks your heart. But trying to go one step past that is when it became incredibly difficult . . . and incredibly complicated."

Philip Shenon, who was relatively new to the Pentagon beat when he started covering the Gulf War story for the *New York Times* last summer, offers another explanation for the lack of interest. "Maybe the people who've been able to jump on this story for years accepted the conventional wisdom," Shenon says. "And the conventional wisdom, as we've learned in the course of the last year, was largely incorrect."

MAKING THE STORY EASIER

When Pentagon officials revealed last June that there was no longer any doubt that chemical weapons had been present on the battlefield, later admitting they had had that information for years, another, less complicated story line emerged. No longer was it a medical mystery; now it seemed like a good old-fashioned cover-up.

"That's a whole lot easier for a newspaper to cover," says Heikes of the *Los Angeles Times.* "That's much more familiar and much easier for us non-scientists to sort out. So at that point, you have a lot more media that became comfortable with the story, and there were then indications that there would be a payoff from great investments of time."

Still, it wasn't until six weeks after the Pentagon's announcement that the *New York Times* began covering the story in a major way. Shenon reported on dozens of veterans who had been stationed near the Khamisiyah chemical munitions blast, as well as on sick Gulf War troops who had reported apparent chemical weapons attacks. He was listening to the veterans, just as reporters at the *Birmingham News,* the *Hartford Courant* and Gannett News Service had done. But there was a difference—this was the *New York Times* giving voice to the veterans' theories and fears.

"Once Phil Shenon started writing about this, he validated the story," says Budahn. "There's still that horrible pack instinct among even major national media. They feel uncomfortable doing the story simply because it's in the *Birmingham News,* even if it has national consequences. But when an issue is being played on page one of the *New York Times,* the rest of the media sits up and pays attention."

And for television, there was finally video: Former Army paratrooper Brian Martin's amateur footage of the demolition at Khamisiyah added a "Rodney King" element to the story. You could actually see the rockets shooting out of the giant black plumes of smoke in that Iraqi desert—with soldiers in T-shirts standing nearby.

While the *New York Times* put several reporters on the story, it was the work of Shenon that attracted the most attention. One important Shenon story included an interview with Dr. Joshua Lederberg, a Nobel laureate, about a 1994 report by the Defense Science Board. The so-called "Lederberg Report" had been touted by the Pentagon as the definitive, independent investigation of possible exposure to chemical and biological weapons in the Gulf War. The panel concluded, "There is no evidence that either high or low levels of exposures of U.S. troops to chemical agents occurred." In a December 10 story by Shenon, Lederberg said that this sweeping conclusion might have been "too firm. . . . Maybe we shouldn't have been so categorical."

SOME HAVE NOT LET UP

Lederberg spoke to the *Times* after *Newsday*'s Sloyan reported that Lederberg served on the board of American Type Culture Collection, a company that exported biological weapons to Iraq before the war. Though that fact had been reported previously by Gannett News Service and *Playboy,* Sloyan's story led the Nobel laureate to speak on the record for the first time since the disclosure of chemical exposure at Khamisiyah—an event his Pentagon-commissioned panel had not uncovered.

The *Los Angeles Times* has published some thoughtful pieces, notably Paul Richter's look at low-level chemical exposure, which reported that it may be years before we know how it affects humans. And the news organizations that have followed the story from the start—the *Hartford Courant,* Gannett News Service and especially the *Birmingham News*—have not let up.

Nor has CBS' Dave Martin, who did a four-minute segment on one key piece of evidence that led to the Pentagon's reversal. Martin reported on a CIA analyst who happened to hear a radio interview with a Gulf War veteran describing a weapons demolition operation. The analyst realized the veteran was talking about Khamisiyah. Before that, according to the Pentagon, while officials had been aware of the destruction of chemical weapons, apparently no one had realized that U.S. soldiers had been nearby.

While low levels of nerve and mustard gas may eventually be linked to some symptoms experienced by Gulf War veterans, that's a long way off. At this point there isn't much evidence linking the various exposures—oil well fires or pesticides or chemical weapons—to veterans' illnesses. But these Gulf War connections certainly can't be ruled out.

"There is confusion," says the *Washington Post*'s David Brown. "You can never prove the negative. And, undeniably, there will be people 30 years from now who will believe what they believe and remain unconvinced—by any intervening studies or otherwise."

STEPPING UP COVERAGE

Some of the confusion may stem from the radically different approaches the media have taken to the story, notably the *Washington Post* and the *New York Times.* Most of the *Post* stories over the years, particularly those written by Brown, lean toward the Pentagon's point of view. Brown's 1994 series on the issue was sympathetic toward veterans who were ill, but all but ruled out any connection between their illnesses and the war.

Brown, who prides himself on his objective, scientific approach, did not dwell on studies linking veterans' illnesses with their service in the Gulf. The headline on one of his stories—about a study of chemical changes in the brain under stressful conditions—illustrates his take on the subject: "A Theory of Chemical Interactions; Study Shows Additive Effects, but Relevance Appears Limited." That story ran as a sidebar to a 3,357-word front page story by Brown that rejected any connection between nerve gas and gulf war illness.

Since the *New York Times* stepped up its coverage of the issue last year, many of Shenon's stories have focused on the experiences and anecdote-driven theories of Gulf War veterans, who feel strongly about the link between their illnesses and exposures to chemical agents.

Time after time, the two newspapers have reported news on the subject in entirely different ways.

When the National Academy of Sciences' Institute of Medicine issued its report on Gulf War health studies last year, the *Times* story on October 19 said that the panel found "*ample evidence* [emphasis added] . . . that some veterans were genuinely sick with a variety of symptoms," but that incomplete and inadequate Pentagon records hampered any definitive conclusions about what had caused them.

The *Post* story, under the headline "Scientists Say Evidence Lacking to Tie 'Syndrome' to 1991 Gulf War," began, "A prestigious committee of scientists, epidemiologists and physicians reported yesterday there is *no evidence* [emphasis added] of a mysterious chronic illness arising from military service in the Persian Gulf War."

The most stark division came in January when the Department of Veterans Affairs released its first findings about soldiers who may have been exposed to low levels of nerve gas at Khamisiyah. The *Post* story stated that the VA study showed that soldiers near the site of chemical weapons did not "appear to have more health problems, or an unusual pattern of problems, when compared to other veterans of the Gulf War."

GOING TOO FAR?

The report's findings looked entirely different in the *Times:* "U.S. Agency Links Chemicals to One Illness of Gulf War Soldiers." The story opened, "For the first time, a federal agency acknowledged today that there appeared to be a direct link between the release of toxic chemicals in Iraq in 1991 and one of the many different symptoms that have come to be called Gulf War syndrome."

The VA maintains that the data released do not constitute a study and says it doesn't draw conclusions from them. The agency takes the position that no single environmental exposure has led to the symptoms Gulf War veterans are experiencing.

There's no doubt whose side Kenneth Bacon, the Assistant Secretary of Defense for Public Affairs, takes in the dispute. He says the media have covered the story fairly, with one notable exception: the *New York Times.*

Bacon says the *Times'* coverage has demonstrated "the best and the worst parts of American journalism. The best: They clearly provided an outlet for veterans of the Gulf War who felt the government wasn't taking their concerns seriously." But Bacon faults the paper for leading readers to believe that Gulf War illness is the result of exposure to chemical weapons. He says the stories don't say this directly, but "are written in a way that leads people to suggest that, particularly the headlines."

"One of the issues we face in this society," he adds, "is, how do we deal with very complex information that is also scary? I think the *Washington Post* has done this quite well with balanced, intelligent treatment that allows readers to make their own conclusions." He says the *New York Times* coverage has been "more exciting than educational," adding, 'it's looked more for villains than answers."

The *Times'* reporting on the subject also draws criticism from other Washington reporters, although not on the record. Bacon echoes what many of these anonymous critics are saying: that the *Times* has focused too heavily on the possibility that chemical weapons are the culprit. "There are 41 possible causes of Gulf War illness," he says. "They've only focused on one."

Andrew Rosenthal, the *Times'* Washington editor and the person who has overseen the paper's coverage, dismisses the criticism, especially from the Pentagon. "It's Ken Bacon's job to criticize the *New York Times* because his organization is guilty of one of two things: incompetence or a cover-up," Rosenthal says. "And both of those are pretty unpalatable choices."

MEDIA CONFLICT/PENTAGON SPIN

As for his colleagues in the media, Rosenthal says the *Times* stories have never been wrong—and that he is proud that the paper has pushed for answers to questions affecting thousands of Gulf War veterans. "What we've been saying is, there's a bunch of sick soldiers. We have proved without a shadow of a doubt that these people were exposed to chemical weapons. The Pentagon and now the president of the United States have admitted that. Every one of these stories has been discussed, every one of these stories has been edited. It [the criticism] is just nonsense."

But he's not surprised at the sniping. "The *New York Times* is a great big, fat, slow-moving target and people love throwing cream pies at us," Rosenthal says. "And trashing what's in the *New York Times* is a great way to explain to yourself and to your bosses why you don't have the story."

Beyond the media conflict and the Pentagon spin, there's yet another school of thought: People who don't see Gulf War illnesses as real. Princeton University professor Elaine Showalter has written a book on "hysterical epidemics in modern media" that lumps Gulf War illness in with alien abductions, satanic ritual abuse and chronic fatigue syndrome.

She says that gulf symptoms are basically "war neurosis" and that the media have exacerbated veterans' fears of war-related sickness. "Perceptions are reported as facts; undifferentiated and unsubstantiated responses are taken seriously as medical evidence," she writes.

A similar view is expressed by writer Michael Fumento, who has written on the subject in *The American Spectator* and *Reason* magazine, among other places. Fumento has also written that the media heavily exaggerated the problem of heterosexual AIDS. Fumento argues that "Gulf Lore Syndrome" is nothing more than "stress-related illness and the normal rates of disease among the 700,000 vets of Desert Storm," as he wrote in a March op-ed piece in the *Wall Street Journal*.

His article sparked an angry response from *60 Minutes* Executive Producer Don Hewitt, whose program's coverage was among Fumento's targets. In a letter to the editor, Hewitt rebutted Fumento's article point by point, dismissing it as a "total farce."

BOTH SIDES MAY HAVE BUNGLED

It took indications of a government cover-up to generate major media interest in Gulf War illness. But shouldn't the media have been pursuing the story more aggressively all along?

"Do I wish somebody had paid more attention to it a couple of years ago? Yeah. Would that have changed things today? I'm not sure," says the *L.A. Times'* Heikes. "If you believe that the reporting of a possible cover-up has forced a response—and the response being not only investigation of the Pentagon but many more scientific studies—then yeah, it would have done some good if we had uncovered this several years ago."

The Defense Department's Bacon certainly doesn't think there has been a cover-up. "The Pentagon has handled this clumsily for a long time," says Bacon. "But we have never been in the business of withholding information on Gulf War illness."

Ed Bradley also doesn't see a full-fledged cover-up. "But it's whatever is just short of a cover-up," the veteran TV newsman says. "Instead of saying, 'Here's everything that we have, here's everything that we know,' it's been more like, 'Oh, we didn't know those reports were here. Oh, we knew about this in 1991 and somehow it was misplaced.' Or, 'We didn't think much of it at that time.' What about this? 'Oh, we lost that. The computer virus ate it up.'"

The irony is that what the Pentagon ruled out so vigorously—exposure to nerve or mustard agents—may not be the villain. The most widely accepted theory is that soldiers were sickened by a combination of chemical exposures—from the flea collars they wore to the nerve-agent pills they took, perhaps combined with low-level exposure to chemical weapons. But it may take years to determine how any of these apply to Desert Storm soldiers. It took decades before the Pentagon acknowledged that the herbicide Agent Orange had sickened Vietnam vets.

"The Pentagon has thoroughly discredited itself on the entire subject of Gulf War illness because of this flap over chemical weapons," CBS' Martin says. "And it may turn out that this entire flap is a red herring."

48

The Video Vise in the Bosnia War

MICHAEL BESCHLOSS

Editor's Note: As we have seen, to fight a war it is necessary for a democratic government to use the mass media to win public support. But it is also possible for the mass media to foment public sympathy for a war and force the government to fight it.

In 1898, William Randolph Hearst forced the American government to declare war on Spain with his front page headlines about events in Cuba. In the 1990s, the American government sent troops to Somalia after the mass media reported on the plight of starvation and disease caused by a corrupt Somalian government.

A similiar situation happened in Bosnia, in the war among various geographic and ethnic divisions in the former Yugoslavia, as this article describes. Indeed, not long after this article was written in 1993, the American government sent troops to Bosnia to help bring peace to the region.

Michael Beschloss is a historian and author. This article was adapted from a report for the Annenberg Washington Program called "Presidents, Television, and Foreign Crises" and published in *The Washington Post*, May 2, 1993, and reprinted with permission.

Recent experience suggests that the genocidal war in Bosnia will be the latest example of an overseas crisis in which haunting television pictures arouse the American people to demand that their government do something. If television did not exist, such public pressure on President Clinton might not be growing; Secretary of State Warren Christopher might not be leaving, as he announced yesterday, to consult with allies on military and other options.

By the same token, one must suspect, in the week after the president dedicated the United States Holocaust Museum, that satellite and video pictures of Auschwitz and Bergen-Belsen in 1943 and 1944 would have moved Franklin Roosevelt, with his preternatural sensitivity to mass opinion, toward expanding U.S. war aims to include the destruction of Nazi concentration camps and the transport lanes that served them.

The new images from Bosnia demonstrate how television rewards crisis management over crisis prevention. Had George Bush used U.S. political and military power to avert the tragedy in Central Europe, he would have had a difficult time overcoming American resistance to the notion of using force for abstract aims in a land few people knew. Prompted and abetted by the television pictures, Bill Clinton will have an easier time explaining why he is acting, if he does, but will suffer the problems attached to making up for lost time.

TELEVISION AND FOREIGN POLICY

In the world of 1993, it is difficult to imagine the age when television did not occupy so central a place in the U.S. foreign policy process. As recently as 1962, European genocide would not have been so easily graven on the American mind. Pictures of overseas events were aired at least one day after they had occurred. Telstar, the primitive first communications satellite, had only just been launched. Sixteen-millimeter black-and-white film had to be developed, edited and flown to the United States, where it was hastily cut to fit into $11\frac{1}{2}$ minutes of black-and-white evening news. The process was so rushed that viewers sometimes saw water marks and strands of human hair on the film.

In that era, a president of the United States enjoyed far greater influence over public information about foreign events. Consider the effect of television on the Cuban Missile Crisis of October 1962. Of that episode, John F. Kennedy's secretary of defense, Robert S. McNamara, could say, "I don't think I turned on a television set during the whole two weeks of that crisis." It is doubtful that his Bush administration counterpart, Dick Cheney, would say the same thing of the Persian Gulf War.

Throughout the Missile Crisis, Kennedy repeatedly benefited from a cocoon of time and privacy afforded by the absence of intense television scrutiny. When the CIA informed the president of Soviet offensive missiles in Cuba, he knew that he had an enormous political problem: He had just assured the public that there were no such missiles there and that if they appeared, it would cause a confrontation of the first magnitude with the Soviet Union.

As the veteran television newsman Sander Vanocur has said, "Now, in the present atmosphere, you have round-the-clock news. You have the beginning of the week with the Sunday morning shows. Then you have the weekdays that begin with the morning shows on the three networks and on local stations across the country. You end it with local television and *Nightline*."

TELEVISION AND VIETNAM

Had the Missile Crisis occurred in the environment of the 1990s, a commercial satellite might have discovered the missiles at roughly the same time the CIA did. The news might have been revealed in a CNN special report, including tape of Kennedy's assurances and pictures of the missiles. On that report and on *Nightline* that evening, angry senators and congressmen would have demanded to know why Kennedy had kept the Soviet outrage a secret from Americans, and called on him to fulfill his pledge by bombing the missile sites immediately.

We now know that had he done so, the act could have quickly led to nuclear war. Instead, benefiting from life in 1962, Kennedy enjoyed six days during which the public was ignorant of the missiles to secretly convene his advisers, deliberate about the matter in quiet and then reveal the problem himself, in his own words, in a way designed to quash hysteria and gain support for his plan of action.

President Johnson presumed that color film of the carnage of Vietnam, aired night after night on newly 30-minute, newly all-color evening news broadcasts, which were gaining more and more millions of viewers, caused Americans to lose their stomach for the war. In 1968, he told the National Association of Broadcasters, "Historians must only guess at the effect that television would have had during earlier conflicts over the future of the nation: during the Korean War, for example, at the time when our forces were pushed back there to Pusan—or when our men were slugging it out in Europe, or when most of our Air Force was shot down on that day in June 1942 off Australia."

Johnson's "lesson" was later cited by President Reagan and his advisers while seeking to ensure that military action in Grenada and Libya was as brief and bloodless (at least on the American side) as possible, and by George Bush and his aides when they did the same thing in Panama, the Persian Gulf and Somalia. Yet, as the scholar Michael Mandelbaum has argued, it is equally plausible that pictures of Americans fighting and dying in Vietnam promoted support for the war by inspiring "the determination to see the way through to a successful conclusion, in order to give meaning to those sacrifices."

In fact, as early as 1969, the networks may have grown slightly bored with Indochina. The percentage of CBS and NBC evening news programs including stories on the war dropped from 85 to 90 percent during 1965–1968 to about 70 percent during the next two years. Determined not to "bug out" of Vietnam, President Nixon was probably aided by his shift in emphasis from the bloody (and photogenic) ground war in Indochina to the more abstract-looking air war, pictures of which were less emotionally provocative. The effect of the distinction between the two sets of images was not lost on military planners under Bush.

TELEVISION, KUWAIT, AND SOMALIA

Saddam Hussein's invasion of Kuwait in August 1990 showed how far television had come from the epoch of 1962. Had Bush wished to follow Kennedy's example of secret deliberations in quiet, he would have been badly frustrated. Even at a time when the Cold War was ending, the Gulf Crisis was the story of the year and it monopolized the airwaves. As Richard N. Haass of the Bush National Security Council staff recalled, "We didn't have six minutes in some ways to contemplate [the invasion of Kuwait], and certainly not six hours or six days, if you'll look at the night when we first found out about it and then at every breaking point since then." Paul Wolfowitz, Undersecretary of Defense in the Bush administration, noted that Saddam's assault was "the first time in history that we had live coverage of a surprise attack."

While planning the Gulf War, Wolfowitz found his colleagues concerned that "you really have to get something like this over with quickly. . . . Perhaps the people thinking this were thinking, and sometimes they would say it, of what the effect of weeks and weeks of television coverage of bombing would do to support for the [anti-Saddam] coalition." Michael Janeway, dean of the Medill School of Journalism, felt that in the Gulf War, the Bush administration was singularly blessed by dealing with a media that was "very conscious of the Vietnam experience. It was conscious of having been the unwelcome messenger. . . . We must question what would have happened if the war had gone on longer, had casualties come more into play . . . if there had come to be many more questions about whether this was a just war or not."

In 1982, during the Israeli invasion of Lebanon, Ronald Reagan had been so disturbed by television pictures of the destruction that he telephoned the Israeli prime minister, Menachem Begin, to demand a halt to the bombing. (As it happened, Begin had already ordered the bombing stopped several hours earlier.) Bush would have scoffed at such "emotionalism." It is unlikely that at the start of the Gulf Conflict, he imagined that the war's endgame would be influenced by television pictures of the "highway of death" and other suffering by Kurds in northern Iraq, and Shiites in southern Iraq, of hundreds of thousands of people who were likely to start dying if nothing were done.

Bush's efforts to relieve that suffering foreshadowed his final foreign policy exercise—after the 1992 election, when he responded to the outrage of the American public over television pictures of the Somalian famine by sending U.S. troops to ensure that domestic turmoil would not prevent food and other supplies from going where they were needed. Bush declined to do the same thing in Bosnia. For this he was badly criticized by candidate Bill Clinton, who found the crisis waiting for him when he entered the Oval Office.

TELEVISION, PRESSURES, AND BOSNIA

In the modern age, television can not only generate pressures on presidents for foreign intervention or for staying out of a crisis; it offers those presidents a superior weapon for framing issues and selling White House policy. It also amplifies public opposition, which, although most presidents forget it, can improve and strengthen their approach to foreign affairs. As demonstrated by the Iraqi invasion of Kuwait and the initial bombing of Baghdad, TV prevents presidents from presuming that they can maintain a monopoly on information for long. One may question LBJ's notion that the Vietnam war was lost on television, but experience suggests that it is in a president's general interest to design U.S. military adventures to be as brief and telegenic as possible.

When Saddam took American hostages in Iraq, Bush heeded the negative lessons established by President Carter over hostages in Iran a decade earlier: Discouraging television attention to such captives and presidential actions to free them lowers their value to their jailer; it also prevents Americans from rating the president on the basis of how quickly he is able to end the crisis. Presidents must always remember that other unexpected events shown on television can have inordinate influence on the American public's perception of a foreign crisis, encouraging, for instance, U.S. military planners during wartime to avoid bombing churches, hospitals and other civilian sites. Had the CNN "boys in Baghdad" been badly injured by American bombs, American public support for the Gulf War would likely have been eroded.

For Clinton, the crisis in Bosnia could prove to be many of these problems rolled into one. Clinton's advantage is that he comes to the problem as the first U.S. president who has lived more than half of his life in the television age. Unlike a Richard Nixon, he does not long for the time before intensive coverage of foreign events. He presumes it. For all of his adulthood, television has been a staple of American foreign policymaking, since the escalation of the Vietnam conflict against which he now-famously demonstrated.

If Clinton does not act in central Europe, he will have to struggle against those television pictures. If he intervenes, it would be one of the cardinal ironies of this moment if the resulting scene shows the forty-second president brooding in the White House, LBJ-style, about strategies to ensure that television does not draw thousands of college students to the Mall, the Ellipse and the Pentagon to fan opposition to his policies or demand premature extrication from the conflict.

ADDITIONAL RESOURCES FOR PART 12

Suggested Questions and Discussion Topics

1. According to Ray Hiebert in "Mass Media as Weapons of Modern Warfare," what was the "press pool," why was it used by the government in the Gulf War, and why did the news media accept it? Should it have been used? Discuss the arguments on both sides.

2. According to "Mass Media as Weapons of Modern Warfare," why do governments need to control or use mass media during wartime? Discuss.

3. In his defense of Gulf War public relations, "The Pentagon Position on Mass Media," how does Pete Williams justify the use of press or media pools?

4. In "The Pentagon Position on Mass Media," Pete Williams suggests that the press and the government each have competing responsibilities during wartime, as summarized in a memo by General Eisenhower in World War II, but does Williams propose a level playing field for the competition? Explain and discuss.

5. In "Missed Story Syndrome" by Kate McKenna, who seems to be more at fault for missing the story of Gulf War syndrome, the government or the press? Explain.

6. In "Missed Story Syndrome," why, according to McKenna, were the big newspapers and broadcast networks slow to report the story of Gulf War syndrome?

7. In "The Video Vise in the Bosnia War" by Michael Beschloss, what is the vise, and who was caught in it? What has subsequently been done about the problem?

8. In "The Video Vise in the Bosnia War," why, according to the author, has television come to play such an important part in the formulation of foreign policy, including the decision to go to war? Discuss.

Suggested Readings

Michael A. Anderegg, ed., *Inventing Vietnam: The War in Film and Television.* Philadelphia: Temple University Press, 1991.

Michael J. Arlen, *Livingroom War.* New York: Viking Press, 1969.

James Aronsom, *The Press and the Cold War.* Boston: Beacon Press, 1970.

George Bailey, *Armageddon in Prime Time.* New York: Avon Books, 1984.

Peter Braestrup, *Big Story: How the American Press and Television Reported and Interpreted the Crisis of Tet 1968 in Vietnam and Washington.* Boulder, CO: Westview Press, 1977.

Bradley Greenberg and Walter Gantz, eds., *Desert Storm and the Mass Media.* Cresskill, NJ: Hampton Press, 1993.

Daniel C. Hallin, *The 'Uncensored War': The Media and Vietnam.* New York: Oxford University Press, 1986.

Susan Jeffords and Lauren Rabinowitz, eds., *Seeing Through the Media: The Persian Gulf War.* New Brunswick, NJ: Rutgers University Press, 1994.

William V. Kennedy, *The Military and the Media: Why the Press Cannot Be Trusted to Cover a War.* New York: Praeger, 1993.

John R. MacArthur, *Second Front: Censorship and Propaganda in the Gulf War.* Berkeley, CA: University of California Press, 1993.

John Sadkovich, *The U.S. Media and Yusgoslavia, 1991–1995.* New York: Praeger, 1998.

Hedrick Smith, *The Media and the Gulf War/the Press and Democracy in Wartime.* Cabin John, MD: Seven Locks Press, 1992.

Jeffrey Alan Smith, *War and Press Freedom: The Problem of Prerogative of Power.* New York: Oxford University Press, 1998.

John Stanier, *War and the Media: A Random Searchlight.* New York: New York University Press, 1998.

Suggested Videos

"The Military and the News Media." New York: Insight Media, 1985. (three volumes, 60 minutes each)

"Lines in the Sand." New York: Insight Media, 1991. (12 minutes)

"Faces of the Enemy." New York: Insight Media, 1987. (58 minutes)

Bill Moyers, "The Press Goes to War." Atlanta: CNN, 1991. (30 minutes)

"Media War in El Salvador." New York: Icarus Films, 1989. (22 minutes)

PART · 13

Minorities

Although some progress has been made since the first edition of this book was published in 1985, mass media in America are still produced mostly by white, male staffs and their content is still culturally biased from a white, male perspective. Many more women are now involved in mass media, as well as more blacks and other minority groups, but much progress remains to be made.

William Raspberry of *The Washington Post* relates the following story about a man driving his 11-year-old son home one night when the youngster asked a question, "Daddy, do white people take drugs?" Of course, the father answered. "Well," said the boy, "I never hear anything about it." That brief conversation, writes Raspberry, stands as an indictment of journalism. He points out that 70 to 80 percent of the consumption of illicit drugs happens outside the black ghettos. "But that knowledge rarely informs our stories and commentaries," writes Raspberry.[1]

On the other hand, a year later a man called *The Washington Post* deeply offended because a TV special on urban crime emphasized black criminals. The caller implied that mass media—especially television—are going out of their way to perpetuate a negative image of young black men, and the result is that these men have come to see themselves only in negative terms. Raspberry, however, points out that although a disproportionate amount of street crime *is* black crime, often black-on-black crime. However, Raspberry writes:

> The media could do a lot more than they are doing to show that people from unlikely backgrounds—from tough neighborhoods, fatherless households and underfunded inner-city schools—are succeeding in any number of fields. . . . The media can help drive home the fact that failure isn't inevitable for youngsters born to unfortunate circumstances—not by refusing to report the truth about criminals, not even by showing that poor kids are sometimes extraordinarily gifted, but by helping to teach our children that commitment and hard work pay off, even for people of ordinary gifts.[2]

One problem is that mass media, by definition, target their messages to the largest common denominator, the majority rather than the minority. All media, it could be argued, are culturally biased; they both reflect and influence the bias of their audience; mass media reflect the bias of the majority.

As Felix Gutierrez argues in this section, however, the new technologies are making it possible for all media to more effectively serve the needs of their own specific audiences. Mass, he says in his book, is giving way to class. And this may provide new opportunities for better representation of all cultures in a diverse society.

Minorities, of course, have long had their own media, and the black press in the past has been particularly strong. However, as mass media have tried to hire more minorities, this for a time weakened the black press, but there are signs of a turn-around in the 1990s. In addition, the ethnic press is growing rapidly.

To be sure, black, Hispanic, and other ethnic media are not going to perceive news in exactly the same way as the so-called "white press" sees it. But this all the more reinforces the knowledge that the white press is biased in its own cultural perspectives, just as much as the minority press might be.

Many minority groups within the larger American society are still not well-represented in the public dialogue. Hardly anyone, for example, mentions Asian Americans, a fast-growing minority, and they rarely raise the subject themselves.

One hope for the future is that young people of all ethnic backgrounds may be less culture-bound and more color-blind and better able to blend into a truly multicultural society in the future, where mass media might better represent us all.

NOTES

1. William Raspberry, "The Drug Problem Isn't Black and White," *The Washington Post,* June 1, 1990, p. A21.
2. William Raspberry, "Minorities, Media, Success," *The Washington Post,* February 25, 1991, p. A9.

49

Advocating Diversity in an Age of Electronic News

Felix Gutierrez

Editor's Note: The new media age might pose some real opportunities to make mass media into better representatives of a diverse and multicultural society. Felix Gutierrez argues that technologies and shifting demographics are transforming the media, creating new opportunities for diversity.

Gutierrez is senior vice president and executive director of The Freedom Forum Pacific Coast Center in Oakland, California. He is co-author of *Race, Multiculturalism and the Media: From Mass to Class* (Sage, 1995). This article appeared in *Outlook,* a publication of the Robert C. Maynard Institute of Journalism Education, Spring 1996, and is reprinted with permission.

A vast transformation is taking place in the communications media, driven by technological advances and by a steady growth in the country's racial and cultural diversity. These two forces—technology and audience demographics—have converged to create a paradigm shift unlike anything the communications industry has experienced in decades.

The changing technical and market realities offer new opportunities for advocates of diversity—particularly as media companies attempt to target information in a variety of innovative ways rather than specializing in one delivery system.

To be sure, over the past three decades, there have been many gains in diversifying news coverage and news employment. Barriers have been broken. Signs of segregation have been overcome. But this is no time to bask in the memory of battles won. Nor is it time to maintain a fixed focus on traditional news media.

Focusing on employment and coverage gains in newspapers in their traditional forms is akin to the publicity given to cities that elected African American and Hispanic mayors in the 1970s. The mayors inherited cities saddled by economic and infrastructure problems, not places that enjoyed the power they once had.

WINNING A BATTLE, LOSING A WAR

Much in the same way, advocates of diversity may win the short-term battle of integrating the nation's newspaper newsrooms only to discover that they missed a new battlefront with even higher stakes—the new media. Today, newspaper companies are rethinking their strategies for long-term growth, looking for the same kind of energy that revived urban downtown areas in recent years. Diversity advocates should follow suit and re-examine the course, content and strategies of their efforts—or risk losing their clout and relevance in the new information age.

Media past give a clue to media future. Concentrating on general-audience media today would be similar to focusing on general-circulation magazines such as *Life, Look* and the *Saturday Evening Post* in the 1960s. These national periodicals once ruled the magazine field. But the magazine landscape changed dramatically with the rise of television as the dominant mass-audience medium. Magazines survived and even thrived by changing their appeal from audience masses to audience classes. Instead of trying to reach everyone with one magazine, publishers now target different magazines to specific audience interests. The audience slice is smaller, but its characteristics are more easily targeted by marketers and advertisers.

NEW MEDIA OFFER OPPORTUNITIES

Today's general-circulation newspapers are at a similar decision point. Like prime-time network television, they operate in a world of mass-audience appeal, albeit an audience sometimes defined by geographic boundaries. Newspaper companies are preparing for change, however, with specialized sections, on-line services and Web sites. Like magazines, newspapers will no doubt survive and thrive in the era of digital news.

The new media offer ample opportunities for diversity and inclusion previously nonexistent in mainstream media. Digital news has, for example, the potential to be an open system, like the telephone, where people can connect and communicate with anyone.

It also offers advocates of diversity a ground-floor opportunity to address inclusiveness at the staffing, content and business level of all the new media organizations, shaping the future of news. Given the nation's growing racial and cultural diversity, it is in the best interest of these ventures to integrate talent, content and audiences representing multicultural America.

But this promise is not yet a reality. "The faces are disproportionately young and male, and almost all are white," said Adam Clayton Powell III of The Freedom Forum Media Studies Center at a journalism conference in 1995. "This is the present face of the [new media] audience. And even more so, this is the present face of the on-line publishers."

THE LANDSCAPE OF NEWS HAS BROADENED

The new media are growing into targeted media, reaching segments of the audience through different channels. They will offer content that reaches a specific audience more quickly and conveniently than other news sources. This capability opens the door to electronic news, commentaries, dialogues and conversations that reach diverse members of the audience and allows them to express themselves. Content is key to the public's adoption of new technologies. Shaping news and editorial content to reach audiences not well served by the existing media will attract new users to on-line media.

The business end of the new media offers opportunities for ownership, advertisers and subscribers. With diversity will come innovative ideas of ways to serve members of a multicultural society at a price that makes sense to both corporations and consumers.

Efforts to integrate the nation's newsrooms are as important today as when the industry began concerted efforts to address racial discrimination in the late 1960s. But the landscape of news has broadened. The best corporate strategies will include all media, not just newspapers and broadcasting. Professional journalism associations and organizations developing new technologies also have a place in the dialogue. Universities should be engaged to prepare their faculty and students for media that are not only technologically, but also racially and culturally, diverse.

50

Black on Black

JIM STRADER

Editor's Note: Once influential and essential, black newspapers have lost many of their readers, as well as their political role and impact. Now they seem to be coming back, largely because they can provide significant local coverage that major newspapers often ignore.

Jim Strader is a wire service reporter in Pittsburgh. This article was originally published in the *Washington Journalism Review,* March 1992.

Forty years ago in Pittsburgh, people couldn't wait to read the *Courier.* Thursday afternoons, "everybody went to the drugstores to buy the *Courier,*" says Ruth White, a reader for more than 50 years. "That's how we got news from across the country." Mayor David Lawrence would send a cab each week to pick up a copy before the ink had even dried. "I can see that cab driver now, wiping the ink off his hands and cussing at Lawrence," recalls former *Courier* Editor Frank Bolden.

In the late 1940s and early 1950s, the *Courier* and other leading black newspapers boasted circulations of a quarter-million or more. Editors whose publications reached far beyond their own cities wielded considerable influence and helped shape the political consciousness of America's blacks.

Now, the readership of those papers has dwindled and competition from the mainstream press and black magazines for both readers and writers has intensified. Papers that once had tremendous presence are shells of what they used to be. Publications familiar to and eagerly awaited by black communities across the country—the *New York Amsterdam News,* the *Chicago Defender,* the *Pittsburgh Courier*—no longer inspire the same anticipation they once did.

A SENSE OF IDENTITY

"It was the old *Pittsburgh Courier* that was the great paper," says Phyl Garland, a professor of journalism at Columbia University who read the *Courier* while growing up and worked there as a reporter from 1959 to 1965. "Now, it's not at all what it was then.

"It gave me my sense of identity and also gave me an opportunity to see and understand what black people had done in the past and see what they were achieving in the present," says Garland. "It was a fine newspaper and my inspiration."

Veteran journalist Chuck Stone also has fond memories of that paper. "I had my consciousness awakened by the *Pittsburgh Courier,*" he remembers. "It was like an umbilical cord that tied us all together. It was powerful as hell and could really affect political decisions in the early days of the civil rights period."

But the black press has changed, says Stone, who was an editor at three black papers and spent 19 years at the Philadelphia *Daily News* before leaving to teach at the University of North Carolina's School of Journalism and Mass Communication. "[The black press] can't represent all African-Americans. It is not as dominant a force as it was 20 years ago.'

ROOTS

The first black papers of any size were published in the 1890s, mostly in the Northeast and Midwest. The *Baltimore Afro-American* first appeared in 1892, the *Indiana Recorder* in 1895, the *New York Amsterdam News* in 1909 and the *Pittsburgh Courier* a year after that. The *St. Louis Argus* debuted in 1912. Roland Wolseley in "The Black Press, U.S.A." estimates that some 3,500 black newspapers have been published since the first, the *Freedom's Journal,* in New York City in 1827.

The advent of most of these papers corresponded roughly with the founding of organizations advocating equal rights for blacks. The National Association for the Advancement of Colored People was established in 1909 and the National Urban League in 1910.

Many black newspapers crusaded for black causes, campaigning first for black freedom and then, after the Civil War, for equality. The *Chicago Defender's* best-known crusade resulted in the migration of 110,000 Southern blacks to the city, Wolseley writes; in 1917 the paper urged blacks to leave the stronghold of the Ku Klux Klan and helped organize clubs that could get group rates on train fares. The *Pittsburgh Courier's* advocacy helped Jackie Robinson become the first black player in major league baseball in 1947. Wolseley notes that *Time* reported in 1949 that the *Norfolk Journal and Guide* "was responsible for the county floating a $750,000 bond issue to improve black schools and for changes in pay scales so black and white teachers were treated equally."

PROVIDING HOPE

Black papers "gave the Negroes hope and did the fighting for them, because they were too weak to fight for themselves," says Bolden.

Black papers of the 1920s also carried news of church, society and sports activities in the black community, items that didn't appear in white-owned publications, as well as occasional reports of national and international events. Garland says they were needed because "black people were invisible as far as the mainstream media were concerned. Maybe there would be a two-inch column in a corner on the back page: 'Afro-Americans in the News.'" Like the white-owned tabloids of the era, many ran sensationalized articles on crimes and scandals.

Over the years, several black papers grew dramatically and became a link for blacks nationally. In the 1930s the *Chicago Defender* distributed 300,000 copies. At its height in the late 1940s, the *Pittsburgh Courier's* circulation was over 400,000, while the *New York Amsterdam News* distributed 200,000. In 1945 the *Afro-American's* national circulation was 137,000.

The papers' readership was by no means limited to the cities in which they published. From Pittsburgh, for example, more than a dozen regional editions of the *Courier* were shipped across the country. The *Defender* and the Baltimore-based *Afro-American* also distributed nationwide.

SPREADING THE NEWS

Distribution was difficult, especially in the South. Bolden says bundles of papers often were burned as soon as they were unloaded from rail cars at Southern depots. In his 1922 book *The Negro Press in the United States,* Frederick Detweiler describes a 1920 Mississippi law that forbade publications advocating equality for blacks.

To circumvent such problems, the *Courier* depended on black railroad porters to safeguard shipments, says Rod Doss, current general manager of the paper, now called the *New Pittsburgh Courier.* Black ministers also agreed to receive the papers and encouraged parishioners to subscribe.

There were other difficulties with putting out newspapers that weren't for the larger, more affluent white population, and high on the list was money. Advertising dollars were scarce for some papers. "Our budget was tight. We didn't begin to make money 'til late," Bolden says. "White businesses don't give you a lot of advertisements when you're criticizing white people."

Photographer Teenie "One-Shot" Harris found a way to live with the *Courier's* tight budget. When he photographed Lawrence, "there were 12 photographers in the building, all shooting pictures," Harris says. "I'd just come in and take one. So he called me 'One-shot.'

"They only paid me for one picture, so why take two?"

LOSING READERS

A number of these papers no longer have their former reach. The *New Pittsburgh Courier* still publishes a national edition with a circulation of 50,000, Doss says. And the local edition, which now comes out biweekly, has a circulation of just 28,500. The *Chicago Defender,* one of only three black dailies—the *Atlanta Daily World* and the *New York Daily Challenge* are the others—has seen its circulation drop tenfold, to 30,000. The *Amsterdam News* now publishes only about 60,000 copies per week.

Some claim the papers' contents have contributed to the circulation decline. "Today's black press does not have the political leadership that the old black press had," says Columbia professor Garland. "A lot of people I know who used to read the *Courier* no longer read it because it's not as tough-minded and it's not as plugged in to the community as it was."

"Today's black newspaper is not the same paper it was 30 years ago at the height of the civil rights period," says Steve Davis, executive director of the National Newspaper Publishers Association (NNPA), a black newspaper organization based in Washington, D.C. "We were the source of telling the story to the public. Now, we've gotten complacent and lost that urgency."

Observers also trace the decline to the emergence of national magazines aimed at blacks. "We now have *Ebony* and *Jet* and you can get the news from around the country," says Garland, a former *Ebony* editor. Publisher James E. Lewis, whose *Birmingham Times* has distributed about 10,000 copies weekly since it was founded 28 years ago, concedes that some functions of the black press a half-century ago have been usurped by the white-oriented media. News about black issues, celebrities and especially athletes now is found in white-owned daily newspapers and on television, Lewis says. In decades past, that kind of coverage was relegated to black papers.

THE ONLY PLACE

"Those papers used to be the only place blacks could read about blacks," says Frederick Benjamin, editor of the Augusta, Georgia, *Focus.* "Now there's competition everywhere."

But Garland says black national magazines, and black television, often devote too much space to entertainment "glitz and gloss." "That presents a distorted view of what is important to us, but it sells magazines."

By emphasizing gossip about black celebrities and the achievements of black athletes, the magazines also neglect the more serious role black newspapers used to play, particularly on political matters, Garland says. "Nothing does that today. It's just unfortunate."

Another drain on black papers is the increased presence of black journalists in the mainstream media. Some, such as Bernard Shaw of CNN, Carole Simpson of ABC News and Ed Bradley of CBS' *60 Minutes,* are in highly visible positions. The result, Stone says, is that the mainstream media now address black issues more frequently.

In addition, minority internships and scholarships offered by media companies steer young black journalists away from the black press. These programs also force black publishers and broadcasters to compete against more established and better-funded rivals for qualified reporters and editors.

"Most of these kids that get these scholarships go into the mainstream media. Very few go into the black press," Stone says. "The increase of black journalists . . . helps the white media."

Black columnists as well are no longer limited to writing strictly for black publications, says Stone, who wrote a column for the Philadelphia *Daily News* before accepting the faculty position at the University of North Carolina. He points to colleagues such as William Raspberry and Clarence Page, who are syndicated nationally, and Vernon Jarrett of the *Chicago Sun-Times.* "We exert as much influence on some issues as the African-American press," Stone says.

LOSING INFLUENCE

But black opinion-writers in the mainstream press have to be careful not to let themselves get pigeon-holed on the basis of race or they run the risk of losing their influence, Stone says. "We can't always write about African-American issues, because people get bored as hell."

Finances were another factor in the decline of the big newspapers. "These newspapers that had vast national circulations—there's just no way to sustain them. It costs too much," says Benjamin.

Readership has also changed, shifting from "practically all of black society" to a segment of the population, says Wolseley. Now, most readers are urban blacks who want news about their own community and "crusaders" of the civil rights movement, he says. "There is a portion of the black community that is indifferent to the black press. Editors don't like to be told this. They have a tough job holding the interest of middle-class blacks."

But G. M. Doss says the *Courier* made changes to keep its main audience, the middle class. "We realigned the product so it gave a more positive reflection of the core readership, which is mostly upscale, better educated, employed, socially and politically active and aware," he says. However, he says the paper remains relevant to its traditional readership—lower-income, inner-city blacks.

Benjamin of the Augusta *Focus* characterizes the future of black newspapers as "pretty bright" but says they can't expect to survive by continuing to conduct business as usual. "Traditionally, black newspapers have taken the audience for granted—they've felt that they had a captive audience. At times, they felt it was enough to keep publishing to keep going."

ALIVE AND KICKING

Media observers and several editors of black papers say that although the black press may have lost its sweeping influence, black newspapers remain vital. They say black communities still need a black perspective on the news and advocacy on black issues.

"The black press finds it necessary to take up a leadership role, because it's not being taken up by anybody else," says the NNPA's Steve Davis.

Many more blacks now trust the non-black media, Lewis says, since the mainstream press has discovered that blacks make news. But that faith is not total.

"Blacks trust CNN. They trust *USA Today,*" Lewis says. "But on the local level, black people do not trust the information that's in the local newspaper as it applies to them."

Hit by the same problems as white-owned papers—decreasing readership and ad revenues—black papers are taking steps to solve the problems. In Augusta, Benjamin says he revamped the design of the *Focus* with a new layout, color photos and graphics, and added special editions on business, culture and social activities.

In 1988 the *Afro-American* chain dropped its national edition. "We looked at our national edition and said, 'That's not our market,'" says Frances Murphy Draper, president of the company that publishes the *Baltimore Afro-American* and papers in Washington, D.C., and Richmond, Virginia. "We said, 'We're a community newspaper.'"

REVITALIZING EFFORT

Draper says circulation of the three local papers has climbed steadily in the past five years. The Baltimore paper publishes about 15,000 copies now, up from 8,000 in 1986; Washington circulation has increased to 10,000 from 4,000; and the Richmond paper now publishes 4,000 copies, up from its circulation of 2,500 five years ago.

In August 1990 the NAACP launched an effort to revitalize black-owned newspapers and television and radio stations. Executive Director Benjamin Hooks, saying black media outlets are "locked in a struggle for survival," called on the nation's 500 largest corporations to devote more ad dollars to the black media, directed the NAACP's 1,500 branches to give more support to black papers and broadcast stations and assigned organization staffers to assist black media owners.

Now more than a year and a half old, the effort has made progress, says NAACP spokesman Jim Williams. He says 250 of the Fortune 500 companies have responded to a letter Hooks sent their CEOs. Half replied that they already were advertising in the black media, and about 10 percent said they would consider doing so. The rest responded that they weren't doing any consumer advertising. Linking those companies with newspapers and stations in their areas is a joint project of the NAACP and the NNPA.

Davis contends that the black press as a whole is healthy, noting that no member of the NNPA has gone out of business in the past four years. But he thinks it should do more.

"People say, 'Where's the black press? They're not out in the streets marching.' Well, maybe we should be."

51

Bad News for Hispanics

MICHELE A. HELLER

Editor's Note: To find out how some of the most prestigious and influential papers in the United States cover the booming Hispanic communities in their respective cities, an analysis was conducted of the *Chicago Tribune, Los Angeles Times, New York Times, San Antonio Light,* and *Washington Post* during the week of August 24–30, 1992.

All stories in all sections of the papers were reviewed, except for obituaries, letters to the editor, play-by-play coverage of athletic games, and special "zoned" sections like the *Los Angeles Times*'s *Nuestro Tiempo.* Any story in which the main subject was Hispanic was put into one of five categories and graded as positive or negative. The author concludes that Hispanics are still almost invisible in America's main newspapers.

Michele A. Heller is an editorial assistant at *Hispanic* magazine, which published this article in November 1992.

How does your newspaper cover the Hispanic community? "I find it a ridiculous question!" declared the metro editor of the long-time standard bearer of the American press, the *New York Times,* when he was asked to rate his paper's coverage of Hispanics.

Until recently, the only Hispanics who made it onto the newsstands were criminals, drug dealers, gang members, or their victims. But with demographic change breathing down their necks, newspapers are slowly opening their eyes to the diversity of the Hispanic community. But regrettably, this revelation doesn't translate into more coverage, as evidenced by this editor's comment.

To find out how newspapers view the Hispanic community, HISPANIC analyzed the coverage of Hispanics in the *Chicago Tribune, Los Angeles Times, New York Times, San Antonio Light,* and *Washington Post* during the week of August 24 through August 30. We counted the number of stories about Hispanics and classified them into five categories—crime, culture, business, people, and issues—and then graded them as either positive or negative.

PRIME COMPONENT IS CRIME AND CONFLICT

We had to look carefully in each paper to find any story—positive or negative—about or including Hispanics. And, when we did stumble across a Hispanic, he or she had a strong chance of appearing in a crime story, as the perpetrator, victim, police officer—or all three. It can be argued that since blood and guts are what keep newspapers in business, the negative stories will always out-number the positive. But, as Melita Marie Garza, ethnic affairs writer for the *Chicago Tribune* and Vice President, Print for the National Association of Hispanic Journalists, explains:

> The prime component of news itself tends to be crime and conflict, so when Hispanics commit a crime, that is news. The problem comes when the only coverage of Hispanics is of Hispanic criminals. That needs to be written, but papers also need to expose the other side. Half of the truth results in a distortion, basically an un-truth. If Hispanics do not appear [in the papers] as experts, as people in the mainstream, as leaders, then the image of Hispanics that rests in the minds of society is in fact negative."

If a foreign visitor spent the week of August 24 in the United States and never came into contact with a Hispanic, save for what he read in the newspaper, here's what he would learn:

The *Chicago Tribune,* serving a metropolitan area that is at least 20 percent Hispanic (all population figures are quoted from the 1990 Census), had only fifteen Hispanic stories, but of those, nine were positive. Even the stories that included a negative stereotype quickly balanced themselves. For example, in an August 24 story about a small town and its booming economy, the first Hispanic we meet is Noe Martinez who is "interviewed as he picked fruit for [greenhouse manager Carl] Ford last week. Martinez, an immigrant from Chihuahua, Mexico, estimated his pay at $200 a week and noted that most places to rent cost more than $300 a month." In just a paragraph the *Tribune* managed to hit at least two stereotypes: Hispanics are manual laborers and they don't make enough money to make ends meet. But a few paragraphs later, Joe Medina, "a local businessman and former Chamber of Commerce president," goes to a city council meeting and relays his opinion on an economic issue important to his community. The story leaves us with the impression that Hispanics aren't invisible in this tiny town, and that they can't be lumped together by profession or any other arbitrary category.

LOW QUANTITY OF STORIES, MANY ERRORS

The problem, though, is not so much with quality as with quantity. "The *Tribune* covers good and bad stories about equally. It's just that there's not sufficient coverage at all," says Mayra Martinez, Director of Communications for the non-profit Latino Institute in Chicago. "Once a year the *Tribune* puts out a 36-page insert called 'Hispanic Heritage Month,' and that's really the extent of its extensive coverage of the huge Chicago Hispanic community. And, of course, they need more than one reporter to cover us."

That one reporter is Garza. Earlier this year she proposed establishing an ethnic affairs beat, and she was subsequently made ethnic affairs writer. Now she not only covers all of Chicago's ethnic and racial minorities, but also serves as a liaison to other reporters in the newsroom who have questions about ethnic issues on their beats.

Martinez describes repeated errors that show the *Tribune's* ignorance of issues important to Hispanics, who number 545,852 in Chicago. For example, the Northwest side of Chicago was mainly populated by Puerto Ricans ten years ago, but now there are as many people of Mexican heritage living there. Yet she finds the *Tribune* continuing to refer to the area and people there as Puerto Rican. In another example, last year most of the stories in the annual Hispanic Heritage insert were about Mexican traditions, leaving the reader to believe that Hispanic Heritage Month was strictly for those of Mexican heritage. She saw some improvement in this year's Hispanic Heritage insert, though.

STEREOTYPES AND CLICHES

The *Tribune* is aware of its shortfalls when it comes to covering the many groups that make up Chicago's Hispanic community. "I haven't seen any major metropolitan newspaper doing a very good job covering the Hispanic community. Papers tend to do stories that give the impression that we've just discovered something a community has known all along," says Reginald F. Davis, a *Tribune* deputy metro editor. "We have improved, but we have a long way to go."

On the other hand, stories about Hispanics are much easier to find in the *Los Angeles Times (LA Times)*. The problem is that they are much more negative. Of the 56 Hispanic stories we counted, 25 were negative. Though the *LA Times* gave extensive coverage to the North American Free Trade Agreement (NAFTA) and other business subjects important to Hispanics, stories specifically referring to Hispanics in L.A. were for the most part about gangs and the after-effects of the L.A. riots. In a city that is at least 40 percent Hispanic, one would think the *LA Times* could have found more Hispanics who were doing positive things.

Even reports of Hispanics taking positive steps in their communities are filled with cliches, leading the reader to believe that most of L.A.'s more than 1 million newsworthy Hispanics live in gang-infested neighborhoods, if they are not gang members themselves. The front page of the August 27 metro section sported a story titled "Making a Bid to End a Bloody Cycle." The sub-headline read: "Violence: Latino gang members meet at USC to talk of Brown Pride and to seek ways to stop the murderous rivalries." After quoting some of the "battle-scarred" members in attendance, the story portrayed the Latino community activists, who helped organize the meeting, as anomalies in a violent Hispanic world. The successful Latinos talked of the dangerous communities and dysfunctional families they overcame, giving the reader the impression that most Hispanics come from such backgrounds.

ISSUES FRAMED IN BLACK AND WHITE

"The *LA Times* had the opportunity to do a solid, positive story. Unfortunately, the story was not representative of what took place," says Gus Frías, one of the meeting organizers and a criminal justice and education specialist for the Los Angeles County Office of Education. "The story had no positive sentence about uniting and doing good for the community." A regular *LA Times* reader, Frías believes the paper's coverage of Hispanics is "degrading, unfair, and racist. They think they are the judges of our community and will decide who our leaders are. They are wrong."

Esther Renteria, National Chair of the National Hispanic Media Coalition, says: "The *LA Times* needs to start covering the Hispanic community, talking with Hispanic organizations, and sending reporters to news conferences called by Hispanic leaders. They totally ignore the growth and importance of the Hispanic community." She cites an example of a news conference that California Hispanic elected leaders called during the L.A. riots. The *LA Times* did not send a reporter. In another example, the sale of Univision was covered extensively by the *Wall Street Journal* and the *Miami Herald,* but the *LA Times* provided very little coverage.

In stories that attempt to include minorities, "Quite often racial and ethnic issues are framed in black and white, and you find Latinos don't exist," observes Cheryl Brownstein-Santiago, an *LA Times* news editor and associate editor of *Nuestro Tiempo,* the *LA Times* bilingual supplement. For example, in *LA Times* stories about rebuilding after the May riots and about minority contract programs, one wouldn't know that Hispanics outnumber blacks almost four to one in the Los Angeles metropolitan area. Often, Hispanic business owners weren't even mentioned in a story filled with black and Asian merchants.

MOVING BEYOND THE SENSATIONAL

However, the *LA Times* recently launched two new editorial features—the *City Times* and *Voices*—aimed at expanding its coverage of multi-cultural communities in Southern California.

Hispanics were also hard to find in the *New York Times (NY Times)*. Of the week's nineteen stories on Hispanics, only eight were positive. Hispanics in New York—where one in four residents is Hispanic—were overwhelmingly portrayed as swindlers, murderers, sex maniacs, and residents of crime-infested neighborhoods. Stories about the decline of Hispanic barrios and increasing crime received front-page coverage on August 28 and 30 and page-23 status on August 29.

The August 28 front-page story headlined "Gunfight Steals Dreams for Rebirth in Bronx" gets mixed reviews. The article begins with a Puerto Rican immigrant who, the reader is led to believe, does not speak English and is the helpless victim of increasing violence that recently climaxed with a shooting spree that wounded twelve bystanders. But the story then moves beyond the sensational shooting and "typical" Hispanic victim to the reasons why this once-hopeful neighborhood is retreating into its undesirable past. The reader is introduced to Hispanic small business owners who have been victimized by the rapid decline of their neighborhoods and Hispanic police officers who knew the area in its heyday. The story quotes Luis L. Suarez, a police detective in the area: "The shooting [Suarez said,] doesn't reflect what's going on in this neighborhood, where most people are not dealers and criminals, but law-abiding, working-class people struggling to rebuild a community." Unfortunately, the reader had to jump from the A section—where the story began with the poor Spanish-speaking Latina—to the B section and then read through 21 inches of text before meeting Suarez and hearing the positive way he portrays the people in his neighborhood.

FAIR AND BALANCED COVERAGE

Suarez was satisfied with the story after it was published, however. "I was surprised the *NY Times* gave a fair overview of the area. We got calls from community groups, and they said they were pleased with the article," says Suarez, whose Hispanic first name, Luis, was incorrectly anglicized to "Louis" by *NY Times* reporter Steven Lee Myers.

But a shopkeeper also interviewed wasn't so pleased. "The *NY Times* wasn't dealing in substance. It could have been a far better story," says the man who immigrated to the neighborhood from Puerto Rico thirty years ago and who didn't want to be identified. "They didn't explain the events that led up to the shooting. They shouldn't just scratch the surface just to get headlines."

NY Times metro editor Gerald Boyd, who thinks it's "ridiculous" to generally rate coverage of Hispanics, believes that his paper's "record speaks for itself."

"I think we have made enormous strides, not just covering Hispanics but all stories relevant to the people in the city," he says.

Smaller and less worldly than the country's leading papers, the *San Antonio Light* has what the others lack: fair and balanced coverage of its population, which is 56 percent Hispanic. With only about half the pages of the giant *LA Times, NY Times,* and *Washington Post,* the *Light* managed to squeeze 49 Hispanic stories into its daily editions. Of those 49, a whopping 37 were positive and only twelve were negative. These numbers indicate that the *Light* knows something the other papers do not: There is more to covering Hispanics than the crime beat. Sure, there are stories about Hispanic crime in San Antonio—it wouldn't be a normal city if there were not. But, as with any population, the number of Hispanic criminals is small compared to the number of Hispanic leaders and cultural events and their positive influence on their community.

REACHING OUT TO VARIOUS COMMUNITIES

For example, a front-page profile on a Hispanic nurse, Paul Rivera, showed the man as professional, intelligent, and active in his community. Save for his name, the fact that he is Hispanic isn't even mentioned in the story, therefore allowing his accomplishments, rather than his ethnicity, to become the focal point of the story. Interviewed after his profile was published, Rivera said the fact that the *Light* interviewed a public employee especially a nurse, was more surprising than the fact that a Hispanic was profiled. "The majority of people in San Antonio are Hispanic, so we get a lot of news coverage," he says. "I would say the *Light* does a good job. They don't just skip over things. They give in-depth coverage to [Hispanic] issues and people."

Light Managing Editor Jeff Cohen explains his paper's mission: "We're constantly trying to innovate and reach out to the various cultural communities in the city. We talk each day about making sure our coverage of people of color, women, special interest groups, and the Hispanic community is complete and representative. I feel we're doing a pretty good job serving our readership."

In contrast to the *San Antonio Light,* the *Washington Post* seems to have forgotten the statistics recently printed in its own pages: The Hispanic population in the Washington area alone doubled from 1985 to 1990. A very conservative estimate counts nearly a quarter of a million Hispanics, about 5.7 percent of the area's population. Only fifteen of the hundreds of stories the *Post* ran in a week were about Hispanics or Hispanic issues. But the *Post* seems to adhere to the argument that quality is better than quantity. The ten of the fifteen stories that can be considered positive show insight and sensitivity to issues affecting the Hispanic community, both in Washington and other areas of the country. Hurricane Andrew coverage dominated the pages of all the papers reviewed, but the *Post* was the only paper to run two stories specifically on the storm's effect on Hispanics in South Florida. An August 26 story reported the particular impact of the hurricane on Mexican migrant workers. The August 29 story on hurricane news being beamed by radio to Cuba to ease the minds of concerned relatives of Cubans in Florida showed sensitivity and familiarity with Cuban-American relations.

A WAY TO GO

But alongside this coverage, the *Post* managed to sneak in a story titled "Immigrant Anglers Line Potomac [River] Banks" on August 25. Hispanics were portrayed as new immigrants, poor, unemployed, non-English speaking, and even ignorant of the law: "For many of the low-income newcomers, some of whom speak little English, the river is an important source of food . . . ." A few paragraphs later: "Police and park officials say it's difficult to determine how many immigrants fish the Potomac each day, in part because most do not buy fishing licenses."

The *Post* acknowledges that it has some way to go in better serving its Hispanic readers. "I think we have improved our coverage [of Hispanics] considerably in the past several years, but I don't think we are anywhere near doing as much as we should be doing," says Milton Coleman, Assistant Managing Editor of the metro section.

Comparing the papers across the country from a Hispanic business perspective, Patricia Rivera, the Washington, D.C.-based public relations coordinator of the U.S. Hispanic Chamber of Commerce, ranks the *NY Times* at the top. "If I was a Hispanic businessperson in Washington, I would not read the *Washington Post* alone. I would definitely get the *NY Times* and the *Financial Times*," says Rivera. "If I had to compare the *Post* to the *NY Times*, the *Times* definitely covers [NAFTA] a lot better." Rivera, who works with media around the country, also has praise for the *Chicago Tribune's* extensive coverage of the Chamber's convention last year, which was held in the Windy City.

THE MAINSTREAM IS NOW MULTICOLORED

Cynthia Muñoz, a partner in San Antonio-based Muñoz y Marín Public Relations, isn't so pleased with the papers that she tries to pitch Hispanic stories to. She explains that when she sends Hispanic-oriented stories to the *LA Times*, the idea is typically not considered for the regular paper but is instead referred to the bilingual supplement *Nuestro Tiempo*, thus effectively segregating the news. "This is important news the general market needs to be educated on. They are withholding news," she says. "But I do praise the *LA Times* for very positive coverage of the Hispanic arts. The *NY Times* is weak all around, the *Chicago Tribune* is pretty good at covering a variety of Hispanic issues, and the *San Antonio Light* is doing the best job of all."

It can be argued that while newspapers have a journalistic obligation to fairly cover Hispanics, this ideal really translates into dollar signs. As newspapers are going out of business left and right, old-time editors blame the 30-second sound bites of TV and the "McNews" of *USA Today*. But they don't blame their own troops for failing to adapt coverage to their changing readership.

"Who a newspaper's public is and who its advertisers need to cater to has changed over the years," says Brownstein-Santiago of the *LA Times*. "The mainstream is no longer what it used to be. It's becoming multicolored. Newspapers have been trying to adapt to this new reality, but not as quickly as some of us would like."

One reason for the slow pace is the low number of Hispanics in the newsroom. The *Chicago Tribune* newsroom is 3 percent Hispanic, *LA Times* is 7 percent, *NY Times* is 3 percent, *San Antonio Light* is 17 percent, and *Washington Post* is 1.4 percent, according to a recent study. Once Hispanics start appearing in the newsroom, perhaps the Hispanic community will start appearing in the paper.

A WIDE DISPARITY

But papers can't rely on Hispanic reporters to act as watchdogs against the negative cliches writers love using. Many reporters and editors need a crash course in cultural awareness, to learn that just because someone only speaks Spanish doesn't mean he is a new immigrant; that gang members aren't all "battle-scarred"; that our countries of origin aren't all "banana republics" ruled by "drug kingpins" who do away with their enemies "execution-style."

Ironically, there seems to be an inverse relationship between the historical prestige of the paper and the quality of its coverage of Hispanics. The more clout a paper has, the less coverage Hispanics get. Perhaps the reason is that papers like the *NY Times, Washington Post,* and *LA Times* are famed and respected around the world for their coverage of national and international issues. Unfortunately, coverage of their own back yard is put on the back burner and the back pages. It takes a quality paper that does not have world recognition, like the *San Antonio Light,* to provide fair, balanced, and quality coverage for and about its readers.

"There's a wide disparity in covering the Hispanic community," says Garza of the *Chicago Tribune.* "Some papers have improved greatly, but others still lag behind with their stone-age perception of Hispanics. The fastest growing segment of the population doesn't see itself reflected in the media."

Hispanics have been invisible in the eyes of newspaper publishers, and therefore readers, for years. Unless this changes, newspapers are in for some bad news themselves. As Garza sums up: "How can the media expect people to read the paper when their community is not covered, or is only covered in a negative light?"

52

A TV Generation Is
Seeing Beyond Color

Nancy Hass

Editor's Note: Perhaps there is hope that the young people in America can bring about a multicultural mass media. At least that's the suggestion of this article, which indicates that young viewers of television tend to cross the color line in their viewing habits, unlike older viewers.

As television aired more non-white shows, targeted to non-white audiences, producers found young people in their audiences regardless of ethnicity or race. Some argue that many non-white programs present an inaccurate picture of African American life, and the number of these shows seems to be in decline at the end of the 1990s, but non-white characters and themes have been accepted and are being incorporated into more multiracial programs.

Nancy Hass is a writer for *The New York Times,* where this article was published on February 22, 1998, and is reprinted with permission.

It's not hard to figure out why, come Mondays at 9 P.M., Anna-Lucille Calabrese can be found parked in front of "Buffy the Vampire Slayer." Like Buffy, the heroine of the hip hourlong drama on WB about a girl who reluctantly takes on the task of ridding her high school of an infestation of the undead, Anna-Lucille, 13, is bright, popular and tinged with teenage irony.

Also like Buffy, whose milieu is the lush environs of Southern California, Anna-Lucille lives in a wealthy suburb—in her case, Montclair, N.J. Her father, a publishing executive, drives a fast black Porsche sports coupe.

"She's smart and in control," says Anna-Lucille of Buffy, whose blond hair and Ivory Girl looks are part of the joke.

But Anna-Lucille is hardly the neat little demographic package that television executives wish for. In fact, during the hour before "Buffy," she does something that not only skews the precarious economics of the multibillion-dollar entertainment industry but also adds a wrinkle to the national debate on race: she flips the channel to watch "Martin" reruns and "In the House," shows with entirely black casts, on UPN.

CROSSING THE COLOR LINE

Like a growing number of young white televisicn viewers across the country, Anna-Lucille crosses the color line daily and barely notices. She and her peers seem not to care much about race, at least wher it comes to the small screen. "They're funny, too," she says of the shows she watches. "They're crazy, but they're funny."

The crossover trend among young televisian viewers is remarkable because it directly contradicts the habits of older Americans. In fact, over all, there is astonishingly little overlap between the most-watched shows among blacks and those among whites.

"E.R." is No. 1 among whites but 18th with blacks. "Seinfeld," a close No. 2 with whites, is an astonishing 54th among black viewers. "Between Brothers" is the most popular show among blacks, but it ranks 107th among whites. In fact, not a single show is in both the top 10 for blacks and the top 10 for whites. Only 4 shows appear on both racial groups' top 20 lists; the one with the highest ratings is "Monday Night Football." Not one is a comedy.

"Blacks generally watch black shows, and whites generally watch white shows," says Dean Valentine, a former Disney executive who became president of UPN last November. "It's a reflection of how fragmented our society has become."

CHILDREN ARE DIFFERENT

Children, however, increasingly seem to be bucking the trend. "Kids are much more color-blind than adults in their television viewing," says Douglas Alligood, who has for the last decade tracked such trends for BBDO, the advertising agency. "And they're becoming more so. They make decisions based on the context of the show, not simply the racial content." Laura Herrold, a white 11-year-old from Ridgewood, N.J., who watches "Sister, Sister" and "The Smart Guy," as well as "Sabrina the Teenage Witch," agrees. "My friends and I don't even talk about whether the people on the shows are black or white," she says. "We watch those shows because they're about people our age."

It's easy to see this news as the harbinger of a new age of racial harmony, led by the youth of America.

On one level, the trends mean that young people are more accepting of diversity than their parents. But while some questions that the crossover brings to mind are sanguine, others may not be. When today's teenagers grow into adults, will they continue this tolerance of diversity and pass it along to their children? Or will they, as their parents did, switch to "segregated" television. Are the series watched by white teenagers the best possible reflections of black culture they can find? And will the young networks that present most of the black series continue to do so, once they've established themselves?

TELEVISION HAS CHANGED

The racial chasm in television viewing is relatively new. That's because until the last several years there weren't enough shows with black casts to fragment the audience.

"Growing up, television was a white medium entirely," says Samm-Art Williams, a black playwright who has written for series like "Martin" and "Good News." "We came of age watching 'Father Knows Best' and 'The Donna Reed Show.' Everyone did." But Fox, WB and UPN have changed that. With NBC, CBS and ABC programming shows with largely all-white casts aimed at a wide swath of middle America, the three upstart networks, each of which has its biggest affiliates in major urban areas, have in the last few years developed more than a dozen sitcoms with all-black core casts.

The result is a slew of new black media images, ranging from warm and fuzzy dads like Robert Townsend on "The Parent Hood" to the feisty 20-something roommates on "Living Single" (which was recently canceled after four and a half seasons).

POLARIZING VIEWING HABITS

But such shows have also polarized America's viewing habits, underscoring the depth of the nation's ambivalence about race and identity. Television dramas like "E.R.," "N.Y.P.D. Blue" and "Chicago Hope" have gracefully integrated their casts (if not, by and large, their audiences). But the races rarely mix on sitcoms. While a few black shows have white minor characters and some of the white shows trot out an occasional black person, prime-time comedy is one of the last bastions of public segregation.

The major networks insist that that's how people, especially older white people, like it. As white viewers get older, the number of them watching sitcoms about black people dwindles to a virtual handful, according to the ratings. Oddly enough, older black people start watching shows that are predominantly white.

"The figures are very stark," says Karen Kratz of A. C. Nielsen, the rating service.

The sole exception to this racial parting has been Bill Cosby, whose audience throughout the years has attracted both blacks and whites. "The Cosby Show," which ran from 1984 till 1992, on NBC was No. 1 in both black and white households. "He is an aberration," says Mr. Alligood. "Cosby," Mr. Cosby's current show on CBS, is 15th in black households and 27th in white households.

BECOMING LESS RACE CONSCIOUS

Even the immensely appealing Will Smith, who starred for five seasons on NBC's "Fresh Prince of Bel Air," was not truly a crossover success. His show, at its height in 1993, was No. 1 among black viewers but never rose above No. 36 with whites.

But if the viewing habits of the current crop of young people are any in-dication, America is slowly becoming less race-conscious. This season, the white teenage viewership of several youth-oriented black-skewed shows rose significantly. "Sister, Sister" had a 42 percent increase in white viewers last year. "The Wayans Brothers" showed a 27 percent rise in its white audience. "Moesha" (starring the pop star Brandy as the girl next door), "Hanging With Mr. Cooper" and "The Smart Guy" saw smaller percentage gains in white viewership.

Although the numbers are still relatively small, industry insiders who have experienced firsthand Hollywood's uncomfortable and often clumsy relation-ship with race are encouraged.

"This is an extraordinary phenomenon," says Stan Latham, a black direc-tor who has worked on virtually every black sitcom from "Cosby" to "The Steve Harvey Show." "I know it sounds excessive, but I really think this could be the salvation of American culture."

WATCHING BLACK SITCOMS

Sociologists say there are several reasons that more white teenagers are watch-ing black sitcoms. To begin with, the shows are there; nearly half of the youth-oriented sitcoms are now made up of largely black casts. In addition, they say, young people of both races are less conscious of color overall and more ac-cepting of diversity.

(Indeed, some white teenage shows—"Sabrina the Teenage Witch," "Buffy the Vampire Slayer" and "Clueless"—have attracted big followings among black teenagers.)

Finally, elements of black street culture have become popular among young whites. For nearly a decade, hip-hop music has outsold rock among white teenagers, and the clothing esthetic that accompanied it—baggy pants, oversize polos with huge logos, expensive sneakers—long ago infiltrated even small-town America.

Notably, it was white viewers who made "Yo! MTV Raps," now the chan-nel's most popular show, a hit in the early 1990s. Before then, MTV had largely ignored rap videos.

"The inner cities weren't even wired for cable when the show took off," says J. Fred McDonald, a University of Northeastern Illinois sociologist and author of "One Nation Under Television: The Rise and Decline of Network TV." "It was white kids who showed the music executives that they would buy that sound."

DIVERSE BLACK IMAGES

These days, rappers are far from the only black entertainers on television. "There is an amazing number of diverse black images available on television these days, from Janet Jackson to Samuel Jackson to Coolio to the dramatiza-tions of the Tuskegee experiment," says Todd Boyd, a professor of critical studies at the University of Southern California's school of cinema studies and author of "Am I Black Enough for You? Pop Culture From the Hood and Be- yond." "That's the sort of environment that kids—black and white—grow up with now. It's no wonder white kids have no problem enjoying black sitcoms."

But the negative side to such a crossover is that it further institutionalizes mediocre programming.

"The problem is that most of these sitcoms with all-black casts are less than spectacular," says Mr. Boyd, echoing a comment often heard in program development circles in Hollywood. Even the network executives who present them agree that virtually none of these shows are in the league of sophisti- cated, and all-white, sitcoms like "Seinfeld," "Frasier" or "Friends." Most episodes of "The Wayans Brothers," on the WB, for example, are little more than 22-minute showdowns to prove which of the lead characters is the bigger muttonhead. "We know the overall quality of these shows is pretty bad, and we aren't happy with many of them," says Mr. Valentine of UPN.

AN ACCURATE PICTURE?

There is widespread ambivalence about such shows among leaders of black or- ganizations. In February 1997, the Hollywood and Beverly Hills chapter of the N.A.A.C.P. issued a statement condemning shows like "Martin" for promoting derogatory stereotypes. And yet just months before, the organization's national board had awarded the show's star, Martin Lawrence, its coveted Image Award.

"Martin," canceled last spring after five seasons, was among the most pop- ular series with young white viewers.

Mr. Boyd and others worry that white teenagers who live in all-white neighborhoods may use the shows as their only reference point in their per- ceptions of blacks. "These shows could actually impair their understanding of the depth and breadth of black culture," he says.

But some writers, including Mr. Williams, take issue with those who be- lieve it is a comedy writer's responsibility to "uplift the race."

"I think black folks need to stop taking themselves so seriously," says Mr. Williams. "It's my job as a sitcom writer to tell jokes, to have fun. If you're go- ing to cure ills, go to the theater."

Ed Weinberger, who wrote for "Cheers" and "Taxi" and more recently created "Sparks," a sitcom about a black law firm, for UPN, says his two sons, ages 10 and 13, love some of the black comedies because the humor is broader and faster moving. But not all pass muster.

"My kids like 'Jamie Foxx' and 'Martin,'" Mr. Weinberger says. "They don't like the quiet comedy of 'The Parent Hood' or 'The Gregory Hines Show.' The thing that sells them isn't race; it's the nature of the comedy. They like it fast and stupid."

BUT BLACK SITCOMS ARE FADING

Quiet, fast, or in-between, the era of black sitcoms is ebbing. Despite the in- flux of new young white viewers, the tenuous economics of running a network are leading some executives to rethink the strategy of catering to urban audiences. "Our advertisers are totally conscious that we be very crossover," says Mr. Ancier. "The message is, if you don't make shows that appeal to white audiences, you fail."

That message was borne out last year. Fox, once a bastion of bawdy black comedy, has nearly completed its transformation to a whiter shade of pale. Added to its successes with "The Simpsons" and "The X-Files," its current home run is "Ally McBeal," a quirky hourlong drama about a white female lawyer in her 20's. The WB's ratings gains this year outstripped any of the six networks, but it wasn't the channel's black sitcoms that made the difference; the gains were made largely on the strength of "Buffy" and "Seventh Heaven," a pious drama about a white minister and his large family. And late in the season Mr. Ancier persuaded the creators of "Moesha" to transfer the main character to a nearly all-white private school. The move was intended to increase the number of white viewers who tune in.

One popular strategy is to concentrate on multi-ethnic shows, integrating the casts in order to hold onto the core black audience while attracting new white viewers.

NEW EMPHASIS ON MULTIRACIAL

Winifred Hervey, a black sitcom writer who is a veteran of "The Golden Girls" and the creator of "The Steve Harvey Show," says she is frustrated by the new emphasis on the multiracial. "A good show doesn't come from someone saying, 'O.K., we want you to write a crossover drama.' The really worthwhile shows spring from a story you want to tell, not from demographics."

But Mr. Valentine says he is determined to satisfy both his advertisers and his audience by "breaking down the ghetto."

"People get really upset about segregation in society, so what I'm unclear about is why they think it's all right on TV," he explains. "We have to bring in a lot of people of all ages and races."

To Edwin Kaplan, a precocious 11-year-old from Montclair, that sounds just fine. "I like shows because they make me laugh," he says. "I don't care if they're about black people like 'Family Matters,' white people like 'Full House' or a family with black and white kids together.

After all, the problems always get resolved in 30 minutes. What's the difference?"

ADDITIONAL RESOURCES FOR PART 13

Suggested Questions and Discussion Topics

1. In "Advocating Diversity in an Age of Electronic News," Felix Gutierrez writes that new media will make things better in the future for minority groups. Why? And How will things get better? Discuss.

2. Discuss how things could be worse for minorities in the future, given the scenario posed in "Advocating Diversity in an Age of Electronic News."

3. According to Jim Strader in "Black on Black," why has the black press in America "lost some of its sweeping influence"? Discuss two of his reasons.

4. According to "Black on Black," the decline of the black press has been tragic, but some of the best black journalists have gone to work in the mainstream press. Has this offset their loss to the black press and black community? Discuss.

5. In "Bad News for Hispanics," what does author Michelle Heller suggest needs to change to get more positive Hispanic news in the newspaper?

6. In "Bad News for Hispanics," the author discusses some of the "wide disparity in covering the Hispanic community." Discuss that disparity and some of the reasons for it.

7. In "TV Generation is Seeing Beyond Color," by Nancy Hass, what are some of the reasons given why more white teenagers are watching black sitcoms? Do you agree? Discuss.

8. What is the negative side to crossover viewership suggested in "TV Generation is Seeing Beyond Color." Why? And do you agree? Discuss.

Suggested Readings

Shirley Biagi and Marilyn Kern-Foxworth, *Facing Difference: Race, Gender, and Mass Media.* Thousand Oaks, CA: Pine Forge Press, 1997.

Christopher P. Campbell, *Race, Myth, and the News.* Thousand Oaks, CA: Sage Publications, 1995.

Gail Dines and Jean M. Humez, eds., *Gender, Race, and Class in Media.* Thousand Oaks, CA: Sage Publications, 1995.

Heather Goodall, Andrew Jakubowicz, and Jeannie Martin, *Racism, Ethnicity, and the Media.* Stuart, FL: Paul & Co., 1994.

George H. Hill, *Black Media in America: A Resource Guide.* New York: G. K. Hall, November 1984.

Yahya R. Kamalipour and Theresa Carilli, eds., *Cultural Diversity and U.S. Media.* Albany, NY: State University of New York Press, 1998.

Beverly Ann Deepe Keever, Carolyn Martindale, and Mary A. Weston, eds., *U.S. News Coverage of Racial Minorities: A Source Book, 1934–1996.* Westport, CT: Greenwood. 1997.

Clint C. Wilson and Felix Gutierrez, *Minorities and Media: Diversity and the End of Mass Communication.* Thousand Oaks, CA: Sage Publications, 1985.

Clint C. Wilson and Felix Gutierrez, *Race, Multiculturalism, and the Media.* Thousand Oaks, CA: Sage Publications, 1997.

Suggested Videos

Stuart Hall, "Representation and the Media." Northampton, MA: Media Education Foundation. 1996. (55 minutes)

Stuart Hall, "Race, the Floating Signifier." Northampton, MA: Media Education Foundation. 1996. (85 minutes)

Lani Guinier, "Democracy in a Different Voice: Race, Politics, and the Media." Northampton, MA Media Education Foundation. 1995. (37 minutes)

Michael Eric Dyson, "Material Witness: Race, Identity, and the Politics of Gangsta Rap." Northampton, MA: Media Education Foundation. 1995. (42 minutes)

"Breaking Through Stereotypes." New York: Insight Media, 1994. (15 minutes)

"Ethnic Notions." New York: Insight Media, 1987. (56 minutes)

"Black and Jewish Images." New York: Insight Media, 1984. (30 minutes)

"Yellow Tale Blues." New York: Insight Media, 1990. (30 minutes)

"Slaying the Dragon." New York: Insight Media, 1988. (60 minutes)

PART · 14

Women, Men, and Children

One of the reasons media aren't quite so "mass" any longer is that audiences have made it clear that the same formula doesn't work for everyone. Audience appetites are always evolving, and different segments want different media content. Also, within media—among those who write, edit, and produce materials for print and broadcast—different points of view brought to the process by employees of different genders, ages, and racial and ethnic backgrounds have transformed a mass formula into many different equations.

Two main obstacles must be resolved before media can accurately reflect the world and the people in it. First, stereotypical characters in entertainment programming and stereotypical treatments in news reporting must be eliminated. Second, employment pathways in news and entertainment media must be opened to groups besides white males, who have dominated mass media decision making.

Progress on these two main issues has occurred, most of it apparent only in the 1990s after two decades of activism and challenges to business as usual. Many more women are now employed at levels of influence and compensated at levels comparable to those of their male colleagues. Many more men are now convinced that this development is right. But it didn't happen because male bosses woke up one morning and decided things should change. It happened because of a series of lawsuits and complaints to the Equal Employment Opportunity Commission in the late 1970s and 1980s, forcing employers to recognize the rights of all their employees, especially those of women. Very few major media institutions escaped legal challenges. Among those who did not were the *New York Times,* the *Washington Post, Newsweek, Time, Newsday, Reader's Digest,* the Associated Press, and NBC.

Although equity in employment has improved as a result of these initiatives, debate about sex stereotyping in news coverage and advertising rages on. So does discussion about the disproportionately small amount of space devoted to news coverage of the activities and issues of concern to women and children. The term coined to describe media treatment that favors stereotypes and omits realistic portrayals of a population subgroup is *symbolic annihilation.* The most frequent victims have been women, minorities, and children.

None of this is to say that men, particularly white men, have not been affected by stereotyping in news coverage, advertising, and entertainment programming. They have. They also have had to contend with competition in the work force from groups that formerly hadn't posed much of a threat. This development has antagonized some men and presents yet another point of conflict that needs to be resolved.

Children, of course, don't make demands in the workplace. But they are an important audience segment with influence over a tremendous amount of spending power—their parents' and, as they mature, their own. Adults in media organizations spend a great deal of time researching and testing ways to reach children and inculcate in them the habit of media use—newspaper and magazine reading; television viewing; and enjoyment of videos, films, and sound recordings. Because children have no organized voice of their own, some adults have become active in urging intelligence in programming directed at children and limiting the advertising such programming can contain. The goal of groups such as Action for Children's Television (ACT), which disbanded in 1992 after two decades of activism on behalf of child viewers, was to raise the quality of children's programming and somewhat restrain the advertisers' bombardment of a young audience. ACT also pushed hard, and successfully, for nonstereotypical treatment of girls and boys in programs and ads.

Media of all types have been enriched by the recognition that there is no such thing as a "mass audience," to be served by only one type of media employee. There are now many more choices for all of us and many more kinds of faces in our newsrooms, production studios, and advertising agencies. These changes have been important, and we can be certain that there will be more.

53

We've Come a Long Way, Maybe

KAY MILLS

Editor's Note: Women have made a good deal of progress in mass media over the past thirty years, both in the way they are portrayed and in the roles they are playing as gatekeepers. Much still needs to be done, especially in getting into high-level, decision-making positions in mass communication.

As an activist woman journalist, Kay Mills has been very much a part of the progress that has been made. She hopes that a new generation will be able to take up where hers is leaving off and complete the work that still needs to be done.

Mills has been an editorial writer at the *Los Angeles Times* and is the author of a book about women in journalism, *A Place in the News* (New York: Columbia University Press, 1990). This article was published in *The Quill,* February 1990.

Some 30 years ago, I walked into the clatter of the Washington bureau of United Press International, an awestruck college freshman thrilled to begin a summer job typing news stories dictated by the reporters from the White House, the Justice Department, the State Department.

I've been in the newspaper business ever since. And over the years, I encountered a host of problems rooted in male resistance to the presence of women in the newsroom, problems I never anticipated and that I never want to deal with again.

I was not alone. No woman who entered the newspaper business in those days of manual typewriters, smudgy carbon-copy "books," paste pots, and cigar smoke could have imagined the changes that were to occur in their professional lives.

Fortunately, changes did occur regarding the acceptance of women in the newsrooms. Women now have a place in the news. Young women entering the field of journalism today often think we who have been around for a while are talking paleolithic history when we bring up our battles against discrimination. They are wrong.

PROBLEMS CONTINUE

There still are problems for women in the newspaper business, problems far more subtle and intractable than the blatant discrimination we faced years ago. These problems, too, should be history, like my hoary war stories of taking dictation from Merriman Smith.

But they aren't history, and they won't become history until the leaders of our profession finally wake up to the fact that they are failing to cover a substantial part of their community and that the only way they can perform that mission is by opening the editorial decision-making process to more than white males.

Some of my best friends are white males, but they do not have an exclusive franchise on news judgment. They covered the savings-and-loan bailout with stories and charts and open pages, but they didn't provide the same depth in covering major congressional debates on child-care legislation.

They rarely cover their areas' black communities systematically. They rely on Asian-American and Latino journalists to understand the distinctions among the various ethnic groups in their communities rather than getting out and learning about them themselves. Or worse, they don't have any Asian-American or Latino journalists on their staffs, which means they provide even poorer coverage.

SMALL INDIGNITIES

If a paper is dominated by white males, the newspaper has little diversity of coverage and it won't get it until it has a better mix of people throughout the newsroom and—especially—at the daily page-one meetings of top editors. Women and people of color are not at those meetings in any numbers yet.

But I have gotten ahead of myself. You see where I am going. Now you have to see how we got where we are.

The day that I introduced myself as the new UPI dictationist, I knew precious little about the history of women in my new profession.

I had watched May Craig of the *Portland Press Herald* on *Meet the Press*. But I didn't know that she had had to crusade to get a women's restroom in the press gallery at the Capitol. I soon took dictation from Helen Thomas, who in my two summers at UPI was the new third person on the White House beat. But I didn't know how many years she had waited to get that job. For that matter, I didn't know that for many years when she covered speeches at the National Press Club, she could not sit on the main floor with the male reporters but had to sit in the balcony.

Indignities such as having to sit in the Press Club balcony seem small today, but they were indicators of the second-class citizenship women had long held in the newspaper business. There had always been a few women in the American newsrooms, but they were so rare that their names come readily to mind.

IN THE PAST

A dozen or so women published newspapers in colonial times. Anne Royall was the first Washington gossip columnist in the early nineteenth century. Margaret Fuller, best known as a member of the Transcendentalist literary set, became the first female foreign correspondent when she traveled to Europe and covered the Italian version of the upheavals of 1848 for Horace Greeley's *New York Tribune.*

Starting in late 1889, Nellie Bly traveled around the world for the *New York World,* beating Phileas Fogg's fictional record of 80 days and sending back stories of her adventures.

In this century, Dorothy Thompson was pre-eminent in the 1930s. She was the first American journalist thrown out of Nazi Germany, and she later wrote an influential political column.

Marguerite Higgins talked her way into an overseas assignment late in World War II, walked in at the head of the column liberating Dachau, served as the *New York Herald Tribune*'s Berlin correspondent, and later shared the Pulitzer Prize for coverage of the Korean War.

But most women in journalism in the nineteenth and well into the twentieth century were either "sob sisters," covering trials and bleeding-heart human interest stories, or they were hired for the women's pages.

In general, male editors seldom let any real news appear on the women's pages, and the staffs of many women's pages were physically segregated from the rest of the newsroom. The newsroom was "no place for a lady."

Indeed, when Kay Harris was hired in the Associated Press bureau in San Francisco in the 1930s, she was mainly assigned to stories outside the office. Today, she suggests that the attempt to protect her sensitivities (or the men's turf, perhaps) worked to her advantage. Being on the street, she had an opportunity to cover a wide array of stories, from union organizing to the treason trial of "Tokyo Rose" to meetings at which the United Nations was chartered.

ELEANOR ROOSEVELT AND WORLD WAR II

These women were the exceptions in the newspaper field. The rule was that women were not hired for the newsroom. But that barrier broke down during three major periods of change for women in the newsroom.

- Eleanor Roosevelt decided that only women could cover her news conferences as First Lady. Since Eleanor Roosevelt made news quite independently of her husband, her decision meant that each wire service, Washington newspaper, and Washington newspaper bureau had to have at least one female reporter.

In many cases, that was *all* they had. But it meant that a succession of talented women got jobs in Washington or held onto them during the Depression, women like Bess Furman, Beth Campbell Short, and Ruth Cowan Nash, who followed one another at the Associated Press.

(Furman and Short eventually left AP because women were expected to leave their jobs when they became pregnant. Some women were fired if they didn't get the message.)

- Just as Rosie the Riveter filled in for men in the shipyards and airplane factories during World War II, so Rosie the Reporter finally got her break in American newsrooms. Helen Thomas got her start at what was then the United Press during the war, as did Eileen Shanahan, later a distinguished economics reporter for the *New York Times.*

Once in the nation's newsrooms, women found there was no special mystique to writing a headline or editing copy or covering a basketball game. Mary Garber of the *Winston-Salem Journal Sentinel* started covering sports then. Flora Lewis of the *New York Times* got overseas in time for VJ Day.

But many women lost their jobs when the war ended, even when servicemen did not return to reclaim their positions. The late 1940s, the 1950s, and well into the 1960s were dreary times for women who wanted to be journalists. As recently as the mid-1960s, after I had worked for UPI two summers in Washington and three years in its Chicago bureau, I tried to get a newspaper or news magazine job. The excuses delight me today but sent me into a tailspin then.

The *Chicago Daily News* already had four women so it couldn't possibly hire another. *Newsweek* had a small bureau and needed someone who could go anywhere. Presumably, I couldn't. Besides, what would I do if someone I was covering ducked into the men's room? Of course no one covered by men would duck into the women's room, because few women were perceived as making news.

THE SIXTIES AND SEVENTIES

- In the '60s and '70s, women on some women's sections began covering the real news of their world—women seeking better educations, women organizing for political influence, women seeking economic parity, women demanding better health care.

Others were campaigning to open the National Press Club to membership and full privileges for women. Others sued their employers, most notably the *New York Times* and the Associated Press.

While these women won only limited gains—and often extra trouble—for themselves (the pioneers-take-the-arrows syndrome), they put their organizations and others on notice that they must hire more women, promote them, and give them better assignments.

Equal opportunity at the Associated Press was especially important beyond the obvious fact that more women got jobs. More women's bylines appeared on the wire and therefore in newspapers around the country; women sometimes did their enterprise stories on issues that affected women; and women were getting the valuable wire-service training that often leads to good jobs at other news organizations.

By the early '70s, more and more women were coming out of college journalism programs, and they simply assumed they could get jobs in newsrooms. Some did.

It took longer for women to be hired in any numbers as photographers, sportswriters, and foreign correspondents, but that has happened, too. However, men still seem to get the benefit of the doubt when these assignments are made; women don't.

SOME IMPROVEMENT

So where are we today and where do we still have to go? Huntly Collins of the *Philadelphia Inquirer* remembers that when she joined that paper only a few years ago, there were few women on the business staff. Now the business page is dotted with women's bylines. When I started out, the only women who covered politics were columnists like Mary McGrory. Today Timothy Crouse could no longer title his book *The Boys on the Bus*.

Marguerite Higgins was a rarity as a war correspondent in Korea. By the 1980s, women often were *the* experts on the guerrilla warfare in El Salvador and Nicaragua.

Solveig Torvik says that when she started at the *Seattle Post-Intelligencer* in the early 1970s, attitudes were such that editors hesitated to send a woman on an overnight assignment or out of town with a male photographer. That has changed, in part because there are now often more women on the city desk than men.

The number of women in middle management constitutes "a dramatic change," Torvik adds, "but that last leap into being final decision-makers is not being made. I'd like to see a woman's name on every masthead of every newspaper worth calling itself that."

BUT NOT AT THE TOP

Indeed, the lack of room at the top is a major problem. A recent survey conducted by Jean Gaddy Wilson, executive director of New Directions for News at the University of Missouri, showed that women now have only 14 percent of the top decision-making editing jobs at American newspapers. They are 18 percent of the directing editors at the smallest papers (under 10,000 circulation); 10 percent at papers of 25,000 to 50,000; 13 percent at papers of 100,000 to 125,000 circulation; and 16 percent at the nation's largest papers (more than 250,000 circulation). They fare less well as publishers, averaging 6 percent of the total.

The higher you look in a newspaper hierarchy, the fewer women you will see. That is partly because women have not been part of the pool of candidates as long as men, partly because some women take themselves out of the running (or are taken out of the running) as they raise their children, and partly because too many newspaper managements still have not done all they can do to recognize female talent the way they are somehow able to spot the bright young man who walks in the door. It may be because he looks like the bosses; we still don't.

"There have to be more voices," says Torvik, now an editorial writer and columnist at the *Post-Intelligencer.* "The task in the 1990s is to broaden newspaper appeal to a vast number of people out there who may not find us very interesting. It's in our own interests of self-preservation to do so."

The question remains: How can the men who run American newspapers be convinced that it is in their long-range self-interest to promote women and thus share power? It's like reinventing the wheel. The men at the top must be constantly convinced that readership exists for broader coverage of issues like child care or women's economic aspirations.

LAWSUITS WORKED FOR A TIME

We've told them and shown them and told them again, but that coverage still isn't second nature to them in the way that coverage of political party conventions and plane crashes is.

We simply must keep covering the stories that we know are there. Women must not be afraid to show how women could survive in Central America or cover dramatic political change in the Soviet Union. Only if newspapers cover a wider range of subject matter will they attract a wider range of readers and thus advertisers. The link between the breadth of coverage to the health of the bottom line seems obvious.

Just as women must do more of the same in terms of coverage, so must we keep up our friendly persuasion on the personnel front. Editors and publishers need to be shown again and again, evidently, the common sense behind promoting women. For their part, women must constantly push their bosses to make changes in what's covered—and who covers what.

Lawsuits, the tool of the 1970s in the effort to end discrimination, will be harder to win in the future. The Supreme Court has chilled that form of attack, but employers who blatantly pass over women for top jobs shouldn't be allowed to feel immune from such threats.

YOUNG WOMEN NEED TO BE MORE INVOLVED

Betsy Wade, one of the women who sued the *New York Times* (and who still works there), says the next fight will have to be waged by the young women, however. It won't be fought by the people who fought it before.

"Everything needs to be done. I don't think we have enough accomplishments to say anything has been done. You look at the hiring lists. You are not seeing what you were seeing when there was legal pressure. It is going to take action of an unrealized sort to make the situation move to benefit women and minorities again.

"We cannot take our daughters and our granddaughters over the waters, much as we would dearly love to do so. They are going to have to muddy themselves."

But first young women have to realize that changes still must be made. I am betting they will wise up when they talk to their friends in other fields about the child-care perks their companies offer and they look at what newspapers don't do for them. And now that women make up one-third of the newspaper work force (and two-thirds of the journalism school graduates), newspapers act at their own risk if they ignore the need.

While child care is, of course, only one issue, employers who do a better job of providing such care would free many women to concentrate more on their work while they are on the job. More important, it would symbolize a real commitment by newspapers to clearing away obstacles to women's progress.

One of these days, younger women are also going to look at their newsrooms and then at their mastheads, and they will want to know why women aren't making it to the top as readily as they have in many other businesses. If newspapers don't change, these young women will vote with their feet, and the profession will lose talent.

WHAT ABOUT NON-WHITE WOMEN?

These younger women also are going to check out the subtle bias in assigning stories and perhaps get to work on that. Or they may concentrate on the nature of the stories that are and are not covered. Or they may more closely examine the language that is still used to describe women as opposed to that used to describe men. Or they may assess the way a paper's resources are allocated to sports as opposed to social problems, and to men's professional sports teams instead of to women's—and men's—recreational sports activities.

They could well raise questions, too, about why black, Latina, and Asian-American women remain even more underrepresented in top jobs on newspapers and about why white women so often forget to include the concerns of women of color on their agendas.

There are individual successes to be sure, such as Pam Johnson, a black woman who is publisher of the *Itheca Journal* in New York State. And there is a growing number of black women who write editorials. But as one of their number said, an editorial writer affects only one editorial on one day, while a black woman at the page-one conference or drawing up a news staff budget can have far more impact on the operation of the paper. It's time for more black journalists to have a shot at running a department or the entire newspaper, but too few organizations seem comfortable with that notion.

We've come a long way from the days of not being allowed to sit on the main floor of National Press Club, but we're not there yet. And we won't be until young women and older women, white women and women of color, stop thinking only of their own careers and form alliances for change at every newspaper in the United States.

54

Is It Just Me, Or Do All
These Women Look Like Barbie?

SHEILA GIBBONS

Editor's Note: Media images of women and girls have received intense scrutiny by women's groups, educational foundations, academic researchers and media activist organizations. Their reports confirm expanded role modeling for women in portrayals in all media, yet females still remain subordinate to males in terms of power, personal authority and freedom of choice.

Sheila Gibbons is vice-president of Communication Research Associates, Inc., and editor of the quarterly newsletter *Media Report to Women*. She also is the co-author of *Taking Their Place: A Documentary History of Women and Journalism* (Lanham, MD: American University Press/University Press of America, 1993).

Someone once said, "the more things change, the more they remain the same," and as an observer of women's portrayal by the media for two decades, I am struck by how true this saying is.

Most who have studied how the mass media portray males and females would agree that the way women are covered in the news and depicted in entertainment has improved. Since the early 1950s, when television began to develop a mass audience, we've seen the appearance of more women newsmakers and more women covering the news. In entertainment, women are among TV's most popular characters and often rise to the top of the recording industry's charts. In Hollywood, male producers and directors still dominate Hollywood film roles and movie content and actors outearn actresses, but even there, women are making inroads.

So what's the problem? It's two-fold:

1. That long-standing definitions of news still tend to diminish the importance of women's achievements and ignore women's voices, even when the stories are about matters important to women; and
2. In entertainment, roles for women and girls, though more plentiful than in the past, are more circumscribed than for men and boys.

In both news and entertainment, "star quality" is required to receive attention. For women, more often than not, that star quality is expected to be wrapped in a comely package, buffed, polished, youthful and most importantly, thin. The result is a very mixed message for women and girls, and for the men and boys around them. The message sent by media to women is that independence and ability are important, but your looks and youthful appearance are the keys to your personal power. If U.S. Secretary of State Madeleine Albright looked like Princess Diana, she'd be on TV every night.

NEWS AND THE CONFLICT MODEL

The conflict model of reporting hushes women's voices. News coverage in American society tends to be conflict-driven, focusing more on the tactics and personalities involved and less on those with a vested stake in the outcome.

The war in Bosnia, for example, was covered in terms of political agendas and military maneuvers. The stories were about prime ministers and generals, armaments and fancy diplomatic footwork. Far too little attention was paid to the disrupted lives and the deaths of women and children caught up in a vicious war, or to women's efforts to rebuild their shattered families and communities.

Similarly, the debate about abortion, which most often is covered by the press as a political or an election issue, tends to reflect the makeup of the players debating it in statehouses across the nation and in Congress. Most of those political players are men. There has yet to be an abortion performed on a man, but you wouldn't know that from the amount of space and air time given to their views on the subject.

Models of news coverage that concentrate on "key players" at the expense of those who must live with the consequences of the players' actions are letting down those with legitimate interests in the issue. All too often, those people are women.

An annual newspaper study by the organization Women, Men and Media has documented how seldom women fit into customary journalistic standards of what is "newsworthy." In its 1996 analysis of the twenty-newspaper sample it has used since 1990, the organization found that references to females were only 15% of all front-page references and only 14% of references on business-section front pages. Fewer than 1% of the references in front-page political stories were to females, and in those instances when such references did occur, they were to political wives and daughters. What news there was of women was quite grim. In most of the sampled newspapers, stories about women who were accused of misconduct or were victims of crime or some sort of disaster predominated on the front and first local pages. In addition, women reporters represented 35% of the bylines on the front pages, but women wrote only 26% of the opinion pieces and commentary appearing in the newspapers.[1]

FEW SOURCES OR EXPERTS

Few national broadcast sources and "experts" are women. Women are minor players on national TV news and public affairs programming as well. In 1996, women correspondents reported only 19% of the stories on evening network newscasts.

Women are the minority of guests on network morning programs such as *Today* and *Good Morning, America.* In 1996, they were only 36% of the guests on these programs, according to a study by ADT Research of New York City. Males dominated as TV experts: they were 86% of all lawyers, 69% of all doctors. (These numbers aren't all bad: Women lawyers, who are 24% of U.S. lawyers, were underrepresented as a group on these programs, but women physicians, who are about 21% of U.S. doctors, were slightly overrepresented.) Only among "real people"—ordinary members of the population invited on to talk about their personal experiences—were men and women invited to be guests in virtually equal numbers (43% women, 47% men, 10% children and teens).[2] On Sunday-morning network public affairs discussion programs, the equation is even more out of balance: more than 90% of the guests are men.

The still-small proportion of women with credible roles in broadcast news and public affairs programming is particularly worrisome, since television is the most popular medium among Americans for obtaining news.

TELEVISION PROGRAMMING, MOVIES AND COMMERCIALS

For better or worse, TV programming is a staple of American society. It's hard to imagine what the nation would be like without it. Because its images and messages are ubiquitous, common sense tells us that TV has an impact on socialization and individual expectations. Just how much, however, no one can say for sure.

Still, no one can argue with TV's singular ability to cue us as to what kind of woman looks good, how her success is measured, how her social behavior is affirmed or rejected and how smart she is. Television does the same for men, and for girls and boys. How impressionable people are, and how big a role TV plays in their lives, has everything to do with how much they will internalize TV's content and take it as a model for their own behavior. The average household's TV is on 7 hours a day; a substantial portion of the day is given over to television. With this kind of dedication from its viewers, TV—along with movies (many of which appear on TV after a first run in a theater or are made for TV in the first place) and commercials—has the potential to be very powerful in contributing to the way that people assign and interpret the roles of the sexes.

Advancing Age Means Diminished Personal Presence and Power

Women have been about one-third of TV's prime-time population since the early 1970s—young women, that is. From 1973 to 1994, women 45 years and older constituted only about 15% of all female characters. (In reality, one in three American women is older than 44 years old, according to the American Association of Retired Persons, which sponsored the TV study.)

Midlife women averaged only 5% of major prime-time characters, and midlife males were more likely to be portrayed in clearly defined occupational roles than midlife females. Major male characters aged 45 to 64 years had undefined occupations only 13% of the time, compared with 54% for females. Older women also were seen as significantly less effective than older men.[3]

Data from the Screen Actors Guild confirms the negative influence of age for women: In 1995, women older than 40 were in only 9.4% of television and film roles, compared with 9.1% in 1991—practically no improvement at all.[4]

The assignment of entertainment roles dramatically underserves the enormous population of vigorous women working and being creative in their midlife and older years. It also perpetuates a stereotype of them that is simply not supported by real life.

The Source of Self-Worth for Women and Girls Is Unclear

Young people are likely to get conflicting messages about women and girls, and from what source they derive their self-worth. Across a wide range of media today, women and girls are more likely to be depicted as concerned with romance and dating, and their appearance is frequently a focus of attention. At the same time, women and girls often are shown using intelligence and exerting independence, according to a 1996 study sponsored by Children Now and the Kaiser Family Foundation. The two organizations studied media used by teenaged girls, including TV shows and commercials, movies and music videos and teen magazines. Their findings included:

- Romance preoccupies women characters in TV and film: 63% of female characters on TV (vs. 49% of male characters) and 65% of female movie characters (vs. only 38% of males characters) were shown talking about a romantic relationship. Teen magazines devoted 35% of their articles to dating, but only 12% to schools or careers.
- In TV shows, male characters were more likely to be shown on the job (41%) than female characters (28%). In movies, men were almost twice as likely (60%) to be shown on the job than women (35%).
- In movies, but also in TV shows and commercials, women's and girls' appearance is frequently commented on: 58% of female characters in movies had comments made about their looks, compared with 28% in TV shows and 26% of female models in the accompanying commercials. Men's and boys' appearance is discussed significantly less: 24% of male characters in the movies, 10% in TV shows and 7% in commercials.
- Commercials aimed at female viewers that aired during the TV shows most often watched by teenaged girls frequently made use of beauty as a product appeal (56%). By comparison, this was true of just 3% of TV commercials aimed at men.

Overall, women were underrepresented (in terms of their proportion in the U.S. population) in all media except teen magazines, in which they are 70% of models in photographs accompanying the articles. They are 45% of female TV characters, 42% of models in TV commercials, 37% of motion-picture characters and 22% of those shown performing in music videos. In all these media, they are subject to exacting (and frequently unrealistic) standards of personal appearance.[5]

CONCLUSION: MEDIA PORTRAYAL HAS AN IMPACT

The lag in depicting women and girls in ways that reflect the majority of their lives may be attributed to women getting a late start in nearly all media. Until the early 1970s, the doors of newspapers, radio, television, ad agencies and magazines were firmly closed to all but a few women professionals. Discrimination grievances and lawsuits opened up opportunities, and after gender-based job discrimination was abolished—at least on paper—women flooded into positions in all media.

Their increased numbers have yet to translate, however, into clout at the top of organizations from which meaningful change can be directed. The glass ceiling—a term I dislike because it sounds like a pleasant, sunny atrium rather than the ugly excuse for discrimination that it is—keeps women from advancing to the levels where ground-breaking decisions are made. If one woman advances to the senior levels of a media organization, that's good, but by herself, she can do little to push for alternative approaches to the coverage or portrayal of women in news, entertainment or advertising. When it becomes uncomfortable for an organization to exclude women from the highest levels and the pipeline opens to the many qualified women now in the media business, that's when we can expect to see some change.

That's also why it's crucial for the consumer who wants more authentic depictions of people in entertainment and news reporting to reflect the concerns of everyone in the audience to push from the outside and demand it. Media executives respond to the market. If enough people in the marketplace say they prefer to see more women with the brains of Barbara Walters than the build of Barbie, we might get somewhere.

KEY STATISTICS ABOUT WOMEN AND GIRLS IN THE MEDIA

News Reporting

TV: Women report 19% of network news stories
Newspapers: Women write 35% of front-page stories

Morning Talk Shows

Women are 36% of guests

Sunday-Morning Public Affairs Programs

Women are less than 10% of guests

TV Entertainment

Women/girls are 45% of female TV characters

Women 45 years of age and older are only 15% of prime-time characters

Women/girls are 42% of models in TV commercials

Women/girls are 22% of performers in music videos

Motion pictures

Women/girls are 37% of motion-picture characters

NOTES

1. M. Junior Bridge, Unabridged Communications, "Marginalizing Women: Front-Page Coverage of Females Declines in 1996," a study of 20 daily newspapers during February 1996 conducted for Women, Men and Media, Washington, D.C.

2. Andrew J. Tyndall, ADT Research, "The Changing News Agenda: New Beats for Men," an analysis of broadcast network morning programs and nightly newscasts, prepared in 1997 for Women, Men and Media, Washington, D.C.

3. Robert H. Prisuta, "Virtually Invisible: The Image of Midlife and Older Women on Prime-Time TV," Washington, D.C.: American Association of Retired Persons, 1996.

4. Screen Actors Guild data, published in *Media Report to Women,* Fall 1996.

5. Nancy Signorielli, "Reflections on Girls in the Media," a study conducted for Children Now and the Kaiser Family Foundation of various media in 1996, released in April 1997.

55

Media Myths and Men's Work

IAN HARRIS

Editor's Note: Although men are much more widely represented in mass media, they too are sometimes victims of stereotypical coverage. This article points out that the picture of most men "enjoying the material benefits of the successful white-collar professional is a media hoax."

As today's economic shakeups threaten their jobs, many men feel inadequate in the face of a media culture that venerates executives in three-piece suits, says Ian Harris, Chair of the Department of Educational Policy and Community Studies at the University of Wisconsin, Milwaukee. This article was published in *Media & Values,* Fall 1989.

The dominant image of the American male portrayed on television, in film and in magazines depicts a white-collar gentleman living in the suburbs in affluent circumstances. These individuals own American Express credit cards and buy the latest model cars. From Ozzie and Harriet to Bill Cosby, these images occupy a powerful place in the American psyche and set standards for male behaviors. They run the media and the large corporations. They speak to us through radios and television. They teach our children. They are not only standard bearers but also the image makers who provide a model for male expectations.

While entertainment programs often create the stereotype of the violent adventurer, advertising campaigns used to promote American products create the deceptive view that the majority of men enjoy the privileges of white-collar professional status. But these images are a myth. In reality . . . few achieve the success portrayed by media images.

Of those men fortunate enough to be employed at all, most work in jobs where they cannot live out the media's version of "the American dream." According to 1981 U.S. government statistics, individuals who fit the category "Males in Professional White Collar Occupations" account for only 15 percent of all employed men, or eight percent of the total male population. Yet certainly they are not the only men satisfied with their professional lives. The non-professional technical occupations, representing an additional 27 percent of employed men, include engineers, skilled craftsmen and other technicians who experience relatively high status and success. Some males in blue-collar jobs and service and farm occupations also earn good salaries and, by their own accounts, feel successful in their work and in their lives. Yet men in all classes are affected by white-collar professional images broadcast through the media and rarely supplemented by images of men in other job categories and occupations. The restriction of work images to wealthy white-collar professional has severe consequences. Raised in a society that honors the Horatio Alger myth, most men believe that a man who works hard will get ahead. Male sex role standards describe a life where American men are supposed to be good fathers, contribute to their communities and occupy positions of power and wealth. The reality of most men's lives, however, is very different from those media-promoted financial and professional success images.

WORKING CLASS MEN

With 71 percent of U.S. men making less than $25,000 annually in 1984, relatively few male workers and their families can approach the standards of consumerism portrayed by television and advertising. The media myth that most men enjoy or have access to the material benefits of the successful white-collar professional is a hoax. Most men will never get status jobs. The vast majority of men either work in occupations other than white collar, are institutionalized, unemployed or have dropped out of the active work force. However, their stories are not told in the media and their plight is ignored.

The 45 percent of working men in blue-collar jobs "man" the factories and other skilled or unskilled trades. Although often taking great pride in their work, many of them labor in positions that offer little or no opportunities for advancement and that may be dull, repetitive and dangerous. Their lives are marked by economic stress, they usually have little or no control over their working conditions and are increasingly threatened by company shifts to cheaper overseas labor and other contractions of the global work force.

Although always the unsung heroes of the U.S. economy, their current media invisibility is something of a change. From 1950 to 1978, this group of men enjoyed some economic security, and media images of the happy, beer-drinking, blue-collar worker abounded in the broad range of ads and commercials and such TV programs as *The Life of Riley.*

Although these men are excluded from the mediated version of the American dream, it is incorrect to assume that men who do achieve some measure of white-collar success necessarily lead more fulfilling lives. The majority of white-collar men spend their lives battling within highly competitive organizations that are so stressful that working within them predisposes them to cancer, heart attack and other stress-related diseases.

UNDERCLASS MEN

Displaced from the labor statistics as they are from society, underclass men lead desperate lives. Seventy percent of these hard-pressed males belong to minority groups. As the migrant workers, prisoners, welfare recipients, homeless street people and patients in mental hospitals, the underclass appears in entertainment programming mainly as criminals. They are seen as a threat to society, but the portraits drawn of them seldom probe the violent worlds that shaped them and their constant fights—often unsuccessful—to survive.

Underclass men do not have regular work. Their hustles for survival include part-time work at low wages, robbery, pimping, drug pushing and other illegal activities. Many end up in prison when they break the law to earn their livelihoods. In fact, prison becomes a sort of brutal haven to escape the viciousness of the street. For the thousands of men of this class, life has no future, few possessions and little purpose. Many are filled with anger at a system that denies them access to the cultural norms of success.

Whether employed or unemployed, whether blue or white collar, men in the United States share a common alienation regarding the conditions of their employment. This alienation is rooted in the realization that a man's work (or lack of work) is at odds with his personal goals.

THE MYTH OF MALE SUCCESS

Unfortunately, male socialization does not help men cope with the realities of the modern workplace. Indeed, male training is designed to create good workers, not full human beings. To cope with deep-felt insecurities, men learn to put up a facade that they are competent and in charge of their destiny. The intense competitiveness of the workplace causes men to be distrustful of their peers, preventing real communication and empathy with others.

These problems in men's lives have become issues for the men's movement. They are also media issues to the degree that the movement seeks to shatter media myths that set sex-role expectations. The mostly white, middle-class leaders of the movement are shaped by the media they see and hear. They are largely ignorant of the problems of most men in the United States, in part because the media seldom, if ever, realistically present underclass and working-class existence.

The media and society as a whole need to bury the popular myth that male success consists of making money. Instead of glorifying male violence, they should portray the pain that causes it. Let's create a new American myth where men are concerned human beings promoting a better life for all creatures on this planet. Liberation is a long and difficult struggle that requires the economic transformation of society as well as the alteration of personal relationships. The media has played its role in creating the problem. It must also be a part of the solution.

56

Boob Tube and Children's Brain Drain

Don Oldenburg

Editor's Note: As shown earlier in this book, television takes up an enormous amount of American's time, including children's time. And to what effect? We have looked at the impact of TV violence and sex on aggressive and sexual behavior. But there may be an even more sinister problem. Some scientific studies are showing that TV viewing may have serious negative effects on the way a child's brain works.

Much research has been done on the effects of television on children. For many years, social scientists accepted the hypothesis that the effects depended on the child; an emotionally disturbed child might become more aggressive after watching violent television, but a normal child would not. Much research funded by television networks came to those kinds of conclusions in the 1960s and '70s. Since the 1980s, much more research has concluded that television has a powerful impact on children's behavior and thought processes. More important, perhaps, has been the cultivation theories of University of Pennsylvania professor George Gerbner and his associates, whose work on the accumulated effects of mass media exposure concludes that the media we use heavily cultivates the way we think about things.

In this article, Don Oldenburg summarizes some of the scientific findings that have led to such conclusions. He is a staff writer for *The Washington Post,* in which this article was published on October 12, 1992, and is reprinted with permission.

Are children experiencing technical difficulties due to television?

Perhaps it should be no surprise that when leading psychologists and scientists who study the developing brain met at a conference in Washington recently to consider that prime-time question, America's top entertainer and babysitter got another bad reception.

Tormenting concerns over what too much TV watching may be doing to our children of course were reiterated. Who can ignore current estimates that the average child watches 22,000 hours of television before graduating from high school—twice the amount of time spent in a classroom? Who isn't troubled by the evidence "from the trenches," as one participant termed the schools, where today's students seem to suffer from an epidemic of attention-deficit disorders, diminished language skills and poor reading comprehension, where teachers report that more than ever children lack analytic powers, creativity and persistence? For that matter, who can organize a conference on television's effects on learning ability without repeating the symptoms?

But if that sounds like a rerun of all the usual suspicions about TV's negative effects, don't touch that dial. Because this daylong high-brow talk show dramatically raised the level of debate over television's undeniable influence—positive and negative—on young minds.

It also raised the ante in what people's worst fears suggest is a potentially devastating game of high-tech Russian roulette: Television's electronic transmissions and programming are blowing out the brains of the remote-control generation.

At the invitation of the U.S. Department of Health and Human Services' Administration on Children, Youth and Families, these researchers, policy makers, educators and clinical psychologists broadened the long-standing question of whether television influences how children use their minds to whether television affects the physiological growth and neural functioning of the brain.

In other words, is television biologically altering—or stunting—the brain power of TV-programmed kids?

WE INTERRUPT THIS PROGRAM

Jane M. Healy refers to the context of such concerns as "our uneasy relationship with a medium that we suspect of rotting our children's brains."

It should be noted that Healy, the conference's moderator, seldom pulls punches when the target is TV's enslavement of children; she prefers to pull the plug instead. One of the nation's most outspoken critics of television's impact on cognitive development, in her 1990 book *Endangered Minds: Why Our Children Don't Think,* she blamed the usually acclaimed PBS program *Sesame Street* for contributing to the death of reading and for misinforming children about the nature of learning.

Generally Healy says she believes television viewing leaves children's growing and pliable brains "disadvantaged" for the learning tasks ahead. She is outraged that any medium possibly that harmful to our progeny has barely been investigated—and is taken so lightly by so many parents.

"Any significant amount of time devoted to an activity has the potential to change the growing brain, [so] what is television doing to or for our children?" asks Healy.

Conceding the TV habit is but one of many influential changes in the lives of children during the past 20 years, she doesn't discount the faster pace of life kids must endure, the fewer models and moments of reflective thinking, the diminishing opportunities to converse with parents and adults. Too often, she believes, teachers and school are unfairly blamed for low achievement scores and learning problems.

"All of this is not attributable to the schools," says Healy, whose work often applies brain research in practical classroom situations. "Teachers are not doing that bad a job, nor are they doing that different a job than they did 10 and 20 years ago. Something is different. The kids appear to be different."

PUMPING BRAIN CELLS

Citing a "Calvin and Hobbes" cartoon showing a slack-jawed, heavy-eyed and drooling Calvin mesmerized by a TV screen, the educational psychologist based in Vail, Colorado, laments, "It is surprising, even shocking, that we can laugh at this situation and draw cartoons about it without demanding the facts. There is virtually no research on the effects of TV viewing on neural development."

Some physiological research does exist, however, that hints of a connection between the kind of experience television provides and a decrease in nerve-cell growth and functioning in the brain. Unfortunately, while that basic research has proven to be significant in demonstrating the incredible changeability of the brain's structure, it only can be speculative about TV's physiological effects. Also, the subjects were laboratory rats, not children.

"Before we did this work, nobody thought the brain could change," says Marian Cleeves Diamond. "It was essentially regarded to be a stable structure except when it deteriorates with aging."

A professor of anatomy at the University of California at Berkeley, Diamond has conducted experiments that compare brain-cell growth in rat pups that are provided with opposite extremes in mental stimulation. While some young rats (equivalent to the age when human children show the most rapid neural development) lived in large cages with playmates and three mother rats, with access to a changing supply of toys, the other rat pups were isolated in small cages without toys or playmates.

Brain samples from the young rats showed increases in every part of the nerve cells measured (dimension of the cerebral cortex, blood vessels, the cell body, nerve branching, synaptic junctions, etcetera) in the enriched subjects and a decrease from the standard measurements in the impoverished subjects.

"This is very simple work to show that with enrichment you can grow not new nerve cells but bigger and better nerve cells," reports Diamond. "And with impoverishment you get less."

TELEVISION VIEWING IS PASSIVE

How do these findings relate to the influence of television? Many critics charge that television viewing is a largely passive experience that steals from children hours of otherwise active and creative play, of reading and other exercises for the mind, of interacting with other children and parents. It could be argued, in other words, that in terms of the learning development of the human brain, television represents an impoverished environment.

"Investigators have shown that if rats sit alone in cages, watching those rats in the enriched environments, their brains do not demonstrate measurable changes," says Diamond. "It is important to interact with the objects, to explore, to investigate both physically and mentally. Mere observation is not enough to bring about changes. A passive existence is not enough."

While psychologist Jane Holmes Bernstein isn't prepared to label television the sole culprit in disadvantaging young brains, she has come to believe that learning disorders rightly or wrongly used as the label for a host of symptoms that plague up to 20 percent of the school-age population—can sometimes result from environmental impact.

"We create them by asking small brains to do things they are not yet ready to do," says the director of the neuropsychology program at Children's Hospital in Boston and assistant clinical professor of psychology at the Harvard Medical School. "And by not facilitating a typical growth or development in the brain."

Although the critical principle "is that of the interaction of brain development and experience," she cautions against rushing to any easy conclusions about television viewing during sensitive periods of brain-cell growth.

"The answer is not going to be simple," she predicts. "Brains are differently influenceable at different times by different events or inputs. So television as a medium, like any other type of input, could be very benign or even positive at one age, and quite deleterious at [another] in the same animal."

But Bernstein worries that high levels of TV exposure in children at the most susceptible ages might be limiting opportunities for the kind of interactive conversation and experiences that promote strong language skills. "The reason why this is important," she says, "is that the active engagement in the processing of language use is crucial to being able to take part in the educational system in the early and later grades."

HOME ALONE (WITH TV)

When examining TV's impact on children, Jerome L. Singer is convinced the greatest influence is if and how parents "mediate" that experience—perhaps supporting the idea that the absence of such interaction is what contributes to the impoverishing effect of television.

"We are seeing some hazards of heavy television viewing. We're talking here of the kind of programs on commercial television . . . particularly the more rapidly paced violent action programs," says Singer, a professor of psychology at Yale University and co-director of the Yale Family Television Research and Consultation Center.

"Most [heavy-viewing] kids show lower information, lower reading recognition or readiness to reading, lower reading levels," says Singer. "They tend to show lower imaginativeness, and less complex language use. We consistently find heavy viewing . . . is associated with more aggressive behavior."

But a most important variable in mitigating those results, says Singer, was parents who were involved in the child's viewing habits. "When parents control television and explain things to the children, we find somewhat dramatic results over years of time," says the coauthor of *Television, Imagination and*

Aggression and *The Parent's Guide: Use TV to Your Child's Advantage*. Children in families with high levels of parental mediation and low levels of TV viewing scored the highest on reading recognition tests, he reports. High mediating families with high television viewing still had "pretty good scores," followed in order by low mediating families and low TV, and at the bottom low mediating families and high TV viewing.

"The situation is a clear hazard for the child who is watching four or five hours or more a day," says Singer. "We have reason to be seriously concerned about those effects. But [with] the kinds of parents who talk to the children, respond to the TV with explanations, you get interesting changes in the overall pattern. The parents who take the trouble . . . are also going to be discriminating viewers of the television and point the kids to child-oriented programming.

"What I think we have to look forward is to a more careful and thoughtful role by adults in helping [the child] deal with the potentially hazardous but also potentially useful medium."

NEW AND IMPROVED

If his colleagues at the conference are pioneers in exploring the impact of television on our brains, Byron B. Reeves has advanced to the next technological frontier.

While they examine the influence of images flickering from standard 19-inch-diagonal screens, the professor of communications at Stanford University who specializes in the psychological processing of television is projecting the effects of state-of-the-art TVs with screens whose diagonals measure 27 inches and may soon stretch to 6 feet. He's concerned about sets with resolution and color nearly the quality of film, with a panoramic-aspect ratio that provides a movie-like horizontal effect, with high-quality sound that surrounds the viewer.

"New changes in television sets . . . may dramatically alter what can be said about how television educates and influences children," says Reeves, who notes with both enthusiasm and caution the significant changes in the size, shape, resolution and sound of TVs in the past decade—with more to come in the next five years. The median diagonal length of TV sets in 1990, for instance, was 22 inches—a 33 percent increase in picture screen area over the standard 19-inch sets of yesteryear. The now-popular 27-inch screen is about a 100 percent increase in picture area over the 19-inch set: One-third of the sets sold in 1990 were larger than 27 inches.

The difference in what happens inside a viewer's head? "It is more likely to be surprising and arousing," says Reeves. "It can be processed without conscious awareness. And it creates a more literal sense of motion—enough to make it more likely to get seasick watching a boat on a big-screen TV. Big screens are also accompanied by big sounds.

"All of these developments," he continues, "make television viewing increasingly lifelike. . . . Our bodies cannot afford to mistakenly dismiss a picture as being inconsequential, even if nothing can actually jump from the screen. The many psychological responses to the illusion of reality can be as powerful as reality itself."

In pilot studies he completed last year on this advanced technology, Reeves found that for adults larger images and higher fidelity increased viewer attention and feelings of excitement, amplified perceptions of people on TV as both more positive and more negative, and inhibited thoughtful processing and produced poorer memory.

"In short," he says, the subjects "liked the experience but they couldn't remember much about it. In children, viewers that we know are even more prone to the influence of visual and auditory form, new televisions could reshape the viewing environment even more radically. . . . Despite the excitement for these new products, they may be introduced without consideration for viewers who will spend the most time using them—children."

PUBLIC BROADCAST

Wade F. Horn considers the impact of television on children's brains an "extraordinarily serious and important" topic. As commissioner of HHS Administration on Children, Youth and Families, and a child psychologist with kids of his own, he's concerned that too many of America's children are arriving at the beginning of their schooling mentally unprepared to succeed—psychologically not equipped with the basic cognitive skills required for learning.

"For good or bad, each of these skills can be influenced by time spent watching television," he says. Horn says he knows there are many contributing factors. But excessive TV viewing is one that parents—with the help of the federal government—can do something about.

"We can begin to focus the attention of the nation on such critically important issues of how television affects the developing mind," Horn says. "And the federal government can disseminate this information to the most important people in children's lives—their parents—so that they can make more informed judgments as to how and what type of television viewing children engage in."

ADDITIONAL RESOURCES FOR PART 14

Suggested Questions and Discussion Topics

1. In "We've Come a Long Way, Maybe," what does author Kay Mills suggest that young women need to do to make further progress in the mass media?

2. In "We've Come a Long Way, Maybe," Mills discusses a number of developments that have improved the role of women in mass media. What do you think are the most important of these, and what are the most important things still to be done? Discuss.

3. In "Is It Just Me, Or Do All These Women Look Like Barbie?" by Sheila Gibbons, the author suggests some potential consequences of misrepresentation and underrepresentation of women and girls in the media. What are they? Discuss.

4. Discuss some ways in which different mass media use different ways of characterizing women and girls and men and boys as described in "Is It Just Me, Or Do All These Women Look Like Barbie?"

5. According to Ian Harris in "Media Myths and Men's Work," what is the myth, and what does he suggest can be done about it?

6. From "Media Myths and Men's Work," discuss the new myth the author suggests should replace the old one.

7. According to Dan Oldenburg's article "Boob Tube and Children's Brain Drain," what happens to each of these five human responses as the television screen gets bigger and the fidelity higher: viewer attention, feelings of excitement, perceptions of people on TV, thought processing, and memory?

8. According to Dan Oldenburg in "Boob Tube and Children's Brain Drain," why are children more susceptible than adolescents or adults to the effects of television?

Suggested Readings

Donna Allen, Ramona R. Rush, and Susan J. Kaufman, eds., *Women Transforming Communications: Global Intersections.* Thousand Oaks, CA: Sage Publications, 1996.

Diane Barthel, *Putting on Appearances: Gender and Advertising.* Philadelphia: Temple University Press, 1988.

Maurine H. Beasley and Sheila Gibbons, *Taking Their Place: A Documentary History of Women and Journalism.* Lanham, MD: University Press of America, 1997.

Daniel J. Canary and Kathryn Dindia, *Sex Differences and Similarities in Communication.* Mahwah, NJ: Lawrence Erlbaum, 1997.

Pamela J. Creedon, ed., *Women in Mass Communication.* Thousand Oaks, CA: Sage Publications, 1993.

Laura Flanders, *Real Majority, Media Minority: The Cost of Sidelining Women in Reporting.* Monroe, ME: Common Courage Press, 1997.

Ellen Gruber Garvey, *The Adman in the Parlor: Magazines and the Gendering of Consumer Culture, 1880s to 1910s.* New York: Oxford University Press, 1996.

Beth Bonniwell Haslett, *Children Communicating.* Mahwah, NJ: Lawrence Erlbaum, 1997.

Cynthia M. Lont, ed., *Women and Media: Content/Careers/Criticism.* Belmont, CA: Wadsworth Publishing Co., 1995.

Marion Marzolf, *Up From the Footnote: A History of Women Journalists.* Belmont, CA: Wadsworth Publishing Co., 1977.

Kay Mills, *A Place in the News: From the Women's Pages to the Front Page.* New York: Dodd, Mead, 1988.

Nan Robertson, *The Girls in the Balcony: Women, Men, and the New York Times.* New York: Fawcett Columbine, 1992.

Suzanne Romaine, *Communicating Gender.* Mahwah, NJ: Lawrence Erlbaum, 1998.

Marlene Sanders and Marcia Rock, *Waiting for Prime Time: The Women of Television News.* Urbana, IL: University of Illinois Press, 1988.

Dale Spender, *Nattering on the 'Net: Women, Power and Cyberspace.* Spinifex Press, 1996.

Julia T. Wood, *Gendered Lives: Communication, Gender and Culture.* Belmont, CA: Wadsworth, 1994.

Suggested Videos

"Women Seen on Television." New York: Insight Media, 1991. (11 minutes)

"Women and the Media." *The News Hour with Jim Lehrer,* November 3, 1997. (15 minutes)

"On Television: Teach the Children." San Francisco: California Newsreel, 1992. (56 minutes)

"Slim Hopes: Advertising and the Obsession with Thinness." Northampton, MA: Media Education Foundation. (30 minutes)

PART · 15

Mass Culture

Culture has two different meanings in this section: one is the quality of a society that arises from its arts and literature; the other is the particular form or stage of civilization that characterizes a society. Here we look at both aspects.

America is, without doubt, the home of one of the greatest mass cultures or popular cultures in history. Americans are known most throughout the world for their movies, music, pop songs, and television serials, not for their poetry, symphonies, or sculpture. Much more of the world enjoys our popular mass media products than our works of noble art.

Some critical observers have divided societies and their arts and literature into high, middle, or low cultures, or into elite and mass. American mass media fall easily and quickly into the middle, low, or mass categories in the eyes of most critics. And yet occasionally some (but not much) of the popular arts and literature of American mass media have achieved a surprisingly high regard among thoughtful critics.

The quality of American journalism is highly regarded by most thoughtful critics in the world, as is the role of journalism in keeping America free. The technological developments that have made the journalistic media strong in America are a source of envy in much of the world. This, too, is part of our culture. But journalism is changing, as we've seen earlier in this book and as we will see now from a different perspective.

To some extent our culture is the product of our media, and as the media change our culture changes. We started as a print media society and have become an electronic media society, a change that is revolutionizing almost everything about our civilization.

Now, to some extent, we are moving from mass media to specialized media, as we will see further in the last section of this book. That development, too, is changing our civilization in deep and significant ways. In fact, this may have been the most important issue concerning mass media in the 1990s.

In this section, four authors look at this from different points of view. They point out that mass media, or at least the new mass media, have separated people into segmented cultures—old and new, male and female, liberal and conservative, etc. And these segmented cultures are increasingly at war with each other, as Bill Moyers points out. The mass media have also spawned powerful new elites and an "elite" culture, as Jonathan Alter writes, but this new "elite" culture, based on mass media and pop culture, is really a culture of vulgarity and the lowest standards, according to Hal Crowther. And Robert Samuelson concludes that this fragmented culture is tearing America apart.

57

"New News" and a War of Cultures

BILL MOYERS

Editor's Note: There is a "new news" today that is replacing the "old news," and it is creating a whole new culture. The "new news" may not be in the newspapers or the other news media, which many Americans increasingly ignore because they feel they are no longer relevant.

Bill Moyers sees this development as foreshadowing catastrophe in our civilization. He is one of the most thoughtful media and culture critics in America today. Former press secretary to President Lyndon Johnson, former newspaper editor and publisher, television journalist and documentary producer, his article here is excerpted from a speech he delivered to the Center for Communication. This excerpt appeared in the *New York Times,* March 22, 1992.

Where is America's mind today? It's in the organs, for one thing. Remember that country song that goes "No one knows what goes on behind closed doors." Now we do.

Americans can turn on a series called *Real Sex* and watch a home striptease class; its premiere was HBO's highest-rated documentary for the year. Or they can flip to NBC News and get "I Witness Video." There they can see a policeman's murder recorded in his cruiser's camcorder, watch it replayed and relived in interviews, complete with ominous music. Or they can see the video of a pregnant woman plunging from a blazing building's window, can see it several times, at least once in slow motion.

Yeats was right: "We had fed the heart on fantasies, the heart's grown brutal from the fare." I wonder if *Real Sex* and "I Witness Video" take us deeper into reality or insanity? How does a reporter tell the difference anymore in a world where Oliver Stone can be praised for his "journalistic instincts" when he has Lyndon Johnson tell a cabal of generals and admirals, "Get me elected and I'll get you your war."

NEW NEWS SETS MORE OF THE AGENDA

Rolling Stone dubs all this the New News. Straight news—the Old News by *Rolling Stone*'s definition—is "pooped, confused and broke." In its place, a new culture of information is evolving—"a heady concoction, part Hollywood film and TV, part pop music and pop art, mixed with popular culture and celebrity magazines, tabloid telecasts, cable and home video."

Increasingly, says the magazine, the New News is seizing the function of mainstream journalism, sparking conversation and setting the country's social and political agenda.

So it is that we learn first from Bruce Springsteen that jobs aren't coming back. So it is that inner-city parents who don't subscribe to daily newspapers are taking their children to see *Juice* to educate them about the consequences of street violence; that young people think Bart Simpson's analysis of America more trenchant than that of many newspaper columnists; that we learn just how violent, brutal and desperate society is, not from the establishment press but from Spike Lee, Public Enemy, the Geto Boys and Guns 'n' Roses. Now even MTV is doing original reporting on this year's political campaign. We are having to absorb, and come to grips with, the news wherever and however we find it.

CONFLICT BETWEEN NEW AND OLD

Once, newspapers drew people to the public square. They provided a culture of community conversation by activating inquiry on serious public issues. When the press abandons that function, it no longer stimulates what John Dewey termed "the vital habits" of democracy—"the ability to follow an argument, grasp the point of view of another, expand the boundaries of understanding, debate the alternative purposes that might be pursued."

But I also know that what Dean Joan Konner said recently at the Columbia School of Journalism is true: "There is a civil war in our society today, a conflict between two American cultures, each holding very different values. The adversaries are private profits versus public responsibility; personal ambition versus the community good; quantitative measures versus qualitative concerns."

And I sense we're approaching Gettysburg, the moment of truth, the decisive ground for this cultural war—for newspaper publishers especially. Americans say they no longer trust journalists to tell them the truth about their world. Young people have difficulty finding anything of relevance to their lives in the daily newspaper.

Non-tabloid newspapers are viewed as increasingly elitist, self-important and corrupt on the one hand; on the other, they are increasingly lumped with the tabloids as readers perceive the increasing desperation with which papers are now trying to reach "down market" in order to replace the young readers who are not replacing their elders.

POLITICAL SYSTEM SEEN AS FAILING

Meanwhile, a study by the Kettering Foundation confirms that our political institutions are fast losing their legitimacy, that increasing numbers of Americans believe they are being dislodged from their rightful place in democracy by politicians, powerful lobbyists *and* the media—three groups they see as an autonomous political class impervious to the long-term interests of the country and manipulating the democratic discourse so that people are treated only as consumers to be entertained rather than citizens to be engaged.

That our political system is failing to solve the bedrock problems we face is beyond dispute. One reason is that our public discourse has become the verbal equivalent of mud wrestling.

The anthropologist Marvin Harris says the attack against reason and objectivity in America "is fast reaching the proportion of a crusade." America, he says, "urgently needs to reaffirm the principle that it is possible to carry out an analysis of social life which rational human beings will recognize as being true, regardless of whether they happen to be women or men, whites or blacks, straights or gays, Jews or born-again Christians." Lacking such an understanding of social life "we will tear the United States apart in the name of our separate realities."

SOCIAL AND POLITICAL PARALYSIS

Taken together, these assumptions and developments foreshadow the catastrophe of social and political paralysis: a society that continues to be governed by the same two parties that are driving it into the pits; a society that doesn't understand the link between two students killed in the hallways of a Brooklyn high school and the plea bargain that assures Michael Milken of being able to scrape by on $125 million; a society that every day breaks open its children's piggy banks and steals $1 billion just to pay the daily bills; a society that responds with anger at check-kiting in Congress but doesn't even know that the executive branch has lost track of tens of billions of dollars appropriated for the savings and loan bailout; a society where democracy is constantly thwarted by unaccountable money; a society where more people know George Bush hates broccoli than know that he ordered the invasion of Panama, and more know Marla Maples than Vaclav Havel, and where, by a margin of two to one, people say the Government's ability to censor the news during the Persian Gulf War was more important than the media's ability to report it.

What's astonishing about this civic illiteracy—some call it a disease—is that it exists in America just as a series of powerful democratic movements have been toppling autocratic regimes elsewhere in the world. While people around the globe are clamoring for self-government, survey after survey reports that millions of Americans feels as if they have been locked out of their homes and are unable to regain their rightful place in the operation of democracy. On the other hand, those same millions want to believe that it is still in their power to change America.

Conventional wisdom says people don't want the kind of news that will bring them back to the public square. Well, conventional wisdom is wrong. Just ask the *Philadelphia Inquirer*. Last fall, the *Inquirer* ran a nine-part series that attempted to find a pattern in the economic chaos of the 1980's. Donald Barlett and James Steele, twice winners of the Pulitzer Prize, spent two years traveling to 50 cities in 16 states and Mexico. They talked to government officials, corporate managers and workers in lumber mills, factories and department stores. And they amassed a hundred thousand documents.

PEOPLE STILL WANT REAL NEWS

When they were done, they had exposed a money trail that helped readers to understand how rule makers in Washington and deal makers on Wall Street connived to create much of the pain inflected on American workers and the middle class.

The series was about tax policy, health care, pension rules, corporate debt and the bankruptcy code—all that "stuff" we usually think no one wants to read about. But it was written crisply and laid out vividly, and when the series appeared so many people thronged the paper's lobby wanting reprints that security guards had to be summoned for crowd control. At last count, the number of reprints had reached 400,000.

People want to know what is happening to them, and what they can do about it. Listening to America, you realize that millions of people are not apathetic. They will respond to a press that stimulates the community without pandering to it, that inspires people to embrace their responsibilities without lecturing or hectoring them, that engages their better natures without sugarcoating ugly realities or patronizing their foibles.

Those of us who are reporters can only hope this generation of publishers understands that what keeps journalism different is something intangible. For all the talk of price-earnings ratio, bottom line, readouts and restricted stock, what ultimately counts is the soul of the owner. The test today for capitalism is whether shareholders have souls, too.

58

The Cultural Elite

JONATHAN ALTER

Editor's Note: America's pop culture, aimed for the most part at the lowest common denominator, has ironically created a cultural elite. Half a century ago, sociologists began to identify an effect of the mass media that they called "status conferral." People who were mentioned in the media acquired status. Ordinary people could become stars (Marilyn Monroe), heroes (Charles Lindbergh), and statesmen (Dwight Eisenhower) if their names got into enough headlines.

The media people who make the stars, heroes, and statesmen have themselves become a new cultural elite. Jonathan Alter examines this phenomenon in this article, published in *Newsweek*, October 5, 1992. Aiding in the research were Donna Foote and Linda Wright in Los Angeles.

Kenny Rogers is not in the "cultural elite." While he still knows when to hold'em and when to fold'em, none of his songs are currently shaping American culture. But Madonna certainly meets the entrance requirements. Ted Kennedy has been expelled. But Dan Quayle is a member.

Dan Quayle? Obviously Quayle would not identify himself as a part of the cultural elite he so actively denounces. He spits the words out, trying to win votes for the Republican ticket by creating a social chasm: *Us* versus *Them,* with the *Them* being dangerous Hollywood and media types inflicting their sinful values on the rest of *Us* regular folks. It's a time-honored, divide-and-conquer approach, and one that's had surprisingly little political bite this year. "We in Hollywood did not audition for the role of Willie Horton, and we're not going to play it," says Gary David Goldberg, creator of shows like *Family Ties* and *Brooklyn Bridge.* Polls show the voters overwhelmingly think the whole fuss is a distraction from their real concern—the economy.

A PROPER POLITICAL ISSUE

But whatever his motives, the vice president is on to something. If the cultural elite isn't a proper political issue, it's at least a compelling sociological one. While the United States has never featured the rigid social and cultural hierarchies of Europe, some kind of elite class has always existed here. It has often produced this country's most brilliant inspirations, from the Constitution to Huckleberry Finn. It continues to ensure that museums and orchestras and other remnants of old culture survive. What's changed in recent years is that the cultural elite has become much less intellectually elite—and much more connected to commerce. With the help of television, that elite has expanded to produce all of America's powerful and highly exportable mass culture—including our worst trash.

Without question, Americans are dissatisfied with the tone of their popular culture. As the wild-and-crazy baby boomers become parents, they are trying to protect their children from being kidnapped by celluloid fiends like Freddy Krueger. According to a *Newsweek* Poll, only 26 percent think parents have the most influence on their kids, a poor second to television's 49 percent. Fully 80 percent believe that movies contain too much violence and sex. But poll respondents conclude that what matters most to the creators of this culture is money, not politics. Only 33 percent agree with Quayle's idea that a cultural elite in the news and entertainment business was trying to push its own values on the public. Nearly 60 percent thought the real motive was just to appeal to the biggest possible audience.

Who are the people who comprise the CE? What are their values? How influential are those values, especially on children? Can Hollywood be persuaded, finally, to take responsibility for the gratuitous sex and violence it produces? Just by generating agitated discussion, Quayle is helping to shape the debate, which is the only real requirement for membership in the cultural elite. You're in, Dan, whether you like it or not.

WHO'S IN IT?

If it's any consolation, *Newsweek* and other major news organizations are also part of the cultural elite, as are academics and government officials who affect the national dialogue. So are smaller publications and cultural hunter-gatherers who move stories up the great media food chain. So are the people who write or publish important books, who produce, direct or "greenlight" movies, who sketch our visual landscape. And prime-time television—where even a flop reaches more people than most movie hits—is at the white-hot center of this universe.

At a recent Hollywood fund-raiser, Bill Clinton said that he had "always aspired to be [in] the 'cultural elite' that others condemn." (That was another sign that Quayle's political punch was not hitting home; if it had, Clinton would never have admitted membership.) Lynne Cheney, conservative director of the National Endowment for the Humanities, acknowledged last week that while the term is so broad as to be almost meaningless, "I suspect that it includes me." Most de facto members are less honest. The usual reaction is, *no, not me, but that person over there is*—just as many Yuppies denied being "Yuppies" in the 1980s. They want the rewards of elitism but not the stigma that comes with it in a democratic idol-smashing society.

The idea of a meritocratic elite has gone by many names over the years. In his once trendy 1956 work, *The Power Elite,* C. Wright Mills wrote of "prestigeful men and women" who "displace the society lady and the man of pedigreed wealth." In those days, the attack on Hollywood came from the left, attacking the TV industry for bland *Father Knows Best* images that were badly out of touch with the diversity of American life. The "counterculture" was just struggling to be born. Now many old hippies run the CE.

It used to be, of course, that "culture" meant serious literature and art. Prof. Alfred Appel of Northwestern University says that at first he thought Quayle's definition of "cultural elite" was a poor use of language: "Opportunistic, greedy, ill-educated, boorish TV and movie producers—is that *culture?*" But Appel concluded: "Movies and TV *are* the center of our culture, alas. The literary culture has become very minor. In the '50s, *Time* could put an intellectual like Jacques Barzun on the cover. Now you can't imagine a newsmagazine cover story that would feature a writer unless it was Stephen King."

NOT AN ECONOMIC ISSUE

For all of its connection to commerce, the new cultural elite is not the same as the economic elite—the people who control this country's wealth. Quayle would never have attacked that elite; it's mostly Republican. Much of the time, anti-elitism is democratically healthy. Unfortunately, it too often takes the form of attacks on intellectuals. When Yale man George Bush condemns Michael Dukakis for being part of "the Harvard Yard boutique" and Bill Clinton for going to Oxford, only a few "eggheads" (the 1950s term of derision) find it peculiar.

Wherever they matriculated, members of the CE are well schooled in hypocrisy. Conservatives who complain about lax family values don't seem to mind when Republican Arnold Schwarzenegger casually wipes out a few dozen men on screen. Concerned liberals almost never manage to speak out about rap music that advocates killing cops. (Imagine their reaction if a group called "KKK" sang about killing blacks.)

The conservative critique is unassailable on one point: the cultural elite is not made up of "average" middle-class Americans, though many were born that way. They are better educated, richer, more liberal, more mobile, less religious and less connected to conventional standards of morality than most of the public.

The citadels of the CE that Quayle identifies—Hollywood, the press, academia—include a disproportionate number of Jews. "We can drop the Republican code for cultural elite," director Mike Nichols deadpanned at the Clinton fund-raiser. "Good evening, fellow Jews." From McCarthyism to rumblings on the far right and far left about the "Jewish-dominated media," resentment against the cultural elite has often boiled down to simple anti-Semitism, though Quayle's Jewish speechwriters could hardly have meant it that way.

In truth, when Jewish studio bosses *really* ran Hollywood—in the old days—the movies were full of traditional values, as Neal Gabler points out in the book *An Empire of Their Own.* Nowadays, there are large numbers of

Jews—many of them nonreligious or intermarried—at all levels of the cultural elite. But at the top, power is fragmented and increasingly shared not just with Christians but with owners back in Japan. The pointlessness of the whole argument is conveyed by the fact that the only TV network owned by a Jew—CBS—is also the network under the most fire (for a *60 Minutes* story) from supporters of Israel.

A more useful way of understanding who comprises the cultural elite is to look at it as a web of interconnected institutions. Each venue uses various spawning grounds—e.g., the *Harvard Lampoon,* the *Yale Daily News,* the USC School of Cinema—but also employs large numbers of people who worked their way up without early connections. The values—or lack thereof—are shared. "There are three elite groups in this country that professionally understand that they must function amorally: Hollywood, the media and politicians," says Howard Suber, cochairman of UCLA's film and TV producers program. Each promotes and feeds off the other, as the *Murphy Brown* hype suggests. It's no wonder that so many Americans think "they" are all in it together.

WHAT DO THEY STAND FOR?

Here are at least three ways to analyze the CE:

Under what could be called the Spiro Agnew analysis, "an effete corps of impudent snobs" injects the culture with condescending liberalism. Clergy and businessmen are generally portrayed as bad guys. Gays and minorities are generally portrayed as good guys. Republicans are people to laugh at. Obscenity is dressed up as "free expression" and sometimes paid for by the government.

Then there's the Thomas Jefferson definition. He described "a natural aristocracy among men. The grounds of this are virtue and talents." This is the cultural elite that Clinton identified as a source of national pride—the social hierarchy in which people get ahead through education and moxie. Begrudging them their status is to denigrate that which is good in American life.

And finally, the Andy Warhol analysis. "Art? I don't believe I've met the man," Warhol said. This is the money first, art second theory. Or as Mike Medavoy, chairman of Tri-Star Pictures, puts it: "We have to make movies that make money, not preach." People in Hollywood, says director John Milius, "don't have a shred of honest ideology among them."

Could the "cultural elite" represent all three approaches? Could it include both cynical purveyors of mindless junk, *and* artistic geniuses? The CE—like any elite—reflects the best and worst of the culture. Both fresh cream and pond scum rise to the top.

Quayle's central point is that the pond scum is the result of value-free liberalism. But when money's at stake, amorality knows no political bounds. The occasional plugs for AIDS prevention notwithstanding, the media are generally so politically *in*correct, that legions of PC professors make careers of deconstructing the racism and sexism they see in it.

Similarly, most TV shows are situated in homey—not hostile—surroundings. Usually, the crook gets caught in the end. Most programs are still about families, albeit extended or untraditional ones. "There's this perception that we sit here and ask, 'How do we change the public's tastes?'" says John S. Pike, president of Paramount's TV division. "We don't do that. We are trying to produce mass-appeal programming." Indeed, several studios promise more "G" and "PG" movies, because box-office receipts show the boomers want them.

In the news media as well, the only meaningful ideology is capitalism. As the conservative William Bennett has argued, liberal reporters will chase anyone for a good story. How else to explain the media feeding frenzies that afflict Democrats at least as often as Republicans? Quayle has undoubtedly taken more media punches because he is conservative. But the cultural affinity between media elites and liberal political elites doesn't always work on behalf of the Democrat. Jimmy Carter received far worse press than Ronald Reagan, and Bill Clinton's press has veered between positive and negative extremes.

HOW INFLUENTIAL IS IT?

The conventional defense of Hollywood comes from Jack Valenti. "Movies reflect society. When people ask why Hollywood doesn't make movies like it used to, my answer is, 'Why isn't society like it used to be?'" Under this theory all the Hollywood cultural elite does is hold a mirror to the world. "The last place any Hollywood producer wants to be is out in front of, or different than the audience," says TV producer Gary David Goldberg. "This is a business that really runs on testing, polling, focus grouping." If they were honest, Goldberg's counterparts in publishing and politics would admit the same thing.

The mirror argument is convenient. But it dodges the question of ultimate responsibility, especially for what children so often see. *Of course* images affect behavior. If they didn't, there would be no such thing as advertising. Barry Diller, retired top executive at the Fox network, says studio executives should take on more responsibility for what they turn out. "There should be a process for companies to be sensitized to what the data tell us. The data says: films and TV have an effect." Apparently the process hasn't yet "sensitized" the coarseness at Fox: shows like *Married . . . With Children* and *Studs* are still very much on the air.

On the other hand, sometimes a laugh is just a laugh. If movies about sex directly affect behavior, why do most of the people who see them lead so much duller sex lives? If the liberal news media have so much clout, why have conservatives been running the country for 20 of the last 24 years? If that changes next month, it won't happen because the liberal cultural elite ordered America to dump George Bush and Dan Quayle.

It may be that the CE is less influential than we imagine—a conditioner of culture instead of its creator. At bottom, says critic Todd Gitlin, "The culture industry can lead, but it can't lead people anywhere it likes. It can take them down the road, but it doesn't build the road in the first place." Building a new moral road (or just voting with your ticket stubs and channel changers)—that's where the American public's ultimate power over the cultural elite comes in. If we build it, "They" will come, with a different set of wares to sell us.

59

Are We Witnessing the Slow Death of Culture?

HAL CROWTHER

Editor's Note: Change is often difficult to endure, especially when it brings an end to things we cherish. Undoubtedly, the twentieth century has experienced the greatest changes to human culture in recorded history, and we can predict that the twenty-first century will see more—and faster—change.

To some extent, mass media can be blamed for changes to the amount of "high culture" seemingly absorbed by the average person. Sales of quality fiction have declined; ratings of soap operas, sitcoms and tabloid TV news have mushroomed. There are many indications, however, that many Americans go to museums and art galleries, attend opera and classical music performances and check books out of libraries, but the general environment of our popular culture leaves many "middle-brows" and "high-brows" feeling discouraged and left out.

Hal Crowther is a syndicated columnist for the *Independent Weekly* in Durham, North Carolina, and a winner of the H. L. Mencken Award for commentary. This essay is adapted from his collection of columns, *Unarmed by Dangerous* (Marietta, GA: Longstreet Press, 1995), and was published in the *Washington Post* on August 27, 1995. It is reprinted with permission.

When a population becomes distracted by trivia, when cultural life is redefined as a perpetual round of entertainments, when serious public conversation becomes a form of baby-talk, when, in short, a people become an audience and their public business a vaudeville act, then a nation finds itself at risk; culture-death is a clear possibility.

—NEIL POSTMAN, "AMUSING OURSELVES TO DEATH"

The death of a culture is a lot like the death of a tree. There's no heart-stopping moment when the line on the monitor goes flat. Each season there are more dead limbs. The foliage grows mangy, the bark turns dry and scaly, creatures burrow deep inside and eat away at the heart. The tree's profile changes, its roots contract. And then one spring there are no new leaves.

Tree surgeons make a science of identifying patients that are past saving, and putting them out of their misery before that final, silent spring. There are no physicians to minister to a dying culture. Just a thousand diagnosticians, each pointing to a different symptom that indicates the end is near.

Pat Robertson preaches that an epidemic of homosexuality will usher in the final days; it says so in the Bible. Me, I began to prepare my kaddish for the culture when Vice-President Quayle attacked the audience and producers of a silly television program as America's "cultural elite"—and the nation laughed for the wrong reasons. Quayle drew the usual catcalls for being so fatally uncool, and the media began a straight-faced debate about the political influence of Hollywood "elitists."

MAKING THE MOST OF SNOBBERY

No one suggested that the American cultural spectrum might still stretch for some distance on the high-brow side of *Murphy Brown.* Or that out there, on that road less traveled, there might still be lonely bands of snobs who'd rather face bladder surgery than a half-hour of staccato close-ups and actors with harsh urban accents shouting pseudo-hip one-liners over a laugh track.

In the spirit of full disclosure, I confess that I'm one of those haughty ultra-elitists who fail to find cultural nourishment on network television. At the risk of cultural excommunication, I further confess that I haven't watched a commercial TV series in nearly 20 years. But I see 60-second samples of these contemporary comedies during commercial breaks in Atlanta Braves games, flying blind with my remote control. I think the one Quayle immortalized is awful—banal, brassy, false-hearted and infuriating with some kind of insider smugness that I'm too far outside to understand. If this program has ever been the guilty pleasure of the cultural elite, we are lost.

If this is snobbery, make the most of it. I don't apologize for despising television. I survived a four-year hitch as a television critic and I feel, like a member of Vietnam Veterans Against the War, that I earned the right to my opinion. Snobs and highbrows are easy targets to hit, but the word "snob" takes on a different meaning during a period of cultural disintegration. A snob may be someone who remembers standards and aesthetic principles that previous generations took seriously.

If you believe you have any taste, any discernment in any area, nurture it. Wear it proudly. Share it with your children. Don't be obnoxious about your standards, but be stubborn, be strict. Keep the flame alive. When a culture is in danger of dying, snobs are its most precious natural resource.

STANDARDS IN FREE FALL

It surprises and amuses me to find myself on the upscale side of the cultural Great Divide. Back-country-bred and culturally disadvantaged as a boy, I became, defensively, a determined low-brow of a type common to ballparks and sports bars. My taste in music, running to blues and bluegrass, is distinctly blue-collar. Even as a salaried critic of cultural events I took an Everyman position that one well-stuffed shirt described as "belligerently proletarian."

I established my ground and held it. But the cultural water table keeps dropping and I find, like many of my friends and role models, that the low ground we held is becoming an aerie. We are becoming mandarins by default. Anyone who reads above the twelfth-grade level and avoids *Geraldo!* has joined the new "cultural elite."

With educational standards in free fall, with students increasingly segregated as much by class and income as they ever were by race, with politicians scheming to abandon public education, it's hard to see where a cultural renaissance is going to begin. Yesterday's outrage is today's commonplace. There are TV commercials in American classrooms now, and the president of Yale University quit his job to work for the man who put them there.

WHAT WE READ

Sixty percent of American households purchase no books at all—not a cookbook, not a sex manual, nada. Of the 40 percent that are up to the challenge of printed material, only a third are up to anything besides "popular fiction"—the stuff with women in torn dresses on the cover and castles burning in the background. Only 2 percent of the books Americans purchase are texts the sneering elitist will acknowledge as "books"—literature, poetry, art, history, non-tabloid biography.

America's literary and intellectual talent is aiming its best efforts at a tiny, shrinking fragment of the population. The largest single bloc of serious readers, ominously, is "over 65." An impressive performance for a serious book is 30,000 copies sold.

Others do much better. Crime stories provide publishers with a steady income. Self-serving celebrity rubbish often sells millions in hardcover, rivaled only by toxic neofascist rubbish culled from politicians and radio talk shows. Innocent twenty-second-century historians may assume that Lee Iacocca and Rush Limbaugh were among the great writers of our era. Cormac McCarthy, widely regarded as the most gifted American novelist, had published five novels before his total sales hit 30,000.

THE FINAL STRAW

Commercial filmmakers, for their part, largely ignore the national literature. A backlog of comic books and campy old television programs provides their most reliable inspiration. Thomas Jefferson based all his hopes for democracy on universal literacy. What he couldn't foresee was a republic that would founder not with illiterates but with aliterates—an American majority that can read but chooses not to.

For many elitists, *The New Yorker* was the final straw. A cultural epoch ended when the last high-brow magazine still afloat in the marketplace was bound over to *Vanity Fair*'s Tina Brown, the crowned queen of celebrity journalism (the perfect oxymoron if there ever was one). It was like hearing that your grandmother was going to pose for Playboy—"Girls of the AARP." Reviews of Brown's regime have been mixed, as they should be. No one misses the book-length profiles of obscure Europeans or the dated, claustrophobic short fiction haunted by "Franny and Zooey." Middle-brow readers feel welcome now, and pedigreed writers are still waiting in line (where else can they go?).

But rude facts linger. Brown's *New Yorker* sent Gay Talese to report on John Bobbitt's penis. A tasteful reading room designed by William Shawn has been redecorated by an O.J.-obsessed editor whose favorite covers for *Vanity Fair* featured nude, obese and pregnant celebrities, and it shows.

UNBROKEN LANDSCAPE OF VULGARITY

Sometimes I can even smell the same lame pseudo-hipness that emanates from *Murphy Brown*. And yet *The New Yorker* at its worst is a paragon of class and intellect, an egghead paradise, compared with the tabloid jungle that devours broadcast journalism. Twenty-five years ago, newsmen at the top of TV's pyramid made fun of Tinseltown gossip Rona Barrett. The late Roger Grimsby called her "Rona-Rooter." Now the network big shots fight for shares of Rona's beat. It was presented as a coup this summer for Barbara Walters, a network anchor when Rona was a joke, to "land" an exclusive interview with a British model whose boyfriend—a popular actor of no particular distinction—wounded her by paying an L.A. prostitute for fellatio. No irony attended this interview, and it earned the second-highest Nielsen rating of any show that week.

To an alien cultural observer like the ones we used to meet on *Star Trek*, America presents an almost unbroken landscape of vulgarity, venality and violence. The three V's should be stamped on our coins, along with a new variation on the national motto: *E Pluribus Nihil*. Count on an elitist to remember a little Latin.

WHO'S TO BLAME?

It's no simple matter to assign blame for this terminal decline. It's easy to see who profits. Media and software conglomerates are already metastasizing into colossal delivery systems for fast-food culture. George Orwell missed the mark by failing to see that techno-capitalism would outlast every political system and usher in a *1984* of its own design. When the mergers and buyouts have absorbed every independent voice, the prolefeed of the twenty-first century will be distributed exclusively by a cartel of pluto-princes scarcely more accessible or altruistic than Big Brother and company.

We know some of their names already: Eisner, Gates, Redstone, Murdoch. TV is still their six-lane highway into your mind. And TV at its lowest—with its daytime talk shows (*Ricki Lake:* Women whose best friends have bigger breasts) and sex-game shows that mate Middle Americans like so many Holsteins—is so outrageously vulgar it defies satire, beggars indignation. It's the grossest of supermarket tabloids come to life in your living room, courting the brain-dead for profit and making no pretense about it. But the music industry, where adults seldom trespass, is the stronghold of corporate criminals who truly get away with murder.

Everyone knows that teenagers, half mad with high-test hormones in the best of times, are angry, confused, alienated and imperiled in these days of imploding families and vanishing value systems. Probably the first measure of decency among adults is whether we try to help these kids or try to make money from their predicament. By that measure, music industry executives are heinous, heartless Fagins who hide behind the First Amendment (and tobacco companies are emissaries from Hell).

WANTING TO BE NOT WITH IT

Tipper Gore may be one of the most misunderstood prophets of her time. If you thought her crusade to police rock lyrics was priggish and ridiculous, you haven't read enough of the lyrics. Employing and manufacturing "artists" who are too old to respond to this gibberish themselves, the swine who run these recording companies sell murder, misogyny, anarchy, rough sex, racism and perversion to 14-year-old nihilists. Crack dealers probably do less harm than the music men from Time Warner. Not 10 percent of these rabid lyrics represent honest political or artistic expression.

With that outburst I guess I reveal conclusively that I am not "with it" or anywhere near it. I suppose it's possible for a person my age to remain with it, to balance indefinitely on the cutting edge. But a revealing measure of a culture's health, it seems to me, is how much you want to be with it. I want to be so far out of it that I can't even smell it decomposing.

You know those old guys you see sitting in parks, or eating in places where old people eat alone? They wear silk bow ties and nice suits cut in antique styles, like extras in Frank Capra movies from the '40s. They look a little foreign; I imagine that they've read Primo Levi and know everything about Rilke and Rachmaninoff, and don't give a damn about anything that's happened since the Second World War.

I want to be just like those guys. And I don't want to wait until I'm 70. I want to start now.

60

The Fragmenting of America

ROBERT J. SAMUELSON

Editor's Note: Mass media of the past brought us together as a family and as a nation. There were fewer mass media, so most of us were audiences for the same messages. Critics pointed out the negative aspects of this process—it "homogenized" us all into one culture.

Now there are far more mass media available, as well as specialized media and personal media. The old critics would like these developments—they allow everyone to be an individual. The new critics decry the new media; they are fragmenting us, destroying our sense of unity, of nationhood, of culture.

One such critic is Robert J. Samuelson, an economist and widely syndicated newspaper columnist. This article appeared in the *Washington Post* and other papers on August 7, 1991.

Who would have thought that the three major television networks could be toppled from their pedestals? But they have been. Between 1975 and 1990, their share of the prime-time TV audience has fallen from 93 percent to 64 percent. It could go lower. Little wonder that network executives whine about how poor and beleaguered they've become. In an odd way, I mourn their plight.

Network dominance never consistently provided quality programming. But it did give us something that's now slipping away: shared experience and a sense of community. People in the 1950s watched *The Honeymooners*. In the 1970s they watched *All in the Family*. As the TV audience scatters to its many new choices—dozens of cable channels, VCR tapes, computer games—we're losing that. It wouldn't matter much, if the networks' eclipse were an isolated phenomenon. But it isn't. It's part of what I call the fragmenting of America.

If you examine recent economic and social trends, you will find that they emphasize (and sometimes exaggerate) our differences. By contrast, the great economic and social trends of the mid-1960s emphasized and nurtured our similarities. The growing awareness of differences is a constant theme in today's politics. It underlies the raging debate over "multiculturalism." There is more to it, though, than race or immigration.

ACCUMULATING DIFFERENCES

We have a deeper sense of accumulating differences. At some level, we don't like it. This explains a barely concealed public hunger for things that remind us of a common national heritage or destiny. Ronald Reagan was so popular in part because he spoke above a splintered society to give voice to traditional (for some, merely nostalgic) values. This hunger also explains why the Persian Gulf War, once won, made most Americans feel good.

When I say that economic and social forces are fragmenting us, here's what I mean:

- *Technology:* In the 1950s and 1960s, television gave us universal entertainment. The explosion in long-distance telephone service shrank distances. So did construction of interstate highways and the expansion of air travel. Now, technology transforms the "mass market" into endless "niche markets." Computers slice us by income, age, education and purchasing patterns into market "segments." Cable TV and direct mail cater to our micro tastes.

- *Economic Equality:* There's less of it. We are more a society of haves and have-nots. Until the early 1970s family income rose rapidly and its distribution became more even. Between 1959 and 1973, the poverty rate dropped from 22.4 percent to 11.1 percent. In 1989 it was 12.8 percent. It's not just income but also the availability of health insurance and pension benefits that's becoming less equal. Coverage, once expanding, now isn't.

- *Regional Convergence:* "Rolling recession" has become part of our vocabulary. In the 1980s, regions suffered severe slumps at different times. First the Rust Belt and the Farm Belt. Then the Oil Patch. And now the Northeast. Until the 1980s regional per capita incomes were converging. Between 1950 and 1980, the South's income rose from 69 percent to 86 percent of the national average. In the 1980s the gap among regional incomes widened.

- *Lifestyles:* Everyone knows that the "traditional" two-parent family with children is on the wane. Marrying later, divorcing more often and living longer, Americans have created new lifestyles, subcultures and market niches. In 1960, 74 percent of households were married couples, and 44 percent were couples with children. By 1990 the same groups were 56 percent and 26 percent of the total.

- *Immigration:* The huge influx of Hispanic and Asian immigrants (legal and illegal) beginning in the 1970s has literally changed the face of America. In the 1980s the Hispanic population of Los Angeles County—to take one example—increased by nearly 1.3 million, reports American Demographics magazine.

To the list, I'd also add the mere passage of time. In the 1950s and early 1960s, all adult Americans had lived through two great traumas: the Great Depression, and World War II. They affected everyone powerfully. Today's

Americans, spanning at least three generations, no longer have common, anchoring experiences of such intensity. Each has its own: For the baby boom, it was Vietnam. The generation gap has become the generations' gaps.

DIVERSITY OR COMMUNITY?

In some ways, the forces pulling America together in the early postwar period were unrepresentative of the economic and social tensions typical of U.S. history. In the 1920s immigration was a great source of conflict. Nor was the "traditional" family so traditional. It was less prevalent before World War II than in the 1950s. We have now reverted to a more normal state. Political calm was shattered in the 1960s by Vietnam and civil rights. Though less dramatic, the changes since then have quietly segregated us. A lot of little things have pulled us apart by creating many more separate worlds in which we all live.

The result is confusion. We celebrate diversity and individuality. We also crave a sense of nation and community. The two seem at odds. The unifying forces of the early postwar era involved a lot of social and political conformity ("bad" in our individualistic culture), but they also created a lot of consensus ("good" in a society that values compromise). Consensus is more elusive now. Too many groups move in different directions, preoccupied by different problems and navigating by different reference points. Politicians survive by offending no one, doing nothing and, in the process, disappointing almost everyone.

Our fragmented society exalts freedom and expands consumer choice. But it also sacrifices a larger sense of belonging. The less we have in common, the more we seek out people just like us. This isn't evil. It's human nature. But it isn't necessarily good, either. It builds isolation and makes more of everyday life strange and alien. There's no conspiracy here. It's history. The TV networks' decline is a small part of the story. Their eclipse is probably inevitable and maybe desirable. Or maybe not. Someday, we may yearn for a bit more of *The Honeymooners*.

ADDITIONAL RESOURCES FOR PART 15

Suggested Questions and Discussion Topics

1. According to Bill Moyers in "New News and a War of Cultures," what is the conflict between new and old cultures, and what role do the media play in that conflict? Discuss.

2. According to "New News and a War of Cultures," where does the author put non-tabloid newspapers in the culture wars? What, if anything, does he suggest can be done about it? Discuss.

3. In "The Cultural Elite," author Jonathan Alter suggests that former Vice-President Dan Quayle maintained that a "cultural elite" in the news and entertainment business was trying to push its own values on the public. What is your opinion? Discuss.

4. According to "The Cultural Elite," how does the movie business in Hollywood defend itself against the charge that it is part of a cultural elite? Discuss.

5. In "Are We Witnessing the Slow Death of Culture?" by Hal Crowther, the author suggests that "high" culture is declining in America. What does he mean, and who does he blame? Do you agree? Discuss.

6. Discuss any three facts from "Are We Witnessing the Slow Death of Culture?" that the author uses to illustrate the "death of culture."

7. From "The Fragmenting of America," discuss three examples given to illustrate the economic and social forces that are fragmenting us.

8. According to "The Fragmenting of America," what is the difference between diversity and community, and what role do media play in creating one or the other? Discuss.

Suggested Readings

Ian Angus and Sut Jhally, *Cultural Politics in Contemporary America.* London: Routledge, 1989.

Arthur Asa Berger, *Narratives in Popular Culture, Media, and Everyday Life.* Thousand Oaks, CA: Sage Publications, 1996.

Alex S. Edelstein, *Total Propaganda: From Mass Culture to Popular Culture.* Mahwah, NJ: Lawrence Erlbaum, 1997.

David Rowe, *Popular Cultures: Rock Music, Sport, and the Politics of Pleasure.* Thousand Oaks, CA: Sage Publications, 1997.

Nick Stevenson, *Understanding Media Cultures.* Thousand Oaks, CA: Sage Publications, 1995.

Kenneth Thompson, *Media and Cultural Regulation.* Thousand Oaks, CA: Sage Publications, 1997.

James B. Twitchell, *Carnival Culture: The Trashing of Taste in America.* New York: Columbia University Press, 1992.

Suggested Videos

Bell Hooks, "Cultural Criticism and Transformation: Part One: On Cultural Criticism; Part Two: Doing Cultural Criticism." Northampton, MA: Media Education Foundation. 1997. (26 and 40 minutes, respectively).

George Gerbner, "The Crisis of the Cultural Environment: Media and Democracy in the 21st Century." Northampton, MA: Media Education Foundation. 1997. (30 minutes)

George Gerbner, "The Electronic Storyteller: Television and the Cultivation of Values." Northampton, MA: Media Education Foundation. 1997. (30 minutes)

Bill Moyers, "The Public Mind Image and Reality in America: Consuming Images [Advertising]." Corporation for Public Broadcasting, 1989. (55 minutes)

Bill Moyers, "The Public Mind, Image and Reality in America: Leading Questions [Market Research]." Corporation for Public Broadcasting, 1989. (55 minutes)

Bill Moyers, "The Public Mind, Image and Reality in America: Illusions of News [Journalism and Politics]." Corporation for Public Broadcasting, 1989. (55 minutes)

Bill Moyers, "The Public Mind, Image and Reality in America: The Truth About Lies [Public Trust]." Corporation for Public Broadcasting, 1989. (55 minutes)

PART · 16

Technology and the Future

As we said at the beginning of this book, mass media are technology-based industries, and these technologies are in a constant state of change. We end by looking at the future and some evolving technologies that have the greatest possible implications for the changes that will affect mass media, the way we communicate, how we live, and our culture and civilization. Given the changes in technology affecting mass media today, we can summarize in a few words the changes that will affect our society: diversity, multiculturalism, individualism, fragmentation.

In an earlier edition of this book, Professor Benjamin Barber of Rutgers University wrote that the "effects of the first age of television [from 1939 through the 1970s] on America's political culture were mixed." But in one clear sense, Barber noted, network television's homogenized programming benefited democracy: It provided a consensus indispensable to national unity.[1]

The new technologies are decentralizing not only television but also all the mass media:

> All this programming diversity and special-interest narrowcasting replaces communication with group narcissism. The tube now becomes a mirror showing us only ourselves, relentlessly screening out any images that do not suit our own special prejudices and group norms. . . . Every parochial voice gets a hearing (though only before the already converted), and the public as a whole is left with no voice. No global village, but a Tower of Babel: a hundred chattering mouths bereft of any common language.[2]

Barber also points out that the very features of the new technology that make it versatile and exciting also make it frighteningly vulnerable to abuse. He is thinking of the use of new technologies to create sophisticated personal media for highly targeted advertising and marketing, using computer files to prepare profiles and dossiers that could make it possible for "big brother" corporations to know all about us, how to get to us, and how to sell to us.[3]

Of course, that is a dismal view, and there may be brighter ways of looking at the future. In this section we present a fairly optimistic view. You must make your own choice.

NOTES

1. Benjamin Barber, "The Second American Revolution," reprinted in *Impact of Mass Media,* 2nd ed. (New York: Longman, 1985), p. 501. Originally published in *Channels of Communication,* February/March 1982.

2. Ibid., p. 504.

3. Ibid., pp. 507–508.

61

The Worst Is Yet to Come

TED KOPPEL

Editor's Note: The new technologies have not necessarily made TV journalism better. In fact, as we've seen elsewhere in this book, TV news has deteriorated over the past decade for a variety of reasons.

In this article a distinguished TV journalist predicts that the future will not get any brighter for TV news. If you think today's television news is bad, he says, just wait!

Ted Koppel is anchor and managing editor of ABC News's *Nightline*. This article is adapted from a speech given at Harvard University in March 1994. This version was reprinted in the *Washington Post*, April 3, 1994.

In the mid- to late-'60s, when I went out to Vietnam for ABC television, we worked hard; but for reasons of technology, if nothing else, we operated at a more leisurely pace than reporters do now. And we focused far more on journalism. My fellow television reporters and I would spend a day, or two, or three in the field; bring the film back to Saigon, perhaps shipping it out the next morning, and 18 hours later—if it was deemed urgent enough—it might be taken off the plane in Los Angeles, processed, edited and then fed by telephone line to New York for use on the evening news.

You write differently when you know that your piece won't make it to the air for another day or two. You function differently in the field when you know that you and your competitors are at the mercy of just one connecting flight out of Saigon in the late afternoon. You have some time to think. You have some time to report. You even have some time, while the film is en route to the United States, to correct errors.

These days American reporters covering foreign wars (or at least those deemed important enough) are accompanied by portable ground stations, satellite phones, and a retinue of producers and technicians who can get you on the air "live" from anywhere in the world at any time. The technological tail is wagging the editorial dog.

MORE LIVE COVERAGE

The network schedule of news programs, or at least news-related programs, is such that a reporter is constantly on call. On major, breaking news there is literally no time for the reporter to go out and report the story. He or she is bound to the transmission point, while producers and camera crews go out and gather material. Frequently, *only* the camera crews actually go out and gather material. And they, for obvious reasons, are more concerned with the visuals.

So despite the fact that more people than ever before are in the field disseminating news, there is less time and less focus than ever before on the actual gathering of editorial material.

The capacity to "go live" also creates its own terrible dynamic. Much, if not most, of the process of good journalism lies in the evaluation, the assessment, the *editing* of raw material. Putting someone on the air while an event is unfolding is clearly a technological tour de force—but it is an impediment, not an aid, to good journalism.

Good reporting is to an event what a good map is to a city: It reduces the original in size and accessibility while remaining faithful to the basic features of the original. To simply train a camera on a complicated event is not journalism, any more than taking someone out on a boat and showing them a stretch of coastline is cartography.

MORE MEANINGLESS JOURNALISM

If you're living in a participatory republic, you need good journalism—but the emphasis is on *good*. Bad journalism is no more useful than a bad chart. Journalism designed for the express purpose of entertaining is no more useful than the exquisite cartouches that adorned many early charts and maps. They were beautiful, but they were strategically placed to cover those areas that the mapmakers had not yet explored. When the cartographers had real information to impart, they didn't muck it up with pretty pictures.

It may shock you—but it will probably not surprise you—to learn that during the most intense two weeks of Tonya Harding-Nancy Kerrigan coverage, television devoted more time to that story than it did to the most intense two weeks after the downing of Pan Am 103 . . . or the collapse of the Berlin Wall.

Let that one carom around the inner caverns of your skull for a moment or two. It is an inevitable consequence of the marketplace bringing its economic forces to bear on journalism.

But we may yet—indeed, I predict we will—look back on these as the golden, halcyon days of television news programming.

In the marketplace today, the three networks still command an enormous share of the audience. While Fox has a number of youth-oriented programs, ABC, NBC and CBS still draw 60 to 70 out of every hundred homes watching television. In *Nightline's* time slot, the arrival of *Late Show With David Letterman* has taken away some audience from *The Tonight Show* (which never recovered from the departure of Johnny Carson), but our audience has actually grown by 25 percent over the past two years.

MORE LOWEST COMMON DENOMINATOR

Are we at *Nightline* in competition with Letterman and *Tonight?* In a de facto sense, clearly—even though theirs are purely entertainment programs and no one at ABC News has ever suggested that we tailor our programming to compete with theirs. But the rules are implicit: In order to be able to produce the kinds of programs that we want to do, including investigative pieces, we cannot afford to ignore the kinds of stories that have always kept us competitive, going back to the days of Jim and Tammy Bakker and all the way through the current travails of Tonya Harding.

We may be in the waning years of mass communication as we've known it over the past 30 or 40 years, but *mass* communication it remains. Our audiences are several times those of our colleagues on cable or public television. For the time being at least, the commercial networks remain what they have always been: the most popular organs of the mass media, dependent upon the size of their audience to determine the size of their income.

Inevitably, that has some impact on the kind of news programming that we produce. Have we reached the level of lowest common denominator? I would argue strenuously that we have not. But are we aware of the continuing need to appeal to a mass audience? Absolutely.

MORE CHANNELS

We are also, however, on the cusp of a massive change. It may take a few years—five to 10 at the outside would be my guess—but the advent of the 500-channel supercommunications highway, and the ability of the audience to interact with its television set, will change our industry forever.

Just as the magazine world witnessed the demise of *Collier's, Life* and the *Saturday Evening Post* as ubiquitous giants of the publishing world; just as *Time* and *Newsweek* now frequently feature cover stories that have nothing to do with the breaking news of the previous week; just as mass circulation magazines have now been largely displaced by literally hundreds of special interest magazines—so too, we in network television news will either adjust or wither away.

The huge salaries being paid to those of us who anchor television news programs are in themselves an adjustment of sorts. As in the worlds of sports and entertainment, the simplest way to draw a crowd is with a recognizable star. But that's just a stopgap, a desperate quick fix.

MORE TIME-SHIFTING

The first major change is already happening: Time shifting. Those of you who like watching *Nightline,* for example, but can't stay up until after midnight, already have the option of taping the program and watching it at your convenience. The lamentable fact, though, is that most of us can't even remove that blinking "12:00" from our VCRs, let alone set the machine to tape a program.

But help is at hand.

Imagine a three-button remote control: An on-off switch, a button that lets you scroll through a menu, and an "enter" button. Turn the set on; scroll through the menu until you come to the word "news"; hit enter. Now scroll through the available options until you come to *Nightline*. Hit the enter button. At your convenience.

You could also, if you wish, scroll through the available *Nightline* programs by date or by subject matter—more than 3,500 of them. And as we all become more "interactively" literate, there will be a whole new world of options available. How about the entire interview that you did with Ross Perot in 1971, Ted? Not just the fragment that you replayed 23 years later on *Nightline*. Play it for me. And I want to see all of your outtakes on that series of programs you did with President Clinton in Europe.

MORE PERSONAL CHOICES

As for you, Peter and Dan and Tom, save me from all that Whitewater nonsense; I'm not interested. I want international news. My cousin, out in South Dakota, wants nothing but farm news. My son is a sports nut, my aging mother is worried about health care. My wife wants nothing but Whitewater. Each of them can shape and craft their own news programs according to their own special interests, and watch them at their own convenience. Gradually, the paternalistic world of television news as presented by a small group of reporters, producers and editors can be replaced by a brave new world of news you can choose.

Will there still be a place for the traditional network news division with its traditional programming? Of course. But probably not three of them anymore. And as programming reaches each home in America through direct satellite transmission, will there still be a need for local stations? Oh, sure. But not more than one or two to a market; and even then, only if they provide wide-ranging local coverage.

Commercials, with their shotgun approach to tens of millions of potential customers, can be far more direct, especially for big-ticket items. Scroll down your shopping list: "Automobiles." Enter. Scroll again. Chevrolet, Dodge, Ferrari, Ford. Enter. Scroll again. Escort, Falcon, Mustang. Enter. And so on, until you find the car you want. Would you prefer a simple one-minute commercial, or a ten-minute introduction to the car? Do you know which options you'd like? Scroll. Enter. Are you ready to talk with a member of our sales staff? Enter. And so on—through the sale, if you're ready to buy, or onto the next car if you're not.

MORE FRAGMENTATION

Why is all of that relevant to the kind of television news coverage you'll be getting? Because we may no longer be sponsored. We may be selling our product to you directly. (*Nightline:* 25 cents a program; 10 cents for the outtakes; a nickel for each old program you dial up.) Gradually, the audience will become more and more fragmented, and the information requested more and more oriented to the specific interests of the viewer. And the economic dynamics that have driven television news for the masses—with all its strengths and weaknesses—will cease to exist.

What I'm offering you here, of course, is simply an opinion, not revealed truth; but it disturbs me that so little attention is being paid to the changes that are all around us. We have traveled, during my relatively brief professional lifetime, from an era during which television news was regarded by its practitioners as almost a calling—when there really was no "business" of television news—to the present, when it is a massive, billion-dollar industry. That has imposed its own drawbacks. But still, there are top-flight professionals gathering, producing and editing excellent, free news programs for tens of millions of viewers.

The era upon which we are embarking, however, will winnow out the well-to-do, well-educated viewers. They will be ordering their news a la carte. They will do their high-priced shopping the same way. What will be left for the less well-to-do and the less well-educated among us will truly be television of the lowest common denominator: a *National Enquirer* of the air, sponsored by those products for whom demographics are irrelevant.

Television, which for so many years has been the great homogenizer in this country, seems poised to go the way of radio stations and newspapers and magazines. And since you were nice enough to ask, I'll tell you: I think it's a lousy idea.

62

The New Journalist

CARL SESSIONS STEPP

Editor's Note: As technology changes, the media change, but the act of journalism is altered as well. In the last decade of the twentieth century, perhaps the most important development for news gatherers and processors has been the Internet and the World Wide Web. The online era is demanding new skills and innovative ways of looking at the profession.

Online users not only talk back to journalists (as audiences always have), but they often do so in real time. This two-way process can shape coverage in new ways. In the twenty-first century, this may yet turn out to be the most drastic change in journalism since the Penny Press gave rise to objectivity and news.

Carl Sessions Stepp is an associate professor of journalism at the University of Maryland, senior editor of the *American Journalism Review,* and frequent coach of writing and editing at newspapers. This article is reprinted with permission from the *American Journalism Review,* April 1996.

When author and college professor Jon Franklin hosted his former editor George Rodgers recently, the two old pals relaxed by the fireplace at Franklin's 50-acre Oregon spread and reminisced about their adventures at Baltimore's late *Evening Sun.* Then they cruised on to cyberspace, where they're master-minding a new pay-per-read site for literary journalism.

Perhaps they seem unlikely new-age pioneers—Rodgers didn't even own a personal computer when he retired last fall. But they have a Web-load of company. As new forms of journalism expand at a Pentium pace, more and more traditionally trained news hands are converting to jobs that were unimaginable when their careers began.

Not long ago, the typical beginning reporter faced a simple choice: print vs. broadcast. Those options remain. But today's growth area is in multimedia jobs that blur and often obliterate the old boundaries. It's a proving ground forging not just new kinds of journalism but a new species of journalist as well.

Expertise and versatility define the members of this new species more than attachment to one specific medium. They can think and work across the widening spectrum from print to television to new information technologies.

POSITIONING FOR ONLINE

Some are wholehearted outriders on the information superhighway, fleeing mainstream newsrooms they consider constipated and obsolete. But many faithfully keep their old-world ties, just branching out a bit for growth and fun.

Above all, whether by accident or calculation, they're positioning themselves to adapt and thrive wherever fickle technology flies next.

The changes already have influenced recruiting for both online and traditional media jobs.

When Associated Press editor Ruth Gersh considers a job prospect these days, for example, she often skims past the cover letter, resumé and references, and zeroes in on another telltale indicator: the applicant's home page.

Gersh, who is developing a new multimedia service for AP clients, demands solid news credentials. But she also looks for signs that candidates can roam comfortably on the cyberbahn.

In the new "technitorial" age, she says, she needs people with a blend of traditional and futuristic skills, who can work imaginatively with the rich swirl of text, photos, graphics, audio and video that multimedia embodies.

"The people who have expressed interest so far," Gersh says, "range from very traditional print backgrounds to people who've come up on the broadcast side, the technical side, the photo side . . . people who've done design, even people who've done marketing.

"Of course," she adds, "what I'm looking for is all of this."

NO FORECAST YET

Editors across the country tell similar stories. At the *Chicago Tribune,* online editor John Lux agrees that applicants with a Web page have "a leg up." It shows their curiosity and commitment, much like previous generations of journalists got noticed by writing for any publication that would have them. One of Lux's recent hires worked for an online union paper. Another volunteered to produce a CD-ROM featuring prize-winning photographs.

And while electronic media—online providers, Web sites, CD-ROMs, e-zines, desktop publishing—have fueled the trend, it spills over into the hunt for journalists of all kinds.

Recruiters for Gannett newspapers, for instance, examine online college papers for evidence their alums have the right flair.

"We're hiring more on potential and brainpower and far less on functional skills," says Mary Kay Blake, Gannett's director of recruiting and placement. The idea isn't to identify computer skills per se, but to recognize that computer-literate people often "show clear thinking, strong analytical skills and connective abilities."

No one can yet forecast whether multimedia journalism will become just one more specialty, or fundamentally remake the mold. But for newspeople restless about the future, taking a taste of new media seems wise.

Youth does help, it appears. But a striking number of veterans are enlisting, from celebrities like Michael Kinsley and Linda Ellerbee (both recently lured to online projects) to long-timers from the news trenches.

What kind of world are they encountering? What kind of skills and attributes do they need? And what early lessons have emerged from this potentially momentous migration?

A NEW WORLD

Journalists infiltrating the new media encounter a world that's frantic, exciting and begging for creativity.

Online coverage is everywhere, from a real-time Super Bowl site visited by millions to CNN's multimedia daily news files to prodigious plans for covering the Summer Olympics and the presidential campaign online. The Newspaper Association of America's Web page lists over 150 newspapers with online services.

When you expand the definition to online magazines, the numbers skyrocket—one list counts 811 available e-zines. These online specialty publications range from crude tracts to sophisticated electronic magazines, and the topics and titles have mushroomed, from Bible study to dream interpretation, from Bad Haircut to Dead Pig Digest.

Online coverage of routine news is becoming, well, routine.

When a Groundhog Day snowstorm white-coated the Washington, D.C., area, for instance, the *Washington Post*'s Digital Ink online service signed on before dawn. Its news team tallied snow totals, updated forecasts, selected photos—and rummaged up a recording of Robert Frost reading his snow poetry to include as a "hot link."

Such is breaking news, Internet style: cross-media, sometimes traditional, often cyber-clever . . . and unfailingly interactive. Digital Ink, for instance, coordinated minute-by-minute snow reports (under the whimsical headline, "Has anyone seen a snow plow yet?") from neighborhood "correspondents," subscribers who messaged in to the central database.

STRONG NEWS INSTINCTS

Charles Shepard, 41, is a decorated reporter who joined Digital Ink last year after 18 years with newspapers. Shepard led the *Charlotte Observer* to a Pulitzer Prize covering the financial troubles of televangelist Rev. Jim Bakker. Later at the *Washington Post* he helped break the story about sexual misconduct by former Sen. Bob Packwood.

Now Shepard is online manager for projects at Digital Ink, where he senses the need for both proven news judgment and imaginative thinking.

"If you think of the people who're most successful," Shepard says, "it's people with strong news instincts, but they also have a feel for the medium and how it's different. They aren't just print journalists wearing slightly different clothes. They can use new media in different ways."

A parallel view comes from Susan Older, 47, managing editor/new content for Nando.net, the widely praised online service begun by Raleigh's *News & Observer*. She looks for good journalists to begin with, but she also likes people who are "risk takers and renegades."

"What makes some journalists just sit in the newsroom, and what makes some break out?" asks Older, who first drifted from newspapers to a CD-ROM project in 1992. "You have to be able to admit that the old way of journalism—hundreds and hundreds of years—is changing."

Such a renegade and risk taker is Jon Franklin, 54, who won two Pulitzers for Baltimore's *Evening Sun* and now teaches writing at the University of Oregon.

Franklin moderates an online literary journalism discussion group, WriterL, and, with George Rodgers, 55, is creating Bylines, an online service to market in-depth articles and stories. A longtime science fiction buff, Franklin began pushing for computers from the moment he showed up in the typewriter-driven newsroom. He's considered himself a pioneer ever since.

People like himself "want novelty," Franklin says. "Sometimes they get into trouble, sometimes they don't. Pioneering is one of the constructive things you can do with that impulse. . . . It's intellectual swashbuckling."

Beyond this open-minded, go-for-it attitude, the new species of journalist needs other qualities as well. Editors and managers see some common traits in the new breed.

A MULTIMEDIA OUTLOOK

They have a multimedia outlook. If anything characterizes the new age of journalism, it will be the need to integrate text, images, sounds and video into understandable packages.

Repeatedly, editors interviewed for this article stressed that they were not looking for hackers or techies (except for the jobs that are strictly technical). Mostly, they want journalists who can draw from writing, editing, design, imaging and broadcasting to meld seamless multimedia messages.

"Increasingly, we're looking at people with multimedia backgrounds, people who think visually as well as in the traditional sense," says Laurie Petersen, editor in chief of Media Central, a Cowles online service covering the electronic media.

At the *Chicago Tribune*'s online service, John Lux uses the term "producer" to describe his electronic news editors. "Writing and editing on the Internet is different," he says. "It's no fun to read on the Internet, so what takes the place of colorful writing is images. What editing is on the Web is not word editing but finding ways to use graphics, images and sounds to tell the story."

A key, according to Older, is leaving behind the old world of linear thinking.

"After years of writing stories that go from the beginning to the end, you find yourself creating something that has tendrils in every direction. If you can't break open your brain and think that way—well, what if someone clicks this way or explores that way—it's going to be hard."

USE NEW TECHNOLOGY

They appreciate new technology and how people use it. Shepard of Digital Ink agrees that technical skills aren't paramount, but he does believe new journalists need to appreciate how computers work in order to master their potential. For Shepard, "the single biggest difficulty has been understanding how a database is constructed and how to build or rebuild one."

If you don't "understand the technical dynamics of the product—what's under the hood," says Shepard, it would be like "running a race car team without knowing what the carburetor is capable of."

Mastering the medium also requires knowing how your audience thinks.

Petersen points out that success depends on understanding how to search the vast Internet, how people actually use online machinery and how they think about processing information. All that requires a bit of technical competence and, she says, "a solid grounding in common sense, having a feel for how people go at things."

WRITING IS IMPORTANT

They have an agreeable online voice and writing style. "Writing is what's important," says Jon Franklin. "Writing, and the ability to see what's going on around you."

Franklin believes that online readers will welcome long stories if they're compelling enough. Bylines, the service he and Rodgers are forming, is based on the assumption that online readers will pay to read extraordinary longer pieces.

Not everyone is sure that they will. Chicago's Lux argues the opposite point firmly. "People who are good writers and know it have to change their mindset that long, elegant stories are good," Lux maintains. "They are no good online, unfortunately. You may only get people for a screenful."

Others point out that the very notion of length is a print concept. Online text is far less linear. Users have many choices. They can stick with a posting for many pages, or "tunnel" to different levels for more details or completely new topics. They can use hypertext links to leap from site to site, or from text to video to audio.

So, while the length question stands unresolved for now, many editors agree that new writing styles will undoubtedly emerge.

As Cowles' Petersen observes, "You have to be a good writer with a voice. Online writing in particular requires a very alive writing style. It's a more personal kind of thing."

Several writers have discovered that, at least in their infancy, online media encourage more humor and conversational writing than traditional media.

Laura Williamson covers health and welfare for the *Atlanta Journal-Constitution*. Her job may suggest one direction journalism will take; she writes stories for the daily newspaper and often files different versions for her paper's Web site.

For example, Williamson has been following several health and welfare issues before the Georgia legislature. For the daily paper she writes stories of general interest. But for the Web site she writes longer, more analytical, even more informal pieces, on the assumption her online audience is already knowledgeable and wants the extra touches.

Williamson thinks the conversational style may keep people moving from screen to screen. "I don't mean flabby writing," she says. "But there's room for a little humor or inside baseball that they would never put in the paper because nobody cares. It's okay to be chatty and okay to be long, but it must be readable."

SHARING CONTROL

They are willing to share control with the audience. "Allowing the user to control what they do is very annoying to some journalists, especially newspaper people," says Raleigh's Older. "But the user is taking over. People don't want to be controlled anymore."

Online users not only talk back to journalists (as audiences always have), but they often do so in real time. That two-way process actually shapes coverage, according to Petersen, and new journalists need to both accept, and anticipate, that interactivity. That means reporters, for instance, have to predict audience questions and gather and present information that accommodates them.

Ultimately—and perhaps ironically, given the high-tech drapings—this all may produce a powerful new kind of community journalism, not unlike old-fashioned weekly newspapering.

"This is a very democratic medium that encourages conversation between producers and users, that has room for all the material you can't fit into the newspaper," says Shepard of Digital Ink.

Like many other developments driving today's journalism, this raises questions about how much new material will be strictly market-driven and how much will reflect editors' concerns about social responsibility. Will new media just feed consumers what they want, or will they devote resources to investigations or serious topics that may have less popularity?

A NEW JOURNALISM

However the mix develops, the potential for reinvigorating community journalism seems high. In fact, Older thinks a stint in community news might be just the thing for the new species of journalist.

"If the Internet is not a community, then tell me what is," says Older, who got her start running a small publication in Bozeman, Montana. "I think community journalism is the best training for doing anything on the Internet, because you find out what community is all about."

So we return to Jon Franklin and George Rodgers, a couple of vets who, as Rodgers puts it, "had our journalistic adolescence at the tail end of the Front Page era."

Now they want to use a new format—the Web—to tell the kinds of meaningful stories they've loved for decades. And they're going at it with true trailblazer spirit.

"A fundamental new journalism?" ponders Franklin. "Oh yes, yes. Probably many of them." ·

63

The Threat and the Promise

PETER F. EDER

Editor's Note: What about the new technologies for advertising and marketing? This article predicts that in the future, they will pose an increasing threat to privacy, but that sophisticated marketing will also lead to more customized products and services.

Author Peter F. Eder is senior vice president of member services for the Association of National Advertisers. Inc., New York. The views expressed here are the author's and do not necessarily reflect those of his association. This article was published in *The Futurist.* May/June 1990.

Advertising and mass marketing are growing more intensive and more invasive, spreading to almost every aspect of our lives. Yet, consumers also have a greater array of media from which to choose and more-sophisticated tools to avoid unwanted commercial messages.

The soaring number of media outlets is spurring this marketing boom. Sixty percent of American homes are now wired for cable television, and the average household can view 27 channels. Some 40,000 journals are published in the United States every year, and more than 10,000 radio stations crowd the airwaves.

Directly tied to the explosion in the number of media is an exponential increase in the number of commercial messages. Since 1965, the number of network television commercials has tripled from approximately 1,800 to nearly 5,400 a year, and this number is increasing by 20% annually, with more 15-second ads and more nonprogramming time. Networks often run five or six commercials in a row, and commercials during prime time average $10\frac{1}{2}$ minutes per hour.

To get an idea of the sheer amount of advertising that forces itself upon us, try this simple experiment: Don't throw away any of the unsolicited mail that arrives at your home—catalogs, special offers, inserts into bill statements, and other "junk mail"—and see how long it takes you to accumulate a foot of material. I suspect that for most readers this would take less than two months.

CONSUMERS BARRAGED

Commercial sponsorship is also becoming increasingly omnipresent. Can you think of a bus-stop shelter, an amusement park, a marathon, a high-school dance, or a neighborhood clean-up effort that isn't commercially sponsored? In all likelihood, the only events left unsponsored are presidential press conferences. Supreme Court hearings, and celebrity funerals.

With the proliferation of sponsorship as a marketing device and the explosion in the number of media messages, the measurements of audience size, profile, and reactions have also increased exponentially. Within the next decade, media operators, manufacturers, and retailers will undoubtedly be able to measure the impact of individual commercial messages. They could assess who saw which television spot and when, what he purchased, how he reacted to the purchased product, and how likely he is to repurchase or switch brands.

But as market research grows more sophisticated, there may be a consumer backlash against it. Researchers are reporting a substantial decrease in consumers' willingness to participate in surveys. The assault of telephone selling—direct marketing disguised as information gathering—has sensitized customers and turned them off. This could create major problems for the data gatherers.

DEATH OF THE MASS CONSUMER?

The growing sophistication of mass marketing isn't necessarily bad news for the consumer: Marketers are learning more about what increasingly heterogeneous customers really want. Thus, products are becoming less mass produced and more customized and specialized. In 1988, 33 new consumer products were introduced each day, not including 3,000 line extensions (modifications of existing products) that year. According to Laurel Cutler, vice chairman and director of marketing planning, FCB/Katz Partners: "The mass consumer is *dead* . . . . The focus of the '90s will be 'intensity' . . . pleasing one person at a time."

Media are becoming increasingly interactive, and there are more media variations to choose from. Three-dimensional television commercials are just the beginning: Viewers can play games with the game-show contestants, select optional endings to dramas, and express opinions by call-in voting.

And despite the assault by an ever growing number of appeals, we as message consumers have powerful tools to use to our advantage. We can not only tune out, but program our VCRs to record programs and even edit out the commercials. To a great extent, we can evade and avoid, and this makes us less homogeneous and more specialized.

We can have someone do the shopping for us, or we can do it ourselves any time of day or night. We can bank without tellers or with private investment counselors. We can purchase cars with an almost infinite array of options and preview on videotape where we want to spend our vacations. With this host of options available to us, we can be "demassified" as we individualize the mass market and the mass media.

Unfortunately, the same options aren't available to everyone, and the gap between the media-recipient "haves" and "have-nots" is widening. Several factors can create dramatically different levels of access to or assimilation of information: the degree of computer access, income and educational levels, geographic location, and ethnic and language barriers. These variations can lead to serious distortions of information, knowledge, and power, and they can ultimately affect our degree of control over our own lives.

Also keep in mind that the same array of tools—and hype—is available to all who have the funds or ability to generate active constituencies. Pressure and special-interest groups are in a position to manipulate information and promotional/publicity channels to their advantage. For example, "Moral Majority"-type organizations have led boycotts against products advertised on television programs with controversial subject matter, language, or sexual situations.

Regulators and organized bodies "acting in the public interest" are increasingly threatening the First Amendment guarantee of free speech to advertisers of legal products and services. In recent months, there have been attempts to ban all advertising and promotion for alcohol at any institution of higher education that receives federal funds. State attorneys general have begun regulating car-rental and airline advertising on a state-by-state basis.

Another area of concern is the potential for invasion of privacy. Marketers today can target mailings not only to ZIP codes, but to streets in a city, to generally defined income or educational levels, and to purchasers of a specific brand at a particular retail outlet. It's entirely within the realm of possibility that Mr. and Mrs. Jones and their 12-year-old daughter could be the source of a database that includes information on every aspect of their lives, such as the videos they rented last week, the causes they contribute to, and their "personal" opinions on everything from reproductive issues to drug use.

Consumers are faced with a barrage of messages, measurements, and solicited and unsolicited appeals, all making extraordinary demands on their attention. For consumers, this becomes a drain on their time and energy that many resent. For communicators, this creates the dilemma of ensuring memorability without causing the audience to tune out.

PREDICTIONS FOR ADVERTISING AND MASS MARKETING

To conclude, here are a few predictions for the next decade:

- We will live in a world of micro everything and macro nothing, with the personalization of media, messages, products, and services.
- We will be assaulted, in every area of our lives, by communications more intensive and more invasive than ever. A substantial portion of our time and probably an increase in our discretionary income will be required to selectively tune in and tune out. A San Francisco firm recently introduced SmarTV, a home-entertainment system that combines a VCR, a personal computer, and artificial intelligence. The system gives the user complete control over the medium in program planning, viewing time, and editing.

- We will run the risk of having special-interest groups intrude upon our privacy, curtail our opportunities, and reduce our ability to make our own choices. We may find our constitutional protections abridged or more narrowly defined.
- Our media, our messages, our products, and our services will be provided by larger and larger firms and by foreign individuals and firms that may not share our heritage, our culture, and our national interest. Bertelsmann of West Germany, the world's second-largest media conglomerate (U.S.-owned Time Warner is number one), owns five major U.S. publishers and two of the largest record companies. The third-largest media conglomerate, Rupert Murdoch's Australian News Corporation, owns *TV Guide, Seventeen,* and 10 other U.S. publications, as well as newspapers in major U.S. cities.

But the 1990s also hold great promise. We will be able to choose as we never have before—where and how we live, what we buy, where and how we consume, what and how we learn, whom we communicate with, what we see, hear, and read. Our array of choices will be limitless. We will be more in control of our lives—where and how we work, commuters and telecommuters alike, and how we spend our leisure time and shape our opinions.

64

The Media in 2045—
Not a Forecast, But a Dream

Claude-Jean Bertrand

Editor's Note: It is fitting to end this book with an ideal version of the mass media. What would they be like if we could make them perfect? Since that proposition seems so remote, however, few have imagined a world in which everything wrong about the media has been made right. In this essay French philosopher Claude-Jean Bertrand provides a dream scenario for what journalistic media could look like at the middle of the next century—if the right steps are taken.

He proposes a quality-control system that could help to ensure quality journalism. His proposed system is not far-fetched. There is nothing fanciful about it: it is a workable system. In the end, we must conclude that the mass media can be improved, and it is up to human beings to see that it will be.

Bertrand is a professor in the Institut Francais de Presse in Paris. This article is a revised version of an essay originally prepared as the Earl English Lecture at the University of Missouri School of Journalism. It is reprinted, with permission, from the *Public Relations Review,* Winter 1995.

A dream as in the "American Dream": in other words, neither something utopian, nor something I know will soon be realized but something which I very much hope may be achieved some day. An ideal.

Like the hero in ancient Greek tragedy, modern human society suffers from a fatal flaw: mediocre media. The media are certainly better than they have ever been, but they are still mediocre. And their further improvement is not simply a change to be desired: the fate of mankind is predicated upon it.

Why? Because only popular participation in the management of human society can insure the survival of civilization.[1] And there can be no true democracy without well-informed citizens. And there can be no well-informed citizens without a quality press.

For centuries, the delivery of news has been hindered by obstacles. First, obviously, material obstacles. Then political obstacles: as soon as the press was born, its development was hindered by the executive and the judiciary; even now, in the most democratic nations,[2] the government will always endeavour to filter the news or to "put a spin" on it.

From the turn of the twentieth century, another barrier to the information of citizens developed: the economic obstacle. Both media proprietors and advertisers treat media as means to make money, as vehicles for advertising: news for them is merely bait to catch a public.

IDENTIFYING THE PROBLEMS

So today, in circumstances when it appears plainly that we are not well informed (like during the 1990–1991 Gulf War), some will accuse the technology; some will accuse the political establishment; and others will accuse the economic establishment. Rightly too. Those three, however, are not the only factors of disinformation. They may not even be the worst, for they are well-known and often exposed.

A major threat, I believe, comes from the media professionals themselves—either because of their own failings, or because of their tolerance of the sins of management. That threat may have become the worst now that the communist pattern of State ownership of the media is no longer a model for anyone; and now that technology produces great media competition in spite of the trend towards concentration. And this fourth threat is rarely exposed.

Quality news media? How to define them. Certainly, political freedom is necessary, but it is not sufficient. It is a condition; it is not the goal—contrary to what some Americans seem to think. Everywhere in the industrialized West, politically-independent commercialized media have been free for many years and they have too often done a terrible job.[3] Certainly media had better be profitable concerns but their goal cannot be *just* to make money.

One great myth is that the central mission of news media is to find and publish "the truth." For one thing, trillions of true events are totally devoid of either importance or interest.[4] Quite rightly such truths are not published. But there is a problem with what *is* published: true and important news is devoid of any value if the reader/listener/viewer shuns it or cannot understand it. Truth, like freedom, is not enough.

For news media to be quality media, they must, on a regular basis, provide all groups with the information that is important to each of them, and that will enable all individuals to be participants in society. And the news must be provided in an understandable, attractive shape.

Quality implies good technology, hence financial resources, obviously—but mainly it implies a concern for the very diverse needs of the public, *before* production. And it implies, *after* production, a concern for the public's evaluation of the product. That is why many observers call good service "the social responsibility of the media" or, more restrictively, "media accountability."[5] Yet "quality control" might be a preferable term—for three reasons: it clearly involves not only newspeople but media owners; it sounds industrial, not moralistic; and the connotation of the phrase is an increase of prestige and profits, not a restriction of freedom.

FINDING SOLUTIONS

Now, to control quality, one needs (1) a definition of quality; and (2) means to check the product and to suggest corrections of defects. Those will be my two topics here.

The easiest way to define quality media is negative: you define what the sins are that they should not commit. That is what codes of ethics usually do and what do most lectures, articles, courses, columns, books, workshops, conferences on ethics.

Most of the violations of ethics that they mention are, in my mind, relatively benign—including inaccuracies, personal bias, invasion of privacy, libel or even minor corruption. Such sins are regrettable but they are not systematically committed—and, mainly, their impact on the public is relatively small.

What I would call the Fourth Great Obstacle to quality news service, the internal obstacle, consists not of a few unethical reporters but, in a combination of narrow-minded media proprietors, of inadequately trained journalists and, above all, of some powerful traditions within journalism.

The media have improved tremendously over the last 50 years. In his nineties one of the fiercest and longest-lived critics of U.S. media, George Seldes, was happy to tell me that in the days when he published his journalism review *In Fact* (1940–1950) he could not have imagined that such progress was possible.[6]

IMAGINE IT'S THE YEAR 2045

So now let us move 50 years forward in time and dream of what the quality newsmedia may be like. What do they do well now, in 2045, that they did not do in the late twentieth century? I have identified about a dozen major improvements, relative either to the selection of information or to the presentation of it. And there are a couple more that relate to the very concept of journalism. The conservatism of the profession has gradually crumbled and many archaic traditions have yielded to the need for better service.

The definition of news has changed—as well as the hierarchy of news. Quality news, as I said, is whatever information any major group in the population finds useful for its well-being. And no longer does tradition limit it to political news, i.e., news about local or national government.

FEWER OMISSIONS

Omission used to be undoubtedly the worst sin of the media. It could be due to the nature of a medium (e.g., radio can use only 24 hours a day), or to an unavoidable lack of resources (e.g., a small daily cannot have correspondents in foreign capitals). But omission could also be due to the greed of owners—or to flaws in the professionals.[7] Proprietors would avoid expensive news or news likely to antagonize friends and clients. Journalists would leave out what they—as young, well-educated, urban, white males, which most of them were—judged uninteresting.

Western media had given almost no coverage to a massacre in the early 1970s when a small ethnic group literally decimated the other (85% of the population), leaving an estimated 300,000 dead. That was probably because the country was Burundi where everybody is black—and there were no whites involved as in South Africa. The same could be applied to apartheid in Malaysia.

All Western media ignored tropical diseases that killed far more people than AIDS and yet got little money and research thrown at them. In France the media seldom dealt with the true cost of alcoholism. And in the U.S., back in the old days, a union or a strike was rarely mentioned in positive language and Department of Defense scandals got little regular coverage.

The U.S. press used to be presented as a model—yet a visitor from overseas, on reading a metropolitan daily, could not help being shocked by the huge proportion of advertising—as compared to the tiny proportion of world news. And, during the 1991 Gulf War, it was a shock to observe—not the predictable military censorship, not the normal amount of lies published—but the absence of background information on Islam, the Arabs, the Middle East and Iraq. There was no excuse for that very serious omission.

Now in 2045, made-to-order news packages make it easier for every minority to be served—but general interest media too carry more diversified information. The improvement was slow in developing. Quality media have by now forsaken most of their traditional prejudices, taboos and sacred cows—those of the proprietors, or of advertisers, or of the newspeople, or of the wealthier part of the audience, or of the majority in the population. All those protagonists are as many obstacles to proper information. But ultimately journalists should be held responsible.

ENTERTAINMENT IS KEPT SEPARATE FROM INFORMATION

Many of the offending acts committed by the news media (like their crude appeal to emotions, their over-dramatization of events or the publication sometimes of pure fiction) belong, in my opinion, to the entertainment side of media—and should be judged by different criteria. They have been common since the invention of printing. People enjoy them and they have little influence—because readers and viewers are no fools.

But in the last decades of the 20th century, such dailies as the London *Sun* or the German *Bild Zeitung* were, regrettably, called "*news*papers." At the turn of the 1990's, commercialism led to a growing confusion between journalism and show business with, on the one hand, glitzy TV newscasts and gossipy front pages even on quality dailies, and, on the other hand, docudramas and reality shows.[8]

One way or another, media now distinguish more clearly between entertaining data and significant data. It has been difficult to make journalists admit that consumers treat much news as nothing but entertainment. By that is meant, not just the early sex life of a Presidential candidate or a divorce in the British Royal family—but also sports results, the eruption of a distant volcano, a plane crash, an attack on a bank—and even some wars, provided they are far away enough. That kind of news is for "event voyeurs."[9] But even an important happening can turn into a fun item if its meaning is not made clear.

Media entertainment is in no way despicable. Entertainment is crucially needed in modern society and most of it is provided by media: it is one of their main functions. But now in 2045, to the extent it is possible, entertainment is not confused with true information; it is not allowed to shove it aside or trivialize it.[10]

MORE GOOD NEWS AND THE HALF-FULL GLASS

A regrettable myth had developed that good news was no news. Could then the end of World War II, the invention of the polio vaccine, the landing on the moon, the fall of the Berlin Wall be labelled bad news? Why should the stress always be on conflict, on drama: "If it bleeds, it leads."[11] The general attitude was negative: if anything can go wrong it will; you're damned if you do and you're damned if you don't.

One quite often had the unsettling impression that journalists were disaster-addicts, that they got high on accidents, failures, massacres, swindles, tornadoes, etc. That they systematically avoided positive phenomena. Was it an attitude forced on the profession by competition and the constant rush? To some extent—but it also revealed an approach that was reactionary, arrogant, masculine, ignorant, lazy and sick.

Thus the public was slowly inculcated a depressive view of the world although life, in the West at least, was undebatably more enjoyable than it had been two or three generations before. Now in 2045, a greater stress is put on positive events, or on a positive interpretation of events—on the half full glass.

INFORMATION IS PROVIDED, NOT JUST NEWS

One cause of the negativism is that little events often are accidents or crimes. But now, in 2045, the media deal not just with the news, which usually is a mosaic of trivial little events. Media are no longer interested in speed and scoops. They convey in-depth information, most often about long-term processes, concentrating on what Ben Bradlee, a famous editor of the *Washington Post* in the late twentieth century, called "groundswell stories." Moreover, as they deal with slow phenomena more than with isolated events, media now never drop a topic after giving it exaggerated attention for a few days or weeks: they keep the public informed of further developments.

NEWS ABOUT THE WHOLE OF MANKIND

An easily explainable but regrettable tradition in every part of the globe was to focus on local and regional news. The nation most guilty of isolationism was the U.S. where in the early 1990's even the best dailies would devote less than 2% of their non-advertising space to foreign news. Now, on the contrary, media deal in knowledge about the wide, wide world and how every individual, every group, every nation fits in it—and how it all came to be so. You might call it history and geography.

Old-timers remember that in 1991 a weekly[12] newsmagazine was launched in France which became very successful among the well-educated: *Courrier International*. It selected and translated articles from dozens of foreign dailies and other periodicals: *Asahi Shimbun* (Tokyo), *Nezavissimaya Gazeta* (Moscow), *Haaretz* (Israel), *Frankfurter Algemeine Zeitung* (Frankfurt), *El Pais* (Madrid) or the *Times of India*. The articles gave the French reader a foreign viewpoint both on his country and others.

In co-operation with the *Courrier,* the public television network FR 3 had a late night and a morning show called *Continentales* which presented TV news shows broadcast a few hours before in nations all over the world—with French sub-titles. It was close to CNN International's contemporary *World Report,* yet different.

In 2045, all media commonly exchange material—and also ideas and techniques.

MEDIA SEEK REALITY BEHIND APPEARANCES

Now the media far more often go and search for the true nature, meaning or implications of events instead of echoing the official line or of braying with the journalistic herd.

A striking illustration of the latter behavior is provided by a South Korean airliner that got into trouble with the Soviets. Not the one that got shot down over the Pacific and triggered a major international crisis. Years before, another plane had lost its bearings over the North pole and instead of flying South to the U.S., it flew South into the USSR. It was spotted from a military base; was shot at and partly disabled by Soviet fighters. But it went on flying for several hundred miles into the Soviet Union and finally landed on the frozen surface of a lake. Was that some trivial incident? Of course not, for it indicated[13] that maybe the Soviet Union was not the tremendous military fortress it was played up to be.

How uncomfortable that must have been for all who had vested interests in the Cold War![14] How else can one explain why the Korean misadventure was underplayed at the time and was ignored afterwards? Then, after communism collapsed, many commentators wondered at the West's forty-year-long misevaluation of the Soviet power.

Not only media must interpret without prompting from special interests—but also reporters should find original news by daring to stray away from the pack and by exploring areas that their colleagues do not even know exist, like Timor in the 1970's and 1980's where they could have helped stop a slow genocide perpetrated by the Indonesians.

MEDIA UNCOVER INVISIBLE PHENOMENA

There is a second, more important, way in which media (now, in 2045) crack their routine and seek the hidden reality. Journalists strive, not merely to report the obvious news (as they have always done), but to uncover important though as yet invisible phenomena evolving below the surface; to point out deep trends and changes before they emerge, often as major problems, sometimes as disasters. How many reporters in France in the seventies had investigated African and North African immigrant suburban ghettos and forecast the crime, the riots they would generate—and the consequent rise of a racist fascist right? That is one aim of the techniques gathered in the 1970's by Philip Meyer under the name "precision journalism," i.e., using computer power to analyze surveys or archives.

MEDIA TRANSLATE KNOWLEDGE

There is still another way of bringing useful information from obscurity into the limelight. The media now more than ever before translate and publicize the discoveries, concerns and thoughts of scientists and other experts.

The old-fashioned trickle down process, from academic journal to local daily, was terribly slow and unreliable. And what the best newspapers, like the *Washington Post* in the U.S. or *Le Figaro* in France, or newsmagazines and television documentaries (e.g., *Future Watch* on CNN) had been doing for years, with little support from advertisers, was far too restricted. Now, all the permanent suppliers of journalism publish clear and stimulating reports on research and development in all branches of science and technology.

Thus the media act no longer just as political message-carriers, but as multidirectional explorers and initiators. Everyone in the twentieth century had the experience of going to the house of new acquaintances or to the waiting room of a new doctor and finding specialized magazines one did not know, and in which one read fascinating stories, serious or entertaining. In 2045, whetting the appetite and diversifying tastes are considered almost as important as providing the food. So there is less and less difference now between journalists and teachers: both contribute to the needed continuous education of all.

PRESENTATION

Anyone with information to convey, pedagogue, storyteller or journalist, knows that *how* you say it matters as much as *what* you say.

NO STANDARD SIZE NEWS PACKAGE OR TIME FOR DELIVERY

In the old days, as media partook of old-fashioned industry, they had to bring out every day a product of almost the same size, with about the same mix of contents—regardless of what happened in the world. So they had to stretch or shrink the news, to ignore important news or introduce a lot of padding so as to fit the immutable newshole in time or space. Inevitably their report was often distorted.

Thanks to the progress of technology, in 2045, there are few or no dailies in the nineteenth century sense, publishing the news of the day before. Now there are few or no old-fashioned news shows interrupting broadcast entertainment programs. The definition of news is different now and the distribution is permanent. News packages of items produced by journalists are tailored by computer to meet the special or regular requests of every subscriber at any time. They also vary in size according to the available news—and are delivered by very diverse channels to diverse locations, of course.

The citizen now can use the all-news radio or CNN type of continuous television service: they became common everywhere in the 1990's. Mainly, the citizen, through his cable and satellite-linked TV set or computer also has access to audio and visual data banks from which he can order his individual mix of information, on every possible topic and region of the globe.

PSEUDO-NEWS MARKED OUT

There are five kinds of information that used to be allowed into the news contents and are now either rejected or tagged with a clear warning.

The worst, but relatively easy to spot, were *advertorials,* ads dressed as regular news items with minimal indication that they were not. Next came "press releases" written by public relations people on behalf of a businessman or a public official and usually containing some proportion of true information; if they were written in the style of a particular journalist, he/she could just add a byline and file it. The third kind of pseudo-news was actually written by a journalist but following some enjoyable junket or other freebie.

The fourth was a major weakness of the old-fashioned media and had been exposed for many years: much of what was reported as news was staged by whoever was to benefit from it. What Daniel Boorstin called "pseudo-events":[15] presidential press conferences, movie festivals or protest marches. Such events had two advantages in the eyes of editors and publishers: they would normally be announced in advance and were pre-processed for use by the media. That kind of news can be useful, even important, but it should be, as it is now, in 2045, carefully filtered and commented.

Last on the list, there are reports on events manufactured by the media themselves: from the antics of paparazzi dogging celebrities, to meaningless investigative journalism exposing non-scandals and violating the privacy of any person caught in the limelight just to satisfy the prurience of an under-educated public.

NEWS MADE UNDERSTANDABLE

Ordinary people are not stupid but they do lack training or motivation in handling the media. In the twentieth century, under-educated people and people not required by their job to keep informed, often found the news media boring, especially the print media—boring largely because to them much of what the media said was incomprehensible. Sometimes the reason was that they did not know the words and concepts that the media used.[16]

And quite often, even if they did keep informed with local middle-brow newspapers or newscasts, most citizens could not understand the meaning of an event: what generated it, or the context in which the event occurred, or the possible consequences of it.

One cause was the incapacity of reporters, itself due to inadequate training. Another cause, especially in Europe, would be sloth: the reporter did not bother to check archives or consult experts. Yet another cause, especially in the U.S., was the cult of objectivity which prevented the reporter from evaluating the news and suggesting interpretations. A last cause could be the tradition of addressing the "happy few," peers or sources or the elite, hence taking sophistication for granted.

To that problem, technology has provided a double solution: on the one hand, basic information has been rendered consumer-friendly (which some U.S. newspapers strove to do in the early 1990's) thanks to a concise, clear and lively style, summaries, photos or infographics. Besides, interactive media now allow anyone who so desires to obtain, easily and immediately, more data, more background, and a lot of analysis and comments on any given piece of news.

IMPORTANT NEWS MADE INTERESTING

The media now, in 2045, consider one of their important missions is not just to make important news understandable, but to make it interesting to everybody—instead of either serving what people naturally like, or addressing only a cultured elite. The media have acknowledged that, for a democratic society to operate properly, *everybody* needs to possess a wide picture of the world that makes sense. So the media must catch and hold the attention of the man-in-the-street.

William Cobbett in the early nineteenth century had opened the way in his *Weekly Register* in which he made politics as exciting as murder or sex. The lower-class London *Daily Mirror* was a pioneer in the twentieth century with its "Mirrorscope" in the 1960s. It was a two-page section in which some serious issue (like the national budget[17]) was presented, in a very attractive fashion. Alas, some Australian tycoon then came along and pulled the whole British popular press downwards further than it had ever been, with a diet of bare nipples, libelous gossip, bloody murder, sports and jingoism—i.e., entertainment.

Making information interesting is not easy: it is a question of approach, personality, style, illustrations, color, etc., while for small media, it is also a question of finding a local peg to hang the story. Traditional journalists in the U.S. were taught a clear lesson in the early 1990's, especially during the 1992 presidential campaign, when talk shows became a major vehicle for serious politicians to convey their ideas and intentions. Merely because the format was fresh and the host was entertaining.

SOME INTERESTING NEWS SHOWN TO BE MEANINGFUL

Conversely, the media now try and show that news which seem to be merely interesting can in fact be important to society. What is required is, not just expertise, but a different concept of journalism—and time to work on the story. For instance: a man has machine-gunned his wife and six children. It looks like no more than a nice little slaughter—but is it not the symptom of some social ill? Alcoholism, loose psychiatric supervision, lack of social welfare, unemployment, easy access to guns? Many human interest stories can serve as catchy introductions to big issues.

Should media only report the news? As early as 1974, the Associated Press Managing Editors association (APME) recommended, in its code of ethics, that:

- "The newspaper should serve as a constructive critic of all segments of society . . .
- Editorially, it should advocate needed reform or innovations in the public interest . . .
- It should provide a forum for the exchange of comment and criticism, especially when such comment is opposed to its editorial positions . . ."

MEDIA STIMULATE THINKING AND DEBATE

In the past, mass media used to cower and yield before the majority or any vocal pressure group such as the NRA or the champions of "political correctness" in the U.S.; and the wine lobby or the Catholic Church in Latin European countries. And they were most often scared of new, unconventional ideas, which consequently often appeared in extremist publications.[18]

Now media consider it a function of theirs not just to reflect public concerns (as the Fairness Doctrine used to call for, in the U.S.)—but to stimulate vigorous public debate on public issues. Thus they serve the long-term interest of the nation and of mankind.

In 2045, media do report and support new concepts and viewpoints. They encourage the discussion of controversial topics, with the participation of minority groups of all kinds, even those that are obnoxious to the majority. This is an expansion of the open policy which from the 1970's led French public television to invite political leaders, from fascist to maoist, and have them grilled by journalists in near-peak viewing time. *USA Today* was remarkable from the early 1980's by the daily publication of pro-and-con opinions. The risk is to offend some people—and to make a little less profit, but the consensus now is that the risk must be run.

MEDIA CAMPAIGN FOR REFORM

Instead of practising local boosterism or keeping prudently bland, media should have a vision. They should advocate solutions and not merely expose problems. They should stay independent, certainly, but be involved. And they should fire people into being active in political and social life.

Many years ago, in 1991, the *Philadelphia Inquirer* published a superb nine-part series[19] investigating the abominable effects of some U.S. policies in the 1980's. At the time, it had seemed incredible, to a European observer, that the U.S. media, known for their aggressiveness, should be so smilingly tame—while strange words and decisions issued from the Reagan Administration.

Now, in 2045, the quality U.S. media would not forget to investigate anything like the Savings & Loans scandal (called the worst financial catastrophe since 1929)—or the looting of pension funds by corporate raiders in the U.S. in the 1980's. They would vigorously campaign for better public services (like education), for gun control, for children's television, for federal assistance to the arts. . . . But those are not issues any more.

MEDIA ACCOUNTABILITY SYSTEMS

How were the media so transformed? By 2045, a number of forces had been at work for some 80 years. Here are four of them.

1. The first factor, in my opinion, has been the ever-growing complexity and integration of the free-market nations in the world: this has made it indispensable to change a number of basic concepts in journalism—and those changes were made possible by technology.

2. Regulation of media has done part of the job. Indisputably, the deregulation of media in the 1970's and 1980's had excellent effects in Europe: the lifting of the State monopoly and governmental control over broadcasting had done much for democracy and for the development of electronic media. But mindless deregulation combined with rampant commercialism can cause disasters.

    It is no sign of fascism (red or black) to believe that humans are imperfect creatures; that unlimited freedom turns society into an ugly jungle; that an individual's activity has to be regulated both by laws and customs and by the pressure of parents, pals and peers.

    Even in the twentieth century, everybody agreed on the need to license broadcasters and cable operators—and on the need for laws to limit concentration of media ownership. Most Europeans agreed on a legal right of reply for citizens or on the need of public subsidies to counter the natural trend towards monopoly in some media fields. Contrary to Americans, they were more afraid of Big Business than of Big Government. By 2045, it is generally accepted, even in the U.S., that true freedom implies regulation.

3. A more educated and militant public realized that the traditional media were not satisfactory, and especially that the conventional concept of news was not satisfactory. And they, the users, could and should do something about it, e.g., pay to get good service—pay directly, not via the advertisers.

    Pressure by the consumers gradually produced media better adapted to the people's needs and wishes. Readers and viewers now realize that good media service is crucial: the media have to fulfill every one of their functions. They must not all, for instance, concentrate on being ad carriers.

4. A fourth factor has been the greater awareness and solidarity of newspeople. In the 1980's, American journalists became more interested in ethics and, after the 1991 Gulf War, it seemed that French and other European journalists had developed a sudden concern for professional morality.

In the early days, however, talk about ethics was popular but action was taboo. For many years, newspeople everywhere ignored, bad-mouthed and resisted all "media accountability systems." Since then, fortunately, they have realized that such systems satisfy the public by giving it a "voice in the product" and a means of access to the media; that such systems increase the social influence and prestige of the profession; that such systems are an excellent shield for them against wild commercialism. And, as a consequence, newspeople realized that media accountability systems (contrary to an old cliché) is a great weapon to protect the freedom of the media.

QUALITY CONTROL SYSTEMS

By 2045, Quality Control Systems, or Media Accountability Systems (MAS), about two dozen of them, have slowly been developed into a vast, flexible, informal network. Some consist in a single individual, others in groups of people; some are publications, others processes. The MAS could be classified into three categories according to their obvious purpose: criticism, monitoring or listening to the public, but actually most systems participate in more than one of the three.

1. Some were well-known (though not very numerous) in Anglo-Saxon countries as early as the late 1960s. Most of those had been started within the media industry but many involved the public too:

   - discreet *liaison bodies* set up by the media and some profession with which they were bound to clash at times (like free press/fair trial committees);
   - *codes of ethics* that media people establish by consensus;
   - *local press councils:* meeting points for media professionals and the community;
   - *regional and national press councils:* informal courts of arbitration set up by the media for citizens with a complaint against a particular publication or electronic news giver;
   - *media ombudsmen,* attached to a particular newspaper or broadcasting network or station;
   - *ethics coaches* in the newsroom to provide continuous training, advice and to organize workshops, etc.;

- *in-house critics* and the "contents evaluation commissions" such as those set up from the 1920's by Japanese newspapers, to scrutinize contents on a daily basis to insure that the code of ethics was respected; and
- *media reporters* that are not content (as most are in France) with giving happy media news—but keep a critical eye on the whole industry.

2. Some MAS were known in the last decade of the twentieth century but were not usually associated with the first category of councils, ombudsmen and such.

Quite a few of them involved decisions by the media industry:

- visible *correction boxes;*
- *letters to the editor* and open forums;
- regular *opinion surveys,* use of readers' panels, etc.;
- *invitation* of readers *to the editorial conference;*
- systematic *pro-and-con presentation* of issues;
- training for working professionals (by one-day *workshops,* week-long seminars and sabbatical fellowships); and
- *books* by professionals and *reviews* specializing *in media criticism,* like the *American Journalism Review* or the *St. Louis Journalism Review.*

Others were external to the industry:

- non-commercial *research,* initiated by academics, by a think-tank, by a foundation, or by a government agency—into bias, audience perception, contents and, mainly, absence of contents (i.e., omissions);
- consumer or media-*consumer associations* (active in the U.S. from the 1960's and flourishing in France after part of television was privatized in the mid-1980's); and
- college-level *journalism education.*

3. Some MAS were so little used in the late twentieth century as to be almost unknown and were then rarely mentioned on one or the other side of the Atlantic:

- *accuracy and fairness questionnaires,* used over the years by a few small U.S. newspapers
- *la société de rédacteurs,* an association of journalists which can own shares in the capital of the medium,[20] hence has a voice in the setting of the editorial policy; the first to attract attention was the one at the French daily *Le Monde,* in 1951; and
- *la société de lecteurs,* which is even rarer, is an association of readers who have bought shares in a newspaper and ask to have some input, even small, in the management of the medium.

CONCLUSION

It is to be hoped that by 2045, without any State intervention, there will have developed in every democracy a loose network of quality control systems whose purpose will be to monitor, analyze, evaluate, criticize, advise the media—and to assist the journalist in his mission.

If the dream comes true, I believe that, at crucial points in the net, one will find universities. For several reasons: universities are a kind of no man's land, more politically and economically independent than any other large institutions; they have communication experts (historians, sociologists, political scientists or semanticists) one of whose missions is to do research, especially long-term team research.

Mainly, universities can both teach journalists that they should engage in the fifteen operations I listed, and teach them how to succeed in it. H.L. Mencken considered the sins of the press derived from "the stupidity, cowardice and Philistinism" of the average journalist,[21] which translates into "conservatism and incompetence." The schools of communication offer the best, bar none, means of improving journalism.

Schools can also provide ethical education. A passion for public service does not come naturally: it has to be sown and nurtured. And a young professional needs to be trained into considering quality control systems as part of his environment. Not many journalists in the 1990's could tolerate criticism, especially from outside the profession.

U.S. journalism schools have done a pioneering job in painfully bringing together the two types of communication experts, experienced media professionals and trained academics—and nowadays they sometimes find both within the same individual. Europe has been regrettably slow in following the example. On the other hand, the U.S. has much to learn in Europe too, and also in Japan. For example: the surviving attachment to media as public services rather than money machines; or the attachment to a balanced division of the audience between public and commercial broadcasting.

So the last wish on my list is that exchanges become more and more numerous between Europe and the U.S. both at the media level and at the academic level. That would contribute greatly to the construction of the media temple of my dream.

NOTES

1. The USSR provides evidence: vast tracts of it have been desertified (like the region around the Aral Sea), or are terminally polluted (like the areas around the paper mills); and thousands of people needlessly died, or will soon die, from what happened *after* the Chernobyl accident. That and much more (from about 60 million people variously massacred between 1917 and the mid-1980s, to the rotting of hundreds of thousands of precious ancient books) would not have happened if the Soviet media had been free, and willing, to report and protest.

2. E.g., in the U.S., where the media were never more manipulated than during the administrations of the so-called "Great Communicator" Ronald Reagan.

3. Constitutionally, the BBC in Britain is less free than ABC in the U.S., but over the years it has served citizens much better.

4. Like the fact that my neighbors' dog died last week or the outcome of a local soccer match 3,000 miles away.

5. Or, even more restrictively, "media ethics."

6. See also his *Even the Gods Can't Change History,* Secaucus: Lyle Stuart, 1976, p. 244.

7. This was well documented in the U.S in the late twentieth century by the annual list of *Ten Best-Censored Stories* established by a panel of eminent media critics and published from Sonoma State University in California.

8. E.g., in 1989 a *Times-Mirror* survey revealed that half the people considered *Most Wanted* (a TV program asking the public to help hunt down criminals) as a news program.

9. A felicitous phrase minted by P.J. Corso in *Editor & Publisher,* 18 January 1992, p. 52.

10. A memorable example of this occurred in 1976 when U.S. media focused all their attention on the brief sex-tinged epilogue of a remarkable *Playboy* interview in which Jimmy Carter presented his presidential platform.

11. A Michael Dukakis phrase, cited in *Broadcasting & Cable,* 17 May 1993.

12. Weekly publication makes it very different from *World Press Review:* it reads like a newspaper.

13. Many years before a German student landed his little plane on the Red Square.

14. Those were the days when at least once a year *US News & World Report* would publish a big scary story on the Soviet armed forces.

15. Daniel J. Boorstin, *The Image: A Guide to Pseudo-Events in America,* New York, Atheneum, 1961, paperback ed. with that subtitle, 1971.

16. In Singapore, in the 1980's, when a newspaper for children was launched, some 11,000 adults cancelled their subscription to the regular paper, because they could understand the new one better.

17. A particular presentation for which it received rare compliments from the London *Times.*

18. E.g., in France, it was the extreme-right that brought up the problem of massive immigration, which parties right and left of center preferred to sweep under the carpet.

19. "America: What Went Wrong?" by Donald L Barlett & James B. Steele, in the *Philadelphia Inquirer,* October 20–28, 1991—later turned into a best-seller.

20. At the daily *Libération,* the *société* owns 62% of the stock. But the *société* at the two big television networks, TF 1 and Antenne 2, which gather 85% of the journalists, do not own shares.

21. Cited by S.L. Harrison in *Editor & Publisher,* 4 July 1992, p. 44.

ADDITIONAL RESOURCES FOR PART 16

Suggested Questions and Discussion Topics

1. From his essay "The Worst Is Yet to Come," discuss three or four of the basic changes that author Ted Koppel predicted in 1994. To what extent have these predictions already come true?

2. In "The Worst Is Yet to Come," Ted Koppel suggests that changes in television are going to make it worse. How will it be worse, and do you agree? Discuss.

3. In "The New Journalist," Carl Stepp describes the new world of on-line journalism. Discuss some of the qualities he suggests will be important to succeed in this new form.

4. In "The New Journalist," what does Carl Stepp mean by "sharing control with the audience"? Why is that different from traditional journalism?

5. In "The Threat and the Promise," author Peter F. Eders says that the "promise" of the future is more and better choices in everything. What are the "threats"? Discuss one. What is your own opinion about the potential danger of this "threat"?

6. In "The Threat and the Promise," what does Eders suggest is a negative outcome of the increased commercial sponsorship he predicts for the future? Do you agree? Discuss.

7. In "The Media in 2045—Not a Forecast, But a Dream," Claude-Jean Bertrand suggests that the future for mass media could be rosy if certain quality control systems, or Media Accountability Systems, are put into place. Discuss any three of his suggestions, and express your opinion regarding the likelihood of their becoming reality. Explain.

8. In "The Media in 2045—Not a Forecast, But a Dream," why does Bertrand recommend more college-level journalism education to make his dream of mass media come true?

Suggested Readings

Diane L. Borden and Kerric Harvey, *The Electronic Grapevine: Rumor, Reputation, and Reporting in the New On-Line Environment.* Mahwah, NJ: Lawrence Erlbaum, 1997.

Joel Brinkley, *Defining Vision: The Battle for the Future of Television.* New York: Harcourt Brace, 1997.

Richard Collins and Cristina Murroni, *New Media, New Policies: Media and Communication Strategies for the Future.* Cambridge, UK: Polity Press, 1996.

Wilson P. Dizard Jr., *The Coming Information Age,* 3rd ed. New York: Longman, 1989.

Carla B. Johnston, *Viewers, Victims, and Victors: The Impact of New Communications Technologies.* Westport, CT: Praeger, 1998.

Sara Kiesler, *Culture of the Internet.* Mahwah, NJ: Lawrence Erlbaum, 1997.

Paul Levinson, *The Soft Edge: A Natural History and Future of the Information Revolution.* London: Routledge, 1997.

David T. MacFarland, *Future Radio Programming Strategies: Cultivating Listenership in the Digital Age.* Mahwah, NJ: Lawrence Erlbaum, 1997.

Sig Mickelson and Elena Y. Teran, eds., *The First Amendment—The Challenge of New Technology.* Westport, CT: Praeger, 1989

Gregory L. Rosston and David Waterman, *Interconnection and the Internet.* Mahwah, NJ: Lawrence Erlbaum, 1997.

Suggested Videos

"The Cable TV Industry and Beyond." New York: Insight Media, 1997. (30 minutes)

"The History and Future of Television." Princeton, NJ: Films for the Humanities & Sciences. (50 minutes)

"To Boldly Go: The Future of Communication." New York: Insight Media, 1997. (22 minutes)

"Cybermedia." New York: Insight Media, 1997. (30 minutes)

"Information Delivery Systems." New York: Insight Media, 1997. (25 minutes)

"The Information Society." Los Angeles: KCET, 1980. (60 minutes)

Ted Koppel, "Revolution in a Box." *ABC Nightline,* November 13, 1989. (30 minutes)

"Digital Debate: Covering Government and Politics in a New Media Environment." Washington, DC: Radio Television News Directors Foundation, 1995. (58 minutes)

"Silicon Summit: Will Technology Affect the News?" Washington, DC: Radio Television News Directors Foundation, 1996. (75 minutes)

"Dollars and Demographics: The Evolving Market for News." Washington, DC: Radio Television News Directors Foundation, 1995. (56 minutes)

Text Credits

"The New TV: Stop Making Sense" by Mitchell Stephens. Reprinted with permission from *The Washington Post,* April 25, 1993, and the author.

"Identity Crisis of Newspapers" by Doug Underwood Reprinted with permission from the *Columbia Journalism Review,* March/April 1992, and the author.

"The Age of Multimedia and Turbo News" by Jim Willis. Originally appeared in the September-October 1995 issue of *The Futurist.* Used with permission froms the World Future Society, 7910 Woodmont Avenue, Suite 450, Bethesda, Maryland 20814. 301/656-8274. http://www.wfs.org .

"The Global Media Giants" by Robert W. McChesney. Reprinted with permission from *Extra!,* Nov.-Dec. 1997, and the author.

"The Leisure Empire" by Carl Bernstein. *Time* Magazine, December 24, 1990. Copyright 1990 Time Inc. Reprinted by permission.

"Video Killed the Red Star" by Dave Rimmer. Reprinted with permission from *The Guardian,* 14 August 1993.

"TV Once Again United The World in Grief" by Tom Shales. *The Washington Post,* Sept. 7, 1997. Copyright 1997, Washington Post Writers Group. Reprinted with permission.

"So Many Media, So Little Time" by Richard Harwood. *The Washington Post,* September 2, 1992. Copyright 1992, *The Washington Post.* Reprinted with permission.

"Tuning Out Traditional News" by Howard Kurtz. *The Washington Post,* May 15, 1995. Copyright 1995, Washington Post Writers Group. Reprinted with permission.

"Is TV Ruining Our Children" by Richard Zoglin. *Time* Magazine, October 15, 1990. Copyright 1990 Time Inc. Reprinted with permission.

"Crack and the Box" by Pete Hammill, from *Media&Values,* Spring/Summer 1992. Copyright 1992 by the Center for Media Literacy. Reprinted with Permission.

"Reflections on the First Amendment" by George Reedy. Reprinted with permission from *The Quill,* July 1991, and the author.

"Keeping the Press Free" by William Rentschler. Reprinted with permission from *Editor & Publisher,* October 25, 1998, and the author.

"The Totalitarianism of Democratic Media" by David Berkman. Reprinted with permission from *Media Ethics,* Fall 1993, and the author.

"Stop Making Sense" by Christopher Lasch. Reprinted with permission from the *Gannett Center Journal,* Spring 1990, now the *Media Studies Journal,* published by The Freedom Forum Media Studies Center.

"Are Journalists People" by James Fallows. Copyright, September 15, 1997, *U.S. News & World Report.* Reprinted with permission.

"Methods of Media Manipulation" by Michael Parenti. Reprinted with permission from *The Humanist,* July/August 1997, and the author.

Index